W9-BYO-783

RESTORING THE CHRISTIAN SOUL THROUGH HEALING PRAYER

Other Books by Leanne Payne

Real Presence

The Broken Image

The Healing of the Homosexual

Crisis in Masculinity

The Healing Presence

RESTORING THE CHRISTIAN SOUL THROUGH HEALING PRAYER

Overcoming the Three Great Barriers to Personal and Spiritual Completion in Christ

Leanne Payne

CROSSWAY BOOKS • WHEATON, ILLINOIS
A DIVISION OF GOOD NEWS PUBLISHERS

Restoring the Christian Soul Through Healing Prayer.

Published by Crossway Books, a division of
Good News Publishers, 1300 Crescent Street, Wheaton, Illinois 60187.

Cover design: Russ Peterson

First printing, 1991

Printed in the United States of America

Library of Congress Cataloging-in-Publication Data

Payne, Leanne.

Restoring the Christian soul through healing prayer / Leanne Payne.

p. cm.

Includes bibliographical references and index.

1. Spiritual life. 2. Spiritual healing. 3. Self-acceptance—Religious aspects—Christianity. 4. Forgiveness of sin. 5. Forgiveness—Religious aspects—Christianity. I. Payne, Leanne. Healing presence. II. Title.

BV4501.2.P3625 1991 234—dc20 91-23574

ISBN 0-89107-625-5

99 98 97 96 95 94 93 92 91

15 14 13 12 11 10 9 8 7 6 5 4 3 2 1

To Mario Bergner, Jean Holt, and Clay McLean,

beloved colleagues in this ministry
who are taking forward the message and ministry
of healing in ways that break new ground.

Table of Contents

Acknowledgments xi

Preface xiii

Part I: The Virtue of Self-Acceptance

1: Self-Hatred: The Traitor Within When Temptation Comes 19

2: First Great Barrier to Wholeness in Christ: Failure to Accept Oneself 25

3: Struggling Through to Self-Acceptance 31

4: Affirmation: What It Is and How It Is Received 45

5: Listening Prayer: The Way of Grace and the Walk in the Spirit 57

Part II: The Forgiveness of Sin

6: Healing of Memories: The Forgiveness of Sin 67

7: Second Great Barrier to Wholeness in Christ: Failure to Forgive Others 81

8: Prolonged Healing of Memories: Abandonment Issues and the Repression of Painful Emotions 103

9: Third Great Barrier to Wholeness in Christ: Failure to Receive Forgiveness 141

10: Conclusion to Healing of Memories 153

Part III: Spiritual Warfare and the Gift of Battle

11: The Use of Holy Water and Other Powerful Christian Symbols and Agencies 163

12: The Gift of Battle 183

13: Cosmic Dimensions of Spiritual Warfare in Christian Organizations 191

14: Wrong Ways to Do Battle 201

15: Restoring the Christian Hope of Heaven and the Grace to Persevere 217

Notes 233

Index 243

Is anything too hard for the Lord?

(Genesis 18:14)

Pastoral Care is defective unless it can deal thoroughly with the evils we have suffered as well as with the sins we have committed.

(Frank Lake, *Clinical Theology*)

Acknowledgments

Restoring the Christian Soul is a book about prayer and its awesome power as we gather in Christ's name. The school of prayer is surely one from which none of us ever graduates in this life. There is always more to experience and learn about prayers of praise, thanksgiving, intercession, supplication, and faith. The kind of prayer we are most concerned with in these pages is prayer for healing of the soul, the forgiveness of sin. This prayer work is not peripheral to Christian practice and the gospel message. It should be and indeed is part of the work of baptism and our initiation into Christ. It has long been neglected, however, and professionals in the healing arts are now dealing with the consequences of this neglect.

To pray effectively for the healing of souls is to see the work of the cross (Christ's passion) made fully manifest in lives and the gifts and fruit of the Holy Spirit flourish within the Body of Christ. It is to see people come into maturity and wholeness and thereby the power to evangelize and to succor a world starving for love, truth, and light. To gather as prayer partners and teams, therefore, is the most exciting thing in the world, for God waits to hear and respond to those who seek His mind on how to pray.

> Again, I tell you that if two of you on earth agree about anything you ask for, it will be done for you by my Father in heaven. For where two or three come together in my name, there am I with them. (Matthew 18:19, 20)

This book then, like my others, is born out of many years of learning to pray with and for others. Therefore, I want to acknowledge first of all the Pastoral Care Ministries Team made up of my prayer partners who also travel with me in the ministry. They are (Revs.) William and Anne Beasley, Mario Bergner, Lynne and Paul Berendsen, (Rev.) Conlee and Signa Bodishbaugh, Connie and Bob Boerner, Patsy Casey, John Fawcett, Jean Holt, Clay McLean, Mary Pomrenning, and Ted and Lucy Smith. What extraordinary fellow pilgrims and prayer partners they are! I thank them for who they are and all that they are. For their courageous, loving hearts and faith, I continually thank God.

A prayer group within the larger prayer team is made up of Lynne, Connie,

Lucy, and Patsy. For over twelve years now, they have met regularly with me for prayer, and I cannot think of many things we haven't faced and prayed through together in these sessions. The faith, love of truth, honesty, and sheer stamina of these remarkable women never fail to bless and sustain me and the other team members. Only eternity will tell what their husbands have given (and suffered!) for this ministry. For a period of time Bob Boerner, for example, stayed home with five teenage daughters and prayed for us while Connie went several times a year to lead the music ministry and pray for others in our healing missions. Now that the children are grown, he joins us on the team when he can manage time off from work. Paul Berendsen, besides doing the huge job of trying to stretch our dollars and keep our accounts in order, has never failed to bless his wife as she, year in and year out, has brilliantly managed the affairs of this ministry. Ted Smith has become the father figure for the whole group, blessing us and everybody else with his gifts of wisdom, guidance, and special faith in prayer.

The Rev. Andrew Comiskey and his Desert Stream team are so often with us that we consider them a part of the PCM family, as is the Rev. Jerry Soviar of Toledo, Ohio. They too are vital prayer partners with us. From thirty or more years ago, I want to recognize Lenora Runge, and from twenty-five years ago, Elinor Price. These precious ones, though long separated by distance, have remained with me in prayer. Gayle Sampson and Carol Kraft, more accessible geographically, are two more whose fellowship in prayer spans the decades. Mike Casey, Dr. Bernie Klamecki, Ivy Upton and John and Mary Stocking are others who never forget to love and pray for this ministry, and they provide a more unique and healing support for me than they realize. We have special prayer partners, translators, and teams overseas, some listed in the acknowledgments to *The Healing Presence*, but the list grows long, and they know who they are. We are so grateful for everyone who prays for and with us. Together we have a wealth of answered prayer, and I could fill books with the miracle of it all.

I trust the Father is magnified and the cross of His Son lifted high in the following pages. If so, His Holy Spirit will bless and heal through them. For this, we thank God the Father, Son, and Holy Spirit in advance.

Preface

But I, when I am lifted up from the earth, will draw all men to myself.

(Jesus, quoted in John 12:32)

This work is the companion volume to *The Healing Presence*, and although it can easily be read on its own, it builds on the theological and psychological foundation laid in that book. These books are not twins. This volume is a continuation of the first, and together they constitute the main body of work and ministry presented in our healing seminars and Pastoral Care Ministry Schools.

In the ministry of prayer for healing of the soul, we are continually helping Christians to hurdle one or another of the three great barriers to personal and spiritual wholeness in Christ. They are 1) the failure to gain the great Christian virtue of self-acceptance, 2) the failure to forgive others, and 3) the failure to receive forgiveness for oneself.

Every time we more fully understand *and accept* our true identities in Christ, forgive another, or confess a sin, barriers to our becoming mature disciples—all we were created to be—fall down. But at times we are unable on our own to understand what is blocking us, much less how to remove it. Then we need the ministry of others in order to walk in freedom. God's love is blocked and unable to flow freely into our brokenness; one of his servants must therefore help us to receive the healing. Part of the discipling process is to help others discern what their barriers are and then through healing prayer to lead them out of the prison house and into the freedom of maturity in Christ.

> Our work begins where God's grace has laid the foundation; we are not to save souls, but to disciple them. Salvation and sanctification are the work of God's sovereign grace; our work as His disciples is to disciple lives until they are wholly yielded to God.[1]

The First and Primary Healing

> True religion is the union of the Spirit of God with the human spirit, and this is effected in and through Jesus Christ. "He that is joined to the Lord is one Spirit." Jesus is the Mediator between God and man. He reveals the Father, unites us with the Father, and comes with the Father to make His home with us (John 14:21-23).[2]

As Oswald Chambers and F. B. Meyer remind us, the first and primary healing out of which all other healing proceeds is the new birth. Once Christ abides within, one with our spirits, then His life can radiate throughout our souls—that is, our minds and hearts—including our memories, our willing (volitional), feeling, intuitive, and imaginative faculties, and beyond that, even to our sensory and physical being. Then, as His light encounters dark places of unforgiveness and woundedness within us, healing can take place.

I will start with the failure to accept oneself, for so many Christians today are stuck at this very point. Once this stumbling block is hurdled, we can then forgive and receive forgiveness from the mature standpoint of who we are *in Christ*. To accept oneself is to be enabled to live out of one's true center, that is, out of the "new man" or the true self in Christ. The true center is the place where we *abide* in Christ. One who dwells there "walks in the Spirit" and is out from under the control of the sinful nature; he *abides* in union with the One who completes him. Such a man or woman wears the robe of Christ's righteousness; he deeply understands his justification and his at-one-ment in Christ and can therefore most truly glory always in the cross of Christ. He or she knows, beyond all shadow of a doubt, that "there is now no condemnation for those who are in Christ Jesus, because through Christ Jesus the law of the Spirit of life set me free from the law of sin and death" (Romans 8:1-2).

Today, there is a multitude of Christians whose failure to accept themselves is accompanied by a needless and ongoing sense of guilt and shame, or even more critically, an intense and even pathological self-hatred. Often these persons have come to Christ out of dysfunctional homes and environments, places where evil has, whether overtly or more subtly, run rampant, ravaging their spirits and souls, if not their bodies as well. These have been robbed of even the most basic childhood pleasures, indeed, of the experience of childhood itself. The problems of shame and self-hatred can be so intense that these persons can hardly receive teaching or even prayer for healing until we have helped them to acknowledge before Christ this self-hatred. It is then in His Presence that the large step of renouncing this hatred is taken. Once this infirmity of soul is faced and dealt with, these persons are able to open their hearts and begin to receive from God the healing they need.

For that reason then—so that *all* can enter into the teaching on self-acceptance and take the necessary steps toward achieving it—I will begin with self-hatred and prayer for renouncing it.

The cross, with its forgiveness of sin and transmission of the very life of God to us through the shed blood of Christ, is the doorway to the removal of all three barriers. Indeed, it is the doorway to all that is authentically Christian.

PART I

THE VIRTUE OF SELF-ACCEPTANCE

It is often said today . . . that we must love ourselves before we can be set free to love others. This is certainly the release which we must seek to give our people. But no realistic human beings find it easy to love or to forgive themselves, and hence their self-acceptance must be grounded in their awareness that God accepts them in Christ. There is a sense in which the strongest self-love that we can have, in the sense of agape, is merely the mirror image of the lively conviction we have that God loves us. There is endless talk about this in the church, but little apparent belief in it among Christians, although they may have a conscious complacency which conceals the subconscious despair which Kierkegaard calls "the sickness unto death."

(Richard Lovelace, *Dynamics of Spiritual Life: An Evangelical Theology of Renewal*)[1]

CHAPTER 1

Self-Hatred: The Traitor Within When Temptation Comes

The old Puritan idea that the devil tempts men had this remarkable effect, it produced the man of iron who fought; the modern idea of blaming his heredity or his circumstances produces the man who succumbs at once.[1]

(Oswald Chambers)

Before a large overseas Pastoral Care Ministries (PCM) conference, Clay McLean was driving across the country toward a city where he was to hold what proved to be very important and fruitful meetings. These were just prior to his joining the rest of the team for the overseas meetings. He was not long on the road when he suddenly found himself enmeshed in spiritual warfare. It was coming in the form of an intense temptation to fall into sexual sin. He actually saw in his spirit dark figures that he thought were not just ordinary demons, but large dark "powers" following him.

On this occasion Clay had to travel alone, something that had always been hard for him. He had gotten into his car for the long journey feeling somewhat anxious. Some of his old feelings of intense loneliness and rejection were plaguing him. He had particularly suffered from self-hatred in the past, and some of this old behavior had returned.

Although Clay wasn't thinking rationally at this point and couldn't see clearly what was happening, the enemy was tempting him to once again wallow in self-hatred and the devastating self-pity that had accompanied it. The accuser of his soul was also reminding him of past hurts and rejections, of sins and grievous failures that had occurred before God began to heal him emotionally and set into him a sense of psychological well-being.

This temptation to fall was a powerful last-ditch attempt to rob Clay of the possessions unique to himself as a person—first, his *oneness* with God and his new self inherent in that oneness, and second, his creative capacity to collaborate with God to bring forth lasting fruit in the Kingdom of God. Oswald Chambers had a firm hold on this phenomenon: "Temptation is," he says, "the testing by an alien power of the possessions held by a personality."

> In the temptation (of Christ) the devil antagonized the same thing that he antagonized in the first Adam, viz., oneness with God.[2]

> Satan does not tempt us to do wrong things; he tempts us in order to make us lose what God has put into us by regeneration, viz., the possibility of being of value to God.[3]

Why Temptation?

There is another side to these occurrences, and that is the sure knowledge that God not only knows about them, but has (even as with Job) allowed them. Why does God allow the Devil to tempt us? First of all, in a fallen world, we are necessarily tempted, not only by the sin without, but the (albeit unconscious) sin within. As Christians who are not sinning consciously and willfully, it is all too easy for us to forget the depth of sin in the human heart. Also, as moderns who are fed on a steady diet of secular psychological wisdom, it is even easier for us to rationalize our own sins and deficiencies and to transfer the blame for them onto others. When we are rationalizing our sins, we are not looking up to God, trusting in Him, and listening for the healing word. It is therefore necessary that temptation and trial compel us to face honestly what is in our hearts. This is, as Chambers says, "in order that a higher and nobler character may come out of the test."[4]

No one with a ministry worth having has escaped this testing, and the tests differ according to our weaknesses—those very things within us that need healing. This is one more reason why, with the greatest of joy and no hesitancy or apology whatsoever, we call people to a radical obedience to Christ.[5] Such obedience requires that we confront, acknowledge, and repent of our sin and propensity toward sin immediately as it becomes conscious. We are thereby spared dreadful suffering, humiliating falls, and perhaps even a lifetime of regret. Too, we discover for ourselves the truth of St. Paul's words: "No temptation has seized you except what is common to man. And God is faithful; he will not let you be tempted beyond what you can bear. But when you are tempted, he will also provide a way out so that you can stand up under it" (1 Corinthians 10:13).

Surely, one of the greatest benefits of learning to undergo the kind of testing that reveals our inner weaknesses is that, if we can correct them early, we can avoid misleading others. David's prayer, offered after acknowledging sin in his life, occupies a prominent place in my prayer journal. Should I forget to pray it, then I will often be reminded: "Let none of those who look to thee be shamed on my account, O Lord God of Hosts; Let none who seek thee be humbled through my fault, O God of Israel" (Psalm 69:6, NEB).

The Way of Escape

In our conferences, I say a lot about creativity. We see people mightily affirmed in their capacity to collaborate with God, and thereby enabled to be the "maker"[6] God has created them to be. This always runs counter to the demonic temptation to self-hatred, self-pity, and to a debilitating sense of shame and inferiority. I have learned to instruct people, as soon as temptation strikes, to invoke the Presence, saying, "Come, Lord Jesus," and then to *practice the Presence of God,* with, within, and all about them. In this way, they immediately get themselves centered; they *abide* in God. They know and affirm their position in God—that they are *in Christ* and He *in them*. Then sometimes immediately, and always amazingly, the demonic force and spiritual warfare recedes. What at first seems overwhelming in its power to overshadow, slime, and hold us in its foul clutches simply fades backward, declawed and whimpering. Oswald Chambers expresses it this way:

> When temptation comes, stand absolutely true to God no matter what it costs you, and you will find the onslaught leaves you with affinities higher and purer than ever before.[7]

This is what Clay did. All this occurred just before God poured out blessing after blessing upon him and paved the way for two more remarkable healings which I will refer to later. In fact, his battle with temptation was all a prelude to the more powerful and effective ministry he now exercises.

The renunciation of self-hatred is no small step to take, especially for those whose personalities have been formed by these attitudes from early on. It requires that we open ourselves wide to the full spectacle and meaning of the cross, that we allow ourselves to be confronted by Christ crucified, not only for our sin but for the evils we have suffered. We cry out, "Lord, I believe! Help thou mine unbelief!" and then go on to receive fully into ourselves all that flows out of His Atonement: justification, sanctification, a full incarnation (baptism or indwelling) of the Holy Spirit, authority in personal and spiritual conflict: i.e., redemption, healing, and full affirmation of who we are in God.[8]

The renunciation of self-hatred is a deliberate (volitional) step we take, and we keep our eyes on the Source of our salvation, not on our subjective feelings, which are unreliable and even "diseased" due to the habitual attitudes we've formed. As we do this, God honors our transaction and showers His grace upon us. We then do battle with all the diseased and negative thoughts and imaginings, lifting them up to Him as they arise in our hearts and minds.

Of course, it takes longer for some Christians—for example, those suffering with over-scrupulousity or perfectionism, or with gross sin and/or perversion in their backgrounds—to finally come out of self-hatred. For them, the root causes underlying their self-hatred, psychological as well as spiritual, are simply more complicated and entangled. As they move toward self-acceptance, these things surface to be spread out before God in prayer.

When Clay first attended a PCM, he sat on the very back row. After about the fifth or sixth one he attended, I asked him to move up front. That is when I found out how he, even as a Christian, "felt about" himself. Though a minister of the gospel who helped those who were the neediest, he felt himself so foul as to fear he would contaminate the ministry team if he sat too close to them.

There are usually (as in Clay's case) several key healings that take place before these deeply wounded ones enter into a full and secure acceptance of themselves as persons. In the meantime, we as ministers and counselors have to help them understand how dangerous and even sinful self-hatred is and how the evil one uses the failure to accept and celebrate the new self in Christ to tempt them to sin. Self-hatred, with its shame and self-pity, is a powerful and compelling means the enemy uses to tempt these precious, gifted souls to step entirely outside the true self and into the old with all its uncreative behavior and sin.

Clay had been delivered out of the hands of Baal, the idol god of sexual orgy, compulsion, and neurosis.[9] Had Clay succumbed to temptation and fallen sexually in his testing, he would once again have found himself in the clutches of Baal. Because of the emotional injuries and deprivations of his childhood, his battle with that loathsome idol had been fierce beyond description and almost claimed his life. And it was these very injuries and circumstances that caused his severe self-hatred. Not only would he have had to once again fight for his sanity, he would also have had the matter of idolatry to deal with, for "temptation yielded to is lust deified."[10]

It is tragic to see Christian leaders fall. There is, even as St. Paul has said, no need to live from the lower self, obeying its drives: "So then, my brothers, there is no necessity for us to obey our unspiritual selves or to live unspiritual lives. If you do live in that way, you are doomed to die; but if by the Spirit you put an end to the misdeeds of the body you will live" (Romans 8:12-13, *Jerusalem Bible*). Christians must, however, acknowledge their need for emotional healing and seek it. Failure to deal with inner insecurities and self-hatred, thereby failure to gain a secure identity in Christ, is the most common underlying weakness in these falls.

Clay has learned the practice of the Presence of Christ, and thereby his at-one-ment with Him. To learn this is to understand the great and grave doctrine of our justification in Him. In a joy that still takes him by surprise, Clay now often phones me from different parts of the globe just to exclaim something like the following: "I'm the happiest man in all Texas. No, in all the world, I'm the most blessed of men!" This is the way one so gifted in Christ and now free to allow that creativity to flow will feel; this is the way any man or woman will feel once released from the hell of self-hatred. This healing is ours in the cross of Christ; it has already been accomplished by Christ's death and resurrection.

We need only receive it, as the full message and efficacy of His cross is applied to our wounds as well as to our sins.

PRAYER OF RENUNCIATION OF SELF-HATRED

> For God caused Christ, who himself knew nothing of sin, to *be* sin for our sakes, so that in Christ we might be made good with the goodness of God. (2 Corinthians 5:21, *J. B. Phillips,* emphasis in Phillips's text)

Prayer of Thanksgiving

Holy Father, I thank You that I am reconciled to You through the death of Your Son, and that through faith in Him as my Savior from sin, my heart is not only washed clean from my own sin, but it can be delivered from its grievous reactions to the sins and shortcomings of others around and against it. Because of Your Son, Father, I can look straight up to You and dare to let all these feelings surface, and I do so now, knowing that Christ is ready to take them and give me in exchange His Life and Your perspective on myself and others. Accept my thanksgiving, O God our Father. I thank You for Christ who has redeemed me from sin and death and who is even now pouring His eternal life into me.

Lord Jesus Christ, Son of the Father, in whom I am to abide, to fully live, move, and have my being (my true and new self), I direct my thanksgiving to You. I bow before You as Lord of my life, and I thank You, Precious Holy One, crucified for me, that Your blood justifies me, that in oneness with You, Your goodness is mine.

Holy Spirit, Thou who dost so constantly and faithfully mediate to us the love of both Father and Son, I thank You now for the grace to receive all that is mine as a child of God. Empower me now as I renounce the sin of self-hatred and as I move toward the goal of wholly accepting my true identity as a child of God the Father, Son, and Holy Spirit.

Pray quietly, giving thanks. If diseased feelings start to surface, simply allow them to flow, one at a time up and out of your heart and mind and into the Crucified One. Note them later in your prayer journal, not only so you can converse with God about them, but recognize and refuse them if and when they return asking readmittance to your heart. Now see Him dying on the cross to take those things into Himself. Then see Him risen again, ascending to the Father, there to intercede to the Father for you, to pour out upon you His Spirit, to send to you words of life that engender in you new and wholesome feelings and attitudes. And give thanks.

Prayer of Petition

You may want to lift, simply and clearly, petitions to the Lord at this time. A prayer such as the following might be in order. It will better prepare you to make your renunciation of self-hatred.

Well you know, O Lord, that I have been unable to appropriate Your holiness and righteousness as I wish; I have been unable to practice Your Presence because my feelings about myself are so diseased. I have looked to You, just now, as my dying Savior, taking into Yourself my sin and darkness, my diseased feelings about You, others, myself. I thank You that You have done this and that in time even my feeling self will reflect this. Heretofore, Lord, I have taken my eyes from You and from objective truth and have descended into and lived out of my unhealed feeling self. This, with Your help, Lord, I will cease doing, and I will note the very moment I am "living out of" that subjective, hurting place and will look straight up to You for the healing word You are always sending. I confess to You the sin of pride that is bound up in my self-hatred. I thank You for Your forgiveness and for full release from it.

For greater understanding of the humility that replaces this pride, see page 49.

Prayer of Renunciation

Now, Lord, in Your Name and with the grace You shower upon me, I renounce the sin of self-hatred.

Quietly give thanks for God's forgiveness.

With this renunciation, a multitude of accusing thoughts or maybe even root causes behind the self-hatred may begin to surface. Simply write them down in your prayer journal, acknowledging them, and then listen for the thought or the illumination God is sending you, for this will be the word from Him that not only replaces the diseased thought pattern but will flood you with understanding.

CHAPTER 2

First Great Barrier to Wholeness in Christ: Failure to Accept Oneself

Jesus then said to His disciples: "If anyone wishes to be a follower of Mine, he must leave self behind; he must take up his cross and come with Me. Whoever cares for his own safety is lost; but if a man will let himself be lost for my sake, he will find his true self. What will a man gain by winning the whole world at the cost of his true self? Or what can he give that will buy that self back?"

(Matthew 16:24-26, NEB)

If you are led by the Spirit, you are not under law.

(Galatians 5:18)

There is a line over which many of us never step. That is the line between

Immaturity
―――――
Maturity

Being under the Law, a law, or many laws
―――――
The walk in the Spirit

Listening to many voices: those within our unhealed hearts, and of the world, the flesh, the devil
―――――
Listening to God

It is the line between bondage and freedom. Accepting oneself is the vital step to be taken in order to cross this line.

One sensitive, loving priest said to me, "I seem to have many who—after making full confession of sin, after healing of memories, after a release of the Spirit in their lives—yet look to me for *something* else. They look up from the Communion cup, from laying-on-of-hands. . . . What is it they are straining for?" I knew the answer: They are straining to come into the freedom that is in fact theirs—but they've been unable to cross over the line. They are still dependent, immature, in some way. They are looking for permission to act, to be.

These folk need to get through the formidable barrier of failure to accept themselves; they need to cross over into the maturity to which Christ calls them.

A person may not accept himself when he is very self-centered, selfish, and has not died to the old self. He experiences real guilt, and it is a good thing that he is sorely afflicted with it. He cannot say with St. Paul and the Christian: "For we know that our old self was crucified with Him so the body of sin might be done away with, that we should no longer be slaves of sin" (Romans 6:6).

It is therefore a mercy that he heartily dislikes and fails to accept that self, that he has honest negative thoughts about himself. But we must differentiate between the self that collaborates with the principle of evil and selfishness, and the self that abides in Christ and collaborates with Him. That is the true self. That is the justified new creation, the soul that is saved and lives eternally. The former self we deliberately and continually die to; the other we joyfully and in great humility and thankfulness accept.

It is true that once we are able to accept and celebrate the new self, we tend to forget this new creation as such, for we are focused on Christ who is our Lodestar, who is (beyond what we can now think or imagine) our life. We are simply too engaged in looking to Him, in obeying and collaborating with Him in His mission to love the world through us. And we say, along with St. Paul: "To me to live is Christ." But it is only with the full acceptance of this new self that we find our true center, that place of quiet strength and solid *being*, that center from which we know and see ourselves to be white-robed in the very righteousness of Christ Himself. It is from this center of oneness with Christ that we can cry out with Isaiah and the saints of old: "I delight greatly in the Lord; my soul rejoices in my God. For he has clothed me with garments of salvation and arrayed me in a robe of righteousness, as a bridegroom adorns his head like a priest, and as a bride adorns herself with her jewels" (Isaiah 61:10).

We need to recognize when this outward focus on Christ has been seriously blocked by the failure to accept ourselves.[1] We need to recognize and do something about the diseased attitudinal patterns toward the self, those formed in the crucible of the various accidents and deprivations of our past.

I can be a Christian filled with the Spirit of God, but if I hate myself, the light of God is going to emanate through me in distorted ways. I will still be seeing myself through the eyes of others around me, those who perhaps could not love or affirm me. I will not be seeing myself through the eyes of God; I

Focus on others

will not be listening for the affirming as well as the corrective words He is always speaking to me, His beloved child. I will be dependent upon others, perhaps grievously bent toward them; I will be seeking their affirmation, their validation, and even their permission for my every move. Failing to accept myself, I will have no solid center, therefore I will "walk alongside myself."[2] I will suffer what the Scriptures name as lack of maturity and lack of freedom and will be a "man-pleaser" rather than a "God-pleaser." Truly, "it is for freedom that Christ has set us free" (Galatians 5:1), but I will know little of the walk in the Spirit; my spirit, unable to soar in the sunlight of all God has done for me, will flutter against the prisonhouse bars.

The other great blocks to wholeness in Christ—the failure to forgive others, and/or to receive forgiveness for ourselves—have to do with more or less specific memories and rejections. In contrast, the failure to accept oneself is an attitudinal block. It has to do with how we perceive and feel about ourselves and others. We develop immature, negative patterns of relating to God and to others when we've failed to come into a mature self-acceptance. Our inner vision of ourselves is diseased. This does not mean that we understand any better than the next Christian the depth of sin in the human heart; in fact, such a deficient view of the self cannot recognize, understand, and fully appropriate its justification in Christ, but is rather turned in on the self in a narcissistic way.[3]

Fr. Michael Scanlon, in his book *Inner Healing*, states that, "We have an attitudinal life which operates from the very core of our being. . . . This life determines broad general patterns of relating to others and to God." He then speaks of five different problem patterns that alert him to a need to pray for what he calls a "heart healing." These are:

1) A judgmental spirit that is harsh and demanding on self and others.
2) A strong perfectionist attitude demanding the impossible from self and others.
3) A strong pattern of fearing future events.
4) A sense of aloneness and abandonment in times of decision.
5) A preoccupation with one's own guilt and a compulsion to compete for position and success.[4]

Enveloping all of these patterns, or overarching them, is the inability to accept oneself and thereby go on to emotional and psychological freedom. In fact, even one of these patterns in a life indicates that the person has not achieved the important step of self-acceptance.

In the more painful cases, I hear remarks such as the following: "I have never liked myself; I hate myself; I was a mistake; I should never have been born; I just don't seem to fit in anywhere."

As Fr. Scanlon has noted, these patterns are present in an otherwise deeply religious life. Usually there is a constant expectation of growth or breakthrough to new spiritual freedom, but it doesn't happen. Why? Because, he says, the heart is hurting. It will continue to hurt so long as the diseased attitudinal patterns remain.

These dear ones often come to me or to some other minister of healing and ask for "one more prayer" for healing of memories. "Please," they will say, "there must be one more memory that needs healing." Their persistence and outright tenacity in looking for healing (which for them would be the magic breakthrough) is amazing in that it seems almost endless. That is because the pain is endless, the heart is constricted, and the pain grows rather than lessens through the years due to the bonds that constitute the failure to be affirmed as a man or as a woman, as a person in one's own right.

How are these people healed? What is their need? Their crying need is to exchange old patterns of relating to life for new ones, to build in new patterns of thinking about themselves and others, of seeing themselves and others, of relating to themselves and others. In order to do this, they must learn to listen—to God and to their own hearts. There is nothing that will bring these souls through the failure to accept the self more quickly and thoroughly than the practice of "listening prayer." Through it, they will begin seeing themselves through the eyes of the Master Affirmer, our Heavenly Father.

This listening involves, of course, coming into the Presence of God and there receiving His Word and illumination as to why we feel the way we do, why we do the things we do. It involves writing down every negative, untrue, and irrational thought and attitudinal pattern as we become aware of it. For some, this is almost a full-time task at first. I've had a number of people exclaim to me, "Oh, but you don't understand! Every thought I have is negative!" Oh yes, I do understand, and all the more reason why such a one has to get his priorities straight and enter into conversation with God as though it were his only lifeline. It probably is. The alternative, a failure to understand why we think or hurt the way we do, is too terrible to think about.

When we write down our diseased patterns of thought, we must always listen to Him for the healing, positive, true words and patterns that are to replace the dark, negative ones! That is how we gain the mind of God and get rid of diseased patterns of thought. We first *acknowledge* we have them; then we find what they are rooted in and why we have them. Finally, we confess and get rid of them by yielding them up to God and taking in exchange the true word He is sending.

In the doing of this, we begin to realize that we are holding onto some of these old patterns, that we have a real resistance to letting them go. We find that they are often, in fact, defense mechanisms against the pain of growing up, of being vulnerable, of being responsible. At first, as Fr. Scanlon has said, we don't usually recognize them for what they are—old wounds used to escape reality, to justify failure, to gain attention and affection.

One of the saints has cautioned us: "Be wary of sickness." I personally have had to be very wary of physical weakness. Its siren song calls me to sit back, to "retire" just a little. Deep in the American psyche is this idea of retiring at a certain age, of resting on our laurels, of "letting other folk do the work." We do indeed need to be wary of a little physical illness and note the ways we allow it to shape our existence. This is even more true, it seems to me, of emotional pain. Whether the weakness is physical, emotional, or spiritual, we need to seek God's face, asking, "What is this pain all about? What are You saying to me through this?"

It is remarkable how often the pain is merely a signal to listen in order that we might know what the next step toward wholeness should be. The following example illustrates this point. A certain young man from a family of high achievers had from early childhood suffered depression and was subject to deep anxiety. The roots of this anxiety and depression were uncovered, and he experienced great healing. He was, in fact, free from anxiety and depression for the first time since he could remember.

One day he got in touch with me, saying that his depression was back. I asked him, "What happened just before you began to be depressed?" With a moment's thought, he said it was after friends had asked him what he needed prayer for, and he couldn't think of a thing. He began to be depressed from that moment on. He was rather taken aback when I exclaimed, "Praise the Lord! We now know what to pray about!"

The next step in his recovery was the realization that he could relate to other people only as a sick person. He had already begun to recognize old coping mechanisms, those that gave him a ready defense against the pain of growing up, that justified his lack of responsibility, and that gained him sympathy and affection. But now this pain signified the valid need he had of learning to relate to others as a person, and not on the basis of his neediness—indeed, learning to accept himself as a whole person. When we learn to listen, we are wary of sickness. We learn to discern what the pain is and what it is saying to us.

CHAPTER 3

Struggling Through to Self-Acceptance

Sally, a young wife and mother, came up to me after I had been speaking on this matter of self-acceptance and told me her story. As a teen, she could not accept her "tall body," as she referred to it. She felt her unusual height would affect her chances of marrying. But she turned the right key early in life, a key every Christian has been given—*she struggled in prayer before the Lord until she accepted her height*. In other words, she came before the Master Affirmer and entered into deep and obedient conversation with Him. In His Presence, listening, she not only accepted her height but made other important decisions, one being that she would not marry at all unless it was to a man who met the qualifications for a good husband. She could not have made this decision had she not first accepted herself. She was lovely, poised, self-assured, and had an especially fine husband, a beautiful marriage, good-looking, tall sons! Others accept her height because she accepts it.

The acceptance of herself made all the difference in the world in her ability to accept the blessings in life God had to give her. When we reject ourselves or any part of ourselves, we communicate that view to others. They most often take us at our own evaluation. It is important to those in the healing ministry to see troubled people as God sees them (the *real* persons behind the phenomenal ones), not as they see themselves.

Romano Guardini, Catholic philosopher-theologian, in his essay "The Acceptance of Oneself," writes:

> The act of self-acceptance is the root of all things. I must agree to be the person who I am. Agree to have the qualifications which I have. Agree to live within the limitations set for me. . . . The clarity and the courageousness of this acceptance is the foundation of all existence.[1]

Nonacceptance ranges from the rejection of some physical aspect of our being to a wholesale hatred or rejection of oneself. Today this failure is being written about in terms such as low self-esteem, lack of affirmation, unmet emotional needs and love hunger as they emerge out of the dysfunctional family, and failing to like or to love oneself.[2]

I use the older term, *self-acceptance,* however, for several reasons. For one, the way I use the term, it includes all the above. Under its umbrella we look at the various traumas and unmet needs that have led to distorted thinking about oneself and others. In the ministry of healing prayer, we are concerned with basic love deficits, those that have rendered us unable to love others or receive love as we should. These gaping holes in people's souls are what God so yearns to gain admittance to, into which He longs to pour His healing life. But in addition, I use the term *self-acceptance* because it stands for a positive goal we as Christians are to reach. It denotes an authentic and necessary Christian virtue, one that is available to all who seek it.

There is yet another very practical reason. We live in a narcissistic age, one in which a sinful and blatant self-centeredness is the *in* thing and is being preached. Some who write on esteeming and loving oneself are confusing sinful and/or simplistic modes with healthy self-acceptance. Others are writing about *self-realization*—something that is not Christian. "We are not called to self-realization but to identification with Christ."[3]

A contemporary example of a mistaken attempt at self-realization is the search for "my lost child," i.e., the girl or boy that I was, or somehow could have been apart from the unhealthy circumstances I faced. There is something ephemeral about the self at any stage of our development. When the person who was neglected or abused in childhood looks to Christ, forgives others, and is forgiven, he or she can find healing of childhood memories. In this way, our Lord does in a very real way come present to the wounded "inner child." But He deals with people as the adults they are, and when He heals our memories (from any age), we simply find a greater integration of who we are in Him. But we will never find "our lost child" by looking for it. Our true self at any stage of our becoming is in Christ. He is the road out of the hell of the self-centered life.

> Your real new self will not come as long as you are looking for it. It will come when you are looking for Him. . . .[4]
>
> In love we escape from our self into Him and into one another.[5]

This, the Christian view, is in contrast, indeed it is antithetical to the various worldly modes of self-actualization and self-realization.

On the other hand, the self-hatred and self-depreciation that accompanies our failure to accept ourselves is not Christian; it is utterly destructive toward the self. Totally pernicious, there is not one good thing in it. It is only after we have accepted ourselves that we are free to love others. If we are busy hating that soul that God loves and is in the process of straightening out, we cannot help others—our minds will be riveted on ourselves—not on Christ who is our wholeness. When we hate the self, we in fact practice the presence of the old self; we are *self*-conscious rather than *God*-conscious. Agnes Sanford, writer on healing prayer, said, "Jesus died for us, not that our souls should die but that they should live! It is only our inherited drive toward evil that is potentially destroyed."

Grievously erroneous and unchristian ideas concerning denying and hating oneself have long been propagated in one form or another in certain Christian circles. These ideas do not distinguish between the two selves—the old self which must be put to death and the new which is to be encouraged.[6] Persons holding these misunderstandings apparently try to combat the wrong kind of self-love by teaching people to love others but not themselves. These errors in thought are unscriptural but firmly entrenched, causing their adherents at times to lash out wildly at anyone who recognizes that there are beautiful as well as dark things within the human breast. The Apostle Paul is often quoted, "I know that within me dwells no good thing," and then, strangely, his qualifying phrase is omitted. Paul's subject here is the old sin nature, and he is saying that within *it* there is no good thing. "I know that nothing good lives in me, that is, *in my sinful nature*" (Romans 7:18, emphasis added).

The simple fact is that if we do not humbly accept ourselves, we cannot love and accept others. If we are hypercritical of ourselves, we will also criticize others. Walter Trobisch quotes the German psychotherapist Dr. Guido Groeger, who states that:

> Because this affirmation is often withheld—especially in Christian circles—a type of Christian is created who loves out of duty and who in this way tortures not only others, but also himself.[7]

These erroneous perspectives not only influence people to disregard and downgrade what is right and good (talents and gifts from God), but train them in the tragic art of killing not the old but the new, creative self. The effects of these perspectives grow more telling with each successive generation.

As counselors, we have to know that:

> At the root of every depression is the feeling of having lost something. . . . The deepest root of depression is the feeling that I have lost myself and have given up hope of ever finding myself again. There is nothing in me worth loving. . . . This means that self-acceptance and depression are closely related.[8]

Recently, after speaking on self-acceptance to a large group of deeply wounded people, we moved into prayer for healing. This particular Pastoral Care Ministries School was sponsored by Rev. Andrew Comiskey and those affiliated with Desert Stream, a ministry to sexually broken people. For a great many of these hurting ones there was a history of depression, the sort that can evolve out of the circumstances of a lost childhood. Then, as Andy Comiskey and Fr. William Beasley stood up with me to pray for them, anguished wails erupted from one young man, and then from others. The deepest root of their depression had been tapped, and the Holy Spirit began powerfully to minister into it. For many there that night, what had been an insurmountable barrier to wholeness was lifted. Christ came present to their worst memories, and they were enabled to yield these up to Him. They walked out of depression and into light.

From a neurotic fixation on the wounded "inner child," then, the suffering Christian's gaze becomes riveted upon the wounds of Christ. Therein is our healing. He takes upon and into Himself our darkness and depression and gives us in exchange His light and life.

In order to accept ourselves, we need to learn with C. S. Lewis the following lesson:

> Since I have begun to pray, I find my extreme view of personality changing. My own empirical self is becoming more and more important, and this is the opposite of self-love. You don't teach a seed how to die into treehood by throwing it into the fire: and it has to become a good seed before it's worth burying.[9]

I have prayed for persons whose parents have, as a matter of religious principle, withheld from them *all* affirmation. Only recently, I prayed with a man who is cut off from his feeling being. He can feel nothing—not sadness, not joy, not anger—though he is often sad, angry, and ever without joy. He learned to cope with his parents' methodical *disaffirmation* by dying utterly to his feeling being. He serves Christ as best he can, but without the power to name or feel emotion. I prayed for the healing of his feeling being, which could not have been more damaged had he been raised by alcoholic or sexually abusive parents.

Parents symbolize God to their young. If the Christian father who teaches his son or daughter about God is himself a stern and unfeeling judge, the child will, apart from some very unusual and happy circumstance, perceive God the Father in that way. If a child's Christian parents are impossible to please, the child will almost certainly perceive God in the same way. Until healing takes place and the damaged psyche is resymbolized,[10] such a one cannot hear God's "well done" spoken over him. He cannot understand and receive the affirmation the Father is continually pouring out upon His children or the promises that they shall have "glory"—meaning approval, favor, appreciation, and even fame with God!

> When I began to look into this matter, I was shocked to find such different Christians as Milton, Johnson and Thomas Aquinas taking heavenly glory quite frankly in the sense of fame or good report. But not fame conferred by our fellow creatures—fame with God, approval or (I might say) "appreciation" by God. And then, when I had thought it over, I saw that this view was scriptural; nothing can eliminate from the parable the divine *accolade*, "Well

> done, thou good and faithful servant." With that, a good deal of what I had been thinking all my life fell down like a house of cards. I suddenly remembered that no one can enter heaven except as a child; and nothing is so obvious in a child—not in a conceited child, but in a good child—as its great and undisguised pleasure in being praised. Not only in a child, either, but even in a dog or a horse. Apparently what I had mistaken for humility had, all these years, prevented me from understanding what is in fact the humblest, the most childlike, the most creaturely of pleasures—nay, the specific pleasure of the inferior: the pleasure of a beast before men, a child before its father, a pupil before his teacher, a creature before its Creator.[11]

In his book *The Healing of Memories,* Dr. David Seamands has two chapters on distorted concepts of God, how they form, and the counselor's need to understand and deal aright with these infirmities within the soul. As he states, the key to understanding the "distorting of God's character" in those whose "love perceptors" are so skewed and damaged is to look at the

> unhealthy interpersonal relationships, especially those which occurred during the early development years of childhood and adolescence. More than any other factor, these faulty relationships cause the emotional damages which distort spiritual perceptions.[12]

For those who need to deal with distorted perceptions of God, I recommend a prayerful reading of these chapters by Dr. Seamands, together with a Scriptural study of the love of God the Father. In addition to looking up the Scriptural references on the love of God, writing them in your prayer journal, and then personalizing them to yourself, you may want to read books such as Robert Frost's *Our Heavenly Father* or *Testaments of Love* (scholarly) by Leon Morris. To begin deliberately celebrating God as the divine Affirmer and the one who bestows favor on you, I recommend a small book entitled *Favor* by Bob Buess (P. O. Box 7110, Tyler, TX 75711) and C. S. Lewis's essay "The Weight of Glory," in his book by the same name.

Molly, Child of Divorce

She was fatherless and unaffirmed. A Christian wife and mother who had a successful ministry to others, Molly (not her real name) was in dire need of accepting herself. She had tried everything she knew to help herself, but had become increasingly mired in emotional and spiritual confusion. She also had serious physical problems which her doctors thought were related to her deep and continuing emotional unrest.

When she finally got quiet enough and gained the courage to face what was in her own heart, the key thing that came up was, "I have always hated myself." She was well versed in the Scriptures, but she could never get past the injunction to "die to the old man." This she had tried with all her might to do, but because she had never accepted herself, she succeeded only in dying to the *real self*.

Molly's parents were divorced when she was quite small. Her father had deserted the family. This was to her a terrible personal rejection that had affected her entire life, but she was largely in denial about it. Needing to maintain some kind of idealized image of the absent father, she projected the blame for her hurt and confusion onto her mother. For example, she charged her with "leaving me and going to work." When questioned, she realized this was irrational. Her mother was forced to work in order to gain their living.

A child takes the loss of a parent, whether through death, divorce, or however, as a personal rejection. Unhealed rejections become seedbeds of diseased "matter" such as bitterness, envy, rage, fear of rejection, and a sense of inferiority. When these things fester inside us, they greatly impact the way we hear and perceive others, who in turn become easy targets of the "missiles" these diseased attitudes and feelings project outward. Like poison-filled arrows, these darts of envy, bitterness, and so on find their mark in the minds and hearts of those we love the most. This is one of the reasons why, until we accept ourselves, we are dangerous to others as well as to ourselves. We are apt to misread their best intentions and slander them. This includes, of course, the way we see and speak of God as well.[13]

Stories like Molly's are legion. In our dysfunctional society, her story, with modifications here and there, is more the rule than the exception. Many children raised in single-parent homes "project" in this way onto the parent who is there to receive it. In Molly's home, the faithful parent was being scapegoated. In the worst way, Molly needed the healing of her early memories of rejection by her father. It is easy to see from this how the wounded child can sustain not only the loss of one parent but, in effect, the loss of both.[14]

For Molly, then, there was no father figure, no protecting, caring male with whom to identify. Every child needs a father to reach up to, and if the father is not there or fails to respond, the child is not lifted up and out of the "nest," up and out of the feminine milieu. The child is not lifted up and out of mother, the source of being on the natural plane. This is a large element in a young man's being unable to accept himself as a man, as well as in male homosexuality, for the young lad is unable to get his identity separated from that of his mother, the feminine. He is barred from the necessary identification with the masculine, and his own masculinity goes "begging." It is not called into life. He is unaffirmed in his gender identity. The young girl is also called up and out of infancy and girlhood and on into a fulfilling womanhood by her father's capacity to affirm her as a feminine person at each stage of her growth. In this way, he helps her separate her identity from her mother's, and he affirms her as a person in her own right. Without the father's help, the struggle is prolonged and heightened.

Dr. Daniel Trobisch says that the masculine principle is one of orientation, direction, order, and responsibility. In loving dialogue with his children, the father "calls them out and points the way to the greater world." The mother, he says, "is like a circle, and the father is the one who draws them out from that circle to a goal."[15] This process of being drawn toward a goal is a psychological reality for the "fathered" child, as well as a physical, spiritual, and intellectual one.

Dr. Trobisch goes on to point out an immensely important and vital truth that we in the twentieth century really do not comprehend: "The father draws the circle (the feminine) as well, into the greater world." In this day, we are chiefly in trouble because men are in full flight from feminine values. (For more on masculinity and femininity, see *The Healing Presence* and *Crisis in Masculinity.*) They are not, as it were, conveyors of meaning (all the feminine values) into the world at large. With a few notable exceptions, the way is barred for the true feminine to enter into and inform the more masculine powers of orientation, direction, order, and responsibility.

So very much of the stuff of psychological healing has to do with something amiss in the identification process. We've failed to bond or to identify with either mother or father or both. On the other hand, we may have internalized the "bad" mother or father and find ourselves so entwined and entangled with their diseased thoughts and attitudes as to be unable to separate our own from theirs. As a consequence, then, we are hurting emotionally, floundering in our relationships, and seriously unaffirmed as persons. This affects every part of our being. Unbalanced and unaffirmed in the masculine and the feminine facets of our personalities, we invariably suffer same-sex and/or other-sex ambivalence as well. In other words, we are irrationally prejudiced toward others and have difficulty relating to them on the basis of their sex. As Dr. Karl Stern points out:

> Compared with the objective reality in which we adults live, the persons of our early life are overcharged with emotional significance. They are larger than life-size. And they have the peculiar property of being able to stain the image of persons whom we encounter subsequently.[16]

Though Molly had little understanding of how the loss of her father figured into her self-hatred, she was all the same suffering the inner deprivation of never having been fathered. Nor could her impoverished, overworked, and unprotected mother provide her a stable home life. She reached adolescence with no affirmation as a woman and as a person in her own right by her own father or a father substitute.

These days it is all too easy for the search for love and affirmation to end in sexual permissiveness. That was the route Molly's need had taken. Because of this, she did things in adolescence that still colored her view of herself. She despised and distrusted herself for those things even though she had long since asked forgiveness and had turned from all consciously known unrighteousness. Yet, she perceived herself as inferior, even base—because of her past. She hated herself. She was trapped in the *unaffirmed position*. Though thoroughly converted to Christ, she was psychologically unhealed.

Obviously, there was a problem with her practical theology. She had failed to *receive* the forgiveness God had long been holding out to her. But she also had failed to accept herself—a psychological as well as a spiritual problem.

Self-Acceptance: A Christian Virtue

Self-acceptance was once taught as a virtue to be attained. Besides teaching the cardinal virtues (faith, hope, love, wisdom, justice, temperance, courage), our forefathers in the faith taught others such as *patience with the self*. Of this great virtue, Romano Guardini writes: "So he who wishes to advance must always begin again. . . . Patience with oneself . . . is the foundation of all progress." Among others taught were the virtues of truthfulness, loyalty, orderliness, disinterestedness, gratitude, recollection, silence, along with this vital one of self-acceptance.[17]

Why was the virtue of self-acceptance taught? Simply because no one is born with the capacity to accept himself. Self-acceptance is now taught (if at all) as a psycho-social developmental step in educational psychology. Psychologists point out progressions from infancy to maturity, which involve many steps of psycho-social development. When we miss a step, we are in trouble.

Ideally, the step of self-acceptance comes just after puberty. It can hardly occur if we have missed earlier important steps in the identification process or if at puberty the affirming masculine father figure is missing. (For more on this topic, see my books *Crisis in Masculinity* and *The Broken Image*.) In these cases, there are unmet basic love needs,[18] and healing and insight is needed in order to clear the way for self-acceptance to take place. There will most likely be serious unhealed memories of rejection in the past.

Puberty and adolescence is the narcissistic stage for all of us. We are mainly concerned about our bodies. We look at ourselves in the mirror, examining every little bump on our faces, every inch of our torsos. We want to know if we have the right kind of equipment for being male or female, and we fear that we don't. Girls don't like the size of their busts (either too small or too large), the shape of their legs, the color and texture of their hair, *ad infinitum*. Boys often focus on their size (their physiques and genitalia), their physical strength, and their competence in sports. In this culture they often suffer a severe sense of sexual inferiority as they compare themselves to others.

To whatever degree we fail to emerge from this adolescent, narcissistic stage, we will be stuck in some form or manifestation of the wrong kind of self-love. Failing to love ourselves aright, we will love ourselves amiss. The rampant morbid practice of introspection[19] is one of the most prevalent of these narcissistic manifestations, and the anxious practice of it can be as pernicious to personality development as masturbation (when carried past puberty) and homosexuality—two of the more obvious examples of a love turned inward.[20] To achieve a healthy personality, we must pass from this self-centered stage to the self-acceptance that is full, secure. Whoever does not accept himself is engrossed with himself.

The myth of Narcissus is the story of adolescence. The youth, Narcissus, looks at his own reflection in the water and falls in love with himself. His attention fixed on his own image, he tumbles into it and drowns. This myth is especially apropos to the twentieth century. The great majority of folk have not emerged out of the adolescent, narcissistic state that C. S. Lewis calls "the dark ages in every life"—that time when "the most unideal senses and ambitions have been restlessly, even maniacally awake." He laments the cessation of the "truly imaginative" as the soul is given over in adolescence to this auto-erotic period.[21]

But the fact that a Christian has not accepted himself, indeed, has not entirely emerged out of the immature, narcissistic state, is not always so apparent. A Christian man, for example, unaffirmed as a man, may very well be fixed on an image of himself as a successful businessman, priest, financial wizard, or whatever. Just as Narcissus of old, he has "fallen into his own image," and the authentic self (with all its authentic desires) is drowned. Such a man does not know his identity as a *person in Christ;* indeed, he does not know himself as an authentic person. He is a masked man, one whose worth and identity are tied up in his role or roles. How he is perceived socially is more important to him than who he *is* privately. His roles obscure his failure to accept himself, but his son or daughter is painfully aware of the truth. Such a father cannot affirm his son or daughter, cannot call them up and out of puberty and adolescence into maturity. He is himself unaffirmed.

Karl Stern writes about what happens to a son or daughter who can identify with a parent only in a role. This happens when there is

> a marked discrepancy between the person's social role and the true person. . . . Such a rift between outer appearance and inner character exists in many of us. Many psychologists have made a distinction between "social ego" and ego proper, between "role" and person. Jung called the social ego *persona* in contrast to the personality. The word *persona* is derived from the concept of the mask. The actors on the stage of ancient Rome wore masks with mouthpieces through which the words sounded (*per-sonare*). The person in his social role is often quite different from the person as he appears in his intimate life. Many people become more dependent on their own *persona.* Their social ego, their role as bank president or railway conductor, has the same function as the exterior skeleton in crustaceae. *They are so united to their social ideal that they would collapse, and very little would remain, if one robbed them of their position in society. Children's growing selves are quite sensitive to this discrepancy. By a number of factors they become identified with social ideals rather than with human beings of flesh and blood.*[22] (italics mine)

> During the process of identification children absorb our sense of values as if by osmosis. If our scale of values is that of an external hierarchy, our children cannot grow. Nobody can grow on synthetic stuff.[23]

Needless to say, women in the church have long been taught, not by the Scriptures but by those who misunderstand the doctrine of the submission of women, to find their identity, not in Christ, but in their roles as wife and mother.[24] We have to deal continually with the sons and daughters of these mothers, as well as with the mothers themselves. When the mother is unaffirmed, and the rift between the real woman and the role-mask is too great, the child identifies not with the woman but with her social ideals about what a woman is. The following will, I trust, illustrate this point.

This woman, now up in years, could not relate to her mother as a flesh and blood person, a problem the other children in the family shared. She was fortunate in that she had a warm, caring father who nurtured his sons and daughters. At the same time, however, she was harmed by the fact that he idealized and idolized his wife as "socially" a step or two above himself. He must have taught his children these attitudes, for they all, though distant from her, respected her for the same reasons.

Later on in life, this daughter had a self-image that was idealized and superficial in spite of a good relationship with her father. This was because she had identified not with her mother, but with her mother's social ideals regarding what a woman is. She acted this out all her life. She could not see a man as a real person, but only as someone who acted out what she perceived as a proper role, in response to the false image she had of herself as woman. Her relationships with others askew, this woman, a devout soul, has struggled all her life to accept herself. Her loyalty to the way her parents saw reality, however, was so strong that she was never able to face the real truth about her need.

If we have failed to accept ourselves, it is vitally important for our children as well as ourselves that we seek and find the great Christian virtue of self-acceptance. To the extent we fail to gain it, we fail to get through the developmental step that ideally comes just after puberty. We will not graduate from the narcissistic period and will be stuck in a wrong form of self-love, if it is only the concern over our own "inferiority" or shortcomings. We will be unable to celebrate our inadequacy, our smallness, knowing Christ to be our full sufficiency. We cannot pass affirmation on to another if we have not received it ourselves. To the extent we cannot accept ourselves, we will be unable to affirm our sons or daughters; we will be unable to see and call forth the real person in others.

The Importance of Fathers to Self-Acceptance

So then, on the human level the key to stepping from adolescence into self-acceptance is the love and affirmation of a father. Sally with the "long body" had an affirming, loving, mature father in the home. He imaged (symbolized aright) God the Father to her. At the same time she was praying through her difficulties in accepting herself, she was receiving the blessing of a Christian father. He was doing what only a father or good father substitute can do—he was affirming her in her womanliness, that which is *other* than himself and therefore crucially complementary to himself and the true masculine everywhere. In so doing, he released her otherness and her "secret"—her true feminine giftedness and wisdom. This then made it infinitely easier for her to settle the whole matter of her unusual height with her Heavenly Father. She could respond to Him, serene in the knowledge that His ultimate blessing too was upon her, and that He had only good gifts for her.

In contrast, Molly's father left when she was an infant, and the few times she had seen him, he was unable to sustain interest in her. He had never in any way been a support to her. The masculine voice and giftedness which should have come through him—all that could first bless and then in awe *hallow* the true feminine within her—was missing. Her "secret" lay untouched by the masculine *other*; it was unawakened, unrecognized, unblessed. There would be no release of the inner being who joyfully responds, in trust and without anxiety, to God and to others. Until healed, she would fear abandonment and even expect that she deserved such.

For Molly, then, there was no release of the true feminine, no fatherly finger pointing the way up and out to the greater world and to a secure place within it. Even though she was Christian, there was little rest in God the Father for her—that which complements the unique feminine capacity to simply be. She had little real understanding that she could look up to Him and receive what had been missing in her life. On the other hand, she felt a compelling need to deny her past and her sinfulness and to transfer blame for it onto others. There was the painful striving to be perfect on her own in order to win God's love and acceptance, and that of others.

A mother, no matter how whole and affirming she is, cannot bridge the gap left by a missing father, or one who is present but unable to love or affirm, or one who is hostile, weak, overinvolved with business. It is extremely odd and irrational that some would think she could.

The father, by the same token, cannot fill the void left by a whole, loving mother. It is in the love of a mother, in a self-giving and secure nurturing by her, that we come to an all-important *sense of being* or of *well-being*. If this is missing, then the best of fathers cannot affirm the child in his or her personal and gender identity until healing takes place.[25] In such cases, there will be an intense sense of deprivation along with bouts of depression and separation anxiety. The painful sense of nonbeing must be addressed in the Presence of God the Father, for only He can create a sense of being where one has had such a difficult start in life.

But just as the mother is so vital to those first months and even years (the infant does not know itself to be separate from its mother, and it is in her love and acceptance that it comes to a secure sense of being), so the father is vital in affirming the child's gender identity.

This is not to say that the love and affirmation of both parents aren't vitally important all along. It is simply to say that in the developmental steps the child takes, the parents do not have the same function. There is a stage between three to six years that is also extremely important to gender identity, and here again, the father is vital. He then, even as later, calls the child up and out of mother—calls it up and points the way outward into the world. Many times when I've prayed with men suffering homosexual neurosis, I found it was at this very point that something traumatic had happened. The memory relived is that of a rejection by the father that impeded their coming up and out of the feminine milieu and gender identity. While achieving a sense of being in a mother's love, the child must separate its identity from her. And the role the father plays here is critical. Needless to say, if a father is present but has no relationship with the child, he will be ineffective in these developmental stages.

During and after puberty, if all goes well, the father must effectively "come between" the son and the mother. In this way he helps his wife to release the son (her main work of mothering is finished). In affirming the son *as a man*, the father enables him to completely separate his sexual and gender identity from his mother's. He does much the same for his daughter, only in the matter of gender identity her need is not so critical as her brother's, for she is the *same* as her mother. But he is key in affirming his daughter as a person in her own right, and with his affirmation she will be secure in her own feminine identity.

It is in dialogue with others that we are called to life.[26] Our parents are our first dialogue partners, and their communication with us from conception on through adolescence is crucial to our development. It either calls us into life or fails to. If our parents were uncommunicative or communicative in the wrong way, we must make up for this deficit in wholesome ways. Our reactions to a parental failure in communication are what we must observe and rectify. We cannot deny gross deficits, but must recognize and come to terms with them. It is essential of course that we forgive our parents.[27] It is our grievous reactions to the shortcomings and sins of others against us that make up so much of the matter to be dealt with in healing prayer. Once these subjective reactions are identified and we set out with the help of God to change them, we are on our way to wholeness. It is in great and good conversation with persons of wisdom, and above all, with our Heavenly Father, that we deal aright with these matters and begin to receive the healing we need. Our inner being, should it suffer a gaping chasm of emptiness and sense of nonbeing, waits to receive (above all) the Word, Christ Himself. And then, with Him, all the *words* of life. Truth, love, understanding, light, joy, faithfulness to the way things really are—all these good things and many more begin to flow into our souls on the wings of real communication with others. It is in conversation with God, with that which is other than ourselves, that we become.

The reason, then, so few come out of puberty and adolescence having accepted themselves has to do with the breakup of the home, the impaired ability of mothers to nurture their infants, and the absence of whole affirming fathers. Additionally, in the social environment of today—with its overheated, even pornographic media, its autonomous and thoroughly secularized public schools, and its culture actively hostile to Judeo-Christian morality and values—young people are called out from under their parent's influence before the necessary affirmation is set in. In these circumstances, the father loses his children to the peer group and to terrible psychological harm from drugs, sex, and so on, before they get through adolescence.

CHAPTER 4

Affirmation: What It Is and How It Is Received

It is in the love and affirmation of those around us as we are growing up that we gain a reasonably self-assured view of ourselves. If those who cared for us approved of us, then, being privileged to see ourselves through their eyes, we feel it is good and right to be ourselves. There are various degrees in the withholding of approval. Thus, the harm done varies.

In one sense we cannot overstate the importance of the loving acceptance and affirmation we need in order to accept ourselves. In another sense, this affirmation is never fully adequate to get the job done. Even if the love is there, the rejections we experience in a fallen world can hold us back from being able to receive it until we are healed. We are like the autistic baby who, no matter how loving his mother, is injured somehow and unable to receive her love; we are like the adopted child, the one so wounded due to loss of natural parents that he cannot love and appreciate the love and nurture his adopted parents long to lavish upon him.

We live in a fallen world; we are fallen. We cannot love as we would even those dearest to us. If we could, they would perhaps make idols of us; we would be their god. This happens even so, and it too is an evil. We all must eventually turn to the Master Affirmer, God the Father, for our true identity, our real, authentic selves. He heals the unaffirmed by sending His affirming word. And we all must receive this, those who are psychologically healthy due to affirmation on the natural plane, as well as those who were deprived of that. We are all unaffirmed in the higher sense until we find ourselves complete in Him.

You might ask yourself at this point: "What person in my life made me feel good about myself?" And then before reading further, write out in your prayer journal what that person did.

An ever-present and always affirming person in my life was my Aunt Rhoda. When I was a small child, an adolescent, and throughout my life, she never failed to make me feel good about myself. There was never a conscious effort on her part to affirm. In fact, the word was not part of her vocabulary. She herself loved to receive compliments, and she accepted them as a child would—with a kind of excitement: "My! That's a great thing to say about someone! Do you think it can be true!" There was joy and grace in the way she received them. In this way she taught me to pass on compliments—an important lesson, I think, and far more important than most people know. So she did not walk about thinking, *I need to affirm this or that person,* a mistaken route some parents take, and the children know it immediately. The act of affirming as a utilitarian method or duty simply doesn't work. It's far too shallow to get the job done.

Aunt Rhoda loved truth and goodness. The reason I always came away from her feeling encouraged was that she somehow managed to see *what was right and good in me* and praised it. Affirming persons praise the good wherever they see it, and they are always looking for it. In this way Aunt Rhoda was very Godlike, for that is surely what He does. Most people think He's looking for just the opposite in us, but in my many years of keeping a prayer journal, I've found He affirms with incredibly encouraging words. I have only the task of receiving them.

Something else characterizes affirming persons. There is not a mean, envious cell or bone in their bodies. Having accepted themselves, they help others do the same. They have no need to level others to a smaller size, thereby making themselves appear larger.

"Folly is bound up in the heart of a child," even as the Scriptures remind us (Proverbs 22:15). In order to see anything good in me, Aunt Rhoda had to look through bushels of foolishness (and God only knows what else) in my childish heart, and then later on in my adolescent and young adult heart. In "looking through" it, she didn't ignore it. She simply called foolishness (or whatever else) by its real name. But she never saw that as the real me.[1]

The truly affirming person, it seems to me, sees the good and the true in a person and calls it forth. Aunt Rhoda was always doing this, not only with me but with everyone fortunate enough to be in her orbit. She, an authentic person, always related to the authentic person in me. She called it forth.

Some may be thinking, "Ah, but Aunt Rhoda's circumstances in life must have been uncommonly good." As a matter of fact, few women would have psychologically or spiritually survived her particular situation. She was married to my Uncle Gus, who was as disagreeable and as prejudiced and as utterly pessimistic about people as my aunt was agreeable, big-hearted, and optimistic. They lived in close proximity to the household in which I grew up, one that consisted of my mother, sister, and grandmother. Because they were childless, they had time and interest to invest in my sister and me. We loved them dearly, but were aware at the same time that Aunt Rhoda was our haven of normalcy and safety from the irrationality that characterized our uncle. Never until I read Tolstoy's *War and Peace* did I ever glimpse another character such as my Uncle Gus. It was old Count Bolkonsky, a man who did everything (or so it seemed to me as I read the book) out of irritation and anger, at least where his daughter was concerned.

My Uncle Gus was far from being a prince, but in his own orbit, he lived as if he were one. Though at odds with the whole world, he was perfectly satisfied with himself. He owned and operated an automotive garage, and if a customer's appearance (for whatever reason) displeased him, he would not work on that person's car. Always too as if that treatment were not enough, he would roundly insult the person in the bargain. Uncle Gus was a "leveler." He leveled others clear to the ground, on principle.

When on occasion I as a child witnessed his irrational mistreatment of another, I was thoroughly mortified. Pained to the very core of my being for the person he wounded, I would press close to Aunt Rhoda for support. Seeing it all occur, she would simply look at him and say, "Now, Gus, if you want to be a jackass, you go right ahead. But Leanne and I, we are not going to let that ruin our day, are we, Leanne?" And at that, her arm around my shoulder, she would look down at me and in her lovely southern drawl say something like the following: "Now, child, you have to grow a niiice, thiiick alligator hide." And then, mixing her metaphors just a little, she'd say: "This is no skin off your nose, you know." Then she would look at Uncle Gus and the person he had just wounded, and she would leave Gus to shoulder the burden of his own asininity.

It was in this way, free from some painful subjective reaction, that she always handled such a situation. She put everything in its right perspective by speaking the truth that not only aptly named the problem, but reminded us that Gus did not have to live from his lower self. If he did, we were not responsible either for his act or to try to change him. It was in calling actions and situations by their real names, then, and not by trying to cover over or "fix" things that Aunt Rhoda ministered deeply to both the injured person and myself. She would then in one way or another give me a lesson in how to handle such things—always, as I realize now—with objectivity.

As the wife of Uncle Gus, it was her lot to live through this sort of scene over and over again. Always when I had been present, she would soon find the occasion to remind me of all my Uncle Gus's good points. "He's a moral man; he is a faithful husband," and so on, something that at the time seemed faint recommendation. My honest, unspoken reaction was, "Who cares that a man is faithful and honest if he's going to act like that!" She would go on to remind me that, "He loves you and your little sister, Leanne," and of course I would try to receive that.

Aunt Rhoda treated Uncle Gus as she treated everyone else—with respect, and never as less than a person. And though I realize this will strain the credulity of some, I never heard her speak a critical word about him or complain about the difficulties he caused. She simply called asininity what it was as it came out in Gus's behavior.

She saw and affirmed the good in him, and she loved him. She somehow saw the real Gus, the man God intended him to be. Therefore, she could forgive him his constant lack of feeling and intelligence. He was what I now know to be a "dry alcoholic."[2] Long before families of alcoholics were taught not to enable drinkers, Aunt Rhoda had a full grasp of the principle. Gus's father had been grievously alcoholic, and had it not been for Rhoda, Gus would have been too. But it was as an unhealed "dry alcoholic" that my Uncle Gus went to his grave. He never knew what normal is and was satisfied always that his mission in life was to level everyone. The miracle was that my aunt, whom he loved as much as he could love anyone, was never diminished by him. She never "bought into" his disease by taking responsibility for his behavior. She knew who she was. She had accepted herself. She stood tall, and even in joy, the whole of her life.

Gus was the one man who was always there in my growing-up years. Had Aunt Rhoda or my mother been at all codependent, i.e., had they subjectively reacted to him and found their lives shaped by his problems, they would have bent into him and crumpled under such a heavy weight. Had they listened to some of their pastors or teachers in that day, they would have tried as women to help him to wholeness through abdicating their true selves and becoming much less than God created them to be. They both knew far better than to put themselves into subjection to the spiritual and psychological darkness that had so diminished him. And because of this, they never sinned against him. Had they been less than who they were, it is questionable how things would have turned out for my sister and me. As youngsters, had we early come under the "leveler" or the "jackass" in my Uncle Gus, it is my belief that we would have been severely emotionally damaged. As it was, however, we had extraordinary models in our aunt and mother. We, like they, ended up loving and caring for Gus to the end of his days. He was a man with virtually no friends or intimates besides ourselves. Aunt Rhoda was able to love him, and then we in turn were—because we were never under any illusion about calling foolishness by its real name, sin by its real name, hard ignorant prejudice by its real name. We were not deceived by erroneous notions about submitting improperly to male sinfulness, and so did not sacrifice the new and true self on the altar of Uncle Gus's infirmity.

God, the Master Affirmer

In the Presence of God the Master Affirmer, the real self in union with Christ comes forward. He sees His Son in me. He calls us forward.

Though Aunt Rhoda, as well as my mother, were affirming, free, whole women who affirmed me in so very many ways, they could not affirm me as a woman and, therefore, as a person. They could not bring me out of puberty and into self-acceptance the way an affirming father or father-figure could have done. I was past thirty when I began working through the failure to accept myself. I learned to come to God the Father for affirmation. He then not only affirmed me as a woman and as a full person in my own right, but ministered into my life the masculine giftedness I lacked because of being fatherless. He gave me the power that enabled me to better contain the feminine world of meaning—to orient it, direct it, order it, and then to take full responsibility for my gift. God has called me, He has gifted me. I cannot deny the gift; I cannot project it onto others and demand they live it out for me. I have permission to be, to move, to walk with God.

Back to Molly

In the case of Molly, she was unable to receive the affirmation her mother and others held out to her. She was far too wounded due to the breakup in her family. As circumstances would have it, a young minister fell in love with her, and she married him. None of this pain had been resolved. She carried guilt and self-hatred over her sexual behavior into the marriage.

It so happened that her husband emphasized the "submission" (meaning subjection) of woman to her husband. He did not teach it as the Scriptures do, but simplistically, as those who have a faulty understanding of authority do. Because she hated herself, Molly willingly, even gladly embraced extreme teachings on submission to one's husband. It was in this way that she submerged her personality in his.

Her husband had been a model Christian boy, a model teenager. He was good, she was foul (or so her thinking went). A kind of spiritual schizophrenia took place: "As I grow more and more in ministry, I hate myself all the more. . . . There are two parts of me. . . . People don't realize this. I can't go on." Molly was trying to minister to others, to "give out," while at the same time she felt, in her own words, more and more split. Having missed the vital step of self-acceptance, she was paralyzed in immature and wrong-headed attitudinal patterns toward the self—to the point there was hardly a self from which to act, to be.

Do you have any idea how many Christian leaders are right here? How many go home after successful ministry and preaching services and suffer the throes of the damned as all the voices of self-hatred well up from their unhealed hearts to accuse them?

With Molly, the self-hatred was so great, her splitness so intense, that her physical body was now showing the effects. There was for her no true self—no solid sense of a center within from which to move.

I meet these Christians everywhere. They may know the Scriptures by heart; they may have their theological lessons down pat. And they can preach to others for a while. Then the pain becomes unbearable. They begin to break apart as the conscious mind wearies and loses its capacity to control and hold down the pain from the deeper levels of the mind and heart. This pain then, like the flame under a furnace, begins to erupt in smoky signals of compulsive behavior. There are falls into sinful, aberrant behavior in order to allay the pain of the unaffirmed, lost self. The failure to accept the self—this is the crisis of the unaffirmed.

Healing for the Mollys in This World

When Jesus read from the scroll of the prophet Isaiah these words: "The Spirit of the Lord is on me, because he has anointed me to preach good news to the poor. He has sent me to proclaim freedom for the prisoners," and so on, He was talking about the Mollys of this world. The good news for the Mollys is redemption, not only from sin, but from the effects of the sins of others. We proclaim this freedom to them in such a way as they can come running, flying, walking, or hobbling on crutches out of their prisonhouses. The pace varies, but the good news is that they are to be ushered out of the darkness of bondage and into the sunlight of identity and freedom.

Some would attempt to usher them into freedom apart from healing them, but this was never our Lord's way. He taught us to heal as well as to disciple His wounded ones. We must first bind up their wounds.

Molly needed healing of the "inner person" in the worst way, though her narrow religious background had prejudiced her against this kind of healing. She needed to understand why she was hurting so badly, and then she needed prayer for healing of memories—a thorough giving and receiving of forgiveness, as we will show in discussing the next two barriers to wholeness. She needed to forgive the very circumstances of her life—all those that went along with being the child of divorced parents and of severe economic hardship. But once this was done, she had to face the theological answer to her dilemma of being unable to accept herself.

Theological Solution to a Psychological and Spiritual Problem

> What our Lord wants us to present to Him is not goodness, nor honesty, nor endeavor, but real solid sin; that is all He can take from us. And what does He give in exchange for our sin? Real solid righteousness.[3]

Having addressed Molly's psychological need, we must now address her crying spiritual need: She would have to confess the sin of pride. Molly must come once again to the foot of the cross and there look up to the Crucified. She must say to Him, "Your death for my sin is sufficient." She would then have to acknowledge Him as her righteousness. "God made him who had no sin to be sin for us, so that in him we might become the righteousness of God" (2 Corinthians 5:21).

She would need to once again confess her sexual sins, but this time, receive the forgiveness. In rejecting and hating herself, she had fallen into pride. Herein is the pride: She wanted to be good enough on her own. It is so abominably hard for people to admit that they are not good enough—that the cross of Christ really was necessary, even for them. Molly would have to take a longer, broader look at the cross of Christ and incorporate into her emotional and spiritual life the great and utterly grave knowledge of our justification in and through the shed blood of Christ. In doing this, she would have to come to terms with the depths of sin in her heart and acknowledge her self-deception.

Just as sons or daughters often will try the rest of their lives to win the love of an unaffirming parent—by great exploits or accomplishments or whatever—so people try to keep the law on their own and thereby win God's love. They want to be righteous by having kept the law perfectly. They want, in short, their own righteousness, not His. And this is where the pride comes in.

The humility that acknowledges ourselves as truly fallen is a first priority in coming to accept ourselves. You may be asking, "Stress humility to the one who hates himself?" Yes, for self-hatred in the Christian is a substitute for humility; it belongs to pride.

I believe the confession of pride here at this point is the foundation of all progress, spiritual and otherwise. We all must confess the pride that refuses to acknowledge that we have indeed lost the divine splendor. We are indeed fallen and have acted out our fallenness.

> The greatest blessing spiritually is the knowledge that we are destitute; until we get there, Our Lord is powerless.[4]

Apart from God we have been and are in many ways monstrous; we do monstrous things. When we are properly related to God, we silence the accuser of our souls by admitting, "Yes, I am capable of the petty; I am capable of the monstrous; and if He should leave me but for a moment, I should do yet worse."

The humble acceptance of myself as fallen but now justified by Another who is my righteousness is the basis on which I can accept myself, learn to laugh at myself, be patient with myself. And then, wonder of wonders, be enabled for at least part of the time to forget myself. "Humble yourselves—feeling very insignificant—in the presence of the Lord, and He will exalt you. He will lift you up and make your lives significant" (James 4:10, *The Amplified Bible*).

St. Paul reminds us, "For [again from Scripture] 'No human being can be justified in the sight of God' for having kept the law: law brings only the consciousness of sin" (Romans 3:20, NEB). Molly was plenty conscious of her past sins—they colored her whole view of herself. Keeping the law (or having kept it!) does not exclude pride, but as the apostle says, "faith does" (Romans 3:27, NEB)—faith in Another who alone is my righteousness.

The Way of Self-Acceptance

> Give ear and come to me; hear me, that your soul may live. (Isaiah 55:3)

No one else can ever accept me for me, or you for you. All of us, like Molly, must confess our pride and then receive the healing word from God in order to accept ourselves. It is imperative that we begin earnestly listening to God the Father, the One who waits to bring us out of fearful, dependent relationships and into right relationship with Himself and others. This will occur quite naturally as we spread out before Him every diseased thought and attitudinal pattern. Then, as His precious chosen ones, we listen and receive the truth and reality He gives to replace them. That is how we bring dysfunctional, sinful, prideful patterns in the thought life and the imagination into submission to Christ. It is in this way that fleshly and demonic strongholds in the mind and imagination are torn down.

As for the Molly in our story, God the Father will in this process affirm her as a woman and as a person. The authentic self, the *real* Molly, will come to the fore quite naturally and more or less unconsciously. If Molly turns inward and introspectively tries to see this affirmation occurring, she will get in the way of her healing. At this point she is rather to note the bent, dependent behavior, especially in the many ways it manifests in her relationship to her husband, but she should not agonize over it. Rather, she is to spread this out before God and learn from Him and from others who are walking in freedom how to come out of what has been an unconscious idolatry. Her attention is to be directed outward in loving, listening-obedience to God, and it is in this stance that she will be receiving all the promises of God, even His everlasting covenant of faithful love and mercy. The hungry, thirsty, unaffirmed places within her will receive food and drink.

> Come, all you who are thirsty,
> come to the waters;
> and you who have no money,
> come, buy and eat!
> Come, buy wine and milk without money and without cost. . . .
> Listen, listen to me, and eat what is good,
> and your soul will delight in the richest of fare. (Isaiah 55:1-3)

In this stance of listening prayer, every thought of the mind, every imagination of the heart, is brought captive to Christ. Much will be utterly obliterated; what remains will be transformed. As her relationship to God is righted, her relationships to others will change, and this can be quite threatening and tumultuous. For example, Molly needed to realize that she had not seen her husband aright. She had idealized him as "the perfect Christian man," relating to him not as the man he really was, but to the "image" or "persona" he had been maintaining. She was fearful of being abandoned by him, while at the same time she was ambivalent toward him—both loving and hating him. This in turn left her open to the attentions of other men, a thing she hated and feared in herself.

Perhaps one of the most surprising things she learned was that he needed as much if not more help than she did. But he was far from acknowledging his need. Hadn't he kept the law perfectly? His rigid, even pharisaical attitudes became apparent as she straightened up from her bentness toward him and found her true identity in Christ. She had to come out of denial and acknowledge that he was emotionally remote and separated in large part from what it means to be human and caring, that he was well on his way to becoming a religious bigot, and that she has been affirming and enabling him in all this.

All this insight takes time, and mercifully, we are not usually required to come out of all of our denial overnight. In order to find wholeness for herself and her marriage, however, Molly had to face all this. She had to fully repent of her part in all of it, acknowledging her self-deception and her responsibility in their difficulties. Listening prayer is an essential for all of us. In the case of the Mollys, those who have in the name of religion put to death the real self, it is like a lifeline thrown to a drowning person. Once they have grasped it, they will come alive both psychologically and spiritually.

Catching Up with St. Paul

Christians, by and large, do not understand Romans and Galatians, which set out their freedom in Christ. Their tendency is either to remain or to come back under law and condemnation rather than to walk in the Spirit, listening to and obeying their Lord.

Paul cried out to the Romans: "There is no condemnation for those who are united with Christ Jesus, because in Christ Jesus the life-giving law of the Spirit has set you free from the law of sin and death" (Romans 8:1-2, NEB).

The occasion for his outcry—the Romans were tending to come back under the law rather than to walk in the Spirit because of the "Judaizers" among them. To walk in the Spirit is to cease striving in our own strength and goodness, and to walk in His. It is to celebrate our smallness, our inadequacy apart from Him. It is to admit that He alone is our righteousness. We cannot keep the law. *Another*, the Holy Other, must do it for us. To walk in the Spirit is to live in the present moment, always looking to Christ, always practicing His Presence, always moving in tandem with Him.

The Role of the Minister

As ministers we can never choose this freedom for another; the person needing it must choose it. We can pray for the healing of a passive and/or a rebellious will,[5] thereby freeing the person who so desires to choose aright. But we cannot coerce another. Jesus never did. As Oswald Chambers has said, "Christ never cajoled anyone." Christian counselors, like parental figures, are often sorely tempted to take such a responsibility upon themselves. But we can never change anyone. We can and must, however, speak the truth. The truth proclaimed in the power of the Spirit is what changes people. They then have the responsibility for listening and for preparing the ground of their hearts to receive the golden grain of truth God is always sowing.

The acceptance of oneself, like all that is great and valid in the Christian faith, can never be a secondhand experience. We must, each of us, apprehend Christ and the fullness of His salvation for ourselves. To so apprehend Him is to come into our full uniqueness. To help others apprehend Him is to point always and unswervingly to Him and to personal communication with Him.

It is in looking to Him that we become like Him! Tyrants, as C. S. Lewis has said, are monotonously alike—their minds are on themselves and their own aggrandizement. But as for the great saints, that is another matter. There is incredible diversity among them. We need think only of the twelve apostles, of Augustine, Luther, Ignatius of Loyola, St. Francis of Assisi, St. Theresa, Dwight L. Moody, C. S. Lewis, to name a few.

I want to be a disciple of Jesus. Adam Clarke, C. S. Lewis, Oswald Chambers, Agnes Sanford, F. B. Meyer, R. A. Torrey, Thomas à Kempis, and especially my own mother—all these (and many more) mean so much to me. I thank God regularly for them. Their faith, their keen minds, their very lives and wisdom have nourished me. They were, however, but ministers to bring me to Christ.

To be a disciple of a disciple is to be pale indeed. I do not want to be a pale Christian. With St. Paul, I say, "To me to live is Christ." With St. John, I lean my head on Christ's breast and hear what He says to me. This is the walk in the Spirit. This is the way we come out from under a law or many laws to abide in Christ. This is the way we cross over into a serene self-acceptance, no matter what our psychological needs have been and into the freedom of the realized true self in Christ.

Slaying Shame

> When you were slaves to sin, you were free from the control of righteousness. What benefit did you reap at that time from the things you are now ashamed of? Those things result in death! But now that you have been set free from sin and have become slaves to God, the benefit you reap leads to holiness, and the result is eternal life. (Romans 6:20-22)

For some, like Molly, once pride is confessed, there is the giant, shame, to deal with. In our Pastoral Care conferences over the years and in counseling, we've seen all manner of sexual brokenness. All of us know shame and have committed shameful deeds. But for the sexually abused and for those who have misused their bodies in promiscuous and/or perverted sex, the shame engendered can be a very large barrier to self-acceptance.

The good news is we have been given the antidote for shame. My prayer partners and I were in prayer, and the word *shame* had not been mentioned. But we were praying about the matter of self-hatred, the fact that so many Christians are stuck in it and fail to move on to a secure acceptance of themselves in Christ. As I was asking the Lord for grace to write of this in such a way that people could come free, Connie Boerner received a strong word from the Lord. It came in the form of a vision that expressed the full meaning of the cross. She shared it with us so vividly that we felt as if we too had seen it.

Connie saw two medieval soldiers in battle. One was filled with light, and his shield was illuminated. He held a sword in his left hand. The name over him was FORGIVENESS.

The other soldier was gray and illusory, almost a vapor, but very powerful. He also had a shield and a sword, but his shield was black. His name was SHAME.

FORGIVENESS stepped forward, plunged his sword into SHAME, and SHAME was slain.

This is precisely the way it is when we finally acknowledge our sin, crying out, "Lord, I have sinned against You and against my own body." We then open fully to receive to the very depths of our being His forgiveness for all our sin, and go on from there to just as deeply forgive and fully release others.

When people feel great shame, they usually also project considerable blame on others. King David, the man after God's own heart, is a great model for us in this respect. When confronted, he immediately accepted full responsibility for his sin.

> Against you, you only, have I sinned
> and done what is evil in your sight,
> so that you are proved right when you speak
> and justified when you judge.
> Surely I was sinful at birth,
> sinful from the time my mother conceived me.
> Surely you desire truth in the inner parts;
> you teach me wisdom in the inmost place. (Psalm 51)

Those struggling with pride and its consequent denial and transference of guilt onto others can be healed through praying the prayers of David in Psalm 51.

This is what the cross of Christ is all about. It causes us to acknowledge our sinful state and allows us to see His atoning death for our sin and His life in exchange for our death.

Several times recently in prayer with the team or alone, I've seen with my heart an exceedingly large cup brimming over (even aflame) with the LIFE of God that is to come to us. Even as we see Christ crucified for us and our sins flowing into Him as we confess them, so we in turn are to receive the eternal life, the eternal cup and bread, from the Risen Lord. We may want to see this huge cup with the eyes of our hearts, the cup he proffers to us even now, saying, "Take, and drink; this is My blood, given for you." This is My LIFE, eternal life, flowing into you, that which cleanses and washes away every stain, that which brings forgiveness and life. No matter how deep the wounding and horrendous the sin, the acknowledgment of ourselves as sinful from birth, the reception of Christ's forgiveness, and the extending of this forgiveness to others releases us from self-hatred and shame. Most truly,

FORGIVENESS slays SHAME.

CHAPTER 5

Listening Prayer: The Way of Grace and the Walk in the Spirit

Do not think that I have come to abolish the Law or the Prophets; I have not come to abolish them but to fulfill them. I tell you the truth, until heaven and earth disappear, not the smallest letter, not the least stroke of a pen, will by any means disappear from the Law until everything is accomplished. Anyone who breaks one of the least of these commandments and teaches others to do the same will be called least in the kingdom of heaven, but whoever practices and teaches these commands will be called great in the kingdom of heaven. For I tell you that unless your righteousness surpasses that of the Pharisees and the teachers of the law, you will certainly not enter the kingdom of heaven.

(Matthew 5:17-20)

The extraordinarily wonderful thing about listening prayer is that it is not only the vital step we take toward self-acceptance, but it is also the same step that begins the walk in the Spirit for all of us, no matter what our psychological needs may be. Three chapters from my book *The Broken Image* deal with listening prayer, and these should be studied in conjunction with the crucial matter of self-acceptance. They are "Listening for the Healing Word" (chapter 6), "The Identity Crisis According to the Scriptures" (chapter 5), and the Appendix, "Listening to Our Dreams."

An Assignment to Help Us Get Started

Remember now that neither I nor anyone else can die to your old diseased attitudinal patterns for you; no one can pray over you the magical prayer that will do the instantaneous trick. But I can introduce you to miracle, that of the creature in holy converse with the Creator.

Once Molly confesses her pride, then she must keep her face turned upward (not toward me or any other human counselor, but to God). When she turns to me, I point her to God and teach her to listen to Him.

The first assignment I give a Molly is to go through the Gospels and personalize every promise and every command of Christ to His disciples. I ask her to write these out, addressed to her by name, in a fresh, new prayer journal. "Fresh" and "new" is stipulated because, if the person needing to accept herself has already been journaling, the pages of her journal will more than likely be filled with introspective musings. It will reflect more or less a "practice of the presence of self" in isolation from the Presence of God and the words He is speaking. It may reflect a losing battle with oppressive thoughts and merely be a record of all the old musings on diseased attitudinal patterns.

But the new journal will reflect true prayer. It will be a place where the person can bring the most diseased thoughts and patterns before God, look at them objectively, and then receive what God is speaking into the situation. The person will be exchanging old ways of seeing for God's way, old patterns for new ones. And the new ones are to be written out. This first exercise, besides bringing the needy one into a two-way conversation with God, will cause the person to deal with all the "I can'ts" in his or her life. It will bring the person into the radical obedience to Christ that prepares us for the other listening we must do.

The Power of Right Thinking

> If your self-acceptance rests on maintaining an image of yourself as a nice, good person who never did anything wrong on purpose, then you cannot allow much truth into your field of vision. True self-acceptance is in stark contrast to this self-delusion. Self-acceptance does not survive honesty; it rests on it. The Christian is not someone who is so brave or thick-skinned that he can face the truth about himself unafraid; rather he is a sinner who can face his sin because he has confidence that God has forgiven and accepted him in spite of it.[1]

When we need healing of our emotional and feeling being, we necessarily have negative, distorted thinking about ourselves and others. We do not ignore or deny it, but we write it out as specifically as we can, just as we do with our sins, and say to God, "Look at this. I don't want this. You take it!" We name it as the distorted thinking that it is. Then we replace it with right thinking—those light-filled thoughts and attitudes in line with truth and the way things *really* are. Remember, nature abhors a vacuum, and other negative patterns flood in when the old diseased ones are not replaced by the true.

Christians, of all people, are to think positively. We alone have reason never to despair. Faith and hope are ours, and they shine like beacons in the darkest circumstances. When our negative thoughts about ourselves are based in unremitted guilt, we immediately confess the sin and petition for cleansing. Then, as we hear what God is saying to us as cleansed souls, we make sure we do not continue to despise ourselves for past failures.

But negative thoughts toward the self that are not based in true guilt come from pride and rebellion rather than from humility (as some think and teach). Our consciences are to be cleansed, made holy and free. Guilt and negativity drive us toward sin and despair, not away from it. Freedom from guilt and full acceptance of forgiveness stop short of libeling the cross of Christ, of saying, "Jesus and His blood are not enough for me." Such is the "humility" of self-hatred, and it is rooted in something other than Christian theology.

In all this, we acknowledge the power of the mind, and we acknowledge the truth of Scriptures, "As a man thinketh in his heart, so is he." It is remarkable what we can do merely through the power of positive thinking toward changing our old negatives into positives.

Hopefully, we realize that we need to train our minds to think. Period. Let us hope, as well, we are not found among those Christians who seem to think that faith excuses them from thinking. Historically, Christians have been accused of *fideism*, the belief that faith *alone*, that is, apart from the exercise of reason, is the basis of knowledge (one of the misguided reactions of Christians to the schism between faith and reason. See *The Healing Presence*, chapter 10). But long before there were confused Christians, Socrates said, "Most are misologists"; in other words, most people hate to think. Some people are very sick indeed because they hate to think; they are too passive and lazy to think through their problems with God. This is mental sloth and should be confessed as such. But in the Scriptures we read: "Come let us reason together, saith the Lord."

And this remarkable invitation from God to reason with Him, when accepted, puts us a grand leap ahead of positive thinking alone. It brings us to the vital matter of listening prayer. We will think positively, all right, with all the faith and hope that is ours in Christ, but as we do this, we will be thinking through all the issues of our lives with God. Then, as we learn to hear God, we will receive from Him the true word, and we replace our old diseased negatives with the positive word He is always sending.

Sister Penelope Learns to Listen

The following example of listening prayer illustrates the way God so powerfully uses the Scriptures we've stored away in our hearts. We sometimes receive messages from Him that are not Scripture, *per se*, but they are always *scriptural*. That is, they are never in disagreement with the Scriptures, but are in full harmony with them and are always to be judged by them.

This story concerns Sr. Penelope, an attractive, saucy nun who had always been at odds with herself. There were, she said, certain sins in her life she had been unable to overcome. She wanted so very much to love God, to do His will ("I have dedicated my entire life to God; I would hold nothing back"), yet she felt rebellious and unlovable. She never felt close to the God she served. She and the other nuns met regularly for prayer in the convent. For twenty years her corporate prayers with the sisters, as well as her private prayers, were filled with negative thoughts about herself and her relationship to the God to whom she had chosen to give all.

She had gone through different kinds of "therapy" for her "problems" when I first met with her for prayer. I was definitely a last resort. She would have continued serving God the rest of her life the best she knew how, though thinking herself alienated from Him and full of hatred for herself.

I prayed with her, helping her to receive forgiveness, and asked her to consciously and deliberately practice the Presence of Christ. This she agreed to do. I then asked her to pay attention to and write out in a new prayer journal her negative thoughts and thought patterns, and then listen to the word God was speaking to her—those words from Him that would replace the negative, diseased patterns of thought. I asked her to discern where the diseased words were coming from—the world, the flesh, or the devil. This she agreed to do. I asked her to confess the pride that had kept her back from self-acceptance, and she did that. It wasn't long before I had a letter from her.

> It didn't take more than a couple of minutes to write down ten negative thoughts to work on. I'm sure I can find more, but that's enough for the moment! I decided to take one a day for cancellation. Wonderful and happy chance! The first black thought to be dissolved was:
>
> *God will never speak to me.*
>
> Obviously, if that couldn't be erased, I'd have a lot of trouble doing anything else! The "answer" was not a direct refutation of the complaint, but rather it was sort of drowned out by that verse in Psalm 85, "I will listen to what the Lord is saying, for He is speaking peace to His faithful people and to those who turn their hearts to Him." The next was:
>
> *God can't do anything with me; I'm too selfish.*
>
> It melted before, "As many as received Him, to them gave He power to become sons of God," and "He will make your righteousness as clear as the light and your just dealing as the noonday."
>
> But yesterday cut and healed at heart level. *I'll never be able to surrender to God* met Ezekiel 36:16-36, but especially verses 25-27. "I will sprinkle clean water on you, and you will be clean; I will cleanse you from all your impurities and from all your idols. I will give you a new heart and put a new spirit in you; I will remove from you your heart of stone and give you a heart of flesh. And I will put my Spirit in you and move you to follow my decrees and be careful to keep my laws."
>
> The surrender issue is of long, long standing. I have felt as though my hands were hopelessly clamped onto my life, control, a driver's wheel, a rope—*something* that had to be let go, but I couldn't pry my grip loose, and confessors who demanded a verbal declaration of surrender made me feel

> only *more* guilty and frustrated and hypocritical because I knew the words couldn't effect the reality. And now—it doesn't matter anymore! It is God's responsibility. I can trust Him to give me the heart and spirit of surrender when it pleases Him. . . .

As soon as she got through the ten negative thoughts about herself, she wrote again, ecstatically:

> Joy continues to well up in me. The negative thoughts just haven't any hooks to hang on any more, and I am becoming less Leah and more Rachel. . . .

Then, in a few more days, I received this remarkable word from her:

> What you gave me was marriage counseling—you got me ready for a wedding!

I then got word from another nun in the convent. The message was this: "Sr. P. is so joyous, the convent is fairly rocking!"

The Mystical Wedding

Here we see the mystical wedding—the wedding of the soul to Christ. That is what listening prayer is all about. That is what any journaling worthy of the name Christian is all about. That is what happens when we decide to quit listening to all the other voices of the world, the flesh, and the devil—when we rightly discern and refute them where necessary and start really listening to God and receiving from Him. This Scriptural promise comes to pass—yes, even in *my* life!

> I will betroth you to Myself forever, betroth you in lawful wedlock with unfailing devotion and love; I will betroth you to Myself to have and to hold, and you shall know the Lord. (Hosea 2:19-20, NEB)

The Crucifix and the Stained-Glass Window

The more we take our place in Christ, the more of our true selves there is to accept. Though the large step of self-acceptance enables us to cross over from immaturity and bondage into maturity and freedom, there is a very real sense in which we continue to die to the old self and accept the new.

To walk in the Spirit is, at the same time, to die to the old man. It is an automatic corollary. (Some people who strive so hard, year in and year out, to die to the old man, simply need to learn to walk in the Spirit! That is the way of getting "filled up" with God, and it spares us the tormenting job of having to "empty out" so often.) Even so, because we are both sinner and saint, we need to work into our lives a regular time for kneeling as sinner before God in preparation for rising anew in our prime identity as a child of God.

For our walk in the Spirit to remain vibrant and alive, then, we need to come present to our hearts, allowing the Spirit to search and reveal them. To do this is to take once again our place in Christ's death and dying. I will be writing more on this in a later chapter, but here would like to tie this in with the matter of self-acceptance and the ongoing necessity of dying to the old self and living to the new.

C. S. Lewis writes as well as anyone I know on the old man or self, that in us which wills to be put first, to be God. It is that gravitation away from God, "the journey homeward to habitual self." When we yield to it, we find ourselves living out of another spirit altogether. This, according to St. John, is the spirit and the nature of the devil at work in us, and if we yield, we will eventually have to hear Jesus say: "You belong to your father, the devil, and you want to carry out your father's desire" (John 8:44). The desire on the part of the created to be as the Creator is the deepest taproot of pride, and we have always to cry out to God to show us our pride that we might confess and yield it up to Him:

> From the moment a creature becomes aware of God as God and of itself as self, the terrible alternatives of choosing God or self for the center open before it. This sin is committed daily by young children and ignorant peasants as well as by sophisticated persons, by solitaries no less than by those who live in society. It is the fall in every individual life and in each day of each individual life, the basic sin behind all particular sins. At this very moment you and I are either committing it or about to commit it or repenting of it.[2]

> In love we escape from our self into one another. . . . The primary impulse of each is to maintain and aggrandize himself. The secondary impulse is to go out of the self, to correct its provincialism and heal its loneliness. In love, in virtue, in the pursuit of knowledge, and in the reception of the arts, we are doing this. Obviously this process can be described either as an enlargement or as a temporary annihilation of the self. But that is an old paradox: "He that loseth his life shall save it."[3]

A terrible thing to note about the old self is that it too can pray, as Lewis's verse so graphically points out:

> *Lord that made the dragon, grant me thy peace,*
> *But say not that I should give up the gold,*
> *Nor move, nor die. Others would have the gold.*
> *Kill rather, Lord, the Men and the other dragons;*
> *Then I can sleep; go when I will to drink.*

(C. S. Lewis, "The Dragon Speaks")[4]

This "fierce imprisonment in the (old) self is but the obverse of the self-giving which is absolute reality":

> For in self-giving, if anywhere, we touch a rhythm not only of all creation but of all being. For the Eternal Word also gives Himself in sacrifice; and that not only on Calvary. . . . From before the foundation of the world He surrenders begotten Deity back to begetting Deity in obedience. . . . From the highest to the lowest, self exists to be abdicated and, by that abdication, becomes the more truly self, to be thereupon yet the more abdicated, and so forever. This is not a heavenly law which we can escape by remaining earthly, nor an earthly law which we can escape by being saved. What is outside the system of self-giving is not earth, nor nature, nor "ordinary life," but simply and solely Hell.[5]

In a city where I once lived, there was a quiet little chapel built to the side of the main sanctuary of a church. It had a wonderful crucifix over its altar, and above that an exquisite old stained-glass window depicting the risen Christ. I had learned to walk in the Spirit and knew the joy of the Lord. The ministry He entrusted me with, however, was growing rapidly. It was then that I learned to work into my life, as Agnes Sanford refers to it, a rhythm of repentance and resurrection. I was so busy serving the Lord and helping others that I usually had little or no conscious knowledge of sin and pride in my heart, but I learned to set aside a time to be very quiet, letting Him show me the repenting I needed to do and the changes I needed to make in my life. At these times, I would go to this little chapel and there look up to the crucifix.

Then when I knew what to repent of, I would in prayer take my stand in His cross with Him and die to it. Sometimes this would take a while. Having died once again with Him to the old man or self, I would (before rising from my knees!) look up to the stained-glass depiction of Him as risen Savior and take my place in His rising, all the while exulting in my forgiveness and true identity in Him.

I no longer have access to this wonderful little chapel, but this practice is firmly planted in my heart. All of us have access to Christ's cross, and to build in such a rhythm of dying and rising with Christ is surely the way we stay spiritually and psychologically healthy. This is also the way we avoid burnout. We never forget that we are both sinner (albeit justified) and saint. Our main identity is that of saint, child of God, but we retain that only by remembrance that we are not yet who we will be when time is no more. Then we will no longer have to concern ourselves with daily dying to the old man. This is all a part of listening prayer and the walk in the Spirit.

That little chapel was a very meaningful place to me, and I think it was there that I learned to ask others to look up to Christ crucified and rising again for them as they confessed their sin and received their healing. Through this process of praying with others, I have become more and more certain of this—our hearts need to picture these great and grave actions of Christ aright, for they image the great story of our salvation. The head may well know Christian doctrine while at the same time the heart is starved for the story and the experience of love and forgiveness that comes with it. It's as if God has been waiting for us to once again be able to see with our hearts the great truths of our faith and receive the healing word and vision He is always sending.

The closer we come to God, the more fully we realize that He alone is our righteousness. To try to get good enough before we accept ourselves is to bypass the way of the cross.

Christ says ever and always, "Give me your pain, your sin, your sorrow. My Life I give in exchange for all that binds you." His vocation, indeed, was to become that sin, that sorrow that has hurt us so badly, whether buried away in our memories or occurring even now in the present moment. And as we take our place in His cross, that is, in His death and dying and forgive even as He forgave, then we become "the righteousness of God" in Him. It is in this way that we can release unto Him and into Him all that has ever beset us, all that has defiled. We can forgive the deepest, most painful rejections and deprivations. We do this, knowing that we too have grievously sinned against ourselves and others. We too are fallen, and we dwell in a fallen world. "I have hurt others, Lord; I have not loved You or others as I should; forgive me, O Lord, even as I forgive others, even as I forgive all the circumstances of my life." This prayer will continue to be part of the walk in the Spirit, and He continually renews us in His love and righteousness.

PART II

THE FORGIVENESS OF SIN

Forgiveness is the exclusive prerogative of Christianity. The schools of ancient morality had four cardinal virtues—justice in human relations, prudence in the direction of affairs, fortitude in bearing trouble or sorrow, temperance or self-restraint. But they knew nothing of mercy or forgiveness, which is not natural to the human heart. Forgiveness is an exotic, which Christ brought with Him from Heaven.[1]

(F. B. Meyer)

Therefore I tell you, whatever you ask for in prayer, believe that you have received it, and it will be yours. And when you stand praying, if you hold anything against anyone, forgive him, so that your Father in heaven may forgive you your sins.

(Mark 11:24-25)

CHAPTER 6

Healing of Memories: The Forgiveness of Sin

The Spirit of the Sovereign Lord is on me,
because the Lord has anointed me
to preach good news to the poor.
He has sent me to bind up the brokenhearted,
to proclaim freedom for the captives
and release from darkness for the prisoners,
to proclaim the year of the Lord's favor
and the day of vengeance of our God,
to comfort all who mourn,
and provide for those who grieve in Zion—
to bestow on them a crown of beauty instead of ashes,
the oil of gladness instead of mourning,
and a garment of praise instead of a spirit of despair.
They will be called oaks of righteousness,
a planting of the Lord for the display of his splendor.
They will rebuild the ancient ruins
and restore the places long devastated;
they will renew the ruined cities
that have been devastated for generations.

(Isaiah 61:1-4)

When you pray, say: "Father, hallowed be your name, your kingdom come. Give us each day our daily bread. Forgive us our sins, for we also forgive everyone who sins against us. And lead us not into temptation."

(Luke 11: 2-4)

Healing of memories means forgiveness of sin. It is the heart's experience of forgiveness of sin at the precise sore spot where it is needed, one that impacts the soul in its totality—in its emotional, feeling, intuitive, imaginative capacities as well as in its more conscious, willing, thinking capacities. This place may be at any level of consciousness or unconsciousness. Nothing illustrates God's Healing Presence more wonderfully than His way of healing man's deepest hurts and memories.

Agnes Sanford coined the term at a time when very little healing was flowing through the church's formal confessional or informal prayer groups. The reason was that the central truth of God's forgiveness of sin, along with all the great spiritual realities of the Kingdom of God, had been largely relegated to the abstract. Victims of the schism between head and heart, we could "talk doctrine" but couldn't *experience* its healing power. We could not get it from our heads to our hearts.

Some could still preach great sermons about the forgiveness of sin, but could not *administer* it to the heart in need of it. In the church today, this is still largely true.

The soul in need of healing is suffering due to this same schism. The head and the heart simply are not working in a complementary fashion. The heart perhaps knows something the head does not, or conversely, the head needs to rightly comprehend and then critique what is in the heart.

The journey of life is, as Fr. Alan Jones has said, "for setting love in order."[1] A large part of that task has to do with setting our "two minds"[2] in order and in harmony, accomplished through forgiveness of sin:

> The truth is that any wound to the soul so deep that it is not healed by our own self-searching and prayers is inevitably connected with a subconscious awareness of sin, either our own sins or our grievous reactions to the sins of others. The therapy that heals these deep wounds could be called the forgiveness of sins, or it could be called the healing of memories. Whatever one calls it, there are in many of us wounds so deep that only the mediation of someone else to whom we may "bare our grief" can heal us.[3]

When someone bares his grief to us, no matter whether we are a priest, psychologist, minister, counselor, or layperson, we are to lead the person in confessional prayers. We may need to learn how to pray for the forgiveness of we know not what in the past history of his family. For example, Nehemiah and other Old Testament prophets offered prayers such as: "I confess the sins we Israelites, including myself and my father's house, have committed against you" (Nehemiah 1:6b). Or we may need to help the person forgive the circumstances of a lifetime. The point I want to stress is that we are hearing confessions of sin, and after these sins are acknowledged and repented of, we must never forget to proclaim the forgiveness of that sin as well as release from the bondage of the sins of others against us. This is the way souls find healing. It is perfectly appalling how seldom this is effectively done, even in the formal confessional.

Most often, the Holy Spirit leads very specifically in what to confess and who to forgive, but when the case is more nebulous (for example, a whole family is sick due to unconfessed sin that goes back through the generations), we need to look to God for direction in forming prayers of confession and forgiveness that will break the power of unconfessed sins over our lives. This is necessary because our woundedness and sin break our relationships. In order for these breaks to be set right, we must confess them. Is the break between myself and God? Myself and others? Within my own inner inner self am I at war? The fallen condition is a *crisis in separation,* and within the trauma of broken relationships resides our illnesses and identity crises. It is through prayer that relationships are mended (or at least forgiveness extended for the brokenness) and that our souls are healed of their grievous lacks due to failed relationships in the past.

King David understood this healing very well: "I acknowledged my sin to you, and my iniquity I did not hide. I said I will confess my transgressions to the Lord (continually unfolding the past till all is told) then You (instantly) forgave me the guilt and iniquity of my sin" (Psalm 32:5, *The Amplified Bible*).

Note the instantaneous nature of what happens when God forgives sin. Healings of the soul that have to do primarily with forgiveness at long last extended or received can be quite dramatic in that the relief is so instant, and in many cases, the joy so exquisite. C. S. Lewis, finally having received forgiveness for something that had bothered him for years, wrote his friend and confidante, Sr. Penelope:

> As for me I specially need your prayers because I am (like the pilgrims in Bunyan) travelling across "a plain called Ease." Everything without, and many things within are marvellously well at present: Indeed . . . I realize that until about a month ago I never really believed (though I thought I did) in God's forgiveness. What an ass I have been both for not knowing and for thinking I knew. I now feel that one must never say one believes or understands anything; any morning a doctrine I thought I already possessed may blossom into this new reality.[4]

At such a time as this, we can think that there is little left for God to do in our souls. But most of us find, on coming back down to earth, that this is the first healing in a series—one that perhaps opens the way for the healing of deeply wounded emotions and/or diseased attitudes.

We need to understand prayer for the healing of memories in the context of prayer for healing in general. To pray for the healing of a person's memories is primarily to pray for the healing of his soul, and this differs from prayer for the healing of his spirit or body.[5]

Man's Spirit

The spirit is sick when alienated from God, and the healing of the spirit takes place when it is united to the Spirit of God. The evangelists, therefore, are the great healers of the spirit in that they broadcast continually the message of salvation. Anytime we introduce a person to Christ, we see this essential healing take place. God's Spirit descends into his spirit, linking the new believer with Himself. One is then "born from above" and now has a place within where the Holy Spirit lives, a holy and righteous base from which He radiates up through the soul as well as the physical body. From the moment of new birth, then, believers can and are to practice His Presence within. This is also the initial and primary healing of man's soul and the basis of his further becoming in Christ.

The Soul

> In reference . . . to man's psychical nature, "spirit" denotes life as having its origin in God and "soul" denotes that same life as constituted in man. Spirit is the inner depth of man's being, the higher aspect of his personality. Soul expresses man's own special and distinctive individuality. The *pneuma* (spirit) is man's nonmaterial nature looking Godward; the *psyche* is that same nature of man looking earthward and touching the things of sense.[6]

The Scriptures use the terms interchangeably, though they differentiate between spirit and soul. To speak of the soul is also to speak of the spirit in that the spirit of a man expresses itself through the soul. Conversely, of course, to speak of the spirit is also to speak of the soul, for the two are wed in man's makeup. We know nothing of a human spirit in isolation from a soul, or a soul in isolation from a human spirit.

To speak of prayer for the healing of the soul is, primarily, to speak of prayer for releasing someone from psychological sickness and emotional pain due to hurts and deprivations of the past. Prayer for healing of memories is in this category. When someone has such a need, he has a psychological barrier to freedom in Christ. Though the human spirit is united with Christ, God's Spirit cannot "radiate" through this problem area until the person gets help to understand and deal with it. This is where the gifts of counseling and healing come in, and people need to open up in prayer to receive them. Until one does, he is being determined by the difficulties of the past and lacks freedom.

There are other psychological barriers to freedom, and they also come under the heading of healing of the soul. They include, for example, the effects of ignorance and terrible poverty. Also, it is possible to be a Christian today and to be ignorant of necessary moral values and virtues—those necessary to our becoming as persons. Obedient to the best we know, we gain a moral self, moral character.

The Scriptures consider man as a whole, and we err if we fall into the trap of trying to separate and define too closely the differences between the faculties of the mind (e.g., conscious and unconscious), or where one leaves off and the other begins. And the same is true of spirit and soul. Spirit and soul differ, the faculties of the mind differ, but to try to differentiate them by separating them too closely is to do what the Scriptures do not do and what great Christian minds such as St. Augustine (in regard to spirit and soul) have failed to do.

Even so, all who pastor souls effectively, from St. Paul to this present day, have to deal with the essential makeup of man. To pray aright and to see healing take place, we have to discern where the need is. We will do a person no good and perhaps a lot of harm if we pray for his salvation (in effect, for the healing of his spirit) when he has in fact already accepted Christ, and his need is for emotional or physical healing. And we do live in a day when the church is in great confusion over these matters. One part of the church actually refuses to acknowledge the need for healing of the soul (as if full sanctification necessarily occurs at the moment of the new birth), while yet another denies, for all practical purposes, even the need for the new birth (the essential healing of man's spirit). To go even further, few Christians can discriminate between the psychological and the spiritual, and they think, like the pagans of old, that the mind is the highest element in man. This is only one more way of saying that we twentieth-century Christians have lost the understanding of Incarnational Reality.

With this in mind, I want to stress the following for all who pray for the healing of persons. It is essential that the Christian who needs healing realize and practice the Presence of Christ within. He must know and be reminded that his spirit is ingodded: it is the "whole place" within him, while the part of his soul that needs healing is coming into the light and being healed. The more wounded the person, the more necessary it is for him to understand and to continually affirm that Christ lives in him.

For example, the Christian who is being healed emotionally due to serious abuse or deprivation of some kind may know the most incredible pain and confusion as his soul is being healed. If he does not know the difference between his spirit and his soul, he may despair, thinking there is no hope for him. Every repressed feeling, memory, and emotion will be surfacing, along with all the dark voices involved. If he thinks of this storm-tossed part of his soul as his essential real self or spirit, rather than that wounded part of his soul that God is healing, then he will be unable to practice the Presence of God within. Indeed, he will think God very far from him. He will think God cannot possibly love such a confused and battered one as himself.

All this changes the moment we lead the person to the quiet place of affirming, "Another lives in me. My spirit is one with His. That is my whole place. All else is raging around me and within me, but I can stand now, confident, and watch as God heals this part of me that is so wounded." The point I am stressing here is that it is dangerous to say that certain things are amiss with the essential spirit of man when the real problem is a need for emotional and psychological healing. It leaves the person paralyzed, crippled, unable to move forward. Even more important, we are not recognizing the key to that person's healing—the practice of the Presence of the One who has redeemed and is even now in the process of healing him.

I've had several occasions recently to see people who are in despair about their lives and on the verge of suicide because they did not recognize this truth. When I asked them to practice the Presence of the Lord, they said, "I can't, my spirit is . . ." and then they would go on to describe some malady of their spirit. As soon as I ascertained they were in fact Christians, I said, "No. That is not so. Christ is within your spirit, ready to radiate up through your inner being. There is a whole place within you. You are the Lord's." They were then ministered to and enabled to withstand the batterings of facing deep woundedness in their souls and lives.

Recently, I prayed with a precious Christian leader who, though she had no conscious confusion over spirit and soul, was in the midst of tremendous psychological strain. From a seriously dysfunctional family, she had repressed her feelings in order to survive. She is now no longer able to repress all these feelings, and they are coming up in a most frightening manner. She was anxious, feeling bereft of God. Immediately I shared the above with her, and she eagerly grasped it, first writing it all down in her notebook. "God is in my spirit; my spirit is whole while my soul is being healed. I can practice the Presence of God, and I will." And she said, "That is exactly what I needed to hear," and her whole countenance changed. We all need to be reminded of this basic incarnational truth.

Ours is an incarnational view of man and reality. Christ is, as F. B. Meyer has said, "the living Fountain rising up in the well of our personality."[7] He is present now. He, our Healer, has already become flesh, has already accomplished the work of the cross, has already poured out the full gift of His Spirit upon us. As long as we dwell in time, there will never be more of Him available to us than now. Our walk with Him, our acknowledgment of Him with us, within us, while remaining fully sovereign—all this in the now—is what faith apprehends. God is available to us; Jesus is indeed, if we are born again of His Spirit, the living Fountain within. We practice His Presence. We keep this truth uppermost in prayer for the healing of the soul, that is, in the removal of blocks to our becoming in Christ.

Man's Body

When man is physically ill due to disease or accident, we pray differently than we would for the healing of the soul. The one effective principle for healing of spirit, soul, or body is invoking and affirming God's Presence with us. "And if the Spirit of him who raised Jesus from the dead is living in you, he who raised Christ from the dead will also give life to your mortal bodies through his Spirit, who lives in you" (Romans 8:11).

The sicknesses of spirit, soul, and body intertwine and overlap. It is not at all unusual to pray for the healing of a memory and see the body healed as well.

Or to pray for healing of the body and find matters of spirit and soul coming to the fore. Prayer for deliverance from demonic activity may (or may not) be needed with any one of these. Healing of spirit, soul, and body is simply, as John Gaynor Banks and Agnes Sanford have said, "answered prayer."

Healing of Memories

In prayer for healing of memories, we not only confess our sin, but we forgive those people and circumstances that have so grieved and wounded us. We often need to stop denying that we have been sinned against.

Sometimes the memories that need healing go far back in time, back before conscious memory. But the heart knows; it does not forget. It banks the memories. There sorrowful, shameful memories are suppressed. They do not disappear, but need healing.

The intellect and the heart, our "two minds," stand in antithesis. Opposite and complementary one to the other, they do not work in ways at all comparable. The heart, as the seat of the memory, is the "feeling mind." It is irrational only in that it "thinks" in symbols. "Feelings are," as Robert M. Doran, S. J., writes, "energy-become-conscious. Feelings are a matter of psychic energy." Furthermore:

> Feelings always enter consciousness through being connected with *some* representation. Now, the most basic form of representation lies in symbols. A *symbol*, [Bernard] Lonergan says, is an image of a real or imaginary object that evokes a feeling or is evoked by a feeling; what this means is that there is never a feeling without a symbolic meaning; never a symbol without a feeling. To *name* one's feeling is to discover the dynamic images, the symbols that are associated with them. To have *insight* into one's feelings is to understand the symbolic association. To *tell one's story* is to narrate the course of one's elemental symbolizing.[8]

In my lectures and counseling I say less about feelings and how to deal with them than most others do. I think that is because I say so much about symbols and how to deal with them. To help a person become aware of and understand the images and pictures his heart is emitting automatically puts him in touch with his feelings. I find it is better to get a person's eyes on the symbol rather than the feeling. In this way, he objectifies the feeling and understands it more quickly. It can't seem bigger than life, "lording it over" him, so to speak.

The heart or "feeling mind," the seat of the memory, is subjective. We cannot reason with it or command it. All who have suddenly blocked on the name of a person they know well, or have been unable to give answers on tests for which they have thoroughly prepared, understand this facet of the unconscious well enough. We can try to reason with it or impatiently command it, and it simply balks.

Agnes Sanford called this, her subjective mind, "Junior," and delighted in teaching people how to treat it. If, she said, you are taking a test and can't remember the answer, just speak softly to Junior (at which point she would pat her hand over her heart as if soothing the balking mind) and say, "That's o.k., Junior, you just fish around and find the answer while I go on to the next question. Then I'll come back and you'll have it." And that is exactly what she would do. And sure enough, "Junior" would come up with it once she stopped trying to force the issue.

Medical missionary and psychiatrist Dr. James Stringham, lecturing on guilt and the need for confession in the healing of the *psyche*, speaks of the unconscious mind as the original computer. If fifty years of one's financial history were computerized, he says, the one time the person failed to pay a bill would be the first datum to come up. And so it is with guilt and experiences of rejection, as well as diseased or unnatural feelings, in the unconscious. The unconscious mind banks our emotions, our feelings of anger, hatred, desire, joy, and love, as well as our memories. And like the computer, it never forgets the "unpaid bill," the unforgiven or the unhealed. Desires or thoughts that the conscious mind has repressed are still very active in the subconscious, and as a further complication, the truly repressed materials come before the conscious mind only in disguised and unrecognizable (that is, symbolic) forms. Such images are not to be taken literally, but are to be read symbolically, in which case they are understandable. As Karl Stern says in his valuable book *The Third Revolution*:

> [T]hat vast dark universe of the "meaningless" which exists outside the world illuminated by logic becomes one meaningful structure once we have introduced certain tentative premises. Before we form concepts, before we think in words, and before we begin to think in logical abstractions, we go through an infantile phase in which the universe of our mind consists of sensation and imagery. The connection between that preconceptual rock bottom and the upper layer of logical conceptual thinking is mysterious. *But it is not unfathomable*.[9] (italics mine)

So the "feeling mind" or deep heart is, so to speak, the seat of the intuitive faculty, of the true imagination, and of the memory.

Memory

The power of the memory to make the past present to us in a very real way is extraordinary. *Anamnesis*, a Greek word used to explain eucharistic theology, best illustrates this phenomenon. It denotes bringing forward into the present an event from out of the past, and like our Lord's statement, "This is My body; this is My blood," it is not merely an act of psychological remembrance.

Even ancestral memories come up at times for healing, and at other times, they are simply, as I found out firsthand, experienced. The first time I went to Scotland, it was after a great deal of travel to the far-flung places of the earth. I happened to be traveling across the Highlands at a time when the mountains were solid purple with heather, and the smell of peat fires wafted across the land. In a profound experience, I somehow knew this place and that I had come home. It was as if my roots went down to the center of the earth there. On my return home, I looked into my genealogy and found that the great majority of my ancestors are Highland Scots. Since sharing this with others, any number of people have shared a like sort of thing with me.

Such an experience has nothing to do with reincarnation, a pagan way of explaining such phenomena. It may well have something to do with genetic imprinting, some basic "memory" written into the very cells of our being. A close friend and associate of mine has a female border collie, one that is now many generations removed from her ancestors who for centuries were bred to move zigzag fashion behind sheep—herding the entire flock forward in the direction the shepherd desired. This remarkable animal, so "humanized" I refer to her affectionately as Beastie just to remind myself she is one, still moves zigzag fashion, whether behind a person, a prey, or just when running in a field exploring. It's written somehow into her brain stem or genetic "memory." Perhaps some small part of what I experienced in Scotland I share with Beastie and the rest of the animal kingdom. But the greater part of the explanation lies in *the nature of time* and in the fact that we, though creatures of time, are made in the image of God. As Christians, these truths apply to us in a special way, for Christ indwells us. C. S. Lewis hints at all these things in this remarkable section on memory.

> Memory, as we now know it, is a dim foretaste, a mirage even, of a power which the soul, or rather Christ in the soul (He went to "prepare a place" for us), will exercise hereafter. It need no longer be private to the soul in which it occurs. I can now communicate to you the fields of my boyhood—they are building-estates today—only imperfectly, by words. Perhaps the day is coming when I can take you for a walk through them.[10]

We now know that when surgeons operate on a certain portion of the brain, their fine instruments "touch off" old memories, memories in which the person relives incidences of the long forgotten past, replete with sounds, colors, smells. This illustrates in a concrete way that the mind does indeed bank the memories. But even more, it illustrates for me the fact that, if surgeons can, by accidentally touching the brain, find a memory, how much more readily can our God touch those memories that need forgiveness and healing.

The Holy Spirit is God's finger on sore memories. If the need for forgiveness of sin goes back generations, how easy it is for God to hear our prayer and touch that ancestral memory. He then lifts from us the burden of that thing that has so wounded our families.[11]

Time

Our memory helps us overcome the limitations we have as creatures of time. Time too is a creature. It is created. That is a mind-blowing concept, but it is true. Jesus, the infinite One, is outside of time, and all times are present to Him.

> To be God is to enjoy an infinite present where nothing has yet passed away and nothing is still to come.[12]

This means that all our times, together with all that we are, are eternally present to God.

Several years before learning how to pray for healing of memories, I had a very unusual experience, one that I did not share for a good number of years. I was on a camping trip in Oklahoma, and in the process of cleaning up the camp, I had walked out onto a huge boulder. The chore finished, I stepped back, and when I did, I stepped back in time. I saw two Indian men, and they saw me. I saw the terrain as it had been hundreds of years ago. I knew instantly that it was long before the white man had come, and that these Indian men had never before seen a white person. We were mutually astonished.

All this happened and was over in an instant. Amazed, I ran back to my old camper wagon and prayed. I asked the Lord what had happened, and I knew it was exactly as it seemed to be. I had looked down through time; they had looked up through time and seen me. I did not understand this experience for a long time, but as I prayed, the Lord assured me that He had allowed it and that it was in no way engineered by the powers of darkness.

At that point in my life, I was deeply perplexed over Edie, a young girl I had prayed for but been unable to help. She repeatedly fell into sexual sin, and then would repent with all her heart, at which times she would ask me to pray with her. I knew beyond all shadow of a doubt the power of God's forgiveness in my own life, and, knowing her desire to change, I couldn't understand her inability to stand in Christ. I did not understand her pain that ended in sexual compulsions, ones that drove her to throw herself away time after time with men.

Edie had been adopted as a young girl, and invariably when we prayed together for any length of time, a painful memory would surface. In it, she and her baby brothers were in a crib, and they were wet, filthy, and hungry. The police came, took her drunken mother one direction, her drunken father another. She never saw her parents or her baby brothers again. She agonized over this, and as the memory would surface, she would sob convulsively. She had taken this loss as the deepest kind of personal rejection. In her heart she felt that if they could not love her, no one could; if they abandoned her, all would. This was the root memory behind her compulsions. Had I known then what I learned later, she would have received a healing that would have enabled her to withstand the psychological storms that blew upon her as her soul was being healed of its deep deprivations.

While on this camping trip, I was asking the Lord why this girl remained so troubled, why she couldn't receive from Him what she needed. The Lord was showing me, both in this experience and in the one I had in Scotland, that all times are one with Him; that He is eternally present to all those moments where forgiveness and healing are needed.

Had I understood then the healing of memories, Edie could have been healed of her sexual compulsions, and then she could have gone on to full self-acceptance. I could have invited God in all His healing power into that memory. It not only contained the root trauma, but it most likely symbolized all the parental neglect and rejection she had ever known. The rejection had left her unable to accept love from God or from others. We would together have confessed the dreadful sins of alcoholism, of deprivation of parental love and care, and so on as the Holy Spirit led, and then, holding her tightly (the tiny infant in her was still crying out for a mother's arms), I could have helped her to forgive her mother, her father, her little brothers for leaving her. In helping her to forgive and then to receive from God both illumination and healing, God could have lifted from her the terrible burden of her parents' sins against her.

God had been with her in that worst of moments, that time when she lost her parents and brothers. Had someone been on the scene who knew how to take hold of God with one hand and her with the other, she could have been been comforted even then. As an infant, she had desperately needed someone to minister Christ's healing love to her, but so few Christians think or know to pray in this way even for the tiny baby. Several years later she was adopted by Christian parents, and under the hearing of the gospel, she had come to Christ. Now Christ lived within her, ready to heal those worst memories and to help her deal with the deep wounds in her soul. But she had needed the understanding and ministering hand of another—one who would not only direct her eyes upward to God, but who would then pray in such a way that Christ could enter into the root memories and bring healing. When that healing did not come, thinking herself fit only to be abandoned, she continued to try to get love, if only for a moment, through compulsively giving her body away to one stranger after another.

Was she responsible for her sin, the way she compulsively attempted to assuage the inner loneliness and pain? Yes. But as a Christian she desperately needed in her behalf the healing power that God has entrusted to the church. However, the church surrounding her had lost its power to heal the soul.

God heals even the traumas we can't remember. He wills to heal all. The good news is that He is present to all our times—past, present, and future. We must simply learn to collaborate with Him in prayer.

Time and Space

To be human is to be gifted with time and space, but it is also to be limited by time and space. We need to understand how the gift of prayer helps us overcome these obstacles. Prayer for healing of memories, that is, for in-depth forgiveness of sin, is the way we overcome our limitations as creatures of time. *Intercessory prayer,* something we are never to neglect, is the means given us to overcome the barriers of space. To intercede for another, no matter where he might be on the globe or even in space is to, in a manner of speaking, be present with him. "Though I am absent from you in body, I am present with you in spirit," said St. Paul, who prayed fervently for the Christians in his care (Colossians 2:5, see also, 1 Corinthians 5:3-5). I insert this admonition to intercessory prayer because it is easy, once we see the incredible results of prayer for healing of memories, to neglect this way of prayer. We then must correct the imbalance. But our illusion concerning time seems to be the most difficult, and C. S. Lewis effectively speaks to this ongoing blindness within the Christian community:

> We have a strange illusion that mere time cancels sins. I have heard others, and I have heard myself, recounting cruelties and falsehoods committed in boyhood as if they were no concern of the present speaker's, and even with laughter. But mere time does nothing either to the fact or to the guilt of sin. The guilt is washed out not by time but by repentance and the blood of Christ.[13]

Time, a creature, does not erase our sin. Only by our repentance and His blood is sin and guilt lifted from both past and present. It is for this reason that when a church, a nation, or an individual repents, *incredible* things happen.

A Warning Regarding False Doctrine

The awesome truth that Christ's atoning blood is sufficient to cancel the power of sin is being seriously obscured by certain ministers of inner healing today. While acknowledging the need for forgiveness and remission of sins, they put forward in their lectures and books something other than this great orthodox teaching. They add to this teaching occult doctrines unacceptable to any branch of the church—Catholic or Protestant. These teachings actually undermine the doctrine of repentance and forgiveness of sin, while at the same time they lead toward universalism and mediumistic practices.

Their main thesis? These teachers jump directly from the all-sufficient Christian truth of forgiveness of sin, especially as it is administered through the Christian liturgy of the Eucharist, to a world of ghosts—of unquiet spirits. The dead, they say, are trying to contact the living. The living have a responsibility to come into an ongoing relationship with the deceased. Rather than offer healing through forgiveness of sin by a holy and just God, they espouse a new *gnosis* (actually a new form of an old occultism) concerning familial spirits haunting the living—a thing that opens unwary people to spiritism and to familiar spirits—demons who impersonate the dead.

These doctrines introduce into the Christian community ideas that have long been part of the Anglo-American occult tradition. Edgar Cayce and Ruth Montgomery would be perfectly at home with what these ministers are practicing.

During World War II when our pilots were flying "The Hump" in the Far East, natives who had long been involved in ancestor worship would run out, getting as close to the propellers as they possibly could in order to relieve themselves of the "spirits" of their ancestors. Often these natives would be killed, and there was not one thing our flyers could do about it. The demonic hold that such practices have, not to mention all the superstitions that go along with them, are something that primitive and pagan races almost always have to be delivered from when they convert to Christ.

A lovely Chinese woman and her family came to one of my conferences. She was deeply distressed that these pagan teachings were flooding into her diocese and that her bishop did not discern the dangers, much less protect his people from them. As a young Christian from the Far East, she had (with great pain and suffering due to demonic oppression) come out of all the deluding practices that have to do with placating the spirits of the dead. She was now amazed to hear such things being taught and recommended in her Christian community.[14]

While this teaching has partially subsided, it still erupts periodically and subtly into Christian circles. We must be aware of it and simply affirm that repentance and forgiveness of sin alone releases us from the effects of our own sins and of others' sins, even when those offenses involve unconfessed sins, curses, and so on that come down through family lines. Christ's blood is enough. It is utterly sufficient. We need add nothing to that. We will then see the miracle of spiritual and psychological healing occur, and with it no bad fruit or seed from the tares sown among the wheat.

Doctrines of demons leave demonized souls in their wake. What we believe really matters. In an age when naturalism with its materialistic ideologies and epistemologies is breaking up and failing, we can expect the muddy mysticisms to flood in. The only protection against the false is the true—the power in the name of Christ that all Christians know as they learn to obey Christ and collaborate with His Spirit to preach, teach, and heal. We move in the *spirituals*, the gifts of the Holy Spirit, and we cease trying to do God's work in our own strength alone. To truly live and move obediently in the Kingdom of God is to move quite "naturally" and joyfully in the realm of *miracle*. But the church, in her capitulation to materialism and the ideologies of this world, has long failed to move as she should in the power that God gives. As this power is being restored, the power of true repentance and the remittance of sin, we will have to deal with the mysticisms that have flooded in to fill in the vacuum. These mysticisms will nearly always contain much of the true, and especially the truths the church is currently neglecting, but they will invariably be mixed and irreparably tainted with something other than *Incarnational Reality,* the reality of Christ with us, forgiving and releasing us from sin, thereby uniting us to the Father by His Spirit within, empowering us individually and corporately as the Body of Christ.

On the other hand, we will have to deal with the rise of the new anti-supernaturalists, dispensationalists, and what not, who are in terror of the true power of God and wildly lump the false and the true together. Christ's teaching on the wheat and the tares is apropos here. (See Matthew 13:36-43.) Such people, dishonestly quoting out of context, with no care for the full body of a fellow Christian's writings and works, are today ignorantly and recklessly pulling up the wheat with the tares. They are themselves sowers of bad seed. They are sowing fear and hatred (among other things) of the true imagination, being ignorant of it it and terrified of the false, and they are sowing fear and hatred of fellow Christians. They are slandering great servants of the Lord whose work and fruit of that work speaks for itself and needs no defense. They are also sowing the seeds of poor scholarship, poor theology, and poor psychology—like those putting forward the muddy mysticisms.

We can no longer naively fail to comprehend the ideologies of the day and the way that Christians who are trapped in them flail about trying to mend things. We can no longer ignore sound theology and the teaching of how truly to move in the power of God. Such was always harmful, but now the hour is critical. Surely there has never been a day when the people (leaders included) could be so easily and fatally led astray. May the Lord strengthen us all to do His will.

CHAPTER 7

Second Great Barrier to Wholeness in Christ: Failure to Forgive Others

For if you forgive men when they sin against you, your heavenly Father will also forgive you. But if you do not forgive men their sins, your Father will not forgive your sins.

(Matthew 6:14-15)

The failure to forgive another is a most formidable barrier to wholeness. One can only begin to comprehend its danger to the soul by meditating on Christ's words above. Most moderns, including Christians, have lost even the language with which to speak of the soul. Therefore, the soul's motions are largely lost to them. For that reason, I will write briefly of what seems to me to be the most common "categories" of this failure in order to help us identify our own needs to forgive, as well as to help us be of greater help to those for whom we pray.

Always, at the bottom of everything that is amiss, we will find pride. We need to confess it. And so it is in our failure to forgive the merely petty things in life. Let's look at that category first.

Forgiving Petty Offenses

We tend to overlook this category when we are praying for folks, but often the need to forgive will be just here. It's the *everydayness* of such irritations and transgressions that gets to us, and we can easily come to despise those who offend us in these ways.

Besides that, we should like to pick and choose those who are eligible to offend us. The implication here, of course, is that the offender is something of a snippet and grossly inferior to us in some way. The remedy is to confess the sin of *pride*, calling it precisely that, and then forgive the offender.

Christ does not see others as we see them. To stop for a moment, practice His Presence, and ask to see this person through His eyes can give us an entirely different perspective. In doing this, we often see strengths we've overlooked in the other person, while at the same time we may be painfully reminded of our own weaknesses and Christ's patience with the petty within ourselves.

I witnessed a remarkable physical healing in a woman who realized her need to forgive a petty offense. This woman was part of a prayer group that met regularly to pray for the healing of the sick. She had become increasingly crippled by arthritis, and no matter how often she received healing prayer, she slowly worsened. Several years into her illness, we were praying once again for her healing when the matter of her upstairs neighbor came forcibly before her. This neighbor was an invalid, and she took lunch to her every day at noon. Invariably, however, a few minutes before she could carry the steaming plate of food up the stairs, the phone would ring, and a whiny voice would moan, "Are you coming?"

Her thoughts toward this neighbor grew darker as this behavior continued, but rather than facing the poor soul with the fact that the daily phone call sorely tried her patience, she simply held her tongue with its growing list of unspoken retorts. But she "thought them" loudly enough. After several years of this, her insides were fairly shouting, "Don't I always come! Do I ever miss!" and so on. She got to the point that she would tense up just before the call came. So things went on, day in and day out.

On the day of her healing, she painfully bent her arthritic knees before the altar, and as we prayed with her, she realized her need to forgive the upstairs invalid and to ask God's forgiveness for her reactions. This she did, and she was instantly healed of her very painful arthritic condition. People who have never seen something like this have difficulty believing it. Such a healing dramatically illustrates the power of forgiveness and the way it can open us more fully to God's Healing Presence.

Humility and longsuffering, those great Christian virtues, are not often expounded or understood these days. Not all who seem to have them (by never thinking about themselves, for example), in fact, do have them. Christians bent toward one another in idolatrous and codependent ways sometimes mistake this condition for one of humility and service to others. In actuality, these conditions merely enable sick and sinful behavior in others.[1] "Humble yourselves—feeling very insignificant—in the Presence of the Lord, and He will exalt you. He will lift you up and make your lives significant" (James 4:10, *The Amplified Bible*).

To confess the sin of pride and to go on to forgive is marvelously simple, but many stumble right here. We find we must enroll in a primary level of the Holy Spirit's school of prayer. "Father, I am nothing apart from You, have mercy on me; I have been seeing *apart from You;* if you leave me for an instant,

I shall be even more prideful, more self-serving." When we learn to pray this prayer, without the least taint of the wrong kind of self-hatred on the one hand or a feeling of superiority on the other, we will be well on our way to maturity in Christ.

Where there are ongoing petty offenses, it is important that we forsake the subjective (reactionary) position and then—listening to God for instructions—step into the free air of an objective position. In this manner, my friend could have dealt honestly with her neighbor's daily whining question and phone call and then ministered Christ's love to the real problem—the invalid's intense loneliness and fear of abandonment.

Failure to Forgive Due to Being Out of Touch with One's Heart

In this day when people's heads are so out of touch with their hearts, many have unforgiveness and do not realize it until, in prayer for healing, the Holy Spirit reveals it.

Often when praying with such persons, I find that a memory of abusive or abnormal behavior by another will come up. The person will not know he needs to forgive the offender. I will have to say, "You must confess this as a sin against you, and you must name it specifically for the sin that it is, and then, before God, extend forgiveness to (offender's name)." The specific naming of the sin and of the offender is important. This is no abstract transaction, but a very real dealing before and with our God.

These persons will invariably be surprised, as if they have never thought about the matter in this light. This is especially true when the need to forgive another involves a parent. But once the deed or circumstance has been acknowledged as an offense, and forgiveness has been extended to that person, healing comes quickly.

Often these people do not know what normal is. They are from dysfunctional homes in which the members do not relate to one another in a healthy fashion. In addition, as children these persons usually were taught to deny their feelings. Even when normal thoughts and feelings were expressed, these were not validated. So there will be a deep inner knowledge of injustice and/or frustration and, at some level of their being, a knowledge of the need to forgive. I know this is so because when they restate (at my request) the offense and extend forgiveness, great anger begins to surface. I then have them raise their hands to Christ on the cross, and they "see" the anger and unforgiveness come up and out of them and flow into the One who, in our stead, takes and carries all our sin and darkness. After this is accomplished, we ask Christ to fill all those spaces where this pain, anger, and unforgiveness have been with His healing love and light.

Judy's story, recounted in chapter 6 of *Crisis in Masculinity*, is a good example of how emotionally sick and confused persons can be when they need to forgive another but do not realize it. The story also shows that we remain tied to parents in unhealthy ways until we extend forgiveness to those parents. In fact, we fail to fully separate our own identity from our parent's and end up hating ourselves.

Forgiving the Unforgiveable

> In all their distress he too was distressed, and the angel of his presence saved them. (Isaiah 63:9)

> Agony means severe suffering in which something dies—either the base thing, or the good. No man is the same after an agony; he is either better or worse, and the agony of a man's experience is nearly always the first thing that opens his mind to understand the need of Redemption worked out by Jesus Christ.[2]

Sometimes we must forgive actions that go far beyond the petty offenses to our pride and prejudice. For the young person, twisted in mind and spirit, robbed of even the simplest pleasures of childhood and youth due to the overbearing hatred and mistreatment of a crazed or perverted parent, forgiving can at first seem impossible. Many and varied too are the more subtle sins against the human spirit and soul that are equally hard to forgive. The minister errs who simply throws out the Scripture "forgive your enemy" to such persons without helping them into the Presence of God in such a way that they can both forgive and receive consolation and healing.

I have often had people say to me, "I cannot forgive." And when they tell me the circumstances, I fully understand their difficulty. In *The Healing Presence,* pages 88-90, I tell about my own experience of forgiving the "unforgivable," how through an entire afternoon I cried out to God for the power to forgive and knew only too well how helpless I was without His grace. As I wrote:

> There were terrible moments in that interminable afternoon when I wondered what I would do if God failed to help me, if I would simply have to cry out like this the rest of my life. Then came a moment when instantly my pleading was interrupted by an amazing awareness of Christ in me, and from that center where He and I were mysteriously one, forgiveness was extended to my enemy. It was as if Christ in and through me forgave the person (who can explain such a thing?)—yet I too forgave.[3]

Note here that it was not until I reached full identification with Christ that I was able to forgive. On the cross He identified Himself with my sin, my suffering—the very pain I was at that moment experiencing. In reaching that place of identification with Him, I could, as it were, stand in the cross and hurt—with Him.[4] One with Him in His dying, I was able to release my unforgiveness, with all its feelings of rage and woundedness, to Him in utter trust. In unison with

Him, I could pray: "Father, forgive them, they know not what they do." All my hurt, fear, inability to forgive flowed into Him, and in exchange He gave me freedom. Having taken my place in His dying, now one with Him still, I took my place in His rising. And I knew joy. There is no better theology than this. It's the message of the cross. And it applies to all of us. This is the way of Christian forgiveness.

On the basis of the Scriptures and from my own personal experience and that of helping many, many others with the worst imaginable situations, I can always assure these dear ones, "Oh yes, you can forgive. And I will gladly show you how. We will go to prayer, and 'you shall receive power' (Acts 1:8)— the power to forgive even your worst enemy." This enemy often will be your "beloved enemy." It is those nearest to us who have the greatest power to wound and maim us.

Johnny's story, first recounted in *The Broken Image*, pages 82-84, and now reprinted below, illustrates the way prayer for healing of memories can help a suffering soul to forgive the "unforgivable." This story also illustrates the vital part Johnny's will as well as his imagination (the way that, in the Presence of God, the heart is enabled to see) played in his being able to forgive an utterly reprobate father.

JOHNNY'S STORY

Johnny was married and in his mid-twenties when his father died. It was then that he, a very needy person, moved into homosexuality, a sexual behavior he practiced for two years.

His deep inner craving still unmet and his marriage in serious trouble, Johnny attempted to extricate himself from his homosexual activity. It was then that he found Christ and, thoroughly converted, became an ardent witness to the faith.

About ten years after his conversion, however, and all of them spent as a devout and wholly committed Christian, Johnny began falling apart. He feared his children would find out what he had been, he feared his wife would leave him, but most of all he had a dreadful fear of failure. In addition to these fears, his homosexual compulsions were once again too strong for his conscious mind to deny or repress, and he feared he was, in truth, deviant. He was in the midst of a nervous breakdown.

It was in this state of collapse that he responded to his wife's concerned urging and came for prayer. His conscious mind, so wearied with repressing all the old fears, denials, and bad memories, had ceased to do its job. Johnny would now have to face his inner loneliness, all the fears and darkness he had so long refused to see and acknowledge.

His story is a terrible one. It has to do with a brutalizing father, and with older brothers who practiced homosexuality as part of the pecking-order syndrome at work in the home.

His father had never had a smile or kind word for him, something he had yearned for all his life. As his sisters grew up, he had to live with the fact that his father was molesting them sexually, and that he could do nothing about it. He also watched his father choose girlfriends for his older sons, and then seduce them himself. These sons, brutalized by their father, spent time in prison, and became involved in the brute kind of homosexuality that prisons are rife with. They would then come home and abuse the younger boys in a similar fashion. Johnny, the youngest, seemed to catch the brunt of their dehumanizing behavior.

No wonder Johnny was breaking apart. All these memories were festering within, as yet unhealed. His masculinity had, of course, been seriously repressed in the environment he had grown up in.

After he had shared his story with me, one that he had never been able fully to tell before, we went to prayer. Although he knew that prayer was the only way, he at first resisted. This was because he thought prayer was more or less an exercise of the conscious mind, and that he would have to try to understand and deal with the whole problem consciously again. And that was precisely what he could no longer do, what he was worn out from attempting to do. That was when I asked him to relax completely and let me do the praying, while he simply looked up to Jesus with the eyes of his heart. His healing illustrates the inestimable value of "picturing" or imagining. Besides being a valid way of "seeing," it opens the heart to any pictures God would send. God sends us His help and truth, and often it comes as a "picture." Johnny's healing also illustrates how closely hate can be connected to love.

Realizing there was hatred toward his father, I asked him to picture his father standing next to Jesus. It is very difficult to look up and see Jesus when one's heart is filled with hate. And it is also difficult to picture the face of the one we hate. We tend to blot it out, annihilate it. Johnny couldn't look up to picture Jesus or his father, but yielding to the Presence of the Lord and with his head bent down almost to the floor, he began to sob uncontrollably as the deep-seated hatred toward his father welled up and out of his heart. He then had to forgive his father, and this forgiveness had to come from the deepest recesses of Johnny's wounded heart. It seemed to him an absolute impossibility. Even so, he knew he had to get through this impasse, for he could not go on in the old tormented way. I assured him that loving and forgiving another is a matter of the *will* rather than the emotions, and that his feelings naturally reflected the abuses of his early years with his father.

Praying that his *will* be strengthened, and insisting that he picture his father, I asked him to *will* to stretch up his hand and take the hand of his father. His head still bent, he slowly lifted his arm up as if to take the hand of his father, sobbing, "I *will* to forgive you, Dad. I *will* to forgive you." I asked him to look up into his father's face and say, "Father, I *do* forgive you." Then, to my astonishment, torrents of repressed love began to pour out. Johnny cried over and over and over, "Daddy, I love you, Daddy, I love you. I *do* forgive you. Jesus, forgive me for hating him. Jesus, forgive me. Jesus, help me." And then, to his dad, "If only you could have said one kind word to me." At this, he slowly looked up to see the face that in life had always appeared so stern and hostile to him. I shall never forget his amazement as he "saw" his dad's face. "My father is *smiling* at me! He is smiling at me!" he exclaimed.

I do not fully understand the smile that seemed to assuage a lifetime of yearning on Johnny's part, but I've seen this sort of thing happen far too often, along with the lasting wholesome fruit it bears, to ever doubt it. Can it be that there is something about forgiving that releases not only the living, but the dead as well? Can the dead know when they are released from another's unforgiveness? This is wonderful to speculate on, and of course we can only speculate. But this I know—when we heal in Jesus' name, He sends us healing pictures as well as healing words. Jesus was in charge of that smile. This also I know—in Johnny's prayer of forgiveness, he came into a relationship with his father, one that he had never been able to achieve in his dad's lifetime.

You will remember that Johnny began to search out homosexual partners only after his father's death. In his heart, he had always yearned to win his father's love and affirmation—that one smile. His dad's death, before any of this happened, left the injured little boy in Johnny crying out for that father-love, crying out for the masculine identity that could come with it. Perhaps he was in part looking for his father in these relationships. He was certainly searching for himself in another. He was in the grip of an acute identity crisis.

In forgiving his father, Johnny set the stage for his release from fear of failure. This fear was no mere weed in the garden of his heart, but a massive choking root that was threatening his entire inner life, and that is how it appeared in the picture that came as I prayed. Prayer for its removal seemed like prayer for the pulling up of an ugly old tree, roots and all. I prayed that the roots be loosened by God's love and power flowing in; and as this began to happen, I saw the fear come up and out of Johnny. I then asked for Jesus to fill with His freeing, healing love all the spaces where the awful root tentacles had been. We waited as we saw this happening, and until there was no fear left in his heart.

Like the lame man who when healed went into the Temple leaping and praising God, Johnny's reaction to finding himself set free was ecstatic. Having long sought the Lord and this healing, he was overwhelmed in its reality. His joy was a blessed thing to see.

In Johnny, we see the unhealed trauma of homosexual rape in childhood, the utter repression of masculinity by a hostile father and environment, and the terrible yearning for a father's love and his own identity all mixed in one. His major healing came as he was released from the repressed hatred toward his father and was enabled to forgive him.

The story of "The Doctor Who Hated His Face in the Mirror," first recounted in *Crisis in Masculinity,* pages 70-76, illustrates the way of helping others forgive the more subtle but equally devastating kinds of sins parents commit against them. In this story, we deal with the childhood oath, and the fear that forgiving may open oneself again to another's power to hurt.

THE DOCTOR'S STORY

A Christian physician, loved by everyone who knows him, had a most difficult time in accepting himself fully. Every morning, as he shaved, he was reminded of this need because he did not like to see his own face in the mirror. He is a man wonderfully used of God, and therefore one who has prayed continuously for the grace to overcome the problem of self-hatred, if for no other reason than in order to accept the vocation God has given him. Anointed by God to pray for the sick, he has *had* to live from the Center, at least part of the time. But he knows the danger of running from God's perfect will for himself when, judging himself unacceptable, he steps alongside and looks at himself with excessive distrust and unlove.

As he grew in the favor and admiration of others, and in success both as a physician and as a Christian serving in the public eye, his self-hatred pained him all the more. All kinds of new fears about himself set in: "Why do I seek out friendships with good-looking, handsome, athletic men?" Before his involvement in Christian ministry, he had kept his feelings, fears, yearnings, needs and loneliness to himself. In fact, before his experience of renewal in the Spirit, he had kept a stern authoritarian control over both himself and his family, a control that kept true conversation with them at a safe distance. Rarely, therefore, could he share meaningfully even with his wife. To do so might mean to look, even for a moment, at his fears, and then he would have to believe the worst of himself. But gradually, as he came present to the Lord, he came present to his own heart and gained the courage to look at his feelings and fears. After hearing me speak and reading *The Broken Image,* he realized and faced the fact that although he did not have a sexual neurosis, he was severely cut off from his masculine side. He simply could not accept himself as a man.

He came to talk to me about his fears, the main one being, "Why am I so desperate for male companionship? Is there really something wrong with me? I have never looked at myself as being masculine; by that I mean 'handsome, rugged, athletic.' I see myself as being different, odd, seeking male approval and companionship. I like to be creative, do gardening, read, travel, dress well, and I am 'people-oriented.' I'm a 'hugger.' And I feel I must apologize for being this way, that I must try to hide my creativity and my gifts."

As we talked, his agitation concerning his father quickly became apparent: "I have never felt loved or affirmed as a son or as a man by my father. I don't ever remember him holding me, telling me he loves me, that I am good, or that he is proud of me."

If ever a man needed to be lifted from the subjective to the objective position where his father was concerned, this good man did. He still yearned for his dad's love and affirmation; he still grew angry with him for not giving it. He looked for his father to change, and he went through all the gamut of emotions over and over again as he reached out to his father and as his father remained precisely the man he had always been: unloving, unreasonable, and always accusing others of neglecting him. At my suggestion that he, the physician, must gain the objectivity to see and accept his father as he in fact was, and that we would pray to this end, the pitch of his voice must have risen an octave: "But you don't know what you are asking! We can't accept him *that* way."

And out came the picture of what it had meant to try to grow up straight in the midst of an evil perversity. His father, a rich man, was also a miser. Although he owned thousands of acres of rich orchards in Oregon, he never gave anything to his wife or children that cost him anything—whether in the way of loving actions or even the lowliest gift. One of the doctor's most agonizing charges against his father was, "He never once gave me a gift. He is a rich man, and for my birthday he gives me coupons that cost him nothing." Throughout his school and college years, the son had spent vacations laboring in the father's orchards. Although he was well-paid, he had no sense of partnership with his father in this enterprise. His father remained as aloof toward him as toward the other workers. Through his work he came to know the magnitude of his father's holdings and remarked to me in bitterness, "My mother died without having even the most common labor-saving devices or a penny to jangle in her pockets. He even did the grocery shopping."

As he shared about his father's words and actions toward himself, I saw him as a miracle sitting before me. A "miracle," true enough, who was not yet affirmed in his masculine identity or as a person, and one who had yet to gain the objectivity needed to creatively handle the problem with his father. But few sons survive such a negation of themselves as this father was able to dish out. A man who negated life and love, this father had failed to snuff out the essential spirit, the *life* in his son. It was almost as if he had tried, albeit unconsciously. He had wounded him dreadfully, and if God had not helped this son, that son could have (by hating or failing to forgive his father) become a little more like him every year.

This is the problem with the childhood oath, with the childhood determination to "never be like my father." Apart from accepting and forgiving our parents *as they are*, we cannot get our identities separated from them and go on to accept ourselves. We are therefore in danger of becoming more and more like them. To fully forgive is divine, and divine intervention is required to do it. "Yes," said the doctor to this insight, "before I found Christ in a deeply meaningful way and began the work of forgiving, I was becoming more like him every year."

Nevertheless, the work of forgiveness to be done was not finished in Dr. L.'s life. He was now face to face with his need to receive the gift of divine objectivity, to be raised from the subjective little-boy position in relationship to his father to one of adult maturity with its capacity to stand above a problem, see it for what it is, name it before God, utterly forgive it, and no longer be grievously entangled in it. It's one thing to suffer a problem while looking down upon it from a free perch, and quite another to suffer it while still having one's feet, like a captive bird caught in the net. For Dr. L. to achieve the objective position, he must now accept his father as the man he in fact is and always has been. After explaining to him his need, I helped him to pray in the following fashion:

"I forgive you, Dad, for being unable to love me, unable to give to me or to my mother, my brother, and my sister. I face the illness and wickedness of your particular brand of miserliness, and I name it as the evil it is, as an evil with the power to wound my mother and my sister (even fatally perhaps, for they both died early of physical diseases), and myself. That you could never see or treat us as *persons,* that you could not affirm the life that was given us, but could only see everything in terms of your own small and even perverted desires, I forgive you. I forgive you for not becoming all God created you to be; I accept you as you have chosen to be, and I will no longer strive uselessly, demanding that you change, demanding that you love me, that you recognize me as a person with needs, feelings, aspirations, and desires. But because I can now truly forgive you, I will no longer give you the power to wound me or my own wife and children. We name the evil, and in the name of Him who is our light and life, we surmount it, we transcend it in the power of the Spirit. We can now bless you as you let us, expecting nothing in return. We do not accept your attempts to scapegoat us, but with the word of truth, that wisdom that comes from God, we turn your accusations and projections back upon your own head, and we leave you to deal with them. We know now that this is love, the love that 'is more stern and splendid than mere kindness.' It is the love, this word of truth, that will help you overcome the evil that binds you to yourself. We do not judge you, Dad, but we do judge the evil that has wounded us all.

"And now, Heavenly Father, I thank You for hearing this prayer, for enabling me to accept and fully forgive my father, and for enabling me to no longer subjectively flail under the evil that has afflicted us all, but to rise into that true objectivity that will perhaps someday enable me to be a channel of Your healing love to my father."

In this way, Dr. L. came into that green and spacious place where he began to know God the Father's affirmation of himself as a son and as a man. He began to hear the voice of the ultimate Affirmer. "On my first eight-day retreat, I heard the Father tell me He loved me, that I was precious in His eyes, and that He needed me to do His work. This permeated my entire being. . . . 'I love you and now call your sexuality [masculinity] into order so that you can grow in My love and then minister to men I call you to.'"

In this way, listening to the affirming words of God the Father, he began to "bond" with Him; he made contact with ultimate masculinity, which in turn struck fire to his own. And he began to gain, slowly at first, the gift of divine objectivity.

Dr. L. could now see that his deep desire for male relationships, never a bad thing in itself but rather needful and healthy for all men, was frightening to him because he had a fear of rejection by other men and such an overwhelming need for their affirmation of himself as a man. He had never bonded with his father and unconsciously sought this masculine bonding through other men. His need for masculine approval and love had been so great, therefore, that he had had to repress it, and rankling as it did, deep in his unconscious, it began to erupt as fear, guilt, odd thoughts, genital responses, impotency with his wife, and finally, as time went on, to an unhealthy fantasy life in order to perform sexually.

As Dr. L. came present to and understood his own heart, all repression of his need for father-love and masculine approval stopped. Then once it moved into the conscious where it could be laid before the Lord, it could no longer erupt in odd ways. He repented of and put to death the fantasy life he had adopted in response to his fears and guilt; his problems with impotency, inappropriate genital responses, and odd thoughts subsided and disappeared.

From then on he could begin to relate to men. He was no longer afraid to put his arms around the man who needed his touch, hold him tight, and pray with him—whether this was in his capacity as a physician treating the ill and diseased, or as a layman called to pray with and for others. Dr. L. had a medical practice in a large West Coast port. His large medical practice brought him all conditions of men and women. As a specialist in his medical field, he is often called upon to treat medical problems that are specific to practicing homosexual males. Before his healing, these patients could bring to life the worst fears he had about himself. Now, however, in his own words, "I can talk with, pray with, cry with" the homosexual person. "I have become more lovingly authoritative or firm in speaking about sexual behavior to the men who come to me." Dr. L. now has, in fact, a most significant ministry to men suffering with sexual neuroses and, because of the cosmopolitan nature of his city, has helped people from many lands.

As infants snuggling in our mother's arms, sons and daughters alike are affirmed in their feminine side. We get in close touch with the feminine within our mothers and therefore within ourselves. Dr. L., having had a loving, understanding mother, was highly developed in his feminine side. And this was a very good thing indeed. But, being insecure in his masculine side, he had been fearful and ashamed of his giftedness. He had even tried to hide the creativity that came directly out of being in close touch with his intuitive, feeling, compassionate self.

"As Leanne and I prayed about masculinity/femininity and their balance, I began to see myself differently. I began to see myself in the light of Jesus. I also saw the balance within Jesus; His masculinity/femininity became more obvious, and His relationships with both men and women." As this physician understood this, he recognized and accepted his own unique gifts.

An important prayer we pray over the one who has been so deeply wounded by the sins and sicknesses of others is one of "binding and loosing" (see Matthew 18:18). In the Scriptures these terms refer to loosing people from their sins and from the effects of being sinned against.

In the effective doing of this, we take an important principle from the prophets of old who, one with their people who had sinned, acknowledged their part in the corporate sin of the nation. Daniel's prayer (9:4-19) is one of the most beautiful illustrations of this principle, as is Nehemiah's prayer (1:5-11).

> I confess the sins we Israelites, including myself and my father's house, have committed against you. (Nehemiah 1:6)

> They stood in their places and confessed their sins and the wickedness of their fathers. (Nehemiah 9:2b)

When praying for someone who is grievously sinned against, we confess those sins before God that have so deeply pierced the soul of the one for whom we pray. This does not mean that the evildoer's sin is hereby remitted. It does mean that with this confession and our extension of forgiveness to the sinning one, the power of that sin to continue to wound and to shape the sufferer is broken.

An extreme instance comes to my mind just now. A woman had undergone the severest kind of ritual abuse as a child, abuse perpetrated by her mother who was involved in witchcraft. By the time she attended one of our conferences, she had received great help through the church, but she had come, hoping against hope, for release from the terror still connected with her memories of torture and abuse. Just to mention "forgiving the unforgiveable" to someone like this dear soul is to see the person begin to relive the terror. And this is what happened to her. She began to scream, saying, "I can't bear the pain; God has to release me," while her eyes, darting in every direction, had the look of an utterly terrorized animal. I held her as tightly as I could while she trembled from head to toe in this traumatized state. Knowing, however, that she had to forgive her mother before she could come into freedom, I pressed on to help her forgive, assuring her strongly of the following:

1) We do not forgive evil (per se).
2) We do not forgive Satan.
3) We do not forgive demons and evil principalities.

But we do forgive *persons* in the clutches of that evil. She calmed a little at that, and then we were able to confess specifically the sins of witchcraft and the sins of her mother's witchcraft against her. With this confession and her forgiveness of her mother (but not without an incredible battle), I was enabled to bind and lift from her the unspeakable sins perpetrated against her and loose her from them. She was freed that very day from the terror of a lifetime. Only in the Healing Presence of God are we enabled to pray this way. But this sin too He has already endured for us and experienced the awful turning of His Father's face from Him as he took upon Himself and into Himself the sin of a fallen world.

A Cleansing Grief

Truly, as Johnny, the doctor, and all of us find out, it is in being humbled to the ground with sorrow and loss that we as Christians can find both the grace and the option of mourning before Almighty God our sins, our sorrows, our grievous losses and injustices. From such a stance, we more deeply recognize the human condition, that we too are sinners, that we too are capable of wounding others. We know that if we do not find the grace to forgive, within our hearts a coldness and a hardness will increase, and we will as sinners grow more monstrous. But if in this state of woundedness and mourning, we cry out to Him for the power to forgive, we receive healing and mercy. Our hearts softened and pliable now in a way for which our greatest successes could never have prepared us, we go on to true victory over the world, the flesh, and the devil. This is why it is not in our successes and victories, but in the fires of sorrow that we find our our truest selves. When we truly forgive (that vital principle at the very heart of Christ's cross and the Christian gospel), we find that He is with us (and has been all along) in the fiery affliction. If I fail to forgive, I turn from Him, and lose the real "I." An icy hardness begins to form in my heart, and I am the loser.

Though suffering is the way we can best learn, not all are helped by it. As Oswald Chambers has said, "it makes some people devils."

> We all know people who have been made much meaner and more irritable and more intolerable to live with by suffering. Suffering perfects only one type of person—the one who accepts the call of God in Christ.[5]

Johnny or the doctor or the woman so injured by witchcraft could have refused to forgive. Thanks be to God, I have seen very few who refuse to forgive once they understand that the grace to forgive and be forgiven is available to them. Once in a while, however, I do see it. It is not something one easily forgets, for of all that is tragic, this is the most. As Oswald Chambers reports:

> There is no suffering to equal the suffering of self-love arising from independent individuality which refuses to submit to God or to its nobler self.[6]

When the Need to Forgive Is at an Unconscious Level

"Forgive your father for dying." I shall never forget these words the Spirit spoke to me the first time I sat under the ministry of prayer for healing of memories.

My father died when I had just turned three, leaving my mother, myself, and my eighteen-month-old sister to grieve his loss.

I was with a group of ministers, religious (nuns, teachers, monks, deacons), and various professionals in the medical, health, and educational fields. We had gathered there as Christians to pray for one another and to learn more about healing prayer. I was already deeply involved in the ministry of praying with others. I had myself received the healing of all known hurts and even disappointments through confession of every known sin in every period of my life, through a wholehearted reception of God's forgiveness for these, through restitution where needed and possible, and through prayerful listening and waiting upon God.

But I was unaware of the deep sense of rejection I had felt at the loss of my father, that it was at the bottom of my need for healing in the first place. I was completely amazed by what happened to me in this healing of memories prayer. Even more important insofar as the healing ministry is concerned, the Lord proved to me beyond all shadow of doubt the validity of prayer for psychological healing—that He not only can, but delights in pointing out and bringing up the root traumas, no matter at what age in our lives they are experienced. And furthermore, it is not something *we* do; rather, it is what we allow *Him* to do!

The minister that day prayed for us, beginning in the present and going down through the years toward birth and conception. Since so much healing had already taken place in my life, nothing happened until we reached age three. Then up popped the clearest voice imaginable from my deep heart: "Forgive your father for dying!" *How ridiculous*, I thought, *to forgive one's father for dying*. But I did it just the same. Most fervently. The clarion quality of that command to me is something never to be forgotten, much less doubted or denied. The fact that children take the loss of parents, however it comes about, as a personal rejection was the subject of the minister's sharing with us on the following day—the very thing God had so clearly shown me.

I was totally unaware that I had experienced the loss of my father as a personal rejection in spite of the fact that throughout my childhood and adult life I had a recurring dream of searching for my father, of finding his casket, and of hoping against hope that he might somehow be alive. But once the memory of his death came to consciousness, the rejection was vividly clear in my mind and heart. Never, since the day Christ touched that memory, has the dream recurred.

With this healing, I finally understood what God was showing me in the camping-trip experience and in the uncanny experience of somehow knowing I had come home when in the Scottish Highlands. God is outside of time; all times are one with the Creator of time. This is a vital part of the Judeo-Christian truth system. It stands over and against pagan and/or occult ways of explaining like phenomena with the concepts of reincarnation, out-of-body-travel, and so on. God was finally able to answer my anguished queries over Edie, the young girl who repeatedly fell into sexual sin. I could see quite clearly how psychological wounds such as hers could be prayed for and healed. It is a wonderful thing to know that God is, even now at this very moment, present to any and all trauma we have suffered. As we learn to invite Him into these places, face the darkness, loneliness, and hurt with Him, and then set our hearts to forgive and receive forgiveness, He heals and sets us free. It is a profound ministry, vitally connected to the Christian confessional, whether formal or informal.

Apart from the healing power of God in our midst, no one can explain a healing of memories and the magnitude of the change in our hearts that can come with it. In simply obeying God and in saying, "I forgive you, Daddy, for dying," I opened the way for Christ to enter into all the ways that I, even as an infant, had responded to the grief and to the drastically altered circumstances of my life at this early stage.

Instantly, as I forgave my father and these accompanying circumstances, I was set free from emotional bonds I'd not hitherto perceived. At this same time, there was also set into me (or freed, I don't know which) a new ministry. It involved special insight into the healing of men. Before I had mostly prayed with women. The connection here, as I later realized, was not only one of churchly custom (women praying only with women), but of an unconscious and even denied fear and distrust of men. All of this was related to the early psychological injury—the traumatic sense of rejection in the sudden loss of my father.

I was like Edie in that, if I'd known my own heart, I would have said: "Daddy, if you had loved me, you would not have left me." My pain and trauma was not nearly so deep or life-threatening as hers. With an alcoholic mother, Edie experienced gaping deficits of the kind of nurturing love that fills and gives an infant a solid sense of being. Unlike me, she was left empty, starving for another's touch and strong, protecting embrace. But she and I would be healed in precisely the same way. It would be through forgiving and then exchanging our old hurt and sense of rejection for the life and light God longs to flood into all the darkened spaces of our souls.

Every traumatic rejection untouched by the vital kind of forgiveness the cross has won for us, whether at a conscious or unconscious level, will be acted out in some negative fashion. We may reject others—before the feared rejection can come our way. I was, in a sense, rejecting men by failing to pray with them. This was never very strong with me and probably represents what most women in this age of unfathered men and women feel, but even so, it subtly shaped the way I ministered. Too, until the healing, I could not receive from men as I needed to. I was now freed to help men as well as women, and—as I grew in understanding—I no longer feared their rejections or transferences. In the process, I began to receive from men the needed masculine input. It awakened great tracts of my spirit and soul, complemented and balanced the highly developed responsive qualities of my own feminine identity.

This healing then paved the way for yet another. It was the removal of a writer's block, and I wrote of that in *The Broken Image,* the "Appendix: Listening to Our Dreams." This healing involved the recognition that there was a part of me that I had never accepted. After a painful period of being "pregnant" with my first book and unable to write it, I realized I needed prayer for enablement to accept that part of me who is a writer—a part of "who I am" vital to fulfilling the work God has assigned me to do.

In a series of six dreams, I came face to face with the writer in me, though I did not at first recognize her. In these dreams, she came right up out of the depths of my deep mind and presented herself to my astonished conscious attention. She first appeared as a feminine figure unprepared, but contemplating a leap over a swollen stream where a bridge had once been but had long ago washed away. Against all odds, she jumped and was gravely, perhaps even fatally, injured in the leap.

This dream and another revealed the inner fears and feelings in which the writer's block was rooted. In the dream the bridge over the stream of life was washed out, and the girl injured in trying to leap across. My father had been that bridge, and the flood of death had taken him away. But the loss of my father formed no part of this or the other dreams. Rather, they consistently revealed the *fear of exposure* along with the concomitant *deep feelings of inadequacy and inferiority* as the direct consequence of being fatherless. And the little girl within me who felt all this was inextricably combined with the writer within.

In another dream, she appeared as a figure prepared to cross a dangerous river, but fearful of exposure. In another, she appeared as an acrobatic dancer skilled, yet fearful of exposure. And finally, she appeared as an acrobatic high-wire artist, performing with skill and precision, exposed but no longer minding exposure. Dreams are terribly frank, and my fear of exposure was symbolized by being scantily clothed—something not unusual in the acrobatic dance or in high-wire artistry. With the last figure, the writer who necessarily exposes herself and I came together. This understanding, along with prayer, brought quite an incredible healing.

The dreams, so briefly alluded to above, revealed that the fear of exposure was rooted in the consequences my family had suffered through the loss of my father. Please note that it was the consequences, and not the loss itself, which had already been touched by God. At the time of his death and thereafter, we were thrown out upon the world, dependent on others for the shelter we needed. The first healing, that of memories, located and touched my sense of rejection; this healing dealt with the mechanisms I had adopted as a way of coping with the loss of love and security. In attempts to overcome the loss, I, like any good stoic, simply denied it. I steadfastly and consistently denied throughout my life the little girl in me who would admit her fear of rejection and exposure, inadequacy and inferiority, in the absence of a father. I successfully denied that valid part of myself. And it was this figure, the stoic in me, who attempted to leap over the swollen river, rather than admit the missing bridge made it impossible.

Therefore, I had to confess pride and receive forgiveness for it. Feelings of inadequacy and inferiority (like those of presumption and superiority), no matter from what psychological injury they stem, are ultimately rooted in pride. I believe that behind every writer's block, indeed, at the bottom of every need for psychological healing, one will find it necessary to confess, "Lord, there is a part of me that has never confessed its need and pride, and therefore that part of me is still trying to be adequate apart from You; it is still fearful and unable to wholly depend upon You."

When my dreams revealed this condition in me, it would have been easy to go on denying these fears (as I had done all my life) rather than to confess them to God. In fact, if I had not written the insights into my prayer journal immediately, they would have slipped back into the unconscious, just as lost to me as if they had never surfaced to consciousness.

I think my healing is fairly representative of what we most often see in these healings. There is the initial instantaneous healing of memories that has to do with forgiving and receiving forgiveness. I can never say what all was done as I forgave my father for dying. It is clearly beyond our merely human powers of knowing or telling. We can never (nor should we) analyze and categorize it too finely. We are all so different, some so ready to receive more, while others less. But the healing of memories, vital in cases of early and unconscious trauma, is the root healing that forms a basis for any later healing needed.

This further healing requires time and process, such as getting in touch with deeply wounded and split-off emotions and feelings—those that surface in separation anxiety and in abandonment depression. One must also deal with the failure to accept oneself and its unconsciously held negative feelings and attitudes resulting from early trauma.

This distinction between the instantaneous and the process is necessary because we in the healing ministry are often criticized for speaking of the quick accomplishment of these profound initial healings. In observing these healings over the years, I find that we more often understate than overstate the magnitude of what God does. At the same time, we recognize the key part these initial healings play in those that come later. Some require agonizing periods of experiencing and working through emotions that have long been repressed as well as sometimes difficult and painstaking attitudinal changes in relating to God, to others, and to the self. For example, I might still be dealing with writer's block had I not learned to listen to God, had I not searched out other wise souls who understood the symbolic nature of dreams and prayerfully helped me read them aright. Also, in this regard, good writing—that which is in line with the way things really are—is hard work and requires sacrifice. I could have been unwilling to discipline myself, and then insisted on calling that failure to pay the price a "writer's block." That too is a facet of human nature that needs prayer help. But my basic message to all and sundry is: "Hope thou in God." "Trust fully in Him." There are answers, there is healing. Keep searching for it.

Prayer for Groups of Christians Seeking Wholeness

In our Pastoral Care Ministry Schools we always conduct a "prayer workshop" in which we pray for healing of memories for the group. This is not something we recommend that others do, but we've been led to do it, and the results are truly amazing. It would be difficult to overestimate the benefit of these prayer sessions and to exaggerate what we see God do when He puts forth His hand to heal His wounded ones. We see healings of prenatal memories, trauma of birth healings,[7] as well as those traumas suffered in earliest infancy and childhood. Deeply repressed memories come up to be dealt with.[8] In these sessions, persons suffering from all manner of emotional problems are ministered to by the Spirit of God.

Even one such need is overwhelming, humanly speaking, and in our meetings there are sometimes several hundred or more people with these deep needs. We know that if God does not come and heal His people, no amount of teaching and preaching about the need will avail. Here is where the understanding of how to collaborate with the Spirit of God comes in. The usual way to approach healing of memories is through counseling and prayer, addressing the need of one person at a time. However, we approach healing of memories from the standpoint of the *charisms of healing in operation within the context of God's gathered community.* Christian mental health professionals and pastoral counselors are amazed and deeply gratified at what they see the Lord do in these healing sessions. The principles of prayer they see demonstrated often revolutionize their practice. They know so well how formidable are the needs that we see the Spirit of God sovereignly deal with. But most will continue primarily as therapists dealing with one person at a time. I say this to stress the fact that not everyone is called to do what we do. But the principles are the same. We pray, "Come, Holy Spirit, come!" And then we invite the needy one into the Healing Presence of God.

When God is in charge, we are never "gift-oriented" or "gift-centered." If we are thinking about operating in this or that gift, we are in trouble and apt to intrude in fleshly ways into what God desires to do. We are always to be "Presence-oriented." If God doesn't do it, it won't be done. Memories, therefore, are not forced up prematurely. Just as important, coping mechanisms necessary to the person's psychological survival are not prematurely removed. In short, there is no manipulation on our part. We collaborate with the Spirit of God as we lift high the cross of Christ with its full message of good news to all who suffer, and as we invite Him to enter into the memories of those ready to forgive and receive healing. This is a ministry that we grow with. In the beginning we did not see full-blown homosexual neuroses healed or repressed memories surfacing. We did begin, however, with the knowledge that behind someone's agonized statement, "I can't love," or "I should never have been born," was a painful set of memories that God wanted to heal, and somehow we could learn to pray to that end.

Infantile Needs

Most people are by now familiar with the "threat-to-life" experiments done by scientists several decades ago. With their fine instruments, the scientists measured the reactions of plant life to hostile acts. The researchers then were amazed to find that plants reacted as well to hostile threats. How much more does the infant in the womb and the young child in our arms. The thoughts, feelings, words we send out bring life or death. We are either channels of God's love, or—in failure to love and accept others—we destroy.

We've come through a long, dark period when there has been little understanding of what constitutes trauma for the embryo, the infant, or the young developing child. The practice of placing an infant with one nursemaid after another, disturbing its capacity to bond with any significant mother figure, is not only a vice of the wealthy or the unavoidable plight of the poor today. Many Christian women holding their babies to their breasts feel as if they are wasting time, that they should be working in some more meaningful or lucrative capacity. Too, we are paying a price for grievously shortsighted and mistaken medical practices that left the newborn uncomforted and separated from its mother immediately after birth. We've not understood the deep rejection that adopted children have experienced in the loss of their birth parents or what happens when a girl is born to parents who want a boy, or vice versa. We've not understood the profound effects of a mother's emotional trauma on her unborn infant, much less how to pray for healing of these later.

My friend, missionary Ingrid Trobisch, loves to tell of a certain African tribe that is dear to her heart. The chief and all his tribe knew that the most important person among them was the pregnant woman. The tribe's future depended upon her giving birth to children who were strong psychologically and physically. The expectant mother was, therefore, given special protection and a place of honor within the tribe.

I'm deeply concerned that Christian parents lack the basic understanding that their infants grow strong psychologically and become enabled to take the crucial developmental steps by identifying and bonding with their parents. The data we now have on these psychological and physical developments, facts that would enable us to avoid some serious errors with our children, seem slow to filter down to the majority of Christian parents. Our misbegotten notions about how the infant and the young child are "spoiled," for example, can lead us into misinterpreting and ignoring their real needs. The time-worn practice of leaving an infant to cry in isolation, even when it goes against the keenest intuitions of the mother, reveals a tragic ignorance of the way that isolation threatens identity in the infant. Writing on the psychological verity that the baby experiences life by identification with the mother, Dr. Frank Lake states:

> So long as the mother is present, and satisfactorily so, the baby experiences its being and well-being in identification with her. It cannot conceive of life going on without her, except for short times when her coming is delayed. So dependent is the baby on her presence that, if she fails to return, the power of being-by-relatedness-to-her is depleted to dangerous levels of hopeless-

ness. Lively expectation gives way to despair and mounting separation-anxiety.[9]

Those of us with long experience in pastoral care know only too well the truth of Dr. Lake's further comment:

> Even though at this point of maximal tolerable panic the mother returns and the experience is split off and repressed, it remains as an indelible aspect of personal identity.[10]

It is no small thing in prayer for healing of memories to have the person bring up infantile memories of this isolation and agonize as they tap into the cauldron of fear and panic that has heretofore been split off and repressed—yet active in ever so deadly a way in the unconscious.

I have had the most wonderful opportunity to watch a young mother, active along with her pastor husband in the life of a growing church, as she relates to her little newborns and then as they grow—one right after another until now there are three. By any standards, she is a busy woman.

I've been astonished, knowing how tired she must be, to see her pick up her infant even when it is not hungry and not crying, when her other children are tugging at her. She just "wools" them around, as the old saying goes. She breast-feeds her babies and is always tenderly caring for them. She knows what weariness is. Bone-deep weariness. But she has the best babies. They hardly cry at all. They laugh and love. She didn't "spoil" them. She gave them the kind of start infants need. She knows intuitively, even as the Indian mother who straps her baby to her back, that the infant's alarm signals mean something and that it needs loving contact in order to grow.

And she will have lots of rest later when mothers who've had less time for their little ones in infancy are spending sleepless nights over their children's difficulties in adjusting and learning and in relating to others.

Christians who misapply the Scripture's warning about "sparing the rod and spoiling the child" can unknowingly create another source of trauma for their children. How easily parents err in this way if they do not understand the rudimentary developmental steps a child takes, or if they attribute evil to the child when no evil was intended. I remember my dismay when one tot, large for her two years, came running toward me. In the process, she ran right over her baby brother sitting in the middle of the floor. Her perception of space was not yet fully developed, and true to her age, all she could see was the goal. Her little brother simply happened to be in the direct path of it. Her mother quickly grabbed and soundly spanked her. Probably even more damaging, the mother verbally interpreted the behavior as stemming from jealousy. I can still see the confusion and bewilderment on the child's face, and I grieve over the knowledge that this child's character will later reflect these types of misjudgment. These parents were not open to exhortation, for they were very strong on not "sparing the rod and spoiling the child." The difficulty was that they were wrongly applying this verse to a very young child and were ignorant of basic developmental stages. Tragically, they had no understanding of the effect their actions had on their children.

These kinds of mistakes, made by well-meaning Christian parents, could be remedied through giving preparation courses in our churches. The stakes are very high. The mental health of our children, not to mention the exercise of simple justice, could easily enough be the fruit. Then our children would be able to receive and benefit by the necessary disciplining we all as parents must undertake.

Our long, dark period may be coming to a close in some ways, for example, in terms of better scientific and medical procedures with the infant. But in other ways it is getting darker still. More and more women are cut off from their true feminine gender identity and are unable to nurture their young. If too many Christian women feel that they are wasting time in the important nurturing process, we will lose not only our healthy children but our capacity to lead in matters of the home, the church, and the state. More truly than we know, it is "the hand that rocks the cradle" that determines finally the fate of a neighborhood, a clan, a nation, or even the world.

CHAPTER 8

Prolonged Healing of Memories: Abandonment Issues and the Repression of Painful Emotions

As we learn more about the processes of healing within the soul, we often find that the power to feel the pain is itself a vital part of the healing. The sufferer has repressed this heretofore and denied it precisely because it was so painful. But now he has to get it up and out. He needs to understand that, if he will stand in the cross and hurt, there is a place for it to go, an end to the pain. This seemingly endless pain is the way he gets in touch with and names the heretofore repressed grief, fear, anger, and shame underlying his depression. In order to come out of certain types of depression, one must feel the most appalling pain and grief. It often seems that death would be easier. But repressed grief and sorrow and loss remain to afflict us in other ways until we grieve them out.[1]

In some of us, our healing requires the pain of getting in touch with soul-shaking grief and loss. The pain, we are stunned to find out, is a vital part of the healing. When we are in the midst of reliving and experiencing the feelings that caused an infantile shutdown of the capacity to receive love from others or of the power to feel at all, even the initial root healing of memories can seem to stretch out interminably. The pain one experiences in such a case is beyond the powers of most to even imagine. At any one time, I will have on my desk letters that express this kind of pain. I'll quote one in full because it illustrates much of what we need to touch on in prayer for such a sufferer. Except for the minor changes that protect this young woman's identity, I am reproducing the letter as she wrote it. Since, however, she mistakenly uses the term "codependency," I will substitute the correct term "emotional dependency" in brackets.

Dear Leanne,

I need your help if you can give it. I have gotten myself into such a mess, and don't know how to get out of it. I've been in law school this past year, suffering more than I ever thought God would let me suffer again in my life. It is hard to write this letter. I am so full of pain, but another part of me says it's my fault, it must be my problem, so quit being melodramatic and self-pitying. I don't know which view is the truth, Leanne. I suspect some of each, but I just pray that the Holy Spirit will give you insight to see and hear the Truth, even where I don't write it right.

I don't know where to begin. . . . I went to the [place name] PCM before going to law school to try to clear up any important remaining "stuff" about my coming out of lesbianism 2¼ years before that. *Nothing* traumatic came up. I felt that the prayer time showed me my real task was the self-acceptance step. So, I began practicing that. But, as I look back, I see things were going a little haywire even before I got to school. I got pretty hooked into a new massage therapist I'd recently met. And I don't know how to describe this, but after this year, I see I did with her what I've done with various "special" women all my life. I needed her. I needed her special beingness to stoke my fires of beingness. To feel alive. It's not that I don't know how, on some level, to separate myself and get back into my separateness; it's that my separateness has no aliveness to it.

Leanne, I have lived through hell this past year. I thought I was following God: many things had worked out divinely, including a housing situation with several other Christian women who love the Lord. But from the beginning, I watched myself slide into a more and more hateful, loathsome place.

I became [emotionally dependent] on one of my roommates: I didn't even want to; I kept doing the things that I knew worked [i.e., to avoid the pitfall of emotional dependency], except they didn't work. Oh, there was one thing I couldn't do which I usually did when troubled with [emotionally dependent] attraction: I couldn't go away. Usually in such a situation, I would/could go away until the [emotionally dependent] attraction, the "craving" stopped. But I couldn't. So I crossed over the line. And it was messy. And Lila [her housemate] was angry and not good about dealing with my "gut-level" processing. . . . I was shamed to see my deepest, most embarrassing, un-okay yearning coming out. We got separate, but through another series of events, I just invested and transferred that energy over to another roomie. Again, it seemed to start out good; when I began to recognize the feelings of craving and longing again, I prayed and resolved even more firmly not to descend into an [emotionally dependent] hell. By choosing like this in the past, I had stayed okay! But no matter. I crossed over the line again. We had to have it out, and I had to just get separate again. This amidst the nonstop pressure of law school, spending by far the most of my waking moments on studies. Of course, I probably overdid it. I probably should have lightened up. But I couldn't. Studying less was more stressful, not less [because] then I was just behind and lost in classes [as well].

I got sick over Christmas vacation. Came back and didn't get well. Nothing really wrong, just a virus. But something, way deep inside me, was so very tired. I started getting pretty nuts—for me anyway. I started going back to AA meetings, just looking for some kind of support group. I started seeing a Christian counselor who works with an ex-gay ministry. I'd just cry. And cry. There was no relief. When I was so depressed and tired I couldn't get out of bed to come downstairs for my birthday dinner, Janice insisted on having everyone come up and pray for me. I could only sob and say, "I don't know what's wrong. I just don't feel good."

Finally, the diagnosis [of the virus]. . . . On to a regimented, incredibly expensive diet. No sugar, no honey, no coffee, no processed foods. . . . I'd cry when I'd eat a piece of fruit: seems that's the only sweetness in my life. . . .

The depression lifts a bit on the diet. I'm not quite so tired. I finish school amazingly, but hell, hell, hell. Right after, I go home for three weeks. I'm so tired. So pent up with all I've been through. But my home church speaks to me. I'm feeling decidedly better by the time I come back—I even feel some lightness in my heart for the first time in months and months and months—but in three days of working full time, I am in unbearable turmoil again. Depressed, tired, screaming to God in my frustration and pain and despair; sobbing, sobbing, sobbing; I can't take it. I want to be well. I hate my life. Finally, I give in. I can't do it. I just can't finish law school. I just can't live like this. If God won't provide the healing and the changes in my life that are so necessary, then I just cannot do law school. I didn't want to be a secretary all my life. I didn't even want to be a massage therapist all my life, but maybe that is all I can really handle, emotionally. That's life.

Sometime after that, (the next morning?), I find I am consumed with a desire to be held, to be loved by a woman. Nothing new about that. I have been living with the almost nonstop craving to be held all year. I cannot look at Michelle or Susan without desiring, wanting, needing to be held. But what is different this morning is that what has not been an option for 3½ years—sex with a woman—is suddenly an option. I cannot help it. How frightening. Now all I can really think about is going back to [her home state] to the first woman I ever really "loved," who likes to take care of people. I want to be taken care of so badly. To be held, loved, kissed, caressed. . . . Or I think about crawling into Michelle's arms, nestling amongst her breasts, putting my lips to them. . . . I have this thing about women's breasts. They evoke in me something so deep. A hunger. A longing so strong. Leanne, isn't there a remedy to this terrible, gnawing hunger for—for a woman's breast— or whatever it is? I cannot live with this hunger, unfed, forever. Leanne, I have been a model, a prize "ex-gay" person these past 3½ years. I truly have. I have not focused on women sexually, my thoughts have been pure, I have not entertained fantasies. Up to this year, Jesus has been enough. But this onslaught I cannot abide. I must have some relief.

God has spoken to me repeatedly in the past that "breasts are but a symbol of the true nurturance I have for you." At times I thought I was receiving that, but these desires have never gone away. They've been muted, even inconsequential at times, but always, always, always there is another snag. Another time of heart-rending pain surrounding it where it feels like I could die, I hurt so badly.

But I have been unable to really feel Jesus' nurturance since last fall sometime. I am resistant now again to male figures. . . . (That's one of the things that seems to make this "my fault"—i.e., if I weren't so stubborn, I'd receive the nurturance I need from Jesus.) It feels like, despite how "well" some part of my mind is, something is bad wrong inside.

Leanne, I realize that on some important level, I have never had an emotional relationship with Jesus. I feel unable to. When Lila and Michelle both were angry about how they felt I was asking something from them that only God could give me—I understood what they meant, but it feels like a cruel joke, because I can't seem to get that from God. I get it from women who are in strong connection with God, but not from God Himself. This seems another area where one could accuse me of just not being diligent enough in my relationship with the Lord. Therefore it's just my fault. My lack of commitment. But I don't think I'm making excuses when I say I can't. When I'm in a good place, then I can have fairly contactful times with the Lord, it seems. But when I get into that hard place, there's just no connection. I can pray for infilling all I want; I just don't feel a thing.

Leanne, I see that my whole life has been spent in finding emotional meaning and aliveness in other women—even after coming to Jesus. Law school was/is an attempt to chart my own course, utilize my own talent, follow my own dream, be alive inside myself. But I'm dying. Physically, I'm sick, emotionally, I am chronically depressed; spiritually, I am despairing and ripe for a fall *which I know shall never fulfill me anyway.*

I beg of you, if it's true, tell me that Jesus can deliver me from this hell. I can't. Leanne, I can't "wrestle this away in prayer." Every time I think I can, I just get knocked down by a flood again.

Isn't it possible that something is still buried in my unconscious that could make this all *livable* at least? Fill up that longing? Make Jesus accessible to me emotionally/spiritually, and not just [through] His women? Or am I just looking for the easy way out? You know, the do-no-work-just-deliver-me approach. I tell you, if it's up to me at this point I am doomed. I just don't have the energy or strength or willingness, hardly.

I cry when I read *The Broken Image* passages of touch deprivation and failing to come to an adequate sense of being. Could that be me? I know of a situation in my infancy that could be the origin. I developed a staph infection

> at three days and was put in isolation for a week before my mom took me home and kept me in isolation there. Of course she also had to stop breast-feeding me, but just knowing of it has not healed me. Please write and tell me you'll pray for me/with me. If my problem is not something that can get really, miraculously handled in prayer, then I am lost. Write me, please. God only knows what continent you're on; you are probably deluged with mail, but please write me fast . . . Please help. God, please help.
>
> Sincerely, (signed) Linda
>
> P.S. I confess that I don't want "healing" so much as I want to be *filled up*. I can't explain that; it just seems that "healing" means the feelings will be taken away, but I will still be left empty. Is that the way it's supposed to be?

Linda is one whose infantile memories hold an intolerable amount of emotional pain due to what for her was an interminable period of abandonment. You may have noticed that it was not until the last of her letter that she got to the real problem—a prolonged infantile isolation from her mother. After having been an embryo nurtured by her mother's womb and heartbeat, then being nursed and loved as a newborn, on day three of her life she was suddenly placed in an utterly lonely, sterile place due to staph infection. That she mentions it as a last resort, even after having read my books and attended a PCM where we deal with these matters, fits in with the way painful emotions arising out of infantile trauma are repressed and denied. Repression and denial, now in the midst of breaking apart, were the coping mechanisms by which she had survived.

Dr. Frank Lake, English psychiatrist-theologian, describes and explains as well anyone can the pain that this young woman was experiencing:

> The roots of all the psychoneuroses lie in infantile experiences of mental pain of such an intolerable severity as to require splitting off from consciousness at about the time they occurred. These have remained buried by repression. The actual cause of the panic may be a time of separation-anxiety endured during the the early months of life, when to be separated from the sight and sensory perception of the source of "being," in mother or her substitute, is tantamount to a slow strangling of the spirit and its impending death. The various patterns of the psychoneuroses comprise and indicate a variety of defences against this separation.[2]

Denial and Repression as Coping Mechanisms

There was strong evidence in Linda's application to the PCM conference she attended, now a year and half ago, that she was dealing with abandonment issues. She was directed, therefore, to see a team member who would understand her plight. On seeing her, this prayer counselor discerned that Linda's mechanisms for coping with her pain were still so strong that she could speak only of "co-dependency," insisting that her problem was in that area. She had a serious problem, indeed, with emotional dependency, a term that would have accurately described a large part of her dilemma, but she could hardly yet even admit to that. The prayer counselor immediately understood that Linda was intensely fearful of facing the deep-seated feelings that were so utterly opaque to her.

As stated in an earlier chapter, it is the Lord's work to gently open a person's memories, and His timing is perfect. Our part is to pray in such a way that the heart of the needy one is opened, thereby giving God the opportunity to heal. It is true that we do not hold back important insight. For example, we did say to Linda, "Your main difficulty is likely to be found within the first months of your life." There was resistance to hearing that, however, and when that happens, we do not overrule—either by force of will or by powerful prayer in the Spirit.

In answer to corporate prayers said over the group, our Lord enters in and gives the insight needed as the individual soul is ready to face it. We can therefore rest in God's timing, knowing His faithfulness. We do not forcibly remove a person's mental, logical coping mechanisms before there's a readiness to face the unbearable, that which was a kind of death to them, that which they cannot remember. This can sometimes be difficult for us, especially when we realize, as in Linda's case, that the feelings, though unconscious and repressed, are still driving the person mercilessly and compulsively, shaping the life and robbing it of freedom.

Professionals in the fields of psychology and counseling are very careful with these repressions. After releasing the prayer of faith—a powerful prayer but one that does not forcibly remove the coping mechanisms—for the healing of someone like Linda, one of the first things we do is to recommend therapeutic counseling and to pray fervently with them to find the right physician. If we can work in tandem with a well-qualified psychologist or psychiatrist, all the better. The professional and the sufferer will need the prayer help and the understanding of the Body of Christ. Likewise, we need the special expertise of those able to provide needed medication and to guard the person through the depressions inherent within an acute deprivation or abandonment neurosis.

In the past, we have not always been able to locate the professionals gifted in this area. Especially when the difficulties have resulted in defense mechanisms associated with male homosexual or lesbian behavior, the things that can go seriously wrong in the professional's office—even the "Christian" professional's office—these days are many and varied. Sadly, at times we have to deal with the wreckage a professional has left, perhaps of one who has forced the irrational belief upon those suffering with lesbian or homosexual neurosis that they are to accept their "sexual orientation," i.e., their defense mechanisms. When these persons have severe gender confusion, and especially when they are breaking, as Linda's letter clearly reveals herself to be, they have little defense against powerful arguments coming from those deemed to be experts who are supposed to be helping them.

Besides these kinds of difficulties, we find on occasion the desperate soul whose mechanisms for coping have been removed prematurely, and the therapist working with the person has had nothing of value with which to replace them—the most notable omission being the gospel of truth with its gift of the grace to forgive and its power to heal. There are also the professionals who disregard early infantile injuries. Still others, even though they do understand them, are fearful of dealing with such repressions at all, and simply prefer to tranquilize and sedate persons. It is no small thing to deal with needs such as these. It requires true wisdom (an empathic and intuitive understanding of another soul) as well as sacrificial giving by the caring, responsible professional and by those who pray and provide pastoral care. At this point in time, we have more and more Christian professionals to whom we can turn. Like the late doctors Frank Lake and Karl Stern, these professionals hold to a thoroughly *incarnational view of man and of reality* and are therefore open to God's healing power coming through prayer and the Word of God. They understand Christ's work on the cross and apply it to the deepest needs of the wounded soul. They know that our best efforts and strictly human sympathy cannot accomplish the full healing, but that divine love can, using us as very human, loving instruments.

In prayer for a group healing of memories, I always ask the Lord to guard such memories until the sufferers are ready to face them and until one of our counselors, well able to deal with this kind of emotional pain, is close. And it is perfectly amazing to see how God always and faithfully hears and answers these prayers. Nothing seemingly is "too large" to come up, but it comes at the appropriate time, place, and with the person needed to assist.

Grief

Linda's healing will involve intense grieving. Her need, then, though it requires healing of memories, is better understood as calling for a *healing of emotions*. In a healing of one's memories, there is always, of course, a healing of emotions going on as well. But in the case of someone such as Linda, the painful facing and working through of repressed emotions is by far the greater part of the task. This involves getting in touch with infantile feelings of grief that were unbearable then—and are now. Linda is ready now, however. Her denial barriers are forever fallen. She can no longer stave off the pain. A year and a half ago she wasn't ready to face the grief. Now she has no alternative.

In the first paragraph of the letter, Linda swings between wondering that God allows her suffering to continue and the fear that she is being self-pitying and melodramatic. In the PCM schools, it is easy for someone like Linda to misapply the teaching on "the bent position" and even on "emotional dependency." These are things Linda was grappling with—with all her might. But her main difficulty lay in the fact that the initial and most important attachment of her life had been traumatically interrupted. The ongoing, trusting relationship with mother that provides the basis for a strong personal sense of selfhood, of *being* itself, was cut off in such a way that she passed a crucial threshold of pain. That left her with a terrible deficit, and there was no bridge back across that threshold into a secure sense of well-being. Until healed, she is left to cry:

> It is always the same, if I am waiting in helpless dependence on someone else to come and pay attention to me, they never come, and the agony of waiting will drive me mad.[3]

Linda, in her heart of hearts, believed herself to be abandoned. She suffered with separation anxiety, and until her primary unmet developmental need was addressed, she would continue to harbor within herself the infantile feelings of abandonment. There would have to be, through prayer and, in her case, special counseling therapy, the healing of these early memories. In such a healing, a kind of trust (not easily achieved) is established with the therapist or the one who prays. This trust allows the sufferer, *as the scene is being replayed in the memories*, to compensate for the original loss—experience, as it were, an "initial" attachment with a trusted "other." Undue fear of being bent toward another could jeopardize the healing.

Note the above emphasis on "as the scene is being replayed in the memories," for it is when the unbearable infantile feelings charge forward that we minister to the suffering inner child. This is what ties all of this in with healing of memories, even though the healing is prolonged. Sufferers are at these times of depression *back in the experience of abandonment* with its associated feelings.

In telling about Edie, the adopted girl, I said that had I understood prayer for healing of memories, I could have thrown my arms about her and held her tight as she forgave her parents. Why the emphasis on holding her tight? Because the tiny infant within her was still crying out for her mother's arms. God could have used me in this way as "substitute" mother in the healing of memories.

This brings us to two important points. First, God takes the loving actions we do in His name and multiplies their effects, even as He did the loaves and fishes to the hungry multitude. It never ceases to amaze me the way He uses such small and seemingly insignificant gestures—in relation to a lifetime of deprivation—to bring about so much healing. The miracle He performed in feeding the multitudes has its absolute counterpart in the healing of hungry and unfulfilled emotional beings.

The second point brings us into the area of what the psychologists call "transference"—the way that we helpers momentarily and at crucial points in a person's recovery *become*, as it were, the parent. In a transference situation, we attract the feelings, both negative and positive, that the sufferer feels toward the parent. This differs significantly from "re-parenting," a practice some people get into, but one that is, strictly speaking, not possible. In a healing of memories where the Spirit of the Lord is mightily moving, the person is so deeply ministered to, both on the human and the divine plane, that an embrace by a "substitute" mother can assuage a lifetime of deprivation and become the channel by which the Holy Spirit heals the deprivation and loss.

Though the capacity for self-pity is a live option with all of us and is for some a chief vice, the feelings Linda suffered from were not of that stripe. Her problem stemmed from the deep inner belief that she was abandoned, and this belief could only be reinforced by thinking she should be able to look only to Jesus and not to persons. Relating to others in the right way was, after all, one of the chief things to be set right. Due to her woundedness, she could not relate intimately with others without her unmet need coming into play. How can we achieve friendship and married love before we've achieved the initial relationship that gives us a secure sense of the self, that the self is in fact there, a self from which we can relate to others? That sense of the self brings with it a feeling of well-being, indeed, of being itself. Dr. Frank Lake speaks of this as the "I-my-self."

> Many of us were fortunate enough to be given the security of our mother's and then our father's continual presence to support our being until it became so much a part of us that we could say I-my-self in such a way that we could carry our mother's spirit and our father's strength about in us. We can always enjoy this tripartite 'I-my-self' nature. Much has been given to us, and there is nothing lacking to our essential humanity that we have not received.
>
> This is not so with hysterical personalities. Faith in one's basic spiritual relationship, in the 'self' which should have been mother, has been shattered. It can be represented only by 'I-my-?' or indeed by 'I-nothing-nothing.' This is what we mean by depersonalization, a sense of the complete unreality of the self when it cannot rely by faith on the other necessary elements of its spiritual totality.[4]

Linda knew only the "I." Due to infantile trauma much of the "my-self"—found in a safe start with mother—was lost in the splitting off of the unbearable feelings. Therefore, friendships were always muddied due to attempts to find the "my-self" in another woman. Linda knew nothing, therefore, of a healthy interdependency upon and with others. She had to swing from the extreme of neurotic attachment (the bentness toward another that sought to make up for the loss of the needed initial attachment) to the other extreme whereby she feared and eschewed all attachment.

Linda experienced the kind of early trauma that leaves one with a sense of being that is either extremely tenuous or missing altogether. There is, even as she describes, an identification with nonbeing itself. Can God heal people like this? Yes, indeed. But we have to understand what it is we are praying for here and how important it is that we learn how to pray aright.

We can see by now why she felt "no aliveness when separate," precisely what the tiny infant in isolation felt. One who did not know herself even to be separate from her mother and who had continuously received her messages of love and warmth, whether within or without the womb, was now unaccountably bereft—dead apart from that "other" whose special beingness told her she was alive.

Linda's letter reflected a need so strong to "connect" with mother (or a mother figure) that there was no room for grieving. She could only endlessly strive toward making the vital connection, that miraculous bridge with woman she missed in infancy. In a sense, therefore, she lived in unresolved grief all the time.

There is often, as Drs. Hemfelt, Minirth, and Meier have noted in their book *Love is a Choice,* a repeating pattern in certain cases. Persons like Linda are often drawn toward those who will abandon them—even as the infant "believes" the parent did. They hope to resolve the original situation by reenacting the abandonment scenario repeatedly until they finally are not abandoned. In these situations, of course, when helpers do not know how to put up the right kind of boundaries, they can get so entangled and then, finally, so discouraged that they have no recourse other than to give up. When we understand neither the problem nor what to do to help, it is better that we "give up" quickly in that we acknowledge we are in over our heads. We then can look and pray diligently for those who can give the needed help. But the point is—it is not difficult for these sufferers to find themselves finally shoved aside—even by the most loving of Christians.

The Breakdown of Rational Coping Mechanisms and the Emergence of Neurotic Desires

Linda speaks of her power to *choose* in the past and thereby flee emotional dependency. This was her swing into no intimacy in relationship to others in order to avoid the overdependency. Her cognitive defenses were very strong—and needful. But when these finally failed, she was reduced to the "sobbing, sobbing, sobbing" and the "hell, hell, hell." When she finally broke and gave in, her awful striving ceased. What happened then? The neurotic compulsions returned full force. All her abandonment issues raced to the fore—the craving for touch, to be held, to nurse. All the unmet infantile desires were then a hunger so strong that she could think of nothing more than attempts to get this gnawing, never-ceasing hunger fed. Just as the young lad who can't accept himself as a man after puberty continues to hurt and seeks this affirmation in various (even neurotic) ways, so she sought to make up this greatest of deficits—a truly awful one. Her lesbian neurosis was little more than a symbolic confusion, a defense against the terrible inner emptiness—the fact that apart from strong, nurturing women, she had no "aliveness," no hope of something to blot out her dread feelings of "nothingness." Frank Lake speaks of this as the "reaction into lust":

An alternative defensive reaction to rage is to substitute for the real mother and her breast a mere fantasy of them as if they were back in possession. This substitution of a real loved object by an imaginary one is termed *libidinal fantasy*. In the Anglo-Saxon sense of the word, this is "lust," an absolute desire for that without which one cannot exist. In the first days of infancy the mind instinctively has a picture of the desired object, the nipple or breast, and a vaguely conceived picture of a desired person's face. In the painful absence of the real person or an acceptable substitute, fantasy "recreates" the longed-for person, or a part of them, or an item of their clothing as a memento, in a mental image. Libidinal fantasy occurs independently of the reaction towards rage.[5]

Anxiety

The anxiety Linda is suffering now is part of a defense mechanism against her split-off feelings—those inherent in an abandonment depression. It is, in effect, the defensive wall in her soul she (and we) can see and that she is painfully experiencing. On the other side of the wall—behind or underneath it—are those things she cannot as yet see—those things she most dreads and fears.

This back side of the defensive wall of anxiety holds back truths people cannot bear to look at, such as those they hold about an idealized mother or father, or fears of annihilation, or repressed memories of traumatic incidents. In Linda's case, the realities of repressed grief, anger, and fear of nonbeing appear to be as yet unfathomed and unnamed. In the economy of the soul, it is better to suffer and deal with terrible and even chronic anxiety than to have to look at something the heart deeply and unconsciously feels is worse.

As this wall of anxiety starts to crumble, the autonomous nervous system kicks into high gear. The body and the deep mind (unconscious level of the soul) are anxious, for they know what the person does not yet know. Some of the severe physical reactions that occur when the break comes include trembling and chattering of teeth, bodies drawn up into contorted positions as muscles respond to the deep inner tension, sweating, and tachycardia (abnormally fast heartbeat). Because the feelings are those of the panic-stricken baby, there will be a heightened adrenalin flow and, therefore, rapid respiration and pulse.

The time may come when we who pray with others are asked to pray for someone whose wall of anxiety is beginning to crack. We will find ourselves attempting to comfort the person as the fear takes hold, and perhaps his or her body will start to shake violently. This state of panic and anxiety can go on for a very long time, even hours.

If when we invoke the Presence of the Lord and lift our voices to Him in prayer, the sufferer can then say, "I can look at this now because God is with me and those I trust are holding me, praying for me," the defensive wall will begin to crumble. If, in other words, the sufferer is enabled to trust that the resources are there with which to face the dreaded infantile memories with all their inherent panic and grief, then healing can come. But when the sufferer cannot in the natural flow of prayer reach this point, we need the help of a gifted physician/psychologist who will, among other things he deems necessary, administer medication as it is needed. This medication will not tranquilize the person to the point of never being able to deal with his grief, but it will grant the merciful reprieve needed so that the sufferer can go on with the dreaded work of facing the inner deprivation and loss.

When we see our fellow Christians suffer in this way, it is terribly difficult to realize that with all our crying out to God there has been little or no relief for the sufferer. Our distress is heightened when we have no understanding of the psychological dynamics—what is going on in the sufferer or what has yet to happen. There can be no relief until the acute anxiety lifts, and then, when it finally does, we are further distressed to see the one we love and want to help plunge immediately into clinical depression. But it is here that the person will begin to relive the infantile memories and thus will get in touch with the split-off feelings. This process can and often does go on for months. What we need to know and what we need to assure the sufferer is that there *is* an end to this suffering. There is light at the end of the dark tunnel. The hurt and pain, unbearable as it is and inescapable as it is, turns out to be a vital part of the healing. It signals that the repression is lifted and that the split-off feelings are coming to consciousness where they can be dealt with. If we know how to pray for healing of memories and help the depressed person to face the worst with Christ, he will in the end be spared a great deal. Healing will not only come, but it will come much faster.

At this point in ministry to the sufferer, relief comes to him as we who pray remember to speak not to the hurting adult before us, but to the suffering infant within reliving the trauma. The ministry the person receives at this time requires the utmost sensitivity and skill on the part of the professional therapist, and for those of us who pray, it requires the same. Our "skill" will differ from the doctor's, but it consists in humility before God in the face of such suffering and in seeking God's guidance, wisdom, and knowledge in every step we take. And He is so faithful, so willing to give it. Above all, our "skill" mainly consists in trust in Him. This trust grows as we see the Lindas, time after time, and in spite of the long, delicate process, set free to enter into joy and into healthy relationships with others.

When the pain is at its worst, though still ministering to the suffering infant, I use the imagery of standing in the cross and hurting. For example, I may pray something like this, "Lord, I stand here at Your cross with this tiny one, and these feelings of panic and fear are so terrible we cannot bear it. But You died to take these feelings into Yourself, and we take our place in Your dying just now. We die with You to the sins and shortcomings of anyone or any circumstance that contributed to it. We forgive them, Lord. We forgive the very circumstances of our lives, Lord. Lord, with You I feel this pain, and now I know it cannot destroy me. In Your perfect being and sacrifice, it has a place to go, and I'm yielding it up to You. Thank You, Lord. Strengthen me to feel in Your good time the other split-off feelings that have to come up, and I will again take my place in your death and dying. Lord, I will stand and hurt in You and then receive Your healing and life in return."

Time

Time is different for the newborn. Minutes are hours, hours are eternities. When persons like Linda relive these early memories, it is as if time itself almost grinds to a halt. The present moment, even as it was then, seems endless, and the pain too great to bear.

In the midst of abandonment depression, there is a loss (as we see in Linda's letter) of the power to function. Linda was crying out to God, but she was unable to feel His Presence ("up to this year Jesus has been enough") or His nurturance. Though she is not yet in touch with the memories, at a deep level she is feeling her mother's absence and the loss of *beingness* she suffered as an infant. She had cried out for mother, and mother didn't come. Now she could cry out for God to come, but she could not, as it were, *be* in His Presence. *Beingness* itself was at risk within her, and so the painful thinking, thinking, thinking and striving, striving, striving. Once this emotional activism peaked, she plummeted down into passivity and depression and then faced the fearful work of getting in touch with what was in her deep mind and heart.

When Kierkegaard cried out that we have forgotten how to exist, to be, and that we can only *think about* being, he was describing Linda's condition. It is evident that he suffered a grief like Linda's—and found no relief for it. He was, therefore, keenly aware of this pathology as it now spreads itself over the church and the Western world.

Our parents in their functioning symbolize God to us, and for Linda there was no nurturing symbolization here. By the time her staph infection was cleared up, she had a far more serious difficulty. She was too wounded to accept in trust the love her mother had to give her. Her reactions now to others would not arise out of a serene sense of having been loved and protected. She could not feel her mother's love and protection; therefore, she could not feel God's help and protection even when it was being given. She never stopped knowing by faith that He was there, but her need to rest in a restored sense of being and to feel safe in the love of God and of others was now overcoming her strong rational defenses.

Touch

Here within the adult person, we see the suffering infant, and for it, as we've noted, time virtually stands still. Its physical sight differs. As these person go into these memories, they sometimes describe difficulty in seeing (hazy or blurred vision), but even so are able to tell us what is happening—or what is failing to happen. Loving human words addressed to the suffering baby and *touch* are what sink deeply into the soul of the inner hurting infant—the very missing ingredients from long ago. Therefore, we comfort the baby within. And the baby responds to touch.

When their worst feelings charge to the surface, they are not relieved by our audible prayer to God but by the comfort given the inner child. (Even in the "Standing in the Cross Prayer" and others that we are led to pray aloud, we are at the same time comforting and relieving the child.) These dear ones find relief as we speak to the tiny abandoned infant and to God for them. We are, in a manner of speaking, back in time—we are ministering to the infant as it was in its initial suffering and wounding. Therefore, we do what we would have done had we been there and understood what was going on. We assure the baby it is safe, that it is no longer alone.

Although our prayer at this time is immensely effective, it is not something the suffering one can yet "think" or "feel." We have ourselves become a prayer—God's love together with ours links the sufferer ever more securely to Himself and to His healing love. When a person is experiencing the hitherto repressed feelings of an infantile trauma and/or emotional shutdown, we are, as it were, holding the inner suffering infant and speaking words of assurance and comfort to it as a mother would. This is where the sufferer can make the vital start—the beginning of trust that *another* is indeed there.

The healings that can take place at this point are nothing short of miraculous. They do not happen, however, apart from our taking great care in the way we minister and pray. The therapist or counselor continues to be important, even pivotal, as the healing proceeds. He or she is the one with whom a vital transference is taking place. But it is good, even ideal, when others (especially family members) can also be involved. The therapist is not always there when the feelings hit. Abandonment depression is intermittent: it comes and goes as the waves of grief come forward. When someone in the family knows how to pray and is also trusted by the sufferer, the whole process can be speeded up. In fact, the major part of a healing can take place with that person.

A husband or a wife, for example, when mature in Christ and trusted by the sufferer, can comfort the inner child when these terrible feelings charge forward. A spouse will need the wisdom and the objectivity at these times never to confuse the situation by introducing conjugal love—a mistake married persons could easily make, but which would be counterproductive at such a time.

Through our prayerful and wise touch, the vital connection missed in those first months of life can be made up for. Some would even say *made*. This much I know, a bridge is built, a new selfhood begins to be experienced in identification and in a truer and healthier interdependence with others.

Transference

> First [still using the feminine for both sexes], the hysteric must be able to posit her insecure selfhood in some Christian person, or better still, a family or group of accepting Christians. Here she can recapitulate with another set

> of parents and brothers and sisters something of what was lost in the vicissitudes of her own unfortunate babyhood. We must interpret this transference activity as a necessary kind of bridge-making bringing her from distrustful isolation (however concealed) back to the reality of the social family. This way she replaces her own neurotic bridge, with the force of forbidden impulse and retributive punishment surging back and forth over it, and substitutes a new and as yet untried bridge of actual trust of a real person outside herself. Only when she has tested the bridge to see if it can carry her weight can she begin to respond in mutual trust again. She has to ensure the new relationship can stand the weight both of the ingratiating attractive side of her personality as well as the unattractive fears and rages and paroxysms of envy and hate that are inalienably part of her tortuous self.[6]

As those who pray, we do not set the stage for a transference. We learn to recognize it when it is occurring. When one who suffers separation anxiety relives memories of perceived abandonment, we who pray with or counsel them are parental figures. We minister into the woundedness. If we've been close to the needy one and they've been looking to us for help, we've likely experienced the ambivalence inherent in a transference situation. Both love and hate can come our way; in other words, we draw toward ourselves both the hysterical and the schizoid reactions in our attempts to minister. Setting appropriate boundaries and knowing the importance of timing and touch are some of the ways we avoid the difficulties.

Bonding

In regard to abandonment depression and deprivation neuroses, I hesitate to use the term *bonding* except to describe what happens between mother and child. That term, it seems to me, carries with it the strong and appropriate image that rightly defines what occurs with good mothering. Used in the context of the healing of someone like Linda, however, it implies that she found something equal to what she lost when the bonding with her mother was interrupted. Therefore, we are in danger of being led astray in several important ways if we use that term in the context of the healing of adult sufferers. Their loss will always be a loss. No one person or ministry can ever take the place of the missing mother or mother substitute. Nothing can replace her love and sensitivity that enables the attachment to her (as well as the healthy detachment later on) as one comes into a sense of being and selfhood. But I know the inestimable value of the healing of memories as one relives in the presence of a trusted soul the trauma one early on faced in absolute aloneness. By placing the trusted one in the parental position as the sufferer relives the past, God makes of him or her a unique instrument of healing and wholeness. And it is a "kind" of bonding, an attachment on the human level that enables God to multiply within that heart and mind the infilling of *storge* (nurturing, familial) love it missed as an infant.

What happens in these instances is truly miraculous. But it is different from what happens in the natural process, and we err if we try to duplicate it.

There is another reason for my hesitation to use—other than very carefully—the term bonding. When helpers take this process too literally, as in the concept of re-parenting, they tend to make cripples of the sufferers. It is too easy to develop emotional dependency on the mother figure. This is especially true when the sufferer tends toward the clinging (*hysterical*) position.[7] The likelihood of emotional entanglement is far less a threat to the counselor when the sufferer tends to fear attachment (the *schizoid* position).[8] Therefore, the counselor may feel that re-parenting is working. But this "attachment" to the parental figure will not necessarily help the person to true interdependency with others nor to overcome his fear of intimacy. It may even inhibit full healing.

This is where the negative aspects of transference take place. In a transference situation, all the delayed hopes for a mother instantaneously rush in. (This could be termed an "instantaneous transference" and should be differentiated from the natural bonding that occurs normally between mother and child, beginning even in the womb.) The miracle of trusting a mother figure is for the first time not only a possibility, but is experienced, and the sufferer feels safe. This is not bonding, though it possibly feels like it. It is the priceless place of safety that allows all the sufferer's memories and feelings of rejection, anger, and abandonment to surface. It is also the place where real trust can take root in the sufferer's heart and a bridge of intimacy be built—one that prepares the way for a healthy normal attachment to occur and then from there interdependence with others to grow. But here the counselor's part grows more crucial.

For this the counselor has been waiting—the emergence of the diseased, repressed feelings. This is not only the critical place of healing for the needy one, but it is the place where the helper needs the most wisdom. Such a sufferer will invariably (from this place of safety) perceive rejection and abandonment on the helper's part because he or she is reliving (at the deepest emotional level) the failed relationship with mother. The woman counselor, as a mother figure, will then be the object of the person's worst fears.

It is for this reason that attempts to re-parent, strictly speaking, lead in the wrong direction. Re-parenting (something the sufferer desperately wants) doesn't work. Though the helper has given the gift of a place of trust and safety where there can be the kind of transference that abreacts these wounds (allows them to surface) and their accompanying fears and feelings, the helper's job at this point is not to be the mother the person never had or a savior from pain. Counselors are not and cannot be either.

Women counselors can, however, especially as Christian women, be serene symbols, icons as it were, of the best and the truest in womanhood. They are indeed sacramental channels of a blessed feminine giftedness into the lives of those bereft of such. They can even be empowered by God in special ways to respond to the wounded. But they cannot be all this to hurting people if they draw toward themselves these persons' fear of rejection and abandonment instead of objectively deflecting these fears into Christ crucified.

They are called to pray and then in the wisdom God liberally gives, they deflect the feelings of deepest dereliction from themselves up to God, who is Mother-Father-Savior. They do this by helping the sufferers to acknowledge before God all these dread feelings, heretofore repressed, and by helping these persons to forgive their parents and the very circumstances of their lives.

This does not happen if the helper has presented herself as the ideal mother, in which case the sufferer will either be bent toward her or demand that various therapists do what the helper has seemed to promise. In the initial stages, the counselor was "the only trusted one." But if the helper does not understand what the later stages hold and how always to call the sufferer to the truth (I am not your mother; you cannot find your identity or sense of being in or through me), the helper will experience the down side of the transference mechanism. Then she will think she has failed and will (apart from some fortunate circumstance) constellate an irrational and hysterical acting out on the part of the sufferer. Even more serious, if the counselor becomes the desired feminine object to the brokenhearted, she then will be an idol, a dead icon that ceases to point to reality.

Some books on deprivation neurosis present re-parenting in such a way that the helper is bound to burn out (perhaps even become codependent or give up on healing prayer in the process), and the sufferers—with their irrational needs either to cling or to flee—will be tempted to stop short of finding their true identity as responsible adults. In focusing too exclusively on the inner suffering child, some have neglected to minister to the responsible adult the person now is. They have over-identified with the "problem" to be healed and under-identified with the true self, the full person who is to be called forward to become all he was created to be in God. In effect, they have lost sight of the person's true identity. It is the adult (albeit one who is suffering greatly due to infantile memories) that we encourage and strengthen to come present to his or her worst memories and see them healed. It is the adult who is to be helped to see and repent of immature or sinful responses, and who is to be led in confession of sin and in prayer for the forgiveness of others.

It's a wonderful thing to watch these adults learn to grieve out their wounded feelings, while at the same time they grow as responsible adults in the midst of their suffering. I've seen the most courageous stability here as they maintain these objective stances, knowing themselves as responsible adults even as they experience feelings of dereliction that few can imagine who've not been afflicted with such depression.

This, I think, is a marvel—but it is part of the grace God gives those who trust in Him. Christian counselors or therapists can get in the way of this grace, however, when they forget the prime identity of the suffering one before them. Some sufferers, of course, those mature in Christ, would never regress and remain in the "wounded child." It would make little difference if we as counselors were unclear in our approach. But there are many more who would continue to live from the center of the wounded inner child rather than from their true center, if they mistakenly focused on their suffering. It is from that true center alone that they as adults take their place in Christ's suffering and in His cross. That is where they die with Him to the pain, releasing it all into Him, and then go on to grow up into the most astounding maturity in Him.

Some of the most balanced and powerful ministers I know have come through these very woundings. My files are full of their joyous letters—letters that proclaim the truth that God turns our worst hurts into healing power for others. Several of these are deeply loved and valued PCM team members. They preach the cross, lifting it high as few others do, for they know its awesome efficacy.

Healing is a delicate process in all these souls, and we who pray for this healing must keep our hearts closely attuned to what God is doing and saying. It is only with the greatest of humility and sensitivity that we can either discern what is going on in the mind and heart of sufferers or continue to simply trust in God with and for them as those inner needs are hidden from us. As we do this, something new and wonderful replaces what was lost in the early trauma, and a new sense of selfhood, of identity-in-relationship comes to the sufferer.

More on Timing and Touch

In prayer for healing that involves deep abandonment issues, I need to emphasize again the vital importance of human touch appropriate to the need, and also timing, that dance-like harmony and rhythm we achieve as we learn to collaborate with God in His healing work.

Inappropriate and lustful feelings associated with touch deprivation often surface in prayers with those suffering separation anxiety, especially when their defense mechanisms have resulted in gender confusion and sexual neurosis. As these feelings occur, we are to help the person note them objectively and then yield them (like all other diseased feelings) up to the Lord. We assure the sufferer he is to feel no shame, but he is to admit rather than deny and repress these feelings, and he is to name them before the Lord as they surface. These feelings are usually related to symbolic confusion, and we need to look at them in that light, thus helping the sufferer to resymbolize the feelings. Often their bodies are stimulated in this process in ways that embarrass and even alarm them. Here too we ask these dear ones to be patient with and speak peace to their physical bodies, which (like the soul) also manifest anxiety and symbolic confusion. It is amazing what can be accomplished in a short time when we help others to this objective stance. We are not ordinarily to eschew touch out of fear of inappropriate responses. Rather we are called to understand the responses, thereby apply the antiseptic of reason, and then ask God to replace unhealthy responses with healthy ones. Prayer, together with honoring the need for human touch, works miracles.

Linda suffered greatly from touch deprivation. After receiving her letter, we put her with one of our prayer counselors. As the counselor prayed for her and held her in the midst of her depression, Linda noted nervously that she experienced erotic sensations. The counselor assured her she was to feel no shame, that they were most likely a leftover association from her former homosexual experiences. When the feelings came up, they acknowledged them together before God and lifted them up to Him. Linda wrote later:

> The fact that [the counselor] did not cringe when I told her nor flinch from touching me thereafter made me know, like nothing else could, that it was o.k. to receive her touch. I was able to receive her touch for the unadulterated nurturance it was and let go of the sexual nuance.

One of the results of this time with the counselor was that touch was resymbolized for Linda.

One can readily see why Linda was so "into" massage and massage therapy. Godly massage therapists who understand all these things can have amazing ministries. Of course, they will not allow others to "bend in to them," but will be pointing those they help always toward identity in Christ. These therapists know their own boundaries and do not allow others to transgress them. Thus they help the sufferers to gain the kind of boundaries *they* need. Those boundaries eventually will form the strong circumference of the "city" of their own unique soul, their own selfhood.

Again it is a continuing marvel to see what God can do with one godly, well-timed, prayerful embrace. Just as Christ multiplied the loaves and the fishes so that all were fed, so He can take the small loving things we do and multiply the healing effects beyond all knowing.

I sometimes have sufferers such as these focus on me so strongly that I cannot minister to them. One young man with a need like this came from a distant country for help. He was bent toward me so strongly, however, that I had become everything. In God we live and move and have our being, but he was far from being able even to imagine this reality. He was centered on me with an enormous compulsion to, as it were, crawl into my sphere of being and disappear into me. Throughout the week of lectures and ministry, his eyes never left my face. There was no way I could minister to him apart from God's bringing him out of this fixation, one that had to do with severe separation anxiety and his lack of personal identity. I sent him to others for prayer, but to no avail. At the very last meeting in the midst of the consecration service, I saw him break. He had lost hope I would minister to him, and this had (together with God's answers to our prayer for him) brought him out of the fixation. I immediately prayed with him, and the Lord seemed to rush in to meet this man's need. It was an extremely powerful moment, and it would have been missed if I had yielded to the powerful hysterical need in him to bend into me. This man, a young physician from a troubled European nation, then told me he had planned his suicide for right after these meetings if he did not get help. As it is, he perseveres in the Lord even in the midst of a torn and tumultuous country.

I share this to emphasize our need to fully depend upon God. In our zeal to help others we can get in the way of what God wants to do. On the other hand, it is through the most commonplace gestures of human love and touch that God often finds a pathway through to the sufferer. Through these small things the power of Christ's love and the full efficacy of His work on the cross issue forth to save the derelict soul, the one suffering the "hell, hell, hell" of which Linda speaks.

Christians gifted in prayer for healing are to pray for the wisdom, the knowledge, and the balance needed here. They must themselves be mature and always maturing in Christ, and their full trust and dependence is upon Him. We know and praise His faithfulness, His lovingkindness. Otherwise, we are in danger of moving unwisely to try to help the needy one escape the pain, the pain that is in these cases part of the healing. We move too quickly to try to meet on the human plane what can only be met on the divine. We thereby find ourselves not the channels of healing, but the objects of idolatry. When we know the work is not ours, but God's, then the person's relief and healing does not hinge upon us. We can celebrate our own inadequacy and smallness, all the while knowing that as we continue to pray, God's will is being done. We learn to collaborate with Him according to His timetable and His knowledge of the soul that is suffering.

With all this in mind, we see how easily touch can be misused. Here we see that a mere touch that seems so insignificant in terms of a person's having had a lifetime of need for it, is used by God to heal touch deprivation. But we also see that there are times when our touch would work against such a person's healing, as in the case of the young physician.

Many, especially those coming out of sexual neurosis, are fearful of touch, as many in the church are. Touch is a volatile thing, and we are careful never to misuse it. But touch is important in healing, and God uses it to a phenomenal extent when and as it is appropriate. It is an exciting thing to follow God's leading in the healing of emotional hurts. On the one hand, we cannot let a soul bend toward us in the wrong way, as Linda would have done had we not helped her with boundaries. On the other hand, we see how God uses so incredibly our human expressions of love and touch. How wonderfully God uses our humanness, how incarnational a thing this matter of healing turns out to be.

The hard thing for many Christians who pray with others to realize is that we cannot always (much less immediately) relieve or even appreciably diminish people's suffering. We cannot get in there and "fix things," not even with an instant powerful prayer (although sometimes we do in fact see God do it!). If we try, taking the initiative out of God's hands, we will fail. We may end up reinforcing neurotic defenses as surely as the physician does who over-sedates. To try to "fix things" or to try to shore-up and defend God's reputation as a loving, healing God allows our own misplaced sympathy and empathy to get in the way of the healing. We cannot magically take away their suffering. No matter how hard we try, we cannot take away their feelings of abandonment. Before healing can take place, their task, hard as it may be, is to face the inner loneliness. It is the same task we all have, only it is excruciatingly difficult for them.[9] Thanks be to God, He knows and understands all this, and He is the righteous judge, too loving to remove the necessary task that precedes healing. As Dr. Lake, writing of the full-blown hysterical personality, says:

> The demands for sympathy and care which the hysterical woman [using the feminine for both sexes] makes are her misunderstanding of the problem. She thinks she needs company; what she actually needs is courage to face aloneness. That can only come when experience of attentive caring has enabled her to possess for herself the reverberating circuits of information within the cortex which enable the normal person to feel, 'I am never alone.' She thinks she needs just a little attention here and a little there. The basic therapeutic task is being evaded so long as she declines to face the depths of her inner solitariness, the infant in utter panic and near dereliction. If these could be repressed again, we might be content, but that is not a very adequate ideal of therapy, for it leaves the personality always on the defensive. Our experience and our confidence is this, that when the infantile separation-anxiety is openly declared, then, in the power of the Holy Spirit's abiding presence, there is an entirely new ability to come to terms with separation-anxiety.[10]

That too is our experience. Over and over again we see these persons not only come through the darkness of abandonment depression into the Light that is always waiting for them at the end of the dark tunnel, but—as they mature within the Body of Christ—we see their wounds turned into the most incredible healing power for others. Their joy, wisdom, and depth of insight are invaluable gifts to the rest of us who've never known the failure to find early on, even in the first months of our lives, a sense of being and of well-being in a mother's love.

When Schizoid Elements Are Strong

The root *schizo* derives from the Greek verb "to split." In this condition there has been a radical split in the ego, in fact in the total person. This took place earlier, and goes deeper than it does in hysterical splitting or depressive splitting. As a result of this overwhelming infantile trauma, the ego, which was beginning to develop a relationship of trust in persons in its environment, is split from top to bottom. Only a semblance of trust remains. A part of the ego splits off and becomes regressive, seeking the intra-uterine security from which it has been ejected. Another part of the ego, forced into continued contact with the "terrible mother," is split off and is identified with a longing for death and annihilation. This ego-splitting experience may be due to "biological pain," such as crushing or distress in the birth passages during a difficult delivery, or to "ontological pain," such as the post-natal suffering of the too-

> prolonged absence of the mother who is the necessary personal source of being.[11]

Because Linda's letter reflects the hysterical elements and the striving to attach rather than fear (even panic) at the thought of attachment, we have illustrated the hysterical condition more fully than the condition in which the schizoid reaction is more apparent.

I would hope that this chapter will encourage all pastoral counselors to read Dr. Lake's book *Clinical Theology,* prepared specifically for them. It is now out in an abridgement of his original 1200-plus-page book. In it he writes of the hysterical, the schizoid, the paranoid, and the depressed as they are in the extreme—the full-blown conditions or personalities—and of the anxiety and related defensive reactions and so on. That is not how I write. I describe persons in whom these elements are to be seen. Linda is not a full-blown hysteric. She is in many ways a mature Christian who is suffering abandonment depression, one with strong hysterical elements that indicate her failure to make the initial attachment. She could easily, however, have fallen finally into the full-blown hysterical position apart from help from the Body of Christ. And in the same way we write of the other elements (such as the schizoid), hoping to help those who pray to understand more about what is going on.

The "Internalized Bad Mother"

Sometimes in our healing meetings, persons suffering in these ways begin to, as we term it, "throw up the mother." Long before I ever heard the term "the internalized bad mother," I knew what it was. We on the PCM team find ourselves holding people as they quite literally gag and spit "her" up and out. We've learned how to spot this as it starts to happen and how to pray for these persons.

The internalized bad mother is the result of emotional and/or physical incest. In cases where the child is forced to meet the emotional needs of the mother, it has had to abdicate any need of its own. The mother has so forced herself on the child that the child has, in a manner of speaking, "swallowed" the mother. Sometimes the internalized critical voice of a mother (or a father, in which case we have the "internalized bad father") is so loud that the personality of the child is crippled or even displaced. There is then the need to get this up and out so that one can hear God. (See case example on pages 136-37.) A great release and healing comes when God enables people to empty themselves of this evil. It was good, therefore, to see in Dr. Lake's book his reference to this phenomenon:

> In deep therapy paranoid patients may spend hours feeling identified with a most "distasteful" experience, as if the mouth were full of a substance so insipid, mawkish or tasteless, and so useless as the food they hoped it was to be, that they will spend hours in abreaction as if spitting out some cloying stuff. This "disgusting" truth compels consciousness to tell a lie and deny that

one could ever have been identified with such an insipid and offensive source.[12]

I remember well one young man in one of the services who began to vomit up the internalized "bad mother" in this way. His mother, the most disgusting of sexual deviates, had been his only companion in growing up. He had been hospitalized on several occasions with depression and had made progress. He eventually married, but then all his schizoid feelings in relation to woman rushed to the fore. One cannot imagine the pain his bride must have endured as she began to receive all his transferences and became the object of his enormous fear of being swallowed up by the female and of his disgust. His spiritual advisors were utterly baffled by the tragic turn his marriage took and could make no headway until they realized what they were dealing with.

Such a person needs expert therapy right away. He is fearful of attachment to woman, and his irrational reactions to her along with his paranoia will only grow until he gets help. If he is thoroughly trapped, say for example, as one whose religious convictions will not allow him to desert her, his sickness in relation to others may worsen. He may begin to irrationally hate and blame other women. Men who are deeply and dangerously misogynous can be formed out of circumstances such as these. It is one thing to "vomit up one's mother," and it is quite another to deal in depth with the dereliction and fearful associations that underlie the fear of attachment, all that must arise when such a one marries.

This young man's need showed up in his face and in his actions. But some whose suffering exhibits the schizoid and paranoid elements can more easily hide their need, appearing quite well integrated, strong, and efficient. Not everyone's face or life on the surface reveals early infantile abuse and abandonment. Probably this is especially the case when the power to feel (the feeling being itself) has been paralyzed. Then, if they have survived the ordeal at all, their cognitive, rational powers are highly honed. Their mental defenses and mechanisms for survival are especially clever and strong. From my perspective and experience, it is more difficult for those of us who pray to recognize what is going on in these cases. We can more easily misunderstand and even find ourselves stricken by their reactions. For example, these persons can be almost uncannily secretive. And even if we've been close to them, we may not realize the difficulties, much less the extent of their needs. These have been too well hidden. Then when the breakdown occurs, we who are close to them will not be the trusted ones. We may even (quite irrationally) be mistrusted.

Unless we recognize what is going on—and that there has to be someone outside what has been the Christian fellowship for this secretive, suffering one—we may feel not only rejected but betrayed by the sufferer. We will be the objects of mistrust. We will be getting the "projections" or the downside of the transference. As mother or father figures who are not trusted, we will be wounded and dismayed if we do not understand the dynamics here.

Regression

I am ministering to a young man, gifted in many ways and not the least in a healing ministry. He ministers to others coming out of severe abandonment depression, even as he himself is still coming out of it. This means he often has the burden of knowing what his needs are, as the inner split-off feelings erupt into consciousness, and of knowing that he could give the help to others while at the same time he is frustrated in attempts to get this help himself.

As anxiety hits, Jason has learned not to run from it. He waits in the Presence of God, there facing the inner loneliness with Him until the feelings come to consciousness and he can do the necessary grieving. He has learned to listen to God. He is strong in the Lord, knowing the Word of God, and His commitment to God is absolute.

However, along with the anxiety and panic, he has often been shamed by the fact that in the presence of his pastor, he nearly always regresses to the hurting little boy. A misunderstood movement or word on the part of his pastor calls forth his most inordinate feelings of rejection, disappointment, and just plain need to be loved and touched by a father. It also calls forth his worst compulsions to somehow get from this man what he was unable to receive through his own father and mother.

This pastor is a "mothering" father figure to him and, therefore, is the object of his transferences. The pastor has the unique power to affirm and even bring him through abandonment depression, but also he is the object of his worst and most paranoid transferences. In order to help him and to straighten out their pastor-parishioner relationship, the pastor needs to understand both Jason's regression in his presence and how to set up the proper boundaries with him.

Jason's compulsions were much more powerful than he realized, and so he was often in danger of depleting his pastor's tolerance and patience. In his constant demands for prayer with his pastor, he was demanding more than anyone has to give. Lest this seem to contradict what we've already said, this situation merely points strongly again to both the timing and the grace of God (His love, not ours) operative in healing prayer.

We then talked again about what Jason already knew—that the pastor, just in existing, had the power with one word or the lack of it to plunge him into joy or despair. He knew this was immature; he knew also that despite his best efforts to rationally control the feelings, in the presence of this man his heart always desired something from him. Wanting "more and more" from his pastor, he would ask for prayer—something he needed but could never be quite satisfied with. He was looking to the pastor for both the healing of abandonment he had suffered with his mother and the protection and affirmation his father had never been able to give. The pastor, with many other responsibilities, was naturally growing weary of this constant demand and draining.

I asked Jason to stop requesting prayer from the pastor and to lift up all his anxiety and feelings of need to God, listening to Him for directions as to what to do next. I told him that when his demands stopped, the pastor would be free, as led by the Spirit, to minister to him effectively. And that is exactly what happened.

Pastors need to understand this regression mechanism and how to put up the needed boundaries to avoid playing into it. Then when they are not at the mercy of the sufferer's neurotic desires and compulsions, they are able to minister the healing with all its needed affirmation as they are led.

In these matters, we see once again how prayer and touch heal when they are appropriate, rightly timed, and come at the leading of God. That healing then prepares the way for the next appropriate prayer and touch. The prayer that attempts to meet neurotic need only works against the true healing. This exemplifies again the fact there is the adult, and there is the inner wounded infant and child. We neglect neither. We minister to the person as he or she is now, seeing him or her as a responsible adult. Even further, in seeing the person through Christ's eyes, we see the full, mature man or woman as he or she shall soon be. It has been necessary to minister to the wounded inner child as memories and feelings have surfaced, but we never forget or neglect to relate aright and with appropriate expectation to the responsible adult before us.

Jason is now largely free from these compulsions. His pastor has ministered deeply into his life, affirming him as a man and in his full personhood. He has helped him through his humiliating regression, an immaturity Jason was rationally so aware of but unable to control or conceal emotionally. Better yet, he helped Jason receive his Heavenly Father's greater affirmation and the manly maturity that goes with his inheritance in Christ.

Fantasy Bond

In prayer for healing of these deepest hurts in the memories, those things that inhibited the crucial attachment to mother, a most incredible window is opened into the emotional life of the infant. Along with the feelings of abandonment, for example, one may relive crucial and traumatic moments when one's emotional life (or the life of the mother) is threatened, or the very moments when the emotional-feeling being shut down. And on occasion, there is the matter of a fantasy bond to deal with.

It seems that if the natural bonding is interrupted, we do in fact bond to something. I've prayed with some who have bonded to the bed, or to the pillow, to some very unlikely object, or even to a shadowy fantasy.

In the first chapter of this book I said I would tell of two other significant healings in Clay McLean's life. One involved getting in touch with the fantasy bond. In the failure to bond with his mother, he had bonded with the dark. This startling knowledge came to light as the team and I prayed with him in response to his fearful bout with temptation and self-hatred. At this time, much healing had already been securely set into his life, but he was still fearful to travel or be alone, especially at night. It was extraordinarily difficult for him to leave home alone, which he often had to do in the ministry.

As we were in prayer for him, I "saw" this fantasy bond and knew instantly what it was. In my spirit I saw it as a black disc and knew (as one can only know by the Holy Spirit) that Clay was yet one with it. Immediately, I cried: "Clay, you bonded with the darkness!" This was surprising to us, for we had not anticipated such a thing, but instantly as I named it, Clay saw the same black disc. He also knew he'd bonded with it. This was a powerful breakthrough for Clay, for we were then able to deal with his failure to come to a sense of being in those first months of life, something he had been in denial about up to this time. To say it was a major healing in his life is an understatement.

From that time forward, he has been able to travel everywhere—and alone. Only a few days after this prayer session, he phoned from his hotel room in a city where he was holding services. He was literally exulting in the fact that he was not only happy alone, but cherished the quiet and the time for reading and prayer. This healing then paved the way for another major one that integrated him with the feminine. It occurred about one year later. Since that time, nothing much has slowed this young man down. From the various parts of the world where he's ministering, I get phone messages such as, "I'm the most blessed man in the world," and so on. He writes songs, extraordinary music and lyrics that exult in the Christian's emerging from darkness into light.

Mira Rothenberg tells of a very troubled little boy who as an infant bonded with the lights in his incubator, and of his uncanny fascination with all light, as well as the remarkable way she helped him get in touch with this fantasy bond.[13] Stories such as hers, of successful therapy carried out in a controlled situation, accurately reported, and proved by its healing results would strain the credulity of many—but not of us who minister in healing prayer to persons with deep abandonment issues.

All his life Clay had had a fascination with the dark. He states that he learned to cope with fear and darkness by becoming fascinated with it. At his birth, there was stress and darkness in his home. His earliest infantile memories reveal intense fear for his mother, a feeling that he needed somehow to protect her but was helpless to do so. These feelings remained with him throughout his childhood and apparently got in the way of his ability to bond with her. Later, as a small child he would make his way through the dark rooms of the house to his mother's bedroom, fearful of the night yet more fearful that his mother had not survived it. Once there he would touch her face—to make sure she was breathing. He played this out, time and again, as attempts to keep her alive. Though afraid of the darkness, he loved and searched out dark, enclosed womblike places. From early on, he had unlimited access to television, and, in his words, "I put faces with my darkness, the faces from old horror movies." He states that he felt a "dark numinous presence" come to him through those dark faces, and a fantasy world grew up around them. His fear of death became a fascination with death. He recalls that "old late night horror movies flooded my mind with concepts, ideas, personalities, and the faces which fleshed out my night specters and filled my inner void. Here again, names like Dracula and Frankenstein had a numinous effect on me. Fascination with these figures would hold my eyes captive to the screen until the screen went black; then the fascination would give way to mute terror as I made my way from the TV set to my bed."

Clay had not achieved a secure attachment to his mother, a woman unprotected and far from being at rest; therefore, his own identification with the true feminine and his own sense of well-being did not develop. The parental inversion came extremely early for him. Rather than the feeling of being nurtured and kept safe in his mother's arms, he was overwhelmed with feelings of dread and the need to protect her. His love and loyalty to his mother prohibited his coming out of denial about the extent of his earliest injuries and what had never been achieved in relationship to his mother. He, like everyone who gets help in these areas, had to come out of denial.

A last illustration of how fascination with certain objects comes as a result of a fantasy bond involves the healing of a *cross-dresser.* We use this term for the heterosexual male who wears women's clothing. The homosexual male who cross-dresses we term a *transvestite*.[14]

The cross-dresser suffers from separation-anxiety and gender confusion related to his failure to make a secure attachment to his mother and thereby gain a strong sense of being or of well-being. This loss has led to a most grievous symbolic confusion in him. The related coping mechanisms (cross-dressing) leave him in the throes of a dread-ridden shame and compulsive behavior.

The cross-dresser, then, is a man obsessed with the idea of putting on a woman's clothing and is either doing it or is experiencing compulsions to do it. Unlike the transvestite who is fixated on his own sex and attempts to bond homosexually with a man, the cross-dresser is not afflicted with homosexual desires, but is fixated on woman. He is obsessed with literal woman and her symbolic representations. He is usually married or desperately desires to be. The Christian men of this type I've seen genuinely love and value their wives and homes, though they are emotionally afflicted and confused and are aware of neurotic aspects in their way of relating to their wives. Unlike the *transsexual* man who cross-dresses and who believes himself to be a woman trapped in a man's body, the cross-dresser knows that he is not a woman. Even so he often desperately yearns to be.[15]

In both the cross-dresser and the transvestite, there is a calming effect in putting on woman's clothes, but only in the cross-dresser is there sexual arousal as well. (See qualifying footnote 14.) He is eroticized in donning feminine attire as well as temporarily comforted, and therefore cross-dressing in him is a fetish.

We should distinguish the cross-dresser from the transsexual at this point. There are no female cross-dressers or transvestites, but there are female transsexuals, those who believe themselves to be men trapped in a woman's body, and they cross-dress. The transsexual male, on the other hand, believes himself to be a woman trapped in a male body.[16] Both male and female transsexuals attempt to live as the other sex while despising their body's sexual features. At times they even try with the help of medicine and surgery to obliterate their sexual organs. Until there is healing, these persons suffer depression, usually with thoughts of suicide, and sometimes there are suicide attempts.

Mary Pomrenning, who is on the PCM team, is one who suffered the transsexual neurosis. From actually thinking herself to be a man, Mary has blossomed into a most effective minister of healing, and having fully integrated with her feminine gender identity, she is a lovely woman as well. (The story of her healing as well as her teaching tapes are available through writing her, care of The Church of the Resurrection, OS 641 Rt. 59, West Chicago, IL 60185.)

Symbolic confusion in cross-dressers is deep. To have the neurosis at all indicates failure in initial efforts to meaningfully relate to their mothers, but some of these sufferers will perhaps seem all too bonded to her. Even so, they suffer intense separation anxiety in relation to her. Together with that, they have never gotten their gender identities, confused as they are, separate from hers. This is the reason why there are no female cross-dressers, for their sexuality and gender are the same as their mothers'.

The immediate need for all these persons is for strengthening of the true self in Christ, their oneness with Him, and then prayer for a sense of being. They always have much shame, and we can help them deal with it as they forgive their mothers and all others who've contributed to their difficulties. (This presupposes the fact that these persons have made a full confession to Christ, repenting in depth and fully for the ways they've sinfully acted out their compulsions.) Some will have no idea that they need to forgive their mothers and will not recognize her part in their painful dilemma.

The following is a classic example of a Christian suffering this neurosis. This case illustrates the need both to recognize and deal aright with a fantasy bond and its later expression in an eroticized fascination with feminine objects. This example illustrates as well the way the cross-dresser's eroticism (fetishism) is connected to separation anxiety, which in the young infant is experienced as tension in the genital area.

For one Christian man whose battle with this horrible neurosis had been particularly severe, the fantasy was of a woman's hair, and he had bonded with that. His mother, herself unable to warmly relate to her children, apparently wished he had been born a girl. A number of memories from his very early life revealed unusual treatment by his mother, but the root trauma changed his life. He was about three and his mother had furtively dressed him in an item of girl's clothing when his father surprised them by arriving home early.

He was badly alarmed, sensing her shame and guilt as she quickly pulled from him the feminine clothing. He remembers feeling acutely ashamed, feelings that never left him after that for long. But it was what had happened just before his father appeared that shaped his whole life into a battle against a compulsion to cross-dress, until these memories were addressed and healed. The feelings he remembered, just before this guilty action of his mother's, were of desperately wanting to please her—wanting to be someone she could love. In a moment that seemed to seal her rejection of him as a male, she tied a woman's scarf about his head and then wondered aloud what he would look like if he had hair like a girl's. This was the root memory to be healed, and the fantasy bond came out of this moment. His attachment to his mother interrupted, he bonded with this fantasy image of himself. It was such a strong moment of rejection for him as a male child, and coming as it did so strongly upon a child still striving to bond with its mother, it left an indelible, even technicolor image of himself with women's hair. If she had crammed down upon his head a girl's wig which for some evil reason could never be removed, she could not have done him more damage. He bonded with that fantasy of a woman's hair, and from that time on, it served as both fetish and bond. It critically shaped and determined the way his personality was formed. He was thereafter compulsively fascinated with woman's clothing and especially woman's hair. His heart was never free of anxiety, guilt, and overpowering compulsions to dress as a woman.

I'll never forget when this dear man received his first healings. They started with his reading of *The Broken Image,* and as he said to me later, "Just having my compulsions named as the symbolic confusion they were gave me power over them and a way to cope with them." He had, of course, repented in depth and fully for the sinful way he had acted out his compulsions in the past. Filled with joy and hope, he wrote me right away, and I invited him to a PCM where he received a great deal more healing. He and his wife were ecstatic, for he was free from his irrational yet compelling desire to be a woman and could cope with occasional compulsions to cross-dress by understanding what was going on. Moreover, as he grew in the Lord, his masculinity was being greatly affirmed.

However, he was still troubled with the symbol (inner and outer image) of woman's hair. The image of himself with long hair would compulsively arise every time he was due for a haircut. He would begin to experience anxiety, and he would have to battle a compelling desire for hair like a woman's. Then, to his utter dismay and sense of having failed God, he would find himself eroticized. There would then be even more guilt over the pleasure involved in the sexual arousal.

When he shared this with me, I sensed we were dealing with a fantasy bond and asked God to reveal it. That is when the specific memory and image of the scarf on his head came to the fore. So much healing had already occurred in him, and he was making great strides forward in his sense of himself as a man affirmed in his masculine identity in God. However, it was not until we dealt with this memory of his mother's acceptance of him only when he had a girl's hair and scarf and we realized that he had bonded to this fantasy image of himself, that the stage was set for his final deliverance from the intense anxiety rooted in his emotional abandonment by his mother. We then understood as well why the symbol of woman's hair held such a fascination for him and why it stubbornly refused to go away with the plethora of other symbolic confusions and fetishes that had plagued him.

Another thing to note in the matter of fetishes is the way great pain can be strangely turned into pleasure for such a sufferer. He has forgiven his mother and even come out of denial about the fact that he didn't love her very much. But for many years before he received healing, he could only wish she had dressed him fully as a girl. The very thought caused a pleasurable eroticism in him. He could not for the life of him feel the need to forgive her; he could only wish she had continued to cross-dress him. (Later, some of these men do attempt to involve their wives in this activity.) But here again, we see the great value of prayer for healing of memories. As he relived the moment the little boy was about to have a girl's scarf put on his head, *he realized the little boy did not want to be a little girl.* He realized that this condition was set into him only after he bonded with the fantasy of himself with a girl's hair. His anxiety over being unable to bond with his mother was then transmuted in a most distressing way to a pleasure in being erotically aroused. This is symbolic confusion, and it is always operating in the person with gender neurosis.

For all those coming out of compulsions to cross-dress, the strengthening of their true gender identity is key. This man's great strides came, even before the uncovering of the fantasy bond, as his true masculinity was affirmed and strengthened, something that always happens when we come into a place of truly trusting and obeying God. For Mary, so critically wounded as the one with a transsexual neurosis is, her true femininity was evident in an amazingly short time as she made her will one with God's. To see gender identity restored is a beautiful thing, and it is necessary if one is to see the full restoration of a person's soul.

A Quick Healing Akin to Miracle

Only a few weeks ago I saw the most wonderful healing of a very great need. I've written this chapter to help Christians realize the long and painful process some have to move through in order to get in touch with repressed feelings, but this story illustrates how quickly a very deep deprivation neurosis can be ministered into by the Spirit of God. This healing came to a lovely, young Korean named K—. She, like Linda, had fantasies of a woman's breast (fear of touching one and being rejected and so on), but with her there was not the complication of lesbian responses. A Christian, she had long suffered with depression and longed to die. She was in a college course I taught, and on the first day in class, I saw the pain in her face.

She was a victim of the type of misogyny (hatred of woman) prevalent in the Far East that prohibits many parents from valuing girl babies, especially as firstborns. These little girls are born to women who due to the longstanding virulence of these misogynous attitudes in their culture are unable to accept themselves as women or to value their feminine giftedness. All of this woundedness within K— quickly came to the fore, even in the first classes. Her face alternately reflected fear and depression. After several days, I received the following note from her, and I quote it exactly, preserving the fact that English is not her first language:

This is K—. My growth group leader encouraged me to see you, Leanne. I sometimes have thoughts of death, and Hopeless, I can find hope only in Christ. I don't have excitement for life, life is so hard & tuff. (but my real life is not hard or tuff). When you prayed for me for self-being, I believe God wants to do something, but I don't know.

Through your lecture, I start to see darkness which I never seen before in my life. Could you help me? Thanks, a lot.

K—

I put off seeing K— because so much illumination and healing was coming to her through the class sessions, and her need was being addressed and ministered to at many levels. Her main and root healing came after two weeks of the classes as we prayed for the group for healing of memories. When we came to those first months of life and prayed for the Lord to set in a secure sense of being and for healing for failures to make the initial attachment to mother, her healing commenced and went on for an hour or so. After several days, she wrote it out:

When Leanne start to speak about "self-being, infant experience" [prayer for sense of being], some kind of pain start to heat my heart with oppression. I start to sob. The pain continually hurt my heart. At that time I start to remember something I didn't think about long time which is my mother had some problem in her brest when I was born, so she need to stay in bed and even she couldn't hold me until she recover from her operation. And she couldn't feed me through my babyhood with her brest, either.

I felt grief is comming out from my heart. I start to cry, and the pain of my heart was getting worse and worse. I start to feel phisical pain in my heart, too. I asked God to help me from this pain, Holy Spirit touched my heart, and I start a little bit relaxed.

At that time Leanne asked Esther [a student but also one of the school counselors] to come over to me for holding. Esther came over and hold me. When she hold me, I felt something touched my heart. Grief start to comming out more, after that, I start to see pictures in front of my eyes.

I see a baby who is in mother's arm nearby mother's brest. I recognize I am the baby, and *mother also is father.* My face is leaning on her brest, and then the baby start to suck mother's nipple. When the baby suck continually I felt something start to fill it up from bottom of my heart and some solid thing start to form inside of my heart. After that, I felt full and relaxed. While I was relaxing in mother's arm, from bottom of my heart "smile" rise up and come to my mouth, and changed my sad-looking lips to smiling lips. Until then my mother was holding me in her left arm close to her left brest. But next moment scene changed. My mother was holding me with her right arm close to her right brest. I suck a little bit more, and rub my face on her brest. [While this healing was going on, she was acting out the motions, and there were long sucking periods.] I wanted to know that she is there. I could feel the nipple. I felt safe and secure. A little bit later I rubbed my face again on her brest and her nipple, I would feel her brest and nipple on my face. I rubbed again, and felt her. I felt so good, safe, and satisfied.

Next scene I saw, I look like between 1 & 1.5 years old. My mother is holding me in her arm close to her brest. I rubbed my face to her brest, and got up from my mother's bosom, and play a little bit, and run toward my mother's bosom. She hold me again, I rubbed my face to her brest, I could feel her nipple.

I felt safe and secure. I rested a little bit in her bosom, and run out to play, and then I come back to her, I did something [this] several times. When every time I came back to my mother's bosom, my time for staying with her was getting shorter and shorter. The last time I came back to my mother, I touched her brest with my hand, and I felt that now I know she is there for me. I felt safe, secure & loved. I run out to play, and I know that I don't need to come back again. This is what God showed to me in front of my eyes. When this picture disappeared, I knew that God did wonderful thing in me. He brought healing, joy, security, life, and freedom from dead-wish. This is more than miracle. Hallelujah! (italics mine)

K— then drew a smile on her note to me, something that until "from bottom of my heart smile rise up in me" she could not have done. I had noticed her frozen emotions, that only with the greatest effort could she attempt a smile. In the two weeks, the attempt never quite made it. The corners of her mouth, try as they may, could turn up only slightly, and then never enough to make the smile. Neither in person nor on paper could she make a smile. In contrast, after this healing, her face was absolutely radiant. For the next week that I was there, it wore an exquisite smile, one that could only belong to a beautiful oriental woman. I'm sure it's still there, and the capacity for it will remain.

Here we see not only a healing of memories, but the way our Heavenly Father moves at times to heal deprivation neurosis. There was no "re-writing of the past," no changing, as it were, of K—'s past history with her mother. There *was* a divine and miraculous move to heal her of deep deprivation. If we can be released from fantasy bonds into the reality of a healing of the failure to make the initial and crucial attachment to mother, how much more can God use a divinely orchestrated fantasy (which is not really a fantasy but only the way our heart pictures what He is doing) to heal us of deprivation neurosis! Here is the P.S. to K—'s note:

I wrote what happened on Thursday morning. Thank you for your obedience to our loving Father. Oh, Leanne, when I saw picture in front of my eyes, I saw mother, *and also she is father*. I asked God what is it. I felt that because I didn't have any close experience with my mother, *heavenly Father became my mother and ministered to me*. Oh, it is wonderful, isn't it? (Italics added)

From being held by Esther, she went right into the arms of God, and He became both mother and father. These are the kinds of healings we see, whether they require time and process or happen immediately as in K—'s case. With K— we say, "Yes, truly, it is more than miracle." These healings do not occur apart from the Healing Presence of God, a Presence that is always with us to heal as we forgive others and the very circumstances of our lives. And the divine Presence does not despise the very human need to suckle. As K— was being healed, we watched her sucking motions as she was, as it were, nursing in the arms of the Lord. Yes, K—, "Heavenly Father" became your mother and healed you.

K— will never, even remotely, be the same. This is not to say she will not have pain as she grows out of many attitudes she has had toward herself as woman and perhaps as she relates to her family. But I've seen enough of these healings to recognize not only their miraculous nature, but their lasting effects. As K— walks in obedience to Christ and learns to listen to Him with her fellow Christians, the next healings will come, and they will come quickly. But abandonment depression and the effects of deprivation neurosis she will no longer have to face.

Physical Movements in Certain Healings

We've referred to K—'s sucking movements, something we've seen often enough to know it is important not to interrupt them. In *The Healing Presence*, page 107, I speak of people who come to us for prayer and then begin to behave in distorted ways—in an attempt to receive from God. They are perhaps trying to reproduce body movements that may have at one time been part of a valid religious experience. These movements are now merely part of a ritualized "liturgy" of behavior or sensory responses. There is no divine action, just reproduced behavior. We on the PCM team can spot this quickly and always stop it in order to help the person receive what God is wanting to do in the present.

Having said this, I want to mention some valid bodily responses that sometimes occur in response to certain kinds of healing. (These do not occur on a large scale, and I hesitate even to write about them for fear someone might try to imitate them. However, to help those who pray with others discern in these matters, I include these responses.) For example, sometimes the person receiving prayer begins to shake or even jerk, almost rhythmically, for long periods of time. As I was writing this section, a colleague, John Fawcett reminded me that this phenomenon occurs in the one whose *true self is emerging*. He said, "It is important that this shaking not become an issue and that it not be seen as demonic. We are to allow the person to feel what he or she is feeling, and we are not to stop the shaking prematurely as the feelings of repression and suppression are being shaken off along with the bodily movements." It is, he says, as if "the true self begins to fill the whole body."

Mario Bergner, a long-time minister with PCM, cautions that this phenomenon should not be tied solely to abandonment issues: "I see these particular movements occur in connection with any severe *suppression* of the real self." He lists some of the most common examples he sees.

The first example involves a suppression of the real self related to sin. Mario then reminded me of the prayer for a priest, one who had purposely repressed the truth in his life and ministry. In his case, the true masculine identity, both as man and as priest, had been denied and suppressed by his failure to obey God and by his continuing in sexual sin. In prayer, as this priest repented and as Mario ministered to him, he began to shake violently. He shook for hours as the true self came forward, and after that prayer, he started to obey God. This man's entire personal life and ministry have changed radically since this prayer.

Mario's second example was that of a woman he and I prayed for who, as a member of a oppressive discipleship movement, had seriously repressed her real self. As we prayed for her, she started convulsing, and she shook for ever so long. Frightened, she looked to me for comfort, and I said to her, "That's o.k, honey, it's just your real self coming forward and shaking off its fetters." As Mario pointed out (and on the front lines in PCM conferences he and John often see this played out), this was not a case involving deep abandonment issues, but one of a deliberate and long-term severe repression of the self in the name of the submission of woman.

A third "category" is one unlike the above. But it has to do with the suppression of the real self through severe practices of introspection, and usually it goes hand in hand with abandonment issues and the failure to come to a secure sense of being. The intermittent shaking can go on for weeks, as the real self comes out from under the control of the conscious analytical mind. In this case, all the intense cognitive thinking, thinking, thinking has all but annihilated the real self. As one emerges out of such suppression of the true self, this shaking goes on.

The person doing the shaking can control it. But to control it amiss is to stop the shaking off of the false and in many cases to prevent the surfacing of the split-off feelings that the one suffering abandonment depression needs to bring to consciousness. The simple truth is that the body works with us!

Earlier on, I wrote of "throwing up the internalized bad mother," and I used an extreme example. But there are more subtle ways in which an infant can be overpowered by a mother, and these are just as serious. Persons affected in this way also at times shake violently as they receive prayer and the true self is coming forward.

One young man, a classic example of the above, received quite a healing as he forgave his mother and "threw up" his internalized version of her. This mother had learned to cope with existence by means of a neurotic perfectionism and a super control of persons and events within her sphere. The pictures we received as we were praying with him reflected this control and revealed that it had affected him from the moment of birth. We "saw" the strongest controlling "tendrils," dreadfully ugly root systems, running throughout his body, and these were stubbornly rooted deep into his male organs. There had been erotic overtones in his mother's behavior toward him, though probably unconscious on her part. These—combined with her general responses to him—had resulted not only in an intense emotional revulsion toward her, but in a thorough repression of his sexuality and masculine gender identity. Through prayer, we called up and out of him this internalized emotional junk, seeing with our hearts these stubborn and deep-rooted tendrils lose their hold. We prayed until the last root came up and out and was yielded up to Christ, and then we prayed into those darkened spaces God's healing light, freedom, and love. This was a major healing, and after this he was able to deal with his fear of his mother and with many other needs in his life.

In this healing, there was *not* the shaking and jerking movements as mentioned above, but a year or so later—as he was in prayer with a Christian brother, the following healing word from the Lord came. It illustrates not only the more subtle ways an infant is overpowered and his own being repressed, but also again the incredible accuracy of the pictures and words that come from God as He moves to heal and call forth the real self.

> As J— was praying for me, and for the strengthening of the true masculine within me, he received this word, and it spoke directly to my abandonment depression and the suppression of myself as a man.
>
> It is as though your head was surrounded by a pillow that would suffocate you. Jesus removes that pillow. It is as though you inhaled your mother's exhalation, the stale air of her own lungs. Jesus is giving you the crisp fresh air of His Presence . . . and a new chest . . . the chest of a man.
>
> I see the cross of Christ, and it extends from the top of your head deep down into your body, and its cross beam fills your chest horizontally. This is your true identity. Over the cross is a purple robe of manly dignity, the mantle of the true masculine, humble yet strong.

As this healing word was ministered, the violent shaking started, and this young man's true self together with his true masculinity made giant strides forward.

This ministry paved the way for the Lord to speak into the next need that was to be addressed. He was yet seriously alienated from woman and had a deep-set sense of gender inferiority that had affected his whole life. This led him to overreact, sometimes with intense fear, to women he perceived as in any way controlling, and irrationally to any who expressed the least hint of a romantic interest in him. A day or two after receiving the word that had so deeply spoken into his entire being and need and left him shaking violently, he was in prayer and in a day vision the Lord moved to correct this inability to relate to woman aright:

> I was standing before the throne of God, and He made me keenly aware that His hands had shaped me and formed me. As I was accepting myself as His good creation, He brought woman to me and asked me if I would receive her as a worthy companion, in much the same way He had brought Eve to Adam. This was not an automatically easy response, since my fear of woman had been so great. In the Lord's presence, though, I knew that He was doing a great healing. So of course I accepted His gift to me. We stood hand in hand together before the throne when I became aware of another man standing next to me. As I looked to the Lord, the woman turned from me and took the hand of the man standing next to me and went off with him. I cried out to the Lord that it hurt me to lose again. Since my mother had emotionally abandoned me, this picture in my heart clearly named my worst fear in relation to trusting woman—that I would love and then lose. The Lord then said to me, "Am I not sufficient security for you? Wait upon me, and I will bring you the friendships and the life-long companion you need in my own time. Do not fear to face the loss of love, for I will never leave you or forsake you."

Once God starts to heal the soul, He does not stop until the full work is done—and this is the fruit of remaining in His Presence. As a last bit of understanding we have to share on this matter of bodily movements and how they are related to the true self coming forward, Jason (see pages 126-27) would shake when receiving touch. Although he of course had often been touched, it was only as he was being healed that he was enabled to *receive* the touch. The touch, now divorced from separation anxiety with its erotic sensory responses, went deeply into him, connecting him in a most wonderful and healthy way with his peers and others.

Discernment in Bodily Manifestations

Discernment is truly crucial in all these cases. Sometimes in our meetings before we can get to a person manifesting in a certain way, someone nearby starts "ministering" to him or her in the belief that the activity is the work of demons. We have to quickly speak to this error. There are of course physical reactions to the expulsion of demons, but with the Holy Spirit's gift of discerning of spirits, these are easily differentiated from the body's reactions to emotional healings and from the ways the body wonderfully works together with the whole of man in receiving God's healing.

Bodily Movements in Misogyny Healings

Those who attend PCM schools see what we've come to term misogyny healings. The related bodily movements as well as the words coming up out of the woman can be frightening to anyone who does not understand what is going on. In these healings, the effects of misogyny (stress, self-hatred, rage toward men as well as women, etc.), often coming down through the generations, are as it were coming up and out of the woman. Often the body reacts violently as the woman spits out, screams out, breathes and prays out the long tendrils of that awful "presence" that is not demonic, but is in effect the expulsion of the hatred toward woman that has taken on almost a presence or identity within her. There are often words such as "I hate you," said with such venom, and these are words stored up in the woman's being, words she has long experienced directed toward herself as woman, and these words are internalized, even as the internalized bad mother or bad father. They are even the words she constantly directs toward herself, hating herself because she has been hated.

Sometimes weeks or months *after* these strong, valid bodily reactions—which must be allowed if the woman is to yield to the healing going on in her entire being—she may experience an awful shaking and think she is going back into a misogyny healing. But that is not what this shaking is all about. It indicates a *weak center,* that is, a very weak sense of identity and of being. Such a one needs to be strengthened in her true identity in order to utterly throw off the misogynous attitudes of a lifetime and in order to know that she is stronger than the emotions that threaten to overwhelm her. Shaking related to a weak center is to be stopped, and the true self is to be ministered to in order that there may be the glorious coming forward of the true woman.

It's a glorious thing to see the true self come forward and fill the human vessel and how wonderfully, as C. S. Lewis says, the body also prays. It is a wondrous creation, and itself receives healing as it works with us to the healing of our souls.

This entire chapter, meant only as an introduction to these subjects, is written to encourage those who pray for others and to help them recognize abandonment issues. I hope as well that it will help many to appreciate the ways God would have those who pray work together with those who are medically and professionally trained. The possibilities here are endless, the rewards so very great.

All the healing here is predicated on the cross of Christ. In fact, such healings are not seen apart from God's intervention, which is available to us because of Christ's Passion. As Dr. Frank Lake so wonderfully puts it:

> There is nothing in the hystero-schizoid makeup of the androcentric man or woman which limits the action of God upon the soul. Rather, since infinite attachment and infinite detachment are already present in such souls, they have, even on the human level, a premonition of the dimensions of the abyss over which Christ was stretched upon the Cross.[17]

CHAPTER 9

Third Great Barrier to Wholeness in Christ: Failure to Receive Forgiveness

But because of his great love for us, God, who is rich in mercy, made us alive with Christ even when we were dead in transgressions—it is by grace you have been saved.

(Ephesians 2:4-5)

If by God's grace we have been forgiven, why is it sometimes hard to *receive* that forgiveness? How do we *administer* forgiveness to others?

It is often harder for us to *receive* forgiveness from God than to forgive even our worst enemies. Have you ever confessed the same sin twice, three times? We can go to God directly, but we do not always obtain the forgiveness Christ died for and freely gives. We can know so well that "if we confess our sins, He is faithful and just and will forgive us our sins and purify us from all unrighteousness" (1 John 1:9)—*but fail to receive it when He hands it to us.*

How do we know when failure to receive forgiveness is the real block? In this failure, a good many things can be involved. The following root causes I find the most common.

Remaining Under Law

"Christ is the end [fulfillment] of the law so that there may be righteousness for everyone who believes" (Romans 10:4). The man "under the law" will always feel guilty. He does not receive forgiveness because he is still trying to be "good enough" on his own merit; he strives to be perfect on his own.

The law, as someone has said, is a fence to make us be good. In Christ, the fence has been removed. The walk in the Spirit replaces the fence. In listening-obedience to Christ and His Word, we are trusting always in His righteousness and doing what we hear Him say. In this way, we do indeed fulfill (not just the letter but) the spirit of the law.

The following is perhaps a helpful way to picture the difference. Under the law a priest wore a breastplate on his robe, and this was anointed. I heard one Jewish rabbi say that when the robe was off, the anointing was off. Since Christ came, we who are His wear the breastplate of righteousness—we have "put on Christ." It is a practice of the Presence.

As ministers, we help others to recognize and put off the "old man" (see *The Healing Presence*, pages 94-95). We watch with them as they confess their sins and put to death all the diseased forms of love: fornication (actual or in the imagination), uncleanness (homosexuality and all other forms of sexual perversion), inordinate affection which is a neurotic dependence or love, evil concupiscence (depraved desire, lust, etc.), covetousness, and all idolatry (all bentness toward the creature). We watch with them as they "put off" anger, wrath, malice, filthy communication, and lying. Then, after proclaiming God's forgiveness for all they have duly confessed, we help them "put on Christ," the New Man. We teach them to practice His Presence, their righteousness, and they are thereby freed from their striving to get "good enough" and from the wrong kind of fear of God. Then, and this is ever so important to get straight in their minds, we assure them on the best Scriptural grounds that they no longer have to practice the presence of the "old man"! "So then, my brothers, there is no necessity for us to obey our unspiritual selves or to live unspiritual lives" (Romans 8:12, *Jerusalem Bible*).

In ministry to others, we need to quickly discern in whose righteousness the sufferer is trusting—his own or the Lord's. Jesus prayed that we might be able in a future Day to stand before the Son of Man (Luke 21:36) and taught us that we do not stand before Him in any righteousness we have earned. We stand in His righteousness, a fact that keeps us always practicing His Presence. Satan, as the accuser, constantly attempts to make us look to our own righteousness. But we have "by the blood of the Lamb" and "the word of [our] testimony" (Revelation 12:11) overcome the accuser of our souls.

Martin Luther is as good an example as we can find here. Until he understood Incarnational Reality, God's righteousness within, he could not receive forgiveness, and he certainly could not accept himself. In the terms of today, he very much needed inner healing. Our counseling rooms are full of people who have this problem. They may not be crawling bare-kneed on sharp stones, wearing hair shirts, or flagellating themselves with whips, but they are doing the psychological equivalent.

Later after his healing, Luther said of the Christian that "he stands at one and the same time a sinner and a justified man." Before Luther understood this, he had been afraid of God. The "righteousness of God" that Paul spoke of in Romans terrified him. He thought of it as the justice of God that judges sinners—as Luther knew himself and all people to be.

Some of the hardest folk to see healed and gotten through to a godly self-acceptance are those who compulsively strive to be perfect. They in effect are denying the necessity of an incarnation of grace, of God's righteousness, and are trying to gain it on their own by their good works and their attention to the letter of the law. Hence, their perspective is askew. Rather than fixing their eyes on God and glorying in the ability He gives us to walk (dance!) before Him in freedom, their eyes are fixed on the "law," wanting to satisfy its demands, something Christ has already done.

Luther was in this terrible place until he came to understand that "the righteousness of God" that Paul spoke of, rather than being a wrathful, legalistic thing, was indeed something we "put on" by faith, that, even more importantly, it is something *in us*—God's life within. When he finally understood this, he cried out: "Faith has the incomparable grace of uniting the soul to Christ as bride to husband, so that the soul possesses whatever Christ Himself possesses." He was thenceforth freed from incredible fear—the fear of always trying to win God's love, of never being quite able to keep the law.

Apart from the need to rightly understand God's grace, there is common to fallen people a terrible passion to be perfect on their own. We need to recognize this for the pride that it is and help men and women confess and come free from it. People prize their autonomy and think of it as freedom. Men, as a rule, have more difficulty than do women at this point. The feminine capacity to worship God and thereby submit and respond fully to Him is an ability a woman often needs to help her brothers in Christ get in touch with.

In addition, there are many "compulsive perfectionists," as they are labeled today. These persons often are the victims of an early training in which love and affirmation was withheld from them apart from good performance. Since a person's performance, no matter how gifted he is, can rarely be perfect, these persons have suffered a deep injury to their souls and have been trained in "the passion to be perfect." Along with helping them "put off the old man," we have to help them replace the law of their parents, a law that still (as a broken record) plays on and on in their minds.

The Need to Acknowledge the "Bad Guy" Within

If Luther could see only his own unrighteousness, the "bad guy" within, before his healing, there are others who deny him altogether. Some people have even been taught this denial, either through inference or bad theology. They genuinely do not understand that Christians, once regenerated (born again of the Spirit) and converted (their wills made one with Christ's), yet need to set apart certain times when they once again kneel as sinners before God and ask Him to show them their sins, conscious and unconscious, that they might confess and be forgiven. Difficult as it may be for many Christian counselors to believe, especially those from the more sacramental traditions, numberless Christians have never been taught to do this on a regular basis.

These Christians, then, denying that the bad guy is there and that they have in fact "practiced his presence," whether consciously or unconsciously, can go through life feeling guiltier and guiltier. They can get on their knees and feel their lives a dreadful mess, but have little insight into what is wrong. They have denied rather than confessed the existence of the "old man," the sinner. So they go about unforgiven. Others, in this same situation, rather than feeling guilty, become prideful and cause other Christians a lot of misery. The Pharisee in them becomes quite strong. Practicing the presence of the old man, they become legalistic and judgmental of others while never seeing their own darkness.

The most dangerous Christians we can ever meet are those who do not know about the bad guy within. More frightening still are the Christians who have a superspiritual religious spirit, deluding them into thinking themselves better Christians than everyone else. I have seen a few of these in my time, and it is wonderful to see them healed. They are not the ones who ordinarily seek help, but cause everybody else who gets involved with them to run for help. There are, of course, different degrees of this problem, but religious tyrants, great and small, come out of this stance. They will always be found slandering other Christians, especially Christian leaders. While accusing others of being demonized, they will often themselves be demonized and will have to be dealt with as such in order to find freedom.

The bad guy in each one of us puts self rather than Christ at the center. The Christian is fully capable of doing this. When he does, he is not living from the center where Christ dwells, but from another center, that of the old man or the bad guy within. As Christians, we can wake up any day of the week and descend into that center. Hence, we will be found practicing the presence of the bad guy. This is why C. S. Lewis can say that if being Christian does not make a man a lot better, it can make him a lot worse.

> For the Supernatural, entering a human soul, opens to it new possibilities both of good and evil. From that point the road branches: one way to sanctity, humility, the other to spiritual pride, self-righteousness, persecuting zeal. And no way back to the mere humdrum virtues of the unawakened soul. If the Divine call does not make us better, it will make us very much worse. Of all bad men, religious bad men are the worst.[1]

That the line between good and evil lies in every human heart was a discovery Alexander Solzhenitsyn made while lying on rotting straw in a Communist prison camp, still a Communist himself, awaiting an operation for cancer. Shortly after this, Solzhenitsyn found Christ.

> Gradually it was disclosed to me that the line separating good and evil passes not through states, nor between classes, not between political parties either—but right through every human heart—and through all human hearts. This line shifts. Inside us, it oscillates with the years. And even within hearts over-

whelmed with evil, one small bridgehead of good is retained. And even in the best of all hearts there remains . . . an unuprooted small corner of evil.[2]

Is it any wonder that the key to healing is repentance and forgiveness?

We must know and acknowledge our two identities—that of sinner and saint. Our prime identity, of course, is that of saint. We are children of God, children of the resurrection. But the rhythm of repentance and reception of forgiveness must be woven into every life. We are always to rise up from confession in our prime identity, having received forgiveness.

When I minister to people whose difficulties are in this area, I lead them in a prayer of confession of specific sin and then help them to receive God's forgiveness. After this initial ministry, I recommend to them ways of setting into their devotional and spiritual practices a regular time for allowing God to search their hearts, a regular time, in other words, to kneel as sinners before Him.

> Who can discern his lapses and errors?
> Clear me from hidden [and unconscious] faults.
> Keep back Your servant also from presumptuous sins;
> let them not have dominion over me!
>
> (Psalm 19:12-13a, *The Amplified Bible*)

> Search me, O God, and know my heart;
> Test me and know my anxious thoughts.
> See if there is any offensive way in me,
> and lead me in the way everlasting.
>
> (Psalm 139: 23-24)

I instruct people always, after confession of sin, whether at home, at church, or wherever, to *receive that forgiveness*. This is an act of faith, a conscious and deliberate reception of God's grace. For many people, the best ongoing way to incorporate this into their lives is in connection with Holy Communion. Before going, they can kneel as sinners before God and listen to Him as He shows them their hearts. They can then take this confession to the Eucharist. There they kneel, having confessed their sins, and as they receive, they take their place once again in Christ's death, dying to their sins and to the world. As they receive the Body and the Blood, they receive forgiveness. They have knelt as sinners. They rise as saints. And they rise prepared to live from that center where God's righteousness abides.

Many ministers of the gospel are today "burned out" because they do not recognize their need for the confessional, their need to receive absolution and laying-on-of-hands by others who love and serve the Lord, their need for regularly acknowledging that there is a bad guy in them.

It is when I have just completed the most successful missions and seen God do the most remarkable things for His people that I need to take several days (rather than hours) to simply wait on God, asking Him to search my heart and soul. We must leave all ministry to others while we are doing this, for we cannot minister to others while in a posture of repentance. This does not mean we cease living from our true center, knowing who we are in Him. It simply means that we acknowledge that we do carry about with us the "old man," the capacity to be the bad guy; we have in very truth sinned and come short of the mark.

Praying, but Not to God

"Prayer was made without ceasing of the church unto God for him" (Acts 12:5, KJV). As R. A. Torrey points out, "The first thing to notice in this verse is the brief expression *unto God.* The prayer that has power is the prayer that is offered unto God."[3] C. S. Lewis expresses it this way: "May it be the real 'I' who speaks, the real 'Thou' I speak to."[4]

Quickly we see that this category of difficulty is related to the disease of introspection (See *The Healing Presence*, chapter 12). In this introspective age, we easily substitute our subjective feelings about ourselves for the objective gift of God's forgiveness. If we are on our knees, hating ourselves, we are not likely to look up and receive forgiveness. We have sunk into an inculcated, emotional state of feeling toward the self, an emotional view we've had so long we hardly notice it. And this is not prayer. It is a common and a serious barrier to receiving the forgiving grace of God.

Lack of Awareness of the Need for Forgiveness

Just as we can be so out of touch with our hearts and feelings that we do not realize the need to forgive another, so it is in the matter of receiving forgiveness. We can be so "heady" that we rise from our knees after confession of a sin we are quite conscious of having committed and fail to notice that we still feel guilty. We do not know the joy of forgiveness, nor do we move from a position of authority and wholeness. We are simply too out of touch with our hearts and feelings to notice. In lieu of having received forgiveness, we become more and more restlessly "active" until the time comes we can no longer control and repress the feeling being.

Inability to Name the Sin

In this category, a person will have a conscious sense of guilt, but it stems from sin at unconscious levels of the heart. It is closely related to what we've already considered—the fact that Christians are both sinners and saints and that there will be those hidden and unconscious faults that they are to ask God to search out on a regular basis. It may or may not also be related in a given person to the fact that "sin consists, not only in the positive transgression of the law of God, but in the want of conformity to His Will."[5] The old Anglican prayer is at once so comforting and so needful: "We have done the things that we ought not, we have left undone those things that we ought to have done." This two-pronged fork is, as Dr. Meyer has said, needful. But most often what we are dealing with here is related to the depth of sin in the human heart and is therefore apropos to all that is considered in this book.

The Christian theologian and historian Richard Lovelace chronicles not only our loss of the understanding of sin, but of its depth within the human heart:

> During the late nineteenth century, while the church's understanding of the unconscious motivation behind surface actions was vanishing, Sigmund Freud rediscovered this factor and recast it in an elaborate and profound secular mythology. One of the consequences of this remarkable shift is that in the twentieth century, pastors have often been reduced to the status of legalistic moralists, while the deeper aspects of the cure of souls are generally relegated to psychotherapy, even among Evangelical Christians.
>
> [T]he structure of sin in the human personality is something far more complicated than the isolated acts and thoughts of deliberate disobedience commonly designated by the word. In its biblical definition, sin cannot be limited to isolated instances or patterns of wrongdoing; it is something much more akin to the psychological term complex: an organic network of compulsive attitudes, beliefs, and behavior deeply rooted in our alienation from God. Sin originated in the darkening of the human mind and heart as man turned from the truth about God to embrace a lie about him and consequently a whole universe of lies about his creation. Sinful thoughts, words, and deeds flow forth from this darkened heart automatically and compulsively, as water from a polluted fountain. "The Lord saw that the wickedness of man was great in the earth, and that every imagination of the thoughts of his heart was only evil continually" (Genesis 6:5). This is echoed in Jesus' words: "Either make the tree good, and its fruit good; or make the tree bad, and its fruit bad; for the tree is known by its fruit. You brood of vipers! how can you speak good, when you are evil? For out of the abundance of the heart the mouth speaks. The good man out of his good treasure brings forth good, and the evil man out of his evil treasure brings forth evil" (Matthew 12:33-35).
>
> The human heart is now a reservoir of unconscious disordered motivation and response, of which unrenewed persons are unaware if left to themselves, for "the heart is deceitful above all things, and desperately corrupt; who can understand it?" (Jeremiah 17:9). It is as if they were without mirrors and suffering from tunnel vision: they can see neither themselves clearly nor the great peripheral area around their immediate experience (God and supernatural reality). At the two most crucial loci of their understanding, their awareness of God and of themselves, they are almost in total darkness, although they may attempt to remedy this by framing false images of themselves and God. Paul describes this darkness of the unregenerate mind: "Now this I affirm and testify in the Lord, that you must no longer live as the Gentiles do, in the futility of their minds; they are darkened in their understanding, alienated from the life of God because of the ignorance that is in them, due to their hardness of heart" (Ephesians 4:17-18). The mechanism by which this

> unconscious reservoir of darkness is formed is identified in Romans 1:18-23 as repression of traumatic material, chiefly the truth about God and our condition, which the unregenerate constantly and dynamically "hold down." Their darkness is always a voluntary darkness, though they are unaware that they are repressing the truth.[6]

When Christians suffer with an ongoing sense of guilt, they need first of all to ascertain whether it is false or real. In prayer for healing of memories, we can often get to the roots of these matters quickly, and then, as ministers, we help those who are suffering discern the false guilt from the real. The real is taken care of through confessing sin and receiving forgiveness. False guilt is taken care of when we help the sufferer to distinguish between violation of an authentic standard as opposed to an irrational or an inauthentic one.

The person who has internalized the "law" of controlling and/or legalistic or perfectionistic parents, authority figures, or communities often needs help to be released from false guilt. The person whose mother died in giving him birth, or the twin who survived at birth when his brother or sister did not, are examples of those who sometimes suffer a deep, unconscious sense of false guilt.

The following story exemplifies how easy it is for us in childhood to misconstrue what we hear and so to pick up false guilt. A woman came up to me after I had been speaking on this topic and blurted out with some desperation that she always felt guilty and had never known why. "I soak up guilt," she cried. Others could do something amiss and she, not they, would feel guilty. I had hardly started to pray, inviting the Lord into any root memory that would shed light on all this, when the knowledge of where it all began came to the fore. On the night she was born, her father had rushed her mother to the hospital, and in all the excitement, he had forgotten to turn off the stove. The house burned down. All her life she had heard, "Oh, the night you were born, the house burned down!" And her heart interpreted this to mean, "It's *your* fault the house burned down." She dissolved in laughter at this knowledge, wondering that she had never seen it before. We then prayed about the false guilt patterns that had formed in her, and she understood that as soon as she was aware of guilt feelings, she was always to place them before the Lord. She was to give them to Him and receive, through listening prayer, the true and right pattern of thinking and feeling in exchange.

There are those who go about for most of their lives with a vague, gray cloud of guilt over their heads. This is not necessary. Real sin is programmed into the memories, and we can usually get to it rather quickly as we learn to pray, asking the Lord to show us any specific sin or complex of sin that we might confess it to Him and receive His pardon. In cases where nothing is revealed, we can confess the "unknown" sin that is behind the sense of guilt. If the guilt is real, it will lift. Usually, it is not long before insight comes and we get in touch with the memory or with the pattern of sinful behavior for which we are feeling guilty.

Failure to Settle the Sin Question

Sometimes we simply have not settled the sin question. While confessing our sin, we may feel, "Oh well, I'll just do it again." In this case we not only fail to receive forgiveness, but we do not like ourselves very well. It is a healthy thing, then, that we experience real guilt, that we get depressed over our sin. It is this despair over what we are and what we have made of our lives that brings us to the end of ourselves and causes us to throw ourselves upon the mercy of God, the "righteousness of God."

There are many, many "unforgiven" folk about who fit into this very category, and one reason is that the organized church itself is full of compromise. Such a church does no better with its prophets than Ahab and Jezebel did; it simply cannot tolerate the true prophet who majors on the grace of God and, therefore, at the same time can preach an uncompromising gospel. Prophets such as these can call the people of God to a radical obedience (radical for the day in which we live) because they know the grace available to those who will walk in the Spirit.

Chapter 14 of *The Healing Presence,* which deals with the renunciation of sexual sin, illustrates the incredible way God's healing power is released when people renounce their idols and take a sure stand against sin. These people gain as well the power to overcome temptation when they truly settle the sin question.

From time to time, I encounter persons who have conscious sin at the top of their conscience, and they have no intention of turning from it. Even so, they will come for prayer, hoping to be healed. I remember one such man about to be hospitalized for emotional problems, who on arriving told me he did not know what lay behind his depression. Realizing that he was too near the breaking point to communicate on the conscious level, I simply laid hands on him and asked the Lord to go to the root problem, the memory where the problem lay. Not one thing emerged. I was led to ask quietly, "What unconfessed sin lies at the top of your conscious mind?" He then told me he was sexually involved with another man's wife. I asked him if he was willing to repent of his adultery and turn from it, and he said no. I then told him it would do no good to pray for him, that he was probably depressed over that and other sin in his life that he had failed to "put to death." I asked him to leave and make a decision about this matter and then return for prayer only if he decided to repent. I have seen him and others, just hours away from hospitalization, healed as soon as they decided to repent. To pray for such people apart from repentance is to waste precious spiritual energy and power. It merely singes them with the flames of God rather than allowing His holy fire to burn away all their impurities. Their hearts are left even more hardened than before.

There are many whose consciences are so seared they no longer feel guilt. They too can receive forgiveness as they *will* to confess their sins, knowing that besides the fact that their consciences have been seared, their feeling being is also out of order. God can restore consciences and the capacity to feel compunction as they confess and deliberately turn from sin.

Conclusion of the Failure to Receive Forgiveness

These "categories" overlap and intermingle, of course, and often we find ourselves ministering to someone whose difficulties fall into several of them at once. We ascertain when failure to receive forgiveness is the block; we provide the needed illumination; we minister the forgiveness with laying-on-of-hands.

In ministering God's forgiveness, as in all prayer with others, we need to be very careful about the person's physical comfort. If we (or an entire group) lay heavy hands on such a one, he may forget his need for forgiveness and be able to think only about how to get his next breath. I nearly always lift the penitent's face up to God, making sure he can get great draughts of fresh air into his lungs. Often, I even ask him to breathe in deeply several times. In this way, he relaxes his body, often breathing out tension and releasing his muscles, and he is thereby all the more ready to receive. Too, I make sure there is room for the person to lift his arms to God when the moment comes for him to receive the forgiveness. The whole person, after all, is interacting with what God is doing. I personally have to remove my large ring since occasionally I have a bit of a heavy touch. The impress of the ring on a person's forehead could distract him during the prayer and inhibit him from receiving the forgiveness.

It used to be that when praying with a woman, I was especially sensitive to her coiffure. Now, having learned more along the way, I am careful with *both* men and women. Often, just before speaking to a group, my prayer team will pray for me. They know not to lay a dozen hands on my head. If I'm worried about how I'm going to look with hair all askew, I won't be able to receive the fullest benefit of their prayers. The same seems to go for most of us.

If there is a crucifix available, I ask the person to look up to it before closing his eyes in prayer. This helps many, for quite a few moderns have imaginations utterly bereft of Christian images and symbols. The person also may be thinking about and perhaps even trying not to picture the thing for which he has heretofore been unable to receive forgiveness. In this way he lifts his eyes from the problem to that which symbolizes God's forgiveness.[7] In a recent PCM, many seasoned church leaders were quite amazed to see how God uses the crucifix not only in deliverance but in healing prayer. The healing ministry can never be understood apart from the cross, apart from the Atonement. Out of the Atonement flows our full salvation: justification, sanctification, the indwelling Holy Spirit, authority in spiritual conflict.[8] The crucifix, rightly used, symbolizes all that is in the Atonement.

The person who has failed to receive forgiveness has most likely confessed the same sin over and over. Even so, I ask such a one to confess the sin once again, this time while "seeing" Jesus, dying on the cross to take that sin upon and into Himself. After the person has confessed it, then I proclaim forgiveness in a way that the penitent can receive it.

In ministering forgiveness, I anoint with oil, making the sign of the cross on the forehead. Then I lay one hand on the forehead and the other at the back of the head. Then, with their confession, I proclaim forgiveness, saying: "Receive God's forgiveness, receive it into the very depths of your being." And it is as if the forgiveness they have never been able to receive before comes right through my hand and into their forehead, and from there, it flows down into the depths of their being: spirit, soul, and body.

At times I have realized that the human spirit is somehow timid and shy, that it is having a hard time opening up to receive the forgiveness. In this case, I then pray very gently that the spirit of this person can open as a lovely bud or flower to receive the forgiveness Christ is sending. And it does.

CHAPTER 10

Conclusion to Healing of Memories

Every time we forgive another, or confess a sin and receive forgiveness, we experience a healing of memories and a cleansing of our hearts and consciences. But there are times when our own "self-searching and prayers" or our "grievous reactions to the sins of others" leave us powerless on our own. It is then we need to pay close attention to words such as we find in "An exhortation for one preparing for Holy Communion" from the *Book of Common Prayer.*

> If there be any of you who by this means [the means of self-examination, repentance, reparation] cannot quiet his own conscience herein, but requireth further comfort or counsel, let him come to me, or to some other Minister of God's Word, and open his grief. . . .

"Surely he took our infirmities and carried our sorrows" (Isaiah 53:4), but sometimes we need the help of one another in order to be enabled to yield up that grief or sorrow. Christ, speaking of Himself said: "But so that you may know that the Son of Man has authority on earth to forgive sins" (Matthew 9:6), and this enraged the religious leaders of the day. But the fact is, He has given us this same power. When we know ourselves as what we truly are, sacramental channels of His healing, His forgiving word, and His Presence, this ministry flows through us.

"I tell you the truth, whatever you bind on earth will be bound in heaven, and whatever you loose on earth will be loosed in heaven" (Matthew 18:18). In the Scriptures, the matter of binding and loosing has to do with loosing people from their sins and from the effects of the sins of others against them. Unfortunately, there is a misunderstanding abroad in sections of the church, especially in the renewal movement, regarding binding and loosing. These Scriptural passages have been taught erroneously as having to do with binding Satan and demons, elemental spirits, principalities and powers, and so on. We do not "bind" and "loose" demons, principalities and powers, etc. In Christ's name we command them to leave, knowing that Christ's death and resurrection have already bound them and that they have no power over us. As long, however, as sin is unremitted in a life, the demons and other dark forces have power in that life. It is the sins and the effects of those sins in the lives that we, the ministers and servants of Christ, are to "bind and loose," that is, lift from the souls of those who truly turn to Christ, repentant and ready to forgive those who have sinned against them.

In the ministry of binding and loosing from sin, we may (even as Christ did) incur the wrath of Christians who misunderstand the priestly role of all Christians as the priesthood of believers. We are to hear confessions of sin and proclaim forgiveness and release to those confessing them (either their own sins or those of others against them). Hostility to the idea of the believers' priestly role is the root of a great deal of the criticism leveled against prayer for the healing of emotional problems, and hence some of the terrible assaults on prayer for emotional and psychological healing. This kind of theological blindness and ignorance catches us up into spiritual warfare, for the accuser of our souls opposes in every way the true ministry of the confessional.

The truth is, Jesus has commissioned us to do His works:

> Again Jesus said, "Peace be with you! As the Father has sent me, I am sending you." And with that he breathed on them and said, "Receive the Holy Spirit. If you forgive anyone his sins, they are forgiven; if you do not forgive them, they are not forgiven." (John 20:21-23)

I never get over my awe at the power of the ministry of healing of memories, that is, of the forgiveness of sin. It is the power of the cross, of the love of the Son of God who made Himself utterly vulnerable, even to the point of crucifixion, to free us from sin.

This ministry of prayer for the healing of the soul is not merely related to the sacrament or ordinance of baptism; it is a vital part of the work of baptism.[1] In baptism we are "buried with Him" and are "raised to life with Him," and this is the crucial imagery in the releasing of the soul from sin and in the calling forth of the true self:

> We were therefore buried with him through baptism into death in order that, just as Christ was raised from the dead through the glory of the Father, we too may live a new life. If we have been united with him like this in his death, we will certainly also be united with him in his resurrection. For we know that our old self was crucified with him so that the body of sin might be done away with, that we should no longer be slaves to sin—because anyone who has died has been freed from sin. (Romans 6:4-7)

Victory over sin in our lives—which is what the healing of memories is all about—is the extension of the work of baptism. It is essential that we who minister in prayer for the healing of the soul not only realize this, but continue to image this healing aright. In that way, the healing of the soul will never be separated from the central doctrine of the forgiveness of sin. The imagery of Christ's death and resurrection and of Christian baptism is absolutely vital to the retaining of a Christian symbolic system,[2] and it is vital in the comprehension of all Christian prayer and healing.

The Interview Preceding Prayer for Healing of Memories

INVOCATION OF THE PRESENCE OF CHRIST

At the very first, before starting the interview with the person desiring healing, we pray, "Come, Lord Jesus, come," asking the Lord to bring up from the person's heart and memories that which needs to come up. We petition God for ears to hear what the person is *really* saying.

GIFTS OF THE HOLY SPIRIT

Effective listening and "listening prayer" are related to the gifts of the Holy Spirit[3] and are key in the ministry of healing. To learn to listen to God and collaborate with Him in healing prayer is to experience the gifts of the Holy Spirit in action. These gifts of wisdom, knowledge, discernment, and so on are not guesswork, but are the fruit of getting the mind of God on the matter.

We who train others in the work of healing prayer are alert for the misguided person who, rather than getting the mind of God on another's need, is still so involved in what God has done in his own life that he wrongly sees his own needs and problems in the lives of others. The counterpart of this we see also in the professional world where therapists fit others into their own favorite theories or methods, and their clients' main difficulties remain unperceived. Every soul is so unique, and even in the cases where needs are similar, the Lord often moves in very diverse ways to heal different persons with like problems.

Here as always, our model is the Lord Himself. The prophet Isaiah spoke beforehand of the power that would rest upon Christ and of the way He would move in it:

> The Spirit of the Lord will rest on him—
> the Spirit of wisdom and of understanding,
> the Spirit of counsel and of power,
> the Spirit of knowledge and of the fear of the Lord—
> and he will delight in the fear of the Lord.
> *He will not judge by what he sees with his eyes,*
> *or decide by what he hears with his ears;*
> but with righteousness he will judge the needy,
> with justice he will give decisions for the poor of the earth.
>
> (11:2-4a, italics mine)

With Christ as our supreme example, we learn to stop speaking our own unaided wisdom and instead seek and find the mind of God.

THE ROOT OR MAIN CAUSE

Although there are nearly always multiple factors and "causes" to deal with (failing to understand this can be a problem), in the interview we often get to the root cause of the difficulty right away. But when we don't, there is no need to pray through the person's entire chronology. Agnes Sanford's method here can hardly be improved upon. She asked the simple question, "Were you happy as a child?" If so, she knew the difficulty did not lie there. The next question was, "Then when did you begin to be unhappy?" As the person told where the unhappiness started, then she knew where to start.

THE DISEASE OF INTROSPECTION

We are alert to recognize this prevalent twentieth-century emotional problem and deal with it right away. Otherwise, the person will continue to tear apart and fragment himself and his thoughts through over-analyzation, destroying the healing work even as it is being accomplished.[4]

THE OLD SELF

We learn to avoid helping someone practice the presence of the "old man" through endless dialogue with "it." We learn to speak to the real person, calling him or her forward, and to teach that one how to shake off the old man or the false self. The old self can talk endlessly and is often today allowed to do so, even though all concerned know that truth is not being spoken. This misplaced empathy and sympathy is not the kind of love that heals.

BENTNESS

We do not allow others to bend toward us, but point them straight up to God. The mark of a great Christian helper or leader is that he is able by the power and assistance of the Holy Spirit to inspire those he helps to be all God called them to be. This means we never draw disciples to ourselves, but help others into full discipleship with Christ. To be a disciple of a disciple is to be a pale Christian, and we help those who have "bent into others" to straighten up into Christ and into their full identity in Him.

THE WILL

We note when special prayer for the will is needed. We remember that sin kills the will.[5]

SIN IS TO BE JUDGED

It is important that we care enough to confront the soul that is hesitant in putting sin to death. We judge not the brother or sister, but the sin that is killing him or her.[6]

THE CRUCIFIX

Many of us need to be reminded that a crucifix is more than a valid symbol for today; it is and always has been a central one. Only as we keep that Christian symbol can we fully retain the equally valid one of *Christus Victor*, the risen Savior. (See chapter 11.)

CHILDHOOD VOWS

We are alert for childhood vows that need be renounced.[7]

TRANSFERENCE AND AMBIVALENCE

We are alert to detect transferences and to name same-sex and other-sex ambivalence as they are revealed either in the interview or in the time of prayer.

For example, if I am praying with a mother who has problems in relating to her son and I know that she experienced rejection by her father, I will ask her, "Could your problems with your son have to do with your unresolved difficulties with your father?" And she will nearly always instantly know if this is a valid insight. In prayer for healing of memories, we get at the root rejections and hurts and the ways that inner negative or idealized feelings and attitudes are irrationally projected onto others.

These come to light as a matter of course because in seeking forgiveness of sin, relationships with others are necessarily coming into the light of the Lord. We do not look for these "projections" or "transferences," but when we discern them, we present them humbly to the person's attention.

TIMING

As in all important matters of the soul, in our zeal to see someone healed we are careful not to move ahead of the Lord or to lag behind. We are quick to acknowledge when we need to bring in wiser, more experienced heads and when special medical and psychological help is called for.

Important Things to Remember in the Prayer

As we go to prayer, once again we invoke the Presence of Christ. We remember that as the memories come to the fore, the key element in the prayer is release from sin and its effects, either the sins of the people for whom we pray or the sins of others against them.

Therefore, we do not forget to function in our capacity as one of the priesthood of believers. It is possible to get so thrilled over the way the Lord moves to heal souls that we fail to fully follow through on the matter of the confession of sin and the full proclamation of God's forgiveness in Christ.

Then, as the Lord uncovers things that need to be confessed:

We direct their eyes to the Lord, and they confess specifically their sins to Him.

We proclaim forgiveness of those sins—so dark and burdensome to the souls confessing them—in the authority of Christ and in such a way as the *heart* can receive it.

We discern false guilt that results from the judgments and suggestions of men, and distinguish that from true guilt that results from consciousness of having betrayed an authentic divine standard.

We bind the sins of others that have so wounded the ones for whom we are praying—leading them to forgive. We then seek to loose them from the effects these sins have had on their lives. This is no small prayer, but is incredibly effective. For example, the man who as a child has seen his father shoot his mother and then kill himself has suffered a trauma that only God can heal. This man will go through life seeing himself as a son of a murderer; he will suffer as a motherless, a fatherless child. In our prayer for him, he is to be "released" into seeing himself as God's child, fathered and mothered by God Himself. He is not to go through life ashamed and hurting, but he is to hold his head and shoulders high, knowing who he is in God. As we pray for the release of his soul and body from the the terrible effects of this sin (after having confessed the sins of murder and suicide and whatever else was amiss), we are to pray in such a way as he will know and receive to the depths of his being the mighty truth that he is not determined by his past, but rather, his wounds are to be turned into healing power for the sake of others.

We discern and send away any oppressing or possessing evil spirits. When necessary, we lead people in a renunciation of idols such as Baal or Mammon.

We pray for God to pour in all the holy love that has been missing and to fill every space where sin, rejection, or a demonic presence has been. The parable of sweeping clean and leaving empty is a meaningful one, far beyond the power of most moderns to comprehend. But the simple truth is, we do not help people rid themselves of darkness and evil apart from helping them to fill up with the light and the life of God. God's glory (fullness of being) is to replace and fill in the space left by the removal of even one fear. "Nature abhors a vacuum," and we scarcely comprehend the vacuum within us left by the removal of sin and darkness. For this reason we are careful not to "deliver" people who are demonized apart from their decision to serve Christ. The demon comes back, even as the Scripture says, bringing others even more evil with it to inhabit the emptied but unfilled space in soul or body.

In the prayer for healing of memories, Jesus journeys into what for us is the past (though for Him all times are one), and He heals the past so that it no longer has the power to shape our present or our future.

As those who counsel and pray with others, we have learned to listen to God and to man. We have discerned the situation and have brought as best we can the light of God to bear on it. In the prayer for healing of memories, we are still with all our beings listening both to God and to the one for whom we pray.

The art of listening is key here. As Christian counselors, the Word of God has been hidden away in our hearts, and, in our obedience, it has taken full root there. That Word is there and active, ready to work with any other word the Holy Spirit may be speaking. God never ceases, in fact, to send the healing word; we need only have the ears to receive it. And it can come as the gift of the word of knowledge, the gift of the word of wisdom, the gift of discerning of spirits, etc. We are carefully, quietly, and gently collaborating with the Spirit of God to see this person released into wholeness.

We know that as emissaries of Christ, His anointing rests on us, that "He hath anointed me . . . hath sent me to heal the brokenhearted . . . to set at liberty them that are bruised" (Luke 4:18, KJV). And Christ does it—through us. As ministers of Christ's healing power, we allow Him to touch others—in a most profound and powerful way—through us.

A disciple is one who has been unchained himself—he then unbinds others. That is what we do when we "carry the cross." We carry God's love and forgiveness into the hearts and minds of others. We are, as Henri Nouwen has said, wounded healers: "Those who proclaim liberation are called to make their wounds into a source of healing power."

It is in forgiving our personal injuries that we learn to pass on to others (the broken, wounded, bound) the forgiveness of Christ. We are channels of Another Life. We listen, we collaborate with God. Ruth Pitter, the English poet, says it this way, in one beautiful line of her poetry, and our hearts resound with it:

"Alleluia all my gashes cry."

PART III

Spiritual Warfare and the Gift of Battle

The reason the Son of God appeared
was to destroy the devil's work.

(1 John 3:8b)

CHAPTER 11

The Use of Holy Water and Other Powerful Christian Symbols and Agencies

Then the Lord said to Moses, "Make a bronze basin, with its bronze stand, for washing. Place it between the Tent of Meeting and the altar, and put water in it."

(Exodus 30:17-18)

Then he shall take some holy water in a clay jar and put some dust from the tabernacle floor into the water.

(Numbers 5:17)

To purify them, do this: Sprinkle the water of cleansing on them. . . .

(Numbers 8:7a)

Jesus answered, "I tell you the truth, no one can enter the kingdom of God unless he is born of water and the Spirit."

(John 3:5)

"And now what are you waiting for? Get up, be baptized and wash your sins away, calling on his name."

(Acts 22:16)

We read of many different ceremonial washings in the Scriptures, water baptism being the foremost for Christians. From earliest times, both within Judaism and the Christian church, the faithful in obedience to God have been seen calling down the grace of God, the "sweet unction of the Holy Spirit" upon water, oil, bread, and wine, and upon holy things and places such as crucifixes and "tents of meeting." The following liturgy illustrates the way the church has prayed since its beginning to set apart and hallow water for the purposes of purification of persons and things. This of course makes it important to the healing ministry. These prayers are taken from *A Manual for Priests* (Society of Saint John the Evangelist, Cambridge, MA, 1978) and are the ones my pastor presently uses.

The Blessing of Water

Salt and pure and clean water, being made ready in the Church or Sacristy, the Priest, vested in surplice and violet stole, shall say:

Our help is in the Name of the Lord.
Who hath made heaven and earth.

And immediately he shall begin the Exorcism of the salt.

I adjure thee, O creature of salt, by the living God, by the true God, by the holy God, by God who commanded thee to be cast by the prophet Elisha into the water to heal the barrenness thereof, that thou become salt exorcised for the health of believers: and do thou bring to all who take of thee soundness of soul and body, and let all vain imaginations, wickedness, and subtlety of the wiles of the devil, and every unclean spirit fly and depart from every place where thou shalt be sprinkled, adjured by the Name of Him, who shall come to judge both the quick and the dead, and the world by fire. Amen.

Let us pray.

Almighty and everlasting God, we humbly beseech thy great and boundless mercy, that it may please thee of thy lovingkindness to bless and to hallow this creature of salt, which thou hast given for the use of men, let it be to all them that take of it health of mind and body, and let whatsoever shall be touched or sprinkled therewith be free from all uncleanness, and from all assaults of spiritual wickedness. Through Christ our Lord. Amen.

Exorcism of the water

I adjure thee, O creature of water, by the Name of God the Father Almighty, by the Name of Jesus Christ his Son our Lord, and by the power of the Holy Ghost, that thou become water exorcised for putting to flight all the power of the enemy; and do thou avail to cast out and send hence that same enemy with all his apostate angels, by the power of the same our Lord Jesus Christ, who shall come to judge the quick and the dead, and the world by fire. Amen.

Let us pray.

O God, who for the salvation of mankind hast ordained that the substance of water should be used in one of thy chiefest Sacraments: favorably regard us who call upon thee, and pour the power of thy benediction upon this element, made ready by careful cleansing; that this thy creature, meet for thy mysteries, may receive the effect of divine grace, and so cast out devils, and put sickness to flight, that whatsoever in the dwellings of thy faithful people shall be sprinkled with this water, may be free from all uncleanness, and delivered from all manner of hurt; there let no spirit of pestilence abide, nor any corrupting air; thence let all the wiles of the hidden enemy depart, and if there be aught that layeth snares against the safety or peace of them that dwell in the house, let it fly before the sprinkling of this water, so that the health which they seek through calling upon thy holy Name may be protected against all things that threaten it. Through Christ our Lord. Amen.

Then the Priest shall cast the salt into the water in the form of a Cross, saying:

Be this salt and water mingled together: in the Name of the Father, and of the Son, and of the Holy Ghost. Amen.

The Lord be with you.
And with thy spirit.

Let us pray.

O God, who art the Author of unconquered might, the King of the Empire that cannot be overthrown, the ever glorious Conqueror: who dost keep under the strength of the dominion that is against thee; who rulest the raging of the fierce enemy; who dost mightily fight against the wickedness of thy foes; with fear and trembling we entreat thee, O Lord, and we beseech thee graciously to behold this creature of salt and water, mercifully shine upon it, hallow it with the dew of thy lovingkindness: that wheresoever it shall be sprinkled, with the invocation of thy holy Name, all haunting of the unclean spirit may be driven away; far thence let the fear of the venomous serpent be cast; and wheresoever it shall be sprinkled, there let the presence of the Holy Ghost be vouchsafed to all of us who shall ask for thy mercy. Through Christ our Lord. Amen.

These are exceedingly powerful prayers, but ones seldom heard in churches across the land. God waits to answer such prayers, and He does so in incredible ways. It is these prayers in conjunction with the charisms of healing that make holy water, when rightly understood and used, a powerful aid to deliverance and healing.

It was out of sheer desperation that I first made use of blessed water, now nearly thirty years ago. The results were at once amazing, and for me personally so overwhelming, that I made sure I was fully prepared before using it again.

The occasion was the need to protect a group of Christian young people from one of their own members who had, in hatred and rebellion toward a minister father, gotten into Satan worship. This emotionally troubled teen had actually begun praying to Satan while on the mission field where her father was ministering.

The situation was such that I could not face it or the youngster directly. A number of rebellious young men outside that Christian group were in league with her, and there was destruction of property, unexplained gunshots, and real danger for the innocent teens under her influence. Had she been faced with the truth, she would have denied it and would have certainly exploited to the fullest the "accusations" against her.

All this was taking place in a summer camp, and the young people were under the immediate authority of intellectually gifted college students. The adults ultimately in charge of the group were far from understanding such spiritual warfare or accepting the workings of the Holy Spirit and would have rejected the Christian who would deal with these dark matters in the only way they can be dealt with. Also, Satan worship, witchcraft, and so on were at that time simply unthinkable for most Americans, except as one might read of it in Haiti, Africa, or some such place. This young girl realized these things and—intensely angry with all in authority—was keenly (even diabolically) clever in manipulating and dominating the situation. Her campmates, many separated from their parents for the first time, were as vulnerable as only adolescents can be. Most had grown up in Christian homes and environments and had been protected from the grosser forms of evil.

Closely associated with this group, I knew that something very dark and mysterious was going on, but could only intercede, asking for God's mercy. I finally found out what was happening when several young people came to me with severe stomachaches and vomiting. The mystery quickly unfolded as their story tumbled out. Jane had stunned them with an aggressive announcement that she prayed to Satan and that he answered her prayers. She had then coerced them by a series of manipulations into "touching their pinkies (fingers) together," and she told them to "pray to Satan for he answers prayers." When they refused, she ridiculed them and accused them of being silly for taking this "game" too seriously or of lacking courage or of being in league with the hated houseparents and so on.

It was just after they succumbed to these pressures that the vomiting began. After having them checked by the physician who could find no cause for the upset, the houseparents sent them to me for prayer and counsel. To say that these young people were terrified is surely an understatement. They had encountered real evil and were in need of deliverance from demonic oppression. They were intensely fearful not only of what was happening to them, but of what would happen should this girl find out they had "told." Before telling me their story, they had secured my promise that I would not go to the authorities, but instead put the whole situation into God's hands. At this point, I reserved the right to share with my trusted prayer partners, including my pastor. They agreed to this after being assured of the confidentiality, even the "seal of the confessional," under which this prayer group operated.

We then went to prayer, and after much repentance and reception of forgiveness, together with laying-on-of hands for the teens, they were much improved. I, however, was then weighed down with the knowledge of what was going on and the urgent need to protect the young people in this camp. My only consolation in being unable to divulge the full truth to the authorities in charge was the knowledge that they would have bungled the situation and that the houseparents of these teens as well as the teens would have suffered the consequences.

I began to pray and intercede, singly and with my prayer partners. Matters only got worse. More property was destroyed; more truly threatening and obscene things were happening. Jane in the meantime was wrapping the authorities around her little finger as they attempted to counsel her in the usual way. She had a way of effectively slandering others in charge, thereby dividing the adults. As in all situations where the demonic goes unchecked, confusion reigned.

Finally, in desperation, I told my prayer partners that I had to do something, but I did not know what. It was then that the pastor suggested the use of holy water, something that utterly amazed me. I was not at all quick to take up the idea but, as he said, "You've tried everything else you know to do. It can't hurt to do this."

After several days and much prayer, in fear and trembling I accompanied the houseparents, whose duty it was to check daily the camp rooms, into this girl's cubicle. Then I sprinkled the holy water, made the sign of the cross over her bed, and commanded any and all demons to come out of her the moment she returned to her room and laid her head on the pillow. The whole procedure took only a few moments.

That very night, legions of demons came out of this young girl. How do I know? I stayed in the camp overnight, and my room was close to hers. These evil things, in this instance all wearing masks, "visited" me on the way out of that place. It was the worst spiritual battle I ever encountered. If God had not opened my eyes to "see" the demons, they might have succeeded in taking my mind.[1] I simply stood my ground, "pleading the blood of Jesus" through what seemed an interminable length of time, and towards morning they had to leave.

It took me several weeks just to recover physically from the battle. The young girl came to Christ immediately, and the terrible things stopped happening.

I had a great deal to learn about this experience, and I remember asking God a multitude of questions about why I was attacked. Foremost, with the use of holy water as in any prayer for deliverance, I should have commanded the demons in Jesus' name to depart the place hurting no one. Perhaps then there would not have been so severe a battle. But after this, I never again questioned the use of holy water in deliverance prayer.

Since this time, I've recommended that this sort of prayer be carried out when, for example, a parent has a youngster whose will is captured by the evil one—perhaps through alcohol, drugs, the occult, or simply through allowing sin and perversion to take deep root in the life. The young girl in the camp situation got to the dangerous place she was in through a deep and abiding hatred of her father, some of which was fueled by an internalization of her mother's resentment of her husband's ministry. To pray in the way I did for her is to gain the gift of time. I don't know how else to say it. For a time, the essential will is freed and the power to choose a better way is given these persons. They then, on hearing the truth as it comes through a parent or minister, can make a better choice. They are freed to accept Christ fully into their lives as they repent and turn from their sinful ways. This prayer, then—once it is understood and administered in wisdom—can yield the highest results. But I always issue a warning in regard to this prayer. I ask the parent or other praying person to use the prayer only after thorough prayer preparation and guidance and not to use it more than once. The reason is that once the demons leave, if sinful and needy persons choose (will) to refuse Christ admittance to their hearts, then as the Scriptures warn, seven times more demons can come in to fill the void in those lives.

Why, you may be asking, have we never heard, much less read, such prayers as those said over blessed water and salt before? In short, it is because, as I've set out at some length in *The Healing Presence,* even Christians today are at bottom rationalists, materialists. We no longer understand the sacraments, much less the use of the sacramentals such as blessed oil and water, or sacramental actions such as the laying-on-of-hands in which we ourselves are the sacramental vessels.

The principle behind sacramental reality is simple yet profound, but as rationalists, we miss it. It has to do with the Presence of God, the "sweet unction of the Holy Spirit," being channeled to us through material means. God does not despise *matter*; He deigns to come to us through the womb of Mary, through baptismal waters, through the Communion cup, through the hands of our brother or sister in Christ who lays them on us and prays in such a way as we are flooded with light and life from above.[2] This understanding of reality is vital to the whole matter of healing prayer. We do not understand the sacraments and the use of sacramentals for the very same reason we have failed to understand and move forward in healing prayer.

The church that omits prayer for healing of the sick in mind and in body is a church that has either become wholly rational or is in danger of becoming so. This state contrasts with being *reasonable*, for the good of reason is preserved in the church only when the windows of our minds and hearts are fully open to God's immediate Healing Presence and Word. When a church is content to remain merely "rational," it inevitably proceeds toward unbelief and apostasy and ironically is eventually given over to the dark supernatural. Pagan superstitions and even the outright occult infiltrate, for they take root in and arise out of the darkness of unbelief. One way we see the pagan and the occult penetrating parts of the church is through the spirituality of C. G. Jung.[3] As John Richards states in his book *But Deliver Us from Evil: An Introduction to the Demonic in Pastoral Care*:

> Jung accomplished more than any other twentieth-century thinker to make occult theorizing respectable, finding his concepts of the "collective unconscious" and "synchronicity" corresponding in many ways with oriental and occult theories. . . .[4]

There are other influences besides Jung, and these will increase until we regain a fully Christian spirituality and by it overcome our rationalism and unbelief as we move to heal the people of God.

Spiritual Warfare in the Modern Christian Institution

Two letters I received from a young seminarian, excerpted below, illustrate the spiritual warfare we get embroiled in when we come under the domination of religious educational institutions that no longer hold the "faith once delivered" but only rationalized and therefore reductionistic versions of it. The loss of freedom to speak the truth in such situations is as insidious a form of tyranny as one could imagine. Sadly, the situations described here are not rare. They point up our need to prepare ourselves to move more effectively in the exorcism of institutions. These letters contain classic illustrations of spiritual bondage—what it looks and feels like, as well as the very real danger it poses to the health of body and soul. This man could have lost his life had he not come out of the bondage. These excerpts also illustrate the effective use of holy water, as well as the struggle that, strangely enough, a man studying for the priesthood had in finding a book containing prayers for use with holy water.

> Dear Leanne,
>
> Spring break is here, and . . . I am definitely on the downhill run in school. I got my GOE scores back two weeks ago and did well in all areas. The same week I came through the faculty ordination vote unscathed (not to be taken for granted here with my theology even though I have maintained a low profile). All I have left is a couple more papers and seminary will be behind me.
>
> It is . . . sad to realize that for all the problems this school has in lack of

direction, lack of vision for ministry, and misguided emphasis upon the sensate and the "demonstrably rational," it is apparently one of the more solid ones in the [denomination]. Of the survivors in my class (we lost over one-third), only a half dozen or so have their feet firmly planted enough in Jesus to really go out and minister. The others . . . will go out as ordained professionals: social workers, mass priests, administrators, or frustrated theologians who are always answering the questions which no one in their congregation is asking. . . .

It is very difficult to succinctly sum up my experiences here. . . . I have obviously gathered a great deal of information about church history, liturgies, ethics, etc., that is necessary . . . but so much has been neglected . . . even denied—that is part of our heritage and so essential for ministry.

The lack of moral absolutes is one of the most distressing aspects of what is taught. While most of my classmates (we are an almost boringly straight group) are exemplary in their conduct, they have continually had their values undermined to the point that few of them feel the liberty to point their congregations to specific standards of conduct. It is all reduced to a matter of relativity. Last week our pastoral theology professor showed us a pornographic homosexual film—ostensibly to desensitize us to "homosexual lovemaking" and to create sympathy for homosexual lifestyles. We spend sixteen hours in required Biblical courses so that we can place this information on an equal par with Shakespeare, Kant, Marx, Nietzsche, and Freud as we search for truth. The fact that the church has survived at all must be the most powerful witness there is to God's continued activity in the world—we surely aren't giving Him much help through the institution itself. I am so thankful for the foundation that God had laid in my life through your influence and that of many others before I came here!

This man had come to Christ through our ministry, received a powerful infilling of the Holy Spirit, and then had gone on to become an effective witness to the faith. From the first, his pastoral gifts were evident, and he knew he was to go to seminary. Midway into his school work, however, he became very ill and phoned me. As I listened, I realized his physical condition was directly related to demonic warfare, so after several days of prayer about the matter, I phoned and asked that he get blessed water and oil and receive laying-on-of-hands at once. Even though before going to seminary he had received such ministry and had effectively ministered it to others, the following (written after his graduation) describes the difficulty he had in praying the prayer that would break the bondage. Months of serious illness elapsed before he could do it:

It is difficult to know where to start in regard to the tremendous inertia which [my wife] and I had to overcome in taking authority with the holy water during my second year. Perhaps I need to go back to the very beginning of my first year. Although I felt that I was well prepared as to what to expect at seminary—emphasis on academics, no three-year spiritual retreat, constantly under scrutiny, etc.—nonetheless I did want to be receptive to what was being offered. After all, these were the professionals which the church had selected to train its next generation of priests. Also, I was lulled to sleep somewhat by [and here he describes the gentle, loving spirituality of one of his profs, one who finally proved to be without power and without mental or emotional health]. All during the first year I rationalized to myself and others that there really must be some purpose and overall design in what we were being required to do that made sense in the context of the historic church. On the one hand, we were told at the outset that religious truth and scientific truth dealt with somewhat different questions and therefore could not be in juxtaposition with one another. We also were told that we would be dealing with questions of faith which could be experienced, but not actually proven one way or the other. Yet, we found the only arguments which were acceptable to the faculty were those which were sustainable by a rational approach which could meet with the criteria of the nonbelieving academic world. (This contradiction between the nature of religious and scientific truths and the methods which were permissible to use in searching for or developing religious truth was something I was unable to get my professors to acknowledge in three years of seminary work.)

Although I felt that intellectually I was remaining true to what God had shown to be true and of value in my life, experientially I was becoming more and more a part of the general atmosphere of the school. My spiritual life was rather barren. It was very easy to find someone with which to drink and party, but that first year [my wife] and I did not find anyone with whom we were at ease to really share our experiences of Jesus and with whom we could consistently pray.

[He describes his "internship" program in a hospital.] . . . where the theology very forcefully presented was that God could not intervene to alleviate the suffering that we encountered on the hospital floors each day. To suggest that He (really She or It) could be anything other than an opiate for those who were suffering met with derision and criticism from the chief supervisors in the intensive, large group meetings. The frequent group sessions were at the best dangerous—lots of amateurish probing and prying with no attempt at healing, and they were at the worst brutal. A classmate . . . struggling with cancer (which was largely in remission and which his doctor thought was very stress sensitive) had to leave when his white count shot out of sight.

Finally, about six weeks into the ten-week program, I decided to take control of my life and began to try to stand up to my immediate supervisor. The road back was more difficult than I even dreamed. Within a week I found myself in the emergency room with the life-threatening condition I later wrote you about. My [internship] ended with a standoff in which we sort of agreed to overlook the negative and accent the positive. My problem was not really with the individual people, but rather with the system that denied that which was the foundation upon which my life was based.

On my return to seminary in the fall, I was determined not to succumb to the system and be seduced in the way I had my first year. However, the work load was so heavy that it really was just a matter of survival without much of a chance to work on my spiritual life and personal growth or actual personal healing. Also, my situation was similar to that of many of my classmates. We had left good jobs or professions in which we had seniority, sold homes, uprooted our families, and put the future of our families as well as ourselves on the line. The criterion for evaluation was much too ambiguous to be able to stand up and make too many waves. The faculty could ask you to leave or recommend that you not be ordained without ever giving specific reasons or being individually accountable for how they had voted.

Although we did establish a good relationship with another couple that fall, our year at school had robbed us of the will to fight with the spiritual weapons with which God had previously equipped us. Our spiritual sensitivity was very low, and we had fallen into the trap of looking for scientifically demonstrable reasons for all that we encountered. Even when we discussed the possibility of there being a demonic element to what we were experiencing, somehow there seemed no way to do anything about it.

When you called . . . and urged us to get the holy water and use it to break the bondage, I could think of many reasons why it wouldn't work and see no way that it could. There was no clergy person to whom I felt I could turn. We had not at that time developed a close enough relationship with our prayer partners to risk such a radical suggestion to them. . . . It was as though someone within me was saying, "You have risked too much to try something this crazy and get called before the faculty for such a thing. You know that this could very easily get you canned in a hurry." Besides, my own spiritual impotence was so pronounced at that time that I could not believe that anything would happen anyway (what a far cry from where I had been a few short years ago!). Why take the risk?

In my journal entry on the day you called, I described myself as beleaguered and confused, and yet, very desirous of being true to God's call in my life. As you know, it took us over two months to get a copy of the prayers from the *Priest's Manual* . . . and then to convince ourselves that we had the authority to act without clergy assistance. An amazingly long time for two people who are normally impatient self-starters, much concerned about my physical health if not our spiritual health. In retrospect it was like being in one of those horrible dreams in which one can see disaster coming, but is unable to move at a normal pace so as to avoid it. When one lives in the midst of a lie long enough, it becomes a part of you whether you want to rationally accept it or not.

We finally, with great reluctance and very little expectancy, blessed the water and used it as you suggested. We did so more out of respect for you than any faith that God would really move. As you know, the result affected more than my serious physical state. It was a turning point for us spiritually and emotionally. It was as though in the next few days the clouds parted, and God's light began to show through for the first time in a long time. The situation at school did not change, but our perspective of it did. Dimly at first, but with increasing clarity, we began to see the struggle which raged around us. We could do battle with the real adversary for a change and allow our anger at individuals and the system to abate. We could see that they were as blind to what was going on as we had been. They simply could not see the way out because they had not been set free. Unfortunately, as long as I was in the position of a student, I did not feel that I could do much to help the situation because the intimidation and prejudice against certain theological positions were real and not imagined.

As I write this to you, I am aware that my resolve to loose myself was not enough . . . I had to get to the point that I could see the problem with my spiritual eyes, and I had to fight the battle with spiritual weapons. My will, my good intentions, and my intellect were not enough. I thank God for the experiences I had prior to entering seminary which encouraged me to take the timid, belated steps which finally led to my being set free. I also thank you for your love and concern which caused you to push us to take the necessary steps.

As I looked over my infrequent journal entries from this period, I came across one which perhaps best sums up what this is all about, "If Satan can spiritually castrate and lobotomize us before ordination, he has little to fear from our ministries."

I want to reiterate how subtle and seductive the attack was in the beginning of our battle: "Does God really expect you to do this or believe that? Is it really so important that you adhere so strongly to that point of view? After all, look at all those who feel differently, and they aren't such bad people, are they?" Eventually we all became targets of, as well as agents for, the deception that was being perpetrated. Like Peter, I sold out all too easily—even before I realized it. . . .

We love you and pray for you regularly.

In Christ, ____________

Could this seminarian have been prayed for, delivered, and healed without the use of holy water? Yes, but not nearly so easily. This takes us back to the point I made earlier about the inestimable value and power of prayer. When we use holy water, we have the force not only of our own prayers, but those of the Church as well. The *prayer of faith* that makes a pathway for the Spirit of God to heal and set the sick free is to be stressed, never the use of holy water per se. But then, that is precisely what makes holy water, when used appropriately, so extremely effective—the prayers said over it.

Besides the fact that we have the prayers of God's people with us when we use holy water, many demonic spirits are quickly, even instantly, routed by it. Working as I do to see people healed and set free from sexual perversions and neuroses, I often have to send phallic demons (unclean spirits) away. These are extremely subtle and seem better able to hide than most. But the fact is, they cannot stand holy water, and they flee from it. Most who have been to our meetings have seen this firsthand.[5]

The following is taken from Michael Green's book *I Believe in Satan's Downfall*. He is an Anglican pastor and theologian, now teaching at Regent College in Vancouver, BC.

> Holy water is another effective symbol, and indeed agency. I discovered its value by mistake, not coming from a churchmanship where the use of holy water was common. One person under the influence of multiple demon possession crowed at me, "Ah, you haven't got any holy water." "I have," I replied, and at once consecrated some water in a glass in the name of the Trinity, and proceeded to sprinkle her. The effect was immediate, electric, and amazing. She jumped as if she had been scalded. The spirit manifested itself powerfully and in due course departed. But I learned a lesson from that. Holy water is a most valuable adjunct to deliverance. The funny thing is that if the person is not possessed, or after they have been delivered, there is no reaction whatever when the water is applied. It becomes a useful thermometer therefore.
>
> It is interesting to reflect on the status of holy water in the church. The Catholic strand of Christendom has retained it, but does not know what to do with it. It had once been dynamic in the days of faith, but became static and fossilized when men no longer believed. The Protestant churches have rejected it as superstition, seeing only its fossilized state and reacting against that. In fact we are fools not to use it both in places and with people who are or may be possessed.[6]

Since my first experience with the young girl who wandered into the unthinkable path of Satan worship, I've used holy water anytime someone is oppressed by evil[7] or invaded by demonic spirits. This was always quietly done—few if any ever questioned it. Many who receive healing prayer expect the anointing with oil that has been hallowed for healing purposes and most likely do not differentiate between it and the holy water. Both the oil and the water are "standard equipment" for most who minister with us in the schools and seminars. I suppose I could fill a book with humorous "holy water" stories, for most Protestants (Catholics too!) simply do not have "holding spaces" in their minds for the kinds of things we see happen with its use.

One man, Pastor John, to give one of the latest examples, a teacher in a Christian Bible school, simply was not going to accept the notion that any good could come of using holy water. He held to this even after experiencing a PCM and seeing its effective use firsthand. But all this changed one day when into his office came a prominent woman who was manifesting demons. Pastor John was beginning to get anxious, for his ministrations seemed to be getting them nowhere. The situation was growing in intensity, along with his alarm.

His secretary, Annie, quietly opened the door and saw immediately what was happening, for it was mirrored in Pastor John's face. Annie could see only the back of the demonized woman, but she knew from the foul words and behavior that demons were manifesting. She had also attended our seminar, and knowing about the use of holy water, she ran to get the bottle she had acquired after the conference. The demonized woman did not hear Annie's quiet reentry, yet she began screaming, "Where's the holy water? Where did it come from?" And her head began spinning around as if it would swing off her neck—all of this under the influence of demons. Needless to say, Pastor John and Annie used the water quite liberally that day, and the woman was set free. Stunned by this, the pastor has since revised his thinking and now has a very large "holding space" in his mind for the use of sacramental helps.

One Jesuit priest, running up to me after a prayer for deliverance from Baal (idols) that had resulted in literally hundreds being set free, said: "I've never seen holy water do that!" We laughed together, for he knew, even as I, that holy water, the crucifix, or anything else can be used perfunctorily and without faith—in which case it is, as Michael Green has stated, merely a fossilized relic. Again, of course, it is never the holy water, per se. It is, first of all, the prayer said over the water—together with the gifts of the Holy Spirit and God's gracious leading in the administration of it—that combine to make the use of sacramental helps such a blessing.

Because of the way holy water is now used in our healing services, its use is apparent and noticed. We realize this is all right and are comforted by the fact that this too is the Lord's doing. It has to do with a vital part of our message—the fact of Incarnational Reality and that God does not despise matter but hallows it. It has to do with healing the rift we moderns suffer between head and heart, reason and faith, and the restoration of both ways of knowing. It also everywhere brings together Protestant and Catholic in ways we'd never envisioned, especially overseas in countries such as Ireland, England, Scotland, and on the continent of Europe where the divisions between these Christians run even deeper than in the United States. Protestants begin to repent of their headiness and their subjective overreactions to what has become for them "Catholic practices"; Catholics receive new understanding and life into the sacramentals they retained, and repent of any perfunctory or superstitious use of them.

Holy Washings

> . . . Christ loved the church and gave himself up for her to make her holy, cleansing her by the washing with water through the word, and to present her

> to himself as a radiant church, without stain or wrinkle or any other blemish, but holy and blameless. (Ephesians 5:25)

Besides the way the Holy Spirit attends the use of holy water in deliverance prayer, we see His power at work in (I don't know what else to call it) "holy washing" prayer. After prayer for healing of memories and for deliverance from false gods, we are often led of the Spirit to ask people to come forward who need the administration of "more holy water." Sometimes this doesn't occur until the last day of a school when we are praying "consecration" prayers with individuals. We know there is yet more cleansing to be done—a cleansing that in a special way ties together all the healings these persons have experienced and enables them to more fully "put on Christ" and to more fully accept the call to minister to others.

The team and I often shed tears as, for example, incest and ritual abuse victims who have received healing of memories cry, "Wash my face, please," or "Wash my hands," or "It's my mind I want fully washed," or simply, "More water, please, more holy water." We then, as led by the Holy Spirit, apply the water, making the sign of the cross over them as we pray. It is as if now not only their memories are touched and flooded with healing light, but the very pores of their bodies and the cells of their minds receive a holy cleansing and release. The skin is washed with that which is holy, and the poisonous effects of having been impurely touched and hated (as only Satan, using another human being, can hate and destroy) are neutralized and lifted.

Those who have misused their bodies sexually have special needs here, and enormous healings occur as those who've been in perverted sexual lifestyles, now set free, come forward crying out for more holy water. As one young man wrote:

> After we renounced Baal and Ashtoreth, I knew that I needed even more cleansing, and when you said to come forward for more of the holy water, I knew the Lord had made the way for this. I asked you to wash my mouth because, in my past sexual activity, my mouth and throat had received the most vile defilement. . . . As soon as you passed the holy water over my mouth, my lips felt so precious and my mouth holy. I felt that there was a word written across the back of my throat which must come out, it was the word *horrible*. For a little while this word stubbornly refused to move, but as you poured more and more holy water over me, this word dislodged and I felt a new word written there. It was my Christian name! Alive with its full meaning!

My files are literally filled with letters chronicling the healings that take place during these holy washings. And they are not just from those who've experienced gross abuse or suffered the ravages inherent in sexual sin, neurosis, and perversion. Many others, when led to come forward, receive additional cleansings, healings and insights. As the following excerpt from a letter reveals, one received a fleeting glimpse of the joy and holiness toward which our cleansing in Christ leads:

> The most amazing thing happened during the washing with holy water. At first, when you announced it, I was in turmoil, as I was thinking of the saying of Jesus, "He who has washed already needs no further washing." Knowing how much washing the Lord has already done in me, my main concern was that I should not dishonor Him in going up. But on the other hand, I was keen not to miss out on any blessing! Finally, I . . . came forward. What happened next was quite extraordinary in its intensity.
>
> You had just finished washing me and tipped my chin up a little. . . . At that moment something clicked in my head and I heard the words, "Washed in the blood of the Lamb." And what I next saw and heard had a split-second quality—it was as if a curtain were momentarily lifted. . . .
>
> I saw people dressed in white with their arms up in the air, praising the Lord, and then I seemed to catch an echo of bells, or singing wafted on the wind . . . the effect it had on me is almost beyond description. I was possessed with a fierce desire, a desperate longing, to get to that Land. The word *Heaven* seems too weak to describe it. The intensity of the experience is almost impossible to convey in words. Indeed I was practically unable to speak of it for months afterwards. Suddenly the rest of my life seemed like a bore—to be got through as quickly as possible. In fact, I have always asked the Lord for a long life, if that is His will, as I want to bear fruit, and I don't want my loved ones to have to grieve me prematurely. And anyway, I enjoy life. So this desire was certainly no kind of death wish. I don't understand why the Lord gave me that experience then, but I do understand why such moments are generally fleeting—we'd none of us be here otherwise!

A year or so ago, after an overseas PCM where we made particularly generous use of holy water, Fr. William Beasley and I were flying home, praising God and talking about the unusual healings we'd seen as God had led in this way, when it became clear to me that we'd had, among other things, a great baptismal service. "William," I said, knowing he did not have a rigid bone in his makeup, but that he nevertheless was a churchman with strong inclinations toward a "proper" baptismal liturgy, "along with all the other washings, it seems to me that we are carrying out the commandment of Christ to go out into all the world, preach the gospel, and baptize. Don't you think some of what was going on in these holy washings were water baptisms in the fullest sense of the word?"

"Yes," he said quietly, "I realized that was happening; in some cases that is exactly what was going on."

Interestingly enough, we got several letters after that conference indicating those who experienced it *knew* as well that this was their water baptism. The young man who received his name (a christening such as occurs in baptism when the Christian name is given) wrote:

> I had once had a "believer's" baptism, but there had been no real repentance. . . . Like a Pharisee, I had gone for the outward show. There had been no change of lifestyle, no bringing forth the fruits that the Lord was looking for. I had worried all week as to whom I could ask to baptize me. After my "holy washing," I couldn't stop laughing. . . . such was the joy. . . . This was my water baptism.

This is in no way to recommend multiple water baptisms. However, this young man's first, deliberately undertaken in unbelief and rebellion, had obviously been farcical. But there can be multiple washings, and God uses the hallowed water in and with the Word to hallow his Bride, the Church.

As Rev. Canon Mark Pearson states:

> God may choose to make use of material objects by which grace, blessing, and healing are conveyed. In Scripture and in Church tradition we read of blessed prayer cloths (Acts 19:11-12) and holy oil (James 5:14). God may also use Holy Communion, holy water, or any number of other objects. The historic term for these things is "sacramentals." One contemporary Pentecostal minister of healing has called them "delivery systems." In addition, the laying-on-of hands is frequently a part of healing and indeed of many different acts of blessing.

And please note the chief reason why this is so: "*The reason for this variation in manner of healing is to keep our focus on God.*" Christian healing does not believe God to be capricious. We can confidently offer prayer, administer the various sacramentals, and lay hands on the sick. But since we are never certain how God will heal or the time-frame in which He will accomplish it, our focus is to be kept on God. There is no "technique of healing," no "magic objects."[8]

It is surely the greatest blessing to be able to hear the Lord say:

> [G]o and make disciples of all nations, baptizing them in the name of the Father and of the Son and of the Holy Spirit, and teaching them to obey everything I have commanded you. And surely I am with you always, to the very end of the age. (Matthew 28:19-20)

And what joy it is to see the myriad ways the Spirit of the Lord uses to send His cleansing flood, and then to engender within the fallen creature His new and uncreated Life. May it be so, we cry, "Come, Holy Spirit, wash us anew. Maranatha! Even so, come Lord Jesus!"

The Use of a Blessed Crucifix

> In addition to Scripture there are other aids we can use. The cross of Christ is of course the great sign of demonic defeat, and I find that few things so provoke the demon to manifest itself and to leave as using a cross to hold before the eyes of the patient. They will often shut their eyes to exclude the sight. Marking the cross upon the patient's person is equally certain to provide a reaction if they are in fact possessed.[9]

In *The Healing Presence,* I have said a great deal about symbols and imagery, that they bind up reality for us, and that we as twentieth-century Christians have lost our Judeo-Christian symbolic system. Christian reality is diminished for us because it has been reduced to an abstraction. Our hearts and minds are bereft of the great Christian symbols and images ("pictures" that mediate a transcendent reality) and contain instead the images and thought patterns of a materialistic or pagan worldview. We've abstracted away the great Christian realities, and we are now at the mercy of alien symbolic systems such as those that form the framework of Freemasonry, the occult, and the various Eastern, pagan, pantheistic, and Gnostic (feminist, Jungian, New Age) systems.

To further compound this loss, many Christians are not only in denial of their intuitive, imaginative faculties, but are taught to be afraid of them by those in extreme reaction to the New Age and related paganisms. As a result, many churchgoers sit in the pews these days, their imaginations furnished with alien images, yet they have learned to hate and deny their own intuitive, imaginative capacities and no longer think in the terms that symbolize the incomparably great Judeo-Christian reality. They may even fear and eschew the crucifix as that which symbolizes Christ's death and resurrection, and ours in and with His—all that pertains to salvation, redemption, justification, sanctification, and spiritual authority over evil.

Interestingly enough, however, the Devil and his demons have not lost the Judeo-Christian symbolic system. They are just in the business of tempting us to lose ours. They cannot stand the crucifix, that which symbolizes our full redemption, the fact that Christ took upon Himself the wrath of God against evil and paid for us the price of His blood.

I'll never forget the deliverance of one grievously possessed young man brought to us. His sexual compulsions were of the worst, and he was, by his own admission, close to murdering his sex victims. Especially memorable were his tormented, blue eyes—eyes that yet retained a beauty Satan had been unable to entirely obliterate and a promise of the true man within who was about to come forward in the Healing Presence of God. He was terrified lest he should hurt me or the ones standing with me, for in other deliverance attempts the demons had caused him to flail about with the strength of many men. He was indeed the sort that would have knocked out the walls of the place we were in had we gone about it in the more popular way of today—with loud speaking and binding of demons, and with no use of crucifix or holy water. But we had a good supply of holy water and a very large crucifix, one we took down from over the altar in the chapel we were in.

As I placed that huge crucifix in his hands, his fingers curled round it in a death grip. Though he remained seated with his hands fixed to the very large upright cross, his head plunged to the floor and he was frothing at the mouth and in agony of the demons. As we prayed and poured the holy water on him, he was gradually able to honor my request that he look up into my face. The crucifix was between him and me, facing him, and as he looked up to me, it was through the face of Christ crucified. It was then I looked into his pain-stricken eyes and called forth the real man, the man who was anxious *to work with me* toward his deliverance. In Jesus' name, we then commanded the demons to leave and to harm no one as they left. Demon after demon tore out of his body as we continued to pour on the water and call forth the true man. Within forty-five minutes this man was delivered. The next day we had extensive prayer for healing of his memories, and we made arrangements for him to have Christian fellowship. Several weeks later, a Christian psychiatrist helped him deal with the serious dysfunctions in his family that had led to such a critically eroticized self-identity. I am happy to report that this man is not only whole today, but he is a leader in the Body of Christ.

What could have taken days took a short time because a ministry team did not focus on demons or darkness, but rather on seeing the true man and calling him forth into the Presence of a Holy God. This, together with the fact that demons cannot stand that which is holy and signifies Christ's death for us, made what would have taken hours and even days into the work of less than an hour.

By reason of the way God put it together, our PCM team is evenly divided between Catholics and Protestants. Patsy Casey, one of our music leaders, is thoroughly Irish and Catholic in background and is, at the same time, gifted in evangelism—ordinarily considered to be more the purview of Protestant evangelicals today. She does not express her special evangelistic gift with some variation of: "Are you ready to make a decision for Christ?" but in a more immediate and colorful way, crying out, "Kiss the cross, brother," and she thrusts out the crucifix.

In our first full London PCM conference, we were in an absolutely packed auditorium. We were about evenly divided between church leaders and truly needy persons. There came a healing moment in the meetings when God was dealing with the most seriously needy, and a good number were being delivered of demons. Patsy was up in the balcony ministering at this moment, and, instantly discerning the demonic, she drew forth her crucifix. One young man, obviously needy and wanting help, began to manifest demons, and she went toward him. The demons within him caused him to hit at her crucifix, knocking it across the balcony. All eyes were on her as she retrieved it and turned to me on the platform, speaking loudly enough for all to hear. In an incredulous voice, as if such a thing were uncommon, she cried out to me: "This man doesn't know Jesus!" She then marched straight back toward him, crucifix in hand thrust toward his lips, saying, "Kiss the cross, brother!" And with no small struggle, that is exactly what he did. He received Christ and was delivered. We saw many, many healings and deliverances that day, but this young man's healing birthed yet another—and it has continued to bear the finest of fruit—that of a vital healing between Protestant and Catholic.

We often see God bless in a signal way the use of a blessed crucifix. It at once images and symbolizes Christ's death for us, the price He paid to deliver all who are oppressed and under Satan's foul heel. Hell and all its minions hate it, for it images the one reality they most fear. For the demon, the Judeo-Christian symbols are clear—and for them, they spell eternal damnation.

Satan's Temptation in Regard to Sacramental Actions and the Use of Sacramentals

The tempting of the Christian in regard to the use of holy water and a blessed crucifix is the same as it is in regard to all things that are true and useful. When we are committed to Christ, our temptations from the evil one are usually the more subtle ones. As Oswald Chambers states, Satan

> does not come on the line of tempting us to sin, but on the line of shifting the point of view, and only the Spirit of God can detect this as a temptation of the devil.[10]

He does succeed in shifting the point of view of some, for example, from the true imagination with its intuitions of the real, including the mind of Christ—to *merely* the picture-making faculty of the mind itself and its power to visualize. For another example, Satan seeks to shift our point of view from the prayers made over the hallowed water and the true principles behind sacramental reality to the water itself and either magical notions about it or the opposite error of seeing it merely as water used by those who are superstitious or in error. As a final example, the enemy would tempt us to shift our point of view from focus on Christ, crucified and risen again for our full salvation as symbolized in a crucifix, to the crucifix itself. *Prayer, the focus on Christ and communion with God, is the reality.* Here again, Oswald Chambers states it succinctly and powerfully, summing it up: "Prayer is the battle," and "Prayer does not fit us for the greater works; prayer *is* the greater work."[11]

We must learn to pray in such a way as to see individuals as well as organizations and programs delivered from the demonic. And when we listen carefully to God, we may find (as our forebears have, generation after generation rediscovering the fact) that sacramental actions, signs and symbols, such as the use of holy water and a blessed crucifix with those needing deliverance, may play a greater part than we would have dared think before the battle grew so grave and we were startled out of our rationalism. The use of what has been hallowed and set apart unto a holy God constitutes one of the ways by which the unhallowed, all that is foul and profane and hates God and His creation, is put to flight.

This chapter is not intended to be a full explication of the use of holy water and other Christian symbols and agencies in spiritual battle. Moreover, it is not an attempt to put forward or push the use of these things. It is, however, a plea for the understanding of symbol and *unction* and explains the unchanging principles behind their use. Both are vitally related to sacramental actions in prayer for the sick. Finally, this chapter underscores the important principle of focusing on God rather than upon demons in deliverance prayer. It is in focusing on Him that the charism of discerning of spirits operates.

As Christian history reveals, the knowledge of how to pray for healing is often lost to the church. It is only in times of the church's renewing that we regain it. This knowledge of healing prayer is one of the first things to be obscured in times of backsliding and the resulting loss of a full understanding of Christian Incarnational Reality.

In the ministry of healing prayer, we often find ourselves trying to reinvent the wheel, so to speak. It is comforting to find information from past ages that confirms, along with the Spirit of God, what we've learned. There have been several such finds in my life, and one of them is a large section on healing prayer from *Liturgy and Worship: A Companion to the Prayer Books of the Anglican Communion.*[12] Dr. Charles Harris wrote the section, and I know of no finer historical overview of healing prayer and the use of the sacramentals in the church. It is well researched and scholarly, yet readable, and retains the good of reason as well as full faith in a God who heals His people through those who pray. Though out of print, this important book can be obtained through libraries.

I found it only a year or so ago, and in reading through the entire section on healing prayer, I was impressed over and over again with the way the Holy Spirit teaches us not only the same truths, but the same ways of following through on these truths. I was especially delighted to find Dr. Harris's report that on occasion instantaneous healings of those with sexual perversions and illnesses occur. Our reports of the instant healings we see in our ministry are at times criticized by some within the church.

Our God is good, and His power is beyond telling. He has always used the small and despised things, such as blessed water and simple faith in Him, to confound the wisdom of this world.

CHAPTER 12

The Gift of Battle

We are not sent to battle for God, but to be used by God in His battlings.[1]

(Oswald Chambers)

Finally, be strong in the Lord and in his mighty power. Put on the full armor of God so that you can take your stand against the devil's schemes. For our struggle is not against flesh and blood, but against the rulers, against the authorities, against the powers of this dark world and against the spiritual forces of evil in the heavenly realms. Therefore put on the full armor of God, so that when the day of evil comes, you may be able to stand your ground, and after you have done everything, to stand. Stand firm then, with the belt of truth buckled around your waist, with the breastplate of righteousness in place, and with your feet fitted with the readiness that comes from the gospel of peace. In addition to all this, take up the shield of faith, with which you can extinguish all the flaming arrows of the evil one. Take the helmet of salvation and the sword of the Spirit, which is the word of God. And pray in the Spirit on all occasions with all kinds of prayers and requests. With this in mind, be alert and always keep on praying for all the saints.

(Ephesians 6:10-18)

Be on your guard; stand firm in the faith; be men of courage; be strong. Do everything in love.

(St. Paul, 1 Corinthians 16:13-14)

Jesus said, "But I tell you, Do not resist an evil person. If someone strikes you on the right cheek, turn to him the other also" (Matthew 5:39). Such a "hard" saying of our Lord's chases many of us time and again to a full study of the Sermon on the Mount. In that discourse, Jesus makes a number of statements like this one, and in doing so, contradicts and overturns the best Jewish wisdom of the day. A study of these words reveals, as Oswald Chambers says,

> the humiliation of being a Christian. Naturally, if a man does not hit back, it is because he is a coward; but spiritually if a man does not hit back, it is a manifestation of the Son of God in him. When you are insulted, you must not only not resent it, but make it an occasion to exhibit the Son of God. You cannot imitate the disposition of Jesus; it is either there or it is not. To the saint personal insult becomes the occasion of revealing the incredible sweetness of the Lord Jesus.[2]

Our Lord's words can never be understood or lived out in the natural. They have to do with the Paschal mystery and with Incarnational Reality, the fact that Another, the One crucified for sin, lives in us and that He is Love. We are to listen for a higher wisdom and collaborate with it. If we are to overcome in spiritual conflict, we must move forward in the knowledge of Christ's Presence with us and in the gifts of the Holy Spirit as these operate through listening prayer. In doing this, more often than not we are sent scurrying back to our Lord's words in this discourse. To experience real spiritual battle is to know what real enemies are. (Many think they are in a spiritual battle when they are merely beset due to lack of knowledge and wisdom as to how to deal with matters.) Nothing will send us back to Christ's words about loving our enemies more quickly than a skirmish with those who truly hate the word of truth (Christ and His gospel) and therefore hate and malign us. We soon find out if we are battling partly in our own strength, and we cry out for mercy to battle only in His.

In *Crumbling Foundations,* Dr. Donald Bloesch writes of our need to pray for the "gift of battle." In a section entitled "Rediscovering the Spiritual Gifts," he reminds us that "Christians can only live out their vocation by discovering and exercising the gifts of the Holy Spirit," and he writes of this additional gift which he says is alluded to in both Testaments. As a theologian and a keen observer of the times, he believes this gift of battle has a crucial significance for our day:

> Christians who are under the cross of persecution need to pray for the gift of battle, the ability to endure under trial, the boldness to challenge immorality and heresy in high places. The gift of battle is properly included in the gift of might or power (Isaiah 11:2). It is the power to enter into conflict and the stamina not to grow weary. It must be accompanied by and fulfilled in the gift of love, since we cannot wage war against sin successfully unless we love the sinner. We must speak the truth, but we must speak the truth in love.[3]

Speaking the truth in a love born of God is, it seems to me, the greater part of the gift of battle. There is nothing weak about this love, for truth—full orbed and aptly spoken—is incredibly powerful.

A first principle in spiritual warfare is the knowledge that we cannot function in the gift of battle without *agape*, the gift of divine love coming from God's life within and issuing forth through us. In such a stance, our trust will be wholly in Him. We will be looking to no other power, no other intervention—but His. This looking straight to God and receiving His battle plan keeps us on a safe ground in another very important matter—we know that we are to hate sin, but we are not to hate our enemy.

The following, a prayer from a Greek Orthodox liturgy, has a permanent and prominent place in my prayer journal. It helps me pray aright for my enemy when the battle is at its height and I am least able to muster up my own words for such a prayer. An absolutely wonderful one, it has within it the true spirit of Christ's Sermon on the Mount.

> Save, O Lord, and have mercy upon those that envy and affront me and do me mischief, and let them not perish through me, a sinner.

Prayer such as this is what loving our enemy is all about.

A second principle is that we cannot function in the gift of battle apart from mature prayer partners. They are the foot soldiers who trudge alongside us, persevering in the same battle:

> Christians who enter the battle against the powers of darkness cannot persevere without a life-support system, without a supportive fellowship that continually holds up its members in intercession to the living God.[4]

Those of us who have these "life-support" systems are deeply grateful for them, but those who do not must pray earnestly for them. The intercessions of the saints who gather together in Christ's name to pray for us are absolutely vital in the Christian walk, and most assuredly so in spiritual warfare. God's gift to us of precious souls that not only intercede for us, but hear and pass on the word that God is speaking when we are sore besieged and fainting is true wealth. All through the years when God would move me from one locale to another, the first thing I besought God for was trusted prayer partners. I often had to train Christians in prayer, but God always sent them, maybe only one for a while. Then another or so would be added. My prayer partners are among my greatest spiritual treasures. To watch God at work in their souls and ministries is an amazing reward in itself, only one of many, many that these "masterpieces" of God's love, these servants of His, bring. I am confounded and amazed to see how rare it is that pastors and leaders have prayer partners such as these. Often they fear to share with others, and there will be no corporate listening for God's voice or intercession for others that is worthy of the name. No one can stand long in battle under these conditions or win the prize of pressing through to victory in the vocations we've been assigned.

I recently prayed with a precious, strong leader in the Body of Christ. She was undergoing the worst spiritual warfare that the archenemy of our souls can muster, and the fierce battle had brought her excruciating suffering. This pain enabled her for the first time to understand what it means to enter into the sufferings of Christ. In coming up against deeply entrenched evil within the church and taking her stand against it, she became the target of astonishing lies, vicious slander, and all manner of verbal abuse. Her very ministry was in question. Weary beyond belief at the strength and the length of the battle, she despaired of surviving the onslaught. *She had strong prayer partners, however, who were standing with her as the battle grew more impossible.* Then as we (the PCM team) came together in prayer with them, we received these incredible words from God. This leader opened her heart and received them, and these words set her back firmly upon her feet and restored to her the vocation (the message of salvation) she has been intrusted with. These are but a few of the words:

> Laura [not her real name] is to lift up her voice; she is to exalt the Lord in the assembly of the people. There will be a glorious vindication—her voice is not to be silenced.
>
> There is a new armor for Laura; it is the armor of love God is going to put on her. She is going to be able to face her enemies with a powerful love. She will be overawed at how this love will come through her. She will go forth in this armor. She is not to strive, for she will feel no need to protect herself.

Most who have suffered in the way this servant of the Lord has would feel the need to put up walls and to take protective measures for themselves and their families. But she is not going to. She has entered into the sufferings of Christ. Therefore, she is facing an enemy whose battle plan is designed to stop her mouth from speaking the truth of the gospel and her entire being from living out the truth that Another, the Holy, All Powerful One, is with her. But she has put on the full armor of God, and has asked for and received the gift of battle.

While the archaccuser of our souls, the enemy who would deceive and bring under dark deception even the elect, plans the full destruction of ourselves as persons, we like Laura battle and overcome under the Lord's banner—His holy cross and its way of love (Hebrews 2:10) and not according to the way the world fights:

> For though we live in the world, we do not wage war as the world does. The weapons we fight with are not the weapons of the world. On the contrary, they have divine power to demolish strongholds. We demolish arguments and every pretension that sets itself up against the knowledge of God, and we take captive every thought to make it obedient to Christ. (2 Corinthians 10:3-5)

The Scriptures refer to this battle that engages the whole of our being as a good warfare (1 Timothy 1:18-19), and "the good fight of faith" (1 Timothy 6:12). It is against "the world" (John 16:33; 1 John 5:4-5), the flesh (Romans 7:23; 1 Corinthians 9:25-27; 2 Corinthians 12:7; 1 Peter 2:11), our enemies (Psalm 38:19; 56:2-4; 59:3), and ultimately, behind and energizing these things, the archenemy of all that God has created and called good, Satan himself (Genesis 3:15; 2 Corinthians 2:11; James 4:7-10; Ephesians 6:12; 1 Peter 5:8-9; Revelation 12:17).

The Scriptures exhort us to diligence in the warfare (1 Timothy 6:12; Jude 3); and it is to be undertaken with faith and good conscience (1 Timothy 1:18-19), steadfastness (1 Corinthians 16:13; 1 Peter 5:8-9; Hebrews 10:23), watchfulness (1 Corinthians 16:13-14), sobriety (1 Thessalonians 5:6-8), endurance (2 Timothy 2:3, 10), self-denial (1 Corinthians 9:25-27), with confidence in God (Psalm 27:1-3), and with prayer (Psalm 35:1-3).

In the ministry God has entrusted to us on the Pastoral Care Ministries Team, we never cease to be amazed at the myriad and unexpected ways God protects (Psalm 140:7), delivers (2 Timothy 4:18), helps (Psalm 118:13; Isaiah 41:13-14), comforts (2 Corinthians 7:5-7), encourages (Isaiah 41:11-12; 51:12; 1 John 4:4), and strengthens (Psalm 20:2; 27:14; Isaiah 41:10; 2 Corinthians 12:9; 2 Timothy 4:17) us in the midst of spiritual battle—even the worst warfare. It is not unusual, when ministering to the most injured, those just coming out of sinful and perverted lifestyles, to see God deliver several hundred people at one time out of the worst sicknesses of mind as well as the related condition of being seriously demonized. Here we are faced with many caught up in the worst spiritual darkness, having lost the battle due to sin and being outside of Christ. In such moments, we know not only the holy Presence of God and His mighty power at work, but at times our eyes are opened and we see the heavenly host working with us! And we are shown different kinds of angels! For example, at times in helping women severely wounded through misogyny, two of the most unusual angels come! We have to go back to the books of Ezekiel and Daniel for the words and images to describe them! These are powerful angels, and they are apparently especially concerned with the evil that women sustain in war and through misogyny. They are there helping us when these women are to be set free! We see through a glass darkly now, but someday our Lord will explain all these things to us. In the meantime it suffices to say that we, as the Body of Christ, have hardly started to draw on the divine resources our God longs to send. There is joy and victory in the midst of real battle and real suffering.

When the Enemy Is the Beloved Enemy

> For a son dishonors his father, a daughter rises up against her mother, a daughter-in-law against her mother-in-law—a man's enemies are the members of his own household. (Micah 7:6)

Often the enemy takes advantage of opposition that arises within our most intimate circles—our close relatives or friends in the Body of Christ—to stir up the most heart-rending kind of spiritual warfare. This especially occurs where an effective ground-breaking ministry is at stake. Always in such demonized warfare, there will be slander and lies. I've yet to see a case like this where a root sin of envy did not have to be exposed and reckoned with as well. Oddly enough, that dread vice is rarely recognized for what it is today.

The tenth chapter of Matthew is concerned with this kind of opposition. When I first began to teach on the healing of relationships through forgiveness of sin, I experienced the most bizarre and irrational opposition, lies, and slander from certain quarters. I would never have expected it to come from that source. The situation was rife with demonic spirits, which also surprised me. Until we've been in the ministry for a good while, we seem to expect these kinds of fierce, obviously demonically inspired battles to happen to other people—not ourselves. I went flat on my face before God. Spiritual battle brings all manner of confusion, so I had a lot of "thinking through" to do with God; and of course I had to forgive and keep on forgiving the same persons, and to intercede and keep on interceding for them. In order to do all this and to keep track of the understanding God was giving me through the Scriptures and the ways He was leading me to pray, I set aside in my prayer journal an entire section entitled, "Beloved Enemies." This section is filled with Scriptures that deeply ministered to me and with prayers God gave me to pray for these dear ones. I can call them that with all sincerity, for they are loved. Had I not learned to pray for them and for the situation effectively, I do not believe I would be able to make that statement. Perhaps I would not have been able to stand in the ministry at all, for the enemy's plan was to bring it down through discouraging me personally. The nature of the warfare would most surely have done that had I not learned to pray for my beloved enemies—those closest to me who opposed the work God has called me to do.

"Painting the Dragon Red"

The Lord delights in showing us how to pray. The earlier we get around to asking Him in each situation, the better off we'll be. When I seemed to be getting nowhere in my battle, I finally cried out in desperation, "Lord, what and how am I to pray for my enemies? Those beloved ones who slander me and the work You've given me to do?"

And God promised to give me a blueprint! Several days later, as I was praying, He did. We on the team call this our "paint-the-dragon-red" prayer. We've helped many other Christians embroiled in spiritual battle by sharing it with them. It contains sound principles that everybody seems to need once the battle is joined:

1) Pray that the eyes of all who surround these persons be opened to see the situation as it really is.

2) Pray that their associates will be given ways to speak truth and light into the situation.

In these first two steps, we are praying for godly illumination and wisdom for the persons who can minister truth and peace into the situation, while at the same time we are praying for their safety. We are asking that these stable people be spared from getting caught up in the dark net of spiritual confusion and deception—a very present danger in spiritual warfare—and that they be enabled to aid others who are ensnared.

As I meditated on these first two ways of prayer, the Lord greatly ministered the story of David and Goliath to me, this truth from 1 Samuel 17:47 in particular: " . . . it is not by sword or spear that the Lord saves; for the battle is the Lord's. . . ." I then asked, "Jesus, what is the smooth stone, slung at your command that will stop the Goliaths of envy, slander, murderous hate, all that is the enemy of Your cross, Your message?"

And immediately I heard in my spirit, "Truth, truth will out—it will hit the mark." Then the following instruction is what caused us to name this way of interceding the "paint-the-dragon-red" prayer:

3) Pray that any demonic power within these persons or within these situations manifest itself—that it may be clearly discerned and seen by all the people.

C. S. Lewis has rightly said that "Love is something more stern and splendid than mere kindness."[5] This is terribly hard on the "beloved enemy," but it is the only way he will be healed. In answer to this prayer, God causes the real enemy of all our souls to be revealed for all to see.

There will, of course, always be some unwilling to see and repent. They blind themselves by continuing to rationalize their sin. It is here that the root sin of envy will often be revealed—the sin that has opened the door for the demonic dragon to enter and has provided a nest from which it can strike within the Kingdom, a nest that can also harbor others of its demonic kind. When this happens, we invoke and practice the Presence of God and find that, "Wherever Jesus is, the storms of life become a calm."[6] We find also that He is doing a work within ourselves that could never have been done apart from the disciplines learned through sustained spiritual warfare.

After this third point, the Lord quickened 1 Samuel 14:15 to me. That Scripture verse gave me further insight into the model for taking the offensive in intercessory prayer. I saw that Jonathan and his armor-bearer, only two men, put the entire Philistine army to flight as they fought for God's people. They stepped out in faith, speaking the word of truth, and the Lord worked with them: "Then panic struck the whole army . . . and the ground shook. It was a panic sent by God."

Here we see so clearly what it means to be used by God in *His* (not our) battlings. When we step out at His command, He sends the panic or whatever else is needed. There is an illusory nature to evil. It attempts to win through bluff—through puffing itself up to horrendous size. One word of truth, spoken in the power of the Holy Spirit, solid as a rock and splendid as eternity, flies swift as the surest arrow to puncture evil's swelled balloon of lies, posturing, and bravado. Then panic sets in. There are times when we pray, "Send Your panic, Lord," and He does. We do not fight with words—we speak and live the truth, and God does the fighting.

The fourth step the Lord gave in this "paint-the-dragon-red" prayer is ever so important. It underlines the fact that our battle is against sin and not against the sinner:

4) Ask that what can be salvaged (in this situation and in the lives of your enemies) be saved, humbled, blessed by the Spirit of God.

With this, I wrote out these instructions from the Lord:

> Pray for the health, the wholeness, of your enemies. Pray for the salvaging of all that is good, beautiful, and true within them. I do a great work, one that will amaze you. Be at rest now from all that besets, offends, attacks—love, write, pray, live in peace in My Presence. Enter the timelessness of My joy and peace.

That our God is faithful to hear and answer all prayer, including these prayers, is something I want to shout from the housetop. With the prophet Micah, I was given the grace to say: "But as for me, I watch in hope for the Lord, I wait for God my Savior; my God will hear me" (Micah 7:7).

And He did. If we are obedient and stand in Him, our God has an incredible way of turning our battle wounds into healing power for others even while He is yet pouring His healing grace and light into the worst of our gashes.

PRAYER

Lord bring us, especially those of us called to lead in the church, to the point where we can truthfully say with St. Paul: "We put no stumbling block in anyone's path, so that our ministry will not be discredited. Rather, as servants of God we commend ourselves in every way: in great endurance; in troubles, hardships and distresses; in beatings, imprisonments and riots; in hard work, sleepless nights and hunger; in purity, understanding, patience and kindness; in the Holy Spirit and in sincere love; in truthful speech and in the power of God; with weapons of righteousness in the right hand and in the left; through glory and dishonor, bad report and good report; genuine, yet regarded as impostors; known, yet regarded as unknown; dying, and yet we live on; beaten, and yet not killed; sorrowful, yet always rejoicing; poor, yet making many rich; having nothing, and yet possessing everything." (2 Corinthians 6:3-10)

CHAPTER 13

Cosmic Dimensions of Spiritual Warfare in Christian Organizations

Dear friends, although I was very eager to write to you about the salvation we share, I felt I had to write and urge you to contend for the faith that was once for all entrusted to the saints. For certain men whose condemnation was written about long ago have secretly slipped in among you. They are godless men, who change the grace of our God into a license for immorality and deny Jesus Christ our only Sovereign and Lord.

(Jude 3-4)

Love is something more stern and splendid than mere kindness . . .

(C. S. Lewis)

Frank Peretti's novel *This Present Darkness* has brought home to many the cosmic dimensions of spiritual warfare and the nature of the suffering that accompanies intense spiritual conflict. In this book and its companion volume *Piercing the Darkness*, Peretti has given back to many Christian minds, formed by twentieth-century materialism, a vital part of their Judeo-Christian symbolic system. These Christians can now "see" the holy angels as well as their fallen, demonic counterparts, and the readers' imaginations are furnished with lively images of the cosmic battle going on "in the heavenlies." Their hearts now have pictures of the way our earthly rulers and institutions are invaded and influenced by the god of this present world. As a result, these Christians no longer abstract away unseen realities. They have a renewed understanding of the value of prayer, the critical part it plays in spiritual warfare. In a manner of speaking, they are enabled to taste again the incomparable "simplicity that is in Christ" (2 Corinthians 11:3, KJV) as they move forward in listening obedience:

> Simplicity is the secret of seeing things clearly. A saint does not think clearly for a long while, but a saint ought to see clearly without any difficulty. You cannot think a spiritual muddle clear, you have to obey it clear. . . . When the natural power of vision is devoted to the Holy Spirit, it becomes the power of perceiving God's will and the whole life is kept in simplicity.[1]

This renewed capacity to see more clearly is one of the gifts that novels written by Christians are especially suited to give. The more profoundly these works emerge out of and reflect Judeo-Christian truth and reality, the greater their value. Such works will always image aright some facet of our earthly situation, and do it against the backdrop of a universe capable of receiving into itself a transcendent order, justice, and harmony. That is, Incarnation (*real* Presence) and Christ's cross (redemption and the possibility of re-creation) will implicitly or explicitly be at the heart of these works. All effective art deals in one way or another with the cosmic battle we are involved in, and with the fact that God, a good beyond our present capacity to fully imagine, has won the ultimate victory.

In the spiritual battle raging within the organized church, we find that not a few of our writers and artists have become infected by the god of this world. When immature and sinful, these artists have an uncommon capacity to mislead others and, like those who teach within the church, will find that much will be required of them at the bar of divine justice (James 3:1; Mark 9:42-50; Matthew 23:1-33). Peretti's novels have had such a great impact on Christians because, within the confines of what these works attempt to do, they effectively image Christian reality. They are thoroughly and unabashedly Christian in a day when some Christian novelists are shy about such things as truth and eternal life, being more concerned with the literary aspects of a work and its acceptance by a secularized church and world. Those of us on the front lines of the spiritual battle today are quite heartily sick of these "artsy" works and the sickly cynicism, however subtle, that leaps up from the pages. Their authors reveal their antinomianism or even outright unbelief along with their inability to paint pictures of good winning over evil as Christians persevere. These defects usually dovetail into attempts to resymbolize sin through psychologizing it in some fashion or another.

For those of us fighting for the souls of men and women, the lack of transcendent meaning and the resulting overemphasis reflected in such art—that of man locked into a narcissistic cosmos of desire, feeling, and so on—is utterly *passé*. It is especially to be deplored in its more refined—that is to say, aesthetic and literary—forms.

We celebrate the art that flows out of a truly Christian imagination and intellect, for it has the power to restore to believers a fully Christian symbolic system. In this century, C. S. Lewis and J. R. R. Tolkien are great models. The images of glory, as well those that depict the true nature of good and evil, continue to reflect the enormous gift that great minds and hearts are to us—with their genius and capacity to mirror moral and intellectual, earthly and transcendent realities to us. Christian writers have always been required to portray truth—to line up with the way things really are—and to come up with images that can at least begin to mediate to the present generation the profound meaning and truth to be mined from God's revelation of Himself. At this time when false prophets, teachers, and apostles or bishops abound, Christians in the arts had better repent their aestheticisms and their need to please a secular public and instead take their place among those whose art flows out of prayerful meditation on and experience of the *real*.

Beyond the shallow, incomplete, and immature writing and art afflicting the church today, some within our church structures and programs are actively given over to an apologetic of evil. These persons are attempting to reconcile good and evil.[2] Some have deliberately set out to destroy the historic faith and are—knowingly or unknowingly—in the service of the enemy of our souls. This being the case, it is no surprise that many Christians faint at the sights, sounds, and smells arising out of the nauseating abominations within the organized church today.

> Woe to those who call evil good and good evil, who put darkness for light and light for darkness, who put bitter for sweet and sweet for bitter. (Isaiah 5:20)

Speaking the Truth

> [I]t matters enormously if I alienate anyone from the truth. (C. S. Lewis)[3]

The old verities, the true nature of God and of His revelation to us in and through Christ, can never be compromised, much less surrendered. There are things we can disagree about, and variously stress, but we must always and earnestly contend for the essentials of the faith. Today, little heresies that will grow to be very large later on are popping up in places we'd never expect to find them. Large ones, too. This has been true throughout the ages, and heresies have served the church in that they keep her humbled and alert, studious and prayerful. They force her to clarify and define for each succeeding generation of Christians "the faith once delivered to the saints" (Jude 3).

But what should concern us most is that one of the things characterizing the current scene is the lack of love for truth itself. One devout, highly respected theologian, after trying to deal with certain well-known writers (also ordained clergy) responsible for spreading error, recently said to me in utter amazement, "They do not care about *truth*!"

What these misguided persons did care about were others' feelings, how others thought about *them*, and how things looked to other people. All this reflects the spirit of the age that loudly proclaims there is no ultimate, objective truth to be known. For these persons, there was only the inner and subjective cosmos of the psyche, with its feelings and desires, to be gratified. Their love for Christ and for others had been sentimentalized and could hardly be called love at all. Care for others was reduced to the level of whatever pop psychology ruled the day. They no longer honored and cared for the truth accessible to the hearts of the faithful and to intellects made holy—enlightened by the Spirit of God in and with His people. Christ, speaking truth to those of like mind in His own generation, said:

> Why is my language not clear to you? Because you are unable to hear what I say. You belong to your father, the devil, and you want to carry out your father's desire. He was a murderer from the beginning, not holding to the truth, for there is no truth in him. When he lies, he speaks his native language, for he is a liar and the father of lies. Yet because I tell the truth, you do not believe me! . . . If I am telling the truth, why don't you believe me? He who belongs to God hears what God says. The reason you do not hear is that you do not belong to God. (John 8:43-47)

The harsh but loving truth that Jesus declares is that we live, finally, by the Spirit of God or by the unholy spirit of this age.

Contending for the Truth

> Buy the truth and do not sell it; get wisdom, discipline and understanding. (Proverbs 23:23)

Apart from the fact that some within the church do not hear the truth and have turned from it, we live in a day when many—though they hold to the truth that is in Christ—find it difficult to contend for the faith once delivered. The spiritual, moral, and intellectual sinew needed to confront and replace the false with the true is oddly disengaged; it is simply missing. I've written about this under the rubric of a "crisis in masculinity"[4]—for that is surely in part what it is. It is the crisis of the unaffirmed and of those unable to initiate and stand for the truth. The good news is that there is healing for this condition, as we've shown throughout this book. Such a crisis involves not only an incapacity to rightly love and honor the truth, but to speak and be the truth in this our day.

To be in touch with one's masculinity (be we man or woman) at the highest level is to be empowered with Truth Himself. It is to be enabled to take one's stand no matter what the circumstances against the lies and the illusions of one's individual life and environment as well as the lies and illusions of one's corporate existence and age. This stand will not be without suffering, even as the lives of Christ and the early apostles illustrate.

When we effectively hear and speak the truth as they did, however, suffering not withstanding, we find true power, true joy, even the true peace that overcomes the world. As one of the great prophets of our age, Alexander Solzhenitsyn, said in his Nobel speech, "One word of truth outweighs the world." What greater consolation can there be than that of being a truth bearer? What greater destiny than to be in league with the God of truth—to have Him for our Father, to have Him name us His children.

Overwhelming Nature of Evil Rampant in Society

> The wicked freely strut about when what is vile is honored among men. (Psalm 12:8)

Christians are overwhelmed by the nature of the evil and ungodliness that are today so highly energized and powerful as they take over civic, political, and church structures. Recently, Illinois newspapers carried articles about concerned parents finding witchcraft and other such obscenities in school textbooks. One friend in a chaplaincy finds herself on a hospital staff with other chaplains who either practice sexual perversion or openly approve it in others. Some of them have an acknowledged and overt hatred of God, and one way this is manifested is through (even as the Beast of Revelation) their blasphemies and slanders against the name of God. This situation, a deeply entrenched one, is in a "Christian" hospital. Unfortunately, such a situation is not rare today and is usually "politically" protected. This chaplain is in the midst of a truly terrible warfare. She sees the unmet needs of the sick and the dying, and when she ministers to them the healing words of Christ's gospel, she receives against herself the bitterest hatred, derision, and persecution. Her situation is desperately difficult, but she is called to be there and is a faithful witness in that place. *She stands firm in the truth she speaks.*

Two other friends, active in a church diocese full of the same darkness and blasphemy, find themselves having to stand alone, often on powerful committees, where not only is sexual perversion approved, but there is continual lobbying for the ordination of actively homosexual priests. All of this is in the face of rampant HIV positive cases and full-blown AIDS among homosexually active clergy who are already illegally ordained.

The experiences of these Christians and of the seminarian quoted in chapter 11 demonstrate that we are not doing very well in the spiritual warfare centered in organizational structures. These precious brothers and sisters in Christ, stepping into these structures where we have hardly even begun to fight the battle, are called to stand in the power of the Holy Spirit and speak truth into the dark heart of demonized warfare. It is not easy, and it can even be, as we saw in the case of the seminarian, very dangerous. As Dr. Richard Lovelace writes, one's authority in spiritual conflict takes

> on a new significance which is much broader than individual defensive spiritual warfare. Not only can we expect to carry out offensive warfare which takes ground away from Satan in the exorcism of persons, we can also undertake, when we have liberty from God to do so, the exorcism of structures occupied by demonic forces—not only fallen structures in the church in the process of reformation and revival, but also fallen structures in society which are instruments of injustice.[5]

The Seminarian's Crisis in Masculinity

We can see the spiritual and physical wear and tear that spiritual warfare inflicts on one such as the young seminarian. In the midst of his conflict and resulting illness, I realized that one of the reasons his blood pressure shot up so high was that he was forced into a situation where his true masculinity and therefore his true self were not only being seriously repressed but killed outright. He went in as a fairly knowledgeable and mature Christian, but due to mistakenly putting himself under the unholy and misguided "law" of that seminary, he reduced himself to an immature and powerless state, and he felt bereft of all moral and spiritual power. He believed he could only wait out his time there. Because he was a mature man, however, one endowed beyond the ordinary with masculine giftedness, he was even more damaged than he would have been if he had lacked true power. By not being free to be himself in Christ, he did grave psychological harm as well as spiritual and physical damage to himself. God has now rectified that and is in the process of turning his wounds into a most effective power to heal others, but his understanding of the psychological damage that occurs when a Christian isn't free to stand and speak the truth is only now becoming clear to him.[6]

Just before his blood pressure shot up, an incident occurred in his CPE (work with hospitalized persons) training, a required course for seminarians. Students from several schools came together in the course. Contrary to what one would expect, the course was not primarily designed to help the students minister to patients in crisis situations. Though they did spend time on the floors with the patients, the real emphasis was on the "confrontational" group sessions they daily had among themselves. Their questions and concerns and encounters with the patients provided the subject matter the students, as "presenters," brought before the group. The object of these daily sessions was not to get at objective ways of ministering truth and reality to patients, but in the manner of twentieth-century insanity, to get in touch with the student presenter's subjective feelings brought up by the encounter with the patient. As one might imagine, this was a way of corporately indulging in the "disease of introspection,"[7] and it had the usual frightful impact. The students and their supervisors questioned, probed, and challenged the presenter's motives and self-perceptions while seeking to discover the root of his or her feelings. The efforts were, as the seminarian said, at best amateurish and at the worst brutal and dangerous. He could hardly believe the amount of emotional pressure brought to bear on the presenter as he or she sat encircled by a group that challenged every response and motive. In every case exposure, not healing, was the goal. He said:

> Oftentimes, I had the feeling that we had laid someone out on an operating table, undressed him, sliced him open, pulled out his guts, and then left him there as we walked out congratulating ourselves on what a fine job we had done. It was assumed that the individual could restore his entrails to their proper places, suture his own wounds, get dressed, and get back on his feet by himself. If this proved too difficult, psychiatric therapy was available at discount rates.

The crowning incident occurred as one student—who had been insecure in his sexual identity and had entered the course hoping to find help—told of trying to help a patient with like difficulties. He told the group that during the patient encounter he had finally realized that he was indeed secure in his heterosexual identity, but he was now deeply fearful that out of his experimental homosexual liaisons (which had been encouraged by his peers in other sessions) he had contracted AIDS. With this admission, the advanced students and supervisors began to berate him severely and almost gleefully for denying his "obvious" homosexual orientation and his alleged fear of admitting it. Their message to him—after an hour of tears and emotional exchanges as he attempted to defend his heterosexual position—was that he should admit he was indeed homosexual and should commit himself to that lifestyle, thus facing "his real fear." At one point, and this seems a scene right out of hell, the student was writhing on the floor, and my friend said it was as if the group had turned into demons, gleefully dancing around this prostrate person, all the while naming him homosexual.

This is a nightmare the likes of which Freud could never have envisioned as coming out of his methods for helping analysts to self-understanding. But this is what spiritual warfare not only *is*, but looks like, and it is flagrantly stepped up within the church today. This warfare is widespread in organizations that purport to be Christian and among those whose vocation it is to prepare church leaders.

My friend, the seminarian, wrote: "My shame to this day is that although I did not enter into the frenzy, I was too intimidated by the process to speak out in his defense." In obeying the law of an apostate structure where profanity and unbelief were the order of the day, he was forced to deny his true masculinity—indeed even his identity as a person and as a Christian in whom the Spirit of God dwelt.

When the great majority of Christians find the above unthinkable, much less acceptable, why do we allow destructive programs and practices in our churches and schools? Why do we permit what is flagrantly sinful and opposed to all that is Christian, moral, or even reasonable? Why do we suffer moral and political conditions known to be destructive? Why, when dioceses are full of this, do we, year in and year out, allow these conditions to prevail?

Sometimes, it is said that we must suffer these things in order to obtain some good—for example, to maintain a degree program. Using the corrupt CPE program as an example, there is nothing inherently wrong with the idea of such a program. But it must be profoundly Christian if seminarians are to be part of it. In this particular case, if we care little about the trainees, we yet have an obligation to the sick and dying in the hospitals where these training courses take place. We cannot idly stand by and watch souls at their most vulnerable left without a witness, much less left in danger of being brought into spiritual warfare, and perhaps even left to die without the help our Lord has died to give them. This will involve creative thinking (listening prayer!) on our part. It also absolutely requires that we understand and admit (rather than deny) not only the fierce spiritual warfare raging in church and political structures, but also our almost total impotence in that warfare. Like the young seminarian, we have been losing the battle, rendered unable to *speak truth* powerfully into it.

We must learn to pray effectively, and then to speak the truth in such a way as to see Christian institutions and programs delivered from the demonic.

Practicing the Presence of the Holy Spirit, the Spirit of Truth

> When the Counselor comes, whom I will send to you from the Father, the Spirit of truth who goes out from the Father, he will testify about me. And you also must testify, for you have been with me from the beginning. (John 15:26-27)

When we find ourselves in decidedly unholy situations, ones rife with and energized by the lies and activities of demons, it is then that—in God's Presence and power—we stand. And it is wonderful at all times, but especially in these hard moments, to reflect on the fact that the Holy Spirit sent to us by Christ is the Spirit of Truth.

In writing on the practice of the Presence of God the Father, the Son, and the Holy Spirit, I've perhaps said less in regard to specific special ways of practicing the Presence of the Spirit. But increasingly, as in situations I've just mentioned, I find myself invoking the Holy Spirit and praising Him as the Spirit of Truth. And this is what I find myself saying over and over again to precious beleaguered brethren: "Do you know that the Holy Spirit is the Spirit of Truth? Invoke His Presence! Speak His truth. It may not be accepted right now, but it will sit on the heads of these people until they acknowledge it." True enough, some will not be converted by what they hear, but one day even they, as the Scriptures say, will bow before God and confess that Jesus Christ is Lord.

What a wonderful and mysterious power truth is. How it sits atop the most resistant head and darts into the darkest heart. That head and heart may not choose to act on the truth or to acknowledge it. The person may even repress it very deeply, but once truth is spoken, there is a place in the human heart that knows it has heard truth, and it will have to wrestle with it from then on. It is the truth, and Truth Himself, who changes people, structures, and nations.

Jesus answered, "I am the way and the truth and the life. No one comes to the Father except through me" (John 14:6). Over and over again, He who is the Truth prefaced His sayings with, "I tell you the truth . . . I tell you the truth . . . I tell you the truth."

In spiritual warfare, those who oppose the truth will nearly always be found reviling His name. The following prayer is a wonderful way of practicing the Presence of Jesus. This prayer is invaluable in all of our life, but particularly in the midst of the cosmic battle.

The Holy Name

To invoke the name of Jesus or to breathe it in prayer (as in the Jesus Prayer that comes to us from the Orthodox tradition) is a special and wondrous way of practicing the Presence. That is because:

> The Name is the symbol and bearer of the Person of Christ. Otherwise the invocation of the Name would be mere verbal idolatry. "The letter killeth, but the Spirit giveth life." The presence of Jesus is the real content and the substance of the Holy Name. The Name both signifies Jesus' presence and brings its reality.[8]

The full prayer is: "Lord Jesus Christ, Son of God, have mercy on me a sinner," but it is best shortened to simply breathing the holy name.

> Before beginning to pronounce the Name of Jesus, establish peace and recollection within yourself and ask for the inspiration and guidance of the Holy Ghost. "No man can say that Jesus is Lord, but by the Holy Ghost." The Name of Jesus cannot really enter a heart that is not being filled by the cleansing breath and the flame of the Spirit. The Spirit Himself will breathe and light in us the Name of the Son.[9]

It is no small joy to leave off breathing the holy name, only to hear the Spirit audibly speak it within.

This prayer, it seems to me, this holding of the holy name, is one of the most precious ways of practicing the Presence. All this was quite forcibly brought to my mind as a way of not only preparing but safeguarding Christians in the advent of persecution for their faith. I had been reading Revelation 13 and 14 and was horrified at the fate of the lost who are destined to wear the name of the Beast on their foreheads:

> The beast was given a mouth to utter proud words and blasphemies and to exercise his authority for forty-two months. He opened his mouth to blaspheme God, and to slander his name and his dwelling place and those who live in heaven. He was given power to make war against the saints and to conquer them. And he was given authority over every tribe, people, language and nation. All inhabitants of the earth will worship the beast—all whose names have not been written in the book of life belonging to the Lamb that was slain from the creation of the world. . . .
>
> He [the second beast] was given power to give breath to the image of the first beast, so that it could speak and cause all who refused to worship the image to be killed. *He also forced everyone, small and great, rich and poor, free and slave, to receive a mark on his right hand or on his forehead, so that no one could buy or sell unless he had the mark, which is the name of the beast or the number of his name.* (Revelation 13:5-8, 15-17, italics mine)

After such a terrifying word and image comes this beautiful one. It is for those whose names are written in the Book of Life, those of whom it could be said that "no lie was found in their mouths." "Then I looked, and there before me was the Lamb, standing on Mount Zion, and with him 144,000 who had his name and his Father's name on their foreheads" (Revelation 14:1).

PRAYER

Lord, may Your name be deeply inscribed on our foreheads even now.

And may Your name be as a holy fire within us, one that not only purifies us, but spills over onto all around us.

May Your name be so glorified in us that we can speak Your truth with great authority and effect, even in the face of slander and persecution. In Jesus' name, we pray. Amen.

PRAYER

Lord Jesus, we lift up to You our remaining time and all that it holds. May we be Your witnesses, filled to overflowing with Your Spirit. May we know the Truth, speak the Truth, be the Truth more powerfully and effectively than ever before, thereby lifting high Your cross for the whole world to see. May the world see the Father in You, in us, and reach up their hands to take His Hand.

Father, we thank You that Your arm is not shortened, Your ear is not deaf. Stretch forth Your mighty arm and rescue all who would acknowledge as truth Your Son, our Lord. Hear His intercessions for us, Your people, and strengthen us to do Your fullest will and slightest bidding. It is in His name we exult and pray. Amen.

CHAPTER 14

Wrong Ways to Do Battle

Finally, be strong in the Lord and in his mighty power. Put on the full armor of God so that you can take your stand against the devil's schemes. For our struggle is not against flesh and blood, but against the rulers, against the authorities, against the powers of this dark world and against the spiritual forces of evil in the heavenly realms. Therefore put on the full armor of God, so that when the day of evil comes, you may be able to stand your ground, and after you have done everything, to stand. Stand firm then, with the belt of truth buckled around your waist, with the breastplate of righteousness in place, and with your feet fitted with the readiness that comes from the gospel of peace. In addition to all this, take up the shield of faith, with which you can extinguish all the flaming arrows of the evil one. Take the helmet of salvation and the sword of the Spirit, which is the word of God. And pray in the Spirit on all occasions with all kinds of prayers and requests. With this in mind, be alert and always keep on praying for all the saints.

(Ephesians 6:10-18)

Although the light of our God shines ever brighter, the darkness has greatly thickened. C. S. Lewis observes this phenomenon, when in his novel *That Hideous Strength,* he puts this observation in the mouth of Dr. Dimble as he converses with his wife:

> Have you ever noticed that the universe, and every little bit of the universe, is always hardening and narrowing and coming to a point? . . . Good is always getting better and bad is always getting worse: the possibilities of even apparent neutrality are always diminishing. The whole thing is sorting itself out all the time, coming to a point, getting sharper and harder. . . .

Mrs. Dimble replies that all this reminds her:

> . . . more of the bit in the Bible about the winnowing fan. Separating the wheat and the chaff. Or like Browning's line: "Life's business being just the terrible choice."[1]

The battle between good and evil is stepped up in this our day, and we are all involved in it, making the "terrible choice" whether prepared or not. Hopefully we are prepared by having put on the full armor of God (Ephesians 6:10-18) and by having asked for and received the true gift of battle. Once this is done, if we are sensitive to the Holy Spirit's leading, we soon become aware that there are many wrong ways to do battle.

Don't Allow Satan to Choose the Battleground

One of the strong temptations we must eschew is the enemy's attempt to get us to leave the positive work of the Kingdom. He works toward luring Christians from their creative, proper, and redemptive work, and down into battle on his own turf, one charged with his negatives: his accusations, rationale, deceptions, and lies. Nehemiah is a great role model for us here, and his story of intense spiritual warfare is one we should probably reread at times when we find our work withstood by our enemies (Nehemiah, chapters 1-6). Nehemiah's enemies were tireless in their efforts to stop the work God had entrusted to him—that of rebuilding the walls of Jerusalem. But Nehemiah simply refused to climb down from atop the walls where he was busy rebuilding and go down to fight with them. His enemies sent this message:

> "Come, let us meet together in one of the villages on the plain of Ono." But they were scheming to harm me; so I sent messengers to them with this reply: "I am carrying on a great project and cannot go down. Why should the work stop while I leave it and go down to you?" Four times they sent me the same message, and each time I gave them the same answer. (Nehemiah 6: 2b-4)

Note that Nehemiah repeats the same answer over and over again through his messengers. This is an important principle in communicating with persons who are determined to destroy us or the work. We let God give us the one word, that one objective word that is difficult for even an enemy to twist or misquote, and then we simply *keep on saying it*.

After that, Nehemiah's enemies began to slander him, with all manner of malice and deceit. But God was with him, and the walls were rebuilt. He was obedient to God, wise as to his enemies' tactics, and he ended up doing the "impossible" task.

Often we do not have the eyes to see the modern versions of Nehemiah's story, the times in warfare when the enemy attempts in much more subtle ways to lure us down onto his plain. A principle to remember is that our archenemy seeks to bring us into endless dialogue with himself through those persons he has deceived. We learn not to entertain the diabolical presence in this way. Such a dialogue is always carried out on the plane of the mind alone—the unassisted intellect or imagination—and we simply do not speak this reduced, desupernaturalized language. It is a language devoid of transcendent meaning and wisdom.

Besides the fact, therefore, that it is foolish to carry on a dialogue with the devil, we cannot translate our language into his. Sadly, however, more people (even Christians) understand this reduced language than the one containing the symbols that mediate to us ultimate meaning, truth, and glory. This is another way of stating that we as Christians have lost the greater part of our souls, together with the language and imagery with which to express the truths of the transcendent and eternal.[2]

I was asked to speak at a large general conference of a church denomination embroiled in spiritual warfare of the most flagrant kind. It was hoped that I would prevail over other speakers who were advocating the acceptance of sexual immorality within the clergy. I declined the invitation, not because I did not want to speak truth into the situation, but because I knew that many of the very Christians who wanted me to speak for orthodox Christianity would not—once the battle was joined—understand my language. And should God have been pleased to move in power, they also would not have understood or approved of the powerful move of the Holy Spirit that it would have taken to bring in the repentance and the healing necessary to really change things in that group.

I knew they would not be like Nehemiah's messengers with one objective word to impart, but that they would get hopelessly ensnared into "loving dialogue" with the enemy as his intents and purposes worked through those under his deception. Our main difficulty in the church battles of today is often with the well-meaning who have learned a spurious kind of empathy, an ersatz way of trying to love their enemies. In other words, these good folk have lost the words and symbols of the Kingdom and speak only the enemy's reduced language.

Another example is the endless church committees on "human sexuality" that meet year after year, endlessly debating and never, of course, coming to any conclusions other than the rationalizing of sin. These committees are often merely a screen for devising an apologetic for perverted sexual behavior. Only the highly trained and very wise heads, those not intimidated by this worldly logic and terminology, who are skilled in disarming patently false logic wherever it arises, should attempt to be the "salt" on such committees. Even then, such persons will often know that they are wasting valuable time, and that the job will simply have to be repeated again the very next year. The enemy tactic consists in constantly repeating the lie and in endlessly pounding away at the moral and spiritual real. The carnal aim is not to uncover and point up truth, but to dishearten those who stand for it. The aim is, through rationalization, to finally make a large entryway for sin into the leadership of the church, and for this the enemy has all the time in the world. After all, he is not engaged in the substantive, creative work of God's Kingdom—only in establishing himself as god.

Rather than go down on the enemy's turf, then, we band together in prayer and receive our instructions from the Lord. We then may well speak a word of truth into a demonized situation and take authority in Christ's name over demons, commanding them to depart. We are not, however, to wear ourselves out, thereby allowing ourselves to become discouraged or even deceived through fruitless and interminable dialogue—dialogue that only too often ends in compromise. Compromise is said to be the art of politics and diplomacy, but wise governments forsake the art when they are facing a murderous tyrant. Compromise spells the death knell in spiritual battle as we face the archtyrant—*Diabolos* himself.

Over and over again, in trying to help Christians embroiled in spiritual warfare, I find myself saying to them, "You are not to dialogue with the old man in anyone! That is merely to bring you into dialogue with the world, the flesh, and ultimately the devil himself!" The carnal old self in those deceived by the enemy has become a mouthpiece for the enemy's lies, slanders, blasphemies, and accusations. Such persons are used to bring the satanic deception they are under upon others. We not only learn to speak, do, and be the truth, but to dialogue only with the truth in another, that is, with the real person and the situation as it really is. It usually takes a good bit of explaining for this to be understood, and I often have to resort to C. S. Lewis's remarkable sketch about the seedy old actor (*The Great Divorce,* chapter 12) to finally make my point. In this story, the actor's wife, Sarah Smith of Golder's Green, would not dialogue with the old, illusory self in her posturing, self-serving husband. She would only speak to the true self, even though it had become almost nonexistent. It finally disappeared entirely as he chose, time after time, illusion and inessentiality over the radiant and substantive reality of heaven that was being offered him.[3] He simply would not leave off his self-pity, and his propensity, always, for shifting blame onto his wife, Sarah, for his unhappiness. Satan is the accuser, and if he cannot distract us in any other way, he would love to usurp all our time and energies in trying to answer his charges. Sarah Smith of Golder's Green did not waste her time or words.

We Are in a Battle That Is Already Won

One of the things to keep in mind in spiritual battle is that the forces of darkness are already defeated by Christ's death and rising, and the evil one's time is strictly limited. Rather than wrongfully striving with him, we are always to be praising, blessing, and thanking our God; we are to be rejoicing in Christ's triumphal train.

> But thanks be to God who always leads us in triumphal procession in Christ and through us spreads everywhere the fragrance of the knowledge of him.

For we are to God the aroma of Christ among those who are being saved and those who are perishing. . . . (2 Corinthians 2:14-15)

Fr. John Gaynor Banks wrote out the following in his prayer journal after meditating on 1 Corinthians 9:25: "Everyone who competes in the games goes into strict training. They do it to get a crown that will not last, but we do it to get a crown that will last forever." Then he wrote the following, a triumphal picture reflecting the true focus in spiritual battle:

MASTER: The saints were great lovers. Love is creative energy. Their love for Me was drawn inward and upward until they became free to serve the Highest. These holy ones, these athletes (1 Corinthians 9:25) of the Spirit, had their battles of course, but they triumphed not so much by any frantic striving with the forces of evil as by concentrating rather on the Sun of Righteousness. They absorbed the rays of My perennial light and heat, and so they literally transcended their lower selves and entered into oneness with the Divine.[4]

Nehemiah's enemies were outside the covenant and the people of God. All too often, our main onslaughts today come from within the organized church itself. And when this is the case, we have to be doubly careful. We must meditate upon Christ's teaching on the wheat and the tares and on His admonitions in the Sermon on the Mount. In this way, and as we prayerfully listen to God, it is possible to be spared from misjudging others, while at the same time we rightly discern and continue in love and unity with our brothers and sisters in Christ. As important, rather than becoming ensnared in misplaced empathy and sympathy with sin, we will be enabled to face issues squarely and name them for what they are.

Wielding the Sword of Truth, Yet Making Peace

Our Lord taught, "Blessed are the peacemakers, for they shall be called sons of God." Barclay, in his commentary on Matthew 5:9, speaks to this word of truth. First of all, it is in the loving, active *facing* of issues that we *make* peace; we can't evade issues and think we are peacemakers:

There is many a person who thinks that he is loving peace, when in fact he is piling up trouble for the future, because he refuses to face the situation and to take the action which the situation demands.[5]

Peacemaking requires that we get the mind of Christ, His love and wisdom replacing our incomplete knowledge and ignorance. At times, it even requires that we take up a whip—after the manner of Christ in the temple with the money-changers. We do all of this, however, with an eye toward establishing right relationships between man and God, and man and man. We are to love our fellows "with actions and in truth" (1 John 3:18). The following, says Barclay, is what Jesus means in this beatitude:

> The Jewish Rabbis held that the highest task which a man can perform is to establish *right relationships* between man and man.[6]

In doing this, however, as we often discover in spiritual battle, there are

> people who are always storm-centres of trouble and bitterness and strife. Wherever they are they are either involved in quarrels themselves or the cause of quarrels of others. They are trouble-makers. . . .[7]

It is no small thing to speak prophetically and to also make peace. We can't always do it. We can never make peace at the expense of truth. True peace comes only with the truth. May we be uncompromising channels of God's truth as well as His peace. In speaking the truth in love, may we plant deep in the hearts of men and women everywhere the seeds of lasting, even eternal peace.

PRAYER

Lord, preserve us from fighting Your battle in our own strength. May we never pull up the precious wheat with the tares. May we triumph, not by frantic striving with the forces of evil, but by keeping our eyes securely fastened on You.

We ask that You make of us expert peacemakers. Help us, in the power of the Spirit, to clear the path of obstacles to making Your peace—real peace—in Your Body here on earth.

Wrongly Personifying Sin

> Then the Lord said to Cain, "Why are you angry? Why is your face downcast? If you do what is right, will you not be accepted? But if you do not do what is right, sin is crouching at the door; it desires to have you, but you must master it." (Genesis 4:6-7)

Here in this remarkable passage, sin is personified. A Biblical commentator explains the origins of this metaphoric speech: "The Hebrew word for crouching is the same as an ancient Babylonian word referring to an evil demon crouching at the door of a building to threaten the people inside. Sin may thus be pictured here as just such a demon, waiting to pounce on Cain—it desires to have him."[8]

Sin within the human heart is a destroyer, and there could hardly be a better metaphor for evil than we have here. This personification of sin enables us to better comprehend its power to devour, and the Scriptural symbols, metaphors, similes, parables, and figures of speech are invaluable in helping us to express these grave matters in such a way as the heart can fully grasp them.

It is one thing, however, to understand sin as figuratively demonic, and quite another to deal with sin in the human breast as though it were in fact a demonic entity rather than a transgression for which the soul is held responsible before God.

In this day when we are so often ignorant of the soul and its motions, many Christians armed with the terminology of deliverance from evil spirits name these motions of the soul (or lack of them) as demons. They identify an absence of the holy graces, good emotions and feelings, together with a corresponding profusion of sinful vices, fantasies, feelings, and attitudes within a soul as demonic infestations. To do this is not only to fail to discern the problem aright—the sin as well as the psychological deficiencies and problems—but even more seriously it is to fail to see the person needing help as human at all. We become thoroughgoing gnostics who spiritualize away the human element—a grievous kind of ignorance that is nowhere modeled for us in the Scriptures. Jesus dealt with *persons*, men and women with full souls, and He helped these souls name and renounce their sins. He never failed to do these folk the grave and great honor of seeing them as persons.

We are souls, with a spirit at our center that either is or is not linked with Christ. In failing to recognize the full soul that is another person, we in effect X out all that is uniquely human about that person's creation. We delete the human. If we fail to see and revere the unique person in the one for whom we pray, we will fail to help that person deal effectively with the real sin and the real emotional difficulties that are there. We may even, in our ignorance and zeal to help the person, name these things as demons and fancy ourselves as "binding" and casting them out. It is the *sin* that is to be bound and the *person* loosed from it. In contrast, the wounds are to be healed. If these have provided a place for demons to hide, we can easily enough expel them once they are discerned.

In ministry that fails to recognize the above, persons are robbed of the great privilege of coming present to their own hearts and there—in the presence of God—finally coming to understand who they are. Rather than helping such persons recognize their sin and repent of it, change their diseased attitudes and allow God to create in them new hearts, we can be in the unhappy position of casting out nonexistent demons of this or that. We will be attempting to "cast out" character traits and deficiencies. Too, and just as tragically, all that is positive within that soul and unique to its creation as a human being will be overlooked. Through ignoring the good, it will go unaffirmed, and, in effect, denied existence. It will not be called into life. A vital step in prayer for this person's healing will have been missed.

Thus today there are well-meaning Christians whose prayers for others are filled with speaking to demons—mostly nonexistent ones.[9] These people need more instruction in the theology of the cross and repentance, as well as clarification about what an authentic gift of discerning of spirits is. All too often, the authentic gifts of wisdom and discernment have been first obscured and then replaced by a faulty theology, often developed from a mistaken exegesis of the Scriptures. A faulty "methodology" quickly follows.

In any one of the three great barriers to wholeness may be found a demon hiding away in a nest that a sin or wound has made for it. In ministry to the person, these demons manifest themselves, and even as Christ would command, "Come out!" or "Be muzzled!" and always simply, "Depart!"—so do we. This is the easiest part of healing prayer once a person has confessed his sin or been released from the effects of another's sins against him. But grievous hurt is done, and prayers for others are needlessly ineffective when, rather than being able to listen to God and to that unique and precious human soul that is looking up to God, we start clamoring about demons and commanding imaginary ones to depart.

It is this unscriptural *practice of the presence of the powers of darkness* and the very grave dangers involved in such a practice that I want to address next. Also, I want to issue a strong warning about the fact that many (again principally those within certain parts of the renewal movement) are failing to understand the planes of spiritual battle that are properly ours and those that properly belong to God and His angelic hosts. All errors here eventuate, not in a practice of the Presence of God, but in the practice of the presence of our archenemy and his minions. And when we practice his presence long enough and seriously enough, he shows up. In focusing on him, we manage eventually to make a pathway for him to come.

Don't Focus on Satan, Demons, or Principalities and Powers

> There are two equal and opposite errors into which our race can fall about devils. One is to disbelieve in their existence. The other is to believe, and to feel an excessive and unhealthy interest in them. They themselves are equally pleased by both errors, and hail a materialist or a magician with the same delight.[10]

Many today who lecture on spiritual warfare start out with the vital statement that we are not to focus on Satan, but then the overall effect of their teachings lead both themselves and their disciples to do that very thing. Often, by way of warning those they are teaching, they will even quote Lewis in his familiar statement of our well-known predicament quoted above, thoroughly agree with it, and then go on in practice to live out something else.

Two practices, both that focus on the demonic, have come together to do the most mischief. One particularly involves "doing spiritual warfare" *against* principalities and powers, done by those who fail to understand what planes of battle are properly ours and those which properly belong to God and His angelic hosts. The other has to do with the misuse of the terms "binding and loosing"—the misapplying of those terms to demons, and then the resulting mistaken practice of *praying against Satan* rather than *to* God. We pray to God for those souls under Satan's foul aegis, helping them to confess their sins and thereby come out from under the control of principalities and powers. This does not mean that we will not from time to time discern strongholds over persons, nations, cities, and communities. But it means we will be very careful of our focus. It means we will always be found ministering to God—singing and speaking to Him in worship, thanksgiving, and praise. We will always be found practicing the Presence of God. In doing this, as demons, principalities or powers are discerned directly in our path, we speak directly to them, and command them to leave.

Planes of Warfare

Because of ignorance about the true nature of our souls, of misteaching, and of failure to abide by the Scriptural model of the gift of battle, it is amazingly easy for Christians to be confused over what it means to "do spiritual warfare." Any confusion here leaves us thinking the battle is ours rather than the Lord's, and we then battle according to our own understanding and strength. To do this even in part, is dangerous, and there is really no excuse for it. The Scriptures are very clear here, not only with regard to the way Christ and the apostles modeled the warfare for us, but also with regard to the plane of battle that is properly ours, as distinguished from that which properly belongs to God and to His angelic hosts.

A Christian who fails to understand this and who puts these misguided notions into practice can become dangerous to anyone who comes under his influence. The enemy, through gaining that Christian's focus, will have found a "landing platform" through which to "touch down" and bring in all manner of mischief and deception.

I saw a very dramatic instance of this in a large overseas base for training young Christians as missionaries. One of the leaders had been sharing about the unusual amount of spiritual warfare they were unaccountably caught up in and was asking for the prayers of the people in order to discern the cause. Several young men were then invited to stand and pray for the group. These men, obviously still in the throes of the "drive toward power," did indeed pray. But not to God. They faced the four corners of the world and with great voice started commanding principalities and powers. I could see they were quite experienced at this and was immediately alarmed as I realized in my spirit that they had made contact with the evil "principality." Dark power crackled down, and bizarre things happened simultaneously on campus. An explosion occurred in one building, while fire broke out in several places on the grounds. Later, as I talked to the leaders on that base, I shared with them how such a practice makes a landing platform for the enemy. They acknowledged that they had experienced all manner of confusion and warfare in connection with the ministry of these particular young persons.

Perhaps one of the most difficult experiences along this line that we as the PCM team have encountered will reveal even further how very dangerous such practices can be. This situation involved intercession and a seriously misguided group's attempt to "bind principalities and powers over a city."

A number of years back, several Christian leaders approached me within a short time span with a word they had received from the Lord in regard to PCM's need to ask for intercessors. One was awakened in the middle of the night to intercede for us and was given visions of the battle we are in, especially in regard to ministering to persons with sexual neuroses. Another had a specific prophetic word that he spoke over the PCM team, a word to the effect that, from this time on, those persons called to intercede for this ministry will play an increasingly vital and even critical part in the work God has for us to do. Part of that word admonished us to: "Pray that an army of intercessors be raised up, and they will go before you, springing the snares and traps of the enemy."

We did this very thing, and through our newsletter we also asked for intercessors. God mercifully raised up many to pray for us, and only heaven will reveal the incredible blessing this has been. We are amazed to see how faithful God is to spring the snares and the traps of the enemy.

In publishing our need, however, we unearthed the dangerous, unscriptural ways of interceding that some persons have gotten into, and unfortunately, we drew them toward us as well. These misguided ones had one thing in common—the idea that to "do spiritual warfare" was to focus on demons and on principalities and powers over cities and to "bind" them. To "bind" them was to take control over them through verbal assertions—spoken out into the airwaves but aimed toward "them"—i.e., the principalities and powers over cities. These folk, influenced by an extreme teaching (referred to by some as "Faith Formula Theology"),[11] attempt to "control" our Almighty and all-knowing holy God in the same way, believing that if they state their objectives in certain ways and affirm them in "faith," they thereby "force" God to do their bidding. (This is not Scriptural faith, but an inducing of a certain psychological mind-set.) These intercessors see themselves as binding demonic powers by talking to them—in effect praying to demons and by repeating over and over such things as, "I bind you, (whatever name the demon or principality or power appeared to have), and I take authority over you." This is what they called being an intercessor or "doing spiritual warfare."

I've just read John Dawson's book *Taking Our Cities for God: How to Break Spiritual Strongholds*. In it there is no practicing of the presence of demons and praying to them. The misguided intercessors I described are trying to do what John Dawson does and teaches, but unlike him, they focus on the demonic rather than on the sin to be confessed. Dawson faithfully publishes the word of salvation in our great cities, places where unconfessed dark sins have kept people from freedom to grow in righteousness. He helps people to discern and repent of the root sins in their cities. Thereby they loosen the city from the power of demonic principalities and forces that have a right to rule because of unremitted sin. John Dawson speaks and teaches on the healing of communities and cities, indeed, even nations, in the same way as we do of the healing of persons. It is through healing their memories—by confessing the sins that bind them—and by loosing the people and their communities into new, substantive, creative life. He stresses praise and thanksgiving to God—an utter and wonderful practice of the Presence. He speaks of intercessions and of listening to God for the healing word He is speaking for that locale, that city.

All of this John Dawson speaks of in terms of "doing spiritual warfare"—of taking souls from the kingdom of darkness and bringing them into the kingdom of light. And true evangelism such as this will always constellate spiritual warfare. But this can as well be named the ministry of the confessional writ large—a ministry that the church has all but forgotten. There are, therefore, many today who "do spiritual warfare," but rather than following Scriptural principles, focus instead on the forces of evil.

The first time the team and I were exposed to the darkness that comes out of these dangerous prayer practices, we were to minister in a church where many had gathered both to learn to pray for others and for help for themselves. Several teachers of these wrong ways of focusing on the demonic had come—not to learn—but to try to impress me and the team. It did not take long for us to be *impressed* in a most negative fashion, for never have we known, in the context of starting out to conduct a prayer and healing service, the unleashing of such darkness. We knew immediately that these persons had inadvertently first invited and then stirred up the darkness and that their practices were exceedingly confusing and dangerous to any naive soul who might get caught up in them.

Before the first service, their leader said to me: "We pray and fast against principalities and powers [meaning demonic forces], in advance, before we ever go to a place, and we have done this for you. You are now safe because we have accomplished this, we have *bound* the principalities and powers in the high places over this city. . . ."

Right away I knew they were in serious trouble, but I could not help them for they spoke only a bleak "spiritualized" language that was overcharged and left no room for reasoned interaction, communication, or fellowship. For them, there was no room for the truly beautiful, either from the realm of nature and the fully human or from the heavenly. There were only demons, and these were to be sought out and dealt with. With these folk, there was no practice of the Presence—only an imagination filled with the demonic.

Unknowingly, these persons were caught up in a spiritual pride beyond the ordinary. In effect, they said to me, "We are the only ones really who know how to 'bind' the devil, how to deliver the seriously demonized person, etc., and that is because we really know how to do spiritual warfare. We seek and engage the 'biggies' themselves, the principalities and powers. We've come to do this for you and show you how it is done."

Thinking themselves to be intercessors *extraordinaire* and the only ones "doing" spiritual warfare, they were in effect practicing the presence of demons. They had drawn the attention of dark powers toward the Body of Christ in that place by *praying to them* and through pridefully seeing themselves as "binding" them. As it turned out, they had become a channel through which a "principality and power"—a ruling spirit over that city—descended into our midst. It was one meant to be withstood in spiritual battle only by the holy angels as we battled properly for the salvation of souls.

As we began the ministry there, our hearts were opened to discern the huge entity. It named itself and threatened each one of us on the team. There were bizarre happenings and unbelievable confusion as we called on the power of God to quell the dark power.

Needless to say, we were brought into a spiritual conflict of unusual proportions, one that need never have occurred. These folk, thinking they were intercessors, had merely succeeded in informing the powers of darkness in, over, and around that city that we were coming! In listening to them proudly relate all their hair-raising tussles with dark powers, I realized they take this "gift" with them every place they go. The way they pray assures that the persons they are involved with will get into dramatic and terrible confrontations with evil powers, and some of them will come under serious demonic deception. This is dangerous error.

I would not tell of this extreme practice except for the fact that it is no longer a rare circumstance. These practices are spreading (usually in milder forms) to well-meaning persons who intercede daily. Too, as one who helps people to wholeness in Christ, I am aware of the many who attempt to cope with life by (usually unconsciously) striving to control events or persons around themselves—named today the codependent personality. Often these persons, in fear of the demonic, attempt to "control" it in these ways of prayer—and thereby hope to stave off the evil. Thus, "talking to the devil" and practicing his foul presence becomes a dangerous adjunct to the codependence from which these people already suffer. Fearing conflict of any kind, they attempt to safeguard themselves through "controlling" character traits in other persons, traits they may come to perceive as demons.

Some, when shown what they are doing will ask, "But how can I pray?" In other words, there are precious Christian souls out there now who no longer know how to pray without talking to the devil. "How," they ask, when embroiled in spiritual battle with their enemies, "do I pray about this lie," or "this slander," or this darkness of any kind? "Shall I get up an hour early and do spiritual warfare?" meaning, "Shall I arise an hour early and focus on demons and bind them?" No, this is never the thing to do. It is great to get up an hour early and focus on God, affirm the fact that He has won the victory, and ask Him how it is we should trust Him in the face of the darkness and slander coming against us. We have no need to try to control that darkness and slander. He's doing it, and we trust our present and future entirely to Him! It is not by focusing on "demons" of lying, slander, etc., by finding names for them, or by "binding" them continually in prayer—that way only brings one into striving and fear at best, and demonic oppression and even deception at worst.[12] Instead we look straight up to God and talk to Him. Christ has bound the enemy, and ours is merely the mop-up action. In showing us how to pray, the Scriptures record no one focusing on demons. Rather, as Christ taught us, we pray, "But deliver us from the evil one." In other words, "You do it, Lord." We don't get involved in "works" prayers to be free of principalities and powers. We trust God and He sends out His holy angels to do the warfare. If a demonic power happens across our path, once we've discerned it, we command it to leave. Only then do we speak to it—a foul presence that the Holy Spirit has shown us is there. And we expel it with a word: "In Christ's name, be gone!"

We won a great victory in the place where this dark incident happened. God is faithful, and people were reborn, spiritually and psychologically. Many there were coming out of the deep darkness that characterizes our culture today. Included were persons with backgrounds in the occult, witchcraft, sexual perversion, and so on. To these circumstances, of course, we are well accustomed and to dealing with any demonic infestation that might happen to be in their lives. But we paid a much higher price than usual, in terms of the intensity of the battle and the sheer physical and spiritual stress such a circumstance exacts; it was absolutely unnecessary.

Two examples here will show how wonderfully a true intercession works. We were to minister in another country at a well-known but liberal seminary in a city remarkably corrupt even by today's standards. We knew we were entering into great spiritual warfare for the souls within that university, and especially for those training for theological professorships and the pastorate in many other nations. As we confessed the sins of that city and university, known and unknown, and cried out to God for His anointing to preach, teach, and heal in His name, our spiritual eyes were opened. The Lord showed us the angelic battle going on over the seminary where we would be. We saw, as it were, before we ever arrived, the holy angels battling and overcoming the evil angels in answer to our prayers. We had a most incredible ministry there, out of which revival continues to spread, and we did not leave there needlessly weakened physically through unnecessary confrontations with evil forces.

Another example is of a time in England when our full conference was being videotaped before a large group. The Lord was mightily stretching forth His hand to heal and to save. Right in the midst of this, Fr. William Beasley's eyes were opened, and he saw an immense and terrible "principality and power." But it was outside attempting to peer in. It wanted so badly to know what was going on, but it couldn't find out. The holy angels were with us as always, and they had certainly done their part ahead of time. And there had been no misguided group of Christians who—by focusing on this evil entity—had made a pathway for it to insinuate itself into our midst.

Jessie Penn-Lewis's book *War on the Saints,* often called a "classic" on spiritual warfare, has influenced people into these erroneous ways of thinking about and "doing spiritual warfare."[13] One of her theses is that revival does not continue because we do not understand spiritual warfare, and she then proceeds throughout her book to focus primarily on demons rather than on sin. For example, speaking of Israel after the time of Moses and Joshua, she writes, "When these leaders died, the nation sank into darkness, *brought about* by evil spirit powers, drawing the people into idolatry and sin. . . ." (italics mine, p. 28). The Scriptural teaching, of course, is that the sin (apostasy) of the people came first and thereby left them open to the powers of darkness.

This reversal is everywhere apparent in her thinking and runs throughout the book, leaving those who follow her ideas to their logical conclusion with an emphasis always on the demonic. The Holy Spirit's gift of discerning of spirits is apparently not understood, and a tortuous system of "deliverance" through "knowledge" (almost scientism) is given to help the person decide if an idea or a bodily movement is a "counterfeit" and the result of demonic deception. She in effect reduces the soul into a battleground between good and evil forces, while at the same time she minimizes the capacity of the Christian's will to determine which will have the victory. She so emphasizes deception that she leaves the believer in great fear as to the reliability of his own understanding of Scripture or his own ability to hear from the Lord.

Though she liberally cites Scriptures, to use her methods would be to indict any one of the Old or New Testament saints. The knowledge she espouses, unfortunately, is one of doubting and analyzing everything and everyone. Any manifestation of the Holy Spirit or even of natural emotion for that matter, as well as all experience, is immediately suspect; it is to be deemed as counterfeit and caused by demons until it can be proven otherwise. Unfortunately, in her system, hampered as it is by a terrible rift between head and heart, there would never be a way of determining this. The "methods" are those of denial (of emotional and physical needs and their expressions) and of over-spiritualization.

She writes that "the Son of God dealt with the powers of darkness as the active, *primary* cause of the sin and suffering of this world" (italics mine, p. 35). The person who adheres to such a theology and psychology will treat every sin and motion of the soul having to do with suffering as an occasion for contending with a demonic entity. This is what has happened with the practice of "casting out" what amounts to perceived character traits and deficiencies as though these were demons rather than sins to be confessed or deficiencies to be remedied through prayer.

Here again, we have to say no. The Scriptures tell us that these things proceed "out of the heart" of man. It is the unhealed and/or unconverted heart that invites demonic participation. Mrs. Penn-Lewis's teaching leaves people either paralyzed or cut off from what is authentically human and deeply suspicious of it. She holds, as well, what amounts to a Manichaean view of the body (pp. 130ff.), not an incarnational one, and therefore especially warns people about practicing the Presence of God. The effect of her teaching is to disable people from living in the knowledge of the Presence of God with us, while at the same time, they are literally to be conscious always of the presence of demons. A sad irony here is that one loses out not only on Incarnational Reality, the Presence of God with us, but also on the power to discern and to deliver from actual demons.

The dark seeds of many excesses regarding the demonic and spiritual warfare that we see today are rooted in the ideas taken from this one particularly influential book. I have been in the ministry long enough to have seen many truly tragic losses as ministers and whole groups came under serious demonic deception after carrying her teachings to their logical conclusions. A serious study and acceptance of what is in this book leads to seeing demons everywhere and in everyone—a real practice of the presence of demons.

People who thoroughly espouse her teachings are hurt and stymied in every conceivable way—a paranoia strikes at their intellectual as well as their intuitive and imaginative ways of knowing. Their imaginations are finally filled with demonic myths—the very thing Penn-Lewis is attempting to avoid.

In many cases, persons become fearful of others, even paranoid, and the grievous sins of slander and pharisaical pride result, all the evil fruit of fastening one's eyes on darkness rather than on God. Those wishing to know where so many of the slanderous cult hunters get their theology, as well as the blueprint for their witch-hunts, need only look at this book in its unabridged form. Anyone with an incarnational understanding of reality and an understanding of God's power to heal emotional and psychological sicknesses will be attacked by these persons. In this way a very real spiritual battle within the church ensues as the work of the Holy Spirit and the practice of the Presence of God are denied and condemned.

Because the ideas in this book continue to influence thinking in certain fundamentalist, evangelical, and Pentecostal circles, inspiring others to write in the same way, these misconceptions keep spawning movements that deeply trouble the Body of Christ. Mrs. Penn-Lewis's exegesis of the Scriptures is faulty in critical respects. Due to the ongoing influence of her book, I hope that qualified theologians and psychologists will fully critique this work and the teachings that have come out of it. I hope these will be critiques understandable to laypersons, for they have been greatly impacted by Penn-Lewis's teachings.

When she wrote her book, it had some value because she recognized the existence of demons in a time when most of the church thoroughly disbelieved the Scriptures in this regard. Often in stressing a lost or neglected truth, people fall into the opposite error of overemphasizing it. In this particular case, Mrs. Penn-Lewis simply did not have the theological and psychological understanding needed to write on these matters and was reacting in fear to the needs multitudes of people coming into revival had for emotional healing and training. Her writings on the cross of Christ have blessed multitudes of Christians, and it is hoped that this critique of her book on spiritual warfare will in no way disparage the good of her writings.

Finding the right words to explain lost concepts to a particular generation is difficult. We who read Penn-Lewis now can easily understand the cultural blindness she and others wrestled with. For example, we know that her culture profoundly suspected the expression of feeling and emotion. Both were severely repressed. When feeling and emotion burst forward under the influence of the healing work of the Spirit, or when the physical body reacted to God's power and Presence, these occurrences appeared to them as unseemly, even as demonic. Manifestations of God's Presence among them, therefore, had to be filtered through the blinders peculiar to their day and age. We are humbled at this, knowing that none of us escape fully the blindness with which our own age afflicts us.

The great theological and spiritual writers manage to see clearly the mistakes of their age and to transcend them. While recognizing and lamenting their own insufficiencies, they allow other ages and times to speak a corrective word to these. In this day of great spiritual battle, may the Lord bless us increasingly with such writers.

CHAPTER 15

Restoring the Christian Hope of Heaven and the Grace to Persevere

Blessed are those whose strength is in you,
who have set their hearts on pilgrimage. . . .
They go from strength to strength,
till each appears before God in Zion.

(Psalm 84:5, 7)

Dear friends, now we are children of God, and what we will be has not yet been made known. But we know that when he appears, we shall be like him, for we shall see him as he is. Everyone who has this hope in him purifies himself, just as he is pure.

(1 John 3:2-3)

To have the hope of heaven restored to the soul is first of all to regain the great hope of Christ's appearing and the mind-boggling promise that we shall be like Him. The power of hope is mysterious in all the ways it ministers life to us, but in this Scripture we see that this hope "purifies us" even now. This is no small promise at any time, but it is especially important for us who live in these closing days of the twentieth century when institutionalized unbelief, with all its inherent unrighteousness, has made such inroads into the Christian symbolic system and into the Christian soul.

The Scriptures are filled with awesome promises to all who hope in Christ, and thereby overcome. We shall, we are told, be given "the right to eat from the tree of life" (Revelation 2:7), and we will "eat of the hidden manna." One of the promises that speaks to my heart is that of being renamed: "I will also give him a white stone with a new name written on it, known only to him who receives it" (Revelation 2:17). Is this our final naming? Perhaps so, since it is written in a white stone. All Christian healing has to do with calling forth the true self; that is, with being named in the Presence of Christ. We are told that Christ will write the name of God and of the holy city upon us (Revelation 3:12) and that we will "be sons of God" (Revelation 21:7) whom "the second death" will not "hurt at all" (Revelation 2:11). We will have God as our God (Revelation 21:7), and be given "the right to sit with" Christ on His throne (Revelation 3:21). In short, we will "inherit all things" (Revelation 21:7). What a wonderful healing it is to regain the capacity to hope and rejoice in all these things and in all the rest that the Scriptures promise to those who persevere in Christ.

The Miraculous Power God Gives to Persevere

> In this world you will have trouble. But take heart! I have overcome the world. (John 16:33)

> Do not be overcome by evil, but overcome evil with good. (Romans 12:21)

There are few things in life more comforting than Christian friends who understand what ministry on a fallen planet is all about. Through the years, Professor Carol Kraft, who teaches the German language and literature at Wheaton College, has been just such a friend. She is a treasured confidant, one in whom I can confide my deepest concerns, for she is not only a trusted friend, but she has learned how to listen. She really *hears* whatever it is I'm struggling with, and then has the knack of finding something that either exactly expresses it or helps me come to terms with it. She gave me the card reproduced below to illustrate the miraculous as we Christians so often experience it.

This, it seems to me, illustrates the power to persevere that is given us along with the unique and great Christian virtue of hope. Surely, it would be difficult to find a truer picture of the sheer grace God gives us not only to survive but also to overcome the impossible. It depicts the very way this grace is experienced—as we inch a straight and steady line through a fallen, hostile world to our true home.

I'm sure some who read these lines have faced or are even now facing the impossible in terms of what God has called them to do and to be. Perhaps calamity, in the form of circumstances so irrational and dark that they could only have been engineered by the powers of darkness, is even now on their horizon, barreling toward them. The enemy's blow is calculated to maim or to crush—to stop them right in their tracks. But God's message to His own is ever the same: "My power and the strength that I give you are sufficient. Call upon it, ask for it, see if I will not cause all grace to abound toward you!"

St. Paul knew and taught with all his might this great truth: "God is able to make all grace abound to you, so that in all things at all times, having all that you need, you will abound in every good work" (2 Corinthians 9:8). It is no small thing to abound in every good work when boulders the size of mountains hit us, but that is exactly what we can do when we place our trust, not in ourselves or in other created things, but wholly in God. We learn to cry out with the psalmist, "You are a faithful God!"

A word St. Paul uses to describe this kind of grace, the very grace of God, is *polupoikilos* which means many-colored. William Barclay, commenting on Ephesians 3:8-13, says, "The idea in this word is that the grace of God will match with any situation which life may bring us. There is nothing of light or dark, of sunshine or of shadow, for which it is not triumphantly adequate." No matter what we are struggling with, as ministers or as suffering persons who desperately need forgiveness and healing, God's grace is sufficient. Jesus, with implicit faith in the Father, said it all when He looked directly at His troubled disciples and said: "With man this is impossible, but with God all things are possible" (Matthew 19:26b).

Obstacles in the Way of Hope

Some, having read thus far, may be shocked at how passive they are about the eternal and fear that nothing can awaken in them this hope. For other Christians, especially those who have not yet been touched by the Spirit's renewing and who are not living on the cutting edge where they see God deeply touching people and putting broken lives back together, the materialism of the past several hundred years has seeped, almost irreparably it seems, into their souls. As C. S. Lewis has said, it has had the effect of removing heaven from their eyes. For others, the passion for man's approval has dimmed their hopes. It seems needful to look more closely at this dread loss and to assure people that God delights in restoring hope to the soul. The hope of heaven may not be regained on the natural level—but we need only seek Him above all else and earnestly petition Him for its restoring.

There is a sense in which we are all victims of a materialistic age, for in our fallen world there is always some very large exterior obstacle to faith. The largest one, however, is interior. There is that within us that prefers, like Milton's Satan, to reign in hell rather than to serve in heaven. Here, as in all that is amiss with the soul, pride must be confronted. We must fight hard against it in the strength that God gives.

The Passion for Fame vs. the Hope of Immortality

> To those who by persistence in doing good seek glory, honor and immortality, he will give eternal life. But for those who are self-seeking and who reject the truth and follow evil, there will be wrath and anger. (Romans 2:7-8)

A passion for earthly glory wars against and annihilates the Christian's hope of immortality and the legitimate heavenly glory he is to seek. An incredible teaching, this: that eternal life is given to those who by persistence in doing good seek glory, honor, and immortality.

> I tell you the truth, unless a kernel of wheat falls to the ground and dies, it remains only a single seed. But if it dies, it produces many seeds. The man who loves his life will lose it, while the man who hates his life in this world will keep it for eternal life. (John 12:24-25)

Christ's teaching here, as the NIV notes state, "rules out ambition" and reveals in the most emphatic terms that "to concentrate on one's own success is to lose what matters." Rather, our Lord speaks of the honor that comes from God and the conditions for receiving such an awesome thing: "Whoever serves me must follow me; and where I am, my servant also will be. My Father will honor the one who serves me" (John 12:26).

John Milton in Sonnet XXII (on his blindness) refers to fame as "the world's vain mask," and having gained it, he hoped to be led through it. He concerned himself with the classical poets' desire for it, realizing how inferior it was to the great Christian hope of reward. In *Lycidas* he alludes to the ambition for fame as "that last infirmity of Noble mind . . ." and says:

> *Fame is no plant that grows on mortal soil,*
> *Nor in the glistering foil [foil: setting of a jewel]*
> *Set off to th' world, . . .*

Tacitus, in *Histories IV,* speaks of "the passion for glory" as "the last from which even wise men free themselves." Nothing so well shows the sordidness and pride in all this, even the mindlessness of it, as C. S. Lewis's "famous artist" in *The Great Divorce*. A bright and holy Spirit, one of the saints triumphant, was sent to invite him to choose heaven and all its incredible light and beauty, but he is only interested in painting it.

> "When you painted on earth—at least in your earlier days—it was because you caught glimpses of Heaven in the earthly landscape. The success of your painting was that it enabled others to see the glimpses too. But here you are having the thing itself. It is from here that the messages came. There is no good *telling* us about this country, for we see it already. In fact we see it better than you do."

But the poor artist cannot be interested in heaven; he can only be interested in his "treatment" of it.

> "No. You're forgetting," said the Spirit. "That was not how you began. Light itself was your first love: you loved paint only as a means of telling about light."
>
> "Oh, that's ages ago, . . . One becomes more and more interested in paint for its own sake."
>
> "One does, indeed. I also have had to recover from that. It was all a snare. Ink and catgut and paint were necessary down there, but they are also dangerous stimulants. Every poet and musician and artist, but for Grace, is drawn away from love of the thing he tells, to love of the telling till, down in Deep Hell, they cannot be interested in God at all but only in what they say about Him. For it doesn't stop at being interested in paint, you know. They sink lower—become interested in their own personalities and then in nothing but their own reputations."

The artist, thinking himself to be not "much troubled in *that* way," nevertheless goes on to ask the shining Spirit if he has met certain artists in heaven, persons who are still famous on earth. He is dismayed to hear that if they are there, the Spirit has not yet run across them (after all, there are a lot of people there, many he has not as yet met):

> "But surely in the case of distinguished people, you'd hear?"
>
> "But they aren't distinguished—no more than anyone else. Don't you understand? The Glory flows into everyone, and back from everyone: like light and mirrors. But the light's the thing."
>
> "Do you mean there are no famous men?"
>
> "They are all famous. They are all known, remembered, recognized by the only Mind that can give a perfect judgment."[1]

All vain ambition, seeking after the approval and honor that comes from man, is only a substitute for reality: the hope of heavenly glory and immortality. This hope comes with keeping our focus on God, thereby maintaining our first love: "Thou shalt love the Lord thy God with all thy heart and with all thy soul and with all thy strength."

We are saddened from time to time to see the work of Christians who seem to be in the same sort of trouble as the artist in Lewis's story. The proper fear of God or hope of heaven is absent from their "seeing"—at least it isn't reflected in their work. Instead we see complaints about suffering here on earth, an elevation of self-pity, and a willingness to blame God. The real power of God is absent, replaced by a need to reduce God to their own size, intellect, and imagination. Today the odd thing is that so few Christians object. Surely this reflects, besides the loss of Christian hope, the loss of the real Presence of God and the awe and the humility that we as creatures know in such a light.

> Have I received a ministry from the Lord? If so, I have to be loyal to it, to count my life precious only for the fulfilling of that ministry. Think of the satisfaction it will be to hear Jesus say—"Well done, good and faithful servant"; to know that you have done what He sent you to do.[2]

> What a revolution would come to us all, if it became the one fixed aim and ambition of our lives to stand before God, and to do always those things that are pleasing in His sight.[3]

Hope, what it is and what it means, is surely a mystery. Who can fully understand these words: "Christ within the believer is the *hope of glory*" (Colossians 1:27) or the truth that ours is "a faith and knowledge resting on the *hope of eternal life*" (Titus 1:2). Glory, another part of the authentic Christian mystery, is intertwined with hope. "Eschatalogical glory," as the NIV commentary on Romans 5:2 points out, "is the hope of the Christian." Glorification, as a theological term, is synonymous with immortality. And Christian hope is to be understood only in the context of glory. We will understand more about hope if we meditate upon the Scriptural references to *glory, glorify,* and *glorified.* Together with meditating on Christ's resurrection and the great Christian hope of immortality, we could ask God to increase our desire for heaven and all it contains and for the anticipation of a future state in which we will have a new body patterned after Christ's glorified body. Then, if we have substituted the favor of men and the things of this world for that which is only God's and heaven's to give, we have the great privilege of asking for the grace to deeply repent. We can be turned around to once again face Him. We are no longer compelled to substitute the shadow for the real, our impressions about glory for the thing itself.[4]

PRAYER

O Lord, be glorified in our midst. Enable us with all our might to exalt and glorify Your name and to give thanks. Fill us, O Lord, with thanksgiving. May the hope of glory be awakened in each one of us.

Hope Is Mythic

One of the reasons we can never closely define hope is because it is mythic; it is mythic in its longing for a good too great to put into words. Such words as *hope* and *glory* require an imaginative response, and the Scriptures are full of such responses. Another reason is because you and I too are mythic—more myth than fact, as Dr. Clyde Kilby[5] would say. We have utterly transcendent dimensions, and words such as *hope* and *glory* reflect this fact. The following quotes from the works of Lewis will flood light on these statements:

> It is perfectly easy to go on all your life giving explanations of religion, love, morality, honour, and the like, *without having been inside any of them.* And if you do that, you are simply playing with counters. You go on explaining a thing without knowing what it is. That is why a great deal of contemporary thought is, strictly speaking, thought about nothing—all the apparatus of thought busily working in a vacuum.[6] (Italics mine)

> Human intellect is incurably abstract. Pure mathematics is the type of successful thought. Yet the only realities we experience are concrete—this pain, this pleasure, this dog, this man. While we are loving the man, bearing the pain, enjoying the pleasure, we are not intellectually apprehending Pleasure, Pain or Personality. When we begin to do so, on the other hand, the concrete realities sink to the level of mere instances or examples: we are no longer dealing with them, but with that which they exemplify. This is our dilemma—either to taste and not to know or to know and not to taste—or, more strictly to lack one kind of knowledge because we are in an experience or to lack another kind because we are outside it. . . . You cannot *study* Pleasure in the moment of the nuptial embrace, nor repentance while repenting, nor analyze the nature of humour while roaring with laughter. But when else can you really know these things?. . . Of this tragic dilemma myth is the partial solution. In the enjoyment of a great myth we come nearest to experiencing as concrete what can otherwise be understood only as an abstraction. At this very moment, for example, I am trying to understand something very abstract indeed—the fading, vanishing of tasted reality as we try to grasp it with the discursive reason.[7]

> What flows into you from the myth is not truth but reality (truth is always *about* something, but reality is that *about which* truth is), and, therefore, every myth becomes the father of innumerable truths on the abstract level. Myth is the mountain whence all the different streams arise which become truths down here in the valley: *in hac valle abstractionis*. Or, if you prefer, myth is the isthmus which connects the peninsular world of thought with that vast continent we really belong to. It is not, like truth, abstract; nor is it, like direct experience, bound to the particular.

Now as myth transcends thought, Incarnation transcends myth. The heart of Christianity is a myth which is also a fact. The old myth of the dying God, *without ceasing to be myth,* comes down from the heaven of legend and imagination to the earth of history. It *happens*—at a particular date, in a particular place, followed by definable historical consequences. We pass from a Balder or an Osiris, dying nobody knows when or where, to a historical Person crucified (it is all in order) *under Pontius Pilate*. By becoming fact it does not cease to be myth: that is the miracle. I suspect that men have sometimes derived more spiritual sustenance from myths they did not believe than from the religion they professed. To be truly Christian we must both assent to the historical fact and also receive the myth (fact though it has become) with the same imaginative embrace which we accord to all myths. The one is hardly more necessary than the other. . . . We must not be ashamed of the mythical radiance resting on our theology.[8]

A great many different views on it [myth] have, of course, been held. Myths have been accepted as literally true, then as allegorically true (by the Stoics), as confused history (by Euhemerus), as priestly lies (by the philosophers of the enlightenment), as imitative agricultural ritual mistaken for propositions (in the days of Frazer). If you start from a naturalistic philosophy, then something like the view of Euhemerus or the view of Frazer is likely to result. But I am not a naturalist. I believe that in the huge mass of mythology which has come down to us a good many different sources are mixed—true history, allegory, ritual, the human delight in storytelling, etc. But among these sources I include the supernatural, both diabolical and divine. We need here concern ourselves only with the latter. If my religion is erroneous, then occurrences of similar motifs in pagan stories are, of course, instances of the same, or a similar error. But if my religion is true, then these stories may well be a *preparatio evangelica,* a divine hinting in poetic and ritual form at the same central truth which was later focussed and (so to speak) historicised in the Incarnation. To me, who first approached Christianity from a delighted interest in, and reverence for, the best pagan imagination, who loved Balder before Christ and Plato before St. Augustine, the anthropological argument against Christianity has never been formidable. On the contrary, I could not believe Christianity if I were forced to say that there were a thousand religions in the world of which 999 were pure nonsense and the thousandth (fortunately) true. My conversion, very largely, depended on recognizing Christianity as the completion, the actualization, the entelechy, of something that had never been wholly absent from the mind of man. . . . [I]f the truth or falsehood of Christianity is the very question you are discussing, then the argument from anthropology is surely *a petitio*.[9]

We need to redeem the term *myth*. Many are confused when they hear the term used in a positive way. Christians, for example, think of the warnings in the Scriptures about turning aside to myths, a needed warning, for false religions (the Manichaean, Gnostic, and Jewish occult, etc.) all have their myths—their symbolic systems. But so does the orthodox Judeo-Christian.

> Those who do not know that this great myth became Fact when the Virgin conceived are, indeed, to be pitied. But Christians also need to be reminded . . . that what became Fact was a Myth, that it carries with it into the world of Fact all the properties of a myth. God is more than a god, not less; Christ is more than a Balder, not less. We must not be ashamed of the mythical radiance resting on our theology. We must not be nervous about 'parallels' and 'Pagan Christs': they *ought* to be there—it would be a stumbling block if they weren't. We must not, in a false spirituality, withhold our imaginative welcome. . . . For this is the marriage of heaven and earth: Perfect Myth and Perfect Fact: claiming not only our love and our obedience, but also our wonder and delight, addressed to the savage, the child, and the poet in each one of us no less than to the moralist, the scholar, and the philosopher.[10]

And the serious problem we now face is that the Christian world has lost its symbolic system (its true myth) and more nearly holds to the symbolic system spun out of atheistic materialism—a myth that denies heaven, the unseen real, the transcendent, and the supernatural, along with the moral good.[11]

Our Pilgrimage in Time

Our journey in time is for the special ordering of our lives and passions. The church wisely has set aside a special time-within-time, the Lenten Season, for us to stop and look at our lives in view of eternity and to check our spiritual temperatures for any worldly virus our souls may have caught. It is not accidental that this period precedes Easter and prepares us for the Feasts of Christ's resurrection and ascension that follow:

> *The grace of abstinence has shone forth,*
> *banishing the darkness of demons.*
> *The power of the Fast disciplines our minds.*
> *Lent brings the cure to our crippling worldliness.*[12]

As Fr. Thomas Hopko writes, Lent stands as the great reminder that:

> We are in exile. We are alienated and estranged from our true country.
>
> To forget God is the cause of all sins. To be unmindful of Zion is the source of all sorrows. To settle down in this fallen world, which is not God's good creation but rather the Babylon which the wicked have made, is death to the soul.
>
> Christians await the "holy city, new Jerusalem coming down out of heaven from God, prepared as a bride adorned for her husband," which is the true homeland of all human beings (Revelation 21:2). . . . They already live in it

> to the measure that they have discovered their authentic humanity made in God's image and likeness in Christ.[13]

There is a dangerous forgetfulness on our part that this world is not our true and final home. This has been greatly exacerbated by the fact that our educational systems, drawing their theories from materialist philosophy, have claimed heaven to be off-limits and have taught us to look within ourselves and to this earth for the ultimate good. As C. S. Lewis points out, this progressive subjectivization has resulted in an

> evil enchantment of worldliness which has been laid upon us for nearly a hundred years. . . . Almost our whole education has been directed to silencing this shy, persistent, inner voice; almost all our modern philosophies have been devised to convince us that the good of man is to be found on this earth.[14]

I think this explains why we have such difficulty in understanding and celebrating Lent in beneficial ways. We are no longer sure deep down that we are exiles, that this is not the promised home. Therefore, we've accommodated ourselves to Babylon and then are overwhelmed at the sickness, fear, hatred, and violence we see here. It is a strange fact that we Christians continue to be unduly shocked and even overcome by the sight and the extent of the evil we discover in the world—as if we didn't know it to be a fallen one.

Lent is to remind us that it is all too easy to settle in here, to warn us that perhaps a "crippling worldliness" has indeed overtaken us.

> See to it, brothers, that none of you has a sinful, unbelieving heart that turns away from the living God. But encourage one another daily, as long as it is called Today, so that none of you may be hardened by sin's deceitfulness. (Hebrews 3:12-13)

This is what the Lenten Scripture readings and teachings are meant to correct in us. They would teach us how we can live in the midst of Babylon and not be destroyed by it, even as Christ prayed:

> My prayer is not that you take them out of the world but that you protect them from the evil one. They are not of the world, even as I am not of it. (John 17:15-16)

Spiritual Discipline of Ourselves

The journey through life then, if made successfully, requires that we order our inner and outer lives. We do this through prayer, and keeping an effective listening prayer journal is the best means I can recommend. For those who have difficulty ordering all that an effective vocation has brought into their orbit, or for those who have grown dangerously passive, slothful spiritually and mentally, you may want to read—on your knees—Richard J. Foster's books *Celebration of Discipline* and *Freedom of Simplicity*, or Gordon MacDonald's book *Ordering Your Private World*. It is essential that we order our lives and our "loves" this side of glory—in time.

We are often said to be creatures of time, and that we are. But time too is a creature. It is created. It will not always *be*. This is, for me at least, an overwhelming concept to grapple with and keep before my eyes; it is one I cannot really "think" or fully grasp. But the truth of the matter is, God is outside of time, and not subject to it. Someday we too will no longer be subject to time. Meanwhile in our pilgrimage, it is important to see time as *gift*, as treasure not to be squandered.

Coleridge in an essay entitled "On Method," makes the following remarkable statement:

> If the idle are described as killing time, he [the methodical man] may be justly said to call it into life and moral being, while he makes it the distinct object not only of the consciousness, but of the conscience. He organizes the hours, and gives them a soul; and that, the very essence of which is to flee away, and evermore to have been, he takes up into his own permanence, and communicates to it the imperishableness of a spiritual nature. Of the *good and faithful servant,* whose energies, thus directed, are thus methodized, it is less truly affirmed, that he lives in time, than that time lives in him. His days, months, and years, as the stops and punctual marks in the records of duties performed, will survive the wreck of worlds, and remain extant when time itself shall be no more. . . .

Such a remarkable idea! That of taking time into ourselves. May God assist us all as we allow time to live in us.

Reminders of Heaven

As a child I had the great good fortune to grow up in the care of a mother who not only lived the gospel, but every day "sang" it as she went about her household chores. She majored on the hymns that celebrated the cross and the hope of heaven. Though she had to be away from the house earning a living the greater part of the day, when at home—if she was not entirely exhausted—the house would ring with the songs of Christ's Atonement, and of His gracious and loving invitation to sinners:

"When I see the blood, . . . I will pass over you."
"There is a fountain filled with blood, drawn from Immanuel's veins."
"The Old Rugged Cross"
"Jesus Paid It All, All to Him I Owe"

These hymns would then always give way to the songs that celebrate heaven and eternal life. Her voice climbed its highest untrained reaches when she sang (which she often did), "When we all get to heaven, what a day of rejoicing that will be." As she sang, heaven, in a manner of speaking, descended to us, became real to my little sister and me, and we often joined in. Our Saturdays were especially wonderful because Mother would be home for a nice, long stretch of time, and together we would sail through the straightening of the house so she could get to her prayers and preparations for teaching Sunday school the next day. With windows wide open, sunshine streaming in, we would be shaking out bed covers, dusting and sweeping, all the while singing and celebrating the story of salvation and eternal life.

My sister and I knew by heart all the Bible stories the hymns were based on, for Mother had told them to us every night at bedtime. She did it in what I now realize to be unique and creative ways. She was a naturally gifted teacher and disciplinarian (the two gifts go together), and she was always *teaching* us—about God, about others, about everything. I've been surprised to see how often in dysfunctional households the children are not taught in this way—it is almost as if the great things are stingily measured out. There seems to be the notion or even fear that children cannot handle truth. I believe they are starving for great and positive input. Though many seem not to realize it, children are from very early on struggling with good and evil and need ways of understanding these and the power to name them. Nothing seemed too great or too high for Mother to tell. So she passed on to us the profound things—early. In marvelous yet simple, down-to-earth ways, the hope of heaven and the understanding of the eternal (ontological) dimensions of *being*, of what it means to be created in God's image and eternal likeness, were passed on to my sister and me—in words and images we could retain. She had, as a widow in her early twenties, done as St. Paul had admonished Timothy: "Take hold of the eternal life to which you were called" (1 Timothy 6:12). And she passed on to us the knowledge of this in story form, along with the *real thing itself.* She was a sacramental channel of the Presence of God and of a most precious faith and hope.

I've shared the above in order to emphasize our plight as moderns. Even with such a heritage as this, I am a twentieth-century person affected by the age and culture in which I live. It is an age that has lost the hope of eternal life and that cannot put up signposts that point the way to heaven. Such an age has lost the capacity even to speak of the soul's longing for heaven and immortality. Therefore, while persevering, and valuing time as gift, I for one need special reminders of heaven. I need to set up personal signposts, those that remind me to pray always for Christ's appearing and to rejoice in my goal of eternal life in Christ and my full inheritance in Him.

Several years ago, I was deathly tired. I had completed *The Broken Image* and *Crisis in Masculinity,* books that had come out of facing great darkness with large numbers of people, and I had experienced intense spiritual warfare and opposition to the work. As I took the last manuscript to copy and mail off, I remember crying out to God, "Lord, I'm fainting, I need a glimpse, an extraordinary one, of heaven. Please, Lord, if I'm to do what you've called me to do,

I need to walk with one foot in heaven and one here! I need reminders of heaven always before my eyes!"

Then I remember thinking, "You'd better be careful praying like that—you may suddenly get caught up to the third (or was it the seventh!) heaven like St. Paul did, and the contrast might make you decide to stay there—unfit you permanently for here!"

Of course, such an experience would have been incredibly healing, but obviously I was not quite ready to ask God for that and was not sure I should. (I don't usually ask God for experiences, per se, for there are pitfalls in doing so, as I write about in *The Healing Presence*.[15] I trust the Lord for the experiences I need, and then only as He wills.) So I wondered if I had crossed over the line at this point. But He answered my prayer—almost instantly—and in a wonderfully down-to-earth way.

Immediately I was surprised to see a small jewelry shop in the same building—one that had not been there a week or so before. On entering, I saw it did not have the usual traditional array of expensive diamonds, gold, silver, and so on. This one carried the work of innovative artists, and their work was not necessarily in precious gems—but in colorful ones, expertly cut, and set into the most pleasingly designed settings, some round, some square, some oblong. All these shapes and colors immediately took on symbolic meaning for me, meaning having to do with eternal life and heaven.

A ring and bracelet suddenly stood out from all the rest. The ring had one large round stone the color of sunshine and one small round ruby. The bracelet had square-cut stones the same as the ring, with several small, square red rubies. The metal was of beautifully crafted silver, with a tiny thread of gold around the jewels in the ring and a matching thread running the circumference of the bracelet. The rubies symbolized the blood of Christ and His cross—the way into the City, while the stones that reflected the color of sunlight, together with their shapes and the beautifully molded metals, spoke powerfully of the City itself. They also spoke to me of another kind of reward, that of our works that will stand the fires of judgment.

Strongly then, the imagery the Apostle John used to describe the Heavenly City and its gates in the book of Revelation (21:18-21) came to me. These very stones of earth suddenly symbolized for me the greater lights and shapes and highways of that City. They seemed to shine with the glory of heaven. I purchased the ring and bracelet and cherish them—I think I always will—for to me they are at once a pointer and a symbol reminding me daily of our great Christian hope and of our eternal reward.

Often as I'm ministering somewhere and there are hundreds of deep needs before me that I know the Lord wants to transform, the stones of my bracelet and ring will suddenly catch the light and speak to me of heaven. The Presence of the Son of God with us in that place, the very Light of Heaven, blesses the myriad facets of the earthly light in ring and bracelet, and becomes for me an awesome reminder of heaven.

It takes a certain amount of courage to share something like this. The one time I told about this in a group, one man cried out, "Now all our wives will want new rings!" So lest husbands feel suddenly protective of their wallets, let me say that God would not necessarily bless the same symbol to every one! In fact, no one has ever shared a like experience with me. Also, I think that if I had overvalued jewelry in the past or valued it for wrong reasons, God would not have blessed it so as a symbol of heaven for me. But I do think that sheer beauty in color, shape, stone, metal, and artistry is a key here. God loves beauty. He created it. He's pleased with the truly beautiful things we craft from His creation, and these things can symbolize Him and His way of salvation for us. Our symbol-starved twentieth-century hearts need, even crave, vital symbols of the eternal home our hearts were fashioned to know and for which they yearn—our incredible Christian hope.

Beyond the way the colors, shapes, and beauty of well-cut stones impress me, the foundation stones of Scripture speak to me far more than I can understand. They tell ultimately of our Lord, the great Foundation Stone, so there is no end to the meaning of what these symbolize. The great hymn "The Solid Rock" nearly always leaves me in tears. As an organist, one of my favorite prelude and hymn pieces was "Rock of Ages." I can't remember playing it when someone didn't start to weep, and I know that was because the hymn never failed to lift me up into thanksgiving and worship. Another is "The Rock That Is Higher Than I," and a modern version of this hymn touches me deeply. This very day, I am listening to it as I write.

Isaiah, foreseeing the first advent of our Christ, writes:

> So this is what the Sovereign Lord says: "See, I lay a stone in Zion, a tested stone, a precious cornerstone for a sure foundation; the one who trusts will never be dismayed." (Isaiah 28:16)

He is the Mighty Rock, seen also as both fountain and cistern, the Stone which at once holds and releases the water of life.

> Whoever drinks the water I give him will never thirst. Indeed the water I give him will become in him a spring of water welling up to eternal life. (John 4:14)

> They have forsaken me, the spring of living water, and have dug their own cisterns, broken cisterns that cannot hold water. (Jeremiah 2:13)

The ring and bracelet that seemed to me to signify the Heavenly City and our Christ, also spoke immediately of our works in time. St. Paul, speaking of his work in the Kingdom, said:

> By the grace God has given me, I laid a foundation as an expert builder, and someone else is building on it. But each one should be careful how he builds. For no one can lay any foundation other than the one already laid, which is Jesus Christ. (1 Corinthians 3:10-11)

He then goes on to describe the work that will last in terms of gold, silver, costly stones. Nothing else will stand the test of fire:

> If any man builds on this foundation using gold, silver, costly stones, wood, hay or straw, his work will be shown for what it is, because the Day will bring it to light. It will be revealed with fire, and the fire will test the quality of each man's work. If what he has built survives, he will receive his reward. (1 Corinthians 3:12-14)

It is necessary to petition fervently that our works will stand the fire of judgment—a worthy goal indeed. As stewards of the Kingdom, we are entrusted with the secret things of God; we are stewards of a wisdom "that human wisdom cannot discover." Have we set ourselves to find this wisdom? God promises it to those who ask for it. In this Scripture, the stones symbolize the purity of the word we pass on to others. These stones rest on the Word, the Foundation who is Christ, and the pure words He passed on to His apostles and to us.

I began this book with the darkness and self-hatred that Christians such as my friend and colleague Clay McLean can suffer until they find the healing that we within the Body of Christ are so uniquely graced to minister. Few can write songs such as his that so deeply articulate and celebrate what it means to come out of the darkness and into the light. Everything in this book is written with the goal of bringing hurting people into just such a transformation. So I close by sharing one of his songs as fruit of the ministry of the healing power of our Lord and as a way of encouraging us all to persevere "against the night."

AGAINST THE NIGHT

When men have lost all reason and evil seems to win,
Then compromise is treason and silence is a sin.
Let all who hate the darkness prepare to stand and fight.
The children of the morning must stand against the night.

When all that wisdom treasures is treated with disgrace,
And idols of Damnation are set up in their place,
When every holy symbol is fading out of sight,
The children of the morning must stand against the night.

We'll do the work of heaven against a setting sun
Until the final darkness when no work can be done.

Then watching for the Bridegroom with oil lamps burning bright,
We'll worship in the darkness and stand against the night.

Against the final darkness no earthly strength can stand.
The evil shall be shattered, but not by human hand.
The Maker of the morning will come in Holy Light
That burns in righteous anger and wrath against the night.

Then comes the final morning when all will be restored,
The shadowlands transformed by the glory of the Lord,
When every darkened memory is washed in Healing Light,
Where there will be no warfare, for there will be no night.

PRAYER

Lord, we would anticipate the very portals of heaven, "each gate made of a single pearl," and what it will mean to pass through such beauty and color and unmitigated light and goodness to receive the reward of those made worthy in the blood of the Lamb. May we pass through with the great hope that our work has survived, that it has indeed been accomplished on and in You, our Great Foundation Stone.

Lord, as You restore our Christian souls, restore to us the hope of heaven. May we once again receive glimpses of the eternal beyond that beckon us as we run this race from the region of time to the healing that only eternity with You can bring. Amen.

Notes

PREFACE

1. Oswald Chambers, *My Utmost for His Highest* (New York: Dodd Mead, 1935), p. 127.
2. F. B. Meyer, *Our Daily Walk* (Grand Rapids: Zondervan, 1951), p. 45.

PART I: The Virtue of Self-Acceptance

1. Richard Lovelace, *Dynamics of Spiritual Life: An Evangelical Theology of Renewal* (Downers Grove, IL: InterVarsity Press, 1979), p. 212.

CHAPTER 1: Self-Hatred: The Traitor Within When Temptation Comes

1. Oswald Chambers, *Oswald Chambers, The Best from All His Books,* vol. 2 (Nashville, TN: Oliver-Nelson Books, 1989), p. 318.
2. *Ibid.*
3. *Ibid.*, p. 319.
4. *Ibid.*
5. This radical obedience is not one of slavish legalism, but that which describes the "walk in the Spirit," that stance whereby we obey God for the primary reason, that of love and awe of Him.
6. *See* chapter 5, "Creative Power," in my book *The Healing Presence* (Wheaton, IL: Crossway Books, 1989).
7. Chambers, *The Best,* p. 318.
8. I recommend Richard Lovelace, *Dynamics of Spiritual Life: An Evangelical Theology of Renewal* (Downers Grove, IL: InterVarsity Press, 1979).

   Today, it is as if many, including leaders, have a remarkably shallow understanding of the Atonement, especially of what justification and sanctification are all about. Many seem to skip from an initial conversion to matters of power—such as are promised in a baptism of the Spirit and in spiritual authority. When we fully receive and live out the doctrines of justification and sanctification, we find we must seek and gain emotional and psychological healing, and we acquire the concomitant self-knowledge that attends such healing. But having lightly skipped over these matters, these persons are not to be trusted with any kind of power.

   In such cases, for example, there will be an exploitation (a "spectacularization") even of true spiritual giftings to the point that they "clang" and become tools in the enemy's hands. Bona fide spiritual power, when in the service of unmet ego needs, quickly becomes corrupted by reason of "admixtures"—i.e., incursions of fleshly and even demonic darkness. The Holy Spirit, offended, does not remain under such circumstances, so that which began in goodness ends in something carnal or even occult. Such Christians are then trapped in a fleshly "drive toward power"—one that has no connection at all with Christ's cross and true spiritual power. In these cases, human pride has been left intact and the extent of sin in the heart unnoticed and unchallenged. One has been too proud to seek and gain the needed psychological and spiritual healing. One has neglected the full message of the cross, and in effect has denied the existence of a Christian soul, one that is in need of restoration.

9. *See The Healing Presence,* chapter 14, "Renouncing False Gods and Appropriating the Holy."
10. Chambers, *The Best*, p. 319.

CHAPTER 2: First Great Barrier to Wholeness in Christ: Failure to Accept Oneself

1. *See* my book *The Healing Presence* (Wheaton, IL: Crossway Books, 1989), chapter 12, "Introspection Versus True Imagination."
2. *See The Healing Presence,* chapter 4, "Separation from the Presence."
3. John Fawcett, a Christian brother and fellow team member who before his healing was trapped in analyzing and hating himself, expresses it this way: "Some who are afraid of the appearance of narcissism in the language of self-acceptance veer dangerously close to self-hatred in their antidote to it, as if a deeper introspective gaze upon our own guilt and sin could bring us to fuller freedom in Christ. But self-hatred is not the opposite of narcissism; rather, it is egocentrism under a different guise—the same mirror of self viewed from another angle. The discovery of the true self encompasses the denial and crucifixion of the flesh, but it is far more than a negative process. We find our true selves positively in relation to God: hearing His loving, affirming Word, we are freed to celebrate the new self He makes. We become enamored not of our own accomplishments nor of our unworthiness, but of the beauty of Jesus. Through His Spirit He descends into us that Christ may dwell in our hearts by faith (Ephesians 3:17), transforming us into His image, from glory to glory (2 Corinthians 3:18)."
4. Michael Scanlon, *Inner Healing* (New York: Paulist Press, 1974), pp. 51-52.

CHAPTER 3: Struggling Through to Self-Acceptance

1. *Die Annahme seiner selbst*, 5th ed. (Wurzburg: Werkbandverlag, 1969), pp. 14, 16. Quoted in Walter Trobisch, *Love Yourself: Self Acceptance and Depression* (Downers Grove, IL: InterVarsity Press, 1976), p. 9.
2. *See* Trobisch, *Love Yourself*; Frank Lake, *Clinical Theology* (Crossroad Publishing); and Hemfelt, Minirth, and Meier, *Love Is a Choice: Recovery for Codependent Relationships* (Thomas Nelson) for solid Christian examples of these writings.
3. Oswald Chambers, *My Utmost for His Highest* (New York: Dodd Mead, 1935), p. 315.
4. C. S. Lewis, *Mere Christianity* (New York: Macmillan, 1960), p. 190.
5. C. S. Lewis, *Experiment in Criticism* (Cambridge: Cambridge University Press, 1969), p. 138.
6. For more on this, *see* my book *The Healing Presence* (Wheaton, IL: Crossway Books, 1989), chapter 13, "Incarnational Reality."
7. Walter Trobisch, *The Complete Works of Walter Trobisch* (Downers Grove, IL: InterVarsity Press, 1987), p. 659.

8. Trobisch, *Love Yourself,* p. 680.
9. C. S. Lewis, *Letters of C. S. Lewis,* ed. W. H. Lewis (New York: Harcourt, Brace and World, 1966), p. 155.
10. *See The Healing Presence,* chapters 8 and 9, "Perceiving God Aright" and "The Imagery Really Matters."
11. C. S. Lewis, "The Weight of Glory" in *The Weight of Glory* (Grand Rapids: Eerdmans, 1972), pp. 8-9.
12. David Seamands, *The Healing of Memories* (Wheaton, IL: Victor Books, 1985), p. 102.
13. As Rebecca Manley Pippert says in *Hope Has Its Reasons,* there is an intentional element in even our worst deceptions, and this is "why we are held responsible for our own condition. We may be deceived, but we are never that deceived." (San Francisco: Harper and Row, 1989), p. 86.
14. There is a good example of this in the life of C. S. Lewis. In his spiritual autobiography *Surprised by Joy,* Lewis describes the grievous effects of losing his mother to cancer (chapter 1). As he writes, his father lost not only his wife at this time, but his sons as well. Lewis struggled for the greater part of his life to understand his deep antipathy toward his father. His life with Mrs. Moore and her family can only be rightly understood as one comprehends the reaction he had to the loss of his mother early in life and then, related to that, the way he could not accept his father. Lewis never had full insight into this, as George Sayer, one of his close and long-term friends, has observed. *See* Fifth Annual Marion E. Wade Lecture, 9/28/79, The Marion E. Wade Center, Wheaton College, Wheaton, IL.
15. Quoted from a lecture given at a Pastoral Care Ministries School.
16. Karl Stern, *The Third Revolution: A Study of Psychiatry and Religion,* Image Books Edition (Garden City, NY: Doubleday, 1961), p. 152.
17. Romano Guardini, *The Virtues* (Chicago: Regnery Company, 1967), p. 6.
18. These would be primarily familial or *storge* needs. For a study of the four basic loves, *see The Four Loves* by C. S. Lewis.
19. *See The Healing Presence*, chapter 12, "Introspection Versus True Imagination."
20. As I show in *The Broken Image*, all categories of homosexuality have this one failure in common—the failure to emerge from puberty affirmed as persons, thereby finding true self-acceptance. All are unaffirmed in their gender identity and have fallen into the wrong kind of self-love.

    As masturbation is always a part of male homosexuality and often a part of lesbian behavior as well, it is extremely important to recognize when this habit is rooted in infantile trauma and is related to severe dread and anxiety. Those feelings accompany the severest psychological injuries in infants. In these cases, a dread-ridden masturbation (in contrast to a merely lustful one) ensues. *See The Broken Image* (Wheaton, IL: Crossway Books, 1981), pp. 54-62, together with pp. 121-136, "Homosexual and Lesbian Behavior Related to Failure of the Infant to Achieve an Adequate Sense of Being" for more on this.
21. Lewis, *Surprised by Joy* (New York: Harcourt, Brace and World, 1955), p. 71.
22. Stern, *The Third Revolution,* p. 149.
23. *Ibid.*, p. 150.
24. *See* my book *Crisis in Masculinity* (Wheaton, IL: Crossway Books, 1985), pp. 130-140 for more on this. When the church faithfully teaches men and women to find their identity in Christ, they will have no difficulty with roles as such. But it is dangerous to teach on the roles of men and women per se.
25. *See The Broken Image*, pp. 121-136.
26. *See The Healing Presence,* pp. 48-54.
27. *See Crisis in Masculinity,* pp. 62-76, for prayers that enable us to forgive even the parent who is the most difficult to honor and forgive.

CHAPTER 4: Affirmation: What It Is and How It Is Received

1. In counseling, it is important to realize that the way of the wounded "inner child" is so often the way of the foolish child: "The way of a fool seems right to him, but a wise man listens to advice" (Proverbs 12:15). We are never to dialogue with that foolishness, but with the authentic person. The writer of Proverbs expresses perfectly what many in counseling desperately need to know and understand: "Do not answer a fool according to his folly [his foolishness], or you will be like him yourself" (Proverbs 26:4).
2. The descriptive term "dry alcoholic" refers to a person who carries the characteristics and personality traits of someone addicted to alcohol. Such a person does not know what normal is, and there may be addiction to other substances. Some of the more obvious traits include manipulative and controlling behavior.
3. Oswald Chambers, *My Utmost for His Highest* (New York: Dodd Mead, 1935), p. 68.
4. *Ibid.*, p. 333.
5. *See* my book *Real Presence: The Christian Worldview of C. S. Lewis as Incarnational Reality* (Wheaton, IL: Crossway Books, 1979), chapter 7, "The Great Dance," for C. S. Lewis on the will; *see* my book *The Healing Presence* (Wheaton, IL: Crossway Books, 1989), p. 64, for a prayer for healing of the will.

CHAPTER 5: Listening Prayer: The Way of Grace and the Walk in the Spirit

1. Dick Keyes, *Beyond Identity* (Ann Arbor, MI: Servant Books, 1984), p. 97.
2. C. S. Lewis, *The Problem of Pain* (London: Collins Fontana Books, 1959), p. 63.
3. C. S. Lewis, *Experiment in Criticism* (Cambridge: Cambridge University Press, 1969), p. 138.
4. C. S. Lewis, *Poems* (New York: Harcourt, Brace and World, 1964), pp. 92-93.
5. Lewis, *The Problem of Pain,* p. 140.

PART II: The Forgiveness of Sin

1. F. B. Meyer, *Our Daily Walk* (Grand Rapids: Zondervan, 1951), p. 142.

CHAPTER 6: Healing of Memories: The Forgiveness of Sin

1. *See* my book *The Healing Presence* (Wheaton, IL: Crossway Books, 1989), pp. 131-32.
2. *Ibid.*, chapter 10.
3. Agnes Sanford, *The Healing Gifts of the Spirit* (Philadelphia/New York: Lippincott, 1966), pp. 126-27.
4. C. S. Lewis, *Letters of C. S. Lewis,* ed. W. H. Lewis (New York: Harcourt, Brace and World, 1966), p. 155.
5. Recommended Reading: chapter 4, "Spirit, Soul, and Body," in my book *Real Presence: The Christian Worldview of C. S. Lewis as Incarnational Reality* (Wheaton, IL: Crossway Books, 1979) and sections entitled "Soul," pp. 1036-37, "Spirit," p. 1041, "Man, Doctrine of," pp. 676-81 in H. D. McDonald, *Evangelical Dictionary of Theology,* ed. Walter A. Elwell (Grand Rapids: Baker Book House, 1984).
6. McDonald, *Evangelical Dictionary,* p. 678.
7. F. B. Meyer, *Our Daily Walk* (Grand Rapids: Zondervan, 1951), p. 169.

8. Robert M. Doran, S. J., "Jungian Psychology and Christian Spirituality: II," *Review for Religious,* 38 (1979/4): p. 510.
9. Karl Stern, *The Third Revolution,* Image Books Edition (Garden City, NY: Doubleday, 1961), pp. 70-71.
10. C. S. Lewis, *Letters to Malcolm: Chiefly on Prayer* (New York: Harcourt, Brace and World, 1963, 1964), pp. 121-22.
11. As an example of a healing of ancestral memories, see David's story in my book *Crisis in Masculinity* (Wheaton, IL: Crossway Books, 1985), p. 51.

    Recommended Reading: David Seamands, *Healing of Memories* (Wheaton, IL: Victor Books, 1985), chapter 1, "The Mystery of Memory," and Lewis, *Letters to Malcolm*, chapter 22.
12. Lewis, *Letters to Malcolm,* p. 109.
13. C. S. Lewis, *The Problem of Pain* (New York: Macmillan, 1962), p. 61.
14. Kenneth McAll's book *The Healing of the Family Tree* was the genesis of this teaching, and *Healing the Greatest Hurt* by Matthew and Dennis Linn and Sheila Fabricant further popularized the notions in McAll's book.

CHAPTER 7: Second Great Barrier to Wholeness in Christ: Failure to Forgive Others

1. For more on this, send for tapes on codependency to Pastoral Care Ministries, P. O. Box 17702, Milwaukee, Wisconsin 53217.
2. Oswald Chambers, *Oswald Chambers, The Best from All His Books* (Nashville: Thomas Nelson, 1987), p. 345.
3. Leanne Payne, *The Healing Presence* (Wheaton, IL: Crossway Books, 1989), p. 89.
4. *Ibid.*, pp. 172-75.
5. Chambers, *Best of All His Books*, p. 345.
6. *Ibid.*, p. 344.
7. For example, *see* my book *The Broken Image* (Wheaton, IL: Crossway Books, 1981), pp. 79-82, "Birth Trauma and Repression of Masculinity," as well as Loren's story, pp. 78-79.
8. *See The Broken Image,* chapter 1, "Lisa's Story: Repressed Memory."
9. Frank Lake, "The Origin and Development of Personal Identity Through Childhood to Adult Life: And Its Significance in Clinical Pastoral Care," Second Year Syllabus, no. 4, Clinical Theology, (The Clinical Theological Assn., Hawthornes of Nottingham Ltd., n.d.), p. 5.
10. *Ibid.*

CHAPTER 8: Prolonged Healing of Memories: Abandonment Issues and the Repression of Painful Emotions

1. Leanne Payne, *The Healing Presence* (Wheaton, IL: Crossway Books, 1989), pp. 173-174.
2. Frank Lake, *Clinical Theology,* abridged by Marin H. Yeomans (New York: Crossroad Publishing, 1987), pp. 4-5.
3. Frank Lake, "Clinical Theological Training and Care," Second Year Syllabus, no. 4 (The Clinical Theological Assn., Hawthornes of Nottingham Ltd., n.d.), p. 5.
4. Lake, *Clinical Theology* (abridged), p. 101.
5. *Ibid.*, p. 41.
6. *Ibid.,* pp. 103-4.

7. The *hysterical* attempt to find or posit an insecure selfhood in another, thus entangling the helper with the sufferer.
8. The inability of the one with *schizoid* tendencies to rest in a healthy interdependence with others.
9. For the fullest, most Christ-centered explication of the personality reactions to the failure to come to a sense of being in the first months of life, I recommend Frank Lake's work *Clinical Theology*, the unabridged edition when available, and the abridged (very fine). The abridged edition omits the excellent work he did on homosexual defense mechanisms. For case examples of these, *see* my book *The Broken Image* (Wheaton, IL: Crossway Books, 1981), pp. 121-136.
10. Lake, *Clinical Theology*, (abridged), p. 99.
11. *Ibid.*, pp. 107-8.
12. *Ibid.*, p. 65.
13. Mira Rothenberg, *Children with Emerald Eyes* (New York: E. P. Dutton, 1987), pp. 27-30.
14. Men who cross-dress, both heterosexual and homosexual in orientation, are typically termed *transvestites*, but *we* use transvestite to identify only those who are homosexual in orientation. According to *Baker Encyclopedia of Psychology,* David G. Benner, editor, homosexuals make up only 10 or 11 percent of those who cross-dress. We use the term *cross-dresser,* then, to refer to the remaining 89 percent who are heterosexual males. Both the cross-dresser and the transvestite receive temporary comfort and alleviation of anxiety when they put on feminine attire. But for the cross-dresser, it is also a fetish—he is sexually aroused by the activity. This is an important distinction in knowing how to pray and in understanding the symbolic confusion in their lives. (We do not find men with homosexual orientation to experience sexual arousal in cross-dressing, but the *Baker Encyclopedia* reports it as a rarity.)
15. At times the heterosexual cross-dresser may deny and camouflage this desire to be a woman. For example, the desire can be covered over by fear and hatred of a mother who cannot love and accept the son, yet who is at the same time possessive, controlling, and overbearing. One cross-dresser I ministered to seemed subconsciously to want to be his mother in order to be strong and enabled to survive the effects of her mental illness. He had a very weak father who could not withstand her or protect his son from her. The son's way of coping with his extreme frustration and pain in dealing with her was finally, in a state of anxiety, to put on her underwear. By putting on her clothes, he was symbolically putting on her "sex." In a manner of speaking, to put on her underwear, was *to be her* in order to survive her. His anxiety at being powerless to withstand her, at being suffocatingly and infuriatingly "under her" (emotionally raped by her), constellated sexual arousal. This eroticism was rooted in anxiety and insecurity. He had overcome his cross-dressing for a number of years, and it wasn't until his fiancée broke up with him that he fell back into the compulsion. Here again, he repeated the pattern. He did not, so far as I know, consciously wish to be woman, but unconsciously he cross-dressed in order to be her (this time, the fiancée). Again, to be her was to have power to withstand her rejection of himself. This understanding, along with healing prayer, freed him.
16. There are transvestites (homosexual cross-dressers) who become female impersonators, and spin a web of delusion about themselves. As they get more deeply into this behavior, they may fall under a demonic deception that they are in fact woman. Such an illusory identity can take on a truly demonic life of its own, and these persons are left grievously demon infested. (See *The Healing Presence,* p. 73 and chapter 9.)
17. Frank Lake, *Clinical Theology* (London: Darton, Longman, & Todd, 1966), p. 9.

    Recommended Reading: Frank Lake, *Clinical Theology* and John Bowlby, *A Secure Base,* Basic Books.

CHAPTER 9: Third Great Barrier to Wholeness in Christ: Failure to Receive Forgiveness

1. C. S. Lewis, *Reflections on the Psalms* (New York: Harcourt, Brace and World, 1958), pp. 31-32.
2. Alexander Solzhenitsyn, *Gulag Archipelago,* ed. Edward E. Ericson, Jr. (New York: Harper and Row, 1985), chapter 7.
3. R. A. Torrey, *How to Pray* (Chicago: Moody Press, n.d.), p. 25.
4. C. S. Lewis, *Letters to Malcolm: Chiefly on Prayer* (New York: Harcourt, Brace and World, 1963), p. 82.
5. F. B. Meyer, *Our Daily Walk* (Grand Rapids: Zondervan, 1951), p. 374.
6. Richard Lovelace, *Dynamics of Spiritual Life* (Downers Grove, IL: InterVarsity Press, 1980), pp. 88-89.
7. *See* my book *The Healing Presence* (Wheaton, IL: Crossway Books, 1989), chapter 11, "The True Imagination," especially pp. 145ff.
8. For an excellent treatment of this topic, *see* Lovelace, *Dynamics of Spiritual Life,* especially chapter 4, "Primary Elements of Continuous Renewal."

CHAPTER 10: Conclusion to Healing of Memories

1. *See* my book *The Healing Presence* (Wheaton, IL: Crossway Books, 1989), pp. 94-95.
2. *See The Healing Presence* in its entirety but especially chapter 9.
3. *See* my book *The Broken Image* (Wheaton, IL: Crossway Books, 1981), chapter 6.
4. *See The Healing Presence,* chapter 12.
5. *Ibid.*, pp. 64, 94-97.
6. *Ibid.*, pp. 182ff.
7. *See* my book *Crisis in Masculinity* (Wheaton, IL: Crossway Books, 1985), pp. 62ff.

CHAPTER 11: The Use of Holy Water and Other Powerful Christian Symbols and Agencies

1. *See* my book *The Healing Presence* (Wheaton, IL: Crossway Books, 1989), chapter 11, for more on the ways our spiritual eyes are opened to see the invisible.
2. For more on the fact that sacramental reality exhibits the principle of the Incarnation, see chapter 3, "Sacrament: Avenue to the Real," in my book *Real Presence: The Christian Worldview of C. S. Lewis as Incarnational Reality* (Wheaton, IL: Crossway Books, 1979).
3. *See The Healing Presence*, chapter 14, for a fuller explication of Jung's gnosticism and its impact on the church.
4. John Richards, *But Deliver Us from Evil: An Introduction to the Demonic in Pastoral Care* (New York: Seabury Press, 1974), p. 28.
5. Phallic demons manifest in the context of Baal worship. *See The Healing Presence*, chapter 14, especially pp. 198-99.
6. Michael Green, *I Believe in Satan's Downfall* (Grand Rapids: Eerdmans, 1981), pp. 141-42.
7. *See The Healing Presence*, pp. 90-94, for a definition of demonic *oppression* as over and against *possession.*
8. Mark Pearson, "Counterfeit Christianity," *Mission and Ministry*, 7, no. 2 (Fall 1989), Ambridge, PA 15003, italics mine.
9. Green, *I Believe in Satan's Downfall*, p. 141.

10. Oswald Chambers, *My Utmost for His Highest* (New York: Dodd Mead, 1935), p. 262.
11. *Ibid.*, p. 291.
12. W. K. Lowther Clarke and Charles Harris, eds., *Liturgy and Worship: A Companion to the Prayer Books of the Anglican Communion* (London: Literature Association of the Church Union, London SPCK, 1932), pp. 472-615.

CHAPTER 12: The Gift of Battle

1. Oswald Chambers, *My Utmost for His Highest* (New York: Dodd Mead, 1935), p. 19.
2. *Ibid.*, p. 196.
3. Donald Bloesch, *Crumbling Foundations* (Grand Rapids: Zondervan, 1984), p. 125.
4. *Ibid.*
5. C. S. Lewis, *The Problem of Pain* (New York: Macmillan, 1962), p. 28.
6. William Barclay, *The Gospel of Matthew* (Louisville, KY: Westminster John Knox, 1975), p. 318.

CHAPTER 13: Cosmic Dimensions of Spiritual Warfare in Christian Organizations

1. Oswald Chambers, *My Utmost for His Highest* (New York: Dodd Mead, 1935), p. 258.
2. *See* my books *Real Presence: The Christian Worldview of C. S. Lewis as Incarnational Reality* (Wheaton, IL: Crossway Books, 1979), "Appendix: The Great Divorce," and *The Healing Presence* (Wheaton, IL: Crossway Books, 1989), chapter 14, "Renouncing False Gods and Appropriating the Holy."
3. C. S. Lewis, *The Problem of Pain* (New York: Macmillan, 1962), p. 85.
4. *See* my book *Crisis in Masculinity* (Wheaton, IL: Crossway Books, 1985).
5. Richard Lovelace, *Dynamics of Spiritual Life: An Evangelical Theology of Renewal* (Downers Grove, IL: InterVarsity Press, 1979), p. 384. *See* pp. 381-386.
6. *See* my book *Crisis in Masculinity*, chapter 4, "What Is Masculinity," for more on the tie-in between true masculinity and the power to speak the truth.
7. *See The Healing Presence*, chapter 12, "Introspection Versus True Imagination."
8. A monk of the Eastern Church, *On the Invocation of the Name of Jesus* (London: The Fellowship of St. Alban and St. Sergius), p. 9.
9. *Ibid.*, p. 2.

CHAPTER 14: Wrong Ways to Do Battle

1. C. S. Lewis, *That Hideous Strength* (New York: Macmillan, 1946), p. 283.
2. *See* my book *The Healing Presence* (Wheaton, IL: Crossway Books, 1989), pp. 80-87.
3. *See ibid.*, pp. 178-180 for more on this.
4. Fr. John Gaynor Banks, *The Master and the Disciple* (St. Paul, MN: Macalester Park Publishing, 1954), p. 135.
5. William Barclay, *The Gospel of Matthew* (Louisville, KY: Westminster John Knox, 1975), p. 108.
6. *Ibid.*, p. 110.
7. *Ibid.*
8. *New International Version Study Bible* (Grand Rapids: Zondervan, 1985), p. 12.
9. Even when there is a demonic infestation, the demons are most often not dislodged through this manner of "prayer," or they will return because the sin or wound hasn't been adequately dealt with. We must learn how to discern (that is, move in the authen-

tic gift of discerning of spirits) the presence of the demonic and learn to bring the finger of God to bear on it. The demonic entity cannot stand the light and has to flee at our command. God in His mercy answers all kinds of "misinformed" prayer, but we as Christians are called to wisdom and to understand the human soul.

10. C. S. Lewis, *Screwtape Letters* (New York: Macmillan, 1962), p. 3.
11. A theology derived from E. W. Kenyon.
12. I know and have ministered to people who have come up with entire mythologies of evil powers, and these are spun out of listening to the demons whose presence they learned to practice. They were, therefore, filled with every evil superstition and fear. Some, so deceived, eventually were into a form of "Christianized" witchcraft. Everyone and everything they could not control was eventually named demonic and as "witchcraft," and a demonic myth was then spun around the unfortunate persons who fell prey to them. Deluded persons such as these can become amateur cult hunters, branding true servants of God as acting in the power of demons. Their slander of the servants of God is always of the most destructive kind.
13. To "do spiritual warfare" is to do the works of Christ; it is to preach, teach, and heal in the power of His name (Presence) and thereby bring people out of darkness into the light of God.

CHAPTER 15: Restoring the Christian Hope of Heaven and the Grace to Persevere

1. C. S. Lewis, *The Great Divorce* (New York: Macmillan, 1946), pp. 80, 81, 82-83.
2. Oswald Chambers, *My Utmost for His Highest* (New York: Dodd Mead, 1935), p. 65.
3. F. B. Meyer, *Our Daily Walk* (Grand Rapids: Zondervan, 1951), p. 76.
4. Recommended reading: "The Weight of Glory," an essay by C. S. Lewis published in a book of essays by the same title. Like his novel *The Great Divorce,* this essay is a classic on longing for heaven and immortality and on the honor and affirmation God so desires to give us. For one of the greatest presentations of glory in Western literature, see *The Lord of the Rings* by J. R. R. Tolkien, especially Lothlorien, the crowning of Aragorn, and the return of Gandolf from the dead with a glorified body.
5. *See* my book *The Healing Presence* (Wheaton, IL: Crossway Books, 1989), chapter 12, "Introspection Versus True Imagination."
6. C. S. Lewis, *God in the Dock* (Grand Rapids: Eerdmans, 1970), p. 214.
7. *Ibid.*, pp. 65-66.
8. *Ibid.*, pp. 66-67.
9. *Ibid.*, pp. 131-32.
10. *Ibid.*, p. 67.
11. For those who desire more understanding of myth as a genre in literature, J. R. R. Tolkien's famous essay "On Fairy-Stories," which could as well have been titled "On Myth," is recommended. It is found in *The Tolkien Reader*.

    Lewis and Tolkien excel in the writing of Christian myth. Their novels reflect a Christian cosmos and reality, and their imaginative genius helps to restore a truly Judeo-Christian symbolic system to the modern so in need of it. Most recently, Frank Peretti's books *This Present Darkness* and *Piercing the Darkness* have met a profound need in many Christians. These writings have restored to them the capacity to imagine angelic beings and the Christian supernatural. Many now pray more, and more effectively to our God, knowing that He, in response to their prayers, sends into action even the heavenly hosts! This is the effect of being *remythologized*, of having an imaginative response to our great gospel restored. Also, chapters 8 to 11 of *The Healing Presence,* as well as chapters 10 and 11 of *Real Presence,* deal with this subject.

12. Fr. Thomas Hopko, *The Lenten Spring* (Crestwood, NY: St. Vladimir's Seminary Press, 1983), p. 9.
13. *Ibid.*, pp. 21, 24, 25.
14. *See The Discarded Image: An Introduction to Medieval Renaissance Literature* (Cambridge: Cambridge University Press, 1964), p. 42, and *Real Presence*, "The Whole Intellect."
15. *See The Healing Presence*, "The Presence of God in Contrast to a Sense of the Presence," p. 24.

Index

Abandonment, 27, 41, 52, 77, 83, 97, 103-39
Absolution, 145, 150-51, 154, 157
Abuse, 32, 34, 54, 71, 84-93, 124-25, 176
Affirmation, 21, 28, 31, 33, 39, 40, 45-55, 112, 126, 127
  by a father, 35, 36-37, 38, 40-41, 42, 43, 85-87, 88-91
  by God, 27, 28, 31, 34, 35, 45, 48-49, 52, 90
  by parents, 34, 42, 126, 143
Against the Night (song), 231
Ambivalence,
  same-sex or other-sex, 37, 138, 157
Anamnesis, 74
Approval (or fame), seeking people's, 27, 91, 192-94, 219-22
Arts, the, 192-94
Atonement, 21, 55, 78, 150, 227
Attitudes, 21, 23, 26, 27, 28, 36, 37, 52, 57, 58, 69, 97, 135, 147, 157, 207

Baal, 22, 158, 175, 176
"Bad" mother or father, 37, 123, 124-25, 136-37, 139
Banks, John Gaynor, 73, 205
Baptism, 154, 155, 164, 168, 177-78
Barclay, William, 189, 205, 206, 219
Beasley, William, 33, 177, 213
Being, sense of, 26, 41, 42, 49, 99, 107, 110-36
Bentness, 25, 26-27, 48, 52, 82, 109, 110, 111, 119, 121, 122, 143, 156
Bergner, Mario, 135-36
Beyond Identity (Dick Keyes), 58
Binding and loosing, 92, 153-54, 157-58, 207, 208-12
Birth trauma, 98, 123
Bloesch, Donald, 184
Boerner, Connie, 54
Bond, 37, 99, 109-12, 117-120, 130, 133
  fantasy, 127-32, 134
Book of Common Prayer
Boundaries, 112, 117, 121, 122, 126, 127
Broken Image, The (Leanne Payne), 38, 85, 88, 95, 106, 131, 228
Brokenness, xiii, xiv, 19, 22, 23, 27, 28, 32, 33, 36, 49, 50, 54, 57, 68-69, 71, 72, 73, 75, 76-77, 84, 92, 93, 94, 103-39, 158, 159, 187, 219
Buess, Bob, 35
But Deliver Us from Evil: An Introduction to the Demonic in Pastoral Care (John Richards), 169

Casey, Patsy, 180-81
Celebration of Discipline (Richard J. Foster), 227
Centered (in God), 21, 144, 145
Chambers, Oswald, xiii, xiv, 19, 20, 21, 22, 32, 50, 51, 53, 84, 93, 181, 183, 184, 222
Child, wounded inner, 32, 34, 87, 110, 116, 119, 120, 127
Children
  developmental needs of, 34-35, 36-37, 38, 41-43, 99-101, see *Affirmation*

parents symbolize God to, 34-35, 37, 40-41, 115
Children with Emerald Eyes (Mira Rothenberg), 128
Clinical Theology (Frank Lake), 107, 111, 113, 116-17, 123, 124-25, 139
Codependent, 48, 82, 119, 212
Coleridge, Samuel Taylor, 227
Collaborating with God, 20, 21, 26, 77, 79, 98, 120-22, 127, 135, 153, 155-56, 157, 158-59, 184
Comiskey, Andrew, 33
Communion, 26, 145, 153, 168, 178
Complete Works of Walter Trobisch, The (Walter Trobisch), 33
Compulsions, 22, 49, 76, 85, 108, 112-13, 126, 127, 129, 130, 131, 132, 143, 147, 179
Confession, xiii, 26, 28, 59, 60, 62, 68-69, 73, 74, 77, 81, 82, 92, 94, 96-97, 119, 130, 141-51, 153, 154, 157, 208, 209, 210, 211, 213, 214
Creativity, 20, 21, 22, 33, 91
Crisis in Masculinity (Leanne Payne), 37, 38, 83, 88, 228
Cross (Christ's), xiv, xv, 21, 22, 23, 25, 50, 54, 55, 59, 63, 64, 72, 83, 84, 85, 95, 98, 103, 109, 114, 120, 122, 137, 139, 150, 154, 158, 179, 186, 192, 207, 215, 229
Cross-dresser, 129-32
Crucifix, 63, 150, 156-57, 164, 175, 179-81
Crumbling Foundations (Donald Bloesch), 184

Dawson, John, 210
Defense or coping mechanisms, 28, 29, 98, 107-9, 112-13, 120, 122, 124, 125, 129
Demons, 19, 21, 52, 73, 78-79, 92, 135, 138, 144 , 153-54, 158, 166-70, 172-75, 179-82, 183, 187, 188, 189, 191, 196, 198, 204, 206-12, 214
Denial, 36, 41, 53, 54, 58, 73, 83, 85, 96, 103, 107-9, 120, 128, 129, 132, 143
Deprivation, 22, 26, 37, 41, 64, 70, 76-77, 103-39
Desert Stream Ministries, 33
Discarded Image: An Introduction to Medieval Renaissance Literature, The (C. S. Lewis), 226
Discipling, xiii, 50, 136, 156, 159
Doctrine (theology), false, 59, 78-80, 143, 171, 208, 210, 214, 215
sound, 50-51, 80, 85, 207
Doran, Robert M., 73
Dreams, 94, 96-97
Dying to the old self, 20, 26, 35, 58-59, 62-63, 142, 143, 145, 149, 156
Dynamics of Spiritual Life: An Evangelical Theology of Renewal (Richard Lovelace), 17, 147-48, 196
Dysfunction, xiv, 32, 36, 52, 72, 83, 180

Ego, 39, 123
Evangelical Dictionary (H. D. McDonald), 70
Emotional needs, 28, 31-32, 37, 38, 41, 42, 58, 64, 69, 71, 77, 95, 103-39
Envy, 188, 189

False guilt, 148, 157
Fantasy, 91, 113, 132
bond, 127-32, 134
Favor (Bob Buess), 35
Fawcett, John, 135, 234
Feelings, 19, 21, 23, 24, 34, 36, 58, 68, 71, 72, 73, 74, 83, 88, 90, 97, 99, 103-39, 146, 148, 149-50, 157, 102, 193, 197, 207, 215
split-off, 97, 100, 107, 109, 111, 113, 114-15, 126, 136
shutdown of, 34, 103, 116, 125, 127
Feminine, 36, 37, 38, 41, 42, 49, 91, 118, 128, 129, 130, 132, 143
Fetish, 129, 130, 131-32
Fideism, 59
Forgiveness, 17
receiving, xiii, xiv, 24, 27, 37, 38, 50, 55, 59, 63, 64, 65-80, 82, 94, 95, 141-51, 153-55, 157-59, 167

obstacles to, 141-50
extending to others, xiii, 27, 42, 50, 64, 81-101, 110, 114, 119, 130, 132, 135, 153, 188
Foster, Richard J., 227
Freedom of Simplicity (Richard J. Foster), 227
Freud, Sigmund, 147, 197
Frost, Robert, 35

Gender identity, 36, 41, 42, 85-87, 88-91, 95, 101, 108, 120, 129, 130-31, 132, 137
Gift of battle, 183-190, 202, 209
Gifts of the Holy Spirit, 79, 98, 138, 155, 158, 166, 175, 182, 184, 207, 214
Glory (favor, appreciation), 34-35, 190, 192-93, 203, 220-23
Gnosticism, Gnostics, 179, 207, 225
God in the Dock (C. S. Lewis), 223
God, the Father, xiv, 23, 28, 34, 40, 41, 79, 134-35, 154, 158, 195
as Affirmer, 34-35, 45, 48, 52, 127
as Healer, 42, 52
distorted perception of, 34, 35, 36
Good and evil, line between, 144-45
Gospel of Matthew, The (William Barclay), 189, 205
Great Divorce, The (C. S. Lewis), 204, 220-21
Green, Michael, 175, 175, 179
Grieve, 103, 109-12, 113, 114, 119, 126, 153
Groeger, Guido, 33
Guardini, Romano, 31, 38
Guilt, xiv, 26, 27, 49, 59, 74, 78, 91, 130, 131, 141-51, 157
false, 148, 157
Gulag Archipelago (Alexander Solzhenitsyn), 144-45

Harris, Charles, 182
Healing Gifts of the Spirit, The (Agnes Sanford), 68
Healing of Memories (David Seamands), 35
Healing of the Family Tree, The (Kenneth McAll), 79
Healing, physical, 72-73, 82
Healing Presence, The (Leanne Payne), xiii, 37, 68, 84, 103, 135, 142, 146, 149, 168, 179, 229
Healing word (God's), 20, 23, 24, 27, 28, 42, 51, 52, 58-64, 86, 87, 109, 137, 158, 169, 211
Heart, xiv, 27, 28, 49, 59, 60, 62, 63-64, 68, 73, 74, 86, 88, 134, 144-45, 147, 157, 191, 206, 207
Heterosexual, 129, 197
Holy Spirit, xiv, 23, 34, 60, 67, 70, 72, 75, 79, 82, 93, 98, 111, 123, 132, 154, 164, 173, 176, 178, 181, 192, 194, 198, 199, 201, 202, 214, 215
gifts of the, 79, 98, 138, 155, 158, 166, 175, 182, 184, 207, 214
infilling by, 21, 26, 150, 154, 155, 170, 200
leading of, 69, 77, 114, 127, 176
power of, 23, 53, 80, 85, 156, 176, 190, 195
Revealer, 83, 108, 138
walking in the, xiv, 25, 27, 53, 57-64, 141-42, 143, 149

Holy water, 163, 164-178, 180, 181, 182
holy washings, 175-78
liturgy to bless, 164-65
Homosexuality, 36, 38, 42, 85-87, 91, 98, 108, 129, 142, 170, 195, 197
Hope of heaven, 217-31
Hopko, Thomas, 225-26
How to Pray (R. A. Torrey), 146
Humility, 24, 51, 59, 82, 144, 222
Hysterical (emotionally dependent) personality, 104-24, 126-27

I Believe in Satan's Downfall (Michael Green), 174, 179
Identification process, 37, 38, 39, 40, 99, 116, 129
Identity, xiii, xiv, 21, 22, 26, 31, 36, 39, 42, 45, 50, 53, 62, 63, 69, 84, 89, 99-

100, 119, 120, 121, 137, 139, 145, 156, 158, 180, 197
Idolatry, 22, 45, 52, 60, 119, 122, 142, 149, 158, 175, 176
Imagination, xiv, 21, 39, 52, 68, 74, 80, 85, 86, 179, 192, 211
Incarnational Reality, 71, 72, 79, 109, 142, 175, 182, 184, 192, 214, 224
Incest, 124, 176
Infants
needs of, 41-42, 91, 98-101
emotional damage to, 95, 103-39, 127
Inferiority, 21, 36, 37, 38, 40, 96, 137
Inner Healing (Michael Scanlon), 27
Intercession, 77-78, 185-86, 189-90, 210, 211, 212, 213
Introspection, 38, 58, 136, 146, 156, 196

Jesus Christ, xiv, xv, 17, 53, 58, 74, 76, 82, 86, 91, 121, 122, 127, 141, 142, 147, 153, 154, 155, 158, 176, 178, 181, 184, 192, 194, 198, 199, 204, 209, 213, 217, 219, 224, 225, 228, 229, 231
atoning blood of, 78, 79
Bridegroom, 61, 178
crucified, death of, 21, 22, 23, 33, 34, 50, 55, 62, 63, 83, 119, 120, 139, 141, 154, 155, 181
Healer, 72, 77, 158, 159
identification with, 32, 62, 63, 84, 120, 145, 153, 154, 179
Life, source, center, sufficiency, 26, 32, 40, 54, 55, 72, 77
name of, xi, 79, 87, 153-54, 164, 168, 180, 199-200
One who frees, 50, 53, 67, 159
righteousness, the believer's, 51, 64, 142
Savior, 23, 24, 53, 64, 79
submission to, 52, 58, 60, 79, 93
temptation of, 20
Word, 42
Jones, Alan, 68
Journal, 20, 23, 24, 35, 45, 46, 58-61, 97, 185, 226
Jung, C. G., 39, 169, 179
Justification, xiv, 21, 22, 26, 27, 50, 51, 142, 150, 179

Keyes, Dick, 58
Kierkegaard, Soren, 17
Kilby, Clyde, 223

Lake, Frank, 100, 107, 109, 111, 112, 123, 124, 139
Language, 81, 194, 203, 206, 211
Law, 26, 51, 53, 57, 141-42, 146, 148, 196
Lenten Spring, The (Thomas Hopko), 225-26
Lesbianism, 104-7, 108, 112, 121
Letters of C. S. Lewis (C. S. Lewis), 34, 69
Letters to Malcolm (C. S. Lewis), 75, 76, 146
Lewis, C. S., 34, 35, 39, 54, 62, 63, 69, 75, 76, 78, 139, 144, 146, 189, 191, 193, 201, 204, 208, 219, 220-21, 223, 226
Listening prayer, 25, 27, 28, 29, 31, 52, 53, 57-64, 77, 83, 94, 126, 135, 141-42, 145, 146, 148, 155-56, 158, 184, 198, 204, 208, 211
Liturgy and Worship: A Companion to the Prayer Books of the Anglican Communion, 182
Love (God's), 17, 32, 35, 51, 64, 83, 99, 109, 115, 116, 122, 123, 126, 141, 143, 158
Lovelace, Richard, 17, 147, 196
Luther, Martin, 142, 143

MacDonald, Gordon, 227
Manual for Priests, A (Society of Saint John the Evangelist), 164, 172
Masculine, 36, 37, 38, 41, 86, 88-91, 95, 131, 132, 136, 137, 194, 196, 197
Master and the Disciple, The (John Gaynor Banks), 205
Masturbation, 38
McAll, Kenneth, 79

McDonald, H. D., 70
McLean, Clay, 19-22, 127-29, 231
Memory(ies), xiv., 26, 27, 28, 32, 34, 36, 38, 42, 50, 64, 65-80, 83, 85, 95, 96, 97, 98, 100, 103-39, 148, 149, 153-59, 176, 180, 211
ancestral, 69, 74-75, 85, 93-95
prenatal, 98, 99
Meyer, F. B., xiv, 54, 65, 72, 146, 222
Milton, John, 34, 220
Misogyny, 125, 132, 138-39, 187
Morris, Leon, 35
Mothering, 41, 42, 43, 99-101, 117
My Utmost for His Highest (Oswald Chambers), xiii, 32, 50, 51, 181, 183, 184, 220
Myth, 39, 147, 215, 223-25

Narcissism, 26, 27, 32, 38-39, 40, 192
Nehemiah, 68, 202, 203, 205
New International Version Study Bible, 206
Nouwen, Henri, 159

Obedience, 20, 26, 31, 52, 53, 58, 63, 70, 79, 132, 135, 136, 141-42, 149, 158, 164, 190, 192, 202, 225
Occult, the, 78-79, 94, 166-68, 169, 179, 213, 225
Oil, 151, 164, 168, 170, 174, 178
On the Invocation of the Name of Jesus, 199
Ordering Your Private World (Gordon MacDonald), 227
Oswald Chambers, The Best from All His Books (Oswald Chambers), 19, 21, 22, 84, 93
Our Daily Walk (F. B. Meyer), xiv, 65, 72, 146, 222
Our Heavenly Father (Robert Frost), 35

Pain, emotional, 27, 28, 29, 49, 71, 84, 103-39
Parenting, 34-35, 36-37, 38, 41-43, 83, 99-101
mothering, 41, 42, 43, 99-101, 117
Pastoral Care Ministry Schools, xiii, 19, 22, 33, 54, 97, 107, 109, 120, 124, 130, 131, 135, 136, 138, 150, 174, 177, 180, 186, 187, 209-10
Pearson, Mark, 178
Penn-Lewis, Jessie, 213-16
Peretti, Frank, 191-92
Perfectionism, 21, 27, 136, 143, 148
Perseverance, 217-31
Perversion, 21, 54, 84, 174, 176, 182, 187, 195, 203, 213
Physical responses to emotional healing, 113, 115, 120, 135-39
Piercing the Darkness (Frank Peretti), 191-92
Pitter, Ruth, 159
Poems (C. S. Lewis), 62
Pomrenning, Mary, 130, 132
Prayer, healing, xiii, xiv, 33, 42, 50, 68, 70, 75, 77-78, 92, 94, 98, 108, 109, 110, 114, 116, 119, 120, 121, 122, 126, 127, 132, 133, 137, 150, 154, 155, 166, 168-69, 174, 182, 208
Prayer, intercessory, 77-78, 185, 189-90, 210, 211, 212, 213
partners in, 185-86
Prayers, 21, 23-24, 90, 114, 146, 190, 199, 200, 206, 222, 232
for enemies, 188-90
Praying amiss, 146
Presence of God, Christ, xiv, 21, 22, 23, 28, 31, 34, 41, 58, 68, 70, 71, 72, 77, 82, 84, 85, 86, 93, 95, 98, 113, 123, 126, 135, 137, 138, 142, 153, 155, 157, 168, 179, 180, 184, 187, 189, 190, 192, 198-200, 207, 208, 211, 214-15, 216, 218, 222, 229
Pride, 24, 50-51, 58, 59, 60, 62, 63, 81-83, 96-97, 143, 144, 211, 220
Priesthood of believers, 154, 157
Problem of Pain, The (C. S. Lewis), 63, 78, 189, 191, 193
Projection, 36, 49, 55, 90, 125, 157
Psychotherapy, 98, 108-9, 110, 114, 125, 128, 139, 147, 155, 157, 180

Rationalization, 20
Reflections on the Psalms (C. S. Lewis), 144
Regeneration, 20, 143
Regression, 119, 123, 126-27
Rejection, 19, 27, 31, 36, 38, 42, 45, 50, 64, 74, 76, 91, 94, 95, 96, 99, 118, 119, 125, 126, 130-31, 157, 158
Re-parenting, 110-11, 118, 119
Repentance, 20, 53, 63, 68, 78, 79, 91, 119, 130, 131, 136, 145, 146, 149, 153, 154, 167, 168, 175, 178, 189, 203, 207, 210, 222, 223
Repression, 71, 72, 74, 85-87, 91, 97, 98, 100, 103-39, 146, 147, 199, 215
Resymbolize, 34, 120, 121, 192
Richards, John, 169
Righteousness, xiv, 26, 50-51, 53, 54, 57, 64, 67, 141-43, 145, 149, 205, 210
Rothenberg, Mira, 128

Sacramental, 143, 153, 168, 175, 178, 181, 182
Salvation, xiii, xiv, 21, 26, 53, 64, 70, 71, 141, 150, 179, 181, 212, 227, 230
Sanctification, xiii, 21, 71, 144, 150, 179, 217
Sanford, Agnes, 33, 54, 63, 68, 73, 156
Satan, 20, 22, 92, 142, 153, 154, 166-68, 173, 176, 179, 181, 183, 186, 187, 189, 191, 194, 196, 204, 208, 209, 220
  tactics of, 202-4
Scanlon, Michael, 27, 28
Schism between head and heart, 59, 64, 68, 83, 146, 175, 214
Schizoid personality (fearing attachment), 111, 112, 117, 118, 123-25
Screwtape Letters (C. S. Lewis), 208
Scriptures, 40, 49, 58-61, 70, 85, 92, 100, 142, 147, 153, 158, 164, 168, 178, 179, 187, 188, 198, 206, 208, 209, 210, 211, 213, 214, 215, 217-18, 223, 225, 226, 230, 231
Seamands, David, 35
Secular culture and ideologies, 20, 43, 79, 147, 168, 170-73, 179, 191-92, 194, 219, 225, 226, 228
Self-acceptance, xiii, xiv, 17, 22, 25-43, 48, 49, 50, 51, 53, 54, 57, 58-61, 77, 88-92, 97, 132, 138, 142, 143
Self-hatred, xiv, 19-24, 32, 33, 35, 37, 49, 50, 54, 55, 59, 83, 84, 88-92, 138-39
Self-pity, 19, 21, 22
Self-realization or actualization, 32
Separation anxiety, 41, 97, 100, 107, 110, 117, 120, 121, 123, 129, 130, 138
Separation from God, others, ourselves, 69, 70
Sermon on the Mount, 184, 185, 205
Serving God, 20, 26, 35, 59, 63, 88, 154, 158, 176, 222
Sexual neurosis, 36, 38, 42, 85-87, 91, 98, 104-7, 108, 112, 120, 122, 129-32, 174, 176, 179, 210
Sexual sin, 19, 22, 33, 37, 50, 54, 76, 85, 94, 125, 136, 149, 176, 203
Shame, xiv, 21, 22, 54-55
Sign of the cross, 151, 167, 176
Sin, xiii, xiv, xv, 19, 20, 21, 22, 23, 24, 26, 27, 49, 50, 51, 54, 55, 58-61, 62, 63, 64, 65-80, 82, 83, 84, 92, 93, 94, 119, 131, 136, 141-51, 153-59, 168, 181, 187, 189, 192, 198, 206-8, 209, 210, 211, 213, 214, 215, 226
Sinful nature, old self, xiv, 20, 22, 24, 25, 26, 32, 33, 35, 60-63, 143-48, 154, 156, 204
  defined, 147-48
  dying to, 20, 25, 26, 35, 58-59, 62-63, 142, 143, 145, 149, 156
Social roles, 39-40
Society, evil in, 43, 194-98, 196, 213, 217, 226
Solzhenitsyn, Alexander, 144, 195
Soul, the, xiv, 32, 69, 70-73, 75, 77, 81, 113, 121, 132, 138, 139, 143, 144, 147, 155, 158, 203, 207, 217
Spirit, human, xiv, 69-72, 151, 207
Spiritual warfare, 19, 21, 154, 166-75, 179-216, 228

defined and described, 187
from people close to us, 188-90
in Christian institutions, 169-75, 181, 191-200, 203, 205
planes of, 208-10
Stern, Karl, 37, 39, 74, 109
Storge love, 117
Stringham, James, 74
Submission, 40, 48, 49, 52, 136
Suffering for Christ, 186, 188, 194-95
Surprised by Joy (C. S. Lewis), 39
Symbol, 34, 40, 73-74, 97, 131, 150, 155, 156-57, 163-82, 191-92, 199, 203, 206, 217, 225, 230
Symbolic confusion, 112, 120, 129, 130, 131, 132

Taking Our Cities for God: How to Break Spiritual Strongholds (John Dawson), 210
Temptation, 19-22, 149, 179, 181
Testaments of Love (Leon Morris), 35
That Hideous Strength (C. S. Lewis), 201-2
Thinking, right, 28, 58-61, 148
Third Revolution: A Study of Psychiatry and Religion, The (Karl Stern), 37, 39, 74
This Present Darkness (Frank Peretti), 191-92
Thoughts, diseased, negative, 21, 23, 24, 26, 27, 28, 37, 52, 58-61, 136, 148
Time, 73-78, 94, 115, 158, 227
Timing, 108, 118, 120-23, 126, 157
Tolkien, J. R. R., 193
Tolstoy, 46
Torrey, R. A., 146
Touch, 91, 95, 105-6, 112, 115-16, 117, 120, 126, 127, 138
Transference, 110-11, 116-20, 125, 126, 157
Transsexual, 129, 130, 132
Transvestite, 129
Trauma, 32, 42, 69, 77, 87, 94, 95, 99, 100, 158
birth, 98, 123
infantile, 98, 99, 103-39
Trobisch, Daniel, 36, 37
Trobisch, Walter, 33
True self or center, xiv, 20, 22, 23, 25, 26, 27, 32, 33, 36, 39, 40, 45, 46, 47, 48-49, 52, 53, 61-63, 88, 93, 119, 120, 130, 135-36, 137, 138, 145, 146, 154, 156, 180, 204, 207, 218, 226
Truth, contending for, 185-6, 189-90, 192-200, 205-6

Union with God, abiding in Christ, xiv, 20, 21, 22, 23, 26, 48, 53, 54, 70, 71, 72, 75, 79, 84-85, 130, 143, 159, 184, 186

Virtues, The (Romano Guardini), 38
Vocation, 64, 67, 88, 184, 186, 197, 226
Vows (childhood), 89, 157

Walking in the Spirit, xiv, 25, 27, 53, 57-64, 141-42, 143, 149
War and Peace (Tolstoy), 46
War on the Saints (Jessie Penn-Lewis), 213
Weight of Glory, The (C. S. Lewis), 34-35
Well-being, 19, 41, 99, 110, 111, 123, 129
Will, the, xiv., 20, 53, 68, 85, 86, 143, 148, 149, 156, 168, 214
Womb, emotional damage to infants in, 98, 99
Woundedness, xiii, xiv, 19, 22, 23, 27, 28, 32, 33, 36, 49, 50, 54, 57, 68-69, 71, 72, 73, 75, 76-77, 84, 92, 93, 94, 103-39, 158, 159, 187, 219

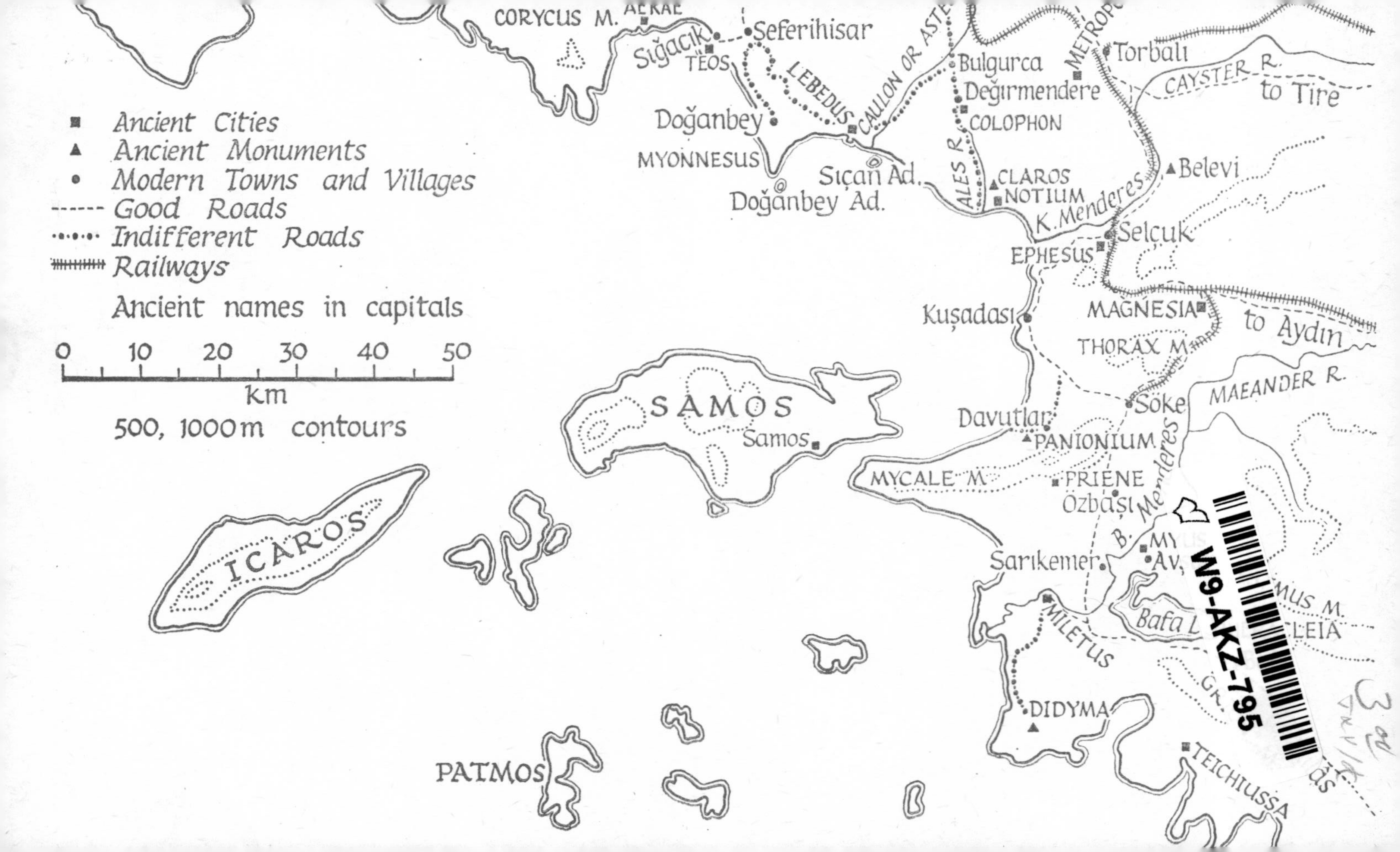

Ancient Cities
Ancient Monuments
Modern Towns and Villages
Good Roads
Indifferent Roads
Railways
Ancient names in capitals
0 10 20 30 40 50
km
500, 1000m contours
CORYCUS M.
Seferihisar
Sığacık
TEOS
LEBEDUS
CAULON OR ASTE
Bulgurca
Değirmendere
COLOPHON
Torbalı
CAYSTER R.
to Tire
Doğanbey
MYONNESUS
Sıçan Ad.
Doğanbey Ad.
ALES R.
CLAROS
NOTIUM
K. Menderes
Belevi
Selçuk
EPHESUS
Kuşadası
MAGNESIA
to Aydın
THORAX M.
MAEANDER R.
Söke
Davutlar
PANIONIUM
SAMOS
Samos
MYCALE M.
PRIENE
Özbaşı
B. Menderes
Sarıkemer
MILETUS
Bafa L.
DIDYMA
TEICHIUSSA
ICAROS
PATMOS

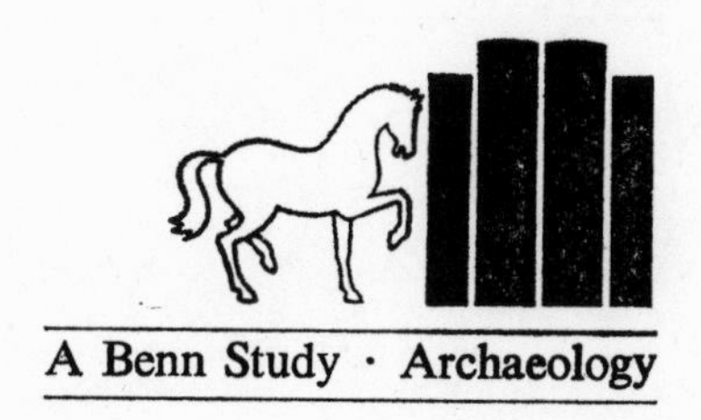

Aegean Turkey

By the same author

Turkey's Southern Shore
Turkey beyond the Maeander
Lycian Turkey

George E. Bean

Aegean Turkey

London · Ernest Benn
New York · W. W. Norton

First published 1966 by Ernest Benn Limited
25 New Street Square, Fleet Street, London, EC4A 3JA
& Sovereign Way, Tonbridge, Kent, TN9 1RW
Second impression 1967
Third impression 1972
Second edition revised and reset 1979

Published in the United States of America
by W. W. Norton and Company Inc.,
500 Fifth Avenue, New York, N.Y. 10036

Distributed in Canada by
The General Publishing Company · Toronto

Printed in Great Britain
by the Bowering Press Ltd.,
Plymouth and London

British Library Cataloguing in Publication Data

Bean, George Ewart
Aegean Turkey. – 2nd ed.
1. Turkey – Antiquities
2. Turkey – Description and travel – 1960–
3. Historic sites – Turkey – Guide-books
I. Title
915.62 DR431

ISBN 0-510-03200-1

ISBN 0-393-01328-6 (U.S.A.)

George E. Bean—a memoir

I first met George Bean in Izmir in 1948 soon after he settled in Istanbul as the teacher of ancient Greek in the University there; and in the next ten or twelve years I was lucky enough to make half a dozen journeys with him in Western Asia Minor. These were archaeological reconnaissances, in which he in particular took over the study of the ancient inscriptions that we found. By this time the younger generation of archaeologists were starting to go round the countryside in jeeps, pausing in the villages only for long enough to enquire whether there were any ancient remains. George was quite different. He was of course enormous—broad in the shoulder and almost six foot six inches tall; and to that imposing exterior he added a perfect command of educated Turkish. Arrived in a village we would take our seat at the coffee-house and for half an hour he would converse in his deep voice with the local dignitaries about crops and topics of the day before mentioning what had brought us there. At first I used to get impatient; but I came to see that by his unhurried procedure he was winning the confidence of villagers and officials and so ensuring that they would do all they could to help us in our search. More than once we came to a village where previous travellers had found nothing and in the end had to stay a couple of days before we exhausted all that came to light.

It was hard work because there was hardly any public transport and our travelling was done on foot. George put up with a good deal of hardship; in a Turkish bus the luggage space at the back was often the only place he could be fitted into, and in hotels he never found a bed that didn't contort him. As he said, things were not made for a full-grown man. But I don't remember him ever being put out of countenance; he took everything in his stride. He was of course a keen sportsman, who had reached the third round in the doubles at Wimbledon and captained Surrey at badminton for ten years.

His travels covered the coastal regions of Asia Minor from Bithynia right round to Cilicia. For twenty-five years he was spending a large part of his vacations in this way. The number of inscriptions that he found and published must run into four figures; in this he had the advantage of an exceptionally thorough knowledge of ancient Greek which he had perfected in the years when he was teaching scholarship Greek at St Paul's. He was very much concerned with ancient sites and their identification, to which he was able to add by his discovery of inscriptions or coins and careful study of the ancient authors. He was a natural choice to collaborate with Sir William Calder on a classical map of Asia Minor in the 1950s, and he was out in Turkey working on a revision of it shortly before he died. Few scholars have discovered and named so many ancient sites as he did.

His later travels were mainly in Southern Asia Minor, where he worked on behalf of the Austrian Academy; and it was from 1964 on that he started on the archaeological guide-books of which this is one. During a quarter of a century he became known in many hundreds of Turkish villages and no one ever forgot him. On the occasions when I have crossed his tracks more recently I have heard of the gigantic, almost legendary figure of Bin Bey and been treated with awe and warm hospitality when it was discovered that I was a friend of his.

His guide-books speak for themselves because he had the gift of writing lucidly and with authority. What his readers may not perceive is that behind the modest *persona* of the books lies an eminent scholar whose massive output in learned journals and monographs makes his name one of the big ones in classical topography and epigraphy.

Edinburgh
May 1979

J. M. Cook

Foreword

Few people, I believe, can pass a pile of ruins without some stirring of interest or curiosity. Turkey is remarkably rich in the remains of antiquity, and especially since the Second World War has been the scene of great archaeological activity, which shows no signs of abating. For the ordinary traveller the west coast in particular is full of interest, but without help much of the interest is lost to him. Many times, in the twenty years I have lived in Turkey, I have been asked, 'Is there no book to tell us about these things?'

Of course there are books. The reports of the old eighteenth- and nineteenth-century explorers, Chandler, Arundell, Hamilton, Fellows, and others, are still excellent reading, but knowledge has naturally advanced since then. In recent times many people have written their 'Turkey books' after longer or shorter visits to the country; most of these are bright and entertaining, but generally unreliable on the antiquities. Two other books have appeared in the last ten years which are addressed to the general public and deal especially with the Greek period in western Asia Minor. The more recent is J. M. Cook's *The Greeks in Ionia and the East*, a scholarly and readable account, from the archaeological point of view, of Greek civilization in Asia. The other is Freya Stark's *Ionia: a Quest*. Miss Stark describes her own journeys, recapturing most sympathetically and successfully the atmosphere of the country; she deals with the historical and literary background more than with the actual extant remains. On the other hand, the *Hachette World Guide* supplies a mass of facts—mostly, but not always, accurate—but has naturally little space for the background.

There seemed to me accordingly to be room for a book, addressed especially to those who have, or would like to have, an opportunity for travel in western Turkey, which should concern itself particularly with the actual standing ruins, letting the traveller know what things there are to be seen and what matters of interest attach to them. This book, therefore, is not written for specialists, who will find in it too much that they know already; rather, the reader is assumed to have an interest in these matters, but no special knowledge concerning them.

My lower limit of time is in general about A.D. 300. Of the Byzantine and Turkish civilizations I have no qualification to write.

The area covered is roughly that which is in comfortable reach from Smyrna. Roads in Turkey are now vastly improved; those shown on the map are all fit for a private car, and others are continually becoming so. A jeep will take the traveller, at least in summer, within a very short distance of all the places discussed. I have myself visited all of these within the last few years, but excavation is proceeding apace and on a number of sites considerable changes will very soon be found to have taken place. Hotels also have improved, and country towns like Bergama or Söke now provide a perfectly tolerable, though simple, night's lodging. Turkey is at last becoming tourist-minded, but it will be many years yet before the atmosphere of the country is seriously spoiled.

Some of the sites included here have very little to show in the way of tangible ruins; but even if the ancient city be regarded merely as a pretext for a picnic and a bathe, so beautiful is the landscape in itself that few, I think, will come away disappointed.

It may be well to draw travellers' attention to the new and severe law in Turkey concerning antiquities. Since 1973 all finds must be delivered by the owner of the property to the appropriate museum, and may not be bought, sold, or exported. Any foreigner found in possession of any antiquity, whether bought or found, is at once suspected of intending to take it out of the country, and if brought to the notice of the police, is liable to arrest and imprisonment. Souvenir-hunting is accordingly illegal and strongly to be discouraged.

My obligations are for the most part to the published works of numerous scholars in the learned journals and elsewhere. I have not thought it necessary, in a book of this kind, to give references for individual statements; in general, these may be found if required in the works listed in the bibliography at the back. I must, however, express my gratitude, first, to Professor J. M. Cook of Bristol University, with whom I have discussed a number of problems, and second, to my wife; the line-drawings, and most of the photographs, I owe to her.

In the spelling of Greek proper names I have used the Latin and English forms which come most naturally to the English tongue.

To write Homeros or Alexandros or Eukleides seems somehow to make a stranger of an old friend. Inconsistently, I have written Claros, not Clarus; but this is simply because in practice no one ever says Clarus.

For Turkish names I use the modern Turkish spelling. In this, as a general rule, the vowels are pronounced as in German, the consonants as in English, except that: c = English j; ç = English ch; ş = English sh. ı is a sound not unlike the indeterminate vowel-sound in 'col*ou*r' or *a*gain'. *ğ* is virtually not pronounced at all. In speaking Turkish names spread the stress more or less evenly over the syllables; in particular, avoid stressing the penultimate syllable.

Publisher's Note

Preparations for this new second edition were put in hand over a year after Professor Bean's death in December 1977. It owes much to the notes he left behind in the event of a new edition, kindly supplied by his widow Jane Bean, and to the help of Dr Stephen Mitchell, of the Department of Classics at University College, Swansea, whose own knowledge and experience of the region have supplemented and revised the text at many points.

Plates 31, 59, and 60 are reproduced by kind permission of Stuart Rossiter.

Contents

George E. Bean – a memoir v

Foreword vii

Publisher's Note xi

List of Plates xv

List of Illustrations in Text xix

Glossary xxi

1 Historical 1

2 Smyrna 20

3 Around Smyrna 31

4 Pergamum 45

5 Aeolis 70

The Smyrna–Pergamum Road 70

6 Westward from Smyrna 99

Clazomenae 99
Teos 106
Myonnesus 115
Lebedus 118
Erythrae 122

7 Ephesus 128

Panaya Kapulu 146
Belevi 148

8 Colophon, Notium, Claros 151

Notium 154
Claros 155

9 Priene and the Panionium 161

The Panionium 178

10 Miletus 181

11 Didyma 192

12 Myus and Magnesia 204

Magnesia on the Maeander 206

13 Heracleia under Latmus 211

14 Sardis 217

Bin Tepe 227

Appendices

1 Eratosthenes' Measurement of the Earth's Circumference 231

2 Thibron's Attack on Larisa 232

3 Achilles and the Tortoise 233

4 The Lydian Language 233

5 The Starting-Gate in the Greek Stadium 234

Short Bibliography 237

Index 241

List of Plates

[In one section between pages 74 and 75]

1 Smyrna. View of the town from Kadife Kale
2 Magnesia ad Sipylum. The true Niobe
3 Magnesia ad Sipylum. Taş Suret. The false Niobe
4 Baths of Agamemnon; the modern installation
5 Smyrna. Tomb of Tantalus
6 Akkaya. Tomb or look-out post?
7 'Eti Baba'. Hittite figure in the Karabel gorge
8 Pergamum. The Asclepieum
9 Pergamum. Round building in the Asclepieum
10 Pergamum. Altar of Zeus
11 Pergamum. Kızıl Avlu
12 Pergamum. Kızıl Avlu; double river channel
13 Pergamum. Theatre
14 Pergamum. Theatre
15 Pergamum. Sanctuary of Demeter
16 Myrina. The site, with Öteki Tepe in the background
17 Hierapolis. Tumulus graves in the necropolis
18 Elaea. Ancient quay
19 Pitane. The Venetian castle
20 Phocaea. Taş Kule; tomb on the Eski Foça road
21 Teos. Ancient quay with mooring-stone
22 Pitane. Archaic statue now in the museum at Bergama
23 Larisa. City wall
24 Teos. View from the theatre
25 Teos. Curiously-cut blocks in the quarry
26 Teos. Re-erecting the columns of the temple of Dionysus in 1964
27 Lebedus. Inscribed stone from the gymnasium

[*In one section between pages 138 and 139*]

28 Erythrae. The city-wall
29 Erythrae. The newly excavated theatre
30 Ephesus. Temple of Hadrian
31 Ephesus. Temple of Hadrian (detail)
32 Ephesus. Relief showing Hermes and the Ram
33 Erythrae. Source of the Aleon
34 Ephesus. Relief showing tripod and omphalos
35 Lebedus. The sea-wall
36 Ephesus. Statue of Ephesian Artemis
37 Ephesus. Theatre
38 Ephesus. Gateway in the newly excavated street
39 Ephesus. Belevi mausoleum; Corinthian capital
40 Ephesus. The newly restored basilica of St John on the hill above Selçuk
41 Ephesus. Marble street and Doric stoa
42 Ephesus. Aqueduct in the valley south of the city
43 Ephesus. Belevi mausoleum; the grave-chamber
44 Ephesus. Belevi tumulus
45 Ephesus. Panaya Kapulu, the supposed House of the Virgin Mary
46 Ephesus. Belevi mausoleum
47 Claros. The Oracular Chamber in 1963
48 Claros. Arm of the colossal statue of Apollo
49 Claros. The newly excavated temple of Apollo, showing the passage leading to the Oracular Chamber
50 Priene. Front seat in the theatre
51 Priene. Wash-room in the gymnasium
52 Priene. The council chamber
53 Priene. Supporting wall of the temple terrace

[*In one section between pages 224 and 225*]

54 Priene. Theatre
55 Priene. Inscribed wall in the gymnasium
56 Miletus. Bouleuterion
57 Miletus. View towards theatre hill
58 Miletus. Covered passage in the theatre
59 Miletus. The baths
60 Miletus. The theatre

61 Miletus. The theatre, with the former island of Lade in the background
62 Didyma. Medusa head from the frieze of the temple
63 Didyma. Temple of Apollo
64 (1) The four 'neocorate' temples at Ephesus. (2) The two ends of the double temple at Sardis. (3) Clarian Artemis. (4) Clarian Apollo. (5) Archaic Heracles at Erythrae. (6) Phocaean seal
65 Myus. The site from the south-east
66 Heracleia. Rock-cut beds for wall-blocks
67 Heracleia. 'Sanctuary of Endymion'
68 Heracleia. The necropolis
69 Heracleia. Market building. Mount Latmus in the background
70 Heracleia. Temple of Athena
71 Heracleia. Walls
72 Heracleia. Walls
73 Heracleia. Walls
74 Sardis. Temple of Artemis
75 Sardis. Ionic capital from the temple
76 Sardis. Temple of Artemis
77 Sardis. Curious rock-formations in the neighbouring hills
78 Sardis. Lydian rock-tombs. Acropolis in the background

List of Illustrations in Text

1 General map 5
2 Districts of Asia Minor 8
3 Smyrna. Joggled arch in theatre 29
4 Karabel. Hittite inscription 34
5 'Tomb of Tantalus' in 1835 36
6 'Tomb of Tantalus' 37
7 'Tomb of St. Charalambos' 39
8 'Throne of Pelops' 40
9 Environs of Smyrna 43
10 Plan of Pergamum 52
11 Plan of Kızıl Avlu 58
12 Plan of Asclepieum 64
13 Plan of Larisa (?). *After Meyer and Plath* 75
14 Yanık Köy 77
15 Plan of Cyme 78
16 Plan of Myrina. *After Pottier-Reinach* 82
17 Gryneum 83
18 Plan of Elaea. *After Schuchhardt* 87
19 Plan of Pitane. *After Schuchhardt* 89
20 Phocaea 91
21 Plan of Phocaea 94
22 Site of Phocaea as conceived by Livy 95
23 Phocaea Road. Taş Kule 97
24 Clazomenae 101
25 Plan of Clazomenae 105
26 Plan of Teos. *After Béquignon-Laumonier* 111
27 Teos. Curiously cut block bearing inscription 115
28 Myonnesus 116
29 Lebedus 118
30 Plan of Lebedus 120
31 Plan of Erythrae. *After Weber* 123

32 Erythrae. Carved blocks 126
33 Plan of Ephesus 136
34 Plan of the Church of the Virgin Mary at Ephesus 140
35 Belevi. Tumulus 149
36 Plan of Notium 154
37 Plan of the temple of Athena at Priene 164
38 Plan of Priene 167
39 Plan of the Sanctuary of Demeter and Core at Priene 169
40 The starting-sill in the stadium at Priene 171
41 Starting-gate in the stadium 172
42 The pancration, from a vase painting 173
43 Plan of the city centre at Miletus 186
44 Plan of the baths of Faustina 190
45 Southern Ionia in early times 193
46 Plan of the temple of Apollo at Didyma 196
47 The starting-sill in the stadium at Didyma 202
48 Plan of Heracleia under Latmus 213
49 Plan of the sanctuary of Endymion 215
50 Plan of Sardis 221
51 Plan of the temple of Artemis at Sardis 224
52 Bilingual inscription in Lydian and Greek 225
53 Runner preparing to start race 235

Glossary

Agonothete. Official charged with the organization of the public games.
Agora. Market-place; the civic centre of an ancient city.
Archaic period. Approximately the seventh and sixth centuries B.C.
Ashlar. Masonry of rectangular blocks laid in horizontal courses.
Cavea. Auditorium of a theatre.
Cella. The main chamber of a temple, in which the cult-statue stood.
Classical period. Approximately the fifth and fourth centuries B.C.
Composite capital. A late style of column-capital combining the Ionic volute with the Corinthian acanthus-leaves.
Corbelled arch. A form of arch in which each course on either side projects beyond the course below, till the two sides meet or nearly meet; the projecting angles of stone are normally cut away.
Corinthian order. A style used in temples and other buildings. The columns are similar to those of the Ionic order, except that the capitals, instead of the Ionic volute, have a drum adorned with sprays of acanthus-leaves.
Cuneus. One of the wedge-shaped sections into which a theatre is divided by the stairways.
Cyclopean. A style of masonry using large blocks of irregular shape laid together without mortar and without courses.
Diazoma. A passage across the cavea of a theatre, dividing it into horizontal sections.
Doric order. A style used very frequently in the temples of Greece, but rarely in Asia Minor. The columns stand directly on the platform without any base, and have normally twenty flattish flutes meeting at a sharp angle. The capitals are of saucer or 'inverted Eton collar' shape.
Hellenistic period. The period from the time of Alexander the Great to that of Augustus—roughly the last three centuries B.C.

Ionic order. The style most used in the temples of Asia Minor. The columns stand on moulded bases and are more slender than the Doric; they have normally twenty-four deep flutes separated by narrow ridges. The capitals are flat; at the front and back (and sometimes on all four sides) they end on right and left in volutes ('rams' horns'), which are the especial characteristic of the order.

Opisthodomus. Rear chamber in a temple, often used to house the temple treasure. Some temples have no opisthodomus.

Orchestra. The dance-floor in a theatre, where the chorus performed, between the stage-building and the cavea.

Parodoi. The side-entrances to a theatre, between stage-building and auditorium.

Pronaos. Front chamber in a temple, usually on the east, giving access to the cella.

Propylon, Propylaea. Monumental entrance gateway.

Proscenium. The part of the stage-building in a theatre which projects in front towards the auditorium; used as a stage in post-classical times.

Stadium. (1) A measure of length, about 180 m., but variable. (2) A foot-race of this length. (3) The long building in which foot-races and other athletic contests took place.

Stele. A narrow slab of stone set upright, generally bearing writing or decoration or both.

Stoa. A long covered portico beside a street or agora or elsewhere.

Vomitorium. Covered passage by which the audience entered and left a Roman theatre.

1 Historical

For the ancients history began in effect with Homer and the Trojan War. Of the two great civilizations of the second millennium lately revealed by archaeologists, the Minoan and the Hittite, only the vaguest memories survived in classical times. There were indeed legends concerning a king of Crete by the name of Minos, who reigned two generations before the Trojan War, conquered much territory, and gained control of the Aegean islands. But of the great Hittite power in central Anatolia virtually nothing was known. Some modern scholars have thought that the stories of the Amazons, who appear in many parts of Asia Minor, may perhaps preserve a confused tradition of the Hittite armies. On Egyptian monuments Hittite soldiers are represented as wearing a long robe reaching to the feet, which gives a distinctly feminine appearance. This is not the case on the monuments of the Hittites themselves, where they are shown dressed in a short tunic; nevertheless, it may help to explain the curious tradition of the formidable female warriors familiar in Greek literature.

There has been much scholarly debate about the historicity of the Trojan War. There is no doubt that its traditional date, 1194–1184 B.C., harmonizes remarkably well with the date *c.* 1200–1170 which archaeologists would assign to the destruction of the excavated settlement known as Troy VIIa. However, there is not the slightest evidence from the soil to connect this destruction with a Greek invasion, and the paltry remains of Troy VIIa bear little resemblance to Priam's splendid city, as described by Homer. If there is any genuine historical background that inspired the epic poets of early Greece, it may have been the confused period of warfare and invasion in the thirteenth and twelfth centuries B.C., which saw the collapse of Hittite power in Anatolia.

Perhaps a century after the Trojan War, and subsequent to the collapse of the Mycenaean civilization and the destruction of the

Mycenaean palaces whose kings had allegedly fought at Troy, a race known as the Dorians, perhaps invaders from the north or a substratum of the indigenous population, came to dominate southern Greece, and as a result of the upheaval caused by them many Greeks left their homes and migrated across the Aegean. The first to make the move were the Aeolians from Thessaly and Boeotia, who settled in the island of Lesbos and in the region between the Troad and the gulf of Smyrna, which henceforth bore the name of Aeolis. They were followed by the Ionians, led according to tradition by the sons of Codrus, king of Athens. These occupied the district south of Aeolis as far as the river Maeander. These settlements seem to have begun in the tenth century, and were certainly spread over a considerable period. It is unlikely that they met with any serious opposition; since the break-up of the Hittite power about 1200 B.C. there was no organized government in Asia Minor, and such resistance as the native inhabitants could offer would be merely local. About a century later the Dorians, too, sent settlers to Asia; these took the islands of Rhodes and Cos and the adjacent coast of Caria to the south of the Maeander, beyond the limits of the present work. The cities founded in the course of these migrations were all on or near the coast. Their relations with the native towns seem to have varied; some at least accepted Anatolians as citizens, but all regarded themselves as Greek cities, and their institutions were throughout antiquity purely Greek.

Herodotus says that the climate of Ionia is the finest in the world; Aeolis has better soil, but inferior weather. Either for this or for some other reason, the development of the Aeolian and Ionian cities was markedly different. Of the eleven Aeolian cities the very names of the majority are unknown to most people other than specialists, and their history is a blank. They remained small, attending to their own affairs and playing little or no part in the main current of events. Smyrna was at first an Aeolian city, but became Ionian at an early date.

Ionia, on the other hand, developed a civilization of quite exceptional brilliance. While Greece was still hardly out of the dark age that followed the Dorian invasion, the Ionian cities were laying the foundation of Greek literature, science, and philosophy. Of the early literary works only those of Homer have survived; they testify to a long tradition behind them. Homer's date and birthplace, and even his existence, have been endlessly disputed; but it is now fairly generally agreed that the *Iliad* and *Odyssey* were composed, or compiled, by one or maybe two poets in the latter part of the eighth century, the *Odyssey* no doubt rather later than the *Iliad*. Tradition said that this poet was called Homer and that he was an Ionian, and the strongest traditions connected him either with Chios or more especially with Smyrna. The civilization depicted in the poems is a mixture of the Mycenaean and that of the poet's own time, but it was the poet's own imagination, not a respect for historical fact, which created the Homeric world of the poems.

Science and philosophy were at first the same thing, and were concerned with the basic structure of matter and the constitution of the physical world. When Thales of Miletus about 600 B.C. made the startling assertion that all things are water, he began a chain of speculation that has led in our time to nuclear theory and the atomic bomb. His successors preferred other basic principles, such as air or fire or even the infinite; the boldness of these conceptions is remarkable at this early date. But Thales' most famous achievement was his prediction of the solar eclipse of 585 B.C. (28 May 585, by modern reckoning). This was not really quite as impressive as it sounds. No one at that time was capable of calculating an eclipse of the sun, but the Babylonian astronomers had noticed that eclipses tended to recur at intervals of about eighteen years, and Thales had his information from them. He predicted in any case only the year of the eclipse.

With regard to the government of the cities at this period we are very inadequately informed. The original system of hereditary kingship did not last very long, and by the seventh century it appears that many of the cities had a primitive kind of constitutional government, with a council and magistrates whose functions were laid down by law. At the same time the influence of the richer citizens and the nobles who claimed descent from the early kings was undoubtedly strong; and in a number of cases the power came into the hands of a tyrant. The word tyrant denotes merely a monarch whose claim to rule was not hereditary; he might have seized power for himself, or he might have been chosen by the people, and his rule might be good or bad. The general standard of living was probably high; populations were modest, not above a few thousand, and most citizens owned slaves; and the art of gracious living was one that came easily to the ancient Greek.

At an early date, apparently before 800 B.C., the twelve major Ionian cities had formed themselves into a Panionic League. The coastal territory was divided among these twelve; the smaller places continued to exist, but without political importance. The League had its religious centre at the Panionium on the territory of Priene, but this bond in no way restricted the independence of the individual cities, who remained free to pursue their own policies and to quarrel among themselves.

The twelve cities were:

Miletus	Ephesus	Teos	Phocaea
Myus	Colophon	Clazomenae	Samos
Priene	Lebedus	Erythrae	Chios

To these Smyrna was later added as a thirteenth.

A number of these cities in due course—mostly in the seventh and sixth centuries—sent out colonies of their own to various parts of the world. The most energetic in this respect was Miletus; in the Propontis (Sea of Marmara) and along the south shore of the Black Sea a string of Milesian settlements grew and flourished. Among the best known are Sinope, Amisus, and Trapezus, all of which have kept their names hardly altered as Sinop, Samsun, and Trabzon. In all Miletus was said to have led no fewer than ninety colonies.

Inland from Ionia lay Lydia, with its capital at Sardis, and beyond this the kingdom of Phrygia. In the eighth century Phrygia was the more powerful of the two; the legend of its king Midas and his golden touch is evidence of its prosperity, and the rock-cut monuments still standing in Phrygia, with their elegant decoration and inscriptions, show that art and literacy were well developed. About the end of the eighth century a new dynasty came to power in Lydia under King Gyges, who at once set about extending his dominion to the north, and also attacked the Greek cities of the west coast. But his plans were interrupted by a sudden invasion of Asia Minor by a horde of barbarians from the north, who for a great part of the seventh century put the civilization of Anatolia in peril.

These were the Cimmerians. Displaced from their home on the north shore of the Black Sea, they moved southward and overran much of Asia Minor. The Phrygian kingdom succumbed to their attacks and never recovered; Sardis also fell to them, and even the Greek cities suffered. The danger of a new dark age was imminent. Deliverance was due to Gyges' successor Ardys, who succeeded in defeating the invaders and expelling them once for all. The Cimmerians disappear from history, but their name survives in Crim Tartary and the Crimea.

Freed from this peril, the Lydians renewed their attempts upon the Greek cities. Priene fell to Ardys, Smyrna to his successor Alyattes; finally Croesus in the middle of the sixth century reduced

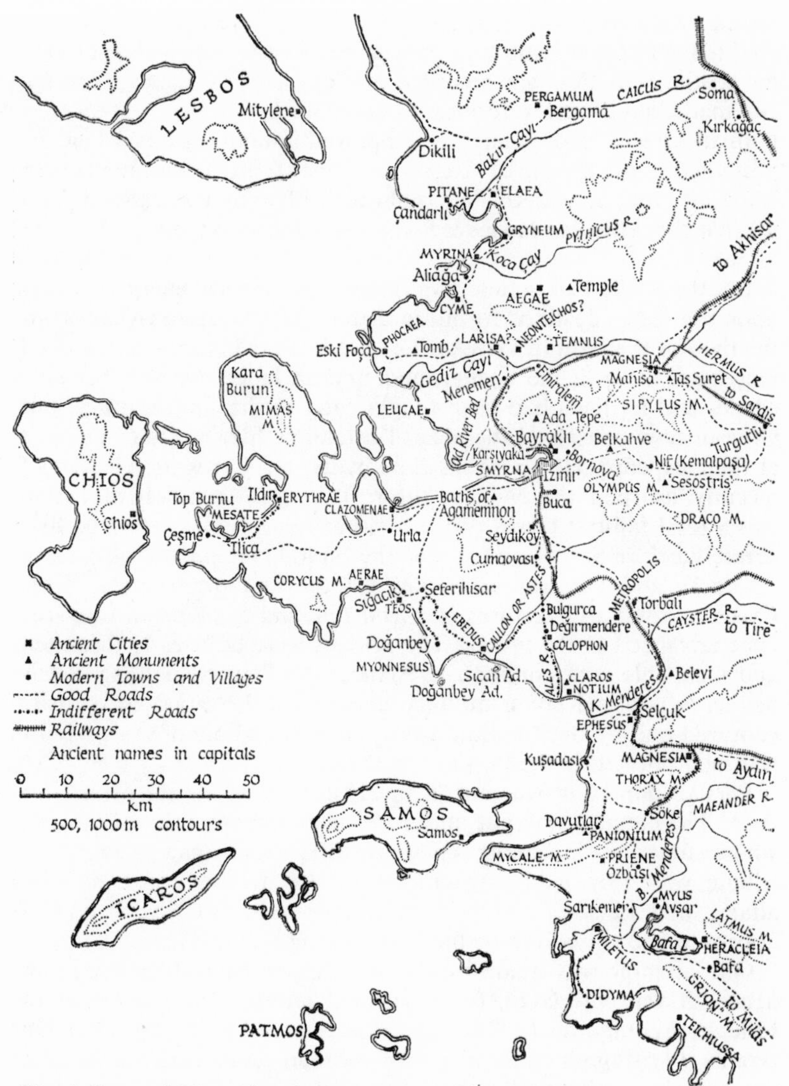

Fig. 1 General Map, showing area covered by this book

them all except Miletus. Long before this there had been intercourse between Greeks and Lydians, and the latter are never spoken of by Greek writers as complete barbarians. The Lydians are, for example, credited with the invention of coinage. Croesus in particular, despite his hostile activities, was regarded more as a friend than an enemy. He made handsome offerings to the Greek temples and oracles both in Greece and Asia; the sculptured column-drums which he presented to the temple of Artemis at Ephesus are now in the British Museum. And it was related (unhistorically, for the dates do not fit) that the Athenian lawgiver Solon visited and conversed with him at Sardis.

But the Lydian supremacy was short-lived. A new enemy appears upon the scene, destined for more than two centuries to overshadow the lives of the eastern Greeks. The Medes and Persians had indeed long been there in the background, and an indecisive war between Medes and Lydians had been fought early in the sixth century; but Croesus now conceived the idea of extending his empire to the east at their expense. He chose his time badly, for Cyrus the Great had recently usurped the Median throne. Croesus' invasion of Persia was a total failure; Cyrus drove him back into Lydia, defeated him severely before Sardis, and sacked the capital (546 B.C.)

Greeks and Persians were now for the first time face to face. Cyrus rejected all overtures of friendship, and the Persian forces at once advanced to the attack. The Ionians were hopelessly disunited and incapable of a common resistance; the Panionian League was neither a political nor a military union, and the cities were easily captured one by one. Within a few years the whole of Asia Minor was incorporated in the Persian empire.

Persian dominion was not in practice onerous for the Greeks of Asia. The country was put under regional governors called satraps, whose functions normally involved little more than seeing that tribute was duly paid; the cities were left to manage their own affairs, and most of them were actually ruled by Greek tyrants approved and supported by the Persian king.

One attempt was made by the Ionians to regain their independence. It was instigated, from personal motives, by the tyrant of Miletus, Aristagoras. In 499 B.C. the cities expelled their pro-Persian tyrants (Aristagoras resigning his own position) and established democracies; with some help from Athens, now a rising power in Greece, they raised an army and advanced to the satrap's capital at Sardis, which was sacked and burnt. But again their lack of unity proved fatal. The revolt was half-heartedly pursued, and the sack of Sardis only provoked the new king Darius to energetic measures. The Greeks at once withdrew to the coast; following a naval defeat off the island of Lade, Miletus was besieged and captured, and the Ionian revolt was at an end (494 B.C.).

Nevertheless, this ill-conceived and ill-managed venture did, in fact, lead indirectly to the liberation of the Greek cities of Asia. The part played in it by Athens induced Darius to embark on a project which he may have had in mind for some time, the subjugation of Greece. The failure of this enterprise, and the Persian defeat at Marathon by Athenians and Plataeans, are familiar (490 B.C.); not less so is the failure of the second attempt by Xerxes ten years later, which came to grief at Salamis and Plataea. The immense prestige gained by Athens in these Persian wars left her as the equal of Sparta in the leadership of Greece, and in particular as the undisputed mistress of the Aegean. The Asiatic Greeks at once placed themselves under her protection, and a league was formed, under Athenian control, with the professed object of maintaining freedom from Persia.

This league, known as the Delian Confederacy, was nominally a voluntary association, and included nearly all cities, Greek and barbarian, on the Aegean coast. Each was required to contribute either ships or an equivalent sum of money. Xerxes, licking his wounds in his distant capital at Susa, had little heart for opposition, and the original purpose of the league was quickly achieved. It might then have been dissolved, but the Athenians were unwilling to forgo the tribute which came in annually from the member states; they severely repressed all attempts to secede, and the league turned gradually into an Athenian empire.

The amounts of tribute collected were recorded at Athens on stone stelae, many of which have survived; they afford interesting information as to the relative prosperity of the various cities at that time.

In 431 B.C. Athens became involved in the Peloponnesian War with Sparta. When this ended twenty-seven years later with a complete Spartan victory, the Delian Confederacy passed into the hands of the victors. But the Spartans had not the qualities required for ruling an overseas empire; the Persians reappeared on the west coast of Asia Minor, and eventually, by the King's Peace of 386 B.C., all the Greek cities of Asia were recognized as belonging once more to Persia.

During this period occurred an episode which, though it had no lasting effects, made an immense impression at the time. In 401 B.C.

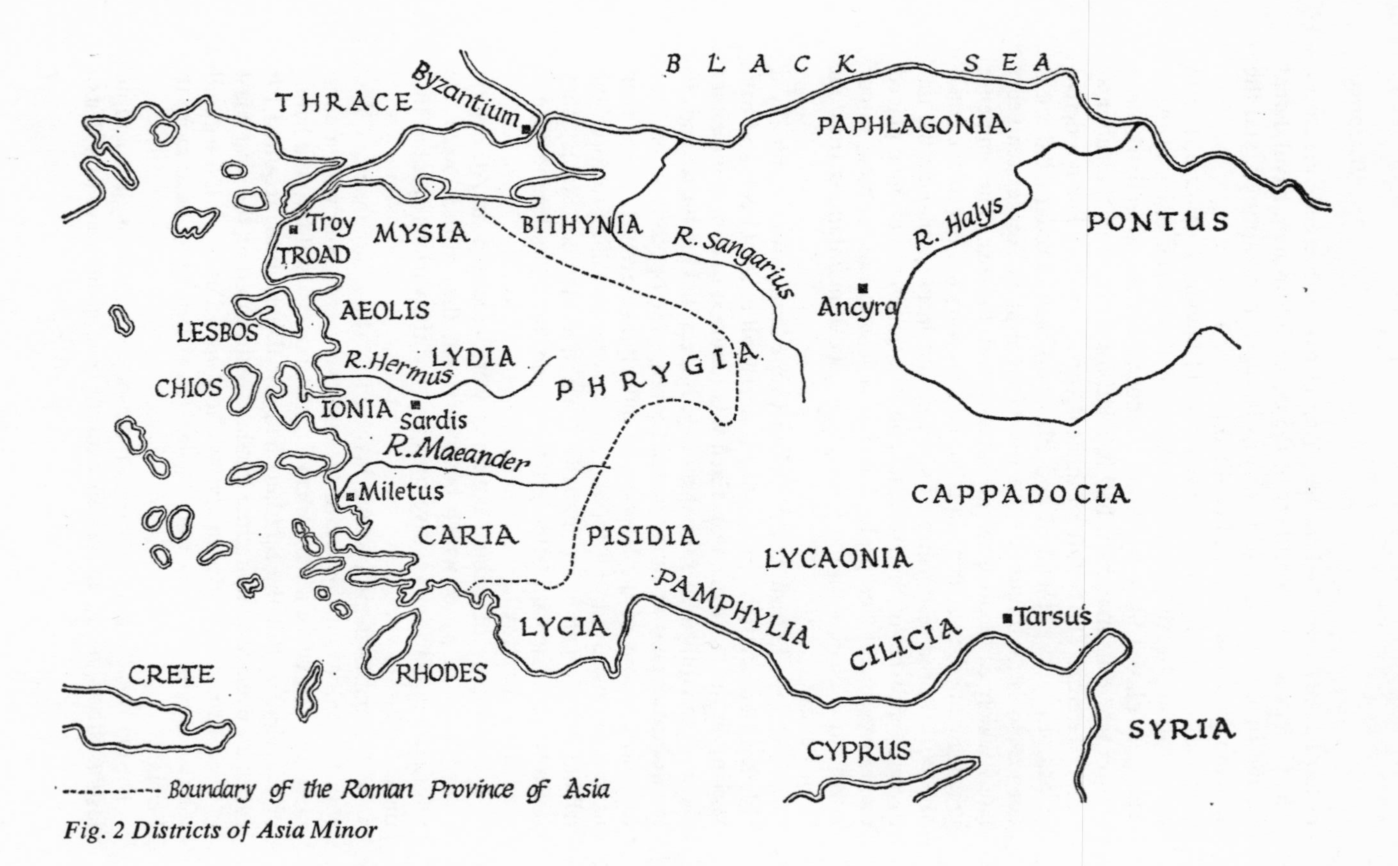

Fig. 2 Districts of Asia Minor

Artaxerxes had lately succeeded to the Persian throne. His younger brother Cyrus, however, desired the throne for himself; collecting a large army, including some 13,000 Greek mercenaries and volunteers, he set forth from Sardis to depose his brother. Among the Greeks was the Athenian Xenophon, who has left us a detailed account of the whole expedition. Slowly the army advanced through Asia Minor and on into the heart of the Persian empire. At length, at a spot called Cunaxa in Babylonia, the two brothers came face to face. In the ensuing battle the Greek troops were in a fair way to win the victory, but Cyrus himself was killed, and his Asiatic forces at once fled and dispersed. The surviving 10,000 Greeks, finding themselves alone and leaderless, refused to surrender to Artaxerxes and formed the plan of marching northwards, through utterly unknown territory, to the Black Sea. Led by Xenophon himself, overcoming every difficulty and danger from the weather and from hostile barbarians, they finally reached safety in the Greek cities of the coast.

For half a century after the King's Peace the Asiatic Greeks lived quietly and contentedly enough under the Persian dominion. Only for a short while was peace disturbed by the activities of Mausolus in Caria. Mausolus' official position was that of Persian satrap, but he had made himself in effect an independent despot and won the allegiance of the Greek islands, allies of Athens, off the coast of Asia. Athenian efforts to recover the islands were repelled, and for a time it looked as if Ionia, too, might be drawn into a Carian empire. But Mausolus died young (353 B.C.) and his ambitions were never fulfilled. He was an able and enlightened man; he reorganized the cities of Caria on the Greek model, and his tomb at Halicarnassus, the Mausoleum, stood throughout antiquity as one of the seven wonders of the world.

With the coming of Alexander a new era opened for Asia and for the whole world. The Macedonians were on the borderland between Greek and barbarian; Philip, by force of arms, had won recognition as a Hellene, and had announced his intention of leading a united Greece to overthrow once and for all the power of Persia. For this purpose he was elected general by the Greeks at Corinth, but he was murdered shortly afterwards and the achievement of his ambition was left to his son Alexander. At the head of an army of some 35,000 Macedonians and Greeks, the young king crossed the Hellespont in 334 B.C. His first act was to visit Troy, where he dedicated his armour to Athena and placed a crown on the tomb of Achilles, whom he regarded as his ancestor.

The conquest of Persia, thus marked as a sequel to the Trojan War, proceeded with extraordinary speed and success. A first engagement with the Persian forces at the river Granicus east of Troy opened the way into Asia Minor. In that same summer and the following winter Alexander overran the whole of the west coast, together with Lycia and Pamphylia; here and there, as at Miletus and Halicarnassus, the Persian garrisons offered resistance, but most of the country submitted readily. A second great victory at Issus in the following year was the prelude to the conquest of Syria and Egypt, and a third at Gaugamela in 331 B.C. brought the final downfall of the Persian empire. The Great King Darius was present in person at both battles, but escaped from both. Alexander went forward to the Persian capitals at Susa, where he laid hands on vast treasures, and Ecbatana; thereafter, induced partly by the course of events and partly by his own instinct for conquest and discovery, he advanced farther and farther into the unknown lands of the east. From the neighbourhood of the Punjab he was forced to turn back when his soldiers refused to advance any longer; on reaching Babylon he was seized by a fever and died (323 B.C.).

Alexander had crossed into Asia as a Greek against barbarians, to avenge the wrongs inflicted on Greece by the earlier Persian kings; but as he saw more of the Persian civilization his views changed, and he began to think of a world empire where Europeans and Asiatics should be on an equality, ruled by a monarch whom all mankind should regard as their own king. It was a new and bold conception, but one which only its originator might possibly have realized.

His successors had other ideas. Upon Alexander's death his generals held a conference at Babylon to determine how to control the vast new empire that had just been won. Alexander was 32 when he died, and left as possible successors from his own family only a mentally deficient half-brother and an unborn son. A move was at first made to reserve the succession for these jointly, but neither was more than a figure-head and before long both were murdered. The power was in the hands of the generals, who proceeded to divide the conquered territories among themselves. For a generation they warred with one another, until finally three main kingdoms were established. The most permanent and stable of these was that of Ptolemy in Egypt; it continued under a succession of kings, all of whom took the name Ptolemy, down to the time of Cleopatra. The second was that of Seleucus, which comprised Syria and, at first, all the eastern regions as far as India; but these latter gradually fell back under various oriental powers. The Seleucid dynasty, under kings named Seleucus or Antiochus, lasted till 65 B.C., when Syria became a Roman province. The third was Macedonia, including Greece. The north of Asia Minor, along the south coast of the Black Sea, where Alexander never set foot, was occupied by smaller kingdoms, non-Greek in origin and established before the Macedonian conquest, notably the kingdoms of Bithynia and Pontus; these maintained themselves against all opposition till the first century B.C., when they, too, were incorporated in the Roman dominions.

Western Asia Minor belonged properly to none of the kingdoms mentioned, but was contested at different times by all of them. After Alexander's death it fell to Antigonus; but his ambitions united the other generals against him, and he was defeated and killed at the battle of Ipsus in Phrygia in 301 B.C. The west coast then passed into the hands of Lysimachus, another of Alexander's generals, who held it till he in his turn was killed in battle in 281 B.C. and his territory annexed to the kingdom of Syria.

At this point a new actor appears on the scene. A certain Philetaerus, finding himself at Pergamum in possession of Lysimachus' treasure, used it to establish a dynasty there (below, p. 46). This Attalid dynasty, as it was called, grew rapidly in power, and Pergamum was before long to be reckoned as an equal to the three main kingdoms. The history of western Asia Minor for the next century is that of the attempts by the various kings to extend their dominion over it. For a time in the third century they were distracted by the activities of the Gauls, a group of three Celtic tribes from Europe which eventually settled in the interior of the peninsula around modern Ankara. Their incursions, which touched most of the Greek cities of the west coast, including Erythrae, Miletus, and Priene, gave the kings much trouble until they were finally suppressed by Attalus I of Pergamum.

Though Alexander's vision of a political union of mankind remained unrealized, his conquests had nevertheless changed the face of the world. One outcome was the great increase in wealth, as the immense treasures of the Persian kings were released; but a more far-reaching result was the permeation of the east by the Greek language and culture. The Hellenistic kings were active in founding new cities of Greek form, named mostly after the kings themselves and members of their families; hence the constantly repeated names on the map of Asia such as Antiocheia, Seleuceia, Ptolemais, and many others. In these Greek was the official language, and in the third century the whole of the hitherto barbarian world was busily learning the tongue of Demosthenes and Plato.

The cultural centre of the Hellenistic world was at Alexandria in Egypt. The vast library assembled by the Ptolemies, variously estimated at 400,000 or 700,000 volumes, afforded unique facilities for literary research and criticism; and if the original works of the Alexandrian poets and prose-writers are not equal in genius to those of the classical Greek age, the achievements of their mathematicians and scientists are impressive. Euclid's *Geometry*, written in the early third century B.C., was still a school textbook in the present writer's youth. To the same century dates the invention of the first primitive machine driven by the power of steam. Alexandrian astronomy is even more striking. That the earth is a sphere was known since before the time of Aristotle; but about 225 B.C. Eratosthenes succeeded in measuring its circumference to within some 200 miles of the truth. There were, in fact, errors in his data, but these happened to cancel out, and his method was absolutely sound (Appendix 1). Heraclides maintained a belief in the daily rotation of the earth, and that Venus and Mercury were satellites of the sun; Aristarchus went further and suggested that the sun was the centre of the entire system of planets. Hipparchus calculated the distance of the moon from the earth as thirty-three times the earth's diameter; the true figure is a little over thirty. Seleucus believed that the tides were caused by interaction of the earth and moon, and was well on the way to discovering the law of gravitation. But the trouble was that in most cases these theories were not at that time capable of proof; they were accordingly not generally accepted, and remained to be rediscovered in comparatively modern times. It is not always realized that most of the major discoveries up to the present century were in fact anticipated by the Alexandrian scientists.

Towards the end of the third century the scene began to be overshadowed more and more by the growing power of Rome. Not that the Romans were eager for conquest in Asia; they were, on the contrary, reluctant adventurers in the east. It was the restless ambition of Antiochus III of Syria that first brought a Roman army across the Aegean. Lately released from their conflict with the Carthaginians under Hannibal, the Romans became embroiled with Philip V of Macedonia, whom they defeated in a pitched battle in 197 B.C. Certain Greeks, dissatisfied with the settlement then imposed by Rome, invited Antiochus to liberate Greece. Antiochus, urged on by Hannibal, who had fled to his court, accepted the invitation. Meeting with no success, he retired to Asia, whither he was followed by a Roman army and decisively defeated at Magnesia-under-Sipylus (now Manisa) in 190 B.C. In the settlement which followed most of Asia Minor was granted to Eumenes II of Pergamum, the Romans having no desire to annex it for themselves. This state of affairs continued for half a century, till the last king of Pergamum, Attalus III, brought his kingdom to an end by bequeathing it to Rome (133 B.C.).

This time the Romans did not refuse. Quickly suppressing a revolt by a pretender named Aristonicus, they organized the territory as the Roman province of Asia. Rome was at this time a republic, immensely powerful in the field of battle, but indifferently equipped for governing a distant province. There is no doubt that Asia was at first badly administered. The supreme authority was in the hands of the governor, appointed normally for one year with proconsular status and assisted by a team of junior officials. In administrative and judicial matters his word was law. Some few governors were honest and upright men, but the majority saw in their province chiefly a means of enriching themselves. A governor was in theory liable to prosecution in Rome for any misdeeds, but his judges were politicians who might one day find themselves in his position, and convictions were hard to secure; a judicious distribution of gifts was normally enough to ensure his safety. A political career at Rome was an expensive business, and it was commonly said that a governor needed to make three fortunes out of his province—one to pay his debts, one to bribe his judges, and one to live on. But a worse infliction for the provincials was the exactions of the tax-gatherers. The taxes themselves were fixed by law, and were probably no higher than had formerly been paid to the kings of Pergamum; but the method of collecting them was unfortunate. The taxes were farmed out at Rome for periods of four years to the highest bidder among the companies of 'publicans' (tax-gatherers); these were left to collect the money for themselves, and any surplus was for their own profit. It was therefore to their advantage to extort the maximum possible; we hear repeatedly of cases where the publicans attempted to tax land which was not properly liable, such as the territory of 'free cities' (see below), or the revenues of fisheries and salt-pans belonging to the temples. On a few occasions their claims were disallowed on appeal to the governor, but in general there is no doubt that they were a sore trial to the province.

Others who found in the province a source of gain were the Roman merchants and bankers who settled in Asia in great numbers. Many of the provincials, both cities and individuals, were before long deep in debt, and were obliged to resort to these companies for loans; security being poor, rates of interest were very high. However, the greatest strain on the province's resources was imposed by the military commanders of the late Roman republic, Sulla, Pompey, and Mark Antony, who requisitioned money and supplies on a huge scale from Asia to support their armies, and who extorted loot and booty from the cities on a scale which dwarfed the worst depredations of the tax-gatherers.

Financial matters apart, it was in general the Roman policy to interfere as little as possible in the administration of the individual cities. Everywhere the daily management of affairs was controlled, as before, by the city council and assembly, and only if the situation grew seriously out of hand did the Roman governor appoint an official to set things right. Certain cities indeed were, in theory at least, entirely independent of the Roman power. Those which had been free under the kings continued for the most part to enjoy their freedom as 'friends and allies' of Rome. These were not subject to the governor's orders and were exempt from tax. Nevertheless, they felt themselves to be very much a part of the province, and most of them possessed a temple and cult of the deified Rome; in some cases this cult had been established before the formation of the province. It was in these cities also that the governor sat to administer justice. Such was the case in Asia with Pergamum, Sardis, Smyrna, Ephesus, and Magnesia.

One last attempt was made to expel the Roman power from Asia. Mithridates VI, king of Pontus, was a man whose huge physique was matched by his ability and ambition. In the course of enlarging his kingdom at his neighbours' expense he had clashed with a number of petty monarchs who enjoyed the support of Rome. Finding himself committed to a struggle with the Romans, Mithridates in 88 B.C. advanced into the province with an army estimated at the unlikely figure of a quarter of a million. Such was the dissatisfaction with the Roman administration that he was almost everywhere welcomed as a liberator; the Roman defence was feeble and the whole of the province was soon in the king's hands. He then proceeded to the step which has made his name infamous. He ordered the massacre of all Romans and Italians in the province, without distinction of age, sex, or status. The order was carried out, apparently with enthusiasm, and in this 'Asian Vespers' 80,000 persons, bankers, merchants, publicans, and their families, are said to have perished. Still not content, Mithridates sent an army across the Aegean to occupy Greece, which now formed the Roman province of Achaea. The Romans, moved to energetic action, sent an army to Greece under Sulla, and the king's forces were quickly expelled. In consequence, however, of political changes at home, Sulla was deprived of his command and even proclaimed an outlaw; a second army was sent under a new commander, Flaccus. But Flaccus was murdered and his command usurped by his subordinate Fimbria; Sulla declined to give up his army, so that the war against Mithridates was carried on by two generals, neither of whom was officially in command. Fimbria defeated the king in Asia, and peace was signed in 85 B.C. on the terms that Mithridates should surrender all his conquests and pay an indemnity, but should be recognized as king of Pontus. Fimbria, afraid to return to Rome, committed suicide at Pergamum.

Twelve years later Mithridates made another attempt, but this time the Romans were better prepared, and the king was unable to advance beyond Cyzicus. The Romans in their turn assumed the offensive, and Mithridates was driven from his kingdom. With the help of Tigranes, king of Armenia, however, he was able to prolong the war until in 66 B.C. Pompey the Great was appointed to the command. Decisively defeated in the field, the king retired to the Crimea, where he died by his own hand in 63 B.C.

This was not Pompey's first success. During the second and first centuries, as the power of the kings of Syria grew steadily weaker, the pirates had established themselves strongly on the south coast of Asia Minor; from there they were molesting sea traffic and even raiding the shores of the province of Asia. In 67 B.C. Pompey, in a brilliant campaign of less than three months, exterminated them so thoroughly that they were never again a serious menace.

But the Roman republic was now entering on a period of internal dissension and civil war which it proved unable to survive. Pompey, Caesar, Brutus, Antony, Octavian, and others played their several parts; under the ultimate victor Octavian, who then took the title Augustus, the republic was converted into the empire (27 B.C.).

For the province of Asia the change was wholly to the good. In the first place, for 300 years the country was entirely free from war. Under the *pax Romana* the cities were able to develop their economy in peace, and most of them prospered greatly. Wealth increased and populations multiplied, till some of the larger cities had something like a quarter of a million inhabitants. The standard of living under the first- and second-century emperors was higher than it has ever been since until quite recent times. The system of administration remained superficially unchanged. A new governor arrived from Rome each year, and not all governors were good; but it was now more possible to obtain redress for injustice. The cities united in a kind of federation called the Commonalty of Asia, so that complaints could be made with authoritative backing, and were indeed frequently successful.

The Commonalty, in fact, conducted all kinds of relations with the imperial government. Important among these was the official worship of the emperor. Augustus himself was reluctant to be deified; but worship of the kings had long been the custom in the east, and the provincials thought of the emperor as they had thought of the kings. They asked permission to establish his cult, and Augustus assented on condition that it be joined with that of the deified Rome, which had long been in existence. Later this was succeeded by a cult of Augustus alone—that is, of the reigning emperor, for all the emperors took the title Augustus. This imperial cult, in fact, played an important part in holding the empire together; it gave the inhabitants of the various provinces a sense of partnership with each other and with Rome, and of belonging to a unified whole.

Another measure tending to the same effect was the grant of Roman citizenship to prominent provincials who had deserved well of their city or of the empire. This privilege was highly prized and extended normally to the recipient's descendants. A climax was reached in A.D. 212, when the emperor, Caracalla, granted the citizenship to all inhabitants of the empire, male and female, except slaves.

By the middle of the first century A.D. the whole of Asia Minor was incorporated in the Roman empire in the form of provinces. Most of these were governed by a legate appointed by the emperor himself; Asia and Bithynia were attached to the Senate, but here also the emperor held the ultimate control. For the first 200 years of our era provincial administration was almost uniformly beneficial, at least as far as the upper classes were concerned; only in the third century did a decline set in. The population continued much as it had always been—mainly Greek in the old Greek cities, mainly Anatolian in the inland parts, with the communities of Roman merchants and bankers spreading gradually to the remoter places. For official purposes the normal language was Greek, though the old Anatolian languages continued to be spoken, and nearly all inscriptions are in Greek; Latin was officially used only in the military colonies which the emperors planted for purposes of security, and even in these Greek inscriptions are also common.

The long continuance of the *pax Romana* brought the cities great wealth and prosperity; on the other hand, it robbed them of the stimulus of armed conflict. Where once the support or the hostility of Ephesus or Smyrna could make or mar the fortunes of a Hellenistic king, the cities were now reduced to striving merely for titles and honours: 'First and greatest metropolis of Asia', 'Four times temple-warden of the emperors', such are the phrases proudly repeated in the official inscriptions. These titles were granted personally by the emperor, and rivalry for them was intense.

Athletic competitions had always been an important feature of Greek life, ever since the foundation of the Olympic games in the eighth century B.C., and they were not less so under the Roman empire. The great festivals of classical Greece continued to be celebrated, and victory at them was still held in the highest esteem; but now every large city, and many of the smaller ones as well, held their own festivals, in most cases once every four years, as also did the provincial Commonalties in the name of the whole province. They included competitions not only in athletics but in music and drama. Sport was by this time highly professionalized; every summer crowds of pot-hunters moved from place to place collecting money-prizes and honours; for those who stood no chance at Olympia or Rome or the Commonalty of Asia, there were plenty of obscurer meetings where victories could be won. Successful athletes were well treated in their home town, for in this field too inter-city rivalry was very keen. The bloodier sports favoured by the Romans had less appeal for the Greeks, but a taste for gladiatorial games accompanied the spread of Roman settlers and Roman rule, and monuments of gladiators are found in many of the cities. In Asia Minor theatres and stadia are thick on the ground, but amphitheatres on the Roman model are on the whole a rarity.

As their wealth grew, so did the cities beautify themselves. Everywhere, in place of the small but handsome Hellenistic buildings, bigger and better structures of Roman type were erected. Temples, theatres, markets, and every kind of public building were constructed, frequently at the private expense of individual citizens; for the richer men were eager to vie with one another in conspicuous service to their city. Except where excavation has revealed the earlier remains, nearly every ancient building which the traveller sees today dates from the Roman imperial age.

The second century, under the 'good' emperors from Trajan to Marcus Aurelius, was the golden age. The third century saw a definite deterioration. In the half-century following the death of

Severus Alexander in 235 no fewer than twenty emperors assumed the purple, many of them barbarians, mostly elected by the army, incapable of ruling an empire, and destined for a short reign and a violent death. The incessant wars in which they were engaged on the frontiers of the empire, though far from the soil of Asia, impoverished this and every other province by the constant passage of armies and the severe drain on the imperial finances. The depopulation which normally follows impoverishment was accentuated by the appalling plague which raged over the whole Roman world for fifteen years in the middle of the century; Gibbon estimates that close on half the human race may have been exterminated. And from 258 to 262 Asia Minor suffered from the repeated incursions of the Goths, whose raids extended at one time as far as the Maeander. This was the first time since the days of Mithridates that a foreign army was seen in the province of Asia.

The following centuries brought a variety of fortunes under good emperors and bad; all was not gloom, but the general tendency was to a steady decline. During the long peace, defence being no longer a consideration, the inhabitants of most of the old hilltop cities had moved for convenience to the plain below; in Asia, Pergamum is an obvious example. Some of them continued in this situation throughout antiquity and down to our own day; but in many cases, as city life lost its importance, the people preferred to scatter into villages to be near their fields; and almost everywhere the old cities on the hills lay deserted and overgrown, to fall gradually, under the influence of time, weather, and earthquakes, into the state of ruin in which we see them now.

The rise of Christianity, and the fascinating story of the struggles of the early Christians with the Roman power, intensely interesting though they are, must be left in the background here. With the adoption by Constantine of Christianity as the official religion of the empire a new era begins which is beyond the scope of the present work.

The sources for the history of Asia Minor are, of course, immensely varied; ancient literary authorities, inscriptions, coins, and modern excavations all contribute their share. It may, however, be useful to say a word about one or two of the ancient writers whose names will figure frequently in the following pages.

Herodotus was born early in the fifth century B.C. at Halicarnassus in Caria. He travelled very widely, not only in Greece and Asia Minor, but in Egypt, Persia, Scythia, and southern Italy. The subject of his history is the wars of Greece and Persia, but he introduces incidentally a vast amount of information concerning the places and peoples he has occasion to mention. He retails for our benefit much that he had seen himself and much that he was told by others; in the latter case he leaves the reader to believe or not as he will. Herodotus was regarded at one time as a credulous dupe of his informants, but the charge is not justified. Modern investigation has tended to confirm much that was thought incredible, and to prove the reliability of his observation. For variety of interest Herodotus' history is unsurpassed.

Strabo was a native of Amaseia, the modern Amasya, and was educated at Nysa near Tralles, now Aydın. His *Geography*, written in the time of Augustus, gives a brief description of the whole of the ancient world, much of which he had visited in his travels. The notes on each place are naturally short, but the description is enlivened by historical comment and anecdotes. He used reliable sources, and his value as an authority is highly esteemed.

Pliny the elder (A.D. 23–79), in his *Natural History*, collected a vast mass of information on all kinds of subjects; he begins with a geographical summary of the known world. This work is an uncritical scissors-and-paste compilation of second-hand matter, and must be used with caution; Pliny sometimes retails information from different sources without noticing that they contradict each other. He nevertheless tells us a great deal that we should not otherwise know.

Pausanias lived in the second century A.D. and wrote an *Itinerary of Greece*, a very full and descriptive guide-book to the southern regions of the country. His work does not cover Asia Minor, but, being a native either of Smyrna or of Magnesia-under-Sipylus, he makes frequent incidental references to that neighbourhood. Pausanias, too, is a valuable and in general highly reliable authority.

2 Smyrna

Smyrna is among the pleasant places of the earth. Its sheltered position at the head of a long gulf, at the seaward end of an easy route from the interior, marks it out to be the site of a flourishing port; when to this are added natural beauty, fertile soil, and an excellent climate, it is no matter for wonder that a city of Smyrna has existed from prehistoric times. The annual rainfall is an inch or two higher than that of London, but most of it falls in the first three months of the year; the summers are hot and dry, though seldom unpleasantly so. Summer temperatures are mostly in the low nineties, but the heat is normally tempered by the sea-breeze, called the Imbat, which rises in mid-morning and blows until evening. When the Imbat fails, conditions are less pleasant. Summer rain is a rarity.

Immediately behind the town, and now largely covered by its houses, rises the hill known in ancient times as Mt Pagus; the Turks call it Kadife Kale, the Velvet Castle. The view from the summit is superb. In front is the thirty-mile (48·3 km.) length of the gulf, half closed at the end by the massive promontory of Kara Burun, the ancient 'rugged Mimas'; to the left are the twin summits of the Two Brothers, clouds upon which are a sure sign of rain; behind to the right is Mt Sipylus, the Manisa Dağı, with its legends of Tantalus and Niobe; to the east is the Nif Dağı, one of the nineteen mountains which in ancient times bore the name Olympus.

The westward view was in antiquity somewhat different. The present northern shore of the gulf is an alluvial deposit of the river Hermus (Gediz Çayı), which until 1886 flowed into the gulf opposite the Two Brothers. In that year it was diverted into its present channel, which seems, in fact, to be its ancient channel, for Herodotus says that the mouth of the Hermus is close to Phocaea, as it is now. When it changed course to the south is not known, but it is certain that in ancient times the coastline ran much farther to the north. A map of 1717, as Cadoux observes, shows Menemen, now some fourteen miles (22·5 km) from the sea, almost on the shore; Chandler in 1764 reckoned the scala of Menemen three hours from the town. The silting process is very visible from Kadife Kale; the navigable channel in the gulf was being rapidly narrowed, and the diversion of the river came none too soon.

The flat-topped hill of Mt Pagus seems destined by nature to be the acropolis of an ancient city. Nevertheless, it was not here that Smyrna was originally founded. The early Greek settlers in general chose for preference two kinds of site, a hill of moderate height close to the sea or a small peninsula joined to the mainland by a narrow neck. Smyrna offered both of these, and the latter was chosen for the original Aeolian city. Beside the present village of Bayraklı is a low hill now called Tepekule (formerly Hacı Muço); this was in antiquity a peninsula, for here too the shore-line has advanced. On this the Aeolians settled, replacing an earlier native settlement dating back to the third millennium. The site was excavated in 1948–51 by the British School at Athens in collaboration with Ankara University, and work has continued intermittently in recent years directed by Professor Akurgal.

Concerning the pre-Aeolian Smyrna various legends were related. One tradition told that this, together with other Aeolian cities, was originally founded by Amazons; it is possible that this is an indistinct reminiscence of the Hittite power (above, p. 1; below, pp. 78–80). Other tales concerned the family of Tantalus, the legendary king of Phrygia; of these more will be said in the following chapter. Yet another tradition said that the coast from Ephesus to Phocaea was held, before the Aeolians came, by Lelegians; this rather shadowy people is located by Homer in the southern part of the Troad, and in historical times in Caria. But none of these legends has received any confirmation from the excavations at Bayraklı.

Of the history of the early Greek town not very much is known. Herodotus tells us that certain Ionians from Colophon, expelled from their city, were received as refugees in Smyrna; this hospitality they repaid by seizing the city while the inhabitants were outside at a festival. By the ensuing agreement the dispossessed Smyrnaeans were accepted as citizens by the other eleven Aeolian cities, and the Ionians kept Smyrna. This narrative is confirmed by other ancient authorities, and the city's change from Aeolian to Ionian is attested by the sherds found during the excavation. Subsequently Smyrna applied for admission to the Panionic League, but the Ionians stood by their resolve to admit no other members beyond the original twelve. These events date to about 800 B.C.

In the seventh century Smyrna shared in the general prosperity of Ionia, and the city expanded considerably; but the country as a whole was much troubled by the aggressive hostility of the Lydians. The first attacks were made by Gyges early in the century; his attempt upon Smyrna was only partially successful, and he was forced to retreat. But a second attack by Alyattes about the end of the century brought the capture and destruction of the city. The site was left in ruins, and for the next 300 years Smyrna, in Strabo's phrase, 'was inhabited village-fashion'.[1] Throughout the whole of the classical Greek age Smyrna was politically non-existent.

Whether Strabo meant that the city was reduced to the status of a village or that Smyrna was represented during this long period by a group of villages, it is clear from the excavations that the site at Bayraklı was by no means wholly deserted. Later in the sixth century, and again in the fourth, habitation there was reasonably prosperous, though it never again rose to the rank of a city. The Delian Confederacy in the fifth century did not include Smyrna. To this 'village-period' also belong the tombs and fortresses on the hill to the north (below, pp. 27–8).

The re-foundation of Smyrna was due to Alexander. According to the story told by Pausanias, Alexander in 334 B.C. paid a flying visit to Smyrna from Sardis and went hunting on Mt Pagus; as he rested afterwards under a plane-tree beside the sanctuary of the Nemeseis on the hill (the Smyrnaeans worshipped not one Nemesis, but two), the goddesses appeared to him in sleep and bade him found a city on that spot, transferring to it the inhabitants of the earlier site. The Smyrnaeans, in accordance with the usual practice before founding a city, sent for advice to the oracle of Apollo at Claros; the god replied:

> Three and four times happy shall those men be hereafter
> Who shall dwell on Pagus beyond the sacred Meles.
>
> (below, pp. 24–5)

Thus encouraged they gladly made the move. Alexander himself had, of course, no time to do more than initiate the work, and Strabo says that the new Smyrna was founded by Antigonus and after him Lysimachus; these no doubt saw to the major part of the building, for Smyrna was not, any more than Rome, built in a day; but Alexander was generally regarded as the founder, and the excavations have shown that the settlement at Bayraklı ceased even during his lifetime. For a short while the new city bore the name Eurydiceia, bestowed on it by Lysimachus in honour of his daughter Eurydice, but after a few years this was abandoned.

Early in the third century Smyrna was at last, on the recommendation of the Ephesians, accepted into the Panionic League as a thirteenth member. During the difficult times of the Hellenistic wars the new Smyrna maintained her status as a free city—free, that is, to lend her support in troops and money to whichever of the kings she preferred. She attached herself first to the Seleucid cause, and was rewarded by Seleucus II with the title of 'sacred and inviolable'; but as the power of Pergamum grew she transferred her allegiance to Attalus I. With the same political acumen the Smyrnaeans were among the first to recognize in Rome the future mistress of Asia, and in 195 B.C. they instituted the first temple and cult of the deified Rome. Their ambassadors were also instrumental in bringing the Roman armies into the east against Antiochus III.

Following the defeat of Antiochus at Magnesia in 190 B.C. the Smyrnaeans lived uneventfully under the Attalids of Pergamum until the formation of the province of Asia. They gave no support to the pretender Aristonicus, and were rewarded by the Romans with the status of 'free city'. When Mithridates arrived, Smyrna seems, no doubt unwillingly, to have submitted to him for a time, since Smyrnaean coins exist bearing the king's head; it is probable that his enforced disloyalty to Rome may have cost the city her 'freedom'.

Smyrna shared with the other cities in the miseries of the province under the Roman republic and in its prosperity under the empire. She was especially famous for her beauty. Strabo calls her the most beautiful of all cities, and other authors agree. Modern writers, too, are enthusiastic about the beauty of the site and its surroundings. But this was not what Strabo meant; he was referring not to the works of nature but to the works of man. Unfortunately, of the many fine buildings which adorned the city in antiquity hardly anything now remains. Strabo mentions particularly that the streets were paved with stone—a rarity in Hellenistic cities—but that the architects neglected to install drains, so that in rainy weather the streets were awash with refuse. The modern city has a somewhat similar trouble, as anyone's nose will tell him who walks along the front at Alsancak on a summer afternoon; the sewage is discharged into the bay, but the prevailing Imbat prevents it from getting away to sea.

Another building at Smyrna mentioned by Strabo is the Homereion, which he describes as a rectangular stoa containing a shrine and statue of Homer. Many cities claimed in antiquity to be Homer's birthplace, but by far the strongest claim is that of Smyrna. In particular, Homer is constantly associated with the river Meles, and the Meles was the river of Smyrna. The name of Smyrna does not occur in the *Iliad* or *Odyssey*, but neither does that of any Ionian city except Miletus—and that only as the home of barbarians.

The identity of the Meles has been much disputed. No fewer than six streams flow into the gulf between Bayraklı and Mt Pagus, but only three of them can reasonably come in question. The most considerable is the Caravan Bridge River (Kemer Çayı or Uzun Dere on the Turkish map), which rises some ten or eleven miles (16 or 17·7 km) to the south of the present city and flows round the base of Mt Pagus into the sea about a mile east of Alsancak Point. This has acquired the name Meles in modern times, but is, in fact, the weakest candidate of the three. A detailed description of the Meles is given by Aelius Aristides, a distinguished citizen of Smyrna, orator and pamphleteer and *malade imaginaire*, who lived in the second century A.D. Many of his high-flown and effusive writings have survived, and will often be referred to in the following pages. If to Aristides' account we add the details supplied by other ancient writers, we obtain the following picture of the Meles. It rises at a number of springs close together in the suburbs of the city and immediately forms a circular lake; it is so short that the whole can be embraced in a single view, rising and joining the sea in the same area; it flows in an artificial channel smoothly and almost invisibly; it never varies in volume or appearance winter or summer; it is navigable even at its source; it has a cave at its springs, where Homer is said to have written his epics. In this description not one single item is appropriate to the Caravan Bridge River, which is twelve miles (19·3 km.) long and varies from a full rushing stream in winter to the merest trickle, or even a dry bed, in summer, and is not navigable in any part. On the other hand, the description applies remarkably well to the stream which reaches the sea a few hundred yards east of the Caravan Bridge River. This rises a little way inland from numerous springs and forms at once a large pool known as Halka Pınar (the Circular Spring), also called the Baths of Diana. From here it flows by an artificial cut to the sea, a distance of 1,300 yards (1188·7 m.). Being fed wholly by the springs, it varies hardly at all with the seasons, maintaining winter and summer a temperature of 75° Fahrenheit. In the last century Diana's Baths were a popular place of resort on summer evenings; today the springs, and part of the stream, are enclosed in the grounds of the Izmir waterworks, and supply the whole of Izmir and Karşıyaka with water. The Circular Spring is now a square pond, in and around which scores of springs well up, probably over a hundred in all. In a corner of the pond are the foundations of a small building with an apse, lying under water; this has no claim to any real antiquity, but several Ionic column-bases and other cut blocks are lying near.

The water of the pond and stream is beautifully clear, but the stream is fouled on its way to the sea by the discharge from factories. The name 'Diana's Baths' seems not to be ancient, but rather to have been attached to the pool in comparatively recent times in consequence of the discovery close to it of one complete statue and the head of another which were thought to represent Artemis. Halka Pınar is still a charming spot, surrounded by trees; and visitors who ask to see it are always most hospitably welcomed.

This Halka Pınar stream corresponds so admirably to the ancient accounts as to leave (in the writer's opinion) no doubt that this is the Meles described by Aristides and other authors of the Roman imperial age. Some scholars have doubted, however, whether it is also the Meles of the early city of Smyrna—that is, Homer's Meles. Two difficulties have been raised. First, there is no natural cave at Halka Pınar where Homer may have sat to write. Second, a passage in a 'Homeric' hymn to Artemis relates that the goddess, 'having watered her horses in deep-reeded Meles, drove swiftly through Smyrna to Claros rich in vines'. Neither author nor date of this little poem is known; but if it says that Artemis, travelling south, came to the Meles before she reached Smyrna at Bayraklı, then the Meles can only be the stream which comes down from the north and enters the sea close to the Bayraklı site. The goddess must in this case have travelled by the road over the summit of the Yamanlar Hills (below, p. 71). We must then suppose that the name of Meles was transferred to Halka Pınar when the new city was founded. Colonists often take the old names with them. But such a transference to a river only two miles (3·2 km.) distant seems most unlikely, and it is far easier to suppose that the hymn in question is, in fact, of late origin and refers to the new Smyrna, in which case no difficulty arises. The 'cave' at the source of the Meles was no doubt an artificial structure which has now disappeared; we may compare the case of the 'cave' at Claros which for so long led searchers for the oracle astray (below, p. 158).

Smyrna has one other Homeric association: here, according to tradition, was made the famous Pramnian wine, the beverage of heroes. Or at least according to one tradition, for there are rival candidates. Pliny, however, is precise: he says it came from Smyrna, from a spot near the temple of the Mother of the Gods. When we hear of it in Homer it is used not for drinking but for mixing in a kind of posset with cheese, meal, and honey. It maintained its reputation in later times, and is described as neither sweet nor thick, but dry and rough and very potent; it was accordingly not popular at Athens, in spite of its aphrodisiac properties. The ancients seem in general to have preferred their wine sweet, and they frequently mixed it with honey; Pliny says that sweet wine, though harder on the digestion, is less intoxicating than dry. If this preference earns them the contempt of modern connoisseurs, this is really no more than they deserve, for there is no doubt that they horribly maltreated their wine. They doctored it not only with honey but with chalk and powdered marble, and they habitually drank it in a weak solution with water. Five parts of water to two of wine was normal; four parts to one was thought watery, and half-and-half very strong. Neat wine drinking was considered quite barbarous; and even in Greece today the popular word for wine means properly 'mixture'. Even more horrific was the common practice of mixing wine with sea-water, which was apparently thought to make it sweeter. The resinated wine familiar nowadays in Greece is not mentioned before Roman times; it seems to have been regarded as medicinal, being (we are told) good for a frigid stomach and causing no hangover. Polite custom required that the water should be poured first and the wine added afterwards. At the same time we hear that at Athens wine already mixed with water was sold in the streets—not dishonestly but for convenience.[2] Altogether one is left wondering what sort of wine the ancients made that called for so much adulteration.

Life at Smyrna proceeded uneventfully under the empire. Apparently unaffected by the great earthquake of A.D. 17, which caused much damage to her neighbours, in 178 Smyrna alone suffered from another earthquake that completely ruined a large part of the city; it was rebuilt with help from the emperor. The year 155 saw the martyrdom of Polycarp, bishop of Smyrna, and the year 250 that of Pionius, both in the stadium at Smyrna. Otherwise, apart from an occasional visit by the reigning emperor, little or nothing occurred to mark one year from another.

The excavation at Bayraklı produced historically important results. It proved beyond doubt that Tepekule is indeed the site of the old Aeolian Smyrna; it confirmed the tradition that Smyrna was at first Aeolian and later Ionian, and it confirmed also the fact and the approximate date of the city's destruction by Alyattes, king of Lydia. The actual buildings unearthed are, however, somewhat unspectacular, and the visitor to Tepekule is apt to be disappointed. Apart from the foundations of a seventh-century temple there is little to be seen. The small finds, on the other hand, are of first-rate quality, and the best of them are exhibited in the Archaeological Museum in the Kültür Park. (It should be noted that there are two archaeological museums in Izmir, the original building near the Basmahane station, which still contains a great deal of material, and the new museum in the park, to which most of the more spectacular objects have been transferred.) Especially remarkable are the fragments of the cult-statue of painted terracotta from the temple, and a column-capital of such unusual form that it was doubted at first whether it was a capital or a base. The most interesting thing on the actual site is the mound of Tepekule itself at the west end of the site. When examined by the excavators down to a depth of 50 feet (15·2 m.) below the summit this mound was found to consist entirely of ancient debris of the seventh century. A pile of this size, rising actually higher than the city wall, cannot be explained as a rubbish-dump; it can, in fact, be nothing other than the siege-mound raised by Alyattes, by means of which he achieved the capture of the city. It is even possible to follow to some extent the course of events during the siege. A mass of mud brick at one point in the mound is likely to have come from the upper part of the city wall, where a temporary breach was effected; at other points carbonized wood and blackening show that the defenders' counter-measures, too, were for a time successful.

During the 'village-period', from the time of Alyattes to that of Alexander, the site at Bayraklı (as was noted above) was by no means deserted. To this period belong the ruins which are still to be seen on the hill to the north. Foremost among these is the so-called 'Tomb of Tantalus' (pp. 36, 37–9 below). Ascribed by early explorers to the remotest antiquity of Smyrna, this remarkable structure is now believed to date to the sixth century B.C.; it is likely to be the tomb of some governor or grandee installed by the Persians. Lower down the hillside to the north-east is a great necropolis extending for the best part of a mile along the slope; the graves are for the most part of the tumulus type, having a general similarity to the Tomb of Tantalus, but on a much more modest scale. Several scores of these may still be seen.

On the summit of the higher hill to the north-west of the Tomb of Tantalus is a fortified enclosure which was formerly believed to be the acropolis of Old Smyrna. Recent investigation has tended to show, both from the sherds found there and from the style of the construction, that it belongs rather to the fourth century B.C. The complex consists of a heavily walled building, apparently a fortified mansion, with an open courtyard adjoining, and a number of lightly walled buildings which seem to be barns or outhouses. The whole is explained as the residence of some influential landlord or Persian appointee.

New Smyrna on Mt Pagus was a city very different from the old. As is often the case, however, when a site has been continuously inhabited from ancient times, very little of the Hellenistic and Roman Smyrna survives. And the enormous growth of the city in the last twenty years has hidden much that was previously visible. Of the wall erected by Lysimachus nothing is now to be seen. The castle, Kadife Kale, at present standing on the top of the hill, is medieval; there are said to be fragments of Hellenic masonry under the existing walls, but the present writer has never been able to confirm this. The statement, quoted by Cadoux, that a tower at the south-west corner is of Hellenic work up to a third of its height seems to be pure fantasy. About a quarter of a mile (402·3 m.) to the west of the castle, close below the modern road, is the long hollow which marks the site of the Stadium, scene of the martyrdom of St Polycarp; it is now completely built over (Pl. 1).

Of the theatre a little more remains. A walk up from Basmahane station through the old narrow streets and houses which escaped the disastrous fire of 1922 brings the visitor to a large hollow in the hillside at about two-thirds of its height. This hollow, approached by street no. 985 from the principal road up the hill, is also filled with recently built houses, but some traces of the theatre may be seen. On the west side a considerable part of the retaining wall of the cavea is still standing, and just inside it one of the vaulted passages to the seats is well preserved. It runs under house no. 11, and may be approached through the garden, with the owner's permission. This passage, or vomitorium, is interesting because it is roofed with a joggled arch. This form of arch, which gives great strength and security against slipping, is exceedingly rare in antiquity. The existing remains of the theatre at Smyrna belong to a reconstruction following the calamitous earthquake of A.D. 178, and the joggled arch technique was no doubt adopted as a precaution against further shocks. A substantial portion of the stage-building is

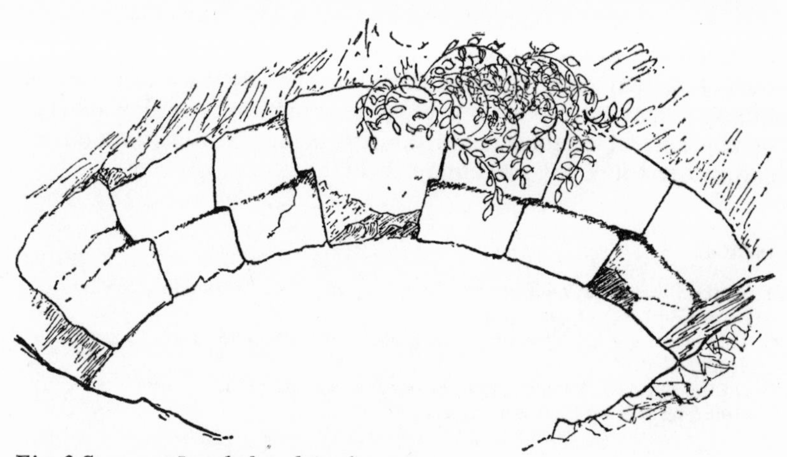

Fig. 3 Smyrna. Joggled arch in theatre

also extant, but it is now lost among the houses fronting the road. If this could be excavated, we should have a handsome addition to the antiquities of New Smyrna.

The agora, or market-place, of the Roman city, called by the Turks Namazgâh, has been repeatedly excavated, and the greater part of it is now cleared. It forms a conspicuous feature of the town as seen from Kadife Kale. The central rectangular space was surrounded, as usual, by colonnaded porticoes, of which many of the columns are standing. On the north side is a large basilica, or hall for the transaction of business; beneath it are very handsome and well-preserved vaults. Statues of Poseidon and Demeter, and a number of inscriptions, came to light during the excavations.

The Baths of Agamemnon lie six and a quarter miles (10 km.) outside the city on the west, half a mile (804·7 m.) south of the main road to Çeşme.[3] The name is ancient; the story ran that the Greeks under Agamemnon, in the course of the campaign in Asia which ended with the fall of Troy, fought a battle with the native inhabitants in the neighbourhood of Pergamum. The Greek wounded were advised by an oracle to resort for healing to the warm springs near the later city of Smyrna. These springs were said to be forty stades, or something over four miles (6·44 km.) from the city; this seems to be an underestimate, but the identification of the spot is not really doubtful. A number of hot sulphurous springs rise in and around a small stream which dries up in summer; the waters, of a temperature up to 160° Fahrenheit, are considered good for rheumatism, sciatica, gallstones, and eczema, and a regular thermal establishment is now installed and much patronized by the local residents. Aelius Aristides, too, frequently resorted there, and he tells us that it was on this spot that Asclepius first began to prophesy. Nothing remains of any ancient establishment; the few miserable ruins around the springs are not of any real antiquity (Pl. 4).

Notes

1 Strabo himself says 400 years, either by a mere slip or possibly reckoning (wrongly) from Gyges' attack.

2 This *eau rougie* in effect took the place of the lemonade and other soft drinks of modern times.

3 On the signpost Agamemnon has become Ağamemnun; in time, no doubt, he will be Memnun Ağa.

3 Around Smyrna

The neighbourhood of Smyrna is unusually rich in small sites and single monuments, some of them of great interest and high antiquity. Two of them in particular even date back to the Hittite empire in the second millennium B.C.; they are the only monuments of that civilization to be found near the coast, and almost the only evidence, except for information found in Hittite cuneiform tablets, that Hittite control—or at least influence—extended so far to the west.

The first is a figure carved in high relief on the steep mountain-side close above the road at Akpınar, about four miles (6·44 km.) east of Manisa. It is a seated female figure and is set in a recess in the rock a few minutes' steep climb from the road. The arms are folded on the breast; the feet appear to rest on two humps, which have been variously understood to represent mountains or footstools; from their rectangular shape the latter alternative seems the more probable. In a panel on the rock to the right, outside the niche, some have thought to discern a hieroglyphic inscription; but this—if indeed it exists— is now utterly indecipherable. The Turks call this figure *Bereket Ilâhesi*, the goddess of fertility, or sometimes merely *Taş Suret*, the stone figure. The whole is badly weather-worn, and the head in particular is much deformed, apparently by incrustations of lime. That the monument is of Hittite workmanship is generally agreed, though full-face figures in high relief are hardly common in Hittite art. It represents no doubt a female deity, probably the mother goddess whom the Greeks later called Cybele (Pl. 3.)

The Hittite character of this figure was suggested as long ago as 1880 by A. H. Sayce; but for a long time both before and after that date a very different identification was in favour. According to the ancient legend, Niobe, daughter of Tantalus, was mother of seven sons and seven daughters, and was rash enough to claim superiority over the goddess Leto, who had only two children, Apollo and Artemis. Thereupon Leto's two slew Niobe's fourteen, and Niobe herself was turned into stone on Mt Sipylus (now the Manisa Dağı), where she continued to weep for her lost children. When scholars first learned of the existence of the Taş Suret they not unnaturally concluded that this was no other than the petrified Niobe. The legend concerning Sipylus is mentioned by Homer and by Sophocles; and if this were our only evidence we might well believe that they had the Taş Suret in mind. That they speak of Niobe as 'on the lonely mountains' and 'on the summit of Sipylus, where the rain and snow never leave her' might be forgiven to poets who, as we are often reminded, are not geographers. But in fact we have much more reliable evidence than this, the accounts of two writers who were both natives of the district. Pausanias is very clear. 'This Niobe', he says,

> I have myself seen when I went up Mt Sipylus; observed from close by it is just a rocky cliff bearing no resemblance to a woman, mourning or otherwise; but if you stand a little way off you will fancy you see a woman downcast and weeping.

Quintus of Smyrna, a poet who wrote perhaps 200 years after Pausanias, agrees with him entirely: seen from a distance the figure resembles a woman, 'but when you come close it is seen to be just a high rock, a fragment broken off Sipylus'. These authoritative descriptions are quite unsuited to the Taş Suret, of which the exact opposite is true; it is only when the observer comes close that he recognizes a carved figure of a woman. Pausanias and Quintus are obviously describing an accidental freak of nature. That scholars were willing, in face of this evidence, to accept the Taş Suret as the phenomenon in question is due to a temptation which constantly besets explorers of the ancient world—namely, before the whole area is thoroughly examined, to identify what is found on the ground with what happens to be mentioned in the fraction of the ancient literature which we possess. In 1938 C. J. Cadoux can still write: 'It is hardly likely that Pausanias' Niobe was a different figure from that known to Homer, or that the latter was other than the Taş Suret; moreover, all efforts to discover a natural Niobe-rock other than Taş Suret have failed'. This last statement, which is really the heart of the matter, was true when Cadoux wrote; but it is so no longer. Immediately after Cadoux's book appeared the true Niobe was found by H. T. Bossert. It is on the fringe of the town of Manisa on the south-west, and hardly higher above the plain than the Taş Suret. From a short distance above the rock presents the appearance shown in the photograph on Pl. 2, from which the reader may judge of the resemblance to a weeping woman. That this is the figure of Niobe described by Pausanias and Quintus cannot be doubted. As for the Taş Suret, it is not altogether unmentioned in Greek literature. Pausanias tells us that the Magnesians of Sipylus possess, 'on the rock of Coddinus', a statue of the Mother of the Gods which is older than any other; and they say it was made by Broteas the son of Tantalus. This can hardly be other than the Taş Suret. After the memory of the Hittites had passed away, it was natural that tradition should connect the figure with the house of Tantalus (below, pp. 35ff.). And the identification with the Mother of the Gods is highly likely to be in fact correct.

The other Hittite monument in the neighbourhood of Smyrna is in the Karabel pass, which leads south from the Smyrna–Sardis road a little east of Kemalpaşa (formerly Nif) to Dağkızılca and the country around Torbalı and Tire. At a point just four miles (6·44 km.) from the main highway the road passes under an ornamental arch; immediately beyond this arch, some 70 feet (21·3 m.) above the road on the left, is a figure cut in low relief in a panel on the rock facing south. It is rather over life-size and represents a warrior holding in his right hand a bow and in his left a spear, wearing a short tunic and a conical cap. Between the head and the spear are some partially obliterated hieroglyphics, not easy to distinguish; the accompanying sketch shows what the writer believed he could see.[1] This figure is similar in style and execution to the Hittite monuments of central Anatolia, and probably portrays a war-god. The Turks call it Eti Baba, the Hittite Father (Pl. 7).

But the Karabel warrior has a particular interest in that he is mentioned by Herodotus. The historian is speaking of Sesostris, king of Egypt in the nineteenth century B.C., and says:

> There are also two figures of this man carved on the rocks in Ionia, on the road by which one goes from the Ephesian country to Phocaea, and on that from Sardis to Smyrna. In either place [*or* on either side] is carved a man four and a half cubits in height, holding a spear in his right hand and a bow in his left . . . and across his chest from shoulder to shoulder is a hieroglyphic inscription saying 'By my own shoulders I won this country'.

When the Karabel figure was first discovered by European scholars about 1840, it was at once recognized as one of these carvings of 'Sesostris'; the other remained for some time a mystery, till in

Fig. 4 Karabel. Hittite inscription

1875 a second figure was found 200 yards below the first, by the left bank of the stream. This second figure was cut on a fallen rock (apparently after it fell) and though badly damaged was apparently similar to the other. It was afterwards thought to have disappeared, but has recently been rediscovered. Under these circumstances it is virtually certain that Herodotus was referring to these two figures, which stood one on either side of the road leading by the Karabel pass. It is true that this spot is not on the road from Sardis to Smyrna, but four miles (6·44 km.) to the south of it; and indeed Herodotus' language suggests that he was thinking of two places on two separate roads; but this (in the present writer's opinion) is certainly because Herodotus had not seen the figures himself and had not clearly understood the information he was given. Hence his other inaccuracies in describing them; the mistake about the weapons held in the two hands is particularly characteristic, confusion between the figure's right hand and the spectator's right hand being especially easy in an oral description. Herodotus' informant was trying to say that the two carvings stood on either side of the road from the Ephesian country to Phocaea, close to where that road crossed the one from Sardis to Smyrna, but Herodotus understood him to mean one carving on each of these two roads.

The mistake concerning the identity of the person represented is easily understood. Herodotus attributes to Sesostris extensive conquests, ranging as far as Thrace, which are, in fact, unhistorical; since the Greeks knew nothing of the Hittites, it was natural to identify the Karabel figures with the supposed Egyptian conqueror. Sesostris is said to have erected, in the lands he conquered, commemorative stelae which Herodotus claims to have seen himself; since he does not make the same claim in the case of the rock-carvings, it is a fair assumption that his information was at second hand (also below, p. 228).

The question remains how a road from Ephesian territory to Phocaea came to pass through the Karabel gorge. From Ephesus itself to Phocaea the way would naturally be through Smyrna, but from the Tire valley, which belonged to the territory of Ephesus, the natural route is not so obvious. The choice would be affected by the lowest point at which the Hermus could be forded, for in the fifth century B.C. there was no bridge. This point seems at present to be at Emiralem, and may well have been so in antiquity (below, p. 71); in this case, the route may have been over the Karabel pass and then westwards, passing north of Belkahve to join the northward road from Smyrna over the Yamanlar Dağı (below, p. 71). If the ford was higher up the river than Emiralem, the easier route skirting the east and north sides of Sipylus through Magnesia would no doubt be chosen.

The region of Mt Sipylus is closely associated with the early legends concerning Tantalus and Pelops, in the days before the Greeks ever set foot in Asia Minor. Some scholars have thought that the names of Tantalus and Sipylus derive from the Hittite kings Tudhaliyas and Suppiluliumas; but in the Greek tradition Tantalus was king of Phrygia and Sipylus was in very early times reckoned as Phrygian. Tantalus was a favourite of the gods, and on one occasion invited them to a banquet; wishing apparently to test their powers of perception, he cut up the body of his son Pelops, boiled it, and served it at table. The gods duly detected the trick with the exception of Demeter, who, lost in grief for her daughter Persephone, absent-mindedly ate a piece of the shoulder. Pelops was restored to life, and Tantalus, either for this or for some other misconduct, was condemned in Hades to the torture which has given us the verb to tantalize. Tormented with thirst, and standing in a lake, he found the waters receding every time he bent to drink. Pelops was later driven from Sipylus and crossed the Aegean to the Peloponnese, which took its name from him.

Pausanias, as a native of the district, has a good deal to say about these legendary figures. 'There are', he says,

> to this day indications of Pelops' and Tantalus' residence in my country—a lake of Tantalus named after him, and a far from inconspicuous tomb, and a throne of Pelops on Sipylus, on the summit [*or* a summit] of the mountain above the sanctuary of the Plastene Mother.

Elsewhere he notes that he has himself seen the tomb of Tantalus on Sipylus, that it is well worth seeing, and that he has noticed white eagles flying around the lake of Tantalus. Other writers record that there was once on Sipylus a city called either Tantalis or Sipylus or Idea, but this was destroyed by an earthquake and its place occupied by a lake. This last tradition was known to Aristotle and survives strongly in later authors.

Since the exploration of the country began in modern times, great efforts and many words have been expended in the attempt to

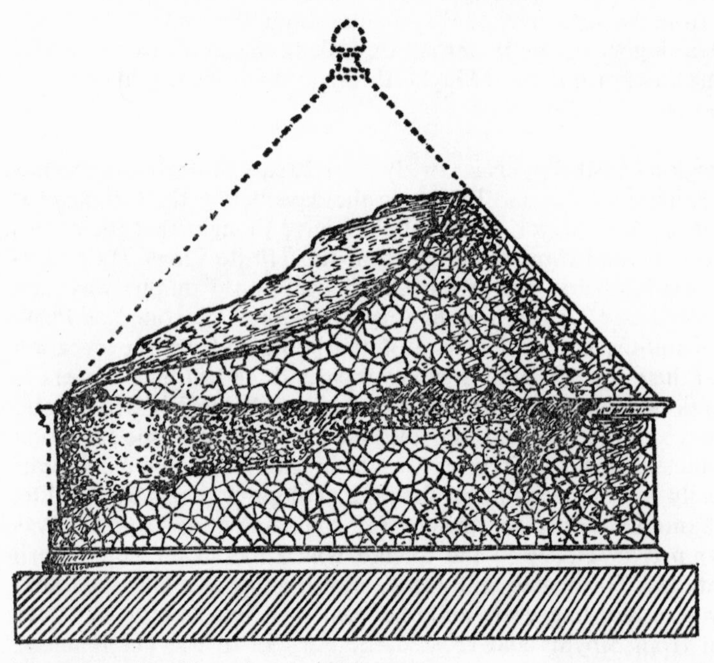

Fig. 5 'Tomb of Tantalus' in 1835

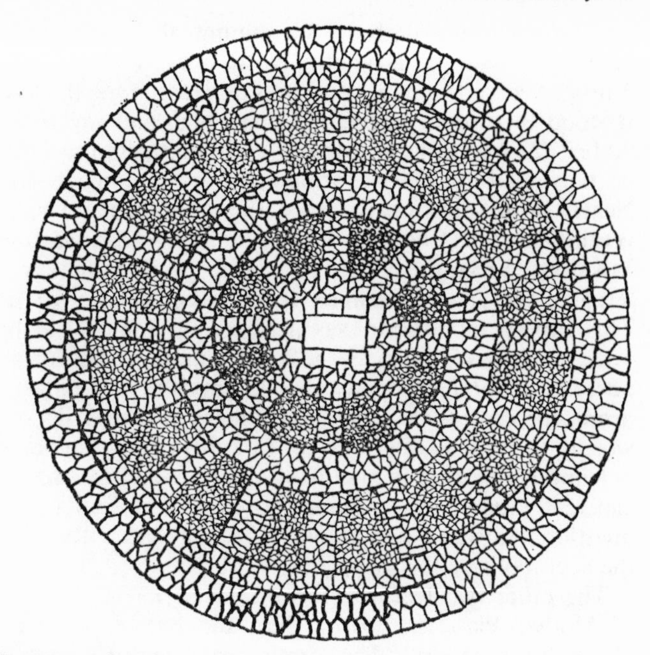

Fig. 6 'Tomb of Tantalus'

identify these various features on the ground. For the city and lake of Tantalus no satisfactory results have been achieved, and the whole problem has been complicated by the uncertainty whether the Yamanlar Dağı can fairly be reckoned a part of Sipylus. There is near the summit of the Yamanlar Dağı a small but deep lake, surrounded by pinewoods and accessible by a bad road from the Yamanlar sanatorium; it is called Karagöl. That there was ever a city in this position is improbable in the extreme; nevertheless it is not unlikely that this is the 'lake of Tantalus' which went under that name in Pausanias' time; the eagles that he saw there suggest that it lay high up.

In the identification of the other items, the tomb of Tantalus, the throne of Pelops, and the sanctuary of Mother Plastene, opinions may be grouped into two schools, the Smyrnaean which finds them all on the Yamanlar Dağı, and the Magnesian which finds them all in the vicinity of Manisa.

The founder of the 'Smyrnaean' school was the Frenchman Texier, who visited Smyrna in 1835. His attention was caught by a fine circular built tomb on the summit of the rise immediately behind the village of Bayraklı; he at once dubbed it the Tomb of Tantalus, which name it continues to bear among the local residents. It stood then some 40 feet (12·2 m.) high and was originally about 90 feet (27·4 m.); it consisted of a circular drum with an outer wall of polygonal masonry, surmounted by a conical superstructure. Nearly in the centre is the grave-chamber, of regular masonry converging towards the top, leaving a gap which was covered by a cap-stone. From this chamber internal walls radiate to the circumference, the spaces between them being filled with small stones. This superb monument was deliberately demolished by Texier in order to discover its mode of construction, an act for which he has never been forgiven; today all that survives is the lower part of the drum, the central chamber, and a mass of stones. That this tomb is worthy to rank as the tomb of Tantalus cannot be denied, and it is not impossible that it may have done so in Pausanias' day; that it can really date back to the supposed time of Tantalus is out of the question. As was noted above, it belongs evidently with the rest of the necropolis on the slopes below (Pl. 5).

The other two features, the throne of Pelops and the sanctuary of Mother Plastene, go together; the throne, we are told, stood above the sanctuary. The 'Smyrnaeans' find them in the heart of the Yamanlar, in the great hollow on the south side of the summit. Close above the village of Sancaklı, on a hill formerly known as Ada Tepe, is a fortified enclosure surrounding two peaks of rock; the southern of these is cut away at one corner to form a kind of chamber open to the sky (below, p. 42). This chamber was identified with the sanctuary of Mother Plastene, and until recently was called locally the 'hiéron de Cybèle', since Plastene is certainly a name for Cybele, the Mother of the Gods. The throne of Pelops was then to be looked for higher up, and was found in a conspicuous peak of rock between Ada Tepe and the summit; seen from below this peak bears some resemblance to a seat with a sloping back. In 1945 the 'chamber' on Ada Tepe was excavated by the present writer in collaboration with Rüstem Duyuran, then Director of the Izmir Museum; it proved to be a cistern, and the whole site is evidently a military outpost. These identifications accordingly fall to the ground, and no others are offered in their place.

The 'Magnesian' school, on the other hand, finds all the monuments in question within a small area to the east of Manisa.

About a mile (1·61 km.) east of the Taş Suret, at the very foot of Sipylus where the mountain meets the plain, is a rock-cut tomb of remarkable, if not unique, design. In front is a platform approached by a flight of steps; from it a door leads to two rock-cut chambers, one behind the other. Both chambers are quite plain apart from a shallow 'pillow' for the dead man's head. Above the door the façade slopes backward, following the line of the mountain-face; all round it a trench is cut in the rock, which has the effect of delineating the monument and of protecting it from the rain-water. This tomb was formerly known as the tomb of St Charalambos, but seems now to have no name. It is undoubtedly very ancient and may well be Pausanias' tomb of Tantalus.

Fig. 7 'Tomb of St Charalambos'

But the 'Magnesians' ' strongest card is the sanctuary of Mother Plastene. This sanctuary was definitely located, at least for Roman times, by discoveries made in 1887 at a point on the plain one hour east of Manisa and some fifteen minutes from the Taş Suret. Two inscriptions were found actually naming Mother Plastene. Unless therefore we are prepared to suppose that the sanctuary was transplanted, any location of it in the neighbourhood of Smyrna is excluded. And since the inscriptions are roughly contemporary with Pausanias, the sanctuary which he mentions as existing in his time can certainly be no other than this. It is likely therefore that Mother Plastene and the Mother of the Gods whose statue (the Taş Suret) was made by Broteas, are one and the same; the sanctuary, for

Fig. 8 'Throne of Pelops'

which there was no room on the steep mountainside, stood a short distance away on the plain.

The throne of Pelops must accordingly be sought on Mt Sipylus not far from this spot, and a plausible identification is, in fact, forthcoming. Some two-thirds of the way from the Taş Suret to the 'tomb of St Charalambos' is a great cleft in the mountainside known as Yarıkkaya; on the west side of this, some 900 feet (274·3 m.) up and accessible at present only by a perilous 'chimney', is an interesting and certainly very ancient site. It is on a steep rock slope some 150 yards (137·2 m.) in length, in which are cut half a dozen cisterns and the lower parts of a score of houses which were perhaps finished with sun-dried brick. And at the very top, in a steeply sloping rock, is a cutting resembling a large seat. This was perhaps originally an altar, but in view of its shape and size it may well have passed in antiquity under the name of the Throne of Pelops. The rest of the site has been claimed as the city of Tantalus mentioned above, but is distinctly exiguous for the part.

On all counts therefore the 'Magnesians' have the best of the argument.

The other sites in the vicinity of Smyrna are military, connected primarily with the new city founded by the desire of Alexander, and form a strong ring of defensive outposts.

The most important is that on Belkahve. Where the main road from Smyrna to Sardis crosses the pass from the plain of Bornova to that of Turgutlu, directly above the road on the left is a conical hill conspicuous from Smyrna and all parts of the plain. The west face is steep, and the hill is more easily ascended from the south and east. The summit is encircled by a ring-wall whose line may be easily traced, though seldom more than a single course is visible above ground. From the summit two interior walls run down to the ring-wall, forming an inner enclosure. Near the summit is a pit which may have served as a water-tank. At various points on the site more than a dozen rectangular sockets have been cut in the rock; these originally held stelae carrying inscriptions. One of these stelae is in the Izmir Museum; it records the presentation of golden crowns by the defenders of the fort to their commander and his family. An inscription to similar effect is still standing on the site, on a stone in the line of the ring-wall near the north-east corner, so weathered as to be almost illegible. It is probable that all the sockets held inscriptions in similar terms. The two mentioned date from about the end of the second century B.C., and the abundant sherds lying around the summit are of similar date. But the site was occupied in much earlier times than this. On the west side a steep glen leads down the hillside, and this is barred at its lower end by a massive wall nearly 20 feet (6·10 m.) thick, of very ancient appearance; in the filling of this wall archaic sherds have been found, and it dates no doubt to the time of the early Smyrna at Bayraklı. Indeed, this site, dominating the approach from the east, is such an essential key-point that its possession must always have been indispensable to the occupants of Smyrna.

The Belkahve fortress was supported by two other strong-points, one to the east and one to the west. About six miles (9·65 km.) south-east of Kemalpaşa, at the north foot of Mahmut Dağı, the ancient Mt Draco, behind the village of Kızılca, rises a high rock of whitish appearance called Akkaya. On the summit of this are numerous rock-cuttings, and on a smoothed rock-wall on the south side are cut inscriptions of similar date and similar content to those on Belkahve. The summit commands an extensive prospect and overlooks the main highway to Sardis and the east. The north face is precipitous, but quite easy to climb; in it is an interesting rock-cut monument whose purpose is disputed. Rough steps lead up to a double chamber divided by a central pillar; at the back is a bench. On the façade, to either side of the pillar, sloping lines have been cut to suggest a pediment; on the right only one line has been cut.

At the left side is a narrow channel in the sloping rock-face, apparently intended to carry off rain-water. This monument has been variously understood as a look-out post or, with greater probability, as a tomb. The absence of a grave-chamber and the inadequate provision for a burial have been explained as due to the tomb being unfinished. Its date is difficult or impossible to determine (Pl. 6).

Just outside the town of Bornova on the north-west, a few feet only above the plain, are the ruins of another fort, now converted into a farmyard. Little remains of the original walls, those now standing being modern; but the foundations of seven round towers are still clearly visible. Nothing else remains. If this structure is genuinely ancient (which some scholars have doubted), it is most naturally explained as a military installation in support of the greater fortress at Belkahve. It can hardly be more than a barracks, as its position is weak in the extreme, being easily commanded from the slope above.

The northern approaches to Smyrna were similarly defended by a group of forts, of which the most important is on Ada Tepe. This site is on a steep hill close above the village of Sancaklı, to which a road leads in about two and a half hours from Karşıyaka through the village of Alurca (formerly Gövdelin). The fort is now known as Sancaklı Kalesi. The hill rises to two peaks of rock connected by a ridge; that on the south forms a sheer precipice over 100 feet (91·4 m.) high, easily visible from Smyrna and called locally Ölüm Kayası, 'the rock of death'. The upper part of the hill is enclosed by a ring-wall of varying style and quality; the best-preserved piece, on the west, is of polygonal masonry with a strong tendency to coursing, a style peculiar to the Hellenistic period. On the summit of the southern peak is a shallow water-trap, and in the eastern corner of this peak is a rectangular recess some 20 feet by 12 feet (6·10 by 3·66 m.), in the floor of which is a cistern of regular masonry. This is the spot which was formerly believed to be the sanctuary of the Plastene Mother (above, p. 38). The cistern was fed by a channel leading down from the water-trap above. It is not certain when this fort was originally constructed, but it is clear from the evidence of the sherds that its main occupation was in Hellenistic times. Placed some 1,300 feet (396·2 m.) above sea-level, about half-way from the coast to the summit of Yamanlar Dağı, it is well situated to command the route over the mountain from the north.

The fort on Ada Tepe, like that at Belkahve, was supported by two subsidiary strongpoints. One of these, now called Çobanpınarı,

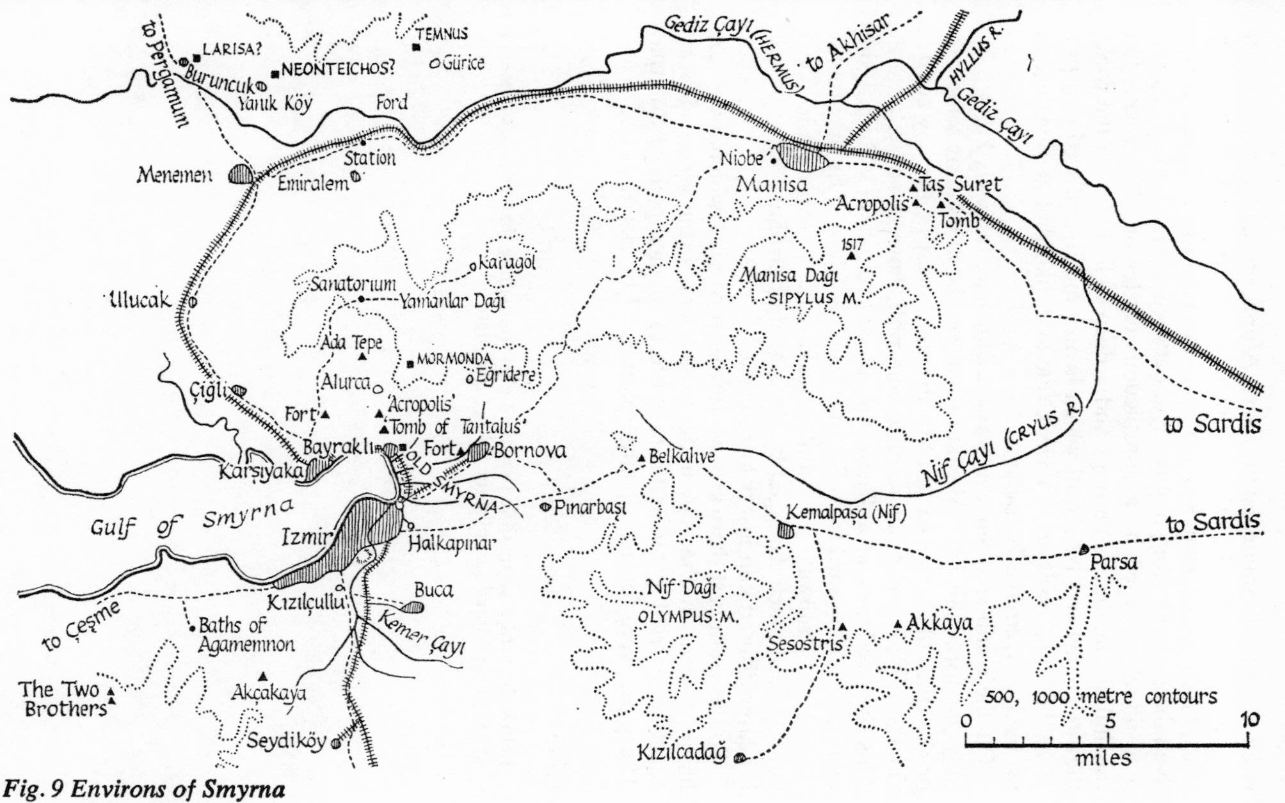

Fig. 9 Environs of Smyrna

is on a steep hill immediately above Alurca on the east; it is small and unimpressive. The other is low down, close beside the modern road which leads from Karşıyaka to the sanatorium. Some forty-five minutes walk from Soğukkuyu, between the road and a stream, is a hillock crowned by a conspicuous cluster of white rocks. On this hill are numerous cuttings and a deep well sunk into the rock; the site is enclosed by a wall which is now mostly reduced to a pile of rubble. The position is a weak one and, like that at Bornova, it probably served as a barracks.

On the south side Smyrna was defended, so far as is known, by only one fort. This is at Akçakaya, among the mountains some five or six miles (8·01 or 9·65 km.) to the south-west of the city centre. On the hilltop are remains of a ring-wall, houses, and a cistern. This site overlooks, at a distance of about two miles (3·22 km.), the main route southward from Smyrna which is followed by the present highroad and railway; it is similar in character to that at Ada Tepe, but has been much damaged by the activities of lime-burners; there is a large disused kiln just below the site.

To the south-east there are two further fortresses, which the writer has not seen, in the region of Arap Dere. From there also an aqueduct carried water under pressure to the acropolis of Smyrna. The pipes were formed of large perforated blocks of stone.

Note

1 Below the bird it is possible in some lights to imagine that one sees the shape of an animal resembling a dog facing left.

4 Pergamum

Of all the cities in this region, the situation of Pergamum is unquestionably the most impressive. The first view of the hill on approaching from the south is not easily forgotten. Smyrna on Mt Pagus is superbly placed, but for sheer power and majesty the citadel of Pergamum is unrivalled. A royal city indeed. Some 1,300 feet (396·2 m.) in height, it rises between two streams, tributaries of the Caicus. Steep, almost precipitous, on all sides but one, it forms a type of city site much favoured in antiquity; Athens is a familiar example. Lying back some distance from the sea, however, it was not occupied by the early Greek settlers in the age of the migration, and played no part in the great upsurge of culture in the archaic period. Sherds found in the excavation show that there was a settlement of some sort on the hill at least by the eighth century B.C., but this was not a Greek city. Its distance from the coast is also the reason why it was not included in the Athenian maritime confederacy in the fifth century.

Pergamum makes a first fleeting appearance in history in 399 B.C. —the year of Socrates' condemnation in Athens. At that time the Spartans, fresh from their resounding defeat of the Athenians in the Peloponnesian War, were disputing with the Persians possession of the west coast. Xenophon, safely returned from his adventures in the interior of the Persian empire, decided to offer his services to the Spartan commander, and Pergamum was the scene of their meeting. The town was held by the descendants of a Greek who had betrayed his city to the Persians at the time of Darius' invasion in 490 B.C., and had been rewarded by the Great King for his treachery by the gift of land in this neighbourhood. His family, though nominally Persian subjects, were in effect independent rulers of their domain, and readily entertained the Greek forces fighting against Persia.

After this incident nothing is heard of Pergamum until after the death of Alexander. When Lysimachus came into control of western Asia Minor and found himself in possession of a vast treasure from the spoils of conquest, he deposited a part of this treasure at Pergamum; the sum is said to have been 9,000 talents. To guard this treasury he appointed a certain Paphlagonian by the name of Philetaerus. When Lysimachus was killed in battle in 281 B.C., the country came largely under the hand of Antiochus, king of Syria; Philetaerus, however, remained in control of Pergamum and the treasure, and no serious effort was made to dislodge him.

From this point begins the emergence of Pergamum as a power in the Hellenistic world. Philetaerus lived until 263 B.C., and devoted his energies to establishing his position. His wealth can hardly be called ill-gotten, as Lysimachus left no heir to claim it, and Philetaerus' title to it was as good as another's; and he used it sensibly. By means of handsome dedications and gifts of money in time of need he won the favour of the neighbouring cities and kept on good terms with Antiochus; at the same time he embellished his city with temples and other new buildings.

Eumenes, adopted son and successor of Philetaerus, was accordingly able to take over a firmly established dynasty. Eumenes is reckoned the first of the kings of Pergamum, though, in fact, neither he nor Philetaerus ever formally took that title. He enlarged the city's territory in the near neighbourhood, but otherwise little is recorded of him. An inscription tells us that the people of Pergamum granted him divine honours; and all his successors, as was normal for Hellenistic kings, were worshipped in their lifetime.

Eumenes was succeeded in 241 B.C. by his adopted son Attalus, whose long reign of forty-four years is a tale of wars and battles. His fame rests primarily on his great victory over the Gauls in 230 B.C. These Gauls were a branch of the central European nation who had migrated eastwards in the previous century. They were invited into Asia in 279 B.C. by Nicomedes, king of Bithynia, who needed mercenaries for his private purposes, and were permitted by him to settle in the district of Asia Minor which from that time bore the name Galatia. Once established, they made themselves a nuisance to all and sundry. Many of the Greek cities suffered from their attacks, for they were a wild and warlike people, and immunity from their attentions could only be had by the payment of tribute. Both Philetaerus and Eumenes had found it advisable to pay this Danegeld, but Attalus felt himself strong enough to refuse. Deprived of this source of income, the Gauls advanced to collect it for themselves. In the ensuing battle Attalus was victorious, and the Gauls were driven away from the west coast. As with many famous victories, legends grew up around this battle. It is said that Attalus' soldiers were terrified at the prospect of a contest with the formidable barbarians; however, when sacrifice was made before the battle, the priest announced that the words 'Victory for the King' had become miraculously written on the victim's entrails. Encouraged by this evidence of divine favour, they fought heroically against great odds. It transpired later that Attalus had written the words backwards on his own hand in ink, and while examining the victim had imprinted them on the liver.

After this outstanding achievement Attalus adopted the titles of King and Saviour. A large part of his reign was occupied, with very varying success, in contesting western Asia Minor with the kings of Syria. At one time he was the most powerful monarch in the east, but by the end of his reign his kingdom was no larger than at the beginning. Towards the end of the third century the Romans began to occupy themselves in Greece, and Attalus became their ally. In this capacity he was associated with the first advent of Romans into Asia. An oracle had advised them to transport the Mother of the Gods from Asia to Rome; having no standing in Asia, they applied for help to Attalus, who received the envoys kindly and handed over to them the sacred stone which was believed to represent the Great Mother.

Though Attalus bequeathed to his successor Eumenes II no larger territory than he had himself inherited, he had made Pergamum a force to be reckoned with, and he had earned the goodwill of the Romans. It was Eumenes who benefited from this. When the Romans became reluctantly embroiled with Antiochus the Great of Syria, and finally defeated him in the crucial battle of Magnesia in 190 B.C., faced with the problem of disposing of his possessions in Asia Minor they handed over most of them to Eumenes. At this point the kingdom of Pergamum reached the height of its power and prosperity; it was a power gained by favour of the Romans, and due to their unwillingness to encumber themselves with territory in the east. Eumenes now controlled the whole of the west coastal region as far south as the Maeander, and the centre of the peninsula as far east as the modern town of Konya.

Eumenes, like Pericles at Athens, used the wealth of which he found himself master for the beautification of his capital. The city had hitherto occupied only the upper part of the hill, above the present car park; Eumenes extended it far down the slope, and enclosed the whole with a new wall. This work involved artificial terracing on a vast scale. At this time were constructed not only the lower agora and the great gymnasium, but also, in the older part of the city, the famous library and the altar of Zeus.

All the rulers of Pergamum were enthusiastic patrons of culture in all its forms. In art, sculpture held pride of place, and an individual Pergamene style developed, of which the Dying Gaul and the friezes of the altar of Zeus are well-known examples. The Attalids made generous donations to the philosophical schools at Athens, and collected at their own court many of the most distinguished poets, philosophers, scientists, and scholars of the day. Of the famous library more will be said below. In this way Pergamum gained a reputation rivalling that of Athens or Alexandria.

Eumenes was not left by his neighbours to enjoy his new prosperity in peace, but was obliged to defend his territory not only against the Gauls but against Pharnaces, king of Pontus, and Prusias, king of Bithynia; the latter was assisted by Rome's old enemy Hannibal. Having reason also to fear attack from Perseus, king of Macedonia, he aided the Romans in their campaign against him; Pergamene troops took part in the decisive battle of Pydna in 168 B.C., which put an end to the kingdom of Macedonia. Towards the end of his reign, however, a certain coolness arose between Eumenes and the Romans, whose favour was conferred rather on the king's brother, Attalus. Long troubled by ill health, Eumenes died in 159 B.C.

Attalus II, already over 60 when he succeeded his brother, made it his firm policy to do nothing without consulting the Romans. His reign of twenty-one years was mostly occupied by a succession of wars. His most troublesome antagonist was Prusias of Bithynia, who at one moment advanced to the outskirts of Pergamum itself; we are told that he offered sacrifice one day at the Asclepieum and the next day carried off the statue of Asclepius. This war was ended by Roman intervention in 154 B.C. Eight years later at Corinth the troops of Attalus assisted the Romans in the campaign which finally extinguished the freedom of Greece. On his death in 138 he was succeeded by his nephew of the same name.

Attalus III, during his short reign of five years, showed himself utterly unlike his predecessors. He was, we are told, cruel and suspicious, hated by the people; he seldom left his palace, but devoted himself to the study of strange sciences; the cultivation of medicinal and poisonous plants was apparently his particular hobby, and these he tested upon condemned criminals. Zoology, husbandry, and metal-working also occupied his attention; his book on agriculture is quoted as an authority by Roman writers on the subject. This portrait of the last king of Pergamum, as drawn by the literary authorities, is to some extent belied by the inscriptions, which show that he did at times take the field, and even won a victory over some unnamed enemy. His crowning eccentricity came last of all. When he died of disease in 133 B.C., it was found that in his will he had bequeathed his kingdom to Rome. For this startling and unprecedented act various motives have been suggested; but however the king's mind may have worked, his famous bequest was really no more than a logical conclusion to the trend of events. Roman influence during the last three reigns had been growing steadily stronger; the annexation, however unwillingly, by Rome of western Asia Minor was, sooner or later, inevitable, and Attalus did no more than hasten it.

The Romans, however, were not permitted to enter peaceably into their inheritance. A certain Aristonicus, reputed to be a bastard son of Eumenes II, at once disputed their claim. Collecting a large army of mercenaries, slaves, and other assorted elements, he defied the Romans with considerable success for three years, and even defeated the consul who was sent against him. In 130, however, he was in his turn defeated and taken captive to Rome.

The kingdom of the Attalids was thereupon dismembered. The outlying portions were attached to the principates or provinces which seemed most appropriate, while the core of the kingdom was converted into the Roman province of Asia. The province thus formed comprised the western coastal area, that is the regions of Mysia, Lydia, Ionia, Caria, and part of Phrygia, and so included all the district dealt with in the present work.

Pergamum itself was left as a free city, in accordance with Attalus' will. But freedom, within a Roman province, no longer meant what it used to mean. When Mithridates, king of Pontus, invaded the province in 88 B.C. as the self-professed liberator of the Greek cities from Roman oppression, Pergamum joined him readily enough, and served for a time as his headquarters; the massacre of the Italians was carried out there with particular unscrupulousness, and even the sanctuary of the temples was not respected. This was the city's last attempt to play a part independent of Rome, and from that time forward the political history of Pergamum is that of the province of Asia.

The city of the Attalids is still not completely excavated, and of the surviving buildings none is standing to its original height; nevertheless it is not hard to imagine how the city must have looked. It is built on a series of terraces, each artificially constructed. The great wall of Eumenes II is best seen at the extreme summit of the hill, where it stands to an impressive height in regular courses of ashlar masonry.

Not far from the top of the hill are the ruins of the famous Pergamene library (C). This stood close behind the temple of Athena, and the association is not fortuitous, since Athena was a patroness of learning. The library comprised a group of at least five rooms, probably more; of these only the easternmost is now recognizable as having contained books, most of the others not being preserved to a sufficient height. Round three sides of this room runs a kind of stone bench, some 3 feet (·91 m.) high and wide, now almost flush with the ground; between this and the walls is a space of some 18 inches (457 mm.). In the fourth wall is the door (not now recognizable), and in the middle of the wall opposite, where the stone bench is widened to receive it, stood a statue of Athena. A row of holes in the walls held staples or hooks to which the wooden bookshelves were fastened. The shelves stood in the space between the walls and the bench, which accordingly covered the lower part of them. The purpose of the stone bench was to keep the public away from the books while enabling the library attendants to reach them. So at least the excavators explain the unusual features of this interesting room.

Books in the classical period consisted of a long strip of papyrus about a foot wide, rolled around a stick. The reader held the roll in both hands, unrolling with one hand and rolling up with the other as he proceeded. Though reasonably convenient for reading a work through, this was highly inconvenient for other purposes—as, for example, finding a reference. No doubt this explains in part why quotations by one ancient author from another are so often inaccurate. For the introduction of the paged book, or codex as it was called, we are indebted to the kings of Pergamum.

Book-collecting was with the Attalids almost a mania. Eumenes II and his successor in particular combed the kingdom for works of all kinds, which they transported, with or without payment, to the capital. The physician Galen, himself a Pergamene, says that manuscripts were forged to satisfy the king's desire for books and more books; and we hear that at Scepsis in the Troad the owners of the precious library of Aristotle, loth to surrender it, were constrained to hide it underground, where the moths and damp got at it, thus accounting for the defective state of the text of Aristotle's works. The results of this collecting-fever were impressive; the Pergamene library is said to have totalled 200,000 volumes. If this is anywhere near correct, we must suppose a considerable annexe; the capacity of the room described above has been estimated at some 17,000 volumes.

The only rival to a library of this size was that at Alexandria in Egypt, and the rivalry seems in fact to have been keen. Egypt was the principal, almost the only, source of papyrus; and the Roman writer Varro tells us that Ptolemy, jealous of the growing Pergamene collection, prohibited its export. Thereupon the king of Pergamum, unable any longer to have manuscripts copied on papyrus, resorted for this purpose to the use of skins, as the Ionians had done long before. From this 'Pergamene paper' comes our own word parchment. Skins, being much thicker and heavier than papyrus, were less suitable for rolled volumes, and it was found preferable to make them into paged books. This new type of book, though more expensive, soon found general favour; for several hundred years both kinds continued simultaneously, but the much greater convenience of the codex led eventually to the abandonment of the papyrus roll. With the development of paper in modern times it has become possible to secure the advantages of both types.

The rivalry between the two great libraries was finally extinguished when the Pergamene collection was presented by Antony, who did not own it, to Cleopatra, who had other things to do than read it. It was taken to Alexandria, where it survived, somewhat diminished, till the seventh century. Then the Caliph Omar, or his significantly named lieutenant, Amr ibn el-Ass, reasoning that if a book was inconsistent with the Koran it was impious, and if consistent, unnecessary, ordered the entire library to be destroyed.

A little lower down the hill stood an equally famous monument, the altar of Zeus (E). Only the foundation is now to be seen on the spot, but enough fragments were found to permit an almost complete restoration. The foundation, some 120 by 112 feet (36·6 by 34·1 m.), comprises a vast criss-cross of walls resembling, as a modern writer expresses it, a huge waffle-iron. On this was erected a solid platform, or podium, nearly 20 feet (6·10 m.) high. Round three sides of the platform ran a wall, the fourth or west side being largely occupied by a broad flight of steps. In front of the wall, on the inner side, stood a colonnade, and in the centre of the court thus formed was the altar itself. The outer wall of the podium was decorated with the famous frieze representing the battle of the Gods and Giants; the blocks composing this were found built into a late

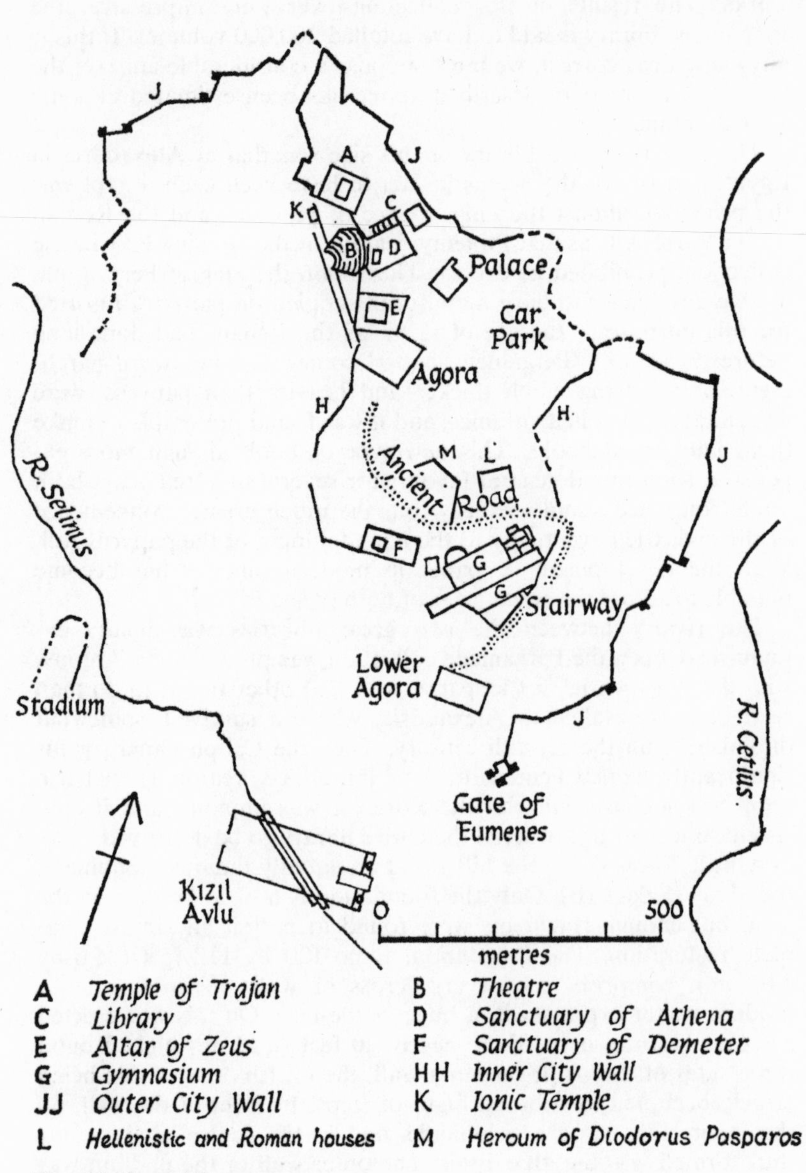
J
A
J
K
C
B
D
Palace
E
Car
Park
Agora
H
H
R. Selinus
M
L
Ancient
Road
J
F
G
G
Stairway
Stadium
Lower
Agora
J
R. Cetius
Gate of
Eumenes
Kizil
Avlu
O
500
metres
A Temple of Trajan
B Theatre
C Library
D Sanctuary of Athena
E Altar of Zeus
F Sanctuary of Demeter
G Gymnasium
H H Inner City Wall
JJ Outer City Wall
K Ionic Temple
L Hellenistic and Roman houses
M Heroum of Diodorus Pasparos

Fig. 10 Plan of Pergamum

wall close by, and are now preserved in the Pergamum Museum in East Berlin. The strife of gods and giants symbolizes the defence of civilization by the kings of Pergamum against the barbarian Gauls. A second frieze adorned the wall of the colonnade; this depicted the adventures of the mythical hero Telephus, ruler of this region at the time of the Trojan War, and later adopted as an ancestor by the kings of Pergamum. This altar, and in particular the friezes, constitute the masterpiece of Pergamene, and perhaps of all Hellenistic, art (Pl. 10).

The suggestion has been made that this altar of Zeus is the throne of Satan mentioned in Revelation in the letter to the church at Pergamum: 'I know where thou dwellest, where Satan's throne is'. But the suggestion is hardly probable. Satan in the Apocalypse, the enemy of Christianity, is represented not so much by the old pagan Greek religion as by the Roman power, which by that time had taken a firm stand against the Christians, and by the custom of emperor-worship. If the throne of Satan really refers to a particular building at Pergamum, the temple of Rome and Augustus is the most likely; but more probably the words mean simply 'where is the central seat of the Roman authority'.

Close to the altar of Zeus is the Greek theatre (B), the most spectacular thing to be seen at Pergamum today. It is built into the steep hillside and faces south-west. The normal shape of the auditorium in a Greek theatre was rather more than a semicircle, in a Roman theatre an exact semicircle; but at Pergamum, owing to the nature of the ground, it is much less than a semicircle. For this it makes up to some extent by its exceptional height; it has seventy-eight rows of seats divided by two diazomata into three horizontal sections (Pl. 13, 14).

Immediately at the foot of the theatre stretches a long narrow terrace, so close indeed that the scene-building stood actually on the terrace. In the oldest form of the theatre, in the early days of the Attalid kingdom, the scene-building was a temporary structure of wood, erected for the performances and removed when the theatre was not in use. The purpose of this arrangement was evidently to avoid obstructing the long sweep of the terrace. The post-holes which form a conspicuous feature of the theatre today were used in erecting this wooden building; at other times they were closed with cap-stones. At this period it is probable that there was no stage, the performances taking place on the level of the orchestra. Some time about the middle of the second century B.C. the wooden scene-building was replaced by a permanent stone structure with a stage, covering up the old post-holes without destroying them; later, in Roman times, this was rebuilt and enlarged. Of these stone buildings very little now remains.

The handsome Ionic temple (K) at the north end of the theatre-terrace is comparatively well preserved. The walls are standing to a certain height, and the flight of steps in front is still in place. Of the columns and the ornamentation considerable fragments survive. The existing structure is a rebuilding of Roman date, but the original temple goes back to the second century B.C. To what deity it was dedicated is uncertain, since of the dedicatory inscription only five fragmentary letters have been found. Asclepius, Zeus, and the deified kings of Pergamum have been proposed; but the proximity of the temple to the theatre suggests rather Dionysus, in whose honour theatrical performances took place. The building was at some period severely damaged by fire, and was eventually rededicated to the Roman emperor Caracalla. Fragments of this second dedication were found during the excavations. The letters of the alphabet carved on the steps on the west side are masons' marks indicating the positions in which the blocks should be placed; they were originally hidden from sight by the blocks above them. The altar of the temple stands in the normal position in front, at the foot of the steps; at its south-east corner is a curious conical stone, now almost buried, with a deep hole in the surface; this may have held a post to which the victim was tied.

The upper and lower parts of the city at Pergamum were joined by a winding paved street which has been cleared for most of its length. Recently the German excavators have concentrated on clearing the buildings to the north of this, and their discoveries have made a substantial addition to our knowledge of the domestic architecture of Pergamum between Hellenistic and Byzantine times. In the Hellenistic period the buildings consisted of a small odeum, a hall designed for a hero cult, and a peristyle house. In the early imperial period the cult shrine was modified and various architectural details added; a set of rooms which appear to have been a library erected beside the odeum, and a large bath-house built further over to the west. The area also contained a number of other private houses. The Hellenistic peristyle house was also converted into a palaestra attached to the baths, but this in turn was roofed over in the late second century A.D. A portrait head of late Hellenistic date was found in the cult room, and the excavators have suggested that it was part of a statue of Diodorus Pasparos, a noted benefactor of the city in the time of the Mithridatic Wars. They interpret the whole complex as a gymnasium for the young men, devoted not merely to athletic, but also to intellectual, pursuits, as was often the way with such buildings. A little to the east of the odeum there were further Hellenistic houses, and these were cleared in the second and third centuries A.D. to make room for a long rectangular building with a wide podium running round the walls. Outside the structure is a large pit which may have been intended to receive blood from sacrifices, and the building may have been intended as the dining-room of a religious organization, perhaps connected with the worship of Dionysus. Still further over to the east the excavations have uncovered a series of shops of the first century A.D., overlying Hellenistic peristyle houses.

Among the buildings lower down the hillside is the precinct of Demeter (F). It is entered at the east end by a propylon dating from the time of Eumenes II, from which steps lead down into the sanctuary. The columns of the propylon are unusual; they have the rare 'leaf capital', a type found elsewhere only in archaic times, and never common; the shafts are flat-fluted at the bottom only, and the usual base mouldings are lacking. Towards the west end of the precinct is the temple of Demeter, with the altar in front of it; temple and altar date from the reign of Philetaerus, in whose time they were outside the citadel. The dedicatory inscription may still be read. Along the north side of the sanctuary runs a long building of which the western part is a stoa, while the eastern part comprises nine rows of stone seats affording space for about a thousand people. Similar seats are found in the Hall of Initiation in the sanctuary of Demeter at Eleusis in Attica, and served for the initiates to watch the celebration of the mysteries; there can be no doubt that the same was the case at Pergamum (Pl. 15).

The Eleusinian mysteries formed an important element in the so-called Orphic religion, which competed strongly in classical times with the official Olympian cult. Its tenets were largely concerned with the after-life. To many people the traditional conception of Hades, the cold and cheerless abode of the spirits of the dead, seemed unsatisfactory, and it was felt that by means of ritual acts combined with purity of mind and body it might be possible to secure a better lot after death. The ritual cult came to be associated especially with Demeter, whose name means probably Mother Earth, and initiation was essential. No one was excluded who was not under a curse or pollution; not only free men, but women and slaves were readily admitted. The details of the ceremonies were kept secret from all but initiates, and the mysteries still remain mysterious; but ritual purification played an important part, and we know that certain 'acts' were performed and certain sacred objects displayed. It is unlikely that any precise dogma was taught, for dogma in general was a negligible element in Greek religion.

Across the path from the precinct of Demeter is the great gymnasium (G), one of the finest specimens of its kind to be found in the Greek world. It comprises three sections, each on a separate terrace. These were assigned respectively, though not exclusively, to the 'young men', youths and boys—'young men' meaning those from 19 years of age upwards to an uncertain maximum of at least 30. The uppermost terrace, that of the young men, is by far the largest of the three. Its main feature is an open rectangular court surrounded on three sides by a colonnade; this is the palaestra, used for wrestling and for athletic exercise generally. Along its north side are three good-sized rooms. The westernmost of these has the form of a small theatre—that is, a lecture-theatre, not for dramatic performances, as is clear from the absence of any stage. The gymnasium in an ancient city served not only for physical training but also as a school and university, and it was common practice to invite distinguished orators from other cities to give lectures. Such a visitor would easily fill the thousand seats in the lecture-theatre at Pergamum.

The next room to the east is the largest of the three. It was the ceremonial hall, used for receptions, prize-givings, and similar official functions. Next again on the east is a room which, from an inscription found in it, was apparently used for worship of the emperor in Roman times, a kind of college chapel. On the east side of the palaestra is an extensive bathing establishment of the normal Roman type. The water for this and other purposes was brought in pipes from the mountains to the north and carried up under pressure to the citadel; this system was first installed by Eumenes II in the second century B.C., and is the most impressive of its kind before the great aqueducts of the Roman period. The smaller rooms around the palaestra were used as classrooms, dressing-rooms, and the like. One of them still contains wash-basins. Along the south side of this upper terrace runs a long, narrow, originally underground building of uncertain purpose, but probably not used for athletics.

The middle terrace is less extensive than the upper and has fewer features. Towards the east end, in the middle, are the foundations of a temple which is likely to have been dedicated to one or both of the gods who in all parts of the Greek world presided over the activities of the gymnasium, namely Heracles and Hermes. Along the north edge of this terrace is a long narrow building lying just below the similar structure on the south side of the upper terrace. This building was in two storeys. The ground floor comprises a long passage with small rooms at its east end; over this, on the upper floor, was a covered stadium, or xystus, used for indoor training during the winter. The stadium proper, where the games were celebrated in the summer, lay in the lower city to the west, between the river and the amphitheatre, but nothing remains of it beyond the mere outline of the elongated hollow.

The lowest terrace is smaller still and consists merely of an open triangular space. It contains no buildings, and served apparently as a simple playground for the boys. Near its east end is the handsome covered stairway, well preserved, which led up to the middle terrace. The ancient road up the hill passes the foot of this staircase. Since neither the lower nor the middle terrace contains classrooms, the boys and youths must have received their education in the rooms on the upper terrace, and the three terraces together form a single great gymnasium.

The lower part of the ancient city is now largely covered by the town of Bergama. In the town itself the most impressive remnant of antiquity is the so-called Kızıl Avlu, or Red Courtyard, a monument of Roman grandeur remarkable equally for its layout and its vast size. The central point of the complex is the great hall, or temple, originally in three storeys, which still stands almost complete; on either side of this is a round tower, also well preserved, with a colonnaded court in front. Of the colonnade hardly anything survives, but in the middle of each court is a long, narrow bathing-pool fed by pipes for hot and cold water. In front of the whole stretches the huge courtyard, over 200 yards (182·9 m.) long and now largely built over. The far wall containing the gateway may still be seen among the houses across the main street. Not the least remarkable feature is that this courtyard is built over the river Selinus, which flows obliquely across it in a double-vaulted tunnel which still serves its ancient purpose (Pl. 11, 12).

The whole colossal structure was certainly a sanctuary of the Egyptian gods, dedicated principally to Serapis (the Egyptian Osiris). The triple form of the building suggests that other deities were associated with him, most probably Isis and Harpocrates. Various features were designed to accommodate different ceremonies associated with the cult. The large forecourt formed the stage for ceremonial processions; the temple itself was divided into an inner sanctum accessible only to priests and initiates, and an outer area

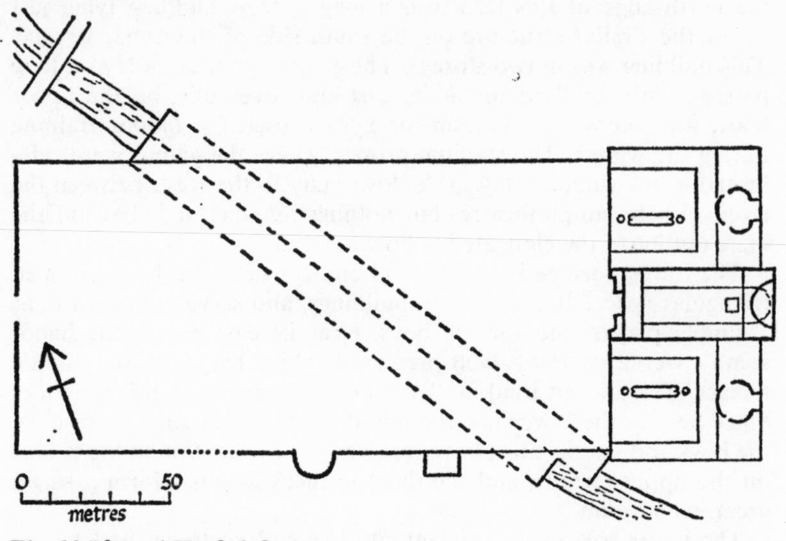

Fig. 11 Plan of Kızıl Avlu

frequented by the generality of worshippers. Beneath the two tower-like structures on either side, there were extensive underground chambers, which almost certainly played a part in the cult since Serapis had close connections with the underworld, and had much in common with the Greek god of the lower world, Pluto or Hades. Furthermore, the bathing pools in the courtyard are explained by the ritual significance of water in the worship of Isis and Serapis, where it was held to symbolize the sacred river Nile, on whose annual flood the wellbeing and prosperity of Egypt depended. The building probably dates to the second century A.D. In later times a church was installed in the central hall, and the present raised floor belongs to this.

The Asclepieum

To many visitors the sanctuary of Asclepius is among the most attractive features of Pergamum. It is outside the city on the south-west, and has been admirably excavated by the German archaeologists; at the time of writing the excavations have been resumed and are still in progress. Here, more than in most places, the visitor can feel himself in intimate contact with antiquity (Pl. 8).

Medicine in the Greek world, like so many aspects of civic life—public assemblies, drama, sport, and others—was under divine patronage; to the ancient Greek, religion was a constant part of his daily existence. Most, if not all, gods had powers of healing, but the god of medicine *par excellence* was Asclepius. In the *Iliad* Asclepius is not a god at all, but the human physician whose sons Podaleirius and Machaon served as medical officers to the army at Troy. It was hardly before the fifth century that he became accepted into the Olympic pantheon. Once accepted, his cult grew rapidly in popularity, and in later times we know of over 200 sanctuaries of Asclepius in all parts of the world. Of these the greatest and most famous was at Epidaurus in the Peloponnese, and it was from here, apparently in the fourth century, that the cult was introduced to Pergamum by a grateful patient. Under the Roman empire the Pergamene Asclepieum ranked in importance as second only to the Epidaurian. Our chronic invalid friend Aristides was naturally a frequent visitor there; several of his pamphlets are directly concerned with it, and in the course of narrating the wonderful cures which Asclepius performed in his case he gives us a good deal of information about it.

The healing art as practised at Pergamum and in other Asclepieia was a curious mixture of the supernatural and the practical. Incubation was the main feature: the patient slept in the sanctuary and either awoke cured or, if he was not so fortunate, related his dreams to the priests, who prescribed accordingly a less spectacular and more mundane course of treatment. Unless the dreams were very precise—as Aristides' often were—their interpretation rested with the priests, who thus performed the functions of physicians; but secular doctors were frequently in attendance also to help with their advice. Galen, the most famous physician of antiquity after Hippocrates, was born at Pergamum and practised in the Asclepieum. He gained his early medical experience as a doctor to a troupe of gladiators, who doubtless performed in the amphitheatre nearby, and provided more expendable human material than most. In fact, the treatment prescribed appears on the whole to have been very sensible and a credit to the profession, at least if we remember the very limited knowledge of medicine available in ancient times. It consisted in the main of three elements, diet, hot and cold baths, and exercise. A characteristic case is that of a man of Mylasa, a dyspeptic, who came for treatment to Asclepius at Epidaurus; he was put on a diet of bread and cheese with parsley and lettuce, and milk mixed with honey, and told to go barefoot, to take a run every day, to coat himself with mud, and, rather oddly, to anoint himself with wine before entering a hot bath. The treatment was successful and his grateful dedication survives as a testimonial.

Coating with mud was employed also at Pergamum. Aristides tells us graphically how at the god's command, one bitter winter's night, he smeared himself with mud and ran three times round the temples, finishing by washing off the mud at the sacred fountain. The cold was so severe that no clothes could keep it out, and of two friends who volunteered to keep him company one turned back at once, while the other was seized by a spasm and had to be carried to the baths to be thawed out. Aristides' own constitution must have been exceptionally strong, despite his constant illness, if we may believe the cures which were worked upon him. On one occasion, after forty days of frost, Asclepius bade him rise from bed, put on only a linen shirt, and wash at the fountain outside. The difficulty was to find any water, as everything was frozen, and the water froze as it issued from the spout. Nevertheless he carried out orders, and felt the cold less than anyone. Another time in mid-winter, when he was in Smyrna, the god appeared in a dream and commanded him to go down and bathe in the river that flows outside the city. The cold this time was such that the pebbles at the river's edge were frozen together into a solid mass, yet after plunging into the deepest part of the stream and swimming and splashing for some time, he felt on emerging a warm glow which lasted the rest of the day. The astonished spectators could not refrain from crying aloud, 'Great is Asclepius!'

Aristides himself was much impressed by the apparently paradoxical nature of these cures; but he must have been a familiar figure at Pergamum, and the priests no doubt realized better than he did himself how much his constitution would stand and how largely imaginary his ailments were. Other forms of treatment that seemed to him paradoxical were the drinking of hemlock juice or of chalk and water, and the relief of constipation by prolonged abstinence from food. A story is told of the sophist Hermocrates of Phocaea that he once gave a recital before the emperor, who was so pleased that he asked him to choose his reward. Hermocrates replied that he was under orders from Asclepius of Pergamum to diet on partridge smoked in frankincense; frankincense being hard to come by in his country, he would ask the emperor for a generous supply. Aristides tells us that Asclepius once in a dream taught a boxer tricks for overcoming a formidable antagonist.

But many of the cures attributed to Asclepius are frankly miraculous. At Epidaurus there stood in the sanctuary in the fourth century B.C. marble stelae inscribed with records of cures effected there, and some of these have survived. One woman, we read, had been pregnant for five years; she slept in the sanctuary, and on emerging in the morning at once gave birth to a five-year-old son. Another woman came to Epidaurus in the hope of offspring, and, when asked by Asclepius in a vision what she desired, replied that she wished to conceive a child. Asked if she had any further desire, she said no, she wished for nothing else in the world. Afterwards she became pregnant, and remained so for three years. On coming again to the god for relief, it was pointed out to her that although specially asked she had said nothing about giving birth. This theme of the ill-expressed wish was popular in antiquity, as in the tales of Midas and his golden touch, and Tithonus who received eternal life without eternal youth. But perhaps the most pleasing case at Epidaurus is that of a certain Pandarus. Having evidently once been a slave, he bore tattoo-marks on his forehead, and came to Asclepius praying to be rid of them. During the night the god tied a bandage round his head, bidding him remove it in the morning and dedicate it in the temple. Next morning it was found that the marks had transferred themselves to the bandage. Shortly afterwards a friend of Pandarus named Echedorus, who was similarly tattooed, came to the god for a similar purpose, bringing with him a sum of money given him by the grateful Pandarus, with instructions to make a dedication to the god on his behalf. Dishonestly he neglected his duty, and when the god appeared to him during the night and asked if he had not received money from Pandarus, he denied it. In response to his request for the removal of his tattoo-marks the god took the bandage which Pandarus had dedicated and tied it round Echedorus' head, bidding him in the morning remove it and look at his reflection in the sacred pool. When he did so, the bandage was found to be clean and Echedorus' forehead to be carrying Pandarus' marks in addition to his own.

These records were compiled and published by the priests, and so have not the authenticity of dedications made by cured patients themselves. Nevertheless, if anyone is disposed to regard them as mythical, let him beware. This was done by a certain man who came to Epidaurus with a withered hand. Reading these cures as he walked round the sanctuary he scoffed at them and declared them impossible. To convince him Asclepius cured his hand, but condemned him to bear for life the name of Doubter, and his case was inscribed on the next stele to be erected.

Such then was the cult of Asclepius, half Droitwich and half Lourdes. But however its results were achieved, whether by autosuggestion or faith-healing or by rational medical treatment, there is no doubt of its immense popularity; and one reason for this was certainly the intimate personal contact with the deity which it seemed to afford. The Asclepieum was not merely a spa, still less a hospital, but a public religious sanctuary, open to all, whether sick or well, citizens or foreigners. Aristides tells us more than once that the distinctly undignified treatment prescribed for him by the god was carried out in front of numerous spectators, and afforded much entertainment.

Naturally, not all patients could be cured overnight, nor in a matter of days, and prolonged visits were often necessary. Indeed, a year seems to have been quite normal. It is not clear where such patients stayed. For really serious cases accommodation on the spot would be desirable, but the excavations have not revealed any buildings clearly designed for this purpose. Patients who could not be moved were perhaps permitted to remain in the incubation-rooms. Against the danger of boredom in less severe cases good provision was made; the sanctuary contains both a theatre and a library. But, in fact, boredom is not likely to have been a real problem. Day by day the sanctuary was full of patients and visitors; we may imagine the learned men, doctors like Galen and others, each accompanied by a group of listeners, strolling up and down, the priests benevolently accessible to all and sundry, and the patients conversing among themselves. In a slave-owning society leisure was abundant and the Greeks knew how to use it; no Greek was ever bored so long as he had someone to argue with.

The ruins of the Asclepieum as they now stand revealed by the excavation date in the main to a great rebuilding in the second century A.D. All that remains from earlier times is the original kernel of the sanctuary, the sacred well, and the foundations of temple and incubation-rooms to the west and south of it.[1] Most of what we see today was erected in the lifetime of Aelius Aristides; but, as it happens, the buildings he mentions are mostly those which have not survived. However, it should be said that excavation has shown that the earliest occupation of the sanctuary dates back to the archaic period and even to the Bronze Age, and it is probable that the cult of the Greek god Asclepius succeeded an earlier native sanctuary.

A visit to the sanctuary begins, as it began in antiquity, at the entrance-gate or Propylon (B). A sacred way from the city led obliquely to a courtyard in front of the gate; a good stretch of this road has lately been uncovered. Immediately to the right, or north, is the library. This is a single square room with niches round the walls. The middle niche on the east side held a statue of the emperor, Hadrian, to whom the library was dedicated as a patron of learning, and who was in large part responsible for rebuilding the whole Asclepieum and promoting it to the first rank among the shrines of the Greek world. Light for reading was supplied by a line of windows above the niches. There is no reason to suppose that this was a medical library; rather it was a collection of classical works for the use of patients. The statue, and perhaps the whole building, was dedicated by a lady named Flavia Melitine.

Adjoining the Propylon on the other side is the circular temple of Zeus-Asclepius (D), the main temple of the existing precinct. Only the lowest courses remain, but the excellence of the masonry is remarkable. At the back on the east was an external staircase apparently giving access to the roof for purposes of repair. In front was a flight of steps symmetrically balancing the steps which led down from the Propylon. The identification of Asclepius with Zeus was considered noteworthy by Aristides; the power of Asclepius, he explains, is great, manifold, and all-embracing, comparable with that of Zeus himself. It was in this temple that Aristides dedicated a tripod in commemoration of a choral entertainment he had organized in the god's honour; each of its three legs carried a golden image, one of Asclepius, one of Hygieia, and one of Telesphorus. It stood under the god's right hand. Hygieia, Health, and Telesphorus, the Accomplisher, of whom more will be said later, were minor deities associated with Asclepius.

On the north, west, and south the sanctuary was surrounded by porticoes, or stoae. These are a constant feature of Greek civic architecture, affording shelter from the sun in summer and from the rain in winter. The best preserved is that on the north, where the columns have been re-erected after the excavation. The order is Ionic, but the ten columns at the end nearest to the library were overthrown by an earthquake, and were, surprisingly enough, replaced by columns with square bases and Composite capitals—that is, capitals combining the Ionic volute with the Corinthian acanthus-leaves.

At the west end of this portico is a small theatre (E). It has the semicircular shape typical of Roman theatres. The auditorium is divided by staircases into five wedge-shaped sections, and horizontally by a gallery, or diazoma. A 'royal box' occupies three rows of the middle section. The stage-building stood originally three storeys high, with a stage in front about one metre high. An inscription records that the theatre was dedicated to Asclepius and Athena Hygieia. Its seating capacity is about 3,500; since the patients in residence at any one time can never have approached this number, it is evident that the general public must also have been admitted.

The west portico was similar to that on the north, but nothing remains of it. Half-way down its length a door and steps led to the entrance of a stoa. This comprised a Doric colonnade, about 131 yards (120 m.) long, backed by a series of chambers and look-

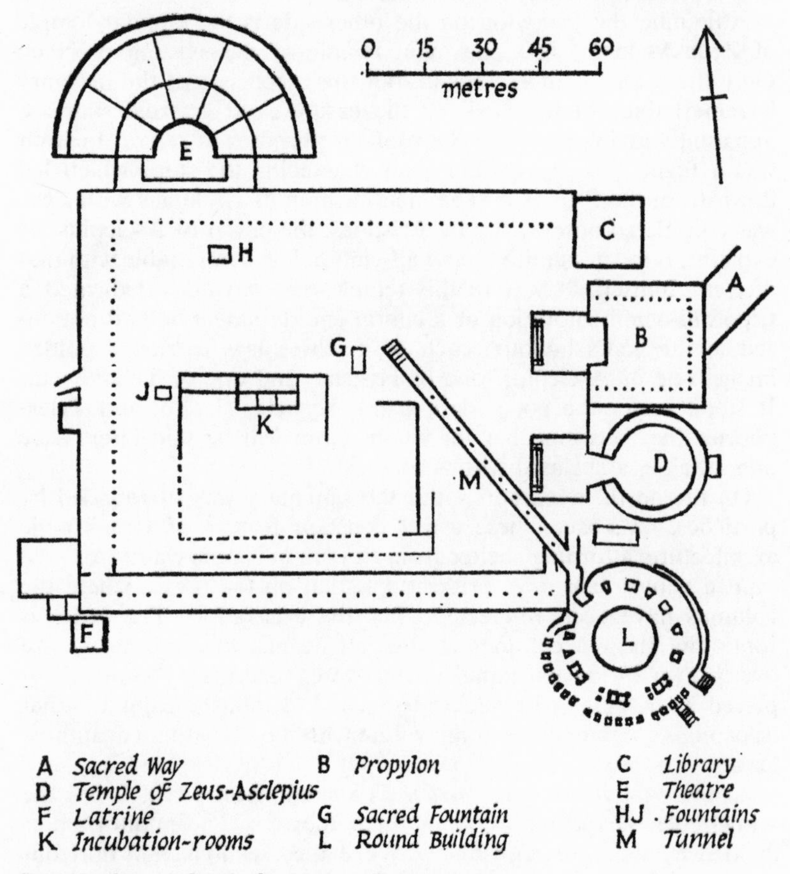

Fig. 12 Plan of the Asclepieum at Pergamum

ing out over an open area which served as a gymnasium, mentioned in fact by Aristides.

The south portico, or at least the stoa itself, is also completely destroyed. The ground being lower on this side, a basement was necessary, and this still survives. It has a row of piers down the middle which helped to support the floor of the stoa, while the basement itself was used as a store-room. At the corner where the west and south porticoes join is an interesting specimen of an ancient latrine (F). The larger room, used by the men, was splendidly furnished with about thirty marble seats; in the middle of the ceiling was a light and air vent with handsome Corinthian pillars at its four corners. These sumptuous latrines are characteristic of the period. Though affording perhaps less privacy than we should consider desirable today, they are beautifully built and excellently equipped. The ladies' room, on the other hand, is smaller and much less magnificent.

The central point both of the sanctuary and of the cult is the Sacred Well (G). It was housed in a simple building and fed by a pipe from a spring. The water was not entered by the patients, but was drawn in vessels either for bathing or more especially for drinking. Aristides is enthusiastic over the virtues of this water, and devotes a pamphlet to its praises. The well, he says, is always full, cool in summer and warm in winter; eyes are cured by bathing with it, chest diseases, asthma, and foot troubles by drinking it; in one case even a dumb man who drank of it recovered his speech. It is not, like some sacred waters—Delos, for example—sacred because no one is allowed to touch it, but sacred in the sense that with the god's help it benefits all who use it.

There were two other fountains in the sanctuary, both of which also played a part in the cure of the sick. One of these (H on the plan) is close to the theatre; it had a marble basin, unroofed, and was probably used by patients who were ordered the cold-bath treatment. The other (J on the plan) is in the middle of the west side; this is a rock-cut basin and was originally roofed over. In winter and wet weather mud collects around this spot; the excavators suggest that the patients coated themselves with this mud, which they subsequently washed off in the basin. If this was the only purpose of this basin, the mud-cure must have been much employed, since the steps leading down to it are deeply worn.

Close to the Sacred Well on the south-west are the incubation-rooms (K). Only foundations survive, and it is not possible to reconstruct the detail of the rooms. The process of incubation involved a strict ritual, some items of which we learn from a mutilated inscription. The suppliant must wash before entering and must wear white clothes, but without girdle or rings; and he must make sacrifice. At Pergamum this was apparently a white sheep garlanded with olive-branches; at Athens, Aristophanes speaks of sacrificial cakes.

In 1958 the German excavators recommenced work upon this central part of the sanctuary. The trenches which they sank remain open, but it is not easy for the visitor to make much sense of them. They produced, in fact, more than one surprise. Under the Hellenistic incubation-rooms there were found walls running obliquely to the otherwise universal north–south orientation; from their style they can hardly be later than the early fourth century B.C. These, together with certain archaic figurines and a very early sherd found close by, suggest that the installation of the Asclepieum in the fourth century was not the first occupation of the site. The excavators suspect that there may have been here a cult of some female deity, for a number of terracotta figurines of a seated woman have come to light in the neighbourhood. These are of later date, so that the early cult (if indeed it existed) must have continued alongside that of Asclepius. But this question is not yet satisfactorily cleared up.

A further surprising discovery was that of a number of simple graves in and around the incubation-chambers. Some still contained the skeletons, and one of these was found to show a severe swelling of the thigh-bone. It is tempting to suppose that these graves are those of patients who let the sanctuary down by dying under treatment and were hastily, perhaps even secretly, buried on the spot.

On the rocky ground to the north of the incubation-rooms stood three small temples, of which only faint traces remain. They were those of Asclepius the Saviour, Hygieia his wife, and Apollo of the Fair Offspring, his father. These are the temples round which Aristides ran three times clad only in a coat of mud. In or adjoining the temple of Hygieia was a shrine of Telesphorus, a boy-deity associated with Asclepius first at Pergamum, then in other parts of the world. He played an active part in the healing cult: Aristides mentions that Telesphorus, that is the priest of Telesphorus, once gave him a balsam with which to anoint himself. On another occasion Aristides was told in a dream that in order to save the whole of his body he must cut off a part of it and dedicate it to Telesphorus; since, however, this would be unduly painful, the priest decided it would be sufficient if he dedicated the ring which he wore on his finger; this would have the same effect as sacrificing the finger itself. There is a convincing air of truth about this story.

In the south-east corner of the sanctuary is a second round building (L) which, after the theatre, is the best preserved on the site. It was in two storeys. On the upper or main floor was a circular room with six large round niches and a wooden roof, but this is now destroyed. The surviving structure is the lower or basement floor. Round a central core of masonry runs a gallery, divided into two by a ring of solid piers placed at intervals. At the foot of some of the piers are set stone basins for washing or bathing. On the south-east are the remains of two staircases leading to the upper floor (Pl. 9).

This building is not mentioned by any ancient writer, and its purpose is not known with certainty. It can hardly have formed part of the original design of the great rebuilding, whose symmetry it destroys. It has somehow acquired the name of Temple of Telesphorus, but this is certainly wrong; as was mentioned above, the shrine of Telesphorus stood elsewhere in the sanctuary. It is not even sure that it was a temple at all. That it had a place in the healing process is hardly doubtful, both in view of the bathing-troughs installed in the basement and because it is linked to the Sacred Well by a long underground tunnel. This tunnel is excellently preserved, with steps at either end; it is lit by a row of holes in the roof. The excavators suggest that it may have served either for the use of the personnel of the sanctuary or as a cool place for patients in summer; but perhaps more likely it afforded a convenient passage for patients, especially in bad weather, from the round building to the heart of the sanctuary around the Sacred Well. We may reasonably suppose that the round building, or at least its basement storey, was intended to meet the need for a place of resort for resident patients in hot or rainy weather. A stone-paved terrace adjoining it on the south would be convenient for invalids to take the sun and air without mingling with the throng of people in the main sanctuary. The guardian who conducts visitors round the site will tell you that the patient was sent to walk alone down the dark and fearsome tunnel, while from each of the holes in the roof a priest-doctor whispered to him, 'Don't be afraid; you are going to be cured'. For this interesting conception there is unfortunately no authority at all.

On two occasions, both during the Mithridatic War, the Pergamene Asclepieum makes a momentary appearance in history. When the king ordered the massacre of all Roman residents in Asia, those in Pergamum ran for asylum to the sanctuary, but were ruthlessly shot down as they clung to the god's statues. A little later the swashbuckling Roman commander Fimbria, unable by reason of his crimes to return to Rome, made his way to the precinct of Asclepius and fell on his sword. Even this he bungled, and was obliged to call on his slave to finish the job.

Towards the end of the third century the sanctuary suffered severely from an earthquake. This disaster, and the rising tide of Christianity, were more than it could resist, and it never really recovered. And yet two hundred years later it was still reckoned as one of the wonders of the world. The list of these wonders had, of course, by that time been greatly extended beyond the original seven; nevertheless, the inclusion of the Asclepieum is a handsome testimony to the splendour it once possessed.

On the open ground between the acropolis and the Asclepieum are the rather scanty remains of the amphitheatre, the only example of its kind in the area covered by this book. The amphitheatre, as its name implies, is a double theatre, that is a circular, or more often oval, building with an arena in the middle and tiers of seats all round. At Pergamum it is built in the valley of a small stream which flows under the arena; of the vast brick structures which supported the seats some rather shapeless masses are standing, but nothing else survives. Amphitheatres were used for the more savage entertainments favoured by the Romans, especially gladiatorial contests and fights between wild animals or between animals and men. In these a good deal of blood was expected to be shed. For the spectators' delectation bears, lions, panthers, and more exotic creatures such as crocodiles were imported from the ends of the earth. On occasion the arena was flooded with water for the performance of mimic sea-fights and other shows; for this purpose the stream at Pergamum was obviously convenient. These sanguinary entertainments did not naturally appeal to the Greeks, but under Roman influence it was inevitable that the taste should be acquired, and in the Greek cities under the empire many theatres and stadia were, in fact, made to serve the purpose of amphitheatres.

The network of trenches on the high ground near the amphitheatre was dug recently by the Germans in an unsuccessful search for the site of the Nicephorium, an important Pergamene sanctuary where a great festival with games was regularly celebrated. Instead, numerous private and one or two public buildings came to light, but there is little to hold the visitor's attention.

Just outside the town of Bergama on the south, to the east of the main road and nearly opposite the side-road which leads to the Asclepieum, is a large tumulus known as Maltepe. The mound, over 500 feet (152·4 m.) in diameter, was originally surrounded by a wall, of which only the filling remains in a few places. On the north side, but not in the diameter of the circle, a passage over 70 yards (64 m.) long leads into the tumulus; it is lined with handsome ashlar masonry and roofed with a vault. It debouches into a cross-passage running right and left, out of which open three grave-chambers; in these, fragments of sarcophagi were found. This part also is handsomely built and vaulted, but is, of course, dark. The method of construction was to erect the masonry first, then to heap the tumulus over it; on the summit stood a monument, but the architectural fragments recovered by the excavators were not enough to indicate its nature. So grandiose a structure was for long believed to be the tomb of a Pergamene king; but, in fact, the lime mortar used in all parts shows conclusively that it must be of Roman date, probably of the second or third century A.D. It carries no inscription, and there is nothing to show what rich and distinguished family was buried in it.

A short half-mile (804·7 m.) to the south-east is another large tumulus called Yığma Tepe. In this case the ring-wall is preserved, and the fine quality of the masonry suggests that this is indeed the tomb of a king. A tunnel driven into it in 1909 failed, however, to find the grave-chamber.

Note

1 The latest excavations are revealing more of the earlier buildings, but their full publication is still awaited.

5 Aeolis

The Smyrna–Pergamum Road

Our friend Aelius Aristides on one occasion made a journey by carriage from Smyrna to Pergamum. He followed the direct main road, whose course was not very different from that of the modern highway. It may therefore be of interest to accompany him along the way. His narrative is lively and detailed; its main purpose is to show the wonderful effect of Asclepius' advice upon his health.

'One summer', he says,

> my stomach gave me a lot of trouble. I suffered from thirst night and day, sweated abundantly, and felt as weak as a rag; when I needed to get up it took two or three men to haul me out of bed. The god gave me a sign to leave Smyrna, where I was at the time, so I decided to start at once on the road to Pergamum. By the time the carriages were ready it was midday and very hot; I therefore preferred to send my servants ahead with the baggage and myself to pass the heat of the afternoon in the suburb. My intention was to spend the first night at Myrina, but beguiled by the charm of the place, and having also some business to transact, we delayed a good while in the suburb, so that we did not reach the inn on the near side of the Hermus till just about sunset.

Where the 'suburb' lay which Aristides found so seductive he does not say; but since it was presumably on the side of the city towards the Pergamum road it is tempting to conjecture that it was by the springs of the Meles at Halkapınar. There is hardly a pleasanter spot in Smyrna today in which to spend a hot afternoon.

Between here and the river Hermus Aristides names no landmark, and this part of his journey is the only part in which his route is at all doubtful. In the second century A.D. the main highroad from Smyrna to the north certainly went, as it does now, round the west end of the Yamanlar Dağı; a milestone found near Ulucak leaves no doubt of this, and Aristides himself on another occasion describes a walk he took in this direction, looking across, as he says, to the city on his left—evidently from a spot between Bayraklı and Karşıyaka. But the matter is complicated by the question of the crossing of the Hermus. As was said above, the river now runs, exactly or approximately, in its ancient course, but in Aristides' time there was no bridge and carriages had to ford the stream. The question is, what was the lowest point at which this could be done? At present, according to enquiries made by Professor J. M. Cook and the present writer, there is a good ford, usable for carriages for most of the year, close to Emiralem railway station, but none is recognized below this. Near the new girder bridge the stream appears normally quite unfordable. If similar conditions prevailed in antiquity, which is likely enough, the high road must have made a considerable detour into the Manisa gorge, and many travellers no doubt preferred the alternative route from Smyrna direct over the Yamanlar Dağı. This is much shorter, but involves quite a stiff climb, nor is it certain that it was ever suitable for wheeled traffic. The English excavators of Old Smyrna found traces of an old carriage road, 8 to 10 feet (2·44 by 3·05 m.) wide, running up from the neighbourhood of Bayraklı to the village of Eğridere, and from there apparently (though this was not actually verified) over the crest of the Yamanlar and down by the lake of Karagöl to the river near Emiralem. It is probable also that a second road led up the west side of the Yamanlar valley, along the line of the present road to the Sanatorium; the small fort beside this road mentioned above (p. 44) suggests that this route was in use. However, it is doubtful whether either of these would, in fact, be any quicker for a horse-drawn vehicle, and we shall probably be safe in picturing Aristides proceeding by the low road through Ulucak and Menemen.

For most of the way to Menemen this road must have run beside the sea. It was originally constructed in 129 B.C., when the province of Asia was formed, and was repaired in A.D. 75 and again in 103, so Aristides should have found it in reasonably good condition. Menemen is not apparently an ancient site, and indeed none is known along this stretch of the road. In the first century A.D. a ferry plied along the coast; and Chandler in 1764 found a busy trade by sea between Smyrna and the scala of Menemen.

At sunset, then, Aristides arrives at the inn by the Hermus crossing, probably not far from Emiralem. The distance from Smyrna is about twenty-four miles (38·6 km.).

I was in some doubt what to do, but when I went inside and saw how intolerably disgusting the rooms were, I decided to push on, especially as my servants were not available, having gone on ahead. By the time we had crossed the river it was quite dark, with a light cool breeze, so that I felt refreshed and cheered; and when late in the evening we came to Larisa I was quite happy to find that we had still not overtaken our train, that the inn was no better than the last, and that there was nothing for it but to persevere with the journey.

Larisa is a common name on the ancient map. There were at least ten places so called, three of them on the west coast of Asia Minor, in the Troad, in Aeolis, and in Ionia. The one in question here was one of the original twelve cities of the Aeolian League, and earlier still, before the coming of the Greeks, had been the principal town of the region. It may indeed have the honour of being one of the very few towns on the west coast named by Homer. In the *Iliad*, among the Trojan allies, we read of the 'warlike Pelasgians who dwelt around fertile Larisa'; their leader, Hippothous, was killed at Troy, 'far from fertile Larisa'. Since Larisa in the Troad is comparatively close to Troy, some ancient critics believed that our Larisa must be meant, and some modern scholars agree with them. In any case, the existence of a Larisa in this region in the second millennium is not disputed.

The Pelasgians were not merely the occupants of the district of Larisa. The name was given by the Greeks to their own predecessors in many parts of the world, not only in Asia but in Greece itself and the Aegean islands. At Larisa legend preserved the name of one of the Pelasgian rulers, Piasus; this man, it was said, fell in love with his own daughter and offered her violence. But the lady had her revenge: catching him one day bending over a cask of wine, she whipped up his heels and drowned him in the liquor.

When the Aeolian Greeks arrived not long after the Trojan War and wished to settle in the country, they found themselves opposed by the Pelasgians; for these, though somewhat weakened by their sufferings at Troy, were still firmly in control of Larisa. The Greeks therefore, as Strabo tells us, built themselves a base some three or four miles (4·83 or 6·44 km.) from Larisa and called it Neonteichos, the New Fort. Operating from here they eventually reduced Larisa, after which they founded the city of Cyme and peopled it with the inhabitants of the region. Both to Cyme and to Larisa they gave the epithet Phriconis, after Mt Phrikion in their native land in Greece.

Shortly afterwards the various Greek colonies in Aeolis, including Smyrna, united into an Aeolian League. As in the Ionian League, there were originally twelve members, but, as related above, Smyrna soon passed into the hands of the Ionians.

During the following centuries the Aeolians, unlike the Ionians, lived more or less untroubled, offering no resistance to the Lydian and Persian conquerors. Larisa makes one or two appearances in history. In 546 B.C. Cyrus, after defeating Croesus, settled some Egyptian allies of the Lydian king in the city, which thus acquired the name of 'Egyptian Larisa'. In the Delian Confederacy it is doubtful if Larisa was ever effectively included. She was assessed for tribute at an unknown sum, but there is no evidence that she ever actually paid. The city seems indeed to have been less wholeheartedly Greek than most, and in 399 B.C. she was one of the few to resist the Spartan general, Thibron, when he came to defend the Greek cities against the Persians—and the only one to resist successfully. Thibron attempted to cut off the city's water-supply, but the citizens defended it vigorously and he was forced to withdraw (Appendix 2).

When Alexander arrived, the whole of Aeolis submitted quietly to him; and when the Attalid kingdom of Pergamum was established, Aeolis formed a more or less permanent part of it. But at some time during the Hellenistic period the existence of Larisa as an independent city came to an end. Perhaps it succumbed to the invading Gauls in 279 B.C. and never recovered; at all events Strabo calls it deserted and Pliny speaks of it as having once existed. Nevertheless, it is clear from Aristides' narrative that a place of some sort still survived in the second century A.D. and possessed an inn, though of poor quality. We should picture Larisa at this date as a village or small town dependent upon Cyme.

Between the Hermus crossing and Cyme, Aristides mentions only one place, Larisa, whereas (if the crossing was near Emiralem) there are two ancient city sites close above the road at Yanık Köy and Buruncuk respectively. Of these, that at Buruncuk has been confidently claimed as Larisa, and was excavated as such by German archaeologists in 1902 and again in 1932–34. Yanık Köy then remains to represent Neonteichos, from which Larisa was originally attacked and captured. These locations agree closely with the distances given by Strabo, namely Cyme–Larisa seventy stades or eight miles (12·9 km.), and Larisa–Neonteichos thirty stades or three and a half miles (5·63 km.).

Recently, however, this view has been called in question. Professor Cook is now disposed to believe that Larisa was at Yanık Köy, while Buruncuk probably represents Cyllene, an obscure Aeolian town of which very little is heard. The problem cannot be fully discussed here, but it is remarkable that the excavations at Buruncuk produced no evidence in favour of Larisa—no inscriptions at all, not a single coin of Larisa, and no Greek sherds earlier than 800 B.C. Yanık Köy has never been excavated, so that no comparison in these respects can be made. Professor Cook points out that Strabo's distances in this region are habitually underestimated, and calls attention to a passage in an ancient *Life of Homer* of uncertain authorship and date and of no historical value, but evidently written by a man familiar with this country. This says that the poet, travelling from Smyrna to Cyme, crossed the Hermus plain to Neonteichos, and from there to Cyme by way of Larisa. Though at first sight this seems to support the generally accepted view, in fact it creates a difficulty; for the writer adds: 'because this way it was easiest for him'. Now, Homer was blind, and the plain implication is that for a sighted man there was a shorter but more difficult road which the poet preferred to avoid; but from Yanık Köy to Cyme the road leads straight by Buruncuk and no alternative short cut is possible. On the other hand, if Yanık Köy is Larisa, where is Neonteichos? The site to the east above Gürice is securely identified with Temnus, and no other seems to be discoverable. Aristides' narrative is unfortunately of little help, owing not only to the uncertainty concerning the exact position of the Hermus crossing, but still more to the vagueness of the Greek expressions of time. He crossed the river soon after sunset, say about eight o'clock; but what is meant by 'late in the evening'? If nine o'clock, then Larisa is Yanık Köy; if ten o'clock, it is at Buruncuk. The problem must be left for the present unresolved; meanwhile the ruins at Buruncuk, though spurned by Freya Stark, deserve perhaps an hour or so of the traveller's time.

The hill, some 300 feet (91·4 m.) high, rises directly above the village and may be ascended on the north side by the ancient road, much of whose paving remains; it led up to the main gate of the city. The acropolis was first fortified about 500 B.C. Before that the town was defended by a wall dating from before the Greek conquest; it enclosed a considerable area, larger than that of the contemporary Troy or Mycenae. Early in the fourth century the whole of the fortification was reconstructed; an extension to the acropolis was built (F on the plan) and the town walls were renewed. The line of the wall L,L may be traced, except where the hill has recently

1 Smyrna. View of the town from Kadife Kale

2 Magnesia ad Sipylum. The true Niobe

3 Magnesia ad Sipylum. Taş Suret. The false Niobe

4 Baths of Agamemnon; the modern installation

5 Smyrna. Tomb of Tantalus

6 Akkaya. Tomb or Look-out post?

7 'Eti Baba'. Hittite figure in the Karabel gorge

8 Pergamum. The Asclepieum

9 Pergamum. Round building in the Asclepieum

10 Pergamum. Altar of Zeus

11 Pergamum. Kızıl Avlu

12 Pergamum. Kızıl Avlu; double River Channel

13 Pergamum. Theatre

14 Pergamum. Theatre

15 Pergamum. Sanctuary of Demeter

16 Myrina. The site, with Öteki Tepe in the background

17 Hierapolis. Tumulus graves in the Necropolis

18 Elaea. Ancient Quay

19 Pitane. The Venetian Castle

20 Phocaea. Taş Kule; tomb on the Eski Foça road

21 Teos. Ancient Quay with mooring-stone

22 Pitane. Archaic Statue now in the Museum at Bergama

23 Larisa. City Wall

24 Teos. View from the Theatre

25 Teos. Curiously-cut blocks in the quarry

26 Teos. Re-erecting the columns of the Temple of Dionysus in 1964

27 Lebedus. Inscribed stone from the Gymnasium

been quarried away, but hardly a stone remains in place; K,K is rather better preserved, though nowhere more than a single course is visible. Remains of all three building-periods may be seen in the north-west wall of the acropolis, showing a mixture of polygonal and ashlar masonry still several metres in height (Pl. 23).

The interior of the acropolis was covered with closely packed buildings, of which only the foundations survive. Chief among them are the two temples B and C and the palace J. One of the temples, probably B, was surely that of Athena, the principal deity of the city. The palace, several times rebuilt, was the residence of the Greek tyrants in early days and later of the Persian governor.

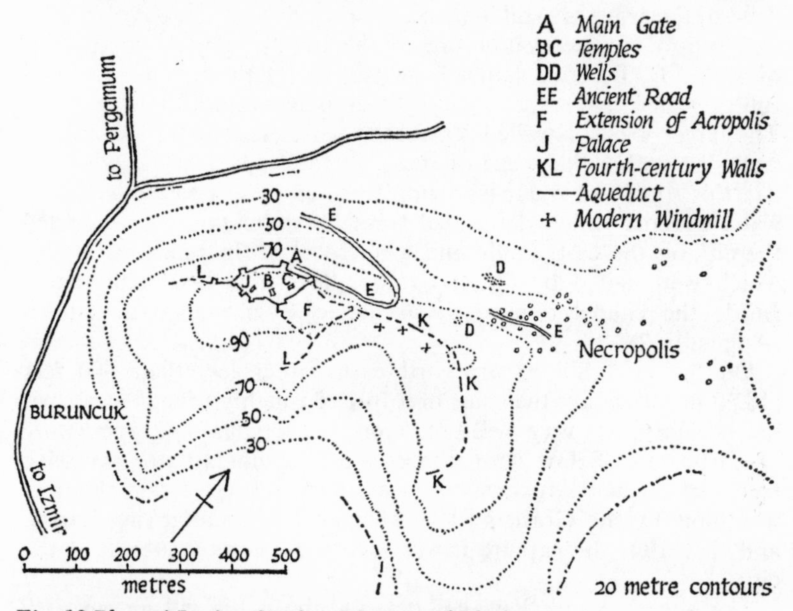

Fig. 13 Plan of Larisa (?) after Meyer and Plath

East of the citadel, beyond the hill with the ruins of three modern windmills, is the main part of the necropolis. About a hundred tombs have been recognized, strewn over the lower slope of the windmill hill and on the saddle between it and the next hill. They were mostly of tumulus type, with a low ring-wall of one or two courses of polygonal masonry surmounted by a conical mound of earth; a tall stone was probably set on the summit. Tombs of this kind, though much later in date, may be seen in the necropolis at Hierapolis (Pl. 17). The grave itself, placed generally near the middle, was constructed of stone slabs set on edge; some tumuli contained two graves. A remarkable feature is the manner in which many of the tumuli have been later enlarged by the addition of one or more segments of circles of varying size; in one case the tomb has been enlarged in this way no less than four times. A few of the tombs are rectangular, divided in some cases into partitions. The whole necropolis is dated by the sherds found in it to the sixth century B.C. All the bodies were buried; no sign of cremation has been observed. Today it is still quite easy to recognize a number of these tombs by a ring of polygonal blocks, and in one or two cases the upright slabs of the grave are still in place.

A supply of water was ensured in the first place by the two groups of wells, D, D, both dating from very early times. They are still full of water, and were in use by the villagers until quite recently. The larger group is called Yirmikuyu, and contains in fact twenty wells, all within the space of some 30 yards (27·4 m.). About 500 B.C. this source of water was supplemented by a great aqueduct or water-channel which descended from the mountain and encircled the city on the east, south, and west. Most of the remnants of this which were noted by the excavators have now been obliterated. Inside the citadel rainwater was collected in numerous cisterns (Appendix 2).

On the next hill to the north-east, rather less than 600 feet (182·9 m.) high, are the ruins of a fort of roughly triangular shape; the masonry, not very well preserved, is polygonal and apparently of early date. Below it on the east and south-east are extensive traces of ancient settlement. The excavators suggest that this fort was built by the Greek settlers when they were attacking Larisa, and that after the capture it was incorporated as a suburb of the city.

The site at Yanık Köy lies directly above the village, an easy half-hour's climb. It is conspicuous from afar by the curious circular rock which forms the citadel. Never having been excavated, it offers little to the visitor beyond a pleasant excursion and a fine view. On the slope towards the village are a number of pieces of handsome polygonal wall, mostly terrace walls; and a long stretch of the city wall, also polygonal, is preserved on the south side of the hill. On the summit is a rock-cut stairway and a little to the north-east some remains of ashlar masonry. The surface sherds range in date from the sixth century B.C. to Byzantine times, the majority being of

Fig. 14 Yanık Köy

the fourth and third centuries. The ancient paved way may be followed from below the village for a considerable way up the hill.

> At midnight or a little later we reached Cyme, where we found everything shut. Still undismayed, I urged my companions to make a further effort and to carry on for the rest of the way to Myrina, pointing out that it was not far to go and that it was much better not to abandon our original intention. When we left the city gates, there was a damp chill in the air and I felt distinctly cold.

Cyme was in Greek and Roman times the most important town of this region; Strabo calls it 'the biggest and best of the Aeolian cities'. Tradition recorded, as was mentioned above, that Cyme was founded by the Greek settlers after the capture of Larisa and the subjugation of the Pelasgians. It served as a centre for the settlement of numerous small towns, many of which did not survive into classical times. The city was said to have received its name, like Smyrna, Myrina, and others, from an Amazon, by name Cyme; some scholars have seen in these traditions an echo of the Hittite invasion of these parts which has left its traces in the Taş Suret and Karabel figures (above, p. 1, pp. 31ff.). Like the Aeolian cities in general, and unlike the Ionians, Cyme was more land- than sea-minded; Strabo says that the citizens acquired a name for stupidity because it was not until 300 years after the foundation that they thought of raising revenue by farming out their harbour-dues—as if it took them all that time to realize that they lived on the sea-coast.

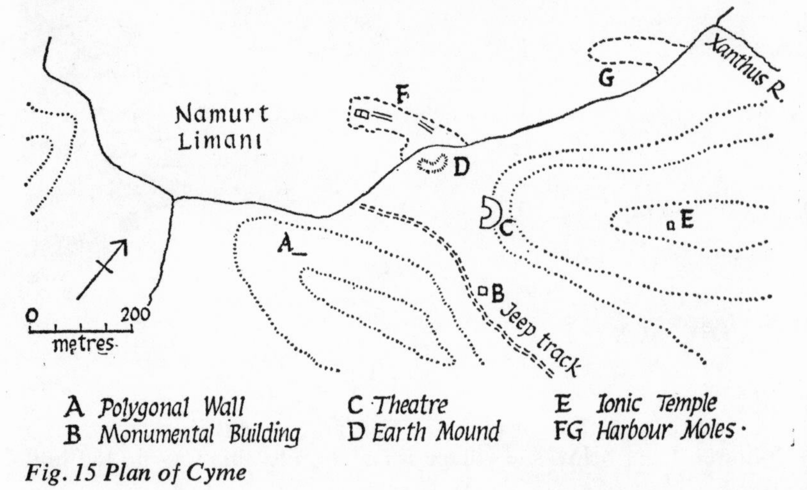

Fig. 15 Plan of Cyme

Stupid or not, the Cymaeans flourished, and were not negligible even at sea. Aristagoras, tyrant of Cyme, led a contingent of his own ships to assist the Persian king Darius in his invasion of Scythia in 512 B.C. (below, pp. 184–5) and when Xerxes invaded Greece in 480, Sandoces, the Persian governor of Cyme, contributed fifteen ships to his fleet. No other Aeolian city was represented on either of these campaigns. In the Delian Confederacy, Cyme paid a tribute of nine talents, not only far more than any other Aeolian town, but more than was paid by Ephesus, Miletus, or any of the biggest cities of Ionia.

The Cymaeans were also not entirely without an answer to the cultural brilliance of Ionia. The epic poet Hesiod, rival of Homer, who lived and wrote in Greece, tells us that his father had emigrated from Cyme, so that if not the poet himself, at least his family was of Cymaean stock. No other Aeolian city could claim as much. The fourth-century historian Ephorus was also a native of Cyme. Strabo says that it was a joke against him that, having no great Cymaean achievements to record in his history, but not wishing his own city to remain without a mention, he wrote: 'About this time the Cymaeans were doing nothing'. So, with the rest of Aeolis, they continued to do under the Hellenistic kings and in the province of Asia, living quietly and leaving little mark on the course of history.

The location of Cyme at Namurt Limanı is abundantly proved by inscriptions and coins found on the spot; but the ruins are scanty in the extreme. Here, as in so many cases on the coast, the ancient stones have no doubt been removed by sea for use in the building of Izmir, Istanbul, and other cities; the fortifications are said to have been destroyed by the Turkish conqueror Mehmet in the fifteenth century.

The site includes two hills, a northern and a southern, of which the latter carried the main habitation. Small-scale excavations have been carried out by Czech, French, and German scholars since the end of the last century, but the remains which they brought to light are not now easily discoverable. At A there is, or was, to be seen a short stretch of polygonal wall of early date. At B, close beside the modern track, are the ruins of a monumental building; two parallel rows of unfluted columns are visible. At E, towards the summit of the northern hill, the excavators unearthed a small Ionic temple dedicated to the Egyptian goddess Isis; this is now hard to find among the dense bushes. Of the theatre at the foot of the northern hill nothing remains but the semicircle of the cavea in the hillside.

Two streams enter the sea close to the city. That on the south has converted the valley into a marsh; that on the north is identified with the river Xanthus which appears on coins of the city. Between their mouths are the ruins of two harbour-moles now under water. The southern, F, is the better preserved and much of its masonry survives. Investigations made recently by German scholars have shown that the sea-level has risen rather more than 5 feet (1·52 m.) since classical antiquity.

Nothing more remains of the biggest and best of the Aeolian cities. Unfortunately in recent years the landscape of the gulf of

Cyme has been much altered by industrial development, and modern oil refineries and petro-chemical works threaten to obliterate the few remaining traces of classical Cyme.

> About cock-crow we reached Myrina, and there we found our men outside one of the inns, still not unpacked because, as they said, they too had found nothing open. In the porch of the inn was a pallet-bed; we spent some time carrying this up and down, but could find no comfortable place to put it. Knocking at the door was useless, as no one answered it. At long last we managed to get into the house of an acquaintance; but by bad luck the porter's fire was out, so that I went in in complete darkness, led by the hand, seeing nothing and myself invisible. By the time a fire had been procured and I was preparing to enjoy a drink in front of it, the morning star was rising and dawn had begun to break. Pride rebelled against going to bed in daylight, so I decided to make a further effort and go on to the temple of Apollo at Gryneum, where it was my habit to offer sacrifice on my journeys up and down the road.

Myrina is a city without a history. Legend told of Myrina, a great queen of the Amazons, who led her victorious armies not only over Asia Minor but to many parts of the world; of the cities she founded one was called after her, and others, such as Cyme, Pitane, and Gryneum, after her lieutenants. Of the Greek settlement nothing is recorded. Myrina appears in the Delian Confederacy with a tribute of one talent, well above normal for the Aeolian cities other than Cyme. Here and there in the historians we find a casual mention of Myrina, but in most cases it is doubtful if these refer to our city at all, for there was a second Myrina on the island of Lemnos.

The great earthquake of A.D. 17 destroyed twelve cities in a single night, of which Myrina was one. The Emperor Tiberius was generous with his help and the twelve cities were rebuilt, Myrina apparently under the new name of Sebastopolis, or Emperor's City; this name was in use in Pliny's time, but the old name afterwards revived. The twelve cities in gratitude erected in Rome a colossal statue of Tiberius, with twelve figures on the base representing themselves. A copy of this monument was found at Puteoli near Naples; the figure representing Myrina is shown not as an Amazon, as might have been expected, but as a priestess of the Gryneian Apollo. In the course of time Gryneum had lost its independence and become incorporated in Myrina, and such importance as Myrina had was mostly due to her possession of this famous sanctuary.

A second destruction by earthquake in A.D. 106 was followed by a second rebuilding; but as the influence of the pagan sanctuaries waned before the rise of Christianity, Myrina sank into utter obscurity, relieved only by the reputation of her oysters.

Like Cyme, Myrina offers little to the traveller in the way of standing ruins. The charm of the site itself is delightfully conveyed by Freya Stark in her description of her visit; she notes that even the few ancient stones that were to be seen were being broken up and carried off for building. But her visit was hurried, and there is, in fact, a certain amount for the energetic traveller to discover (Pl. 16).

The site lies at the mouth of the Güzelhisar River, the ancient Titnaeus or Pythicus. It is reached by a very bad track which turns off the main road half a mile north of the river; the distance is a mile and a half. The city occupied two hills, formerly known as Epano Tepe and Kato Tepe, but now called merely Birki Tepe and Öteki Tepe ('the One Hill' and 'the Other Hill'). Birki Tepe formed the acropolis, and was defended by a polygonal wall, of which two pieces were noted by the French excavators, but they are not now easy to find. On the other hand, a piece of Byzantine wall, E, is conspicuous to the visitor arriving from the east. On the west slope is a hollow, C, which probably held the theatre. There is nothing to be seen on the summit, nor on the Other Hill, though the latter is terraced and was evidently occupied in antiquity.

At F is a small landing-stage, of which the seaward side is formed by the remains of an ancient quay. Several of the blocks project into the sea and are pierced by round holes for the purpose of mooring vessels. Similar blocks are also to be seen at Teos (below, p. 114).

On the north slope of Birki Tepe and the hill facing it on the north between 4,000 and 5,000 tombs were excavated in 1880–82; of these the great majority were hitherto unopened. Most are simple rectangular graves, taking a single occupant, sunk into the chalky rock; sometimes two or three are superposed. There is no rule about orientation. A few are circular, and a few are smaller cavities holding a cinerary urn; but cremation is exceptional and inhumation is the normal practice. Over many of the graves stood a tombstone inscribed merely with the name of the dead person and his or her father; in other cases a slip of bronze in the grave itself gave the same information. These inscriptions date the necropolis as a whole

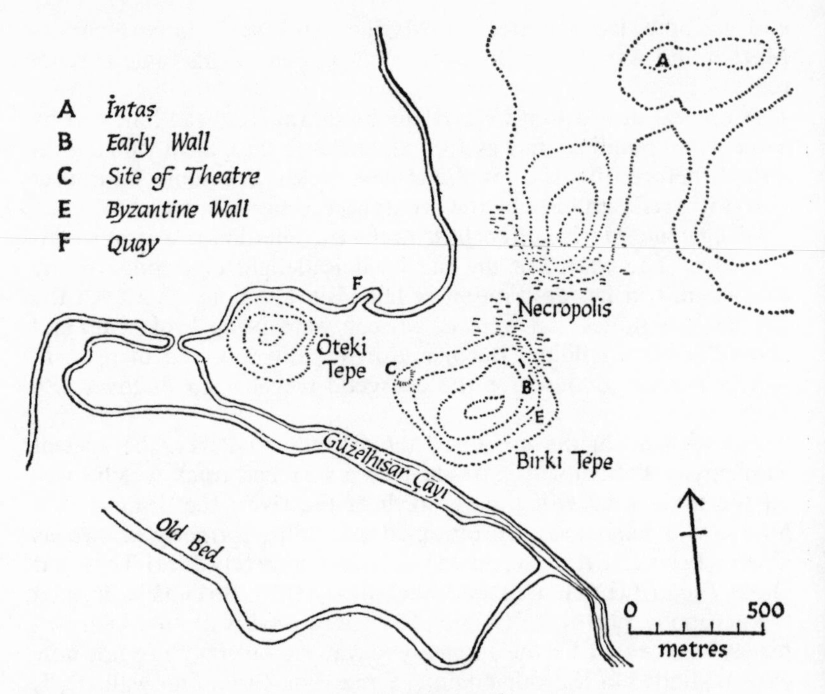

Fig. 16 Plan of Myrina (after Pottier-Reinach)

to the late Hellenistic period, approximately the last two centuries B.C.

The tombs varied greatly in the richness of their contents. Some were almost or quite empty apart from the corpse itself, others contained a variety of objects deposited at the time of burial. Many of these were deliberately broken, seemingly with the purpose of discouraging tomb-robbers.[1] These objects fall into several categories. First, nearly every grave was found to contain one or more coins. The original custom was to place an obol (say a penny) in the dead man's mouth to pay his fare in Charon's ferry over the Styx into the underworld; at Myrina the coins used are all bronze of small value, though not actually obol-pieces. Inflation had been at work in the interval and Charon's prices had gone up with the rest. These coins are nearly all of Myrina itself, and date from Alexander to Tiberius. Next in importance are the plates for the dead man's food and the bottles for his drink. These are in many cases token offerings only; some of the clay bottles are merely an inch or two high and quite solid. Third come the objects used habitually in life—lamps, mirrors, needles, perfume-boxes, and many others. Jewellery, however, is scarce. Finally come the famous terracotta figurines, of which a thousand or so were found by the excavators and entitle Myrina to rank with Tanagra. They include all kinds of figures, men, women, children, gods, and animals; Eros and Aphrodite are especially popular. There are also grotesque and comic figures, and tragic and comic masks. The purpose of these figurines has been much disputed, but it seems that often they have no particular significance, being merely favourite possessions of the dead during life.

Of all these graves nothing whatever is to be seen now, the ground having long since been ploughed over.

Some half a mile to the north-east of the acropolis, in a conspicuous yellow outcrop near the top of the second hill in that direction, is a rock-cut chamber-tomb known as Intaş (A). The main chamber has a vaulted roof, and from it ten vaulted niches some 6 feet (1·83 m.) deep open off. There are numerous other rock-cut tombs of more modest character in the neighbouring hills, which the local shepherd-boys will readily point out.

> On reaching Gryneum I made my sacrifice and occupied myself in my customary way; then proceeding to Elaea I put up there for the night, and on the following day arrived in Pergamum.

Strabo observes that Apollo was held in especial honour all down this coast; and of all his seats of worship in these parts the oracular sanctuary of Gryneum was the most famous.

Gryneum was one of the original twelve Aeolian cities, but nothing is recorded of its foundation by the Greeks. Tradition spoke

Fig. 17 Gryneum

of an earlier town named after the Amazon Gryne, who followed Queen Myrina on her campaigns and had the honour, or misfortune, to be violated by Apollo. The city first appears in history in the fifth century as a member of the Athenian maritime confederacy, in which she paid the modest sum of one-sixth of a talent, later raised to one-third. By the end of the century Athens, defeated by Sparta in the Peloponnesian War, had lost control of this region to the Persians, and about 405 B.C. we hear that the Persian satrap was drawing revenues of fifty talents a year from Gryneum. The figure is astonishingly high in view of the city's humble assessment in the Delian League, and is likely to be wrong.

The country was still in Persian hands in 335 B.C., when the Macedonian general Parmenio, sent ahead to prepare the way for Alexander's crossing into Asia, captured Gryneum by assault and enslaved the inhabitants. This event did not put an end to the city's independent existence, for the rare coins of Gryneum date from the third century; but at some time during the Hellenistic period it became a dependency of Myrina, noted henceforth mainly for the sanctuary of Apollo.

Of this sanctuary we have short descriptions in the writers of the Roman period. Strabo mentions the ancient oracle of Apollo and a costly temple of white marble. Pausanias speaks of a most beautiful grove of Apollo with trees, some cultivated for their fruit, others such as give no fruit but are pleasing to the sight or smell. These are still represented today by the olives and by the great expanses of pink oleanders which adorn the site. Pliny, who says there is now nothing but a harbour where Gryneum once existed, clearly does less than justice to the place.

We read in Virgil that it was Gryneian Apollo who urged Aeneas, after the fall of Troy, to go to Italy, where he became the legendary ancestor of the Romans. Apart from this somewhat unhistorical case, despite the fame of the oracle not a single response of Apollo at Gryneum was known until the present writer found at Caunus in Caria an inscription recording a consultation by the Caunians in the second century B.C. The Caunians ask to what gods they should sacrifice in order to obtain fruitful harvests. Of Apollo's reply in hexameter verse only the beginning is preserved; it is involved in suitable oracular obscurity, but advises that honour be paid to Apollo and Zeus.

Pliny mentions the oysters of Gryneum along with those of Myrina; and, in fact, both oysters and mussels are frequent on this coast. The coins of Gryneum show on one side the head of Apollo and on the other a mussel, thus commemorating the city's two chief claims to distinction.

The site of Gryneum is marked by the little promontory of Temaşalık Burnu, rather more than half a mile (804·7 m.) south of the village of Yenişakran. On this headland the temple of Apollo is supposed to have stood, though no very clear traces of it have been found. At present a rectangular mound or platform may be seen on the highest part of the peninsula, which may represent the sacred precinct; a dozen or more unfluted column-drums lie around its perimeter, but nothing more is visible. Even these are not of white marble, so cannot come from the temple; and indeed they seem to be of Byzantine construction. There are no signs of any ancient harbour-works; though Pliny finds the harbour worth mentioning, it can never, in fact, have been usable by any but very small boats, as the Mediterranean Pilot makes clear.

The peninsula is too small to carry a city, even a modest one like Gryneum, especially if a large part was occupied by the temple precincts. The main habitation must have been on the mainland. A few years ago there came to light, close beside the main road, a cemetery with sarcophagi dating to about 500 B.C. and a handsome mosaic pavement of late Roman date. Nothing else, and in particular no acropolis, has yet been found.

On the little Temaşalık Burnu, then, we may picture Aristides making his sacrifice and occupying himself 'in his customary way'. What this may have been he does not say, but if we imagine him chatting with the priests, telling them the news from Smyrna and the condition of his stomach, and making a thank-offering to Apollo, we may not be far from the mark.

Elaea differs in several respects from the other cities of Aeolis. It has the distinction of being apparently the earliest Greek foundation on this coast; tradition said that it was settled at the time of the Trojan War by Menestheus, leader of the contingent from Athens, a hundred years or more before the Aeolian migration from Greece. For this or some other reason it was not included among the twelve members of the Aeolian League, and in classical times was a place of little account; its assessment in the Delian Confederacy was very low, no more than one-sixth of a talent. The city's importance began in the Hellenistic period, when most of the Aeolian towns were sinking into obscurity, and was connected with the rise of the Pergamene kingdom. Being situated at the nearest point on the coast to the capital, it was made into a port and naval station by the Attalid kings, and in this capacity it is mentioned from time to time by the historians. With the conversion of the kingdom of Pergamum into the province of Asia this importance was largely lost. Elaea furnished a bed for Aristides in the second century, and was still existing in early Byzantine times. Oysters are not mentioned here, but Galen of Pergamum speaks of a thyme-covered hill not far away which produced the most excellent honey. Elaea means 'olive', an obviously appropriate name which is repeated today in the village of Zeytindağ some three miles (4·83 km.) to the north-east.

Little more remains at Elaea than at Gryneum, and the site has never been excavated. It is reached by a rough road turning off the highway at the coffee-house of Kazıkbağları, rather more than four miles (6·44 km.) north of Gryneum.

The principal surviving remnant of antiquity is the harbour wall D, now called Taş Liman. Still solidly preserved, this runs out for some 200 yards (182·9 m.) into a melancholy waste of mud-flats. It is constructed of large blocks laid horizontally and secured with metal clamps; the clamps themselves are gone, but the holes remain. The other walls of the harbour and quay are not now in evidence (Pl. 18).

The acropolis A is a low hill barely 60 feet (18·3 m.) high. Nothing remains standing on it, but ancient marbles are frequently turned up by the plough; a number of these are collected at the coffee-house. Sherds are abundant all over the hill; lamps, tiles, and sometimes coins may be picked up. Those who enjoy searching for fragments of antiquity will find here a happy hunting-ground.

The line of the city wall B,B is traceable in places, especially between the acropolis and the main road, as a ridge in the ground, but nothing appears above the surface except a few stray blocks. German scholars sixty years ago were able to determine its thickness at 11 feet (3·35 m.), and to date it to 234 B.C. by an inscription on one of the blocks. Of the gate H the position is identifiable in a dip between two hills close above the road, but the gate itself is not visible.

The necropolis seems to have been in the neighbourhood of N; here at least were found two inscribed funeral stelae which are at the time of writing in a private house near the café at Kazıkbağları.

No sign of a theatre or stadium has been found, and apart from the wells G,G nothing more is at present to be seen of ancient Elaea.

At Pergamum we take leave of Aristides, cured of his disorder

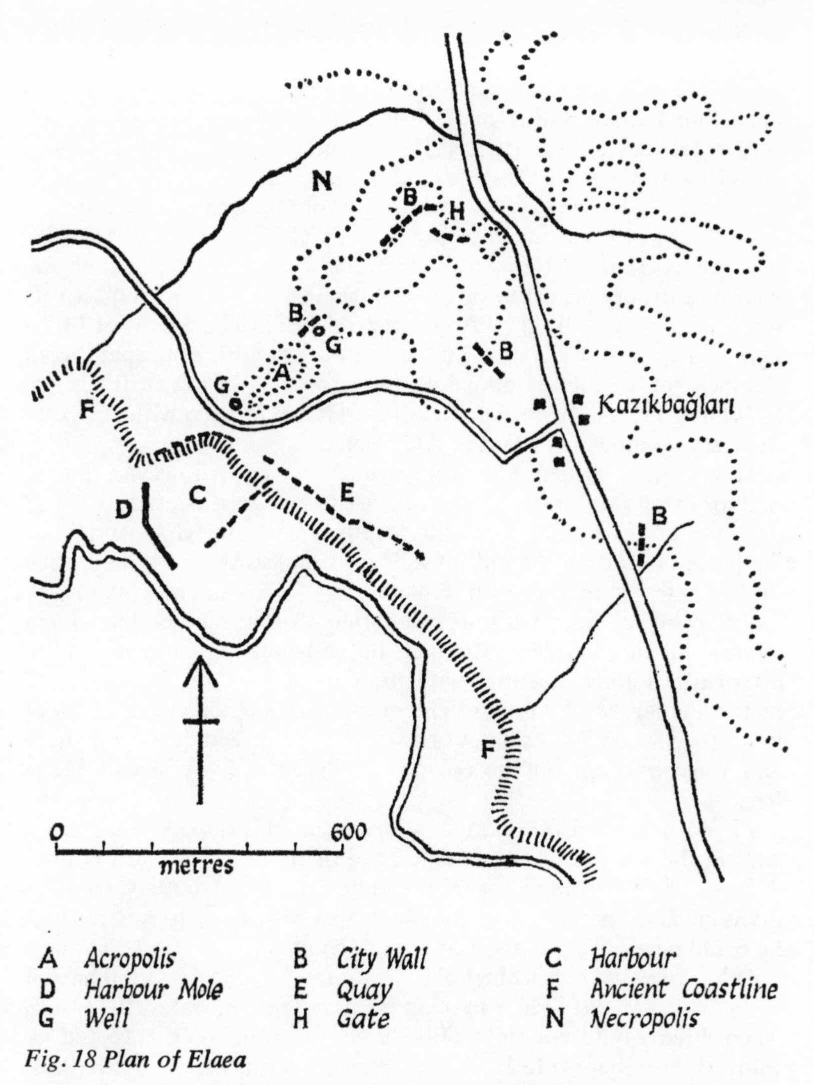

Fig. 18 Plan of Elaea

by the mere effort of the journey. On the way back to Smyrna we may turn aside to look at one or two sites which lay off his road.

A little to the north of Elaea a road leads westward to Çandarlı, site of the ancient Pitane, on its tongue-like peninsula. The excursion is worth while if only for the fine Venetian castle which stands in the town. Pitane was the northernmost of the members of the Aeolian League, but no Greek foundation-legend survives. The town itself was far older than the Aeolian colonization; pottery has been found there dating back to the third millennium. The Greek settlement was not unopposed, for we hear that the native people, called as at Larisa 'Pelasgians', succeeded in recapturing the city, which was only recovered with the help of the men of Erythrae.

In later times Pitane was noted for its vicissitudes of fortune, so that the expression 'I'm a regular Pitane' became proverbial of one who had experienced the ups and downs of fate. These varied fortunes were related by the fifth-century historian Hellanicus of Mitylene just across the water; but his works are lost, and apart from the incident mentioned above we know nothing of the early history of Pitane. The city was included in the Delian League with the same modest assessment as Elaea and Gryneum.

Despite this evidence of comparative poverty, however, Pitane had an extensive territory, and at least in the third century was not destitute of funds. She was able to purchase from King Antiochus I a piece of land on the gulf of Adramyttium to the north at a price of 380 talents; to this sum Philetaerus of Pergamum, anxious to secure good relations with his neighbours, contributed perhaps forty talents out of the 9,000 of which he had possessed himself. Soon afterwards Pitane, together with most of Aeolis, was incorporated in the Pergamene kingdom. The city appears again for a moment in history when Mithridates, hard pressed by Fimbria, fled there and was besieged; but he escaped easily enough by sea to Mitylene.

Pitane produced one famous citizen, the philosopher Arcesilaus, who in the third century became head of the Platonic Academy at Athens. He was noted for his readiness to plead both sides of a question and for reserving judgment—so much so, it is said, that he could never bring himself to write a book.

Otherwise, the city's chief claim to fame was her bricks. The soil being volcanic and lighter than an equal volume of water, the bricks when dried would not sink. This statement of Strabo's, repeated by Pliny, does not seem to have been verified in modern times; indeed, the ancient pottery found there is remarkable for its fine hard clay, and nothing is known at Çandarlı of any floating bricks.

Little now remains of ancient Pitane; the ruins have been thoroughly plundered for the building of Çandarlı. The peninsula was fortified by a wall of irregular masonry 8 feet (2·44 m.) thick, running round close above the sea: some very battered remnants may be seen here and there on the west side. Strabo refers to the city's two harbours; that on the west is formed by a mole now under water, running out to a tower on an islet. No such harbour-works are visible on the east, but this side being protected against the prevailing wind it is probable that none were needed.

Of the city's public buildings nothing survives, but the site of the theatre is recognizable about half-way down the east side of the peninsula; and a partly artificial terrace near the southern point seems to mark the position of a stadium. The Venetian castle is said to stand on ancient Greek masonry visible here and there (Pl. 19).

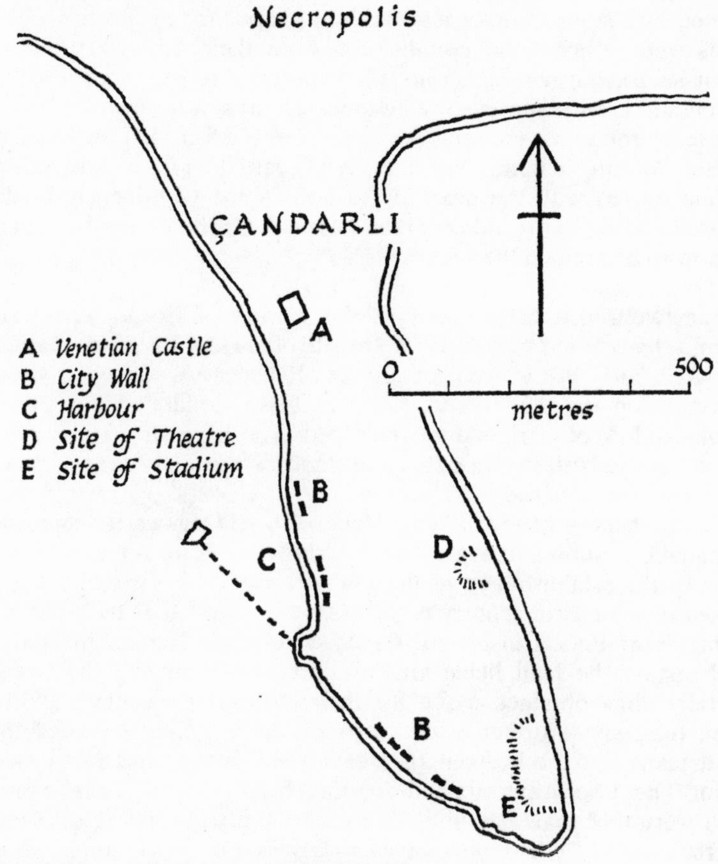

Fig. 19 Plan of Pitane (after Schuchhardt)

In 1958 an archaic statue of Ionian type was found by the villagers near the base of the isthmus, and is now in the Bergama museum. It is a life-size figure of a young man, naked apart from a mantle thrown over his left shoulder, 5 feet 4 inches (1·63 m.) in height. The very low relief of the features (which are, however, somewhat rubbed away), and the rigid upright posture, are typically archaic. The statue is dated to the latter part of the sixth century B.C. (Pl. 22).

This discovery led to an excavation by Turkish archaeologists in the following year, and a necropolis, dating in the main to the sixth century B.C., was brought to light. The custom here was to cremate the dead body and put it into a plain urn, of which the mouth was closed by a stone more or less carefully shaped for the purpose. The urns were either stood upright or laid on their side, according to their shape, but here again no rule is observable with regard to the orientation. In some cases a number of urns were enclosed by a circle of rough stones some 10 to 15 feet (3·05 to 4·57 m.) in diameter, forming a family burying-place. Many handsome vases were found buried with the dead in the urns; some of these are in the museum at Bergama, others are in Istanbul. Of these burials nothing is now to be seen on the spot.

Some two and a half miles (4·02 km.) north of Buruncuk a road turns off westward to Eski Foça, the site of ancient Phocaea. Though situated fairly in the Aeolian country, Phocaea was always Ionian; Smyrna, on the other hand, being at first Aeolian, to this extent Ionia and Aeolis originally overlapped. The harbour at Eski Foça is one of the best on this coast, and Phocaea was at all times a place of some consequence.

In the history of Greek colonization in Asia, Phocaea was a late foundation, subsequent not only to the occupation of Aeolis but also to the establishment of the Ionian League; this would bring it down to the eighth century B.C. The tradition was that the colonists came from Phocis in central Greece under the leadership of two Athenians; the land being already apportioned among the Greek settlers, they obtained a site for their city by agreement with the men of Cyme—further evidence of the un-sea-mindedness of the Cymaeans, for the harbour they gave away is far superior to their own. The Phocaeans applied for membership of the Panionium, and were told that they must first take kings from the descendants of the sons of Codrus who played so large a part in the colonization of Ionia. They accordingly took three from Erythrae and Teos and

Fig. 20 Phocaea

were admitted to the league. It is likely, however, that this tradition is false and was invented at a later date to explain the name Phocaea by a supposed connection with Phocis. Modern scholars think it more probable that the city was a secondary foundation from Erythrae and Teos, and received its name from the humpy, seal-like appearance of the off-lying islets; for *Phoce* is the Greek word for a seal. The coins of Phocaea, and especially the earlier issues, commonly bear the image of a seal (Pl. 64).[2]

Profiting from its fine site and the enterprise of its citizens, the city quickly rose to a place of eminence. The Phocaeans, like the Ionians in general, were great mariners, and their adventurous spirit led them to the west, where they were the first to explore the Adriatic and the western Mediterranean, even as far as Tartessus near Cadiz. Hereabouts they founded a number of colonies, of which the most famous was Massalia, the modern Marseilles. In this connection a curious little tale was told. The Phocaean adventurers arrived hoping to establish a city, and found the country in the possession of a local chieftain by the name of Nannus. This man was on the point of marrying his daughter off, and invited the Greek leader to attend the ceremony. The custom was for the girl to enter the room where the suitors were assembled and to offer to the man of her choice a cup of wine and water. She, however, 'whether by chance or for some other reason' (one wonders which), gave the cup to the Phocaean visitor. Nannus, seeing in this erratic behaviour the hand of the gods, made the best of the situation; he accepted his Greek son-in-law and gave him the land on which to found Massalia. The colonists were afterwards able to be of service to their mother-city.

When at Tartessus the Phocaeans struck up a friendship with the king of that country, who urged them to leave Ionia and settle where they liked in his dominions. Their refusal gave him so little offence that, on learning from them that the Persians were then growing dangerous, he gave them a sum of money to fortify their city. 'He gave with no niggard hand, for [says Herodotus] the wall they built was not a few stades in length and all of large stones carefully fitted'. Of this wall nothing remains today.

In due course (544 B.C.) the Persians arrived and laid siege to the town. Their commander Harpagus offered remarkably easy terms, merely demanding that the inhabitants should demolish one breast-work of their wall and consecrate a single house to the Persian king. The Phocaeans asked for one day to think it over. Harpagus replied that he knew very well what they had in mind to do, but would nevertheless grant the delay. While he withdrew his army, the citizens hastily put on board their wives, children, and movable property, together with most of the statues and offerings from the temples, and sailed away to Chios. Next day the Persians marched into an empty city. From Chios, where they found themselves unwelcome, the Phocaeans set sail for the island of Corsica, where they had a colony called Alalia; but on leaving they put back into Phocaea and slaughtered the garrison left there by the Persians. Thereupon they swore mighty oaths to stick together on their migration, and threw a lump of iron into the sea, vowing never to return till it should reappear. No sooner had they left, however, than more than half of them, overcome by longing for their familiar haunts, broke their oaths and sailed back to the city. How they made their peace with the Persians for the murdered garrison we do not hear, but Phocaea was permitted to exist. The others meanwhile made their way to Corsica, and from there after a time to Rhegium, and finally to Elea in the south of Italy. The city they founded there became rapidly one of the greatest of western Greece, and developed in the fifth century the Eleatic school of philosophy; the best known of its professors is probably Zeno, whose notorious paradox of

Achilles and the Tortoise, and his other puzzles concerning motion, were famous in antiquity and are still none too easy to explain away (Appendix 3).

The loss of half its population had the natural result of reducing the prosperity and commercial activity of Phocaea; for several decades the coinage appears to have ceased. By the end of the sixth century, however, the city had so far recovered that she could venture to take part in the Ionian revolt against the Persians, though her modest contribution of three ships to the Ionian fleet at Lade in 494 is evidence of her continuing weakness. So in the Delian League her tribute is assessed at only two to three talents, less than one-third of that of her neighbour Cyme. During the fifth century Phocaea issued an abundant coinage of electrum, an alloy of gold and silver, but this money seems to have had a bad reputation, perhaps because the gold content was too low.

In the fourth and third centuries little is heard of Phocaea. Later, when the Romans came to Asia in their war with Antiochus III of Syria, the Phocaeans were reluctant to see in them the future masters of the country and preferred to take the king's part. The Romans accordingly invested the city in 190 B.C. The fine wall admired by Herodotus, now over 300 years old, was not proof against the Roman battering rams, and was breached in two places; the citizens, however, repelled the first assault and continued to resist with such fury as to provoke the Roman commander Aemilius to remark that by fighting on they seemed more determined than the Romans to ensure the city's destruction. When reasonable terms were offered, and no help was forthcoming from Antiochus, the Phocaeans at length opened their gates, on condition that they should suffer no hostile treatment. But Aemilius proved unable to contain his men; his commands were disregarded and the city plundered by the Roman soldiery. Afterwards he restored it to its owners, together with its territory and its independence.

Sixty years later the Phocaeans were guilty of a second error. When Aristonicus contested the Roman inheritance of the kingdom of Attalus, they made the mistake of supporting him. The Romans this time were less forbearing, and Phocaea was condemned to destruction by the Senate. The Massaliotes, however, came to the rescue of their mother-city; they interceded with the Senate and secured a pardon for the offenders. In the Mithridatic War nothing is heard of the Phocaeans, and it may be presumed that they had learned their lesson.

The site of Phocaea at Eski Foça has never been in doubt. It is

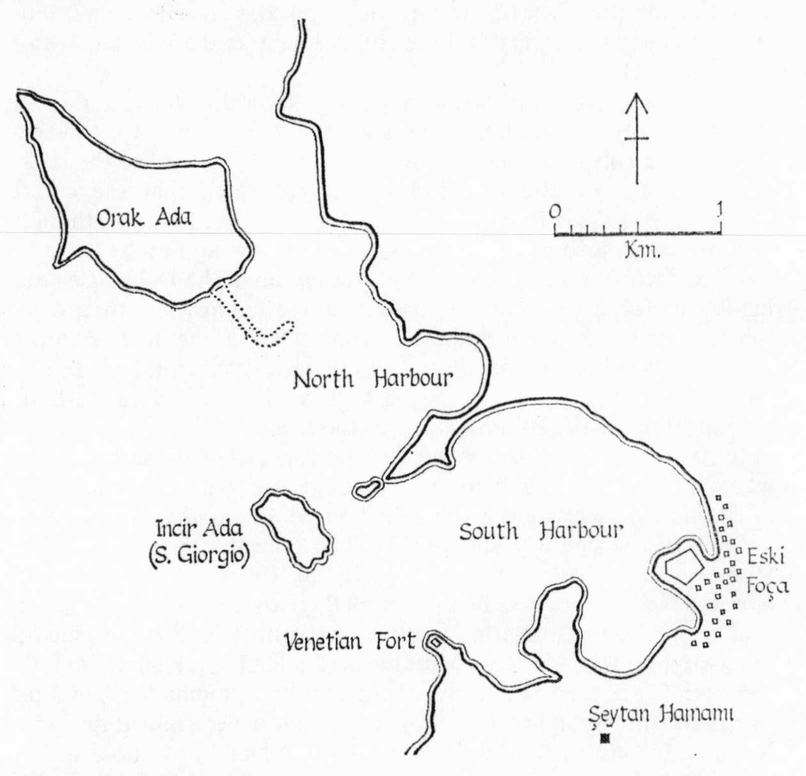

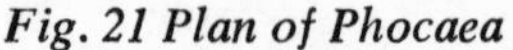

Fig. 21 Plan of Phocaea

amply proved by the survival of the name, by the Phocaean coins found on the spot, and in particular by the description given by Livy in narrating the events of 190 B.C. 'The city', he says,

> is of oblong shape and situated at the head of a bay. The wall encloses a space of two and a half miles, then runs in from either side to form a kind of wedge, which the natives call Lampter. There is at this point, a width of twelve hundred paces. Next, a tongue of land a mile long runs out and divides the bay approximately in the middle; where it joins the narrow entrance it forms on either hand a very safe port. That on the south is called Naustathmus because it will shelter a vast number of ships; the other is close by Lampter.

There can be no doubt that this account refers to Eski Foça, of which it has often been called an exact description. Nevertheless it is not easy to relate all the details to the actual terrain. Livy's text is no doubt taken from his Greek authority; he does not write from personal knowledge. Lampter must be the little peninsula on which the modern town stands, and the tongue of land a mile long must be the spit running out towards the island of San Giorgio (now Incir Ada), though, in fact, it is little over half that length. This spit runs out from a spot twelve hundred paces across the harbour from Lampter, which is approximately correct. The two harbours are then the present harbour (Naustathmus) and that beyond the spit which the Admiralty Chart calls the North Harbour. So far, so good; the difficulty lies in Livy's last few words. How can the other, i.e., northern harbour, be said to be close by Lampter when Lampter is at the very heart of the southern harbour? This difficulty is so severe as to wreck the whole description, and some have even been led to identify the two harbours with the little bays immediately north and south of the Lampter peninsula. Since Lampter means a lamp or beacon, we might then suppose that a beacon or lighthouse

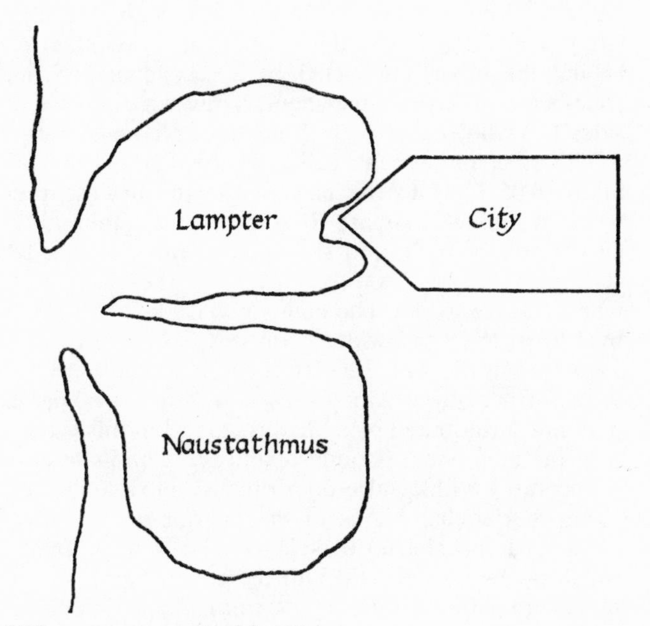

Fig. 22 Site of Phocaea as conceived by Livy

stood on the north side of this peninsula, so that the northern harbour might be said to be 'hard by the beacon'. But we are not really any better off; the tongue of land a mile long will not fit in at all. Livy's account is certainly faulty; he seems to have imagined that the spit was to the south of Lampter, with the harbour of Naustathmus beyond it, somewhat as in the adjoining sketch; his description will then hang together.

Hardly anything remains of classical Phocaea. That the ancient city stood in part on the small peninsula which is the centre of the modern town was proved by the excavations undertaken in 1913 and 1920 by the French archaeologist Sartiaux, but his discoveries were limited to sherds and other small finds. A further investigation by Turkish archaeologists, begun in 1953, located a temple (probably that of Athena) on a rocky platform near the tip of the peninsula; but in general the ancient remains lie deeply buried under the modern buildings.

The surviving monuments consist principally of two tombs. Outside the town on the south-west, a short distance up the hillside, not easy to find without a guide, is a rock-cut chamber tomb known as Şeytan Hamamı, the Devil's Bath. The arched entrance is approached by a passage cut in the rock, with a recess on right and left just in front of the door. Inside are two plain chambers, one behind the other, connected by a second arched doorway. Each chamber contains two rectangular graves let into the floor on either side. The whole tomb is very neatly carved and well repays a visit.

The other monument, called by the Turks Taş Kule, stands five miles (8·05 km.) to the east of the town, close beside the road where it crosses a stream. It consists of a tomb entirely cut out of an outcrop of rock, and still stands nearly 20 feet (6·10 m.) high. Its appearance has been compared to that of a small country church with a square tower. The main cube is about 28 feet (8·53 m.) long by 19 feet (5·79 m.) wide; upon this base, at its east end, are four steps leading up to a smaller cube on which there stood originally some further object which is now broken away—perhaps a stepped pyramid surmounted by a phallus-stone, but this is uncertain. Otherwise the monument is quite plain except on its eastern face, which is decorated with a false door divided into four panels.

The burial-chamber is in the interior of the cubical base. The entrance is on the north side and leads to a small antechamber which opens on the right into the grave-chamber itself. Both these rooms are plain, with flat roofs; in the floor of the inner room is the actual grave, a simple rectangular trough.

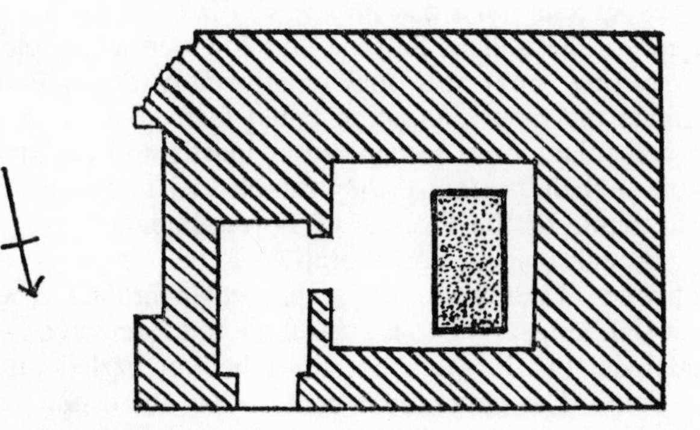

Fig. 23 Phocaea Road. Taş Kule

There are numerous cuttings in the rocks around the tomb and in the bed of the stream close by. These latter may have been used for washing clothes, in the manner of Nausicaa—as indeed the present writer has actually seen them being used.

Nothing whatever is known about this remarkable tomb. No expert who has seen it doubts its great antiquity, and its general style is reminiscent of the early monuments in Phrygia, dating to the time of the Old Kingdom in the eighth century B.C. This was a time of good relations between the Phrygians and the Greeks, when King Midas was the first barbarian to make an offering at Delphi. Later, when the Lydians and then the Persians intervened, Phrygian influence in Ionia is hardly to be expected. There seems no reason why this tomb should not date back to this early period; it may indeed be earlier than Phocaea itself (Pl. 20).

A little farther down the coast is the site of Leucae, at a spot now called Üç Tepeler, the Three Hills. A curious story is told concerning the origin of this city. Diodorus says that it was founded in the fourth century, not long after the King's Peace, by a Persian officer Tachos, and that after his death Clazomenae and Cyme quarrelled for the possession of it. After some indecisive fighting they agreed to consult the oracle at Delphi, and the god decreed that Leucae should belong to whichever of the two peoples should first make sacrifice there—the conditions being that each party should march from its own city at dawn on an appointed day. Leucae being by land much nearer to Cyme than to Clazomenae, the Cymaeans expected to win easily, but the Clazomenians were equal to the occasion. After agreeing on a day for the sacrifice they sent a party of colonists across the gulf of Smyrna and founded a city close to Leucae; by starting from this they comfortably forestalled the Cymaeans. Since the new foundation could fairly be called 'their city', the Clazomenians were recognized as masters of Leucae, and to commemorate their ingenuity they established there an annual festival by the name of the Festival of Forestalment.

This story, though it lacks corroboration, is perhaps less suspect than it might seem. Tachos was at the time engineering a rebellion against the Persian king, and Leucae was no doubt founded as a base for his operations; but in the event the rebellion fizzled out and nothing was done. The subsequent contest for possession of the place may also be historical; at least, the Festival of Forestalment must be an historical fact, and there is nothing to prove that the explanation given is not the true one.

The town itself was never of any great consequence. In the latter part of the fourth century it was sufficiently independent to strike its own coins, bearing the type of a swan; this is the normal type of the coins of Clazomenae. It makes one momentary appearance in history when, after Attalus III had bequeathed his kingdom to Rome, the pretender Aristonicus persuaded the men of Leucae to support his cause and used the town as a base. What penalty, if any, the inhabitants were made to pay to the Romans we do not know.

The site of Leucae lies on the great expanse of alluvial land created by the Hermus River. This region has for many years been a prohibited zone, and it is not normally possible to visit it, at least without special permission. The coastline has, of course, advanced since antiquity. When founded, Leucae was on an island; by Pliny's time this had become a headland, and it is now some way from the shore.

Notes

1 So say the excavators; but the breakage may well have had a ritual purpose, as was certainly the case in other countries, e.g. Central America and Egypt; see for example L. Cottrell, *Lost Cities*, p. 186. We may compare the custom of breaking the glass after drinking a toast.

2 We may compare the islands at Erythrae known as 'The Horses' (below, p. 125).

6 Westward from Smyrna

Clazomenae

For twenty miles (32 km.) west of Smyrna the south coast of the gulf offers nothing in the way of a harbour. The present Izmir–Çesme highroad, once past the Baths of Agamemnon, follows the coast below the Two Brothers, and in the neighbourhood of Kızılbahçe (formerly Kilisman) enters the territory of ancient Clazomenae. The city itself is six miles (9·65 km.) farther on, situated on a small island joined to the mainland by a causeway. This island carries a quarantine station, and is also occupied by a hospital specializing in diseases of the bone; visitors desiring to wander over the island may therefore be somewhat coolly welcomed, and a letter of introduction from the Kaymakam of Urla is a useful precaution.

Clazomenae, like Phocaea, was a comparatively late foundation in the Ionian settlement of the coast. Pausanias observes that the sites of these two cities were uninhabited until the Greeks came. In the case of Clazomenae this is not strictly true, for pre-Greek sherds have been found on the little hill just to the east of the scala of Urla (A on the plan); this, however, was not the spot chosen by the Ionians. Pausanias tells how a group of the Greek settlers, later comers than the rest, took a leader from Colophon and founded a city under Mt Ida in the Troad; this they soon abandoned and settled for a while on the territory of Colophon, then finally occupied the land which became their permanent home, and built a city called Clazomenae on the mainland. The move to the island came later, 'through fear of the Persians'.

That Clazomenae was originally on the mainland, not the island, is certain from other evidence as well. Strabo notes a place called Chytrion on the mainland, 'where the Clazomenians were once settled'; there will be more to say of this place later. Over a wide area several miles long and broad there have been found large numbers (certainly over a hundred) of the distinctive painted terracotta sarcophagi which are peculiar to Clazomenae. One or two specimens of these may be seen in the Izmir Museum, but most of those which were taken to Izmir were destroyed in the great fire of 1922. These sarcophagi date in general to the sixth century B.C., and none appears to have been found on the island. The exact site of this early Clazomenae has been determined with great probability by Professor J. M. Cook. About a mile to the south-west of the hill A, in a small enclosed valley (B on the plan), he found much pottery of sixth-century and earlier date clearly indicating habitation at that time; no remains of buildings are now visible here, but some eighty Clazomenian sarcophagi were unearthed in the immediate neighbourhood by the Greek excavator G. P. Oikonomos in 1921–22. The acropolis of this early city must have been the hill C, on which stands an isolated house; it is low for the purpose, but no more so than, for example, the acropolis of Elaea. We should nevertheless have expected a rather stronger site; for about 600 B.C. the Lydian king Alyattes, fresh from his capture of Smyrna, invaded Clazomenae and was severely defeated. This seems to argue either very strong walls, of which no trace survives, or great valour on the part of the citizens.

From here the Clazomenians moved to the island 'for fear of the Persians'. This would naturally suggest a move at the time of the Persians' first descent to the coast after the fall of Croesus in 546 B.C.; since, however, the pottery on the archaic site continues till the end of the sixth century, it appears that the move must have been rather in connection with the ill-fated Ionian Revolt of 500–494. At this time there was no causeway; and throughout the fifth century Clazomenae continued to be strictly an island-city. In the Delian League her normal tribute was one and a half talents, a sum which puts her little above the level of the humblest in Ionia; but during the Peloponnesian War it was suddenly raised, first to six talents, then to no less than fifteen. Moreover, it appears that these amounts were, in fact, paid. It is not known what the reason may have been for this startling increase; the Athenians needed money for the war, but this in itself would not enable the Clazomenians actually to pay, and no cause is known why the city's fortunes should have taken such a turn for the better. However this may be, a few years later Clazomenae was easily persuaded by the Spartans to revolt from Athens; the citizens crossed to the mainland and fortified a small place called Polichna as a refuge. Shortly afterwards the Athenians attacked and captured Polichna and moved the Clazomenians back to their island; Clazomenae rejoined the Athenian alliance, and a subsequent Spartan assault was unsuccessful.

By the terms of the King's Peace in 386 B.C., when peace was made between the Greeks and Persians, it was laid down that 'the Great King deems it right that the cities in Asia should belong to him, and of the islands Cyprus and Clazomenae' (an oddly assorted pair). From this we should naturally infer that the causeway was still not in existence; and, in fact, we have the testimony of two ancient writers that the idea of the causeway was due to Alexander the Great more than fifty years later. Pliny says that, Clazomenae being an island, Alexander ordered it to be joined to the mainland across a space of two stades. Pausanias says that Alexander intended to make Clazomenae into a peninsula by means of a mole from the mainland to the island. This explicit evidence has, however, been called in question in recent years—in the writer's opinion, mistakenly. The problem may be set forth briefly.

Fig. 24 Clazomenae

In the years before the King's Peace, Clazomenae was disturbed by internal dissensions, apparently of long standing, to which we have three separate items of testimony. An Athenian decree of 387 B.C., preserved on stone, permits the Clazomenians to decide 'whether they will or will not make a truce with those at Chyton, and also what to do with the hostages they hold from among those at Chyton', and refers to 'those who fled and those who remained'. Aristotle, writing about 330 B.C., observes that faction in cities sometimes arises owing to the nature of the ground, when the physical conditions are not suited to a single city, and two separate cities would be more appropriate, 'as for example at Clazomenae between those at Chytron [*sic*] and those on the island'. Evidently the men of Chyt(r)on on the mainland found it difficult to get on with their fellow citizens on the island, and when a split occurred on the island, probably between democrats and oligarchs, one of the parties had withdrawn thither expecting to find sympathy, and no doubt widening the breach between the two parts of the city, so that hostilities resulted. It is no doubt to these events that Ephorus refers in a fragment of his history dealing with this same period: 'those from Clazomenae settled in a place on the mainland called Chyton'. This place is presumably the same as Strabo's Chytrion, where the Clazomenians used to live.

The place in question has given rise to much controversy. First, which is the true form of the name, Chyton, Chytron, or Chytrion? The presence or absence of the 'r' affects the meaning of the word. In a question of this kind preference is naturally given to the inscription, which is an original document, over the literary passages, which are liable to the hazards of corruption. Suppose, then, that Chyton is right. This word is used in literature of earth heaped up into a mound or dyke, and some scholars have seen in it an allusion to the causeway; they accordingly place Chyton at or near the landward end of the causeway. In further support of this view they point to the words of Pliny, who appears to say that Clazomenae was at one time called something like Chytoporia; this would mean 'the passage by the dyke', which could hardly be other than the causeway. But the reading is uncertain, and the passage is corrupt in other respects too. These considerations are not, in the present writer's opinion, sufficient to displace the definite statement of two authorities that the causeway was due to Alexander. Moreover, as Professor Cook rightly points out, Aristotle ascribes the trouble at Clazomenae to the nature of the ground being unsuitable for a single city; this would naturally imply not only some distance between the two parts but also a difference in their situation liable to give rise to an incompatibility of outlook. Clazomenae being an island city, Chyton should be looked for inland, not by the shore at the end of the causeway. Remembering Strabo's Chytrion, 'where the Clazomenians used to live', we might suppose that the place in question was simply the original city (B on the plan), which may well have continued to exist as a deme of the island city; but Professor Cook prefers a site still farther inland, on the plain to the south-west of Urla. Here he found sufficient sherds to indicate settled habitation, though again no traces of buildings are to be seen. We can then easily understand that the men living here, occupied mainly with agriculture, found it hard to achieve sympathy with the maritime preoccupations of the islanders. If this is right, as appears probable, we are not obliged to choose between the various forms of the name; if Chyton is the true form, the reference may be to some other dyke or mound not now identifiable. When Strabo says the Clazomenians were formerly settled at Chytrion, he need not mean that this was the original site of the city; he may mean merely that it was no longer inhabited in his own day. This problem is of a kind that frequently faces those who are concerned with the topography of the ancient world; its solution, or probable solution, is one of the many services that Professor Cook has rendered in this branch of science.

Clazomenae was not backward in the field of learning; two of her citizens at least were distinguished philosophers. Anaxagoras, born about 500 B.C., was reckoned the last of the Ionian Physicists. These men, the fathers of Greek philosophy, sought to discover the basic elements of matter, the material of which the world is composed; more will be said of them below (p. 183). Whereas his predecessors had looked for a single basic element, such as water, air, or fire, Anaxagoras broke new ground by admitting that the elements of all substances existed from the beginning, and were sorted and arranged to form the substances we know by a controlling principle which he called Mind. By thus introducing an intelligent rather than a mechanical causation he paved the way for the yet more enlightened views of Plato and Aristotle. Anaxagoras taught at Athens for thirty years, counting Pericles and Euripides among his pupils; but some of his views, for example that the sun was a mass of red-hot stone, were too much for the conservative Athenians, and he was prosecuted for impiety. This could be a capital offence, as was later shown in the case of Socrates, and Anaxagoras was only saved by the personal intervention of Pericles. He was obliged to withdraw from Athens and ended his days at Lampsacus on the Dardanelles.

The second Clazomenian philosopher was the sophist Scopelianus, who lived more than 500 years later in the time of Domitian. His name is hardly known now, but he was a man of distinction in his day. He lived and taught in Smyrna, and when the Clazomenians urged him to return and adorn his native city he declined to do so, on the elegant plea that the nightingale will not sing in a cage. He had personal reasons, too, for not wanting to live in Clazomenae, for he had quarrelled with his father. The old man desired to take a second wife out of matrimony, and took his son's disapproval in bad part. The lady declared that Scopelianus was in love with her himself, and a rascally slave joined in with a tale that he had bribed him to poison his father's food. Shortly after, when the old man died, it was found that he had left all his property to the slave.

In A.D. 92 Domitian issued his notorious edict that all vines in Ionia should be destroyed and no new ones planted. In this the emperor was credited in antiquity with prohibitionist motives, but it is no doubt more probable that he wished to encourage the cultivation of corn. Viticulture being, then as now, a main industry in the region of Smyrna, there was consternation in the province, and Scopelianus was chosen to lead an appeal at Rome. Such was his success that he brought back from the emperor not only permission to plant vines but penalties against those who failed to do so. This was certainly something of a triumph, for Domitian cannot have been an easy man to plead with.

The island, now again under its old name in the form Klazümen, has a little more to show in the way of ancient remains than the mainland sites, but still not very much. The famous causeway still exists, close beside its modern successor. Chandler in 1764 rode across it on horseback, and had some difficulty in getting back when the Imbat got up in the afternoon. It is doubtful whether this could be done today; normally only a few of the blocks are visible above water. Chandler estimated its width as 30 feet (9·14 m.); the length of the modern causeway (slightly longer than the ancient) is 700 yards (640 m.), so that Pliny's 'two stades' is a distinct underestimate.

The harbour was in the bay at the waist of the island on the west. On the north side of this bay at J are clear remains of harbourworks, now nearly submerged, containing good squared blocks and apparently ancient. At the northern tip of the island there are also remains of a quay, now almost flush with the water, and the sea is full of blocks fallen from it; just above the waterline are two small intercommunicating basins, one of which has been used as a kiln. On the shore at this point is a short stretch of the city wall, in ashlar masonry of smallish blocks; the rest of the wall has disappeared. After the construction of the causeway, that, too, would afford a convenient landing-stage, on east or west according to the wind.

On the north slope of the northern hill was the theatre, of medium size, but virtually nothing remains of it beyond the hollow in the hillside. When the writer was there in 1946, numerous well-squared blocks had recently been dug out, but these have since been removed. On top of the hill above the theatre, at the highest point on the island, is a corner of the foundation of a rectangular building, neatly cut in the rock. Of the building itself nothing survives; in this situation it is likely to have been a temple. As with other sites on islands or peninsulas with easy access to the sea, Clazomenae has suffered terribly from stone-robbing. It was easier and cheaper for the architects of Byzantine and Ottoman Constantinople, not to speak of cities nearer at hand, to send their ships to the ruins of cities like Cyzicus, Clazomenae, or Iasus (to name only three of the worst sufferers) and remove carved blocks from the ancient buildings, than it was to quarry fresh marble or limestone.

Quite close to the shore, at F, is a cave containing a well. As its name Ayazma implies, this has in the past been regarded as a holy place. The steps leading down to it are not ancient, but the masonry over the entrance is good and regular. The cave is said to consist of four communicating chambers; these were cleared out some thirty-five years ago, but in the process the roof fell in, and only one

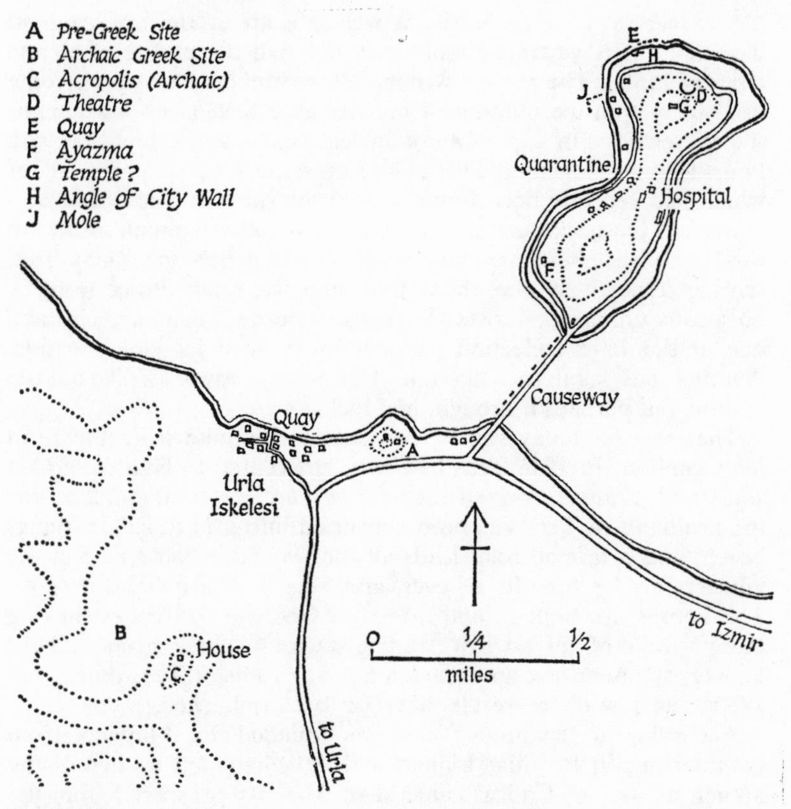

Fig. 25 Plan of Clazomenae

chamber and part of another are now visible. This one contains the well; its roof, only about 5 feet (1.52 m.) high, is of rock and is supported by two rock-cut pillars. There are several niches in the walls. The well is about 5 feet deep; the water, though not salt, is unfit for drinking. Pausanias, speaking of the various noteworthy features of Ionia, says that the Clazomenians possess a cave which they call the 'Cave of Pyrrhus' mother'; Pyrrhus was a shepherd, and there was a tale told about him—but he does not tell us what the tale was. Whether this may be the cave just described we cannot know; at least no other remarkable cave seems to have been noticed on Clazomenian territory.

Teos

'There is', says Freya Stark, 'a welcome about the approach to Teos. . . . It is where I should live, if I had the choice of all the cities of Ionia'. The present writer well remembers his own welcome in 1946; within ten minutes of his arrival in Sığacık he found himself presented with a quantity of ancient vases, lamps, figurines, and knucklebones, together with a bag of some seventy coins, all of which had recently been found among the ruins of Teos. Knucklebones are the neck vertebrae of a sheep or other animal, and were used as dice; there are four surfaces on which they may rest, scoring respectively one, three, four, and six. Loaded dice were by no means unknown; Aristotle speaks of 'leaded dice', and, in fact, one of the 1946 collection has a lump of lead let into one side. Another has scratched upon it 'Herostratus loves B.Z.'—a little cryptic, but perhaps it brought him luck.

The traveller today can hardly hope to be quite so fortunate in his reception. In 1946 Teos had only just ceased to be a forbidden zone, and strangers were a rarity; now they are commonplace, for the headland of Teos has been converted into a N.A.T.O. bathing-beach, and a tarmac road leads all the way from Smyrna. But the villagers are as friendly as ever, and Sığacık is a delightful spot.[1] The houses are built in and around a Genoese fortress occupying the position of an ancient landing-stage. A party from Ankara University undertook an excavation in the ruins of Teos during the 1960s, but few of the results have yet been published.

According to tradition Teos was founded by Minyans from Orchomenus in Boeotia; Ionians and Athenians led by two of the numerous sons of Codrus came later. The city prospered from the beginning and led a number of colonies overseas, though most of these remained obscure. About 600 B.C. Thales of Miletus proposed that the twelve Ionian cities should establish a common political assembly at Teos, as being centrally situated. The idea was a good one, for the Panionium was religious only, and the lack of a common policy was the Ionians' great weakness, as was to be proved in the time of danger; but the proposal was not adopted. When the Persians came and Teos fell with the rest, the citizens, 'unable to endure the Persian arrogance', set sail in a body for Thrace, and there founded the city of Abdera. This, though the best known of the Teian colonies, was not a great credit to them, for its inhabitants were later noted for their stupidity, and Abderite became proverbial for a simpleton. Many of the colonists, in fact, soon returned to the mother-city, and at the battle of Lade in 494 B.C. were already able to muster seventeen ships.

The early prosperity was quickly regained, and in the Delian Confederacy Teos was assessed at six talents, a figure which places her among the richest of the Ionian cities. Her wealth came surely from seaborne commerce; Smyrna was at this time reduced to village status, and Teos must have taken a large share of the trade that would otherwise have gone there. Indeed, when Hamilton visited Sığacık in 1836, he expressed surprise that its harbour was not even then more used in preference to Smyrna, to avoid the long trip up the gulf and the much more difficult return journey against the prevailing Imbat.

In the year 304 B.C. the whole of Ionia was shaken by an earthquake. Perhaps in consequence of this Antigonus proposed to transfer to Teos all the population of Lebedus and to fuse the two cities into one. His elaborate plans for this 'synoecism' are preserved in a long inscription found at Seferihisar; but they were never put into action, for Antigonus lost Teos to Lysimachus in 302 and was himself killed in battle in the following year. Lysimachus had other ideas; he needed men to fill the new city of Ephesus which he had just founded, and he transplanted thither a number of the citizens both of Teos and of Lebedus.

The principal deity of Teos was Dionysus, and the great sanctity of this god led, about the end of the third century, to a notable accession of dignity for the city. Teos was chosen as the residence of the Asiatic branch of the Artists of Dionysus, and her territory was recognized as sacred and inviolable. These Artists were a professional guild of actors and musicians which supplied paid performers at the dramatic and musical festivals held all over the Greek world. In addition to the centre at Teos there were local branches at many other cities to serve the surrounding country and to compete for the prizes given in the contests for tragedy, comedy, music, singing, and the rest. Drama being always under the patronage of Dionysus, his Artists were a religious as well as a professional body, and enjoyed certain privileges universally recognized, notably freedom from taxation and safe conduct for their person wherever they went. Each branch had its own organization and was largely independent of the city to which it was attached; relations between Artists and city were regulated by agreement in each case. But the artistic temperament is notoriously difficult. Indispensable as they certainly were, the Artists seem to have been overconscious of their own importance, and they had a bad reputation as troublesome customers. Philostratus calls them 'a very arrogant class of men and hard to keep in order', and one of the Aristotelian Problems is devoted to the question 'Why are the Artists of Dionysus in general bad men?' The suggested answer is that too much of their time is occupied in loose living, and that their arts are practised not for art's sake but in order to earn a livelihood, leaving little or no time for the acquisition of wisdom.

The history of the guild in Ionia does nothing to contradict this judgment. At first all was well; the Teians bought a piece of land of the value of one talent and presented it to the Artists with compliments and prayers for their wellbeing. But before long quarrels broke out and became frequent; about the middle of the second century the Artists were obliged to move to Ephesus. They seem to have been no more popular there, and Attalus II of Pergamum transferred them to Myonnesus. Whereupon the Teians complained to the Romans of this accession of strength to a town on their frontier, and the Artists were moved on once more, this time to Lebedus. Here at last they found themselves welcome, for Lebedus was meagrely populated and glad of any addition to its manpower. Mark Antony moved them again to Priene, but this was only a temporary measure for the benefit of Cleopatra, and they were soon back in Lebedus.

In 190 B.C. there occurred an incident which has an especial interest owing to the topographical detail with which it is described by Livy. Antiochus III and the Romans were at that time contesting possession of the coast, and the Teians had collected considerable supplies, including five thousand jars of wine, which were destined for the king's forces. Learning of this, the Roman admiral put quickly into Teos, anchoring in the northern harbour behind the city, and began to plunder the Teian territory. When the Teians complained of this conduct, he gave them the choice of surrendering to him the provisions collected for Antiochus or being treated as an enemy. After deliberation they decided to do as he wished. Meanwhile the king's fleet lay a few miles to the south at the island of Macris (now Doğanbey Adası). Its commander, hearing of the Roman activities, conceived the design of trapping them in the harbour; for, says Livy, the entrance is so narrowed by projecting headlands that two ships can hardly emerge together. This is certainly an overstatement: the channel is, in fact, scarcely less than half a mile (804·7 m.) in breadth: nevertheless, the plan of stationing ships at the headlands to attack the Roman vessels as they made their way out against the wind was no bad one and might well have succeeded. Before it could be put into operation, however, the Roman admiral decided that for purposes of taking on board the wine and other provisions it would be more convenient to move the fleet to the southern port close in front of the city. When this was done and the men were ashore collecting the stores (and especially, says Livy, the wine), news was brought that the king's fleet was preparing to put out. Great was the alarm; amid the utmost confusion the men were recalled and hurried on board; Livy compares the scene to a sudden outbreak of fire or the capture of a city. In the subsequent engagement, however, the steadiness of the Roman fighters prevailed, and Antiochus was reduced shortly afterwards to suing, unsuccessfully, for peace. This incident lives again vividly for the visitor to Teos. It constitutes in effect the last appearance of Teos in history, for with the establishment of the Roman province she disappears from the current of events.

As notable citizens of Teos, Strabo can name two men. One is, of course, the lyric poet Anacreon, the first, it is said, after Sappho the Lesbian to make love the theme of his poetry. This charming hedonist, whose statue in Athens showed a man singing in his cups, was Teos' only contribution to the early culture of Ionia. The second, Apellicon, was not a great man at all, and is remarkable only for the part he played in the curious history of Aristotle's library. On his death Aristotle bequeathed his books, the only library hitherto collected, to his successor Theophrastus, who in turn left them to his pupil Neleus; this man carried them to Scepsis in the Troad, where they passed to his descendants, unscholarly men who neglected to look after them, and to avoid surrendering them to the library of Pergamum (above, p. 50) hid them away in a damp place underground where they suffered badly. Consequently, when the books were sold about 100 B.C. at a high price to Apellicon of Teos, he found the texts defective in many places. Being a bibliophile rather than a scholar, he copied the texts on to fresh sheets, filling in the gaps with his own conjectures, and so published the books full of errors. Apellicon's library was later carried off by Sulla to Rome, where the texts were re-edited by a keen Aristotelian scholar named Tyrannion. Strabo adds that mistakes continued to be common owing to the rascality of the booksellers, who employed inefficient copyists and neglected to check the copies.

The site of Teos is in some ways unusual. It is of the peninsula type, but the acropolis was not on the headland itself but on a separate hill in the middle of the isthmus, half-way between the northern and southern harbours, about a mile from each. The earliest fortifications are on the acropolis hill; some remnants of polygonal wall survive, but the whole is much overgrown and little can be made out. The town extends on the south side, between the acropolis and the harbour, and was fortified in the third century B.C. with walls of regular ashlar; the ground being level, the walls run in straight lines at right-angles to one another—a highly unusual feature. Little of them is visible above ground, but a short stretch of the western wall has been excavated close to the temple of Dionysus and gives a good idea of the masonry.

The south harbour has been much silted up since antiquity by a small stream which flows into it, but a part of the ancient quay survives on the inner side of the southern spit; at intervals are projecting blocks pierced to form stone rings to which boats might tie up. Hamilton reasoned from their position just above water that there can have been no great change in the sea-level since ancient times; in fact, however, it has risen by nearly a fathom (above, p. 79), and the rings must have stood well above the waterline. In the northern harbour, too, there are remains of a mole or landing-stage running out underwater from beneath the Genoese castle (Pl. 21).

The famous temple of Dionysus, the great deity of the Teians, stood on the west side of the city just inside the wall. It was first excavated by the Society of Dilettanti in the eighteenth century, after which an enterprising Smyrniote set up business in the sanctuary as a marble quarrier, with the result that when French scholars dug the site in 1924, little remained beyond the foundations. The architect was Hermogenes of Priene, who built it early in the second century B.C.; it was perhaps his first important work. It was evidently a completely new building, for no traces of an earlier temple have

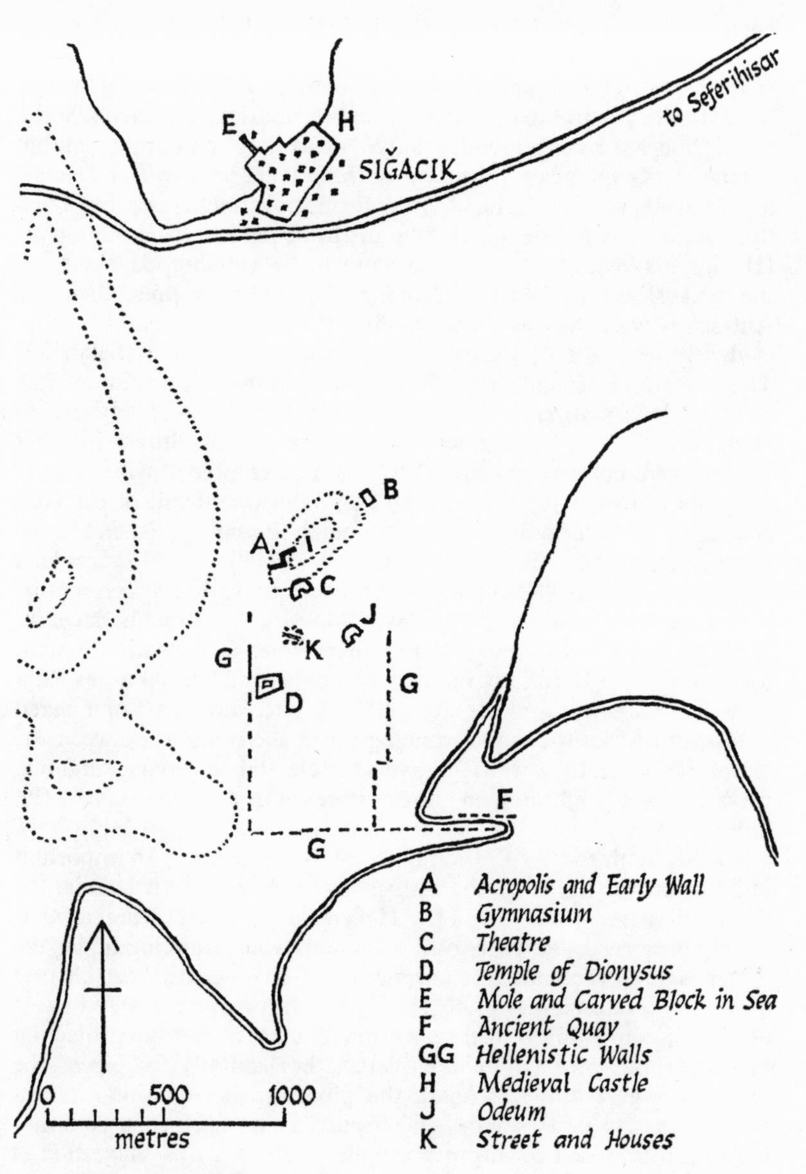
to Seferihisar
E
H
SIĞACIK
B
A
C
J
K
G
G
D
F
G
A Acropolis and Early Wall
B Gymnasium
C Theatre
D Temple of Dionysus
E Mole and Carved Block in Sea
F Ancient Quay
GG Hellenistic Walls
H Medieval Castle
J Odeum
K Street and Houses
0
500
1000
metres

Fig. 26 Plan of Teos

been found beneath it. The order is Ionic and the plan is normal, except that the surrounding enclosure is, surprisingly, of trapezoidal shape. In Roman imperial times the temple was renovated with a fresh dedication to the emperor, probably Hadrian; fragments of the inscription have been found. Dionysus had here the curious epithet Setaneios, which means normally 'of the present year' with reference to the fruits of the earth. A recently discovered inscription from the temple provides details of honours to be paid to King Antiochus III and his sister Laodice, who were to be worshipped alongside the god Dionysus himself. Among the offerings prescribed for Antiochus were specimens of the first fruits of each season's crop, evidently also one of the regular offerings to Dionysus Setaneios. This inscription found in the Turkish excavations is a mine of fascinating information concerning the cults that were offered to Hellenistic rulers, and shows the way in which rituals in their honour were deliberately embedded into and combined with existing religious practices in the city. We may note one detail of the rites connected with Laodice, that a fountain in the agora should be consecrated to her, and that its water be specially used in sacrificial rituals, in washing the bodies of the dead, and for the ceremonial bath of girls on their wedding-day. Dionysus, the Roman Bacchus, was at Teos, it seems, the god of the new wine. The Turkish excavators have now begun to re-erect a number of the columns, and between the temple and the city wall have uncovered part of a paved street with a water-channel running down the middle. Between the temple and the theatre they have also cleared an area containing private houses and another narrow street with a water-channel (Pl. 26).

At the south foot of the acropolis hill is the theatre, an important building in the home of the Artists of Dionysus. As it stands, the theatre is a reconstruction of a Hellenistic building. The cavea is poorly preserved, but parts of the vaulted gallery running under the upper seats still remain. The stage-building has recently been cleared by the excavators; it is of Roman type, with a stage about 14 feet (4·27 m.) from front to back. A curious feature is that the projecting blocks of the proscenium are pierced horizontally by pipes; the blocks being several feet apart, the pipes are not continuous, and it is not easy to understand their purpose. It has been suggested that they were intended to improve the acoustics, but this suggestion is perhaps hardly probable. The acoustics of Greek theatres were always excellent, as any visitor may prove for himself; and in ancient times they were further assisted by sounding-vessels placed in the auditorium. It was recommended that these should be of bronze, thirteen in number, tuned to intervals of a fourth or fifth, and placed upside down in a horizontal row round the cavea. No such bronze vessels have actually been found in ancient theatres, but earthenware vases apparently intended for this purpose have occasionally come to light.

The view from the theatre at Teos has aroused the enthusiastic admiration of modern writers. It embraces the site of the city, the harbour, and the coast as far as the promontory of Myonnesus. 'How intensely', says Hamilton, 'the contemplation of such a scene must have heightened the enjoyment of the spectator during a performance of the Agamemnon or the Medea'. Ximinez, in his *Asia Minor in Ruins*, goes even further: 'In choosing the position of a theatre the Greeks' first thought was for the landscape they would have before them'. This, in the present writer's opinion, is a misconception. Most Greek theatres have certainly a good view, because they were built on hillsides, and the Greek and Anatolian scenery is naturally beautiful. But this view could be enjoyed any day of the year, and from better viewpoints than the interior of a theatre; from the lower seats at least the stage-building would cut off any view at all. Performances in ancient theatres were special occasions, confined to a limited number of days in a year; the spectators assembled to watch a play, and it is unlikely that they gave a thought to the scenery familiar to them all their lives. Indeed, it is doubtful if a view of this kind would have impressed them much. Sea and shore, mountains and blue skies are commonplace in Greek lands; we think them beautiful, but the Greeks preferred a good well-watered arable plainland. The writer once commented to a peasant in Attica on the beauty of the scenery; he smiled at my quaint foreign enthusiasm and replied: 'Too many stones' (Pl. 24).

A handsome addition to the attractions of Teos was made in 1964, when the excavators cleared the odeum (J). This is a small theatre-like building with eleven rows of seats largely preserved; two tall statue-bases carry inscriptions in honour of distinguished citizens of Teos under the Roman empire. Odea were used for musical recitals and, in some places at least, for rehearsals of dramatic performances intended for the theatre.

A short distance to the north-east of the acropolis are the ruins of a large building (B on the plan), identified by an inscription found in it as a gymnasium. The inscription is interesting for the information it gives about schooling in the second century B.C. It records a donation by a rich citizen for (among other things) the appointment of staff in the gymnasium. The children, boys and girls, are divided into three classes, to be taught their letters—that is, reading, writing, and literature—by three masters drawing salaries from 500 to 600 drachmae per annum. Two physical-training instructors draw 500 drachmae each. Such payments are not below average for the time; in a school at Miletus they are respectively forty and thirty drachmae a month. The music master is somewhat better remunerated at 700 drachmae. A drill-sergeant and an instructor in archery and the javelin are to be engaged from outside for two months at a fee of 300 and 250 drachmae respectively. A provision which strikes an echo today is that made for possible overcrowding of classes; if necessary, extra classes are to be held in the council chamber. Salaries on this scale seem meagre nowadays, but it is only in quite recent times that the profession of schoolmaster has been held in any high esteem; the sums mentioned are comparable with those paid only a few years ago to a Turkish village schoolmaster.

The buildings of Teos were constructed of a hard blue local limestone of the quality of marble. The quarries from which it, or some of it, came are to be seen on a small but steep isolated hill a mile from Seferihisar on the road to Sığacık. This hill is, in fact, being used as a quarry at the time of writing. Half a mile to the northwest is a small lake, reached by a rough road turning right off the main road 500 yards (457·2 m.) beyond the hill. Across the road from the lake, in a hollow, were lying a hundred years ago fifteen or twenty quarried blocks of marble of huge size, cut into such extraordinary shapes that Hamilton observed he had never seen anything so remarkable. Many of them contained 10 or 12 cubic yards (13·08 or 15·7 cubic metres) of stone. Most have now been removed, but two or three may still be seen close to the road, and others are hidden among the bushes. The style of the cuttings is shown in the accompanying sketch, but no two were alike in detail. Some carried inscriptions in Latin recording the date (by the Roman consuls of the year), the place (indicated by a numeral) from which they were quarried, and the name of the quarry-owner or the official in charge of the quarrying operation. Hamilton imagined they might be intended as stands for the display of cups, statues, and other objects in a temple treasury; but the true explanation is more commonplace. A similar block is still lying half above water in the sea beside the ancient quay at Sığacık, where it evidently fell while being loaded into a boat; these stones were clearly intended for export, and were trimmed in this curious way for reasons of

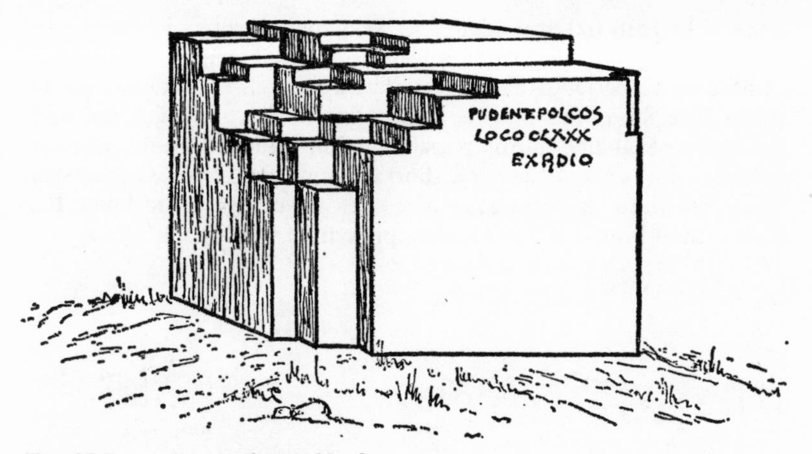

Fig. 27 Teos. Curiously cut block

economy, to lose as little material as possible, short of sending out the stone as a mere jagged block. Teian marble was, in fact, well known and highly valued. The consuls named in the inscriptions are those of A.D. 165–166, from which it appears that at that date the quarrying activities for some reason came to a sudden end, and the blocks were left where they were cut. The one now lying, a good deal water-worn, in the sea is of similar dimensions to the rest; it is remarkable that the exporters, with comparatively primitive tackle, preferred to transport and put on board blocks weighing upwards of 30 tons rather than cut them into more manageable sizes. Large blocks were evidently in demand. Remarkable, too, that the stone, instead of being blocked out at the quarry to suit the customer's ultimate purpose, was apparently exported simply as bulk material (Pl. 25).

Pliny surprisingly lists Teos among the islands. On this evidence some scholars have believed that a canal was constructed, probably by Alexander, joining the north and south harbours; but no trace of such a work has ever been seen, nor does Livy's narrative of the events in 190 B.C. favour its existence. It is more likely that we have merely another of Pliny's numerous mistakes.

Myonnesus

An attractive excursion, though not very easy, is that to Çıfıt Kale, the ancient Myonnesus, or Mouse Island.[2] The island itself is a steep rock 190 feet (60 m.) high and very picturesque, joined to the mainland by an ancient causeway now under water. It lies about a mile north of Doğanbey Point. The approach by land is difficult; from Seferihisar the road is respectable as far as Doğanbey, after that very rough and hardly possible to find without a guide. To reach the island it is also necessary, short of swimming, to cross the causeway; the water at most seasons comes about up to the knee. It is easier therefore, if possible, to approach by boat from Sığacık.

Fig. 28 Myonnesus

Myonnesus makes one or two appearances in history. As was mentioned above, it was for a short time the seat of the Artists of Dionysus, till the Teians objected and they were moved to Lebedus. Some years earlier than this, in 190 B.C., Antiochus III of Syria was attempting to hold the coast against the Roman fleet. The Romans, in search of supplies, were one day making for Teos when off Myonnesus they caught sight of a dozen or fifteen vessels which they supposed at first to be part of the king's fleet. Soon they realized that they were, in fact, pirate vessels loaded with spoils from a raid on Chios, and accordingly gave chase; the pirates, however, having swifter craft and a good start, reached Myonnesus in safety. Loth to abandon a rich prize, the Roman commander decided to put in and carry off the vessels from the harbour. This he did, says Livy, in ignorance of the nature of the place; and the historian proceeds to give a description of Myonnesus which could hardly be bettered. 'The hill', he says,

> rises like a pyramid from a broad base to a sharp point; it is surrounded by cliffs so eaten away by the waves that in some

places the overhanging rocks project further seaward than the boats sheltering under them.

The Romans therefore, for fear of rocks dropped upon them from above, dared not come close, but abandoned the attempt and went on to Teos. There followed the events described above (p. 108), ending with the battle of Myonnesus and the defeat of Antiochus.

From this narrative alone one would naturally infer that the rock of Myonnesus was nothing more than a pirates' hide-out, for which it is well enough adapted. Other notices, however, make it clear that Myonnesus was a proper town, if not a city. Hecataeus of Miletus about 500 B.C. apparently called it a city; Artemidorus of Ephesus, on the other hand, about 100 B.C., called it merely a 'place'. Pliny says it was once a town, but had perished in his own time. It is in any case obvious that the Artists of Dionysus cannot have been settled in a mere pirates' nest. But the habitation, whatever it was, has almost entirely disappeared.

The rock itself is utterly inadequate to support a town, having virtually no level ground at all. It is split in the middle by a great cleft running east and west, only a few feet wide; on the portion to the north of this is a stretch of fine ancient wall still 9 or 10 feet (2·74 or 3·05 m.) high in places. The masonry is of the type that used to be called 'Cyclopean', with very large blocks of irregular shape; one block measures almost 8 feet by 4 (2·44 by 1·22 m.). This wall has a very archaic appearance, and belongs no doubt to Hecataeus' 'city'. This is the sole surviving remnant of ancient Myonnesus; the rest of the hill is covered with ruins, but they are nearly 2,000 years later, for Myonnesus had a part to play in Turkish history too. The three cisterns lined with red plaster at the top of the hill are undatable, but are likely to belong to this later habitation.

The town, and the seat of the Dionysiac Artists, must have been on the mainland opposite. Here there is a valley, reasonably fertile and now rather patchily cultivated, which must represent such territory as Myonnesus possessed; the surface is thinly strewn with sherds, but no trace of any ancient building has ever, it seems, been observed. Since the country is almost deserted for miles around, it is likely that stones have been removed by sea, but the total absence even of foundations suggests that Myonnesus never possessed the massive buildings which are familiar on the larger sites. The Artists, one would suppose, can hardly have managed without a theatre; but none has ever been discovered.

Lebedus

Of the twelve Ionian cities two were noticeably humbler than the rest; these were Myus and Lebedus. Their ruins are among the scantiest, and both are very rarely visited. Myus was ruined by the mud and mosquitoes of the Maeander; Lebedus lived quietly on her peninsula and played no significant part in history.

The foundation legend is of the familiar kind. The country was originally occupied by Carians, till in the course of the Ionian migrations another of the sons of Codrus and his followers drove them out. His name is variously given as Andraemon or Andropompus; this latter name, 'escorter of men', is suspiciously appropriate to the leader of a colony, and may safely be regarded as mythical.

Fig. 29 Lebedus

Lebedus is a characteristic example of the peninsula type of settlement. The peninsula itself is low and rocky, some 300 yards (274·3 m.) across, joined to the mainland by an isthmus about a furlong (201·2 m.) broad. On the mainland opposite is a hill some 200 feet (61 m.) high which formed the acropolis. The country around, though thinly populated now, was considered in ancient times to be good fertile land, and it had the special peculiarity of possessing the finest and most abundant thermal springs on the Ionian coast. But the city's position precluded it from ever growing really prosperous. Completely cut off landward by the territories of Colophon and Teos, its wealth could come only from the sea; but it lacked a good harbour and, with the far better favoured Ephesus and Teos to north and south, could attract little in the way of seaborne commerce.

Consequently the early history of Lebedus is a blank. So far as we know she never led a colony overseas, nor did the great age of Ionian civilization bring forth any Lebedian poet, philosopher, or scientist; indeed, Lebedus never in any age produced a famous citizen. To the Ionian fleet at Lade she contributed no ships at all. In the Athenian maritime league in the fifth century (the Delian Confederacy) Lebedus was at first assessed at three talents, but this proved to be altogether more than the city's resources could meet, and the assessment was quickly reduced to one talent. Alone among the cities of Ionia Lebedus struck no coins in the classical Greek period.

In Hellenistic times the city makes two or three appearances, but they hardly show her in any brilliant light. Antigonus' plan for merging Lebedus into Teos has already been mentioned (above, p. 107); it seems to have involved the complete abandonment of the site, but was never actually put into execution. Lysimachus, on taking over from Antigonus, is said to have uprooted Lebedus entirely and transferred its population to Ephesus. Despite these attempts to erase it from the map, the city managed to survive; about 266 B.C. it came into the possession of Ptolemy II of Egypt, who carried out some form of refoundation under the new name of Ptolemais. This name continued only for some sixty years.

In the second century Lebedus became the permanent home of the Ionian branch of the Artists of Dionysus. These troublesome associates, expelled in turn from Teos, Ephesus, and Myonnesus, were welcomed at Lebedus purely as an accession of manpower; shortage of men had always been a trouble there. There at all events they stayed, except for a brief sojourn at Priene, and in Strabo's time they were celebrating annually at Lebedus a festival with games in honour of Dionysus. Horace, writing shortly before Strabo, surprisingly refers to Lebedus as a deserted village, but this is clearly an error, or at least an exaggeration; the city, in fact, continued to exist, and struck coins down to the end of the second century A.D.

The peninsula of Lebedus is now known as Kısık; on earlier maps it is called Xingi. Ürkmez village lies a short distance to the northwest. The most pleasant approach is by boat from Sığacık, but the site is also easily accessible by land. Leave Seferihisar by the Doğanbey road, and a quarter of a mile out of the town fork left where a tall iron gateway stands on the right, with a well opposite. The road is dusty but passable for a car. Beyond Lebedus it con-

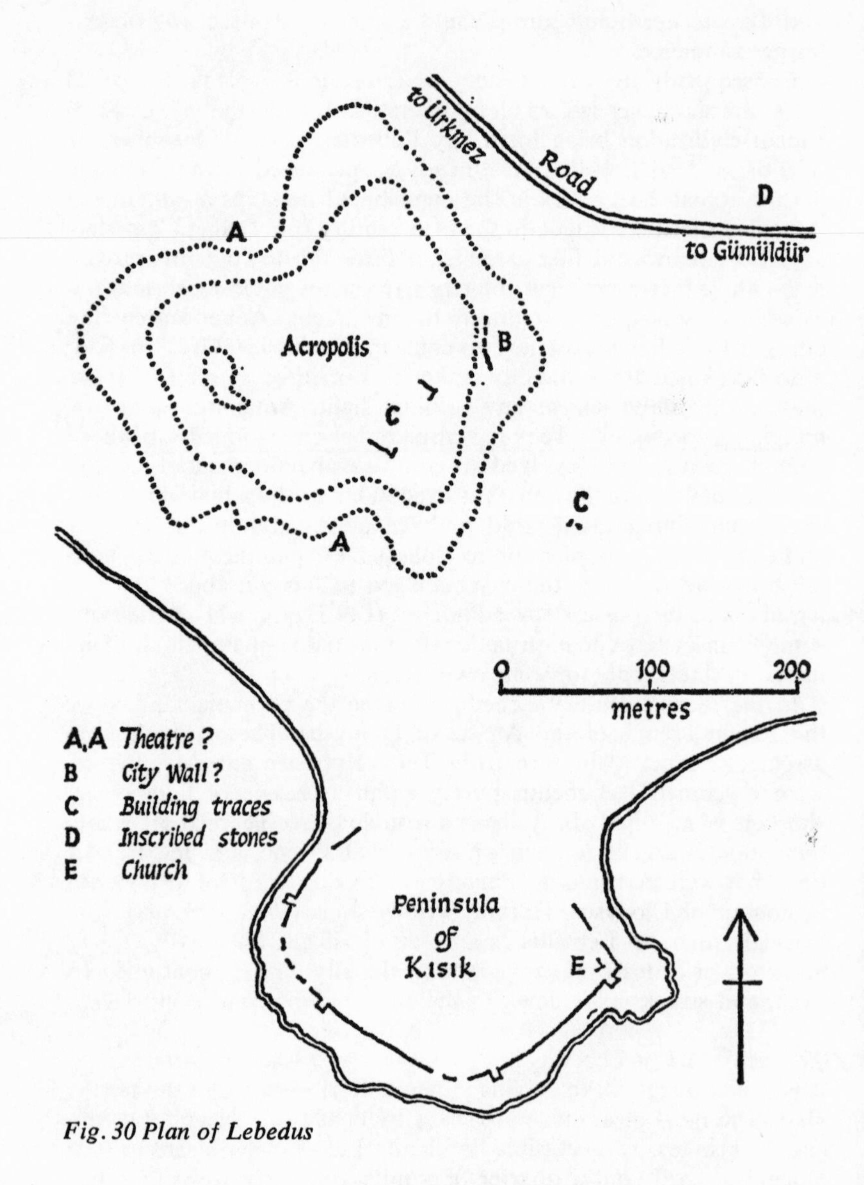

Fig. 30 Plan of Lebedus

tinues by the Gümüldür gorge to Bulgurca and Cumaovası, so that the round trip from Smyrna to Teos and Lebedus may be made in a long day in either direction.

Lebedus has never been excavated, and the visible ruins are scanty. By far the most striking is the wall around the peninsula, which is still preserved to a height of three or four courses. It is some 7 feet (2·13 m.) thick, of good regular ashlar constructed in the familiar fashion with an inner and outer face of squared blocks and a filling of rubble. It has four towers and three gates opening directly on the sea; to that on the south-east, which is the best protected from the prevailing Imbat, a rock-cut ramp leads up from the water. No trace is to be seen of any quay or mole either on the peninsula or on the isthmus. The wall does not at present continue across the isthmus, though it presumably did so in antiquity; here as at Myonnesus it is likely that many stones have been removed by sea in modern times, and the villagers of Ürkmez admit to taking them as required for building. Inside the wall are fairly numerous traces of ancient buildings, but only the foundations survive. At the east corner is the foundation of an old church of basilica form with three aisles, of which little can now be made out; a bishop of Lebedus is recorded in the Byzantine lists (Pl. 35).

But the main habitation was certainly on the mainland opposite. Here the ground is thickly strewn with sherds, and the slopes of the hill carry many vestiges of buildings. Here and there short pieces of wall may be seen, but whether they are terrace walls or belong to a defence wall is not easy to decide. Just below the summit is a broad platform; at the edge of this, on the south and south-east, are foundations of large buildings, or perhaps of a single large building, of uncertain purpose. The permanent seat of the Artists of Dionysus must presumably have possessed a theatre, but as at Myonnesus none has been found. Several hollows in the hillside would afford a suitable site, in particular one which looks towards the peninsula and one on the north-west side, but no clear traces of theatre building are to be seen.

Lying close to the north side of the road, opposite to the isthmus, are two blocks of stone, one of which carries a cross; the other once formed part of the wall of a gymnasium, and on it are roughly cut the names of various students. These were cut by the boys themselves, to reserve the places: 'Eikadios son of Menas, his place' and the like (Pl. 27). This same proceeding may be observed again at Priene (below, p. 176).

As was said above, the territory of Lebedus was noted for the abundance of its thermal springs. One of these is at a spot called Karakoç, ten and a half miles (17 km.) from Seferihisar on the road to Ürkmez, just below the road on the right. The water is good for rheumatism, and varies in temperature from about 104° to 120° F.; the mud baths and hot-water baths are much patronized in summer, even by visitors from as far afield as Ankara. Close beside the modern installations are the ruins of the ancient baths. Other medicinal springs for bathing and for drinking exist on the shore to the west of Lebedus; they are reached by a road forking right about a mile (1·61 km.) north of Karakoç.

Erythrae

Legend said that a statue of the deified Heracles was launched into the sea on a raft from the Phoenician city of Tyre, though no one could say why. The raft floated to the shores of Ionia and came to land on the headland of Mesate (now Top Burnu) half-way between Chios and Erythrae. The Chians and Erythraeans used every endeavour to bring the statue to their own country, but it could not be persuaded to move, until a blind fisherman of Erythrae had a remarkable vision: it was revealed to him in a dream that the women of Erythrae must cut off their hair, from which the men should plait a rope to draw the raft to their shores. The noble ladies flatly refused to co-operate in so absurd a proceeding; but the Thracian women, both slaves and resident foreigners, readily consented, and with the rope thus made the Erythraeans secured possession of the raft and statue. The fisherman recovered his sight and a sanctuary was built for the statue of Heracles; into it no women were allowed to enter save Thracians. The rope of hair was preserved and could still be seen in the time of Pausanias. Statue and sanctuary, he says, were both of great antiquity, and the statue was more Egyptian than Greek; both are shown on coins of the city (Pl. 64).

Erythrae retains its ancient name in the form Ildır; the intermediate forms Ritri and Litri are recorded. Top Burnu is, in fact, just half-way between here and the town of Chios; but it is not certain that Erythrae was always in this situation. Professor J. M. Cook has recently suggested that the city may have moved its site about the middle of the fourth century B.C. from the small peninsula of Kalem Burnu just to the west of Ilıca. He points out that about that date the signs of habitation, especially sherds, cease at Kalem Burnu and begin at Ildır; and further that a fourth-century inscription found at Ildır provides for the laying-out of a network of streets as if in a newly founded city. A recently discovered archaic deposit of sherds and other objects on the acropolis may, however, prove an obstacle to this theory.

The original foundation is said to have been due to a party from Crete under the leadership of a certain Erythrus, who gave his name, 'Red', to the city; but such 'eponymous' founders are invariably mythical. Later, a son of Codrus named Cnopus collected a band of Ionians from the other cities of Asia and whether by force or by agreement (the accounts differ) introduced them to Erythrae. This early city is described as rich and prosperous, but not much is known of its history. Herodotus says that Erythraeans and Chians spoke the same dialect of Ionic; but this produced no amity between them, for in the seventh century Erythrae was at war with Chians and Milesians combined. Relations between the cities were, however, constantly changing; a little before this Erythrae had joined with Miletus in founding the colony of Parium on the Sea of Marmara.

At the battle of Lade in 494 B.C. Erythrae contributed eight ships

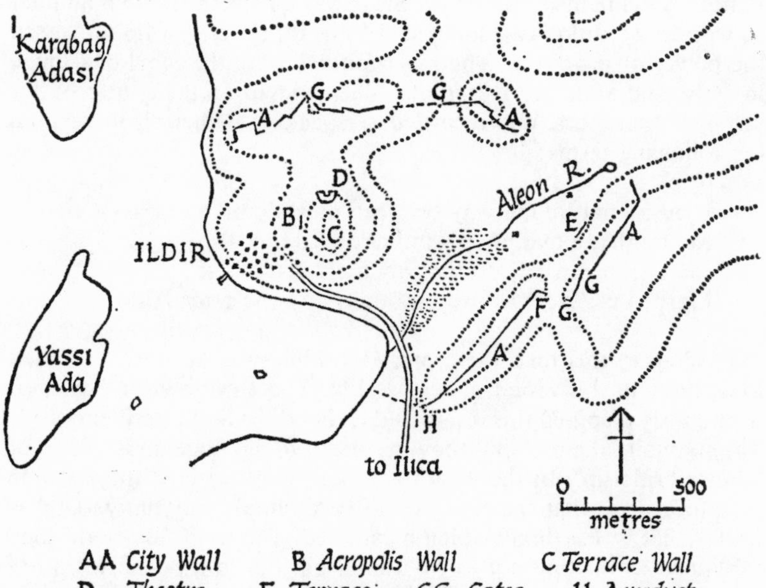

Fig. 31 Plan of Erythrae (after Weber)

to the Ionian fleet, as compared with a hundred from Chios. In the Delian Confederacy the Erythraean assessment was seven talents, equal to the highest among the Ionian cities; in this case no comparison with Chios is possible, for Chios never paid tribute in money to Athens, but preferred to contribute ships, of which the number is not known. The wealth of Erythrae was no doubt due to the same causes as at Teos (above, p. 107).

Fourth-century inscriptions found at Ildır give us tantalizing glimpses of the city's history which our information does not allow us properly to understand. One is a decree in honour of Mausolus, dynast of Caria, who is called a benefactor of Erythrae, but we cannot tell why. Another refers to defacement by certain oligarchs of the statue of a patriot who had slain 'the tyrant'; but again we cannot fill in the details. A third is particularly frustrating; it honours a citizen for providing funds 'for the sending out of soldiers and the demolition of the acropolis'. We should like to know where the soldiers were sent, and why the acropolis required to be demolished, especially if at that time it had only just been built; but we are reduced to conjecture.

Among the city's titles to distinction was the possession of the famous Sibyl named Herophile. Sibyl was a name given to a number of women in antiquity—some said four, others ten—who possessed the power of prophecy. The most famous were the Sibyl of Cumae in Italy, and after her Herophile. This woman, in the course of her inspired utterances, was recorded as speaking of herself in verse in the following terms:

> I am by nature midway between mortal and goddess—
> My mother a nymph, my father an eater of fish—
> Ida-born from my mother; my native land is red
> Marpessus, sacred to my mother, and the river Aidoneus.

According to this text, therefore, Herophile was born at red-soiled Marpessus in the Troad under Mt Ida. The Erythraeans, however, strenuously disputed this origin and claimed the Sibyl for themselves. To maintain their claim they resorted to an ingenious piece of 'higher criticism'. In the passage quoted they rejected the last line as spurious, so that the text should read simply 'my native land is Red'—that is, Erythrae, which means red. The term 'Ida-born' they explained as relating not to Mt Ida at all, but to a poetic word *ida* meaning wooded country. Their own account was that Herophile was born in a cave on Mt Corycus in the territory of Erythrae, that she travelled widely and lived for 900 years. In the year 1891 the actual seat of the Sibyl was found at Ildır, in the form of a fountain-house containing a number of inscriptions of the second century A.D. In one of these the Sibyl strongly reasserts her Erythraean origin as against the claim of Marpessus. Unfortunately this discovery was involved in a good deal of secrecy, and the spot seems to be no longer identifiable.[3]

The ruins of Erythrae are in general scanty, largely owing to systematic plundering of the stones by contractors in the nineteenth century. The site itself is a fine one; the acropolis, 280 feet (85·3 m.) high, rises directly from the shore, well isolated from the surrounding hills; the harbour is admirably protected by an off-lying islet, one of the group called in ancient times Hippi, the Horses. The wall-circuit, two and a half miles (4·02 km.) in length, follows the low ridges to the north and east. The territory thus enclosed is watered by a stream which rises at a spring just inside the city wall on the east; its total length is less than a mile. Its water, however, is bitter and unfit to drink; it is usable for crops, but not good. In its lower course this stream forms a marsh; it has an abundant flow and turns two mills on the way. Its ancient name is not certain; inscriptions speak of a river Aleon, and this is confirmed by Pliny, who notes that it has the unusual property of causing hair to grow on the body. On the other hand, coins of Erythrae show a river-god with the name Axus. If these are two different streams, which of them is the stream just described, and where the other may be, remains uncertain. The water being undrinkable, the city was supplied by earthenware pipes laid on or under the ground; many of these have been found on the site. The aqueduct H is of much later date (Pl. 33).

The circuit of the city wall may be followed for the greater part of its length, a pleasant walk of an hour or so. The wall is a strong one, of beautiful ashlar masonry, from 12 to 17 feet (3·66 to 5·18 m.) thick, with gates and towers at intervals. At F is a particularly striking piece, where the pale, almost white, limestone is diversified by two courses of dark brown stone; the effect is most unusual. The wall ends on the north side at a rocky knoll, forming almost a second acropolis; along the shore no trace of it remains (Pl. 28).

Of the inner citadel wall defending the acropolis very little is now to be seen, except for a few pieces above the village at B; the masonry is similar to that of the outer circuit. At C is a short stretch of polygonal wall which appears to be rather a terrace-wall than a fortification; the masonry is of the 'coursed polygonal' style which dates generally to the early Hellenistic period. Nothing survives on the summit but the ruins of a Greek church.

The theatre is cut into the north slope of the acropolis hill, but its state of preservation is not more than moderate. An excavation was undertaken here in 1963 in the name of the Izmir Museum; it has revealed that the stairways of the cavea are quite well preserved, but of the rows of seats hardly more than the foundations remain. Nothing is visible of the stage-building. The theatre faces north, an arrangement of which Vitruvius approved; a south aspect he regarded as undesirable, not because the sun would be in the spectators' eyes (a point which he does not mention) but as being unhealthy, because the hot air would become imprisoned in the auditorium and dry the moisture from their bodies. In practice Vitruvius' rule was by no means always followed, and Greek theatres, in fact, face in all directions; those of Miletus and Priene face due south, those of Teos and Cyme south-east and south-west. The main consideration seems to have been merely the existence of a suitable concave slope in a convenient position. If anyone really believes that the Greeks' first thought was for the view which the theatre would command, let him consider the theatre at Erythrae, where east, west, or south the view is greatly superior. It is not known when the theatre was originally built; a theatre is mentioned in an inscription of the second century B.C. (Pl. 29).

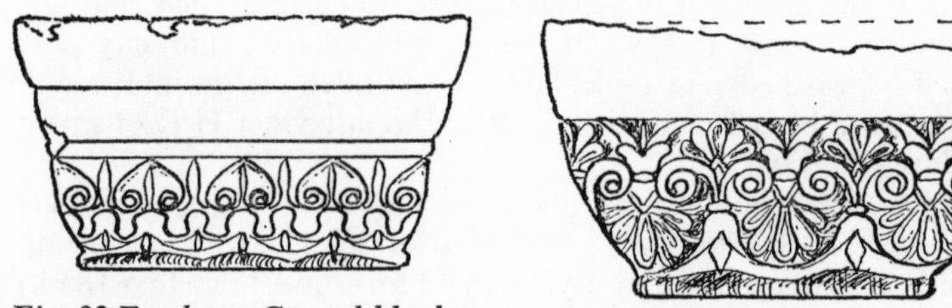

Fig. 32 Erythrae. Carved blocks

At E on the plan is a stretch of handsome wall supporting a terrace (not easy to find without a guide); its masonry is a mixture of polygonal and ashlar. Ionic architectural fragments found close by, and a number of votive niches in the rock to the south, indicate that a sanctuary stood here; Hamilton thought this might be the famous temple of Heracles, but others have considered the situation, so far from the sea and the oldest part of the city, to be unsuitable. If Erythrae was indeed transferred from another site in the fourth century, this objection loses most of its force. But, in fact, we do not know where any particular temple of Erythrae was situated; the ruins have been too thoroughly despoiled. We do know that they were numerous; an inscription records the official sale by the city authorities of some forty priesthoods.

North of the village, not far from the theatre, is a well-preserved mosaic floor; the building to which it belonged is destroyed. Other mosaics have been found in various places, but these are no longer to be seen. A small museum has been built in the village to house the smaller objects found in the recent excavation. These include the rather unusually decorated blocks shown in the accompanying sketch.

Erythrae is now less inaccessible than it used to be. A respectable road has recently been constructed from Ilıca to Ildır; alternatively, travellers may charter a motor-boat at modest expense from Ilıca, the journey occupying about an hour and a half each way.

Ilıca itself is not an ancient town, but represents the site of the thermal springs for which the territory of Erythrae, like that of Lebedus, was famous; it is now a popular seaside resort, much frequented in the summer by the people of Smyrna. Ildır on the other hand presents a melancholy spectacle. Most of its houses are empty shells, deserted since their Greek inhabitants left in the great exchange of populations after the First World War.

Notes

1 The name is now written Sığacak on the signposts.
2 This name is now transferred to Sıçan Adası, a little east of Lebedus.
3 It is described as 'at the east foot of the acropolis hill, close on the left of the road as you approach from the south'—which is hardly intelligible with the line of the road as it now is.

7 Ephesus

Before the Second World War a visit to Ephesus was something of an adventure. 'Ephesus', says H. V. Morton, writing in 1936, 'stands dignified and alone in its death . . . with no sign of life but a goatherd leaning on a broken sarcophagus or a lonely peasant outlined against a mournful sunset. Few people ever visit it. Ephesus has a weird, haunted look'. In 1939 the road from Smyrna was so bad that the vehicle in which the present writer was travelling was unable to follow its course and finished up in a cornfield. Conditions are different now. A fast highway brings the motorist from Izmir in something over an hour; visitors in the season are numbered by scores or hundreds every day, and are able to refresh themselves at a restaurant close by the entrance to the enclosure. The Austrian excavations, first begun in 1896, have lately been resumed and are in progress at the time of writing. In recent years Ephesus has become the showpiece site of the west coast.

Ramsay calls Ephesus the city of change. Its history is varied, and the nature of the ground has changed; and like many other Greek cities—we have already seen the cases of Smyrna and Clazomenae—it did not always stand on its present site.

The foundation legend as told by Athenaeus (VIII, 361) is somewhat picturesque. The founders, he says, being at a loss for a site, consulted the oracle, who told them to choose the spot which a fish and a wild boar should point out. It happened that some fishermen were roasting fish for their lunch near the later harbour, and that one of the fish jumped out of the brazier with a live coal attached and set fire to some shavings; the fire spread to a thicket in which a boar lay hidden; the boar rushed away in alarm and was pursued and finally shot down where the temple of Athena afterwards stood. In memory of this remarkable fulfilment of the oracle the effigy of a wild boar stood as late as A.D. 400 beside the main street of the city.

These founders, according to Strabo and Pausanias, were Ionians led by Androclus, another of the numerous sons of Codrus, the legendary king of Athens. They found the region occupied by Carians and Lydians living around a sanctuary of the great Anatolian mother-goddess; with these they came to an amicable arrangement, founded a new city, and adopted the native goddess under the name of their own Artemis. This earliest city of Ephesus occupied the north slope of the theatre-hill—anciently Mt Pion, now Panayır Dağı—and the land at its foot, which at that time was on the coast; the sea then came up past the city as far as the modern Selçuk. The archaic cemetery lay beneath the main street and upper agora of the Roman city. In this neighbourhood presumably stood the temple of Athena, but it has not been located. Of this early city nothing now remains with the exception of a small piece of polygonal wall high up on the north slope of the hill.

Here the city remained for the first 400 years or so of its existence. It had two advantages which gave it a prominent position among the Greek settlements in Ionia; first, its harbour, conveniently situated in the middle of the west coast of Asia Minor, at the mouth of the river Cayster, and second, the sanctuary of Artemis, a place of pilgrimage from prehistoric times. By the sixth century Ephesus was in a prosperous way; perhaps for this reason it was the first object of attack by the Lydian Croesus. The Ephesians defended themselves by tying a rope from the temple of Artemis to the city, a distance of about three-quarters of a mile (1,207 m.), so placing themselves under the goddess's protection; this pious measure was, however, unavailing. Croesus, never a bitter enemy of the Greeks, treated the sanctuary well; the sculptured column-drums which he presented towards its reconstruction may be seen in the British Museum with his name carved upon them. The city itself, however, he could not permit to continue as it was; he destroyed it and transplanted the inhabitants farther inland, to the level ground south of the temple of Artemis.

That this was its position through the classical period has been proved by soundings, but no proper excavation has yet been attempted there. Excavation will, in fact, be difficult, owing particularly to the rise in the water-table since antiquity. This classical city was unwalled and militarily weak, but its harbour and its sanctuary remained; first under the Lydians, then under the Persians, then as a member of the Athenian maritime confederacy, its prosperity continued undiminished. Its normal tribute in the confederacy, six or seven talents, puts it about on a par with Miletus, Teos, and Erythrae; the only city on this coast with a considerably higher assessment is Cyme. With the King's Peace in 386 B.C. Ephesus fell back with the rest under Persian dominion until the coming of Alexander. Ephesus throughout its history always had a large and influential Persian population, which must have given it a more distinctly oriental character than the other cities of Ionia.

In the course of this period the great temple of Artemis underwent numerous vicissitudes. The earliest building of which traces have been found seems to date to the eighth century and to have been destroyed by the Cimmerians; it was replaced by another of which the architect's name was Chersiphron. This was still unfinished in the sixth century when Croesus arrived and made his contribution to it. In 356 B.C.—tradition said on the very night when Alexander was born—this temple was set on fire and destroyed by a lunatic named Herostratus, apparently with the object (which, in fact, he has achieved) of perpetuating his memory. The Ephesians at once set to work to raise a still finer structure, under an architect whose name is variously given as Deinocrates or Cheirocrates. The work was still going forward when Alexander reached Ephesus in 334 B.C.; much impressed by what he saw he offered to defray all expenses, past and future, of the building, if he might be permitted to make the dedicatory inscription in his own name. This handsome gesture was courteously declined, on the ground that it was not fitting for a god to make a dedication to another god.

The temple, finished eventually by the Ephesians' own efforts, later ranked as one of the seven wonders of the world. The list of these wonders was not drawn up before Hellenistic times; it included, besides the temple of Artemis, the pyramids of Egypt, the Colossus of Rhodes, the statue of Zeus at Olympia, the hanging gardens of Babylon, the lighthouse at Alexandria, and the Mausoleum at Halicarnassus. Later, certain alternatives were admitted, and later still the list was greatly extended beyond the original seven (above, p. 68).

After Alexander's death Ephesus came with the rest of Ionia into the power of Lysimachus. The harbour at this time lay between the north end of Panayır Dağı and the mouth of the Cayster away to the north-east, and the silt brought down by the river was already impeding it; the process was observable even in Herodotus' time. Lysimachus, perceiving that the city in its then position was doomed to inevitable decay, undertook a complete rebuilding on a new site. For this great benefit the Ephesians displayed a regrettable lack of gratitude; as always happens, they were reluctant to leave their homes, and the king was obliged to resort to a stratagem. Taking advantage of a heavy downpour of rain, he blocked up the water-channels of the old city and rendered the houses uninhabitable. It has recently been suggested that this reluctance to move may have been due to a superstitious fear of occupying the area of the archaic cemetery of Ephesus which lay directly beneath the later Lysimachean city.

The site chosen by Lysimachus was that where the ruins now stand, though of its original buildings hardly anything still survives. It was on an impressive scale, with a circuit-wall not far short of six miles (9.65 km.) in length. The old harbour was abandoned in favour of a new one in the bay (as it then was) below Mt Pion on the west. In the wars of the Hellenistic kings Ephesus was not remarkable for the consistency of her allegiance. After Lysimachus' death she supported first the Seleucid kings of Syria, then for a time the Ptolemies of Egypt; she served as headquarters to Antiochus the Great, then after his defeat at Magnesia in 190 B.C. passed into the power of Eumenes of Pergamum. When Aristonicus attempted to dispute the Roman inheritance of the Pergamene kingdom, the Ephesians took the Roman side and with their own forces defeated the pretender in a sea-battle near Cyme. On the other hand, when Mithridates arrived as a professed liberator they readily supported him and joined whole-heartedly in the slaughter of the Roman residents.

As the capital city of the province of Asia, and normal residence of the Roman governor, Ephesus flourished exceedingly. Strabo, writing in the time of Augustus, observed that it was increasing daily in prosperity and was the greatest trading-centre in the whole of Asia west of the Taurus. Its population under the early empire is estimated at something like a quarter of a million. In its inscriptions the city calls itself 'first and greatest metropolis of Asia'. There was, however, one perpetual menace with which the Ephesians had to contend, namely the constant silting-up of the harbour by the river Cayster. A misguided attempt to meet this danger had been made by Attalus II of Pergamum, who tried to deepen the channel for large merchant-ships by constructing a mole at the harbour entrance; this, however, had the opposite effect to that intended, and by the first century of the empire the situation was serious. In A.D. 61 the proconsul of Asia under Nero had the whole harbour dredged; and in the next century Hadrian attempted a different cure by diverting the course of the Cayster. An inscription from the reign of Antoninus Pius contains an edict of the Roman proconsul designed to prevent harbour-users from stacking heavy timbers, or sawing up blocks of marble on the dockside, which might cause it to collapse and further aggravate the problem. In the third century, as an inscription tells us, a private citizen made a donation of 20,000 denarii for the cleaning-out of the harbour. But nothing could permanently avail; the silting continued, and the port of Ephesus is now a good three miles (4·83 km.) from the sea.

The fame of the temple of Artemis continued undiminished. Among its privileges was that of asylum, which conferred sanctuary and complete inviolability on any person taking refuge in the temple. Alexander extended the limits of the protected area to a distance of one stade all round the temple; Mithridates determined them by shooting an arrow from the corner of the temple roof, and was judged to have slightly exceeded a stade—a shot of some two hundred yards (182·9 m.). Mark Antony, emulating the action of Julius Caesar at Didyma, doubled this distance, so actually including a part of the city itself; but this was found to be unsatisfactory, as putting the city at the mercy of malefactors, and it was rescinded by Augustus. In A.D. 22 Tiberius instigated a thorough investigation of the claims to asylum maintained by the various Greek temples, for complaints of abuse were becoming frequent; the cities were invited to send delegates to Rome to defend their claims. The Ephesians, relying on the recent edict of Augustus, had the satisfaction of heading the list of those who were accepted.

The pre-eminence of the cult of Artemis was without prejudice to the cult of the emperors. All the leading cities of the province were eager to build a temple for the imperial worship; but this could only be done by permission of the emperor himself, and competition was severe. The privilege, which carried with it the title of Neocorus, 'Temple-Warden', was granted to Ephesus four times in all by different emperors; but one of these, Caracalla, 'in his modesty [as he expresses it himself] made over his neocorate to the goddess', so that no new temple was built to him, but the title was granted by virtue of the existing cult of Artemis. Ephesus' proud position as 'four times Temple-Warden' is illustrated on the third-century coin of the city shown on Pl. 64. Of the four temples and statues represented, that on the top left is of Artemis, the other three are emperors. This exceptional compliment paid to the old Anatolian goddess illustrates the readiness of the Roman government to encourage the long-established institutions of the eastern world.

But the enemy who was finally to humble the proud Ephesian

Artemis was already at hand. Christianity took root quickly in Ephesus. St Paul arrived in A.D. 53 and found a small nucleus of converts. St John, accompanied or not by the Virgin Mother (below, p. 147), was in Ephesus and other cities of Asia certainly by 67 and perhaps a good deal earlier; it may well have been he who founded the churches later visited by St Paul. St Paul himself lived in the city for three years; the success of his mission is clearly shown by the story told in the nineteenth chapter of Acts. A certain silver-smith, by name Demetrius, made his living by manufacturing silver shrines of Artemis, and he found that Paul's preaching was seriously damaging his business. Calling a meeting of all those engaged in his and similar trades, he pointed out to them the danger not only to their livelihood but also to the dignity of the goddess herself. Roused to anger, they created a clamour that quickly spread through the city; the people rushed to the theatre, taking some of Paul's companions with them. Paul himself would have gone too, but was dissuaded. In the theatre uproar prevailed; for more than an hour the people, many of whom had no idea what the matter was, continued to shout, 'Great is Artemis of the Ephesians!' The tumult was finally quelled by the secretary to the city council, who came out on to the stage with words of severe commonsense. 'The greatness of Artemis,' he said,

> is not in dispute, and these men have committed no indictable offence against her; if anyone thinks they have, let him apply to the law courts in the proper way. If this riot continues, we shall be held to account by the Roman authorities, and shall have no defence.

The incident thus passed off, but Paul immediately left Ephesus.

The general decline of the empire in the third century affected Ephesus like other places. Moreover, the silting of the port was rapidly becoming unmanageable; when Justinian in the sixth century founded the great church of St John, he built it not in the city, but on the hill to the north-east above the present town of Selçuk, which thenceforth became the centre of habitation. The connection with the sea was broken, and the great days of Ephesus were over (Pl. 40).

The modern visitor to Ephesus may begin appropriately with the site of the temple of Artemis. It lies a few yards to the north of the Kuşadası road, and is marked by the mound of the excavators' spoil. It presents a melancholy spectacle. Among the reeds a few foundation blocks rise above ground, submerged or not according to the year's rainfall. In recent years the Austrian excavations have uncovered the altar of the original archaic temple, along with large quantities of bone from the animals sacrificed there. The occupation layers of the site range from the seventh century B.C. to Roman times, but the site, sunk below the modern ground level and always liable to flooding, remains obstinately unspectacular.

The discovery of the famous temple was due to an English engineer, J. T. Wood, who had made it his life's ambition. The position of the temple was quite unknown, except that it was sure to be deeply buried, and for a long time no clue was available. Wood worked at Ephesus from 1863 to 1874, and spent a considerable private fortune in more or less random soundings in various parts of the plain. The clue was at length provided by a long but fragmentary inscription found in the theatre, containing a regulation that whenever a performance or an assembly was held in the theatre, the sacred images should be carried there from the temple and afterwards returned. The route prescribed was by the sacred way from the Magnesian Gate. It remained to find the Magnesian Gate, which would naturally face in the direction of Magnesia, and to follow the sacred way. This Wood successfully did; the street, deep under ground, proved to be quite well preserved, with a marble paving 12 yards (11 m.) wide; it led to the precinct wall, and so to the temple itself, 15 feet (4·57 m.) below the surface. This discovery ranks as one of the romances of archaeology. Wood, however, did not excavate the temple to its lowest level; this task remained for D. G. Hogarth in 1904, when the fabulous foundation-deposit of objects in gold came to light.

The unimpressive situation of the Artemisium on flat ground outside the city has often been remarked. Leake, however, pointed out that the greater Ionic temples of Asia Minor, almost without exception, are similarly placed; he believed the reason to be that the tall and slender Ionic order shows to better advantage on flat ground, whereas the comparatively squat Doric temple calls for an elevated position. We shall see further examples at Magnesia, Sardis, and Didyma; but Claros is an exception.

Artemis of the Ephesians never became a truly Greek goddess, but always retained a large measure of her oriental nature. Her non-Greek character is evident enough from the form of her representation in art (Pl. 36). The feet and legs fused together give the statue the effect of a pillar. The rows of egg-shaped objects across the chest have been understood to be breasts, but the most recent opinion is that they are in fact eggs, the egg being a familiar symbol of fertility. These features are quite unsuited to the virgin huntress of the Greeks. On the other hand, the numerous beasts portrayed on the lower limbs—bulls, lions, sphinxes, and others—might be thought to represent the animal world which the Greek Artemis loved and protected; though here again the inclusion of the chimaera gives a definitely eastern touch.

Similarly, the cult of the goddess was served by orders of ministers most of which were utterly strange to any Greek hierarchy—some of them not Greek words at all. At the head was the Priest (or priests, whether one or more is not certain), a eunuch with the title of Megabyxus; this word is Persian, meaning, 'set free by God'.[1] The Megabyxus, as Strabo tells us, was always chosen from abroad, no doubt from the non-Greek nations, and was held in great honour. Assisting him was a numerous body of virgins, compared by Plutarch with the Vestal Virgins at Rome. They were divided into three classes, the Priestess-to-be, or Novice, the Priestess, who performed the actual ritual, and the ex-Priestess, whose function was to instruct the novices. A further order of priests was known as the Essenes. This again is a non-Greek word, used with the meaning 'king'; whether it may be Semitic and have some connection with the Jewish sect of Essenes is not clear. It has been suggested that the Ephesian hierarchy was built up around the bee, the bee being the national symbol of Ephesus, appearing regularly on the city's coins and on the effigies of Artemis. According to one ancient interpretation the word Essen means properly 'king-bee'—that is queen-bee, for the Greeks were in error on this point—and some have thought that the virgin priestesses were called Melissae, 'bees'. It is known that certain priestesses of the Mother Goddess had this title, but there is no actual evidence for it at Ephesus, and this whole theory must be regarded as dubious. The Essenes appear to have acted as intermediaries between the religious and the civic sides of the city's activities; they offered sacrifice to Artemis in the city's name, they assigned new citizens to a particular tribe, and they organized the public banquets that followed the religious ceremonies.

Another college of priests attached to the service of Artemis was the Curetes. In Greek mythology the Curetes were demigods associated primarily with Zeus; but a local Ephesian legend told that they assisted Leto in giving birth to Artemis—which event the Ephesians located in the neighbourhood of their city—by scaring away Hera, who was jealously watching to do what mischief she

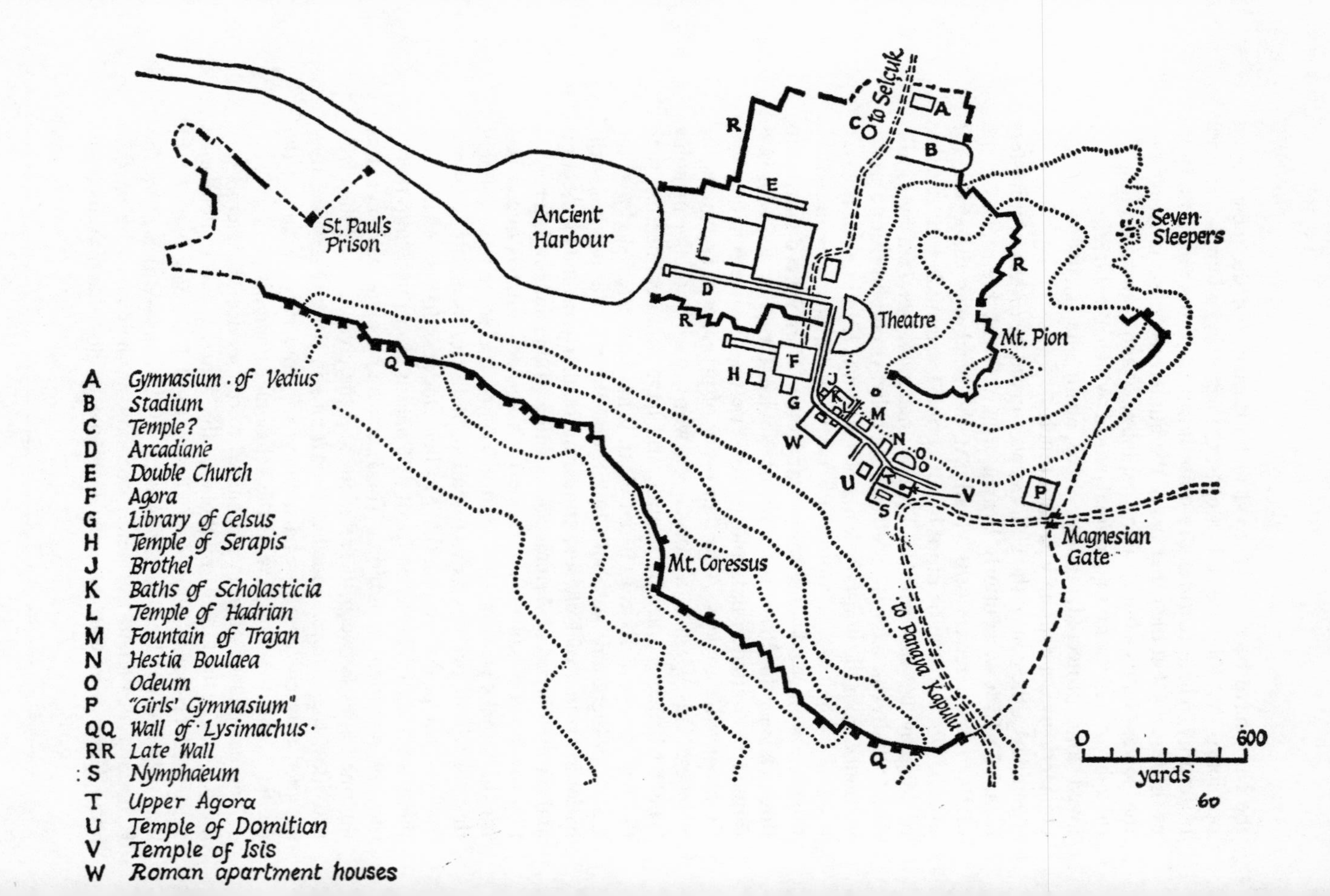

St. Paul's Prison
Ancient Harbour
to Selçuk
Theatre
Mt. Pion
Seven Sleepers
Mt. Coressus
Magnesian Gate
to Panaya Kapulu
0
600
yards
A Gymnasium of Vedius
B Stadium
C Temple?
D Arcadiane
E Double Church
F Agora
G Library of Celsus
H Temple of Serapis
J Brothel
K Baths of Scholasticia
L Temple of Hadrian
M Fountain of Trajan
N Hestia Boulaea
O Odeum
P "Girls' Gymnasium"
QQ Wall of Lysimachus
RR Late Wall
S Nymphaeum
T Upper Agora
U Temple of Domitian
V Temple of Isis
W Roman apartment houses

could. This event was celebrated by an annual festival, at which the human college of Curetes held sacrifices and banquets.

Yet another order had the curious name of Acrobatae, or walkers on tiptoe. Why they walked in this way we do not know; all we learn of them is that they were twenty in number and performed sacrifices. These again are peculiar to Ephesus.

Strabo's language suggests that not all the exotic features of the cult of Artemis survived unchanged in his own day. Indeed, it is remarkable that the goddess and her hierarchy resisted the influence of Hellenism so long and so successfully as they did.

The surviving ruins of Ephesus belong almost exclusively to the Roman imperial period. The outstanding exception is the circuit-wall built by Lysimachus. On the low ground it has largely disappeared, but it still stands along the crest of the 1,100-foot (335·3 m.) mountain, now called Bülbül Dağı, to the south of the city, and provides a recommended excursion for those with half a day to spare. With its towers and postern gates it affords an excellent example of a Hellenistic fortification wall. When it stood complete it contained, by Miltner's calculation, not less than 200,000 cubic metres of stone, exclusive of the towers. Where it descends at its west end to the ancient harbour it contains a very handsome tower set on a low hill, which has, for no good reason, acquired the name of 'St Paul's Prison'. It is conspicuous from the city. An inscription in the tower identifies the knoll on which it stands as the 'Hill of Astyages'; who Astyages may have been is not known.

The road which diverges to the ruins from the Kuşadası highway brings the visitor first to the Gymnasium of Vedius, constructed in the second century A.D. as a gift to the city by a rich citizen named Publius Vedius Antoninus. The visitor enters it from the rear. The standing remains are those of the baths which were normally attached to gymnasia in the Roman period; we have seen the case of the upper gymnasium at Pergamum. The palaestra, the open area for gymnastic exercise, lay to the east, with a well-appointed latrine in its south-west corner.

Just to the south is the stadium. In its present form it is not earlier than the third century A.D., and its poor state of preservation is due to plundering of the stones for the Byzantine fortification on the hill above Selçuk. The starting-lines are not preserved, and the most interesting part of the stadium is at the east end, where a circular area has been enclosed to serve as an arena for gladiatorial and similar contests, and rooms are installed for the apparent purpose of housing the wild beasts. As in most Greek cities, there is no amphitheatre at Ephesus; and since the substitute thus produced was certainly no part of the stadium as it was built, it was evidently only at a late date that the need was felt to stage this kind of display.

Directly across the road from the stadium is a low mound on whose summit there once stood an octagonal building, of which only the rock-cut parts remain. It was probably a temple, and has been thought to belong to the early Ionian Ephesus, before the time of Croesus, but there is no real evidence either of its nature or of its date.

Farther to the south is the great theatre, a good example of the so-called Graeco-Roman type, that is to say a theatre of Greek form reconstructed in the Roman fashion. The original building dates from the time of Lysimachus or shortly after; from this period there survive the main core of the scene-building and the general form of the cavea, rather over a semicircle, with its twelve stairways, eleven cunei, and two diazomata. A noteworthy feature is that the steepness of the cavea slope increases above each diazoma, thus improving the view of the spectators at the back. The ground floor of the stage-building consists of a long hall running north and south, with eight rooms lying to the west of it; the two end rooms at north and south opened on to a narrow terrace behind the building, the others open into the hall. A passage runs through from the terrace into the orchestra. All of this is preserved. Of the upper storey, which formed a background to the stage, little now survives. The stage itself is calculated to have been 8 feet 6 inches (2·59 m.) in height and about 10 feet (3·05 m.) in depth; it sloped from back to front, like a modern stage, with a gradient of about 1:25 (Pl. 37).

In the classical period, as is now generally agreed, the theatre had no stage; the actors in the plays of Euripides or Aristophanes performed on the same level as the chorus in the orchestra, or at most were raised above them only by a low dais or platform. In the Hellenistic period, when the importance of the chorus was much reduced, a high narrow stage for the actors was introduced, making them more audible from the upper seats without being less visible from the lower. This Hellenistic stage is generally some 8 to 10 feet (2·44 to 3·05 m.) high and about the same in depth; a good example is preserved at Priene (below, pp. 165–6). In the Roman period all the action took place on the stage, which was accordingly increased to about double in depth from front to back; the orchestra,

28 Erythrae. The City-Wall

29 Erythrae. The newly excavated Theatre

30 Ephesus. Temple of Hadrian

31 Ephesus. Temple of Hadrian; detail from the façade

32 Ephesus. Relief showing Hermes and the Ram

33 Erythrae. Source of the Aleon

34 Ephesus. Relief showing tripod and omphalos

35 Lebedus. The Sea-Wall

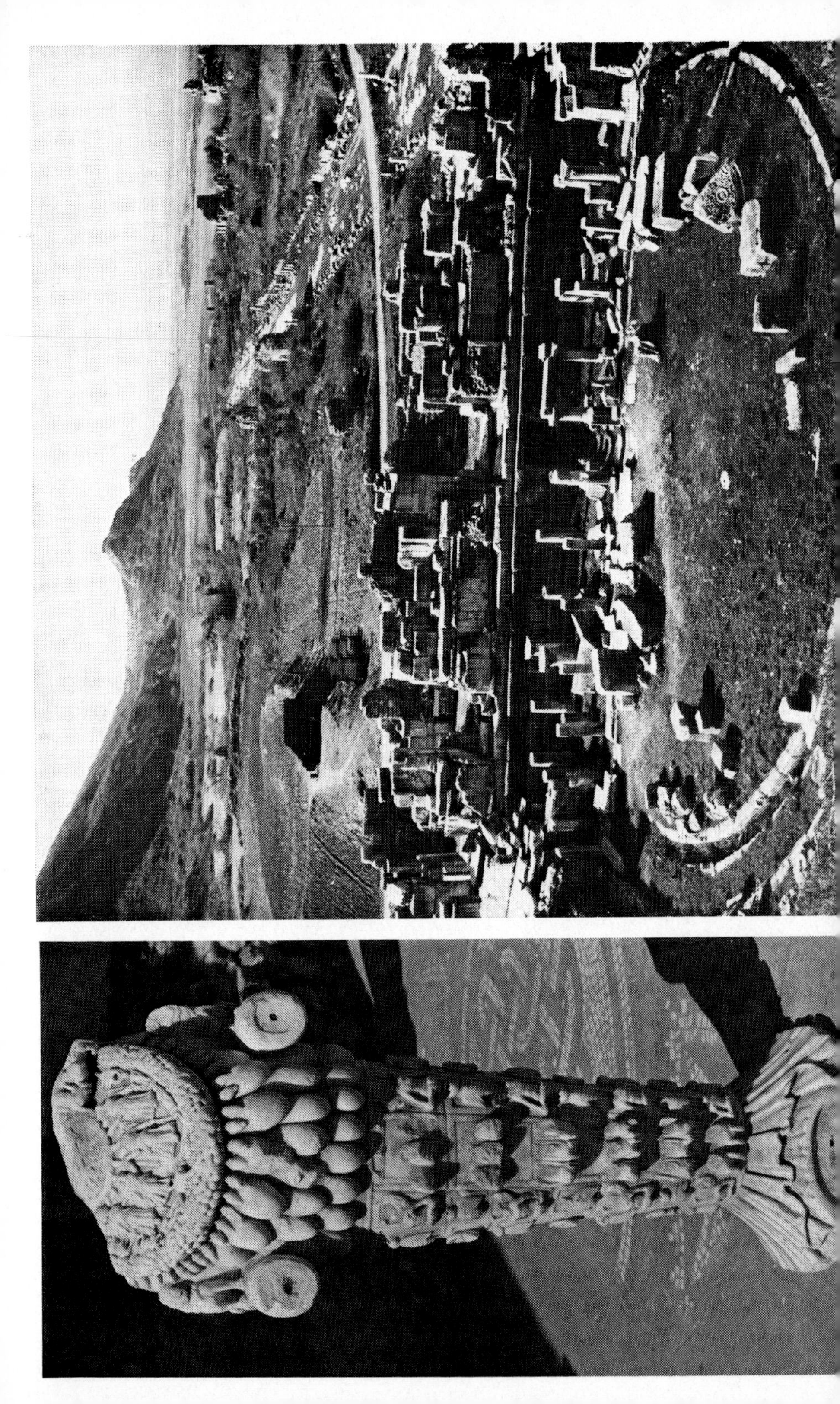

36 Ephesus. Statue of Ephesian Artemis

37 Ephesus. Theatre

38 Ephesus. Gateway in the newly excavated street

39 Ephesus. Belevi Mausoleum; Corinthian Capital

40 Ephesus. The newly restored Basilica of St John on the hill above Selçuk

41 Ephesus. Marble Street and Doric Stoa

42 Ephesus. Aqueduct in the valley south of the city

43 Ephesus. Belevi Mausoleum; the Grave-Chamber

44 Ephesus. Belevi Tumulus

45 Ephesus. Panaya Kapulu, the supposed House of the Virgin Mary

46 Ephesus. Belevi Mausoleum

47 Claros. The Oracular Chamber in 1963

48 Claros. Arm of the Colossal Statue of Apollo

49 Claros. The newly excavated Temple of Apollo, showing the passage leading to the Oracular Chamber

50 Priene. Front Seat in the Theatre

51 Priene. Wash-room in the Gymnasium

52 Priene. The Council Chamber

53 Priene. Supporting Wall of the Temple Terrace

now useless to the performers, was occupied during the performance by chairs for the more distinguished spectators.

During the first century A.D., therefore, the theatre at Ephesus was subjected to an extensive reconstruction to bring it up to date. The stage, still of the same height, was carried forward another 10 feet (3·05 m.) into the orchestra and supported on the two rows of columns and one row of square pilasters which are still standing. In the front of the stage-building, behind the stage, a great façade was erected, rising in three storeys above the stage and decorated with columns, niches, and statues. The long hall in the ground floor was now roofed over, in place of its old wooden ceiling, with a stone vault resting on walls placed against the side walls of the hall; their handsome blocks were probably taken from a dismantled part of the Hellenistic theatre. A second row of eight rooms was also added on the west. The side entrances to the orchestra, called parodoi, were in the Hellenistic theatre open passages between stage and cavea; these were blocked by the new constructions, and fresh covered entrances were built, of which that on the north side is well preserved. These changes involved a reduction of the cavea at its two extremities by about 5 feet (1·52 m.) and the construction of new retaining walls; an inscription was found recording the dedication of this huge work to the Emperor Domitian in A.D. 92.

These massive alterations were begun about A.D. 40 and completed some seventy years later. They were accordingly in progress when St Paul was at Ephesus in the fifties. To visualize the riotous assembly caused by Demetrius the silversmith we should picture the stage-building enveloped in scaffolding and the astonished workmen looking on during an unexpected rest-period. We must also imagine the rows of seats extending right down to orchestra level, for the lowest six rows were removed at a later date and the present semicircular wall constructed.

The acoustics of the theatre are, as always, excellent, and were further improved in ancient times by placing bronze or clay sounding-vessels at various points in the auditorium—a remarkable anticipation of the loudspeakers used today at Wimbledon and elsewhere (above, pp. 112–13). The spectators were shaded, at least partially, by a huge awning stretched from side to side of the cavea.

From the hillside above the theatre an excellent view may be had of the greater part of the city. In front, a little to the right, a marble-paved street runs straight for some 600 yards (548·6 m.) to the ancient harbour, whose shape can be distinguished by the different colour of the grass. There was always a street in this position, but the present paving dates only from about A.D. 400. It is some 35 feet (10·7 m.) wide and had a stoa on either side. The name of the street is given by an inscription found in it, which says: 'Arcadiane contains in its two stoas, as far as the wild boar, fifty lamps'. The wild boar, as was mentioned above, recalls the foundation legend of the city. The provision for street-lighting is interesting and a great rarity; Antioch had it in the fourth century, but in the first century, even at Rome, the streets, as we learn from Juvenal, were unlighted. The name Arcadiane, given in honour of the Emperor Arcadius (A.D. 395–408), tells us the approximate date. Another inscription found beside this street gives interesting information concerning charges payable to the Record Office. For example, a parsley-vendor's licence, 1 denarius; a salt-vendor's licence, 1 denarius; proclamation of a victor in the games, 6 denarii; registration of birth, 1 denarius—but if the mother is of a prohibited class (such as a priestess or a slave), the charge is 100 denarii. Evidently possession of a birth-certificate in such cases conferred certain privileges and was worth paying for.

From Arcadiane a short walk to the north brings the visitor to the Church of the Virgin Mary, sometimes called the Double

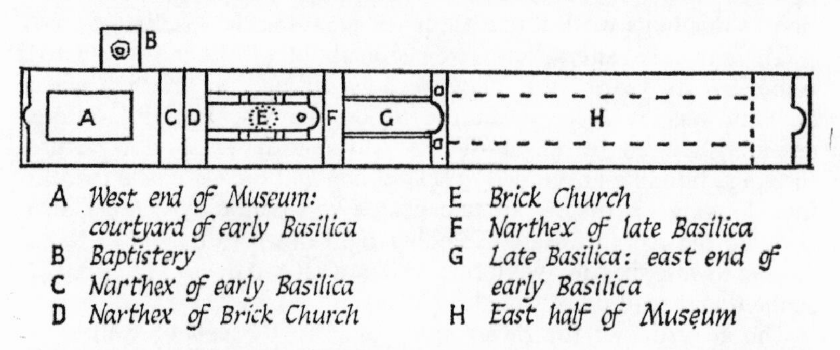

A West end of Museum: courtyard of early Basilica
B Baptistery
C Narthex of early Basilica
D Narthex of Brick Church
E Brick Church
F Narthex of late Basilica
G Late Basilica: east end of early Basilica
H East half of Museum

Fig. 34 Plan of the Church of the Virgin Mary

Church. The original building was not a church at all but a secular building of unusually elongated form, some 100 feet (30·5 m.) wide and about eight times as long, with an apse at each end and a row of small rooms along each side. This was the Museum—that is, not what is now understood by a museum, but a Hall of the Muses, used for lectures, disputation, and higher education generally. This building was destroyed by fire, and in the third century A.D. the ruins of its western half were converted into a church of basilica form with a courtyard in front on the west (A–G on the plan). In this church, dedicated to the Virgin, was held the stormy third Ecumenical Council of A.D. 431, where the Nestorian heresy was condemned. On the north side of the courtyard a baptistery was added; this is comparatively well preserved, and has in the floor of its central room a font for baptismal immersion, with steps leading down on each side. The form of this early basilica is not now easy to recognize, owing to later alterations. At an uncertain date a domed church of brickwork (E on the plan) was installed in the western half of the basilica, with a new apse at its east end; and later still, after the destruction of this church, a small basilica G was inserted between it and the east end of the early basilica. The remains of these later churches have almost completely overlaid the church of the Virgin. The courtyard A, however, remains unaltered; a number of inscribed blocks have been re-used in its paving. The eastern half H of the original museum was converted into dwelling-houses.

Below the theatre, at right-angles to Arcadiane, runs a similar marble-paved street. Wheeled traffic was permitted along it[2] as is shown by the ruts in the surface. This paving is probably of similar date to that of Arcadiane; but the handsome Doric stoa on its west side was dedicated in the middle of the first century A.D. (Pl. 41).

Beyond this stoa on the right is the library of Celsus, probably the finest surviving specimen of its kind, which has been restored in recent years with meticulous care by the Austrian excavators. The process of restoration has provided new insights into the techniques of ancient architects, and hitherto unnoticed constructional details have come to light. For instance, it appears that in designing the façade the columns and capitals at the edges were made smaller than those in the middle, thus making the whole frontage appear wider than it actually is. Following the rule laid down by the Roman architect Vitruvius, it faces the east, so as to take advantage of the morning light. From the courtyard in front steps led up to a two-storeyed façade with windows in the upper storey and an inscription naming the building as the 'Celsian Library' and recording that Gaius Julius Aquila left 25,000 denarii for its upkeep and for the purchase of books. This Aquila was son of Gaius Julius Celsus Polemaeanus, proconsul of Asia in A.D. 106–107, in whose honour and as whose tomb the library was built. Statues of Celsus stood on the wings of the front steps, with honorific inscriptions in Greek and in Latin which may still be read.

The interior consisted of a single large room 50 feet (15·2 m.)

high, surrounded by galleries, in three storeys; it has a number of features in common with the library at Pergamum. In the middle of the back wall is a semicircular niche which probably contained a statue of Athena. At the foot of the walls is a platform 3 feet (·91 m.) high and rather more broad, which carried columns supporting a gallery above. In the walls are ten rectangular niches which held the books; similar niches, with a narrow gallery in front, no doubt stood in the second and third storeys. Round the exterior of the walls runs a passage 3 feet (·91 m.) wide, serving to protect the books from damp. On the north side this passage leads round to the grave-chamber of Celsus, situated directly under the semicircular niche in the back wall. This chamber is generally kept locked, the guardian holding the key. It contains a marble sarcophagus in which is the actual coffin of lead, still unopened. Tombs in ancient times stood normally outside the city; the privilege of burial in the city was a considerable distinction.

From the courtyard in front of the library a three-arched gateway leads through to the agora on the north. This gate, built almost entirely of marble, was dedicated in 3 B.C. to Augustus and his son-in-law Agrippa by two rich freedmen, Mithridates and Mazaeus. The inscription, which originally stood above the gate, is now placed along the side of the agora. This Mithridates has, of course, no connection with the famous king of Pontus. In the wall between the gate and the courtyard is an inscription of the third century A.D. praising a certain market-inspector for keeping down the price of bread: 'Fine bread', it says, 'was sold at 4 obols for a 14 ounce loaf; inferior bread at 2 obols the 10 ounce loaf'. A century earlier prices had been about half of these; in the meantime the currency had been debased, and inflation had done its work. Inscriptions of this kind bring the ancient city to life more vividly perhaps than many more imposing monuments; so, too, does a graffito roughly scrawled in a niche of the same gate on the opposite side: it says 'Whoso relieves himself here shall suffer the wrath of Hecate'.

Behind the library to the west are the ruins of the temple of Serapis, built in the second century A.D. Serapis, the sacred bull Apis, was an Egyptian deity; but Ptolemy I built him a temple at Alexandria in which the god's statue was given features resembling those of Pluto, the Greek god of the underworld. This was an attempt to establish a cult which should be acceptable both to Egyptians and to Greeks; the Egyptians, in fact, soon dropped it and reverted to the old worship, but its success with the Greeks, and even with the Romans, was remarkable. Under the Empire almost every city of note in the eastern provinces had a cult of the composite Serapis, frequently associated with Isis and other Egyptian deities.

The Serapeum at Ephesus is notable especially for its massive architecture. It had columns only in front; eight in number, these were formed each of a single block of stone. The diameter is nearly 5 feet (1·52 m.), and the height about 46 feet (14 m.), so that each column must have weighed not far short of 60 tons. The achievement of transporting and erecting these monoliths, and of placing on them the capitals and the heavy entablature, all with the utmost precision, is impressive in the extreme. Of the richness of the decoration an idea is given by the block lying in front of the temple-steps. Quarter-circular grooves in the floor show where the heavy double door opened into the interior. Several of the surviving stones, including the columns, show traces of the red paint with which they were originally coloured; temples and statues were normally painted in antiquity. Red and blue are the colours most used; of these the red pigment employed was the more durable, and not infrequently survives, whereas blue is rarely to be seen.

Opposite the library the paved street turns to the east and rises gently to follow the south foot of Mt Pion to the Magnesian Gate. This part of the city is in process of excavation by the Austrian archaeologists at the time of writing. Among the new discoveries the visitor's eye is perhaps most attracted by the temple of Hadrian, fronting the street on the north side (Pl. 30). The façade has been re-erected from the architectural fragments found. It appears that this attractive little building was not the temple which earned for Ephesus its second 'Temple-Wardenship', but a shrine privately dedicated to Artemis of Ephesus, Hadrian, and the people of Ephesus in 117–118 or 118–119. The title of 'Temple-Warden' for the second time did not come to Ephesus until 130–132, and the temple associated with this new honour has yet to be identified. In the fourth century the building was damaged by fire or by an earthquake; the reliefs in the porch, or pronaos, belong to the restoration which was then undertaken. (Those now in position are casts; the originals are in the museum.) That on the right (east) side is particularly interesting. It shows a group of thirteen figures; on the extreme left and right stands Athena with her round shield; after her on the left come six other Greek deities, then a group of five representing the Emperor Theodosius and his family on either side of a figure of Artemis. If we remember that Theodosius was among the fiercest opponents of paganism, this acceptance of the pagan goddess, as it were, into the bosom of the royal family is remarkable indeed, and leaves no doubt of the strong hold which Artemis still had upon men's minds, even at this late date.

Further evidence to the same effect was found by the excavators in the temple of Hestia Boulaea adjoining the odeum higher up towards the Magnesian Gate. In this sanctuary burned the eternal fire, which was never permitted to go out; it formed the political centre of the city. This building was found, when excavated, to have been systematically despoiled in antiquity and its contents removed; nevertheless it still contained two statues of Artemis carefully preserved where they lay. The statues might be overthrown by the Christian destroyers of the temple, but respect for the goddess still forbade that they should be carried off to the lime-kiln.

The despoiler of this sanctuary is, as it happens, known. Behind the temple of Hadrian are the so-called baths of Scholasticia. This lady, commemorated by a statue found in the building, restored the baths in the fourth century, perhaps after the same earthquake which damaged the temple of Hadrian. She used for the purpose material taken from the temple of Hestia Boulaea. That this is so is especially clear from the thick solid columns which stand in the front hall of the baths. These are covered with inscribed lists of members of the College of Curetes; similar lists are found on the outer walls of the temple of Hestia, to which accordingly it is safe to suppose that the columns also originally belonged.

Adjoining the baths of Scholasticia is a room identified, from inscriptions and from the erotic character of certain figurines found in it, as a brothel (Aşkevi on the notice-board). In essence the building was a typical peristyle house of the first century A.D., to which additional rooms for customers were added in the third and fourth centuries. As a great port and a city which attracted a huge number of visitors of all types, the brothel would surely never have lacked for clients.

Among the inscribed stones lining the street, about 30 yards (27·4 m.) below the temple of Hadrian, lying flat behind the upright row, is a statue-base erected by the Sacred College of Silversmiths —the same to which Demetrius belonged.

Just above the temple of Hadrian is the elaborate fountain of Trajan, and farther up the paved street other buildings are being brought to light. On the saddle at the top of the rise the odeum has long been known; it is a small theatre-like building, in very decent preservation, used for musical performances and perhaps for lectures and rehearsals.

The odeum looks south over the upper agora, or market-place, of Roman Ephesus, 175 yards (160 m.) long by 63 yards (58 m.) wide. This was surrounded by shaded porticoes, or stoas, where stalls could be set up. On the west side was a raised platform area, and in the middle of it a small Doric temple has been found. Only the foundations survive, but they indicate a peripteral temple with six columns across the front and ten down the sides. Small finds from the area suggest that it was dedicated to the Egyptian goddess Isis in the second half of the first century B.C. Nearby, the head of a colossal statue has also been discovered, strongly resembling portraits of the Roman triumvir Mark Antony. Antony visited Ephesus at different times between 42 and 31 B.C., on one famous occasion entering the city in the guise of the god Dionysus accompanied by a procession of ecstatic Bacchic worshippers. His connection with Egypt through Queen Cleopatra is also well known, and the excavators have made the attractive suggestion that he was responsible for building and dedicating the temple.

Opposite the odeum is a large fountain, or nymphaeum, which served for the distribution of water to the city. It was fed by an aqueduct of which a part remains, crossing the valley three miles (4.83 km.) to the south of Selçuk, immediately below the present main road. It is a handsome structure in two storeys, and is dated by its inscription to the time of Augustus. Farther on still is the Magnesian Gate, of which hardly anything is left, and close beside it the Girls' Gymnasium—so-called not because it was for the use of young women but because of the numerous female statues found there (Pl. 42).

If the visitor will continue from here round the east foot of Mt Pion, he will come in about half a mile upon an impressive necropolis in a gully of the hillside. In addition to numerous single graves, large vaulted halls of brickwork have been constructed, with sepulchral niches and chambers in their walls, often in two or more storeys. The whole installation is of Christian date, and grew up around the burial-place of the famous Seven Sleepers of Ephesus. These young men, so the story ran, were Christians who lived in the time of the Emperor Decius, about A.D. 250. To escape the obligation of having to perform sacrifice in the temple of the emperor they left the city and lay down to sleep in a cave. When they woke up and went back into the city to buy bread, they found that they had slept not one night but close on two hundred years, and that Christianity was now the accepted religion of the Roman world. The emperor, Theodosius II, was informed of this remarkable occurrence and at once recognized in it a proof of the doctrine of bodily resurrection, a question which was at that time agitating the Church. When the young men eventually died, their bodies, miraculously preserved from decay, were given splendid burial and a church was built over their resting-place.

Excavation has, in fact, revealed a small church, and beneath it a rock-cut gallery with chambers opening off it, on the walls of which are scratched invocations to the saintly young sleepers. From a desire to be buried as close as possible to them the surrounding necropolis was gradually extended in subsequent centuries, and the place has ever since been regarded as holy.

Digging continues. Among the most impressive of the recent discoveries are the private houses on the steep slope above the paved street. They are in several storeys, and many of them contain wall-paintings still in good condition; most of these are kept locked.

Panaya Kapulu

Just outside the city on the south a recently made road leads to the so-called Panaya Kapulu, or house of the Virgin Mary, Meryem Ana in Turkish. This is a small building now converted into a chapel, set in a pleasant spot with terraces and an abundant fountain. Whether this is really the Virgin's home, and even whether the Virgin really lived and died at Ephesus, are hotly debated problems (Pl. 45).

The canonical tradition holds that Mary died in Jerusalem at the age of 63. But the foundations of this tradition are neither very early nor very strong. The principal evidence is a passage of St John of Damascus, written in the eighth century, which relates that in A.D. 458 the Empress Pulcheria wrote to the bishop of Jerusalem asking him to send the body of the Virgin to Constantinople. The bishop replied that he was unable to do so, as according to a reliable tradition she was buried at Gethsemane, and the tomb was found empty, three days later, by the apostles. There is reason to suspect, however, that this passage has been interpolated into the text of St John; and it is curious that earlier writers such as Eusebius and Jerome make no mention of this tomb at Gethsemane. The scriptures themselves are completely silent concerning the latter part of the Virgin's life.

The rival tradition, which goes back at least to the Council of Ephesus in 431, maintains that Mary came with St John to Ephesus between 37 and 48, lived there and died there. Christ on the Cross entrusted His mother to His beloved John; 'and from that moment the disciple took her into his home'. It is to be assumed, say the Ephesian partisans, that from that time on the two were inseparable; when John came to Ephesus, Mary must have been with him. John was certainly in Asia from 67 onwards; but if Mary died at the age of 63, she cannot have lived until that date, and it is necessary to suppose that John paid an earlier visit to Ephesus. This must have been before 48, in which year he is known to have been in Jerusalem. Between 37 and 48 we have no information as to where he was or what he was doing, and this silence is well explained by the theory that he and Mary were at Ephesus, far from the centre of events in Palestine. We can then understand how it happened that St Paul in the fifties found churches already established in Asia.

Nothing therefore prevents our believing that Mary lived for some time, and died, at Ephesus, and a tradition that she did so recurs repeatedly from the fifth century onwards. But the situation of her house and of her tomb was, of course, unknown, and the house was likely to have perished long since. Its discovery, against all probability, was due to the publication in the middle of the nineteenth century of a Life of the Virgin as revealed in visions to a certain Catherine Emmerich. This invalid German lady, who for twelve years had not left her bed, and had never in her life been near Ephesus, placed the Virgin's house on a mountain above that city and described its appearance in considerable detail. In 1891 a search was organized by M. Poulin, Superior of the Lazarists, in the hills around Ephesus, and resulted in the discovery of a ruined house which answered exactly to the description—so exactly that, in one observer's opinion, the house and its surroundings might have been laid out according to Catherine Emmerich's directions. This was the Panaya Kapulu. The masonry of the house is agreed to be characteristic of the sixth or seventh century, but competent scholars have been prepared to say that the foundations might quite possibly go back to the first century. Moreover, the search-party learned that every year, on 15 August, the Orthodox Greeks of the neighbourhood, and even from a considerable distance, had long been in the habit of assembling there to celebrate the Dormition of the Virgin, whom they believed to have died at that spot. This belief had been inherited through the generations, and might well be very ancient.

Such is the case for Panaya Kapulu. It at once won the approbation of the archbishop of Smyrna, who in 1892 authorized the celebration of the Mass in the building and pronounced it a place of pilgrimage.

Since then numerous wonderful cures have been recorded, and in a corner of the chapel are collected the crutches, sticks, leg-braces, and other implements dedicated by grateful sufferers who have been enabled to discard them. Faith in the healing powers of the place continues still; when the present writer was there in the early 1960s, an old gentleman sorely afflicted with rheumatism was painfully exercising his crippled limbs inside the chapel, until obliged to return to his wheel-chair. Until lately there were also to be seen in the chapel hundreds of fragments of cloth hung up by visitors either in gratitude for a cure effected or in hope of a cure to come. This practice is observed in many places in Turkey which are reckoned holy.

As for the Virgin's tomb, it was declared by Catherine Emmerich to be at a distance of something over a mile from the house; all efforts to find it have so far been unsuccessful.

Belevi

Some ten miles (16·1 km.) from Ephesus, near the village of Belevi on the Izmir road, are two monuments of comparatively early date, well deserving of a visit. They stand about two miles (3·22 km.) from the village beside the rough road leading to Tire.

The first, which is close beside the road on a slight eminence, is a mausoleum of most unusual construction. The core of the monument consists of a cube of living rock about 80 feet (24·4 m.) square and nearly 50 feet (15·2 m.) high, formed by cutting away the hillside from around it. This was faced with solid marble blocks, with steps at the foot and a Doric triglyph-frieze at the top. On this massive base was erected a chamber, also of marble, surrounded by a Corinthian colonnade. Along the top of this colonnade stood winged lions arranged in pairs on either side of globular urns. The roof over the chamber was probably of pyramidal shape, with perhaps a chariot-and-four at the summit (Pl. 39).

The grave itself was not in this chamber, where it might be expected, but was secreted in the rock-cube on the south side facing the hill. To form it, the rock-cube was cut away from top to bottom, the two sides of the cut sloping inwards towards the top; the grave-chamber was then installed in the lower part of this cut, leaving a trapezoidal area above it. Inside was the sarcophagus (now in the museum at Ephesus), elegantly carved and decorated with a relief showing eleven Sirens; the detail of the wings and birds' feet is finely rendered. On the lid of the sarcophagus the dead man is represented reclining on his elbow. This chamber was completely invisible from outside, as the marble facing was carried without interruption across the cut in the rock (Pl. 43, 46).

Only one man was ever buried in this tomb, and in view of the vast expense incurred he must have been a distinguished personage; but no trace of an inscription was found, and it is not known who he was. At first it was conjectured that he might be Antiochus II of Syria, who died at Ephesus in 246 B.C. under suspicion of having been poisoned by his wife Laodice. It would be normal for the king's body to be taken back to Syria, but in the conditions of war prevailing at the time it might possibly have been decided to bury him near Ephesus. However, the more recent opinion is that the mausoleum dates to an earlier period, probably in the fourth century while the country was still under the Persians. The form of the winged lions in particular suggests Persian influence. The occupant of the tomb will then have been a local dignitary of wealth and position; it is not possible to say more.

The second monument is also a tomb, but of utterly different character. It stands on the hill next to the west of the mausoleum. It has the form of a tumulus, but the tumulus in fact consists merely of the summit of the hill itself. Round it runs a wall of elegant cushioned ashlar masonry. To resist the thrust of the earth each block has in its upper surface a groove into which fitted a corresponding projection on the under-side of the block above. The entrance, on the south, leads to a tunnel 20 yards (18·3 m.) long

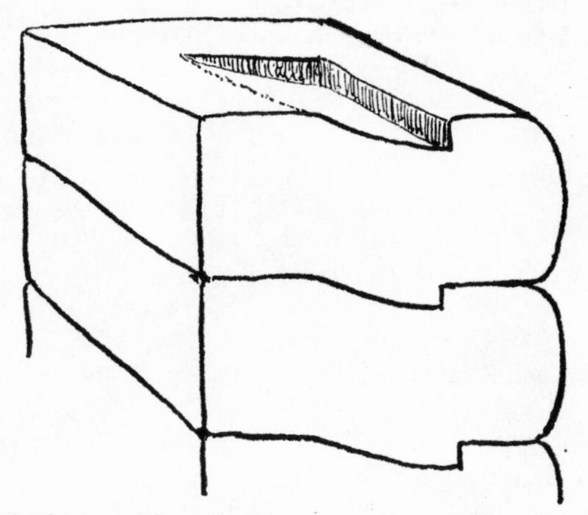

Fig. 35 Belevi. Grooved blocks from the tumulus

running into the hill, at the end of which, nearly at the centre of the tumulus, are two grave-chambers. The ring-wall was carried past the entrance, which was accordingly invisible from outside. Both tunnel and grave-chambers were constructed by cutting down through the rock from above, then lining with masonry and roofing over with large slabs. The tunnel is at present encumbered by piles of earth and stones thrown up by treasure-seekers. The chambers are rectangular, and the roofs are carefully built to prevent collapse. In the outer room the roof-span is reduced by laying blocks obliquely across the corners; in the inner room the roof is formed of a 'corbelled' arch, each course on either side projecting beyond the course below. Above the ceiling of each room is a relieving chamber to reduce the pressure from above; these were not originally accessible, but a hole has been cut in the roof of the inner chamber by tomb-robbers. No sarcophagus or other trace of the actual burial has been found, nor is there any inscription. On the top of the hill are lying a number of squared blocks, showing that some kind of monument stood there. The quarry from which the wall-blocks were cut adjoins the tumulus on the south-west (Pl. 44).

Very varying dates have been proposed for this tumulus, which, like the mausoleum below, must have been the tomb of no ordinary person. The latest opinion is disposed to place it in the fourth century B.C., perhaps a little earlier than the mausoleum.

Notes

1 Or perhaps 'given by God'.
2 Or at least along part of it.

8 Colophon, Notium, Claros

These three places lie close together in the same valley and were always closely associated; Colophon and Notium were cities, Claros was not. Colophon was a member of the Ionian League; its foundation legend concerns Claros and will be recorded below. Notium, on the other hand, was not in origin Ionian at all; it is included by Herodotus in his list of the Aeolian cities. Some scholars have found it surprising to have an Aeolian city isolated so far south from the rest, and have suspected either that Herodotus is in error or that he refers to another city of the same name. The name Notium, meaning 'southern', is one that might well recur on the map. No second Notium is actually known, however, in this region and the tradition need not be doubted; Magnesia on the Maeander was also an Aeolian foundation, equally distant from Aeolis, and like Notium was never included in the Ionian League. The name Notium may indeed refer to the situation of the city far to the south of Aeolis proper. (The alternative is that it means 'south of Colophon'.) However this may be, Colophon and Notium were certainly in close relations from very early times, as indeed they must be if both were to survive. When the Colophonians led a colony to Myrleia (now Mudanya) on the Sea of Marmara, they must have sailed from Notium; and, in fact, we hear that Colophon in early days possessed a powerful fleet.

Colophonian territory extended to the east over the great plain of Cumaovası, perfect country for cavalry; it is no surprise that the city was famous for its horses. So much so that in any doubtful engagement the intervention of the Colophonian cavalry was at once decisive; hence, says Strabo, the expression 'to put the Colophon on it', meaning to settle the matter out of hand. The explanation is dubious, as the word *colophon* means a summit or culmination (whence its use in English for the end-plate of a book), and there need be no reference to the city.

In battle the Colophonians used squadrons of dogs, finding them, says Pliny, the most reliable auxiliaries, with the additional advantage of not requiring pay. If the animals were anything like the Anatolian sheep-dogs of today, we may well imagine they were formidable adversaries. Interestingly enough an inscription from nearby Teos mentions the use of dogs at guard-posts in the city's territory. The dog played another part also at Colophon, for there as at Sparta, and nowhere else in the Greek world, it was used as a sacrificial animal. So at least Pausanias tells us. When the Greeks sacrificed an animal, the flesh was normally eaten afterwards by the animal's owner and any whom he might invite; a specified portion was the priest's perquisite, and the god received some of the hair or fat or other part which made a fragrant smell, this odour being fortunately what the gods particularly enjoyed. The Greeks rarely ate meat except after sacrifice—that is to say, they sacrificed their meat before eating it. To offer a dog was therefore a sacrifice in every sense, not merely an occasion for a good meal. At Colophon the custom was to offer a black bitch by night to Hecate, that strange three-headed deity of the underworld, sender of ghosts and haunter of cross-roads. At Sparta the offering was made to the war-god.

Rich territory and a strong navy together brought great wealth to Colophon, so that before long it could be quoted as a city where the rich were actually in a majority. Affluence had its common effect, and the Colophonians sank into luxury and effeminacy; as many as a thousand of the citizens, we read, used to attend the market-place in purple robes worth their weight in silver and drenched with perfume; this and their extravagance at table caused them to be compared with the notorious Sybarites of southern Italy. By this profligacy, say the historians, they and their city were ruined; in the early wars with the Lydians, Colophon was the only Greek city besides Magnesia that Gyges was able to conquer. Later, of course, it fell to Persia with the rest, and never afterwards regained its former prosperity. When the Persians were expelled after Salamis and the Delian Confederacy established, we find Colophon paying a normal tribute of three talents, only half as much as, for example, Teos.

In these early times little is heard of Notium. Thucydides calls her 'Notium of the Colophonians', and her assessment in the confederacy was as low as one-third of a talent, or less than was paid by many of the small Carian townships. It was always paid separately from Colophon. During the Peloponnesian War an incident occurred which is interesting for the light it throws on the ideas and methods of the time. Not all Colophonians were content to be tribute-paying members of the Athenian maritime confederacy; many preferred the old conditions under the Persians. These therefore banded together and called in the Persian forces, who occupied the town. Their opponents, the anti-Persian party, fled for refuge to Notium; but before long similar trouble arose there too, and the city was divided into two camps. The pro-Persians walled off a large part of the town and called in those of the same mind from Colophon; the other party applied for help to the Athenians. The Athenian commander Paches thereupon invited the commander of the Persian party, by name Hippias, to a conference, promising to return him safe and sound to the city if no agreement was reached. When Hippias responded, Paches put him under detention, and by an unexpected assault captured the city. He then restored Hippias according to the letter of his promise, and as soon as he was inside the walls seized him and put him to death. Notium was given back to the pro-Athenian party, but Colophon remained in Persian hands, and continued so almost without interruption till the coming of Alexander.

Aristotle, writing in the fourth century, quotes Notium and Colophon as an example of faction arising owing to the ground not being suitable for a single city, presumably because the places were too far apart; it is a fair inference that before his time Colophon was joined in a political fusion with Notium, so as to form one city. This was certainly the case in the third century. The year 299 B.C. was important for Colophon; having the temerity to resist Lysimachus, the city was captured by him and destroyed; its population was transferred to help man the great new city of Ephesus which he had just founded. The tomb of the Colophonians who fell in this battle stood, says Pausanias, on the left of the road as you go to Claros—possibly one or both of the two tumuli still visible about a mile north of the village of Çile.

After the death of Lysimachus in 281 Colophon was restored, with a new wall several miles in length. But the new city was never of very much account; in Hellenistic times the emphasis was on seaborne commerce, and apart from Notium, Colophon was nothing. The two cities were now one; Colophon was called the Old Town, Notium was New Colophon or Colophon-on-Sea, and her own name fell into disuse. Even the two combined, however, could not compete with Ephesus, and soon ceased to play any part in history. Such prosperity as they had was almost entirely due to the fame of the oracle at Claros.

The three sites are easily visited by motor transport in a day from Izmir. The road is good as far as Cumaovası, after that poor. The ruins of Colophon at Değirmendere, apart from one or two stretches of the Hellenistic wall, are scanty, difficult to find, and unrewarding when found. Most travellers will be content to pass on to Claros and Notium.

Notium

Notium is a typical early Greek settlement site, on a hill directly above the sea, with a river close at hand and a modest territory in the valley. The ruins are not spectacular, as very little is actually standing, but the site is very attractive. The hilltop is about a kilometre in length and comprises two eminences with a saddle between. The whole is surrounded by a ring-wall over two miles (3·22 km.) long, of similar date to that at Colophon; considerable stretches of this are quite well preserved.

On the western eminence is a small temple (A), with an altar in front on the east and surrounded by a stoa; surprisingly, the stoa is not parallel with the walls of the temple. This building was at one time conjectured to be the temple of Clarian Apollo; when excavated by French archaeologists in 1921 an inscription was found proving it to be a temple of Athena.

The agora (B) is on the slope towards the saddle; adjoining it on

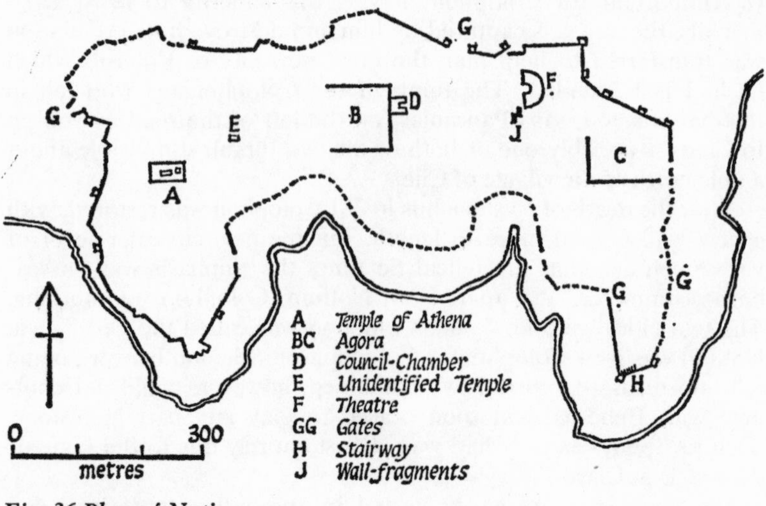

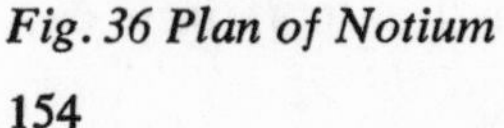

Fig. 36 Plan of Notium

the east, at D, are the scanty ruins of a building containing rows of seats, which the excavators suggested might be a court of justice. The arrangement of the seats on three sides of a square, as also the situation close to the agora, are strongly reminiscent of the council chambers at Priene and Heracleia (below, pp. 168, 214) and it seems more probable that this was the function of the present building also.

On the eastern eminence is a second agora (C) now featureless, and the theatre (F). This is small, with only twenty-seven rows of seats, and has never been excavated. The form of the cavea is Greek, being rather more than a semicircle, but it has been reconstructed in Roman times; part of the southern retaining wall is preserved, with a vaulted passage. There are considerable remains of the stage-building, but they are now buried.

It would be interesting to identify the wall built by the pro-Persian party, during the principal appearance of Notium in history (above, p. 153), to fence themselves off from their opponents. Its approximate position is hardly doubtful; it must have run across the waist of the site between the theatre and the agora B. A few scraps of wall are now to be seen here, in particular at J, close to the theatre; but they are scarcely convincing. It appears highly likely that the wall was removed, as an unwanted impediment, immediately after the crisis was ended.

On the western slopes of the hill next to the north of the town is a fairly extensive necropolis; the tombs are either sunk into the ground, or cut horizontally into the rock, or in a few cases constructed of masonry above ground. To the west of the town, on the opposite side of the river and close to the shore, is a cave some 50 feet (15·2 m.) wide and deep and about 10 feet (3·05 m.) high. At the back is a spring of poor but drinkable water with an arched coping above it and various niches cut in the rock near by. This spot was probably sacred in antiquity, but we have no information concerning it. In 1963 its floor was strewn with tin cans, old newspapers, and other rubbish, for an attempt is being made to convert Notium into a bathing resort, and two restaurants are now installed on the beach, where the visitor may refresh himself with a scanty meal at extortionate cost.

Claros

South of Colophon, and about one mile (1·61 km.) from Notium and the sea, is the site of Claros. There was never a city here; the site is on the territory of Colophon and contains the famous temple and oracle of Apollo with its associated buildings. Like most of the great temples of Asia Minor, it stands on flat ground; but the explanation is not in this case that the Ionic order appears to better advantage in such a position, for the architecture is, surprisingly, Doric. The sanctuary lies in the valley of a small stream called in antiquity the Ales or the Halesus, and said to be the coldest in Ionia; this now overflows every winter, and in the course of centuries had buried the ruins deeply under its silt, and until recently the exact site of the temple was unknown.

The Colophonians maintained that the sanctuary and oracle of Clarian Apollo were very ancient. Our earliest mention of the sanctuary is in the Homeric hymn to Apollo, which may perhaps date to the seventh century B.C.; a second mention in the short hymn to Artemis may be a good deal later. Neither of these refers to the oracle. Nor was Claros among the oracles consulted by Croesus in the sixth century, and, in fact, there seems to be no recorded activity of the oracle before early Hellenistic times.

On the other hand, the spot was traditionally associated with divination from the remotest antiquity. Even before the Trojan War, it was said, the Sibyl Herophile came there and uttered her predictions, one of which was that Helen would be the ruin of Europe and Asia. The original Carian inhabitants were first displaced by Greeks from Crete; later a party of Thebans, including the prophetess Manto, came to settle, and Manto married the Cretan leader. Their son was the famous seer Mopsus. After the Trojan War the equally famous seer Calchas arrived at Claros, and a contest in divination took place. 'I wonder', said Calchas, 'how many figs there are on this tree; can you tell me the number?' Mopsus replied, 'Ten thousand; and if you measure them with a bushel measure, there will be one over which you cannot get in'. This answer was judged to be correct (nothing is said of the method of judging), and Calchas thereupon died of grief, as he was destined to do when he should meet a greater seer than himself. An alternative version made Calchas put before Mopsus a pregnant sow and ask how many young she was carrying; Mopsus replied, 'Three, including one female'. This also proved correct (and much less disputable than the other), with the same melancholy result.

Virtually nothing is heard of Claros in classical times, though the sanctuary certainly existed. The temple seen today was built early in the Hellenistic period; one of Apollo's first responses from his new house may have been the advice he gave to found the new

Smyrna across the Meles (above, p. 22). Like so many other sanctuaries, Claros suffered from the pirates; the oracle seems to have declined for a while, but revived brilliantly under the Roman empire. The temple was rededicated by Hadrian towards the end of his reign. At this period delegations came regularly from many parts of the world—Caria, Phrygia, Pisidia, Pontus, Thrace, Crete, and even Corinth—to consult the god and to sing hymns in his honour. Records of these visits are carved in hundreds on the steps of the temple, on the Propylaea, on the bases, and even in the flutes of the columns, and elsewhere; Ionia is represented only by Chios and Phocaea, and it seems that the neighbouring cities for the most part preferred to give their custom to Didyma.

For the method of consulting the oracle we have Tacitus' description of a visit paid by Germanicus, the adopted son of Tiberius, in A.D. 18. 'There is no woman there as at Delphi', says the historian;

> rather a priest, after hearing merely the number and names of the clients, goes down into a cave; there he drinks from a secret fountain and, though generally illiterate, issues responses in verse concerning the various matters in the consultants' minds.

This trick of answering the enquirers without hearing their questions seems peculiar to Apollo at Claros. Pliny also mentions 'a pool in the cave of Clarian Apollo, a draught of which inspires wonderful oracles, but shortens the life of the drinker'. From the inscriptions we learn that the envoys sent to consult the god were commonly initiated into the local mysteries, but as to the nature of these mysteries we have unfortunately no information. The Clarian oracle was one of the last to survive in Christian times; the temple was finally overthrown by an earthquake and the ruins gradually buried under the river mud.

All remained to be rediscovered. In 1826 the Rev. F. V. J. Arundell saw two marble columns just projecting from the earth; by 1907, when the Ottoman Museum undertook an excavation, these had completely disappeared, and were only found again when a peasant reported that he frequently struck his plough against a block in the ground. The excavation revealed a building which was thought to be the temple, but proved later to be only the Propylaea, or entrance gate to the sanctuary. Nothing more was done; the river got to work again, and when the writer visited the site in 1946, all that could be seen was an overgrown hollow and the tops of one column and one pillar. A thorough excavation was finally undertaken by the French in 1950; the temple of Apollo was found and cleared, and a number of other buildings brought to light.

From the words of Tacitus and Pliny quoted above it was naturally thought that the oracle was not in the temple of Apollo but in a cave outside. Just opposite the sanctuary a side valley opens on the east from the main valley, and about half a mile up this is a cave high in a cliff, accessible only with tackle. When entered in 1913 it was found to contain a spring of water and numerous stalactites, also sherds of pottery ranging in date from the third millennium to the Roman empire. This cave was confidently hailed as the oracle of Apollo. Tacitus' words 'goes *down* into a cave' might perhaps have caused misgivings, and, in fact, the oracle has now been conclusively located inside the temple. Nevertheless, the cave was evidently important, and probably sacred, in antiquity; and if anyone cares to believe that this was the original holy place at Claros, before the temple was built, he can hardly be contradicted.

The French excavations were conducted under difficulties owing to the high water-table, and pumps were necessary for the lower levels; it is to be feared that the mud will before long cover the site again. In the rainy season the water may reach up to the level of the temple pavement.

From the Propylaea a sacred way, lined with monuments but only partially excavated, led north-west to the temple. The latter is large, and of the Doric order; its east front is the best preserved, the blocks at the west end having been largely robbed for later buildings. Towards the west end was placed the colossal cult-statue of Apollo, of which fragments were found and remain on the temple platform; the right arm measures over 11 feet (3·35 m.). The god was represented seated, with a laurel branch in his right hand, just as he is shown on imperial coins of Colophon. On his right was Artemis, his sister, on his left Leto, his mother; the three figures also appear on coins. Fragments of the female statues also were found (Pl. 48, 64).

But the most interesting part of the temple is certainly the adyton, or holy of holies, where the oracles were delivered. This part was especially difficult to excavate, but the work was fortunately helped by the occurrence of two exceptionally dry seasons in succession. All this part has now filled with water again, but in 1963 the plan was still visible on the spot (Pl. 49).

From the east front a stairway leads down on either side, with a double bend, to a narrow corridor running under the length of the temple. Making four more right-angled turns on the way, this leads for 100 feet (30·5 km.) to the two oracular chambers, roofed with vaulted arches and barely high enough for a man to stand. The inner chamber, directly under the statue of Apollo, held at the back a large basin of water contained by a breast-high parapet; here the prophet entered alone to draw inspiration from the sacred water. This then is the 'cave and secret fountain' which deceived explorers for so long. The outer chamber, joined to the inner by a passage through a thick wall, was probably for the use of the clergy attached to the temple. Clients were not, it seems, admitted to the adyton itself, although the circumbendibus by which it is approached seems naturally adapted to bewilder a suppliant and reduce him to a fitting state of humility in presence of the god. The titles of the clergy are known from the inscriptions; in addition to the prophet they included the priest of Apollo, a thespiode, and one or two secretaries. The function of the thespiode was to render the oracles into verse; it appears that Tacitus was deceived in thinking that this was done by the illiterate priest. In this outer chamber a remarkable discovery was made, namely a stone some 2 feet 3 inches (·69 m.) high, of bluish marble, in the form of half an egg. This is the omphalos, or navel-stone, of Apollo, which is properly a feature of Apollo at Delphi. Legend said that Zeus, to determine the centre of the earth, set two eagles to fly from its opposite ends; they met at Delphi, which was accordingly known as the navel of the earth. A navel-stone was in fact found there by the excavators, similar in shape to the one at Claros. It appears that in course of time the omphalos came to be regarded as belonging to Apollo rather than to Delphi, and similar stones have been found in other places where he was worshipped (Pl. 47).

Some 30 yards (27·4 m.) from the front of the temple is the great altar of marble, 58 feet (17·7 m.) long. On its surface were found the marks of two separate tables for offerings, one for Apollo, the other for Dionysus. This sharing of the worship is again reminiscent of Delphi, where during the three winter months Apollo withdrew to enjoy the sunshine with the Hyperboreans beyond the north wind, and Dionysus reigned at Delphi in his place. Lying near the altar is a well-preserved sundial dedicated to Dionysus.

A little to the north-west of the main temple is another smaller temple in the Ionic order, belonging to the Clarian Artemis. It was identified by an archaic statue found by the altar in front of it; on the statue is an inscription in letters of the sixth century dedicating it to Artemis. Since the dedicator himself was the first priest, the foundation of the temple will be of that period. No cult-statue has been found in this temple, but it appears from the coins that Clarian Artemis had a distinctly un-Greek form, reminiscent in its general outlines of the Artemis of Ephesus (Pl. 64).

A certain number of responses by the Clarian oracle are recorded. The god's advice concerning the foundation of New Smyrna has already been mentioned. Germanicus in A.D. 18 was warned of his approaching end; and, in fact, he died in Syria the following year, poisoned (as was believed) with the connivance of his adoptive father Tiberius. We read in Pausanias that when the Roman emperor diverted the course of the river Orontes in Syria, there was found in the dry bed a gigantic coffin and a skeleton more than 11 cubits in height. The Syrians applied for enlightenment to Claros, and the god declared it to be the body of Orontes, an Indian by race. This Orontes being utterly unknown, Apollo's pronouncement had the great advantage of being unverifiable while at the same time providing an origin for the name of the river. At the time of a severe pestilence in the second century A.D. the men of Pergamum sent to Claros (rather than the neighbouring Gryneum) in the hope of relief. Apollo's advice was characteristic: divide the citizens into four groups for the worship of Zeus, Dionysus, Athena, and Asclepius; offer to these certain prescribed sacrifices and prayers for salvation. This is by far the commonest form of oracular advice: sacrifice to particular deities. The French excavations have not brought to light any new responses, which were evidently not set up at the shrine (as they sometimes were at Didyma), but only in the city to which they were addressed. However, the full publication of the inscriptions and other finds from Claros is still awaited. When it appears, it may perhaps enlighten us also concerning a curious statement of Tacitus; that the Colophonians normally chose a Milesian to be priest of Apollo—a surprising allegation for which no supporting evidence whatever has hitherto come to light.[1]

Note

1 It is indeed contradicted in the case of the poet Nicander, who is said to have held this priesthood in the third century B.C. It was, we are told, hereditary in his family. But Nicander was a Colophonian.

9 Priene and the Panionium

For many travellers Priene is perhaps the most attractive of all the ancient sites on the west coast. Not only are the ruins comparatively well preserved, and admirably excavated for the visitor's benefit, but above all they give a feeling of intimacy greater than is easily found elsewhere. Priene is small, and its buildings are small likewise; they date for the most part to the earlier days of the city's existence, and the massive Roman structures familiar on so many sites are conspicuous by their absence. The visitor, wandering among the public buildings, streets, and private houses, can feel himself back in the days of Alexander. Priene is above all a *Greek* city.

The present site beside the village of Turunçlar is not, however, the original site. Where that may have been is quite unknown. Tradition said that the city was founded during the Ionian migration by Aepytus, a grandson of Codrus, the last king of Athens, who was later joined by a party of Thebans under one Philotas; Priene, in fact, always looked to Athens as her mother-city. This early city was from the first a member of the Ionian League, but no trace of it has ever been found; it lies no doubt deep under the Maeander mud. Its history, too, is scanty in the extreme. We know that it suffered severely from the Persian conquest, and for a time hardly existed; it recovered, however, sufficiently to provide twelve ships against the Persians at the battle of Lade in 494 B.C. No inscriptions, and only a single coin, of the old Priene are known.

Two circumstances, however, gave the city an importance disproportionate to its size. In the first place it produced one of the Seven Sages of antiquity, namely Bias, who is famous for two pieces of advice which he gave. When Croesus had overrun Ionia and was beginning to build a navy to attack the islands also, Bias, hoping to save them, went to Sardis and reported (falsely) to Croesus that the islanders were preparing a force of cavalry to attack him. The king was delighted: 'Nothing would suit me better than that islanders should engage the famous Lydian cavalry on land'. 'What then', said Bias, 'do you imagine the islanders are thinking, when they hear that the land-power of Lydia is intending to engage them on the sea?' Croesus saw the point and abandoned his shipbuilding. Later, when Persian rule had replaced the Lydian, Bias advised the Ionians assembled at the Panionium to abandon their cities and sail in a body to Sardinia, where they might found a new city and prosper in freedom. The Phocaeans had, in fact, already followed similar counsels, and the Teians did so shortly afterwards, but the Ionians as a whole could not bring themselves to leave their homes. So great was Bias' reputation that there was afterwards in the new Priene a building called after him, the Biantium; a similar honour was given also at Priene to Alexander, and at Smyrna to Homer.

In the second place, it happened that the site chosen for the Panionium lay on the territory of Priene, and the Prienians were largely responsible for its management; they had, for example, the privilege of appointing the president at the various meetings. The coastal strip on which the Panionium lay was, however, claimed also by the Samians, and this quarrel lasted for centuries, with Priene on the whole getting the better of it.

All the while the silt of the Maeander was pushing the coastline farther to the west, and for this reason no doubt it was eventually decided to refound the city on a new site, where its ruins now stand. It appears that this new site was the same which had previously served as the harbour of Priene, called Naulochus; Strabo says that Priene was originally on the coast, and that in his own time it was forty stades, or rather over four miles (6·44 m.), from it. If this is correct, the rate at which the coastline was advancing at that period must have been (as indeed is natural enough) much greater than it has been since (below, p. 181).

Building of the new town was begun at the time of the visit of Alexander the Great in 334 B.C., who apparently transferred the inhabitants from the nearby port of Naulochus. Concerning the temple of Athena, he made the same proposal that he had already made at Ephesus, which was to undertake the cost of the building in return for the privilege of making the dedication. The Prienians were less proud and independent than the Ephesians—or perhaps they were merely less wealthy—and the offer was accepted; Alexander's dedication was found by the first excavators and is now in the British Museum. It stood on the temple wall; the architrave over the columns would have been a more natural place, but the building had perhaps not yet reached to that height.

In the second century, while Priene was under the rule of Pergamum, a peculiarly undeserved misfortune befell her. Ariarathes, king of Cappadocia, was deposed from the throne by his brother Orophernes; the latter, in the course of his reign, deposited 400 talents for safe keeping at Priene. Later, when Ariarathes, with the help of Attalus II, succeeded in expelling Orophernes, he demanded the money back. The Prienians replied that they were bound to return it only to the man who had deposited it, whereupon Ariarathes, with Attalus' consent, sacked the Prienian territory. The citizens appealed to Rome; they had, says the historian, high hopes of keeping the money themselves, but they were disappointed, being required to give back the 400 talents to Orophernes, and having meanwhile suffered severely for their loyalty to him.

As a city of the Roman province of Asia, Priene, like the others, had much to bear from the tax-gatherers and from the hardships of the Mithridatic Wars; and when better times came under the empire, Priene, for whatever reason, did not share in the general upsurge of prosperity. The harbour Naulochus had by then been long since unusable; even if another had succeeded it, the city must have suffered from the competition of her mighty neighbour Miletus. However this may be, Priene sank into insignificance. No gigantic structures rose to overlay the simpler buildings of earlier times, and Priene remains as the best example we have of a Hellenistic city.

The town is situated on sloping ground at the south foot of a mighty cliff of rock. Above this, on the mountain-top, is the acropolis, called in antiquity Teloneia. It housed a permanent garrison, whose commandant, elected for a period of four months, was forbidden to leave it during his term of office. Nothing remains on the summit except some ruins of the fortification-wall, and the chief reward for making the climb is a superb view over the city and the plain, with the Maeander meandering into the distance. The ascent may be made by a narrow rock-path up the precipitous cliff-face; the path is not exactly dangerous, but calls for a good head for heights. On the way up it passes an attractive little sanctuary containing rock-cut reliefs and statue-bases. The alternative route is by the valley on the west.

The principal sanctuary of Priene is that of Athena; when the temple was standing, it dominated the town. The English excavators in 1868–69 found the temple walls still in place to a man's height, but the blocks were later plundered by the local inhabitants, and until recently little more than the foundations was to be seen. The architect of the building was the Carian Pytheos, who had earlier worked on the Mausoleum at Halicarnassus; he afterwards wrote a book, taking the Athenaeum at Priene as a model of temple-construction. This book was still used as a textbook in Roman times.

The plan of the temple is, in fact, typical of Greek temples of the classical period. The antechamber, or pronaos, on the east, is entered between two columns; from here a door leads into the main chamber, or cella, at the back of which stood the cult-statue. At the rear, but not communicating with the cella, is a third chamber, the opisthodomus, also entered between two columns. In many cases this rear chamber was used to house the temple treasures, in which event the spaces between the columns and side walls were closed

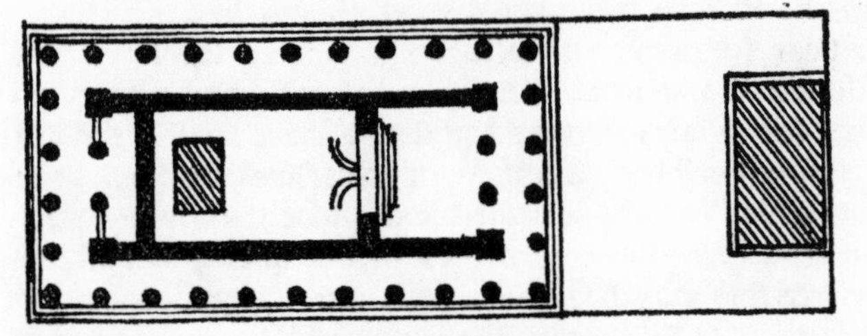

Fig. 37 Plan of the temple of Athena

with grilles or marble slabs; traces of such a closure can still be seen at Priene. The whole building was surrounded by a single row of Ionic columns; the drums of these, being less convenient for house-building, have not been removed by the villagers, and many are lying on the temple terrace and on the slopes below, where they were thrown apparently by a violent earthquake. In 1964 a number of them were re-used in re-erecting half a dozen of the columns; this has resulted in a great improvement to the appearance of the temple.

Ancient temples were not used, like modern churches, for congregational services. The building was conceived as a house for the deity, and on ceremonial occasions was entered only by the priests and others who had a special function to perform; the congregation remained outside.

As was said above, the temple at Priene was dedicated to Athena by Alexander in 334 B.C. Later a second dedication was made to Augustus, so that the temple henceforth belonged jointly to him and to Athena. Architrave blocks carrying this new dedication are still lying on the temple platform. At this time also was built an entrance gateway on the east of the precinct; one side of this is still standing. The altar is in the normal position in front of the temple on the east; in its general form it was similar, though on a smaller scale, to the great altar at Pergamum, but the existing remains give little idea of its former appearance (Pl. 53).

The theatre is another building that goes back to the early days of the city's existence. The alterations to which, like all the rest, it was subjected in Roman times have not destroyed its Greek character; it gives an excellent idea of what a Hellenistic theatre was like.

Only seven or eight rows of seats in the cavea were originally excavated; since the 1960s several more have been cleared, but the appearance of the theatre has been little if at all improved. The front row consists of five marble thrones of honour spaced at intervals round the orchestra; similar thrones in the theatre at Athens were reserved for the priests, and the same may have been the case here. In the middle of the fifth row is a 'Royal Box', but this is not a feature of the original theatre. In the middle of the front row is the altar of Dionysus, to whom sacrifice was made whenever the theatre was used. The cavea is more than a semicircle and is supported at the ends by retaining-walls (analemmata) of handsome cushioned ashlar, well preserved. Between these and the flanks of the stage-building on either side are open passages (parodoi) which served as entrances for the public and, during the performance, for the chorus; at other times they were closed with gates. An interesting feature, peculiar to the theatre at Priene, is the water-clock which stood at the west corner of the orchestra. Only the base remains in position; the cuttings in it provided for the flow of water, but it is not easy to see exactly how they worked. We hear nothing in literature of any time-limit on dramatic performances, and it is more likely that the clock was used during the public assemblies which also took place in the theatre. A time-limit on speeches was certainly normal practice in the law-courts at least—and, in fact, it is not impossible that the theatre was actually used as a court of law (Pl. 50).

The stage-building consisted of two parts, a rectangular two-storeyed building containing the property-rooms, dressing-rooms, and the like, and a narrow single-storeyed structure projecting in front. This latter is the proscenium; nowhere else is a Hellenistic proscenium so well preserved as here. Its front consists of a row of twelve pillars, ten of which have Doric half-columns attached, surmounted by an architrave and triglyph-frieze; from this stone beams were laid across to the front of the main building, and wooden boards laid between the beams. The eleven spaces between the columns were variously filled: the two at the extreme ends were closed merely by iron bars forming a very wide-meshed grille; the third, sixth, and ninth held double folding doors; and in the remainder were inserted painted panels of wood. The holes and sockets for these various fixtures may still be seen on the pillars. Numerous traces of colour, blue and red, survive on the epistyle; but the red colouring of the columns and capitals was done at a much later period (Pl. 54).

What was the purpose and use of this proscenium building, which dates from the third century B.C.? On this question scholars are not yet agreed. We know from inscriptions that tragedies were produced at Priene in the fourth century; in these, actors and chorus alike must have performed at orchestra level in the classical fashion, and it is commonly supposed that even after the erection of the proscenium this continued, for some time at least, to be the case. The three doors then served for the actors' entrances and exits, and the painted panels between the columns could represent the scenery. The flat roof of the proscenium would be useful for the appearance of the *deus ex machina,* or when it was required to show a character on the roof of a building. Others, however, maintain that the proscenium roof *looks* like a stage (which can hardly be denied) and must always have been used as such. Many visitors to Priene will probably share this feeling; on the other hand, the doors and panels between the columns then become rather meaningless. It has also been argued against this opinion that the marble thrones in the front row must have been intended to give the best view, which they would only do when the performance was on ground level; but, in fact, with so narrow a stage, the loss of view is negligible. It is interesting to test this on the spot, remembering that the actors wore high buskins.

At all events, it is generally agreed that by about the middle of the second century B.C. the performance took place on the proscenium roof, the actors entering by three wide doors in the front wall of the upper storey of the main building. At this time probably the 'Royal Box' was installed to restore to the previous occupants of the marble thrones the slight advantage of a horizontal view. The high stage made the actors better visible and better audible to the spectators as a whole, but it had one inconvenience in the awkward separation of the actors on the stage from the chorus down below in the orchestra. Not that this mattered in the dramas produced by the contemporary playwrights, which made little or no use of the

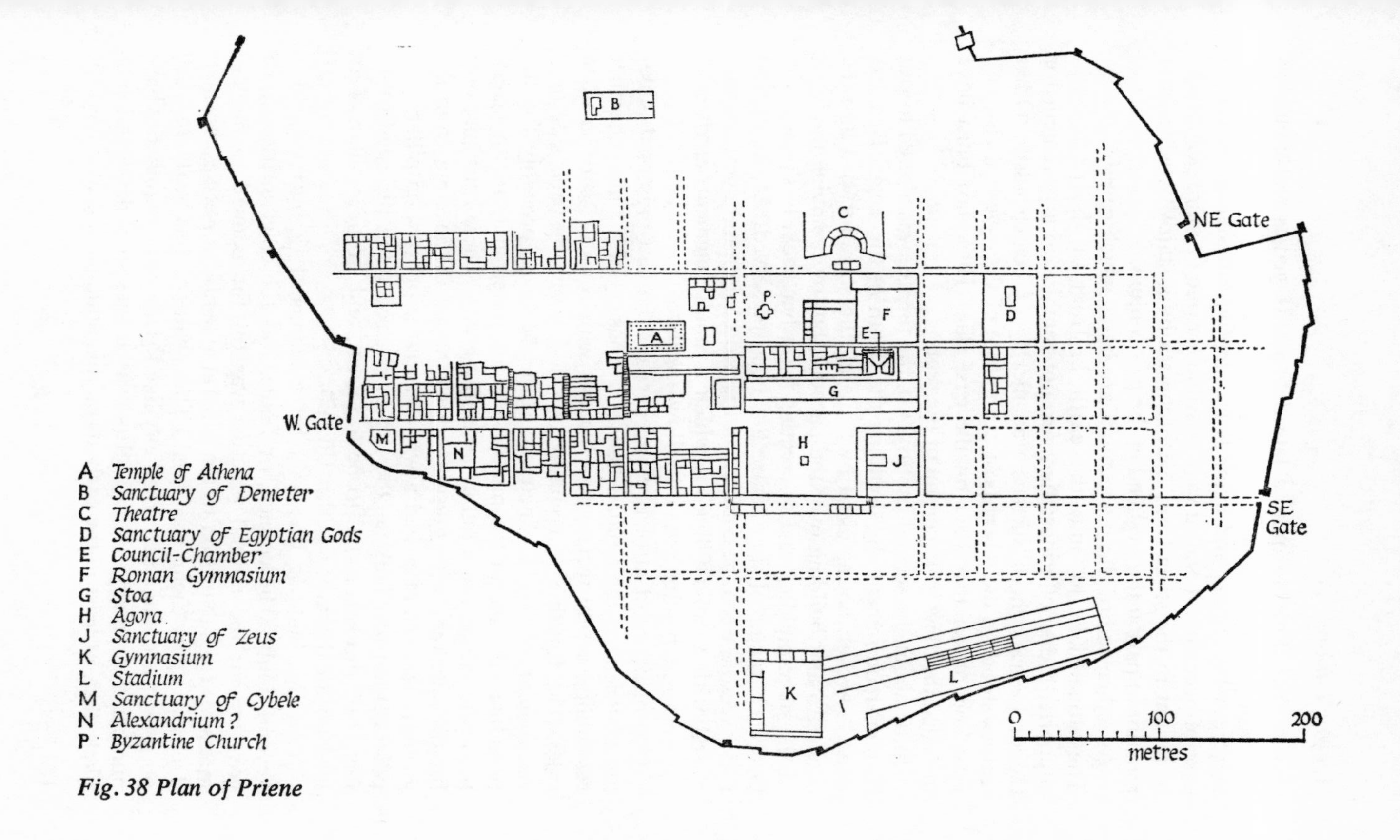
B
C
NE Gate
P
F
D
A
E
G
W. Gate
M
N
H
J
SE
Gate
K
L
0
100
200
metres
A Temple of Athena
B Sanctuary of Demeter
C Theatre
D Sanctuary of Egyptian Gods
E Council-Chamber
F Roman Gymnasium
G Stoa
H Agora
J Sanctuary of Zeus
K Gymnasium
L Stadium
M Sanctuary of Cybele
N Alexandrium?
P Byzantine Church

Fig. 38 Plan of Priene

chorus; but down to quite a late date the tragedies and comedies of the old classical masters were regularly revived, and in these contact between chorus and actor is frequently required. However, in case of necessity, it was always possible for one or more performers to mount to the stage from the orchestra by a stairway, which still remains in part at the west end of the proscenium.

At either end of the proscenium are bases which carried statues. The stone slabs let into the earth in front of the proscenium supported other offerings; they are not remains of a pavement for the orchestra, whose surface was merely of beaten earth. Other statues stood on the newel-post at the foot of the cavea on east and west and on another base on the east side. These last must have impeded the view from certain of the seats.

In or about the second century A.D. the theatre was altered to suit Roman requirements by doubling the depth of the stage. This was done, however, not as usual by bringing the stage forward into the orchestra and building over the parodoi, but by removing the front of the stage-building and re-erecting it farther back. In this way the Greek character of the theatre has been preserved. At this period the spaces between the columns of the proscenium were permanently closed with a solid filling of which a small fragment survives at the west end, painted red and yellow on white.

One of the most attractive and perhaps the best-preserved building in Priene is the council house. It consists of a single chamber resembling a tiny rectangular theatre, with rows of seats on three sides. The fourth side contains two doors, one on each side of a rectangular recess in which are stone benches, probably for the presiding officials. In the middle is a decorated altar for the sacrifices with which every public assembly began. There is no platform for the speakers, who presumably addressed the meeting from the ground. The chamber had a wooden roof supported on pillars; the pillars stood originally at the top of the seats, but the span of 47 feet (14·3 m.) was found to be too great, and stronger pillars were later installed nearer together (Pl. 52).

That this building was used for meetings of the city council is beyond doubt. The council, or boule, was the chief instrument of government; the normal practice was for the council to prepare measures for submission to the general assembly, or ecclesia, whose decision upon them was final. The chamber has seats for 640 persons; the council in a small city like Priene can certainly not have numbered so many—even at Ephesus it was only 450—and it is likely that, at least in the early days, this building was also used for the general assembly. It is perhaps surprisingly small for the purpose: 600-odd enfranchized citizens would imply a total population of some 3,000: but we have no reason to suppose that Priene in the fourth century was any larger than this. In later times it is probable that the general assembly was held as usual in the theatre.

Visitors who are not unduly pressed for time should make the short climb to the Sanctuary of Demeter and her daughter Core, that is Persephone. This, too, dates from early Hellenistic times, and possesses a number of unusual features; for Demeter, the Earth Mother, was not like the other Olympian gods, and her sanctuaries have a character of their own.

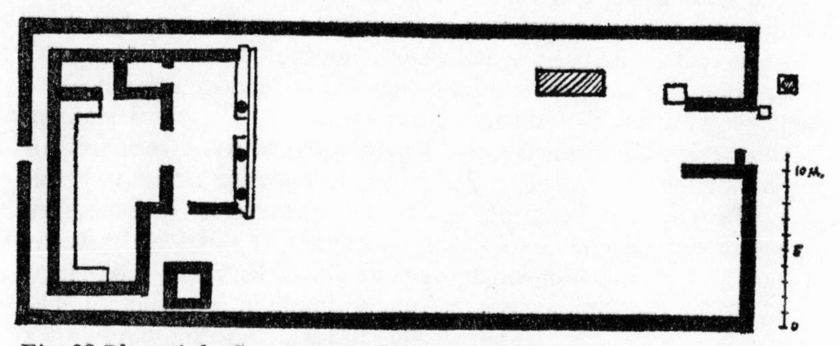

Fig. 39 Plan of the Sanctuary of Demeter and Core

The entrance is on the east. Just beside the gate stood two statues of priestesses, one of which was found and removed by German excavators; the base of the other remains. The central part of the sanctuary is an open space; though it contains no rows of seats as at Pergamum and Eleusis, it may be assumed that mysteries were celebrated here also. The temple stands, as at Pergamum, at the west end of the enclosure, but its form is highly exceptional. In front is a porch with three Doric columns between the side walls, forming a kind of pronaos. From this the main room, or cella, is entered; its length is strangely from north to south. At the north end are two small rooms side by side, of which the eastern opens into the porch. Along the west wall of the cella runs a high stone bench, used for displaying votive offerings, as is shown by the sockets cut into its surface. The east wall is broken by a double right-angled turn. Round the temple, between it and the enclosing wall of the sanctuary, runs a narrow passage. Almost every feature of this building is alien to the normal form of a Greek temple, and not less interesting is the sacrificial pit sunk in the ground outside the temple on the south-east. It is square and carefully lined with masonry, and was covered by planks, laid across between stone blocks of flat triangular shape, one of which remains. Pits of this kind served for pouring offerings, especially the blood of sacrificial victims, to the deities of the underworld, among whom Demeter and Persephone were pre-eminent; the custom is familiar, but the actual pits are very rarely preserved. At a much later time an altar of normal form was installed, towards the east end of the sanctuary on the north side; its Roman date is shown by its inferior masonry. Until then the victims were apparently slaughtered at the mouth of the pit.

The stadium lies close against the southern wall in the lowest part of the city. It was constructed in the second century B.C.; but there must have been a stadium at Priene from the beginning, for in the inscriptions a front seat at the games is awarded as a privilege to benefactors from the fourth century onwards. The word stadium denotes originally a measure of length equal to 600 Greek feet, or approximately 200 yards (called in English a stade; 182·9 m.); this being the length of the sprint, the shortest distance run in the official games, the word comes to mean a foot-race of this length; finally it is used of the arena in which the races and other games took place.

At Priene the stadium is exceedingly simple in construction. The course is a level space 20 yards (18·3 m.) wide and something over a stade in length. Spectators sat on the north side only, owing to the nature of the ground; for the same reason the stadium had not the usual rounded end. Stone seats were provided only in the middle part; at the two ends either wooden seats were installed or, as at Olympia, none at all. All races finished at the eastern end, and to improve the view of the finish from the far end the western part makes a slight angle with the rest.

The starting-sill for the stadium race is partially preserved at the west end. It consisted originally of a row of ten square pilasters with Corinthian capitals and an architrave. The bases remain in position, resting on a long stone foundation; the cuttings in these present an interesting problem: how was a simultaneous start obtained? In the surface of the long foundation, through all its length, even under the pillar-bases, is a channel 9 inches (229 mm.) wide and 6 inches (152 mm.) deep; in the open space between the two central columns, which is wider than the others, two short side-channels turn off it at right-angles. The bases have in their sides, over the channel, rectangular cuttings about 4 inches by 6 (102 by 152 mm.); these are found on both sides of the two central bases, on the inner side of the two end bases, and on the outer side of the other six bases. A narrow ledge cut along the upper rim of the long channel suggests that some sort of covering was laid over it. Fragments of the entablature over the pillars found by the excavators showed a similar horizontal channel and vertical perforations.

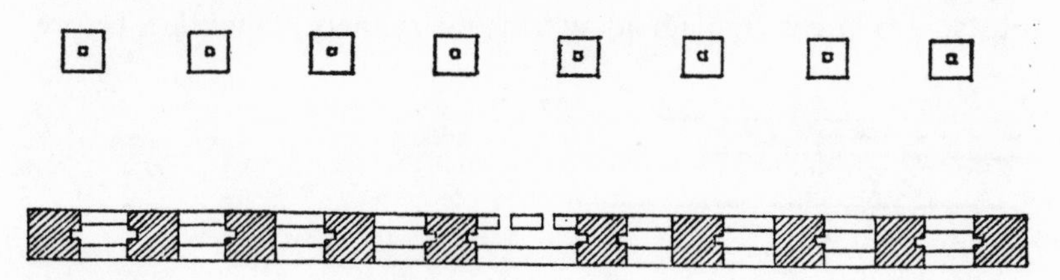

Fig. 40 Starting-sill in the stadium

How are these facts to be interpreted? No complete explanation has been advanced, but certain possibilities suggest themselves for consideration. In most Greek stadia where the starting-sill is preserved we find that two grooves are cut in the sill one behind the other, from 4 to 7 inches (102 to 178 mm.) apart, to hold the runners' toes at the start; their closeness together argues an ancient starting-technique different from the modern. Since the sill at Priene is, as it stands, utterly unsuited for a start, it seems likely enough that boards or stone blocks carrying grooves of this kind were fitted over the long channel between the pillars; a breadth of 9 inches (229 mm.) allows ample room for grooves only 4 inches (102 mm.) apart. Place would thus be provided for eight runners; the central space was not used for this purpose. The long channel itself is nothing more than a drain, to avoid the danger of a slippery start in case of wet weather. To the further question, how the starting-gate was manœuvred, the evidence will hardly furnish a complete answer, but here again a suggestion may perhaps be offered. The function of the vertical cuttings in the bases was apparently to hold upright wooden posts against the sides of the pillars; we may suppose that these posts held horizontal bars working up and down like signal-arms; cords attached to these arms could then be passed up through the hole in the entablature and along the channel to the central space where the starter stood; holding the ends of the cords in his hand he could, by releasing them, drop all the eight 'signal-arms' simultaneously. A method exactly similar in principle to this was certainly used at the Isthmian Sanctuary at Corinth, where clear traces of it were found by the excavators. It may be noted, however, that no function is thus assigned to the extra cuttings in the middle and end bases. (See Fig. 41 and Appendix 5.)

In any case it is certain that this comparatively elaborate starting-sill was not in use in very early times, and at Priene is probably not earlier than Roman. In the fifth century B.C. there was no physical obstacle in Greek stadia holding back the runners at the start; before

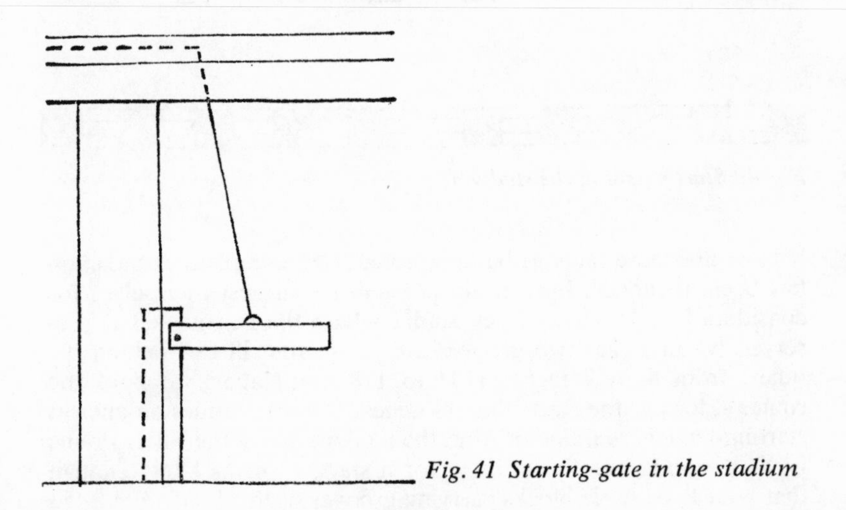

Fig. 41 Starting-gate in the stadium

the battle of Salamis in 480 B.C., Themistocles, who was eager to engage the Persians without delay, was rebuked by the Corinthian general: 'At the games, you know, Themistocles, those who "jump the gun" get a stroke of the rod'. And even at Priene, where the stadium is not older than the second century, we have apparently the remains of an earlier and simpler starting-sill. Some 6 feet (1·83 m.) in front (to the east) of the sill described above is a simple line of eight square stone slabs let into the ground; in the centre of each is a square hole evidently intended to hold a post. Nothing more survives, and the details of the starting-method employed are no longer recoverable.

The athletic events contested in the stadium at the official games in the Greek cities were: foot-races, wrestling, boxing, the pancration, and the pentathlon. Horse and chariot races were held separately in the hippodrome. All athletic events were divided into age-groups, generally men, youths, and boys.

Foot-racing was in three categories, the stadium-race, the diaulos, and the long race. The first was a simple sprint from one end of the course to the other. The diaulos was a double stadium, that is, up the course and down again, with a hairpin turn at the end. For this a second starting-sill was required at the other end of the stadium, but at Priene this has not been found. The long race seems to have varied in length at different times and places; we hear of seven stades and twenty-four. Time-keeping was of course unknown, water-clocks and sand-glasses being obviously inadequate, so that we cannot tell what sort of standards were achieved. Victory was the thing that mattered; second prizes for athletics were rarely given, although inscriptions do sometimes record that a runner, wrestler, or boxer had competed 'with distinction', implying that he had gained glory from his performance despite failing to win the prize.

Wrestling was of the 'upright' kind—that is, a fall was counted as soon as any part of the body above the knee touched the ground; the bout was not continued on the ground. The contest was probably

Fig. 42 The pancration, from a vase-painting. One man has his thumb in the other's eye; this being a foul, the steward stands by ready to administer a stroke of the rod

best-of-five, three throws being necessary for victory. The so-called 'Graeco-Roman' style of wrestling is not, however, ancient. The pancration was a form of unarmed combat, not unlike all-in wrestling; it was not decided by falls, but continued on the ground until one man surrendered. Punching, kicking, and strangling were permitted—indeed, all means except biting and gouging. One pancratiast had a trick of winning by breaking his opponent's fingers, and this device was even copied by a wrestler.

Ancient boxing was very different from the modern. The gloves used had a ridge of hard leather over the knuckles, and were intended not merely to protect the striker's hands but to render the blow more severe. There were no ring and no rounds; as in the pancration the bout continued until one man admitted defeat. Classification was by age only, not by weight; hence in practice only heavyweights competed in the men's class. The rules also were probably different from ours, though we have, of course, no actual statement of them, and the vase-paintings may not be reliable evidence. If these could be trusted, it would appear that blows were aimed almost exclusively at the head; in general the hands are held high. On the other hand, there is some rather uncertain evidence that kicking may have been permitted.

The pentathlon was a combination of five events, three peculiar to the pentathlon, namely the jump, the discus, and the javelin, and two, running and wrestling, which had their own separate events as well. In the discus and javelin only distance counted: there was no question of aiming at a mark: it was only required that the missile should not fall outside the level arena into the spectators' seats. The javelin was thrown with the aid of a thong wound two or three times round the shaft and allowed to slip from the hand at the moment of throwing; this use of a thong permits slightly better performances than the ordinary modern method.[1]

The jump was a long jump; high jumping was not an event in the games, and seems hardly to have been practised by the ancients. But it was not a simple long jump as we know it today, and its nature has been much disputed. In the first place jumping-weights were used, made of stone or metal and weighing from 2 to 9 lb, held one in each hand throughout the jump. In the second place jumps of 55 and 52 feet (16·8 and 15·8 m.) are recorded, admittedly exceptional. Since a long jump of even 30 feet (9·1 m.) has never been achieved in modern times, it has been thought that the ancient jump was really a hop, step, and jump, and it was on this supposition that this event was included when the Olympic Games were revived in 1896. The present world record is 58 feet 8½ inches (17·89 m.). But experiments have shown that a triple jump *with weights* is exceedingly cumbersome and that 35 feet (10·7 m.) is about the limit of possible achievement. For a *standing* long jump, on the other hand, weights are a distinct advantage, and a recent theory is that the ancients practised a fivefold standing jump, that is five successive leaps, each from the spot where the previous one landed. Ten feet (3·05 m.) being a very good single jump under these conditions, a world record of 55 feet (16·8 m.) is possible enough. This theory is attractive at first sight; on the other hand, ancient vases exist which seem clearly to show a jumper *running* with his weights. In this case a standing jump is excluded, and the latest suggestion is that of a double jump—that is, a step and a jump.[2] No such jump is ever practised nowadays, so that no records are available, and the effect of carrying weights is uncertain; all the arguments cannot be discussed here, but this last solution is perhaps the most probable yet offered.

How was the winner of the pentathlon decided? This fascinating problem, too, has been vigorously debated. Again it is not possible here to present all the evidence and all the arguments, but a number of points are reasonably assured. It is quite certain that the modern system of awarding marks for each event and adding these up was not employed in ancient times. Victory again was the thing that mattered, and three outright wins in the five events was always enough to determine the victor. Recent discussions have further established that the number of competitors—so long as no one had three outright wins—was successively reduced in three stages; that is, after the first three events (which were the three field events peculiar to the pentathlon) only those who by their performance had earned the right to do so competed in the fourth event, the foot-race. Again after the foot-race only a limited number proceeded to the wrestling. As soon as any one competitor gained three clear victories the pentathlon came to an end; failing this, the winner of the wrestling was the final victor. On the difficult question of the principle by which the number of participants was reduced agreement has not yet been reached.

Conveniently adjoining the stadium at Priene is the lower gymnasium. Chance has preserved for us an inscription recording the decision to build this gymnasium; it is dated soon after 130 B.C. A resolution, we learn, had earlier been made to erect the building, relying on contributions promised by certain of the kings; owing, however, to changes in their fortunes, the money had not been forthcoming, and the expense is now undertaken by a rich citizen named Moschion.

The gymnasium consists as usual of an open palaestra for athletic exercise, surrounded by a stoa and rooms for gymnastic and educational purposes. Best preserved are the rooms on the north side. In the middle is the ephebeum, used here as a lecture-room; benches for the students ran round the foot of the walls. The upper part of the walls was adorned with Corinthian half-columns. This room can hardly fail to appeal to any visitor who has ever carved his name on his desk at school, for the wall is covered with names of students. 'Phileas son of Metrodorus, his place; Epicurus son of Pausanias, his place'—more than 700 names may still be read (Pl. 55).

As was seen at Pergamum and Ephesus, it was normal in Roman times to have full-scale hot baths (thermae) adjoining the gymnasium. At Priene we see the simpler Greek practice, for the washroom at the west end is well preserved. The row of basins at the back survives, fed—with cold water only—through lions'-head spouts from a channel in the wall. Two other basins, for washing the feet, stood one on each side of the entrance. The floor is covered with a paving of smooth pebbles (Pl. 51).

The other rooms on this side, if they followed the normal rule, should have been used respectively for the wrestlers to coat themselves with fine sand, for the boxers to practise with a punch-bag, and for the athletes generally to anoint their bodies with oil. Vast quantities of olive-oil were consumed in this way, and its provision was a favourite form of endowment by public-minded benefactors: 'So-and-so oiled the citizens for a year', is the rather quaint expression used in the inscriptions.

The streets and private houses are certainly among the most attractive features of Priene. The streets are laid out on a rectangular plan, with main streets running east and west, joined by numerous lanes running north and south. Owing to the steep slope of the ground, these latter are frequently stepped. Each block, or 'island' as the Romans said, contains normally four houses.

The houses are of a type still commonly seen in Mediterranean countries, being shut off from the street by high walls affording no view in from outside; these outer walls, which are still standing often to a man's height, are in general of very good masonry, comparable with that of the public buildings and dating from the early days of the city.

The interior arrangements are on the whole remarkably uniform, though not now so easy to follow on the ground as when they were first excavated. The street-door, often set in the side-street, leads through a vestibule to an open courtyard; beside the door stood commonly an altar for family sacrifice and a herm, or truncated image of Hermes, the god of good luck. On the north side of the courtyard is an antechamber open in front, and behind this the main living-room of the house; at the side of this and of the antechamber there are generally two more rooms, one of which is the dining-room. Upper storeys are not preserved, but traces of stairs occur in a few houses. There is no indication of separate women's quarters; possibly the women lived upstairs, as sometimes in classical Athens. The rooms were high, as commonly in hot climates, often 15 to 20 feet (4·6 to 6·10 m.); they were heated in winter by portable braziers. Kitchen hearths are sometimes found in the antechamber. Only one bathroom was found by the excavators; it is tiny, some 6 feet by 3 feet 6 inches (1·83 by 1·07 m.), and accommodates one person sitting with his feet in a basin-like hollow. Latrines occur only in three or four houses, nor have any public conveniences been found at Priene. Windows in the houses are not preserved, but probably only because the walls are not standing high enough; light was also admitted through the doors from the courtyard, but in general the interiors must have been distinctly dark. Wall-decoration is simple, and mostly imitates architectural forms; wall-painting consists merely of plain geometrical designs.

The early date of these houses is proved by the many coins found in them, most of which are of the third century B.C. Some of the houses were later converted to the 'peristyle' type favoured in Roman times, but for the most part they remain as they were when the city was first built.

Finally a word may be said of an interesting little sanctuary among the houses in the third block from the west on the south side of the main street leading to the west gate. It has the general from of an ordinary house, with an entrance from the side-road on the west into a courtyard; on the left door-post was found an inscription recording the holding of a priesthood, and adding: 'No admittance to this sanctuary except to the pure, and in white raiment'. On the north side of the courtyard is an antechamber, badly ruined, and beyond this a large room, in the north-east corner of which is a stone bench for offerings, similar to that in the sanctuary of Demeter. In front of this bench, over a natural crevice in the ground, stood a marble table; its supports were in place when excavated, but have now collapsed, and the whole condition of the building has been allowed to deteriorate. Among a number of statuettes found here is one that appears to represent Alexander the Great, and some have accordingly supposed that this sanctuary is the Alexandrium mentioned in an inscription and not found elsewhere in the city (above, p. 162). Alexander-worship is well attested. On the other hand, the sacrificial table over a crack in the ground suggests rather offerings to some subterranean deity, and on the whole it is safer to reserve judgment.

The Panionium

Mention has been made above more than once of the Panionium, where in early times the religious assembly of the Ionians was held and accompanied by a great festival, the Panionia. The sanctuary was sacred to Poseidon Heliconius, so named from the town of Helice in Greece where his worship was established and transported to Ionia. The place being on Prienian territory, it was under that city's management and it was customary for a young man of Priene to be appointed as priest. According to Strabo it was reckoned a good omen here if the sacrificial victim uttered a bellow during the ceremony, and some ancient scholars believed that Homer was alluding to this when he wrote: 'he bellowed as a bull bellows when dragged to the altar of Lord Heliconius'. They may well have been right; and their conclusion, that Homer must have lived after the Ionian colonization of Asia, was certainly correct.

Some time during the fifth century it became impossible to celebrate the Panionia owing to the constant hostilities, and it was transferred to a safer place near Ephesus; Thucydides refers to it under the name of the Ephesia. Diodorus, who records the transference, says that nine cities took part, not twelve; this statement lacks ancient corroboration and has generally been supposed to be a mistake. For a hundred years, under Persian rule, the activities of the Ionian League were in abeyance; Alexander's conquests brought a revival, and the Panionia continued to be celebrated in its original place down to Roman times. Its importance was, however, diminished by a second Federal festival which the Ionians instituted in honour of Alexander himself, held on the territory of Erythrae; and, in fact, the Panionia never really regained its early brilliance.

The site of the Panionium has only recently been finally determined and excavated. The approximate position is described by Herodotus as on Mt Mycale facing north, and by Strabo as the first place north of the Samos strait, three stades from the sea. In

1673 an inscription naming the Panionium was found in the village of Güzelçamlı; it was seen again by Chandler in 1764 in a church by the shore, but the church is now destroyed and the inscription lost. The exact site was conjectured by the German scholar Wiegand at the end of last century, when he saw on the hill of St Elias near Güzelçamlı the remains of eight rows of seats, as of a theatre, cut in the hillside. These seats were still visible when the present writer was there in 1946, but subsequently became hidden and were only with difficulty rediscovered in 1957. In that and the following year excavations were carried out by a team of German archaeologists. The hill has meanwhile changed its name. It was used in the First World War and the ensuing Greco-Turkish War as a machine-gun post, whence its present outlandish name of Otomatik Tepe.

On top of the hill, which is quite low, are the scanty remains of the sacred enclosure. The surrounding wall is partly preserved on the north, west, and south, though nowhere to a height of more than three courses; the entrance is distinguishable on the west. In the middle, running north and south, was a long narrow structure some 57 by 14 feet (17·4 by 4·27 m.); it is now completely destroyed, and is recognizable chiefly by the cuttings and dowel-holes in the surface of the rock. This was evidently not a temple but an altar, and, in fact, the ancient authorities make no mention of a temple at the Panionium, but speak consistently of sacrifices. These scanty relics are not datable in themselves, but are attributed by the excavators on other grounds to the late sixth century B.C.

Some fifty yards (45·7 m.) to the south-west of this enclosure is a large cave about 30 feet (27·4 m.) deep and the same in width. Nothing significant has been found in it, but since the whole site was dedicated to Poseidon, the Earth-Shaker, it is likely that the cave, too, was sacred to him, and may have played a part in the cult.

Below the cave, at the foot of the hill, is the theatre-like building mentioned above. When excavated it proved to have eleven rows of seats, and never apparently had any more; its total diameter is a little over 100 feet (30·5 m.). Where the stage of a theatre would be, there is only the rock, in part artificially levelled, and where the side-entrances (parodoi) would come, transverse blocks are laid across. It is accordingly clear that the building cannot, in fact, be a theatre, appropriate though this would be on the site of a great festival, and there can be no doubt that we have the remains of the council chamber in which the delegates from the Ionian cities met to take decisions in the interests of the League. Here it was that Bias stood to advise the Ionians to migrate to Sardinia. Thales of Miletus would have had a common council of the Ionians at Teos, nearer the centre of the country, but his recommendation was not adopted. The excavators thought to discern in the arrangement of the front row of seats some confirmation of Diodorus' statement that only nine cities participated, but this is not easy to make out on the ground.

About 200 yards (182·9 m.) to the west of this spot is a small hill or mound carrying the ruins of a structure of Roman date, apparently a tomb.

Notes

1 The difference is about 4 per cent on average, but for the best throws may be as much as 16 per cent.

2 H. A. Harris, *Greek Athletes and Athletics*, chap. IV (c).

10 Miletus

Great changes have taken place in the Maeander valley during the last few years. Whereas formerly the river used to flood the plain every winter, and Miletus was approached by a rough track, renewed annually, and a primitive grind across the Maeander, now a large part of the plain has been reclaimed, a fine new road has been driven across from Söke to Milâs, and cars may reach Miletus all the year round. The ancient site was formerly occupied in part by the village of Balat—that is, Palatia, with reference to the Byzantine castle on the hill above the theatre; but this village was destroyed by an earthquake in 1955, and a new one, Yeniköy, has been built a mile (1·61 km.) to the south on the road to Didyma.

Miletus tends to produce a sense of strangeness, even of unreality, in the modern visitor. He may feel, as the writer felt on his first visit, 'This is not what I expected'. When the name of Miletus is mentioned, the hearer thinks at once of the great maritime city of the archaic period, mistress of the Aegean and birthplace of science and philosophy; but of this city most visitors see nothing. Roman Miletus, whose ruins meet the eye today, was, of course, a great city still, but somehow it does not satisfy as Ephesus, for example, does. This feeling is greatly accentuated by the complete change in the landscape due to the silting process of the Maeander. This river is what Herodotus calls a 'worker'; it has been, and still is, advancing the coastline by an average of some 20 feet (6·10 m.) in a year, so that Miletus, in classical times a city on a headland at the mouth of a broad gulf, is now nearly five miles (8 km.) from the sea. The island of Lade, of sinister fame, now stands high and dry as a hill on the plain, and the Latmian gulf has become the freshwater lake of Bafa. Standing on the hill above the theatre, it requires a strong effort of the imagination to picture Miletus as it once was.

Miletus has the unique distinction among the cities of Ionia of receiving mention by Homer. It was the home of 'Carians of uncouth speech' who fought against the Greeks at Troy.

In archaic times there was a strong Carian element in the population and the father of Thales himself bears the Carian name Examyes. Miletus is one of the cities which has produced very early evidence for Greek settlement in Asia Minor. Some of the earliest pottery has affinities with material from Minoan Crete, and there was a substantial Mycenaean settlement here between 1400 and 1200 B.C. The main occupation was on the stadium hill, where excavations have recently revealed a *megaron* and associated buildings. Pottery kilns have also been found. Around 1200 a fortification wall of casemate construction, which resembles the defensive walls of Boğazköy, the Hittite capital, and also those at Enkomi in Cyprus, was built round this hill, reflecting the unsettled condition of western Anatolia at this period. The later Ionian colonization was said to have been led by Neileus, a son of Codrus; he found the place occupied by a mixture of the native Carians and certain Cretans who had migrated from a town of the same name in Crete. The Ionians, says Herodotus, slaughtered all the male inhabitants and married their wives, having brought no women with them; wherefore the women of Miletus, then and afterwards, bound themselves by oath never to sit at table with their husbands nor to call them by name.

Ionian Miletus prospered exceedingly and was in early times beyond question the greatest city of the Greek world. A favourable position, combined with a spirit of enterprise derived from their Athenian founders, gave the Milesians the leading place among the sea-traders of the time. By land the city's communications were poor. It might appear today that Miletus served as a terminal to the great caravan route down the Maeander valley; but a glance at the accompanying sketch-map will show that in antiquity this was far from being the case. Priene and Myus were better placed in this respect; but, in fact, this route seems rather to have led, as it does now, to Ephesus (p. 193, Fig. 45).

But by sea the Milesians were unequalled. As early as the eighth century, and especially during the seventh, they founded numerous colonies on the shores of the Hellespont, the Sea of Marmara, and the Black Sea; the total number is put as high as ninety. Obviously these cannot all have been peopled solely by Milesians; the mother-city must have served as a centre for disaffected persons, exiles, and others in search of a new home. These would gravitate to Miletus and join the next group that was sent out. However this may be, preferential terms of trade with these colonies undoubtedly contributed to the wealth of the city.

Material prosperity was accompanied by brilliant intellectual achievement. Not that Miletus was alone in this: Heraclitus of Ephesus, Bias of Priene, Xenophanes of Colophon, and others prove the contrary: but Miletus certainly led the way. First and foremost comes the name of Thales. His dictum that 'All things are water', and his prediction of the solar eclipse of 585 B.C. have been mentioned above; he is credited also with diverting the course of the river Halys to allow Croesus' army to cross. When someone taunted him that for all his brains he was still a poor man, Thales' answer was practical and effective: his study of astronomy enabling him to know that next year's olive harvest would be a bumper one, he cornered all the olive presses in Miletus; by letting these out at a high rental he proved that philosophers can if they wish grow rich, but (says the historian) this is not their aim. Thales also, we read, was the first man to succeed in inscribing a right-angled triangle in a circle; in celebration of this he sacrificed an ox—which means in effect that he stood himself a good dinner.[1] Another of his achievements was to calculate the height of the Pyramids in Egypt by measuring their shadow at the time of day when a man's shadow is equal to his height. Among his sayings the most famous is 'Know thyself', which was inscribed on the temple at Delphi. Less acceptable to modern ideas, perhaps, is his remark that he thanked the gods for three things, that he was human and not an animal, a man and not a woman, a Greek and not a barbarian. The list of the Seven Sages in antiquity varied enormously, but three names were unanimously included, those of Thales of Miletus, Bias of Priene, and Solon of Athens.

Thales was followed in the field of physical science by his countrymen Anaximenes and Anaximander. The former found in air the basic substance of the universe; by a process of condensation and rarefaction this produced all other forms of matter. Anaximander preferred a different basic principle, which he called the Infinite. Or perhaps—since it was both finite and material—the Unlimited would be a better word: unlimited, that is, by any characteristics or qualities, and so capable of breaking down into the various material substances of the world we see.

Milesian, too, were the fathers of geography. Anaximander produced the first map of the world; based upon supposed principles of symmetry in the disposition of the continents, seas, and rivers, it was grotesquely inaccurate to modern ideas, nor does Anaximander himself appear to have travelled. Such was not the case with Hecataeus, whose *Geography* was a commentary on his fellow citizen's map. He travelled a great deal, and could supplement his own observation from the constant stream of visitors to Miletus from all parts of the earth. Where we can check the fragments of his work that survive, they are found to be very reliable. Hecataeus is frequently quoted, and rather uncharitably criticized, by Herodotus. One famous saying of Hecataeus epitomizes the new spirit of enquiry after truth which characterizes Greek and especially Milesian thinkers of the sixth and fifth centuries: 'I write what appears to me to be true, for the tales the Greeks tell are many and ridiculous'. Readers of Hecataeus' successor Herodotus will certainly feel that the world would be poorer for lack of these Greek tales, however ridiculous.

Intellectual and material prosperity had no softening effect upon the Milesians. 'Once upon a time', said the later proverb, 'the Milesians were brave men'. They successfully resisted the attacks of the Lydian kings Gyges and Alyattes, and even Croesus was content to make a treaty with them. The Persians were too strong for them, but they, too, consented to make terms; Miletus was the only Ionian city thus distinguished. Tribute had to be paid, and the tyrant ruled only with Persian consent, but otherwise Miletus was more or less free.

In the ill-starred Ionian revolt of 500 B.C. the part played by Miletus was bound up with the romantic career of Histiaeus. The story begins in 512, when the Persian king Darius undertook his disastrous expedition against the Scythians; his force included a naval contingent led by the tyrants of the Greek cities, including Histiaeus, tyrant of Miletus. On reaching the Danube he crossed on a bridge of boats, leaving with the Greek captains a cord in which he had tied sixty knots, with instructions to untie one every day, and if he had not returned by the time they were all untied, to sail away home. He then advanced into the wilds of Scythia. The Greeks waited the sixty days, but the king did not appear. While they were hesitating what to do, a party of Scythians arrived and urged them to destroy the bridge, so ensuring Darius' ruin and their own freedom—for the king meanwhile had been suffering serious reverses in Scythia. The Greeks were tempted to fall in with this proposal, but Histiaeus restrained them and preserved the bridge. When Darius arrived hard pressed and found the bridge surviving after the allotted period, he was so grateful to Histiaeus that he allowed him to choose whatever he wished. Histiaeus asked for Myrcinus, a small town in western Thrace with silver-mines close by, which he proceeded to fortify. Darius, however, warned that a Greek stronghold here was highly undesirable, summoned him to the Persian capital on the pretence that so valuable a friend was needed at his side. Histiaeus accordingly languished in Susa for eleven years. Meanwhile his son-in-law Aristagoras was ruling in Miletus in his place; having failed lamentably in an attack on the island of Naxos which he had persuaded the king to let him undertake, his stock was low. At this point Histiaeus, weary of enforced Persian hospitality, secretly sent a slave to Aristagoras bearing tattooed on his head the message 'Rouse the Ionians to revolt'. This he did in the expectation of being sent by Darius to quell the revolt when it should occur. Aristagoras, who had himself been contemplating this same means of retrieving his fortunes, acted accordingly. And sure enough Histiaeus appeared on the scene, professedly sent to help the Persian satrap to suppress the rebel Greeks. The satrap, however, was suspicious and declined to work with him, whereupon Histiaeus fled, and occupying Byzantium turned his hand to piracy. Not long afterwards he was captured and put to death by the Persians. Such is the story as told by Herodotus; modern historians have no difficulty in pointing out its improbabilities.

The battle of Lade in 494 B.C., the collapse of the revolt, and the Persian capture of Miletus put an end to the city's golden age. Never before had she been taken by force, and the event was recognized as a major calamity. When an Athenian dramatist put on a tragedy entitled 'Fall of Miletus', the audience burst into tears and the poet was fined 1,000 drachmae. According to Herodotus the city was destroyed, most of the men slain, and the women and children enslaved. Nevertheless, within a generation Miletus was on her feet again. Following the defeat of the Persians in Greece and the liberation of the Greeks of Asia, the city was rebuilt on the site which she was to occupy for the rest of her existence, and by the middle of the fifth century was paying five talents a year as a member of the Delian Confederacy, a sum only a little less than that paid by Ephesus. At the same time she was issuing an abundant silver coinage.

Despite this remarkable recovery, Miletus was never again the force that she had been. The Athenian naval supremacy deprived her of her commanding position as a trading nation, and there was nothing to take its place. In general the city's fortunes followed those of Ionia as a whole. In the fourth century there is evidence of close relations between Miletus and the Carian dynasts Mausolus

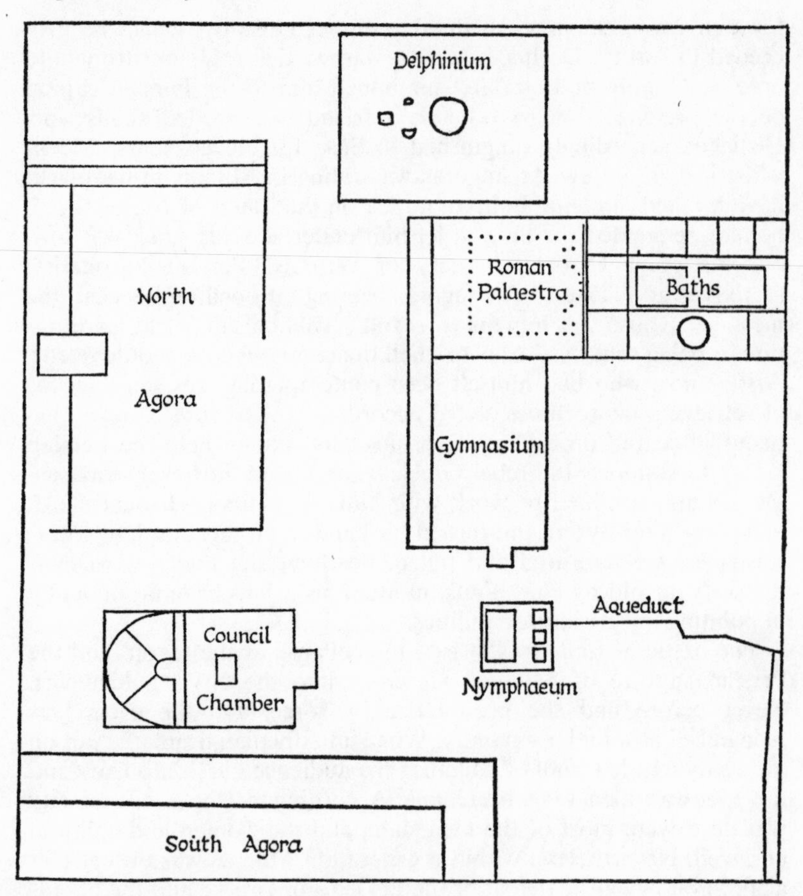

Fig. 43 Plan of the city centre at Miletus

and his father Hecatomnos, and the city may have been actually in their power for a time; Milesian coins exist bearing the inscriptions EKA (tomnos) and MA (usolus). Be this as it may, when Alexander arrived in 334 B.C., a Persian garrison was in control, and Miletus was the first city to offer him resistance. He at once laid siege to it; his ships forestalled a Persian relieving fleet, and the city fell to a vigorous assault.

In the Hellenistic era Miletus experienced the usual vicissitudes, coming in turn under the power of Antigonus, Lysimachus, the Seleucids of Syria, the Ptolemies of Egypt, the Attalids of Pergamum, and finally, of course, the Romans. In the province of Asia, Miletus was a 'free' city, rich and prosperous like the rest, with many fine buildings. But the threat of the Maeander silt was growing serious; some time about the fourth century A.D. the coastline passed the Milesian promontory, and before long Lade, too, ceased to be an island. Mosquitoes swarmed, and the once great city slowly sank to become the fever-ridden village of Balat.

Concerning the earliest, pre-Greek settlement at Miletus a certain amount has been learned from the recent excavations. It lay on the level ground to the south-west of the existing city, and dates back to Mycenaean and Minoan times, about 1600 B.C. The considerable quantity of Cretan pottery found there supports the tradition which said that Miletus was founded from Crete. If this is in fact true, it must have been occupied, not as a trading-station—for, as was said above, Miletus' land communications were poor—but as a port of call on the route to the further east. During the fourteenth century, about the time when the Minoan power in Crete came to an end, the settlement at Miletus was fortified with a solid wall over 14 feet (4·27 m.) thick; this may perhaps indicate that the place had passed from Minoan hands into those of some Asiatic dynast, whose descendants may represent the 'Carians of uncouth speech' who fought at Troy.

The subsequent course of events has not yet become clear. The great wall did not stand for very long, and in course of time the archaic temple of Athena was built by the Greek colonists directly over its ruins. Somewhere about 800 B.C. a fortified settlement was built on the hill now called Kalabaktepe, some two miles (3·22 km.) to the south-west of the present ruins, but the excavators are not now disposed to regard this hill as the acropolis of the early Greek Miletus; it is not, in fact, yet determined exactly where this archaic city lay. The region of the pre-Greek settlement continued to be occupied right down to the destruction of Miletus by the Persians in 494 B.C., as is shown by clear traces of burning found in the excavations; but not enough ground has yet been cleared to show whether this was indeed the site of the city of Thales and Hecataeus. Kalabaktepe was excavated in 1904–08, when strong walls 12 feet (3·66 m.) thick with gates, and numerous foundations of houses and a small temple, were brought to light. By no means all of this can still be seen today. Sherds reveal that the hill was occupied from about the eighth century till the Persian capture in 494, and was not altogether deserted even after that.

Among the ruins of the later city all else is overshadowed by the magnificent theatre. In its present form this was built about A.D. 100, replacing an earlier theatre on the same site. If Priene gives us the best surviving Hellenistic theatre, Miletus undoubtedly has the finest of the Graeco-Roman type. The stage-building is of similar form to that at Ephesus; the cavea is semicircular in the Roman fashion, and the seats are completely preserved up to the first diazoma. The vaulted passages under the seats, and the vaults and stairways of the vomitoria, are also in excellent preservation. The 'Royal Box' is marked merely by two pillars. On some of the front rows of seats, from the third to the sixth, are a number of inscriptions reserving the places for certain persons or groups of persons: in the fifth row is the 'place of the Jews also called the God-fearing', and in the third row the 'place of the goldsmiths of the Blues'—with reference to the factions of the Blues and Greens familiar in Byzantine history. On a block of the wall at the top of the stairway at the west end of the upper diazoma is an interesting inscription relating to a labour dispute which arose in the course of the construction of the theatre. The workmen—evidently free agents, not slaves—became dissatisfied with the terms of their employment and were considering abandoning it and seeking other work elsewhere. The matter was referred to arbitration, the arbiter being Apollo at Didyma. His recommendation, in hexameter verse, was to make proper use of building technique, to seek the advice of a skilled expert, and (characteristically) to sacrifice to Athena and Heracles. In other words, 'Get someone to teach you how to do the job economically, and you will find it will pay you well enough'. The men were not mere labourers for hire, but a group of artisans who, in accordance with the normal ancient practice of paying by piecework, had contracted for the job as a whole; owing (apparently) to their own inefficiency, they found it unsatisfactory and were thinking of breaking the contract. This is about as near to a strike in the modern sense as is found in ancient times. Apollo's advice was presumably followed with success, or the matter would not have been recorded on stone (Pl. 57, 58, 61).

The centre of the city lies to the east of the theatre on the low ground, where the ruins are flooded every winter. The Delphinium, or precinct of Apollo Delphinius, was the principal sanctuary at Miletus apart from the great temple at Didyma. It was also very ancient, for the cult was brought from Athens by the original Ionian settlers. Inscriptions found in it date back as far as the sixth century B.C., having apparently been brought from the earlier city; one may be seen built in under the wall on the south side of the court. The name Delphinius is derived from the Greek word for a dolphin, and has only an indirect connection with Delphi; an early legend, seeking to explain the name Delphi, related that Apollo, needing priests for the temple he intended to build there, espied a Cretan ship on the high sea, and changing himself into a dolphin, guided the sailors thither. The existing remains at Miletus are those of a Hellenistic building reconstructed in Roman times; the extensive use of a pinkish stone gives them a distinctive appearance. In the course of the excavation nearly 200 inscriptions were found of the greatest interest for the city's history.

The bouleuterion, or council chamber, is among the earliest buildings surviving at Miletus, being built between 175 and 164 B.C. It consists of a semicircular assembly hall, fairly well preserved, and a badly ruined forecourt. In the middle of the forecourt are the foundations of a rectangular structure which has recently been identified as an altar dedicated to the cult of the Roman emperors. Its position opposite the entrance to the bouleuterion is interesting, since it demonstrates the close connection that existed between the local government of a city like Miletus during the Roman empire, and the expression of loyalty to the emperor required of its citizens and formulated in the rituals and worship of the imperial cult.

Opposite the council chamber stood the nymphaeum, from which water was distributed to the city, but the existing ruins give little idea of this once fine and ornate building. Above the three vaulted niches which now catch the eye were two reservoirs fed by the aqueduct which leads to the building from the rear. From these the water was conveyed partly to channels spreading to various parts of the city, and partly to a large basin in front and below. This basin was framed by an architectural façade of three storeys at the back, with columns, niches, and statues, and at either side a two-storeyed colonnade. Of this ornamentation nothing remains but fragments found during the excavation.

Apart from the theatre, the best-preserved building at Miletus is the Baths of Faustina. The Faustina in question is probably the younger of that name, wife of the Emperor Marcus Aurelius, a lady noted for her profligacy with other people's money. The whole complex is really a gymnasium with baths attached in the usual Roman way, and the stadium close by. The palaestra is at the time of writing a cultivated field; from its east side is entered the main chamber of the building (2 in the plan), a long hall running north and south, with small rooms along each side, and an apsed chamber at the north end (1 in the plan). Statues of Apollo and the Muses were found in Room 1, indicating that it was used as a lecture-room; the small chambers of Room 2 served for small classes and discussion. Some of those at the south end may have been changing-rooms for those intending to use the baths. Rooms 1 and 2 together have a striking

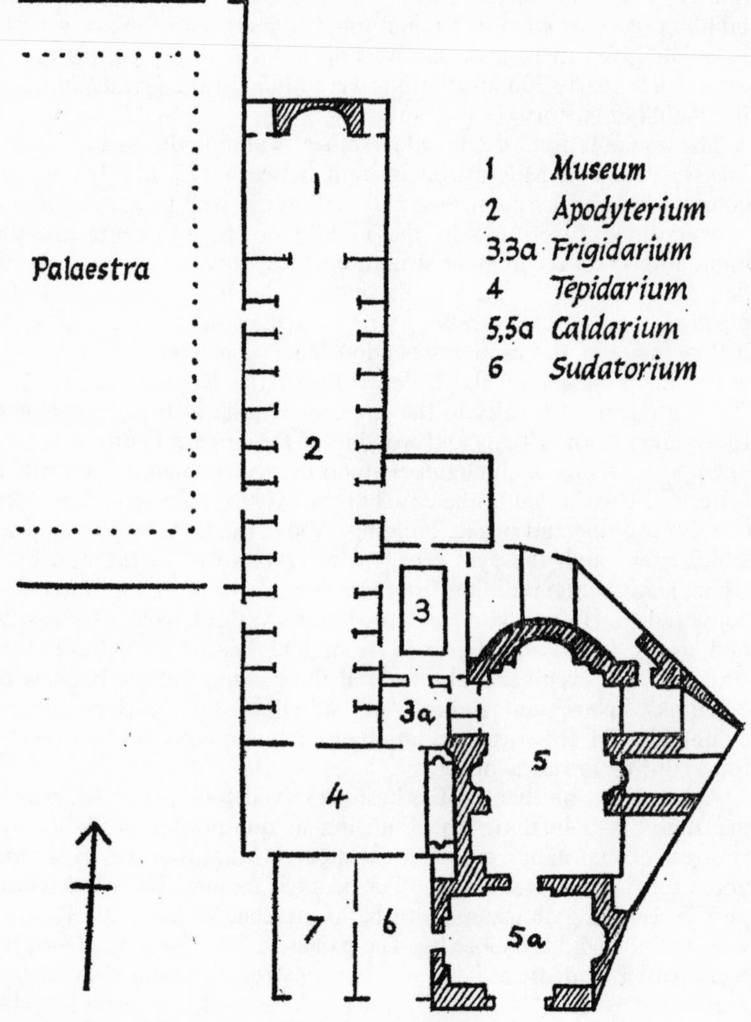

Fig. 44 Plan of the baths of Faustina at Miletus

resemblance to the original Museum which preceded the Double Church at Ephesus (above, p. 141). The baths, adjoining on the east and south, comprise as usual a series of rooms heated to varying degrees, much as in a Turkish bath, which is indeed a direct descendant of the Roman thermae. Room 3 is the frigidarium, or cold plunge, a simple rectangular basin of cold water; at one end was placed a reclining statue of a river-god, no doubt the Maeander, and in the middle of one side a marble lion. Water was admitted through the base of the statue and through the lion's mouth. This room is in good preservation and the statues have been left in position. A smaller frigidarium 3a adjoins on the south. Of the other rooms the coolest was the tepidarium (No. 4); it was slightly heated by a basin of warm water at the east end. Rooms 5 and 5a are the hot rooms, or caldarium. They were heated by a hypocaust; that is, the floor was raised some 2 feet 6 inches on supports and the space below filled with hot air from an adjoining furnace. Flues also ran up the walls between the niches. In the hottest room of all, the sudatorium, or sweating-room (No. 6), flues ran continuously all round the walls. The northern half of this room was later converted into a water-basin, from which the bathers might pass into the cool room 4 and finish with a cold plunge in the frigidarium. The adjoining room No. 7 was probably similar to No. 6, but has not been excavated.

Note

1 There is something wrong here. The least mathematically-minded can inscribe a right-angled triangle in a circle. Unless we should read 'equilateral triangle', the meaning is probably that Thales first proved that a triangle inscribed in a semicircle is right-angled.

11 Didyma

Beyond Miletus, in the extreme south of Ionia, stands what is probably the most impressive single ancient monument on the west coast, the temple of Apollo at Didyma. It is remarkable for its huge size, for its unique plan, and not least for its fine state of preservation. Over a hundred years ago Sir Charles Newton could write: 'Two giant columns supporting a piece of architrave, and a third unfinished column are all that remain standing of the Temple of Apollo, of which the mighty ruins lie as they originally fell, piled up like shattered icebergs'. Today, thanks to the French and German excavators, the building stands exposed, except for its colonnade, virtually complete. In size it is hardly exceeded by any temple of the Greek world. Planned in Hellenistic times, it serves as a reminder that vastness in architecture was not purely a monopoly of the Romans.

Like Claros, and unlike Gryneum, Didyma was never a city; the temple with its oracle belonged to the territory of Miletus, and its priest was an important official of that city. The name is not Greek but Anatolian, like Idyma in Caria, Sidyma in Lycia, and others; but its accidental resemblance to the Greek *didymi*, 'twins', gave rise to the idea that it referred to Apollo and his twin sister Artemis. Some ancient writers actually use the form Didymi. Artemis had, in fact, a temple and cult at Didyma, but it was of minor importance compared with that of Apollo.

Pausanias says that the oracle existed even before the arrival of the Ionian settlers. It is certainly very ancient; the earliest inscriptions found on the site go back to about 600 B.C., and one of them is a fragment of an oracular response. The clients appear to have asked if it was right for the younger generation to engage in the practice of piracy, and the god replied, 'It is right to do as your fathers did'. In these early days the cult was in the hands of the

Branchidae, a noble family claiming Delphian origin; and Branchidae is often used as an alternative name to Didyma.

When Croesus in the middle of the sixth century was contemplating an invasion of Persia, he thought to take the advice of an oracle; and to make sure of having the best advice he devised a preliminary test. He sent messengers to a number of the best-known oracles, of which Didyma was one, to ask on a particular day what King

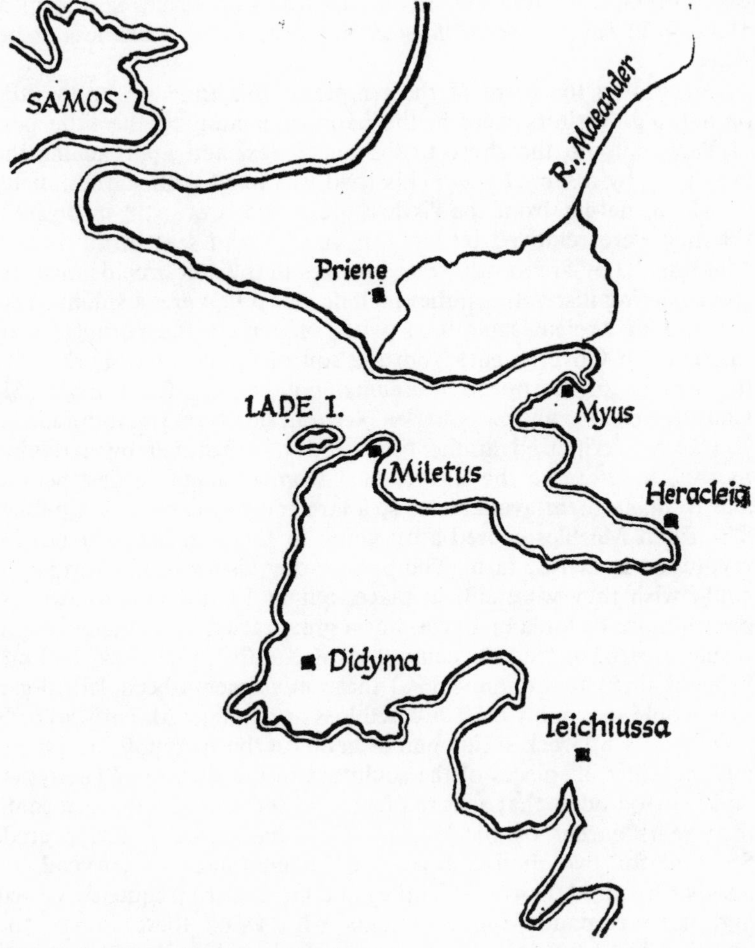

Fig. 45 Southern Ionia in early times

Croesus was doing at that moment; he was, in fact, boiling a tortoise and a lamb in a bronze cauldron. Apollo at Delphi found the answer, and another oracle also received honourable mention, but Didyma failed to rise to the occasion. Croesus was nevertheless a good friend to the Branchidae and made splendid offerings to the god—the same indeed that he made to Delphi. These latter are described by Herodotus; they comprised 10 talents of pure gold and 226 talents of 'white gold' (electrum), a total of close upon 2 cubic metres; two huge bowls of gold and silver; four large jars of silver; two sprinklers of gold and silver; his wife's necklaces and girdles; and a gold statue, about life-size, supposed to be a likeness of his cook.

Concerning the form of the temple at this time we know little or nothing. Visitors were in the habit of landing at the little port of Panormus on the shore to the north-west and approaching the sanctuary by a sacred way. This road was lined with statues, many of which, dating from the sixth century B.C., were still in position till they were removed by Newton in 1858 and sent to the British Museum. They are mostly seated figures in the stiff archaic posture, some bearing inscriptions; they include also a lion and a sphinx. This removal of ancient sculptures (with, of course, the permission of the Turkish Government) from the soil of Greece and Turkey for the benefit of European museums, notably by Lord Elgin, Sir Charles Fellows, and Sir Charles Newton, has been often criticized. It was not criticized at the time, and was justified by a double motive, to preserve the monuments from damage or destruction, and to make them available to scholars and to the educated public. The Elgin Marbles caused a sensation in England and produced a revolution in artistic taste. The present-day visitor to the Parthenon could wish they were still in place, but in 1800 a visit to Athens, or still more to Ionia or Lycia, was a great rarity. How many people would ever have seen the sculptures of Xanthus if Fellows had not brought them to London? Had these monuments been left alone, they would inevitably have suffered loss or damage; Mahaffy records how he saw a Greek sitting gun in hand on the Acropolis at Athens and shooting off pieces of the sculpture in the theatre of Dionysus; and Newton notes that a seated figure on the sacred way, seen some fifty years earlier by Sir William Gell, had already disappeared. Survival for two thousand years is no guarantee of survival for another hundred. Now that Turkey and Greece are frequently visited and have responsible governments who value these things, the question has reasonably been raised whether they should be given back; meanwhile, as at least a temporary measure, casts can be installed, and in some cases this has been done.

The early phase in the history of Didyma came to an end with the destruction of the temple by the Persians. Herodotus tells us that after the collapse of the Ionian revolt and the fall of Miletus in 494 B.C. Darius sacked and burnt both temple and oracle; Strabo and Pausanias, on the other hand, say that this was done by Xerxes on his return from Greece after his defeat at Plataea in 479. The Branchidae on this occasion were guilty of sad disloyalty to the god; they willingly surrendered his treasures to the Persian king, and to escape the consequences of this treachery they fled with him to Persia, where he settled them on a site in Sogdiana. A hundred and fifty years later Alexander came upon this settlement still existing; after asking the Milesians in his army how he should deal with it, he destroyed it utterly. So, as the historian does not fail to point out, the sons paid the penalty for their fathers' sins. Later still, Seleucus I of Syria found in Ecbatana, the Persian capital, the bronze statue of Apollo that Xerxes had stolen, and restored it to Didyma.

It was long before the oracle recovered from the destruction by the Persians; for the rest of the fifth century and most of the fourth it is silent. With the coming of Alexander, however, we learn that the sacred spring, the fountain of prophecy at Didyma, which had long been dry, gushed again; the oracle, coming to life, announced that Alexander was a true son of Zeus and foretold his victory at Gaugamela. But the real revival of Didyma was due to Seleucus. About 300 B.C. he began to build, on the site of the old temple, the vast structure which is still standing today. The new sanctuary quickly became rich, but in 278 B.C. it suffered severely from raids by the invading Gauls. Among the inscriptions found by the excavators is a temple-inventory for the year 277 B.C.; it records that there survived 'from the war' in the treasury of Apollo one ornamented bowl and a silvered ox-horn, and in that of Artemis one censer lacking the support under one of its legs, two smaller censers, and three girdles: nothing more. But the unfinished building still stood, and for the next two hundred years the Milesians themselves worked to complete it; a further plundering by the pirates about 70 B.C. was quickly made good. The temple never, in fact, received the finishing touches, as the visitor today may readily observe; for example, many of the blocks were never finally smoothed, and the fluting of the columns was not completed.

The plan of this temple is unusual, or even unique, in a number

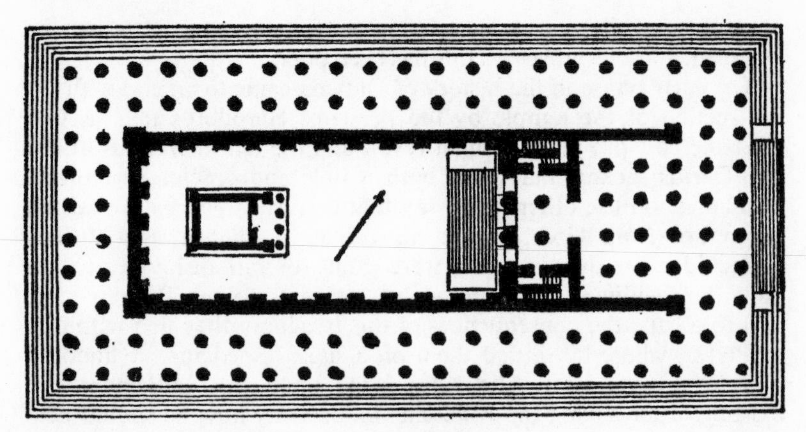

Fig. 46 Plan of the temple of Apollo at Didyma

of respects. The order is Ionic; the type is 'dipteral decastyle', that is the building was surrounded by a double row of columns numbering ten across the front and back. The pronaos, or forecourt, is filled by twelve more columns, making a total of 120. Between the pronaos and the cella, or main chamber, is an antechamber containing two more columns; this has a door opening on to the pronaos, but it was not used as an entrance, since the sill is 4 feet 9 inches (1.45 m.) high. This antechamber is a quite exceptional feature, and its purpose will be discussed later. From it three doors open on to a flight of stairs leading down to the cella, which lies 18 feet (5·49 m.) below. The cella itself is like a great open courtyard, with walls over 70 feet (21·3 m.) high; its unusual length is due to the absence of a rear chamber (opisthodomus). Owing to its size, as Strabo tells us, it was never roofed. From the pronaos the cella is reached by two sloping tunnels, one on either side, a unique arrangement. It was customary for the cult-statue in a Greek temple to stand towards the rear of the cella; at Didyma, since the cella was open to the sky, the statue of Apollo was housed in a small Ionic temple, of which only the foundations remain; this temple also contained the oracular spring. The upper part of the cella walls is decorated with pilasters; between their capitals ran a frieze carved with griffins and lyres. One or two fragments are lying against the north wall. A further unusual feature is the two staircases built in the wall on either side of the antechamber; they lead up to the top of the cella walls. The temple was richly and variously ornamented; mention may be made of the varied decoration of the column-bases in the pronaos, and of the Medusa frieze which ran above the architrave. At the west end a fallen column has been preserved by the excavators, with the drums overlapping, exactly as it fell when overthrown. The temple platform is not exactly horizontal, but slightly raised in the middle; the convexity, though only of a few inches, is clearly visible by squinting along the steps. This curvature is normal practice in Greek temples, to correct the optical illusion by which a long, dead flat line appears to sag in the middle. It is said that the Parthenon does not contain a single straight line (Pl. 62, 63).

An ancient privilege of the temple was that of asylum. Just as Antony extended the asylum at Ephesus, so Julius Caesar extended that of Didyma by two miles. In spite of this, when the Emperor Tiberius held his investigation into the claims of the Greek temples (above, p. 132), the Milesians relied not on Caesar's action but on a letter written by Darius I in the ancient days of the Branchidae, with the result that Didyma was placed only in the second class, namely those whose claims were doubtful by reason of their antiquity.

In general the Roman emperors showed themselves good friends to Didyma. Trajan in A.D. 100 paid for the construction of a road from Miletus to the sanctuary, a distance of some eleven miles (17·7 km.); hitherto the Milesians had been in the habit of sailing to the port of Panormus. The reason for Trajan's beneficence is to be found in the writings of the contemporary philosopher and orator Dio of Prusa (modern Bursa), who tells us that the oracle at Didyma prophesied to Trajan early in his career that he would one day become emperor. Trajan also paid Apollo the compliment of accepting the office of prophet, an honour which was later repeated by Hadrian. It is not, of course, to be supposed that these emperors listened to the inspired utterances of the prophetess at the sacred spring and turned them into verse for the benefit of the clients; all that is implied is that the expenses attached to the function of prophet were defrayed by the imperial treasury. In the second century, under the 'good' emperors from Trajan to Marcus Aurelius, Didyma enjoyed great prosperity and the oracle flourished; of the oracular texts found by the excavators the majority date from this period.

Decline set in in the third century. In A.D. 262, when the Goths came marauding down the coast, the temple of Apollo was hastily converted into a fortress, of which the ruins remained to be cleared away by the modern excavators. At this time, as we learn from an interesting inscription, the people, penned inside the temple walls, suffered from thirst until Apollo revealed a spring in the sanctuary and so saved them. This can be no other than the sacred spring itself, which must accordingly at that date have been utterly neglected, if not altogether lost. At the time when the inscription was written, about 290, it had once more fallen into decay, and was repaired by order of the proconsul; but again it is spoken of as a quencher of thirst rather than as a source of prophetic inspiration.

The cause of this decline was unquestionably the spread of Christianity, which seems to have taken an early hold at Miletus. The oracles, as one of the main strongholds of paganism, were bitterly attacked by the Christian writers; by the anti-Christian emperors they were naturally defended and patronized. Diocletian sent to Didyma to ask Apollo how he should deal with the Christians, accompanying the question with a present of statues of Zeus and Leto; it is not surprising to learn from our Christian source that the god 'responded as an enemy of the divine religion'. Julian the Apostate was another emperor who, as he tells us himself, was prophet of Apollo; and on learning that a number of chapels of Christian martyrs had been erected at Didyma, he ordered them all to be burnt or razed. But the tide was not to be stemmed by these means, and the end came in A.D. 385 with the famous edict of Theodosius, that 'no mortal man shall have the effrontery to encourage vain hopes by the inspection of entrails, or (which is worse) attempt to learn the future by the detestable consultation of oracles. The severest penalties await those who disobey'. The final humiliation was the erection of a Christian church in the holiest part of the temple itself.

For the actual working of the oracle at Didyma we are moderately well informed. The classical authors speak consistently of a prophetess and of a sacred spring as the source of her inspiration; we learn also that prophecy was by means of words—not as at Ammon in Libya by nods and signs, nor as at Dodona by the rustling of the winds in the trees. Our only detailed account comes from a writer of the fourth century A.D., the philosopher Iamblichus. His words are puzzling. The woman, he says, either holds in her hand a staff 'given by a certain god', or sits on an *axon*, or wets either her feet or the hem of her robe in the water, or inhales the vapour from the water; by all these means she prepares herself to receive the god's inspiration. He adds that she is required to live in the sanctuary, and before prophesying to bathe and to abstain from food for three days. It is hard to know what to make of this, or how reliable the information is. What the *axon* may be is quite unknown—possibly some kind of swivel seat—and the staff is equally obscure. But there is at least no mystery about the spring of water. It was discovered by the excavators in the interior of the cella, where it may still be seen in the little Ionic temple. In fact, three springs or wells have been found inside the cella; the repeated disappearance and rediscovery of the sacred spring in ancient times may perhaps be due to its shifting its position from time to time.

The clients were not permitted to come into the presence of the prophetess; the oracles, rendered into hexameter verse, were delivered to them in writing by the prophet of Apollo. The prophet was the highest official of all at Miletus; he was appointed for one year by a mixture of choice and lot, and while in office was required to live at Didyma. He was assisted by an official called the *hypochrestes*, the subordinate oracle-giver, whose duties are not explained; it is not unlikely that it was he who put the oracles into verse, a task which not all prophets may have been well qualified to perform. Only one oracle of Didymean Apollo is known to have been in prose. The hypochrestes may also have performed the functions of the prophet in years when that office was held by an emperor.

From the inscriptions we learn further of the existence of a building called the *chresmographeion*, or oracle-office. It is not known where this stood. The French excavator Haussoullier supposed it to be the antechamber at the top of the stairs which lead up from the cella, between it and the pronaos. This room is not a normal part of a Greek temple, so that it was natural to regard it as relating to the special feature of Didyma, the oracle. The German excavators on the other hand believe the chresmographeion to be identical with a building which no longer exists, but whose blocks were found scattered in great numbers in and around the temple; these blocks were inscribed with the names of prophets, who evidently had the right to immortalize themselves in this way. Something like 200 names occur. The original position of this building is uncertain, but there is reason to think it was not in the temple itself. This was no doubt where the versification was done, perhaps also where copies of the oracles were kept. The room between the cella and the pronaos may have been a waiting-room for the clients while the business of prophecy was going on.

The crop of oracular inscriptions revealed by the excavations is disappointingly meagre—hardly more than a dozen texts, and mostly so wretchedly fragmentary as to suggest they were deliberately smashed by enthusiastic Christians. From the literary sources we learn a little more. Under the Branchidae, high though Apollo's reputation was, his recorded responses hardly show him in a very brilliant light. In one case he appears to condone his clients' leanings towards piracy; a second case is his failure—or perhaps his refusal?—to meet the test prepared by Croesus. A third was that of Pactyes the Lydian. After Cyrus' defeat of Croesus this man attempted to raise the Lydians against their Persian conquerors, but was compelled to fly to Cyme, where he asked for political asylum. The Persians at once demanded his surrender. The Cymaeans, torn between respect for a suppliant and fear of the Persians, asked the advice of Apollo at Branchidae, and were told to give Pactyes up. A certain citizen, however, by name Aristodicus, suspecting that the envoys had falsified the oracle, persuaded them to send others, including himself, and ask again. The god's reply was the same as before. Whereupon Aristodicus proceeded to walk round the temple driving out the sparrows and other birds which were nesting in it. At this a voice was heard from the sacred precinct saying. 'What impiety is this—chasing out the suppliants in my temple?' Aristodicus replied, 'Lord, you protect your suppliants, yet urge the Cymaeans to surrender theirs?' Apollo, fairly trapped, did the best he could. 'Yes, I do—that you may for the impiety perish the sooner, and learn never again to consult the oracle about surrendering a suppliant'. The Cymaeans, now in a worse dilemma than before, evaded it by sending Pactyes to Mitylene.

In later times Apollo scored some notable successes. His forecast of Alexander's victory at Gaugamela was mentioned above; at that same time, while Seleucus was still only an officer under Alexander, the oracle hailed him as king. Furthermore, when Seleucus asked about his return to Greece, the god replied, 'Be in no hurry to reach Europe; Asia is for you far better'. And in 280 B.C., when Seleucus crossed the Dardanelles to set foot in Europe for the first time since Alexander crossed into Asia, he was stabbed to death by his enemy Ptolemy Ceraunus. Apollo's advice regarding the labour troubles at Miletus has already been mentioned. When the emperors Licinius and Constantine were fighting each other for the mastery of the world the former approached the oracle at Didyma concerning the outcome; the god replied, 'Old man, youthful warriors are pressing you sorely, while your strength is undone and hard old age is upon you'. This pessimistic estimate was justified soon afterwards, when Licinius was decisively defeated and deprived of the purple. Later, when asked whether Christ was god or man, Apollo is said to have answered, 'He was a man in the flesh'. This judgment was no doubt predictable, and on the whole Didymean Apollo may be thought to have deserved his reputation. Some of the most interesting oracular texts from Didyma, preserved either on stone or in the literary sources, date to the third century A.D., when Christianity was beginning to make an impact on the eastern Roman empire. At the same time pagan philosophers and intellectuals were responsible for sophisticated refinements of the old pagan beliefs, and monotheistic ideas were becoming increasingly prevalent. The oracle at Didyma seems to have served as something of a mecca for those interested in these theological and religious questions, and played an important part in inspiring and furthering these developments.

A question which is more often asked than answered is, how did the oracles manage to maintain their reputation for knowing the unknowable? How did they succeed in satisfying a multitude of clients for hundreds of years? The enquirers ranged from kings to peasants, and the enquiries from the highest matters of state to the most trivial personal affairs; even if we bear in mind that in such matters one striking success will make up for many failures, it is remarkable that people continued to be willing to make long journeys to consult the prophetic gods and heroes. With regard to questions of policy there is perhaps no great mystery. The priests of a great shrine like Delphi or Didyma, listening day after day to queries on affairs of state from all over the Greek world, were well placed to know what was going on; even without sending out intelligence agents (for which there is no evidence), they must have been well able to offer shrewd and reliable advice. Oracles have a reputation for obscurity, and it is true that they tended to avoid a direct reply. Croesus on a famous occasion was told that by attacking Persia he would destroy a great empire, and did, in fact, destroy his own, but such downright ambiguity is exceptional; more often the client is given some general advice, or advice which he may interpret for himself. Or again, when a woman asks who has stolen her gold earrings, or who is putting the evil eye on her daughter, she will seldom receive a straightforward answer, but will be advised to sacrifice to this or that deity. Nevertheless, mere evasion and obscurity cannot be satisfactory for long, and it is perhaps not excluded that genuine inspiration may have played a part. At all events, the preparations undergone by the priestess, the abstention from food, the inhaling of vapours, and the rest, combined with the general atmosphere of expectation, must have put her in a highly receptive frame of mind.

But the oracle was not the only activity at Didyma. Every

fourth year there was celebrated the festival of the Great Didymeia. Instituted at least as early as 200 B.C., this festival was especially popular under the empire. In addition to the usual athletic events there were contests in oratory, music, and drama; these were presided over by the prophet, but the organization was, as usual, in the hands of the agonothete. We learn that the festival was held only partly at Didyma and partly in Miletus; curiously enough, the contest in tragedy was held in the sanctuary, where no sign whatever of a theatre has been found, while the splendid theatre at Miletus remained for this purpose unused.

The stadium, on the other hand, is still extant. It lies immediately beside the temple on the south side, so close indeed that the steps of the temple actually served as seats for the spectators. The lower steps are covered with names carved upon them to reserve places for particular persons; close on 200 names may still be read, some carefully engraved, some merely scratched. The names are thickest on the lowest steps, which were evidently regarded as the best seats. They are all names of individuals, singly or in groups; no places are reserved for any officials in their official capacity—not even for the prophet or agonothete, who must nevertheless have had their special seats.

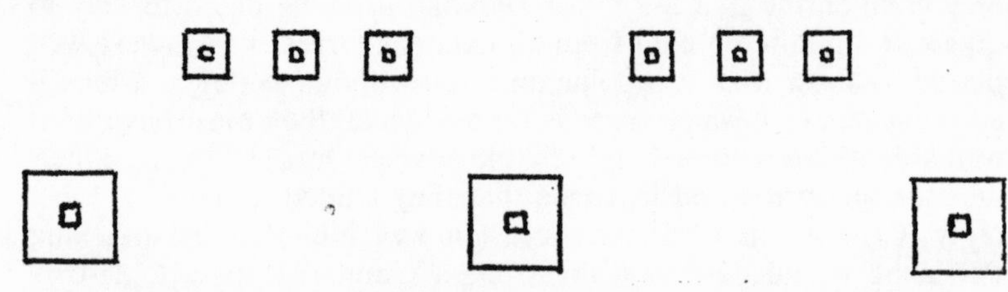

Fig. 47 The starting-sill in the stadium at Didyma

The starting-line for the foot-races is preserved at the east end of the stadium. It differs in some respects from that at Priene. The remains consist of nine stone blocks, three large and six small, pierced with holes for holding upright posts, set in a double line across the stadium. The three large blocks are placed at intervals of about 16 feet (4·88 m.); the six smaller ones are set in two groups of three in the spaces between the large blocks but a little in advance of them. The adjoining sketch shows the original arrangement; but as the stones are set merely in the earth, those on the north have shifted their positions. The excavators explain that the actual starting-line was formed by a cord stretched across between the three large posts; the smaller posts served merely to space the runners equally at the start. In this way the stadium would accommodate eight runners at a time. But the matter may not be as simple as this. The central large post seems to serve no purpose on this theory; moreover, this block has also a horizontal perforation which remains unexplained. Nor is it clear why the smaller posts were not set in line with the larger in the natural way. The starting-lines of the many stadia in the Greek world show such a variety of forms, and offer so many problems, that it is safer to reserve judgment.

A conspicuous feature of the temple is the letters carved in great profusion on the walls and steps of various parts of the building. Much speculation has been aroused as to their purpose. They fall into three groups: (1) the letters IE, (2) one or more abbreviated personal names, and (3) both of these together. Various explanations have been offered, but it is now proposed to regard the personal names as those of slave-owning citizens of Miletus who hired out their men to the temple authorities to work on the construction of the building. IE then denotes slaves of the hieron or temple itself. Where two or three marks appear on one stone, slaves of different owners worked on that block—not necessarily all in the temple itself, perhaps also in the quarry or the workshop where the stones were trimmed. The purpose of the marks is then to indicate to whom payment is due for the handling of that particular block by his slaves; payment was made, as usual in antiquity, by piecework. The marks were, of course, intended to be shaved off when the stones received their final dressing; but the temple was not finished, and this stage was never reached.

Recent excavations at Didyma by the German Archaeological Institute have uncovered a substantial stretch of the sacred way (the visible paving dates to the time of Trajan), with buildings on either side of it, including Roman baths and another structure which appears to have housed a secondary sanctuary. The dedicant, however, is still unknown.

12 Myus and Magnesia

Among the twelve cities of the Ionian League Myus was probably the poorest and most insignificant; Lebedus alone might rival her in this respect. The site now lies solitary and deserted beside the Maeander, well away from normal traffic routes, and is scarcely ever visited. The surviving ruins indeed may be thought not to justify the trouble of reaching them; but anyone who is attracted by out-of-the-way, end-of-the-world places will find the excursion rewarding. Myus lies half an hour's walk to the north-west of the village of Avşar, and may be reached by a tolerable road from Sarıkemer; there is also an alternative approach from the village of Özbaşı, crossing the river by a ferry. The site was dug by the Germans at the time of the excavation of Miletus; in 1964 the work was continued on a small scale, but without producing any striking change in appearance.

Myus was founded, according to legend, by yet another of the sons of Codrus; but the site was poorly chosen and it is likely that almost from the beginning the city was affected by malaria. It may well be due to the depressing and enervating effects of this disease that Myus played no part in the great flowering of Ionian civilization, nor, ever, so far as we know, produced a famous citizen.

A story is told that when Themistocles, the Athenian hero of Salamis in 480 B.C., later fell into disgrace and exile, he made the friendship of the Persian king, and was given by him three towns to supply him with a livelihood—Magnesia for his bread, Lampsacus for his wine, and Myus for his *opson*. This Greek word has no equivalent in English; it is translated in Turkish by *katık*, and means 'something to eat with your bread', whether meat, fish, cheese, olives, or anything else. It illustrates an interesting difference in dietary habits: whereas we eat bread with our meat or fish, the ancient Greeks, like the modern Turks, ate meat or fish with their bread.

Bread was indeed the staff of life; and a Turkish countryman will seldom eat less than the equivalent of half a loaf with his meal. In the case of Myus the *opson* supplied to Themistocles was no doubt mainly fish, for, as the historian Diodorus rightly says, the sea around there was rich in fish; the *dalyan*, or fishery, a few miles to the south-west will bear witness.

Curiously enough, this was not the only occasion when Myus was given as a present by a king. In 201 B.C. Philip V of Macedon was overrunning Asia Minor with his army; being short of supplies, he approached the Magnesians, who gave him a quantity of figs, for they had no corn. When later he laid his hands on Myus, he presented it to the Magnesians in payment for the figs. There can surely not be many free cities which have suffered the indignity of being twice given away to others.

The history of Myus is in the main the story of the Maeander silt. In 499 B.C. a fleet of 200 warships could anchor there, although five years later at the battle of Lade the city could provide no more than three ships, a figure equalled only, among those who were present at all, by the half-city of Phocaea. In the Delian Confederacy, Myus paid a normal tribute of one talent, again equal to the lowest among the Ionian cities. In 390 B.C. she was still at least an independent city, for she was involved in a quarrel with Miletus over a piece of land; by 201 B.C. she was sufficiently reduced to be given away in return for figs; and early in the second century she appears as a mere dependency of Miletus, for we find that city claiming a piece of territory on the grounds that it was sacred to Apollo Terbintheus, the principal deity of Myus. Malaria and the Maeander mud were steadily doing their work; the population became so reduced that by Strabo's time Myus was no longer able to function as a city and was fused in a political union with Miletus. At that date Myus could no longer be reached by sea, but by sailing in small boats some three miles (4·83 km.) up the river. Pausanias tells us graphically what finally happened. 'There was close to Myus a small inlet of the sea'—now represented apparently by the Azap Gölü—

> which the Maeander converted into a lagoon by blocking the entrance with mud; as the sea receded and the water of the lagoon became fresh, such innumerable swarms of mosquitoes arose from it that the inhabitants were obliged to abandon the city. Taking with them all their movable property, including the statues of their gods, they moved to Miletus, and when I was in

Myus, there was nothing there but a white marble temple of Dionysus.

The foundations of this temple may still be seen today, but virtually nothing is standing. The site is marked by a conspicuous Byzantine castle on a knoll beside the river; the lower slope of this hill has been fashioned into two rock-terraces one above the other. The upper of these is flanked by a rock-wall containing a shallow chamber, or niche, with a number of cuttings. This terrace carried a large temple in the Doric order, some 56 feet (17·1 m.) in width; this was probably the temple of Apollo Terbintheus, Lord of the Terebinth. The foundations of one side-wall survive in part, and a row of round holes parallel with it, as if to hold the columns of the peristyle. Supporting this terrace and flanking the lower is a wall of large blocks in the 'Cyclopean' style; on this lower terrace stood the temple of Dionysus seen by Pausanias. There remains only a part of the foundations, a supporting wall, and a single white marble column-drum.

The main habitation was on the next hill to the east, on which are numerous rock-cut houses, tombs, and cisterns.

The extreme scarcity of cut blocks on the site, despite the excavation and the absence of any considerable modern building in the neighbourhood, is explained by their removal to Miletus for constructional purposes there. Be this as it may, it is certain that no other excavated site in Ionia offers so little to the visitor's eye. Myus had presumably public buildings like any other city, but apart from the scanty fragments mentioned no trace of them has come to light (Pl. 65). An exception, although of later date, is the small Byzantine castle called Avşar Kale, standing on the crest of the ridge on which Myus lay.

Magnesia on the Maeander

Cicero remarked that all the Greek colonies in Asia were washed by the sea, with the single exception of Magnesia. The statement is not quite accurate, as Colophon and the other Magnesia are also some way from the coast, but inland settlements are certainly the exception. In actual fact the original site is not known, for Magnesia, like Priene and so many others, changed its position in classical times. The city is remarkable in another way, too: though situated in the heart of Ionia it was, like Notium, founded by Aeolians, and was never a member of the Ionian League. These founders came from the original Magnesia in northern Greece; they are said to have travelled first to Delphi, then to Crete, and finally to Asia. In a later inscription the Magnesians claim to have been the first Greeks to cross into Anatolia.

The scanty history of the early city is mainly a series of calamities; and, in fact, the 'sufferings of the Magnesians' became proverbial. In the seventh century, when Gyges, king of Lydia, was attacking the Ionian cities, Magnesia contrived for special reasons to incur his particular enmity. The story was that a foppish poet of Smyrna, named by a coincidence Magnes, in the course of his travels aroused by his good looks the affections of many men and women, and especially of King Gyges. In Magnesia he made a particular hit with the women, many of whom he seduced; their menfolk thereupon, on the plea that Magnes had slighted their city in his poems, set upon him, tore his clothes, cut off his long hair and generally beat him up. Enraged by this treatment of his favourite, Gyges repeatedly attacked Magnesia and finally captured it. Yet worse was to follow; soon afterwards the city fell to the Cimmerian invaders and was almost annihilated.

But the principal fame of Magnesia in early times lies in its connection with Themistocles. Of the three towns presented to him by the Persian king Artaxerxes (above, p. 204), Magnesia was the one which he chose as his residence. It was to supply him with bread; as we learn that the king had been drawing a revenue of fifty talents a year from the city, Themistocles had certainly no reason to go hungry. He was, in fact, greatly honoured by the citizens; he built a temple of the Mother Goddess and appointed his daughter as priestess. Of his death various accounts are given; Thucydides says he died of disease, but others say he deliberately took poison because he felt himself unable to fulfil his promises to the Persian king. The later version was that while sacrificing a bull to Artemis he collected a bowlful of the blood, drank it, and so died.[1] He was given public burial at Magnesia, and a handsome monument to him was erected in the market-place.

Chiefly owing to its inland situation, Magnesia was never a member of the Delian Confederacy, and its next appearance in history is in 400 B.C., the year following the adventure of Xenophon's Ten Thousand. The Spartan general Thibron, attempting to secure the freedom of the Asiatic cities, succeeded in capturing Magnesia from the Persian satrap; seeing that it was unwalled, we are told, and fearing that the satrap might retake it during his absence, he transferred the city to the neighbouring Mt Thorax (the present Gümüş

Dağı). The site chosen, where the ruins now lie, was the little town of Leucophrys, 'Whitebrow'; it is militarily a very weak one at the foot of the mountains, and moreover the city continued to be unwalled. If greater security was really Thibron's motive for changing the site, he must have been relying on the sanctity of the place, for there was there an ancient and venerable shrine of Artemis, surnamed Leucophryene—the same, in fact, at which Themistocles was sacrificing when he met his end. It seems, however, probable that, as in the case of Priene, the advance of the Maeander silt was at least a contributory reason for the move.

The new city, of course, fell quickly back with the rest into Persian hands, and remained so till the coming of Alexander, to whom it surrendered without resistance. In the troubled Hellenistic times the city seems to have prospered quietly, without playing any significant part in history. An inscription of Magnesia found near Davutlar, if it is in or near its original position, implies that early in the second century Magnesian territory extended to the west coast beyond Mt Thorax. If true, this is surprising: this land was disputed by Priene and Samos, whereas Magnesia looks naturally to the east: it seems more probable that the stone bearing the inscription has been carried from farther east for the construction of the mosque into which it is built. Stones are often carried considerable distances in this way, and these *pierres errantes* frequently cause trouble to students of historical geography.

From early times the Magnesians were often at war with the Ephesians, fighting best, we are told, when inspired by the song of the cicada. The chirruping of this insect, which many people tend to find irritating, seems always to have had an exhilarating effect on the Greeks. Magnesian cavalrymen, like the Colophonians, took hunting dogs into battle with them; these they used as their first line of attack, followed by their servants armed with javelins; the horsemen themselves formed the third line.

When the province of Asia was overrun by Mithridates, the Magnesians were among the minority who declined to accept liberation at his hands. For their loyalty to Rome they were rewarded with the title 'free', and Magnesia became a leading city in the province and a judicial seat of the governor. On a coin of the third century A.D. she describes herself as 'seventh city of Asia'.

Among the distinguished artists of Magnesia was a certain Anaxenor, a singer to the lyre. This man was one of the crowd of artistic youths with whom Mark Antony surrounded himself in the east; he was highly honoured in his own city, and his statue was erected in the theatre. The inscription on the base ended with a quotation from Homer, and Strabo tells us that the stonemason, for lack of space, omitted the final iota of the last word, thereby converting a dative into a nominative and bringing on his city a reputation for illiteracy. The German excavators, digging in the theatre, had the good fortune to find this base still largely intact—an exciting discovery. They report that there is, in fact, just room at the edge of the stone for a narrow letter, and that the surface actually shows a mark there which might be taken for a badly written iota, but is probably only an accidental defect in the stone. Alternatively we might suspect that some Magnesian, tired of the jeers at his city's scholarship, carved the missing letter with his penknife. The stone itself was taken to Berlin.

The principal excavations took place in 1891–93, but the ground is flooded every winter by the neighbouring stream, the ancient Lethaeus, and most of what was unearthed is now buried again. There is indeed little to be seen apart from the ruins of the temple of Artemis Leucophryene, which lie in a flat heap close beside the road.

Artemis had a temple here from at least the sixth century B.C., for remains of that date were found under the present building. This latter was the work of Hermogenes, architect of the temple of Dionysus at Teos, and dates from the early second century B.C. The plan may be traced, with some difficulty, among the jumble of blocks. Interesting features are the internal columns in the pronaos and cella, and the placing of the external columns at twice the usual distance from the temple walls. To this latter feature the term pseudo-dipteral is applied, as if the object were to give the appearance of a double row of columns without the expense of the inner row. Another peculiarity is that the temple faces west, contrary to the normal rule. It is in the Ionic order and stands as usual on flat ground.

Shortly before Hermogenes' temple was begun, in 220 B.C., there occurred a remarkable epiphany of the goddess. In what way exactly she manifested herself we do not know, but on the matter being referred to Apollo at Delphi the god declared that the city and territory of Magnesia should be regarded as holy ground. The Magnesians therefore decided to establish a great quadrennial festival under the name of the Leucophryena, and sent ambassadors all over the Greek world inviting the cities to attend it and to recognize the sanctity of Magnesia in accordance with Apollo's words. The favourable replies of some seventy cities were found by the excavators inscribed on the walls of a hall in the market-place. The inviolability thus conferred finally removed any need for the Magnesians to fortify their city; the walls now to be seen date from early Byzantine times, when Apollo's pronouncements no longer passed current.

The theatre lies at the west foot of the hill just to the south of the temple, but there is very little to see. The curve of the cavea remains, and a fragment of the supporting wall, but the seats are gone; of the stage-building only the top of an arched door and a couple of column-stumps are visible above ground. This theatre nevertheless is, or was, interesting, as it is one of the half-dozen in which a tunnel was installed leading from the stage-building to the middle of the orchestra. These tunnels were presumably used for the appearance of actors rising from the underworld, as is required in one or two of the surviving Greek tragedies. When the present writer first visited Magnesia in 1939 the tunnel was visible in the form of a deep trench, lined with masonry and filled with brambles, leading out from under the stage into the orchestra and branching right and left in the form of a letter T. It has now been filled in, no doubt in order to avoid the nuisance caused by animals falling into it; that this can easily happen was proved by the writer's companion, who had the misfortune to do so himself. The only other tunnel of this kind in Asia Minor is that at Tralles, the modern Aydın, but long occupation of the acropolis hill by the military has obliterated this also.

Higher up to the south are some scanty traces of a smaller theatre or odeum, and farther to the west the outline of a stadium can be discerned; for the rest the ruins of Magnesia are once again covered by the mud.

Note

1 This method of suicide, though seldom if ever actually imitated, was reckoned perfectly possible in antiquity. Pliny says that bull's blood coagulates and hardens very quickly, and is therefore considered poisonous to drink fresh, except that at Aegira in Greece the priestess drank it before descending into a cave to prophesy. How much truth there may be in this the present writer is not able to say.

13 Heracleia under Latmus

Until the last few years Heracleia, tucked into the far corner of the lake of Bafa, was highly inaccessible and rarely visited. The writer in 1946, and Freya Stark in 1952, made the journey in a small boat from the west end of the lake; and this may still be done. But the recent opening of the fine new tarmac road from Söke to Milâs has made things easier. Skirting the south shore of the lake, and towards its east end, the road passes a small landing-stage, with a coffee-house across the road opposite; from here a motor-boat may be hired to Kapıkırı and Heracleia. By land a passable road leads from the village of Bafa in six miles (9·65 km.) to the site; it crosses at one point a causeway and bridge over a marshy stream. If the bridge is not in good repair, a pleasant half-hour's walk brings the traveller to his destination. The village is deserted in high summer, when the inhabitants move to their *yayla*, or summer quarters, about a mile along the shore of the lake.

It is safe to say that no one who makes the excursion to Heracleia will be disappointed. Though situated on the Ionian coast—for the lake of Bafa was in antiquity an arm of the sea—the city belongs, in character as in history, to Caria. The scene is dominated by Mt Latmus, whose serrated crest has given it the name of Beş Parmak, the Five Fingers. Some 4,500 feet (1371·6 m.) in height, this wild and rocky mountain sends down a spur towards the village of Kapıkırı, and up this ridge run the walls of Heracleia, in beautiful masonry unusually well preserved. They rise, in fact, about 1,600 feet (487·7 m.) from the lake, but they seem to climb into the sky, twisting and turning in a fantastic wilderness of rocks. The visitor who follows them up and up finds himself, says Freya Stark, 'curiously uncertain as to where the confines of reality end or begin'. The contrast with the rich lands and gentle contours of Ionia is complete.

The city was Carian from the beginning. In early times it bore the name of Latmus, distinguished only in gender from the mountain above, and under this name it paid a tribute of one talent a year in the Delian Confederacy in the fifth century. This assessment puts it among the more important of the non-Greek townships of Caria. Mausolus, dynast of Caria in the fourth century, captured it by a rather mean trick, after winning its confidence by a pretence of friendship and enticing the citizens to open their gates as his army marched by. Mausolus probably atoned for this attack by building the fine walls round the old city of Latmus (M on the plan). However, the great fortifications of Heracleia itself should date to the period after Alexander the Great, *c.* 300 B.C., and may be compared with the Lysimachean fortifications of Ephesus. Heracleia was never, in fact, a city of much account. With little in the way of territory, its prosperity must come from the sea; and with Miletus at the mouth of the gulf its prospects were poor. As the Maeander gradually converted the gulf into a lake, Heracleia became completely cut off.

Nevertheless, Heracleia-under-Latmus has at least one claim to fame in its association with the enigmatic figure of Endymion. The legends concerning Endymion are confused and contradictory to the point of relating apparently to two different characters. Some say that he was a king of Elis in the Peloponnese, that he set his sons to run a race at Olympia to decide who should succeed him, and in this way originated the Olympic foot-race. But the better-known stories tell how he was loved by the moon Selene and slept eternally on Mt Latmus. Zeus, it was said, was fond of the handsome lad and gave him leave to choose whatever he wished; Endymion chose to sleep for ever deathless and ageless. The choice appears a strange one; but there was perhaps more in it than meets the eye. It was whispered that Endymion had an amour with Hera, and when this came to Zeus' notice, it may be that the choice he offered was similar to that offered in more recent times between gun, rope, and poison-cup. At all events Selene saw him sleeping on Latmus and came down to him and kissed him, and some say she bore him fifty daughters. This might be thought enough to wake him; and, in fact, his sleep cannot have been really eternal, for the men of Heracleia pointed out his tomb in a cave on Latmus, and his sanctuary also on the mountain. A later account rationalizes the story. According to this, Endymion was the first man to discover the true orbit of the moon; having done nothing with his life but study for this, he was said to have slept for thirty years. Let other scientists take note. Later still, certain Christian writers declared that Endymion was a Carian mystic who desired to learn from the moon the name of God; on learning it he died, and his mortal remains were preserved to that time in Caria, where his coffin was opened every year and the bones were observed to emit a humming sound—presumably in an effort to communicate the name of God to man.

The outstanding feature of the ruins of Heracleia is undoubtedly the great city walls. Taken in their entirety they show, still standing intact, almost every feature of a classical fortification. Towers and curtains, roofs and windows, gates and posterns, internal stairways leading to the parapets, all are in excellent condition; here and there,

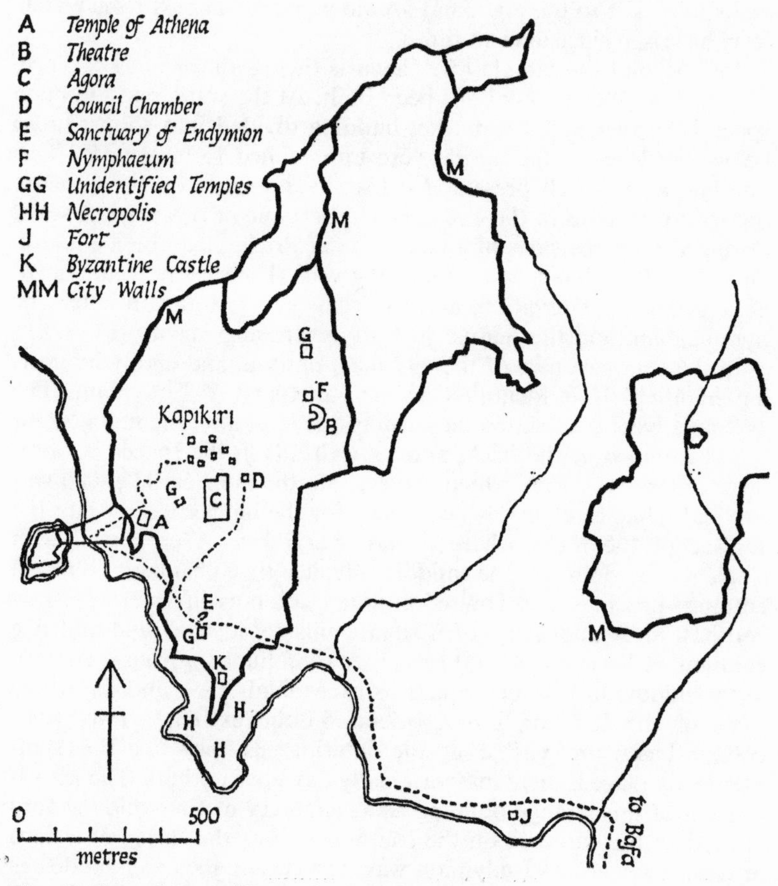

Fig. 48 Plan of Heracleia under Latmus

where the wall is gone, the beds for the blocks may be seen climbing the steep rock-faces like stairs (Pl. 66, 71, 72, 73).

But the lower town, too, has much of interest to show. To the traveller approaching from the lake the most conspicuous building is the well-preserved temple on the bluff above the landing-stage. It is identified as the temple of Athena by an inscription still lying beside it. The form is simple, merely a cella with walls standing to their full height, and a pronaos; there were columns in front, but none at the back or sides (Pl. 70).

The little island opposite the landing-stage was a peninsula in antiquity and was included in the fortifications; the remains of the walls joining it to the mainland are now under water, for the water-level has risen since ancient times.

Just beyond the temple of Athena is the agora, or market-place, on which a village school has been built. At the south end the open space is supported by a market-building divided into shops; those below the level of the agora were approached from outside. This building also is well preserved. Close to the agora on the east are the scanty remains of the council chamber; one or two rows of seats, arranged on three sides of a square as at Priene, may be made out, and part of the handsome supporting wall. The theatre to the north is in poorish preservation, and the ruins of the fountain-house, or nymphaeum, and the temple just above are also scanty (Pl. 67).

In the southern part of the city is an unusual and highly interesting building. It is identified as the sanctuary of Endymion. The accompanying plan shows the form of the structure; the main chamber is rounded at the back, and its wall fills in the spaces between large outcrops of rock which project into the interior. The wall was originally higher than it is now; beds for the blocks are cut into the surface of the rocks where it ran over them. A cross-wall with originally a door in the middle divides this chamber from an entrance-porch with a row of unfluted columns in front; the row consists, most unusually, of a square pilaster at each end and five columns in between. An odd number of columns, giving a column in the middle instead of a space, is exceedingly rare, and the whole form of the building is exceptional in the extreme. Two other column-bases are visible in the interior; as they are not symmetrically placed, there may originally have been others. The identification of this strange building as a sanctuary of Endymion is very attractive; the entrance on the south-west suits the shrine of a hero or demi-god such as Endymion was; temples of gods and goddesses were entered from the east. As was noted above, Endymion had a

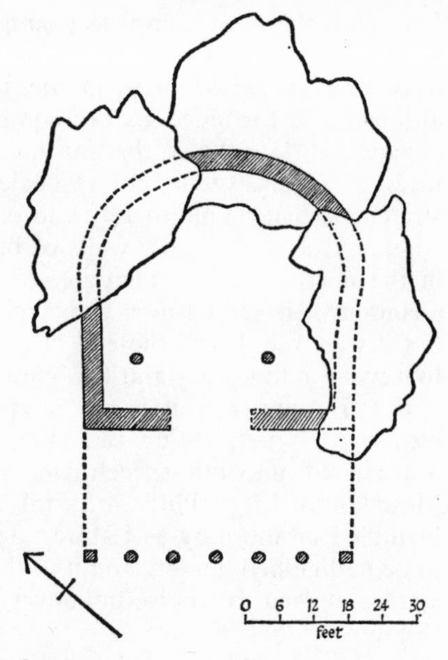

Fig. 49 Plan of the sanctuary of Endymion

sanctuary on Mt Latmus; either this is a second shrine, or the spot is counted as being on the mountain (Pl. 67).

If the visitor will walk a few minutes south from this sanctuary to the headland beyond the Byzantine castle, he will look down on one of the strangest cemeteries he has ever seen. The graves are of the Carian type, a rectangular hole sunk in the rock and covered with a separate lid. The surface of the rocks is pitted with scores of these tombs, many of them side by side in pairs; a few of the lids are lying close by, but all the graves have, of course, long since been opened and plundered. Some of them are now visible under water, submerged by the rise in the level of the lake (Pl. 68).

To the east of the city of Heracleia lies another fortified enclosure, which is certainly the site of the older foundation of Latmus, occupied until the fourth century when the inhabitants were moved to Heracleia (M). The walls are substantial, and especially notable are two small fortresses (*tetrapyrgia*), one in the north curtain wall, the other free-standing in the north part of the town. This was probably the house of the ruler of Latmus. Inside the walls public and religious buildings can be distinguished, as well as many houses.

Latmus is the most complete example of a pre-Greek Carian town in Asia Minor and is therefore of very great interest. It seems to have been occupied between the sixth and fourth centuries B.C., although the fortifications are comparatively late in date, perhaps erected by Mausolus in the fourth century. The walls consist of two faces of regularly cut and embossed blocks, laid as headers and stretchers, that is, alternately end on and side on. They have been compared in style to the walls of buildings attributed to Mausolus in the nearby Carian sanctuary of Labraynda. After Latmus was abandoned, it served as a cemetery for the new city of Heracleia, but it was resettled at the end of the Byzantine period, as is shown by several late houses and two churches at the centre of the site.

But first and last it is the mountain that stays in the visitor's memory. Homer, listing the allies of the Trojans, refers to the 'Carians of uncouth speech who dwell around Miletus and the Mountain of Lice' (Phtheiron); this curiously named mountain was identified in antiquity as Latmus. Some, however, feeling the name to be undignified, understood it as the 'mountain of the Phtheirians', a tribe of men otherwise unknown. The villagers of Kapıkırı deny strenuously that lice are to be found among them. Scorpions there certainly are, and we have it on the authority of Aristotle himself that the scorpions of Latmus never sting strangers, but only the local inhabitants. For this the present writer cannot speak, but he can answer for it from painful experience that the same does not apply to bees.

Latmus was always a holy mountain, and in the Middle Ages it was a favourite resort for anchorites and other holy men. Numerous monasteries and hermitages which they founded may still be seen; but in general they are high up among the wastes of rock, and are virtually inaccessible to the ordinary traveller.

14 Sardis

About the year 700 B.C. the kingship of Lydia was held by a certain Candaules. This man had the curious fancy to fall in love with his own wife, and it was his habit to extol her loveliness, especially to his favourite minister, by name Gyges. Dissatisfied, however, with the degree of enthusiasm shown by the prudent minister, he was one day moved by an evil genius to address him thus: 'Gyges, it is clear that you doubt what I tell you of my wife's beauty; seeing is believing, so we must contrive that you see her naked'. Gyges was horrified, but the king reassured him:

> Don't be alarmed; she will not even know that you have seen her. I will place you behind the bedroom door; there you can watch her as she disrobes, and as she walks to the bed with her back towards you do you slip out without being seen.

Gyges, seeing there was nothing for it, reluctantly consented, and all took place as the king had arranged—except that as the minister left the bedroom the queen caught sight of him out of the corner of her eye. With great self-control she neither screamed nor gave any sign; but next morning, in the presence of the most faithful of her retinue, she summoned him to her and said: 'Gyges, you have seen me naked; you must therefore choose one of two courses. Either you must kill Candaules, marry me, and be king of Lydia, or you must perish here and now'. Finding entreaties vain, Gyges elected to save himself. That night the queen installed him behind the self-same door, dagger in hand, and when the king was asleep, he crept out and struck him dead. In this way the throne of Lydia passed to a new dynasty. Not, however, without disturbance; many of the citizens took up arms in the cause of their murdered sovereign, and civil war was imminent. Finally it was agreed to abide by the decision of the oracle at Delphi, and this proved to be in Gyges' favour.

The vast 'Gygian treasure' of gold and silver afterwards preserved in Apollo's sanctuary testified to the new king's sense of gratitude.

The new dynasty, thus (according to Herodotus) inaugurated, lasted for a hundred and fifty years, during which period the Lydian nation enjoyed its great age of prosperity. Of its earlier history little is known with certainty. Homer makes no mention of Lydians; but among the allies of Troy he speaks of certain Maeonians who lived about Mt Tmolus and Lake Gygaea—that is, in the later Lydia. Herodotus says that these Maeonians voluntarily changed their name to Lydians at an early date, but this is now generally agreed to be an error. Much more likely the Lydians were a separate nation who at some unknown period invaded and occupied Maeonia; even in antiquity the two races were regarded by some writers as distinct.

A strong tradition, led by Herodotus, said that Etruria in Italy was colonized from Lydia. In consequence of a long famine the nation divided into two halves, one of which stayed in Asia while the other sailed to find a new home in the west. Modern research has, in fact, tended to confirm this colonization from the east, and dates the settlement to about 800 B.C. At that time Rome was not yet founded, and for centuries the Etruscan civilization was far in advance of any other in Italy.[1]

Of Lydia and its capital Sardis under Gyges and his successors a good deal has been said above. The gradual subjugation of the Greek cities of the coast by Gyges himself, Ardys, Alyattes, and Croesus is already familiar. Despite these generally hostile relations the two races entertained a mutual respect and admiration, and each learned much from the other's civilization. Lydia had relations with Assyria too: Gyges is readily recognizable in the 'Gugu of Luddi' who sent ambassadors to Assurbanipal.

Lydian customs, says Herodotus, were much the same as the Greek, with one notable exception. Girls normally earned their dowries by prostitution, a practice which carried no reproach. The Lydians claimed to have invented all the games which were common to them and to the Greeks—not athletic games, but such pastimes as dice, knucklebones, and ball. The very ancient game of *pessoi*, a kind of draughts or chess, they did not claim as theirs; and the claim to the invention of ball-play was certainly not justified; ball-games were familiar, not only to Nausicaa, in the *Odyssey*, but in early times in Egypt. Rather surprisingly, we hear next to nothing of them in classical Greece.

A more important invention which was attributed, apparently with

54 Priene. Theatre

55 Priene. Inscribed Wall in the Gymnasium

56 Miletus. Bouleuterion

57 Miletus. View towards Theatre Hill

58 Miletus. Covered Passage in the Theatre

59 Miletus. The Baths

60 Miletus. The Agora

61 Miletus. The Theatre, with the former island of Lade in the background

62 Didyma. Medusa head from the frieze of the Temple

63 Didyma. Temple of Apollo

64 (1) The four 'neocorate' temples at Ephesus. (2) The two ends of the double temple at Sardis. (3) Clarian Artemis. (4) Clarian Apollo. (5) Archaic Heracles at Erythrae. (6) Phocaean Seal

65 Myus. The site from the south-east

66 Heracleia. Rock-cut beds for wall-blocks

67 Heracleia. "Sanctuary of Endymion"

68 Heracleia. The Necropolis

69 Heracleia. Market Building. Mount Latmus in the background

70 Heracleia. Temple of Athena

73 Heracleia. Walls

71 Heracleia. Walls

72 Heracleia. Walls

76 Sardis. Temple of Artemis

74 Sardis. Temple of Artemis

75 Sardis. Ionic Capital from the Temple

77 Sardis. Curious rock-formations in the neighbouring hills

78 Sardis. Lydian Rock-Tombs. Acropolis in the background

justice, to the Lydians is that of coined money. Certainly earlier civilizations such as the Hittite and Egyptian seem to have made no use of coinage, though metal bars and rings were used in some places as currency; the Greek word 'drachma' meant originally 'a handful' of these. But of actual coins of precious metal guaranteed in weight by the government stamp we know no earlier specimens than the Lydian. These, with very few exceptions, bear no inscription, but merely the lion's head which was the royal emblem of Sardis. They were made at first of 'electrum', an alloy of gold and silver; tests have shown that the gold content varied from about 36 to 53 per cent. This variation may have shaken public confidence, and it was perhaps for this reason that Croesus, the last Lydian king, introduced coinage of pure gold and pure silver. The new invention was at once adopted by the Greek cities of the coast, and indeed spread rapidly over the whole world.

The gold for these Lydian coins was obtained, in part at least, from the river Pactolus, a small stream which flows down from Mt Tmolus (Bozdağ) through Sardis to join the Hermus. From this and other gold-bearing rivers an early method of collecting the dust was to lay sheepskins in a shallow part of the stream to catch the particles of gold; the legend of the Golden Fleece is supposed to have arisen in this way, for Colchis, too, had its gold-bearing river, a branch of the Phasis. The Pactolus itself was quickly exhausted, and even in Strabo's time had ceased to yield any gold. It had, however, sufficed to make the names of Gyges and Croesus proverbial for wealth.

With Alyattes' expulsion of the Cimmerians from Asia Minor the Lydian power rose to new heights. Phrygia, disastrously weakened by the northern barbarians, was annexed and Smyrna was destroyed, though Alyattes failed before Clazomenae and was only partially successful at Miletus. Under his successor Croesus the Lydian empire was extended over the whole Anatolian peninsula except for part of the south coast. Croesus was the last and most famous of the Lydian kings, and many tales, more or less historical, were told about him; a number of these have already been related.

The annexation of Phrygia brought the Lydians into immediate contact with the Persian empire, with only the river Halys (the Kızılırmak) between them. Learning of the increasing power of the Persians under their new king, Cyrus, Croesus determined upon an attempt to check it. Encouraged by his wrong interpretation of Apollo's oracle (above, p. 201), he crossed the Halys into Persian territory. Following an indecisive battle, he thought it wise to retreat and collect a larger force; but Cyrus, with unexpected vigour, passed to the offensive, invaded Lydia, and after defeating Croesus' forces outside Sardis penned them up in the capital. The siege lasted for a fortnight before the city fell; of its capture Herodotus gives the following account. An earlier Lydian king, by name Meles, had a concubine who bore him a lion; the soothsayers, consulted about this prodigy, declared that if the lion were carried round the fortifications of Sardis, the city would be impregnable. Meles therefore had this done, but omitted one part on the south side which seemed so precipitous as to need no supernatural protection. It happened that a Lydian soldier dropped his helmet at this point and had to clamber down the rock to retrieve it; a Persian observed this, and the following day, with a large number of companions, scaled the acropolis at the same place and took the city by surprise (546 B.C.).

Croesus himself was taken prisoner and by Cyrus' orders placed in fetters on a pyre to be burned alive. As he waited for the fire to be lit he groaned and uttered three times the name of Solon. Cyrus' curiosity was stirred and he bade the interpreters ask who this Solon might be. Croesus replied that he was an Athenian who had formerly visited Sardis and made light of Croesus' wealth and prosperity, bidding him reckon no man happy so long as he lives, but to wait for the end. Cyrus, impressed, ordered Croesus to be taken down from the pyre; but by this time the flames were ablaze and he could no longer be approached. Thereupon he called on Apollo to save him, and at once a storm gathered from a blue sky and a violent downpour extinguished the fire. Convinced by this that Croesus was more than an ordinary man, Cyrus ordered his fetters to be removed and bade him sit beside him. After a long silence Croesus asked, 'What are those men doing over there?' 'Plundering your city', replied Cyrus, 'and carrying off your wealth.' 'Not mine any longer', said Croesus; 'it is *your* property they are pillaging'. Cyrus at once ordered the plunder to cease.

Such is Herodotus' version of the end of the Lydian monarchy. Other ancient accounts differ considerably, but the existence of these legends, with their miraculous elements, only a hundred years later, is striking evidence of the impression made by Croesus on Greek minds.

The end of the monarchy was the end of Lydian greatness. Hitherto formidable warriors, the Lydians are henceforth regarded, together with the Phrygians, as effeminate and fit only to be the slaves of Greeks. This was due (again according to Herodotus) to deliberate policy on Cyrus' part. Angered by Pactyes' attempt to organize a revolt (above, p. 200), the Persian king had a mind to sell all Lydians into slavery. Croesus, however, interceded and urged him merely to forbid them the use of arms and make them bring up their sons to shopkeeping and the practice of music. Thus their warlike spirit was subdued, and in later times the Lydian and Phrygian were among the principal musical 'modes' of the ancients. The Phrygian was considered exciting and emotional, the Lydian decorous and educative, but we do not really know what they were like. Ancient music is a difficult subject, and was regarded almost as a branch of mathematics; in general it was simple, its elements merely melody and rhythm. 'Harmony' to the ancients meant a scale or harmonious succession of sounds; in its modern sense of a harmonious blending of sounds it was hardly known to them. One or two ancient hymns have been found inscribed on stone with the musical notation entered above; converted to modern notation (supposing this to have been correctly done) they sound thin and strange to European ears.

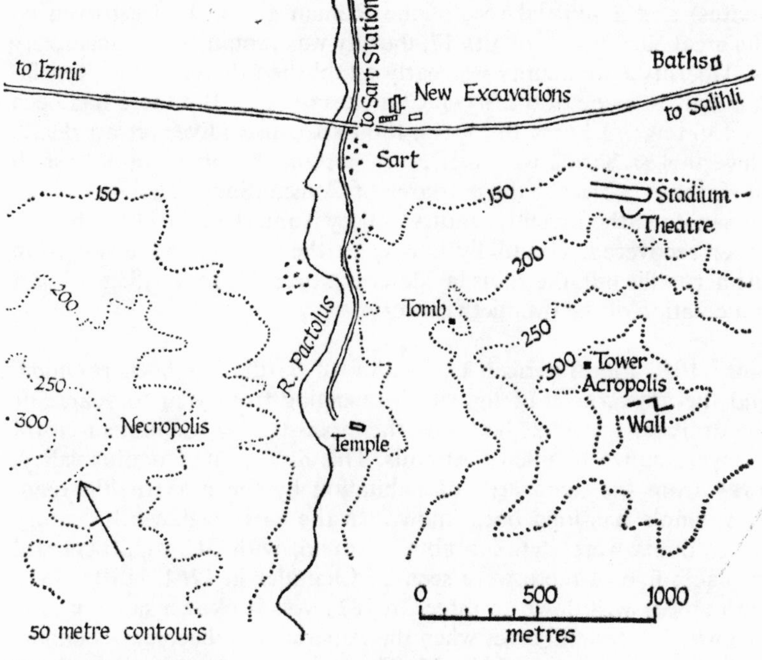

Fig. 50 Plan of Sardis

Sardis nevertheless continued to be an important city. First as the residence of the Persian satraps, then under the Hellenistic kings, it was always a place of consequence. In 213 B.C. Achaeus, a member of the Syrian royal family, had proclaimed himself king in Asia Minor; hunted down by the legitimate king, Antiochus III, he shut himself up in Sardis. Then occurred an almost exact repetition of the capture by Cyrus. A Cretan named Lagoras in Antiochus' army noticed a precipitous place with a gully below, into which dung and corpses of animals were habitually thrown by the inhabitants, so that the place was constantly full of vultures and other carrion birds. He remarked acutely that these birds when replete used to perch on the city walls above, and inferred that the walls must normally be unmanned at that point, which was accordingly selected for a surprise attack. It is not now possible to identify the place, or places, where these attacks were made. The soft friable rock of the acropolis has crumbled and washed away, carrying most of the fortification with it. The knife-edge hills so characteristic of the region are due to this peculiarity of the ground.

In the province of Asia, Sardis was the capital of a district (conventus) and a judicial seat of the Roman governor. Destroyed by the great earthquake of A.D. 17, the city was rebuilt by the generosity of Tiberius. Christianity was early established there, and in Revelation Sardis is one of the Seven Churches of Asia. But there had been backsliding: 'I know thy ways; thou art called alive, yet art dead'. Nevertheless Sardis was later an important bishopric, ranked sixth of all those subject to the patriarch of Constantinople. Sacked by the Sassanids in the seventh century and by Tamerlane in 1401, the city never recovered. Gradually buried by the soil washed down from the acropolis hill, the ruins lay deserted; even the little village of Sart is a creation of the twentieth century.

Since 1958 the American excavation of Sardis has been resumed, and the appearance of the site is changing from year to year. For the ordinary traveller, however, the most striking monument is still the well-known temple of Artemis. This lies up the Pactolus valley, away from the main area of habitation by the modern highroad. The temple has long been known. In the early eighteenth century six columns were standing above ground, with the architrave still in place; five of these were seen by Chandler in 1764, but by 1812 the number was down to three. In 1824 von Prokesch saw only the two which were still erect when the American archaeologists undertook the excavation in 1910–14. The task was a vast one, requiring the removal of a 30-foot (9·1 m.) depth of earth at the east end; the original ground-level may still be seen (Pl. 74, 76).

In 499 B.C., during the course of the Ionian revolt against the Persians, Sardis was sacked and burned by the Greeks; on this occasion Herodotus mentions that the temple of the native goddess Cybebe (that is Cybele) was destroyed by fire. Cybele being the principal deity of Sardis, her temple would surely be rebuilt, and the early explorers in modern times supposed the extant building to be no other than this. It was therefore something of a surprise when the first excavations revealed numerous inscriptions, in Greek and in Lydian, proving the temple to be that of Artemis. More remarkable still, one of these inscriptions refers to 'those who dwell in the sanctuary of Artemis *and Zeus*'. And in fact the building proves to be indeed a double temple, divided into two nearly equal parts by a cross-wall, close to which are the bases for two cult-statues, back to back. It was accordingly supposed that the two halves belonged respectively to Artemis and Zeus—Artemis on the west and Zeus on the east. Much later, in the second century A.D., the cult-statues of these deities were replaced by statues of the Emperor Antoninus Pius and his wife Faustina, to whom the temple was presumably rededicated. The latest investigations, however, have caused these views to be reconsidered. Zeus' share in the temple is now discredited, and the partition of the cella is believed to have been first made by Antoninus Pius, who joined a cult of the deified Faustina to that of Artemis. An interesting coin of Sardis, struck under the Emperor Elagabalus (A.D. 218–22), shows two temple-fronts, each of eight columns, seen obliquely; above each is its cult-statue in a shrine. One statue is female, the other of uncertain sex. It is probable that this coin shows the two ends of the double temple of Artemis and Faustina (Pl. 64).

The building is in the Ionic order, standing as usual on low ground, with eight columns at the short ends and twenty on the sides. There were also fourteen interior columns, none of which remain, and a further six in each pronaos, two of which are slenderer than the rest and stand on high pedestals. These four are the only columns actually found whose fluting was carried out. The high pedestals are unique in Greek architecture, except possibly in the Artemisium at Ephesus, and may be a Lydian feature. Of all these columns two are still complete, and thirteen others stand to a part of their height. The temple was pseudo-dipteral on the flanks, with the columns at twice the usual distance from the cella walls. The Ionic capitals are among the most beautiful known, and the decoration on the bases is reminiscent of that at Didyma (Pl. 75).

At the west end, just outside the line of the north wall of the cella, excavation revealed a flight of steps which may still be seen. They belong without doubt to the existing temple, but their position is utterly abnormal. The arrangement of steps at the west end was evidently unusual; a conjectural attempt at a restoration was made by the excavators, but the question is so uncertain that on the plan, Fig. 51, it has been thought wiser to show only the steps whose position has actually been determined by excavation.

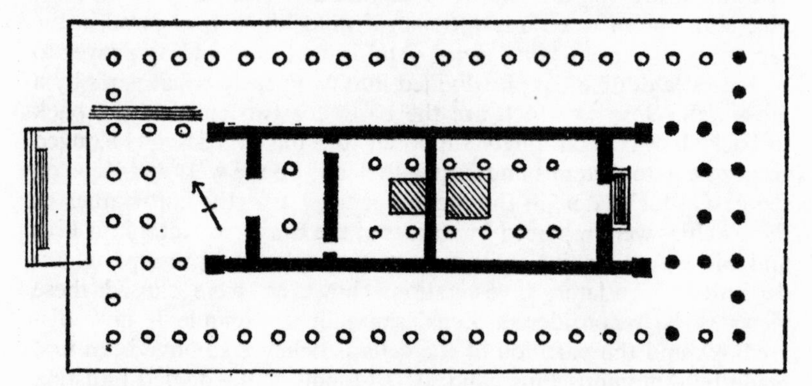

Fig. 51 Plan of the temple of Artemis at Sardis

Also at the west end of the temple is an earlier structure which was evidently an altar. Since it is not quite in alignment with the temple walls, it was formerly thought that it must be the altar of an earlier temple on the same site; but this view also is now disputed. The present belief is that the altar, constructed probably about 400 B.C., stood alone during the greater part of the fourth century; for generations the worship of Artemis was centred only upon this. The existing temple—the only one ever to have stood on the site—was begun about 300 B.C. Contrary to the normal rule it faced towards the west; given the already existing precinct this was natural, or even inevitable, to avoid making it look eastward into the slope of the hill.

By the end of the third century the cella at least was built and in use; a long inscription of about that date carved on the cella wall relates to a loan of money issued by the temple treasury. In the second century construction continued and a start was made upon the surrounding columns; but the work proceeded very slowly, or perhaps came to a complete halt, until the Roman imperial period. It was no doubt set back by the severe earthquake of A.D. 17, from which Sardis, we are told, suffered more than any other city. A metrical inscription on the base of the fourth column from the north

ΝΑΝΝΑΣΔΙΟΝΥΣΙΚΛΕΟΣΑΡΤΕΜΙΔΙ

Fig. 52 Inscription in Lydian and Greek

at the east end records that that column was the first to be erected; since the style of the script indicates the second century A.D., it is likely that the work was restarted by Antoninus Pius (138–161) when he joined the cult of his wife to that of Artemis. Even then the temple was never quite finished, as appears from the absence of fluting on the columns.

The temple of Faustina was entered from the east by a door still partly preserved. Its threshold lies 6 feet (1·83 m.) above the level of the temple platform, and was approached by a flight of six steps between projecting wings; of these nothing now remains in place.

Standing on the north side of the temple, towards the west end, is a tall pedestal bearing an inscription in Greek in honour of a woman who is described by the Lydian word *kauein*, a priestess. Lying on the slope to the north of the temple, farther to the east, is a statue-base of the fourth century B.C. with a bilingual inscription in Lydian and Greek (see Fig. 52 and Appendix 4).

Close beside the north-east corner of the temple is a small church or chapel which may date back to the fourth century.

The hills around Sardis, and especially those to the west of the Pactolus, contain hundreds of Lydian tombs, the earliest of which belong to the seventh century B.C. Many of these were cleared by the first excavation party, but most have become buried again by the constant shifting of the soil. The standard type comprises a passage leading to a door about 6 feet (1·83 m.) high, closed by a slab or slabs of stone; at the outer end of this passage stood tall stelae with floral decoration and probably painted inscriptions. Inside the door is the burial-chamber cut out of the solid hillside, with gabled roof and funeral couches on either side and at the back.

These couches held tub-shaped sarcophagi of terracotta, painted red, white, and black. A group of three tombs recently re-excavated may be visited by following up the side-valley which opens on the west about a quarter of a mile (402·3 m.) to the south of the temple; the tombs are on the south side of the hollow in which the valley ends, close above a vineyard. (But it is advisable to take a guide.) This excursion is worth while if only for the attractive views of the acropolis which it affords, and for the remarkable pinnacles and buttresses into which the soft rock has been eroded (Pl. 77, 78).

A tomb of quite different type stands on the west slope of the acropolis hill. It has the form of a stepped pyramid, but only the lower part is preserved. The style of the masonry shows that it dates to the period of Persian domination in the fifth to fourth centuries B.C. Perhaps 900 years later than this is another tomb in the east bank of the Pactolus some 500 yards (457·2 m.) south of the main road. It consists of a vaulted chamber with wall-paintings of peacocks and other birds.

The recent excavations have taken place chiefly in the Pactolus valley by the modern village and on the plain to the north. Lydian remains have come to light in every part, and it appears that the city of Croesus was actually greater in extent than the Hellenistic and Roman cities which succeeded it. At the time of writing the principal excavations are on the north side of the main road some 200 yards (182·9 m.) east of the Pactolus bridge. Some of the buildings, notably the gymnasium and the synagogue, have now been strikingly restored, and convey the splendour, grandeur, and scale of Roman city-building in a way which may surprise the visitor used to the usual display of foundation courses and broken columns. The small finds are full of interest, and it is intended eventually to exhibit them in the museum at Manisa.

The chief building-complex immediately beside the road comprises a gymnasium and adjoining structures. The gymnasium has a north and south hall, with an impressive entrance building on the east; farther to the east was the open court of the palaestra. The gymnasium as a whole dates to the second century A.D.; the marble façade was added under the Emperors Caracalla and Geta in A.D. 212. A Byzantine reconstruction about A.D. 400 is recorded by a metrical inscription written round the sides of the court.

Immediately to the south-east of the gymnasium is the Jewish synagogue, identified by the inscriptions found in it; this building appears to have been originally constructed in the third century and repaired about A.D. 400.

Adjoining the gymnasium on the south is a row of Byzantine shops, and between these and the present highroad the excavators have uncovered a stretch of the ancient street, a part of the great Royal Road which led up from the coast to the interior of the Persian empire. The street, of late Roman date, is about 30 feet (9·1 m.) wide and paved with marble blocks; it had a colonnaded sidewalk on either side. This road was later superimposed by another of Byzantine date, and this in turn by the Ottoman road which remained in use till the construction of the present highway in 1952.

Nearly a mile farther to the east, again close beside the road, is a vast structure of Roman date which the recent excavations have shown to be a bathing establishment. Of the theatre and stadium the positions are recognizable, but nothing remains standing. The numerous fragments of city-wall which are visible in various places belong to the fifth century A.D., when it seems that the city was deliberately reduced in size. The early fortifications have almost entirely disappeared, but on the north side of the acropolis, not far from the top, a handsome tower is preserved in its lower part. At first believed to be Hellenistic, built perhaps by Antiochus III, this is now regarded as being probably of Lydian construction.

In 1965 an interesting and unusual feature of the city came to light. Enclosed by a high wall, the excavators found an area half an acre in extent occupied by shops and workrooms—a striking anticipation of the *souqs* and oriental bazaars familiar today. Not least remarkable is the date of this complex, which belongs to the period following the expulsion of the Cimmerians in the early part of the seventh century B.C.

Among the many recent discoveries not the least interesting is an installation on the right bank of the Pactolus where the gold from the river was refined from the early sixth century onwards. Elsewhere much restoration has been done.

Bin Tepe

Some six miles (9·65 km.) to the north and north-west of Sardis, on a ridge between the Hermus plain and the Gygaean Lake (now Marmara Gölü), is the great Lydian necropolis called by the Turks the Thousand Hills. These tumuli are conspicuous from the Sardis road. A thousand is an exaggeration, but there are probably over a hundred. They are more easily visited now than formerly, since the construction in recent years of a new bridge over the river just to the east of Ahmetli. Beyond the bridge the roads are bad and only fit for a jeep; except in summer they may be impassable.

Three of the mounds are noticeably larger than the rest. The largest of all, at the east end of the ridge, is identified with the tomb of Alyattes described by Herodotus, who was much impressed by its vast size. The base, he says, is formed of huge blocks of stone, the upper part being a mound of earth; on the summit are five pillars. He estimates the circumference at over three-quarters of a mile. The monument was erected by the tradesmen, artisans, and prostitutes of Sardis, and the five pillars were inscribed with a record of the work done by each class; the prostitutes' share was found to be the largest.

The existing mound answers very well to Herodotus' description. Its general appearance must have resembled that of the 'Tomb of Tantalus' at Smyrna; there is in each case a circular wall of masonry at the base, surmounted by a conical pile. Of the inscribed pillars, however, nothing has been found; instead, there lies on the summit a spherical stone, 10 feet (3·05 m.) in diameter, attached to a rectangular base. This is thought to be a sort of phallus, such as frequently stood on sepulchral tumuli. The mound was first examined archaeologically in 1853, when a marble burial-chamber was found in the interior, approached by stone-lined passages; it had, as usual, been plundered. The excavators have recently closed the entrance to these passages, and the tomb-chamber is not ordinarily accessible.

Herodotus' description is not the only ancient notice of this monument that we have. A fragment of the satiric poet Hipponax, who wrote perhaps a hundred years before Herodotus, is addressed to a friend in Lydia bidding him join the poet in Ionia. The fragment is corrupt and difficult, but according to an accepted text it says:

> Traverse, Tearus, the whole road to Smyrna; cross through Lydia past the tomb of Alyattes and the monument of Gyges and the great city and the stele, past the memorial of the great king Tos, turning your belly towards the setting sun.

On the strength of this passage the three largest mounds have been called respectively the tombs of Alyattes, Gyges, and Tos, in order from east to west. But the last two of these names are not really more than a convenient means of designating those particular tumuli. It has been suggested alternatively that 'the stele and the monument of Tos' refers to the Hittite figure in the Karabel Pass.

To the present writer this suggestion is unattractive (above, pp. 33–5).

In 1964 the Americans began an exploration of the second tumulus, called the tomb of Gyges. Here, too, a circular wall exists within the mound, and the architecture is interesting as resembling that of some Etruscan tombs. Future discoveries here may well be of great importance. A number of the smaller mounds also have been examined and found to contain a sepulchral chamber, situated generally away from the centre to make discovery more difficult. Some of them have more than one chamber. Whether there was in all cases a circular retaining wall at the base does not seem to have been determined.

Note

1 Many scholars, however, prefer to keep an open mind.

Appendices

1 Eratosthenes' Measurement of the Earth's Circumference

Beginning with the information that at Syene (Aswan) at noon on midsummer day the sun's rays reached to the bottom of a deep well—that is, that they fell vertically—Eratosthenes erected at Alexandria, also at noon on midsummer day, a perpendicular rod; from the shadow of this he was able to read off the angle between the rod and the direction of the sun's rays as 7° 12′, or just one-fiftieth of a complete circle. A simple geometrical construction will then demonstrate that the distance from Alexandria to Syene (a known quantity) is one-fiftieth of the earth's circumference. For the mathematically minded:

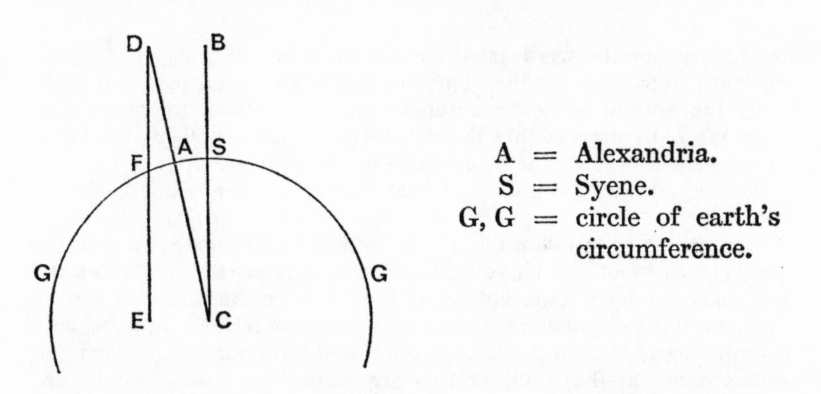

Produce the line of the rod at Alexandria (DA) and the line of the well at Syene (BS) till they meet at C; since both are vertical at the earth's surface, C must be at the earth's centre. From the top of the rod at D drop a line DE through the end of the shadow at F; this will be parallel to BC (since the rays of the sun are parallel to one another).

Since DE and BC are parallel, and are cut by the line DC, the alternate angles EDC and BCD are equal; therefore the angle BCD =

7° 12′, the known value of EDC. This being equal to one-fiftieth of a circle, the arc AS which subtends it must also be one-fiftieth of the circle of which it forms part, that is of the circumference of the earth.

In fact, Eratosthenes' figures for the angle of the shadow and the distance from Alexandria to Syene were not strictly correct, but as was said above, it happened that the errors cancelled out instead of accumulating.

(The above construction is slightly simplified from that actually used by Eratosthenes.)

2 Thibron's Attack on Larisa

Xenophon (*Hellenica* III, 1, 7) gives the following account of the attack in 399 B.C.

> As for the 'Egyptian' Larisa, as it is called, when he [Thibron] failed to win it over, he proceeded to invest it. Finding himself unable to take it by other means, he cut out a tank and dug a tunnel, with the object of depriving the defenders of their water. When these made frequent sorties and threw wood and stones into the excavation, he constructed a wooden shed to protect the tank; however, the Larisans issued out by night and burnt this down. As it was clear that he was making no headway, the ephors sent him instructions to abandon Larisa.

In this passage the word 'tank' has caused some difficulty. The meaning must apparently be that Thibron dug a square pit (called a tank) from the bottom of which a tunnel might be driven under the city wall. We must suppose that the defenders' water-supply was contained in a cistern just inside the wall, which he hoped to pierce. The Larisans replied by throwing stones and branches into the pit to impede the diggers.

If we attempt to relate this to the terrain at Buruncuk, the result is not very satisfactory. There is, in fact, a large cistern just inside the wall near the main gate, but the ground outside the wall falls steeply away on this side, whereas Xenophon's narrative seems to call for only a gentle slope. Moreover, the cistern in question is only one of many on the acropolis at Buruncuk, and its loss would not in any case be immediately fatal to the defence.

Thibron's scheme, to be successful, requires rather special circumstances. The city wall would, of course, be founded on rock; but to cut through rock would be a formidable task indeed. He must have intended, as in normal mining operations, to dig through soil to the base of the wall and then to pierce the masonry below ground. A fair depth of soil is therefore needed. Such a proceeding is quite out of the question on the north slope at Buruncuk, nor do the necessary conditions appear to exist elsewhere on the hill. How things were at Yanık Köy we cannot know till the site is excavated; meanwhile, visitors to the two places may be interested to try their hand at making sense of Thibron's operations.

3 Achilles and the Tortoise

Zeno's professed object was to prove the unreliability of the senses. Achilles runs a race with a tortoise, giving him, say, 100 yards start and running ten times as fast. The spectator's sense of sight tells him that before long Achilles overtakes and passes the tortoise, but reason shows that this is, in fact, impossible. For consider: by the time Achilles has made up the 100 yards start, the tortoise is 10 yards ahead; when this is made up, the tortoise is still one yard ahead—then a tenth of a yard, and so on indefinitely. Every time Achilles catches up, the tortoise is still just a little ahead, and the gap can never be reduced to nothing.

By reflecting that all these motions are, in fact, actually gone through, it is possible to reduce oneself to a state of bafflement over this problem. Perhaps the simplest exposure of the fallacy is that by the system adopted the race is in effect limited to a distance of 111·1 yards, and in this distance it is perfectly true that Achilles cannot pass the tortoise.

Even more subtle is Zeno's paradox of the Flying Arrow. We see an arrow fly from the bow to the mark, but again reason tells us that this motion is illusory. By way of analysing the arrow's flight, let us take as our unit of time (call it a moment) the space of time during which the moving arrow is in one place. There must be such a unit, for to say that the arrow is in a given place on its route for *no* space of time is equivalent to saying it is never there at all, which is absurd. How, then, does the arrow contrive to move from one place to another? It cannot, by definition, move *during* a moment; and it cannot move *between* the moments, because the moments are continuous; there cannot be gaps in the arrow's course. Obviously, then, the arrow cannot move at all, and our eyes are deceiving us.

The fallacy lies, we are told, in the assumption of a 'moment' during which the arrow is in one place only. Reasonable though this seemed, space and time cannot, in fact, be so divided into compartments. The arrow is never *stationary* in one spot; even as it is entering a given place it is at the same time leaving it, and the whole process is continuous. This is, of course, right; nevertheless, one takes off one's hat to Zeno.

4 The Lydian Language

In 1873 it could still be said: 'We do not know that the Lydians had any alphabet or literature of their own' (L. Schmitz in Smith's *Diction-*

ary of Greek and Roman Geography). Since then more than fifty inscriptions in Lydian script have come to light, the majority during the excavations at Sardis. Of anything that could fairly be called literature actually written in Lydian we have still no specimen, but as some of the inscriptions are couched in a form of verse, it may fairly be assumed that a Lydian literature did exist.

The alphabet consists of twenty-seven letters, of which more than half are readily recognizable from the Greek. The remainder were added by the Lydians themselves, either by adopting characters from other languages or by simple invention. The phonetic values of most of these have been more or less satisfactorily determined, and some progress has been made towards an understanding of the language. In this task great help has been afforded by a small number of bilingual inscriptions, one of which is illustrated above on p. 225. Lydian proves to be a language of the Indo-Germanic family, having affinities with Phrygian, Lycian, and Etruscan; this last would, of course, be expected, if the tradition of the colonization of Etruria from Lydia is historical. Apart from the alphabet, it seems to owe little or nothing to Greek. Much use is made of 'sonant' consonants, and letter-combinations such as vqb, nsrs, kml are frequent. Nasalized vowels seem also to be used.

The text illustrated on p. 225 is a dedication to Artemis, consisting of a line of Lydian, written (as usually, but not invariably) from right to left, and a Greek translation below. The Lydian is transliterated

Nannas Bakivalis Artimul

and the meaning is determined by the Greek: 'Nannas, son of Dionysicles, to Artemis'. Bakivalis, as the equivalent of Dionysicles, is evidently formed from Dionysus' alternative name Bacchus. Dionysus was, in fact, an Asiatic deity before he became Greek.

In the Lydian inscriptions the name of the city is written Sfard. It is therefore probable that the Sefarad mentioned in the twentieth verse of Obadiah may be identified with Sardis.

5 The Starting-Gate in the Greek Stadium

The general nature of the ancient starting-gate (called in Greek *hysplex*) is not doubtful, but the details certainly differed at various places and times. It was not in use at all in 480 B.C. (above, p. 172), but was introduced not long after that date. The occasional references in ancient writers make it clear that the general principle was that of a signal-arm, and that in Roman times at least this normally operated by falling, making something of a clatter in the process; it is said of a slow runner that 'the sound of the *hysplex* was in his ears'.

If the interpretation I have suggested of the arrangements at Priene is correct, the runner's feet at the start were directly under the bar of

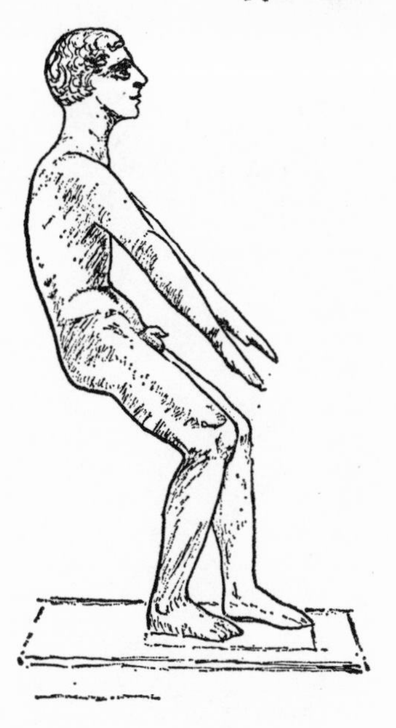

Fig. 53
Runner preparing to start race

the *hysplex*. This would prevent him from leaning forward while waiting for the starting signal, or even standing upright; but this is not such a difficulty as it might seem. There is, in fact, good evidence that the runner did actually lean backwards. Plato (*Phaedrus* 254 E) compares a charioteer reining in his team to a runner 'leaning back from the *hysplex*', and this is graphically illustrated by a bronze statuette in the Metropolitan Museum of Art. The attitude of this figure is shown in the accompanying sketch, in which the position of the feet explains why the grooves for the toes were so close together. The backward lean is pronounced, and the arms are held forward to preserve the balance; the bar of the *hysplex* should be imagined about the height of the man's chest. No runner would, of course, wish to be leaning so far backwards at the actual moment of starting; we must suppose, I think, that he would have a second or so notice of the falling of the bar, whereupon he would immediately throw his arms back, straighten his knees (so allowing room for the bar to fall) and begin his forward motion. A curious method of starting, but the evidence is hard to explain otherwise; wherever the double grooves for the toes are preserved (as at Olympia, Epidaurus, and Delphi) they are directly in line between the posts which held the 'signal-arms'.

The alternative explanation that the 'signal-arm' may have been raised rather than dropped (as with the starting-gate of a modern horse-race) is not supported by the ancient testimony, which refers more than once to its falling. The bar would need to be heavy, to avoid danger of sticking, and the eight falling together would make a characteristic noise.

The old idea (above, p. 202) that the start was effected by means of a rope stretched across in front of the runners is certainly false; there are indeed one or two references to a rope in connection with the start, but they concern the hippodrome, not the stadium.

Short Bibliography

General (with a preference for works written in English)

R. Chandler, *Travels in Asia Minor and Greece*, 3rd edition (London, 1817).

R. Chandler, N. Revett, and W. Pars, *Ionian Antiquities* (Society of Dilettanti, 1769).

Charles Fellows, *Asia Minor* (London, 1839).

W. J. Hamilton, *Researches in Asia Minor* (London, 1842).

C. T. Newton, *Travels and Discoveries in the Levant* (London, 1865).

W. M. Ramsay, *Letters to the Seven Churches*, 2nd edition (1906).

S. Ximinez, *Asia Minor in Ruins* (English translation, 1925).

B. D. Meritt, H. T. Wade-Gery, and M. F. McGregor, *The Athenian Tribute Lists I*, Chapter IX (Cambridge, Mass., 1939).

Freya Stark, *Ionia: a Quest* (London, 1954).

J. M. Cook, *The Greeks in Ionia and the East* (London, 1962).

2 Smyrna

C. J. Cadoux, *Ancient Smyrna* (Oxford, 1938).

J. M. Cook in *Annual of the British School at Athens*, Vol. 53–54.

RIVER MELES: W. M. Calder in Ramsay, *Studies in the Eastern Roman Provinces* (1906), pp. 95–116.

3 Around Smyrna

G. Perrot and and C. Chipiez, *History of Art in Phrygia, Lydia, Caria and Lycia* (English edition, 1892).

C. J. Cadoux, *Ancient Smyrna*.

NIOBE: H. T. Bossert, *Altanatolien*.

SESOSTRIS: J. M. Cook in *Türk Arkeoloji Dergisi*, VI, 2, pp. 3 ff.

LATER MONUMENTS: G. E. Bean in *Journal of Hellenic Studies* (1947), pp. 128–34 (Ada Tepe), and *Jahrbuch für Kleinasiatische Forschung*, III (1955), pp. 43 ff.

4 Pergamum

Altertümer von Pergamon (Berlin, 1885–1937): publication of the German excavations on the upper citadel.
E. V. Hansen, *The Attalids of Pergamon* (New York, 1947).
E. Boehringer in *Neue Deutsche Ausgrabungen* (Berlin, 1959), pp. 121 ff.
ASCLEPIEUM: O. Deubner, *Das Asklepieion von Pergamon* (Berlin, 1938).

5 Aeolis

ARISTIDES' JOURNEY: W. M. Ramsay in *Journal of Hellenic Studies*, II (1881).
LARISA: Boehlau-Schefold, *Larisa am Hermos* (publication of the German excavations).
J. M. Cook in *Annual of the British School at Athens*, 53–54, p. 20.
CYME: C. Schuchhardt in *Altetümer von Pergamon*, I, 1 (1912), p. 95.
MYRINA: E. Pottier and A. J. Reinach, *La Necropole de Myrina* (Paris, 1887).
C. Schuchhardt, op. cit., pp. 96–98.
GRYNEUM: Schuchhardt, op. cit., p. 98.
ELAEA: Schuchhardt, op. cit., pp. 111–13.
PITANE: Schuchhardt, op. cit., pp. 99–100.
E. Akurgal in *Türk Arkeoloji Dergisi*, X (1960), pp. 5–6 (in Turkish).
PHOCAEA: F. Sartiaux in *Comptes Rendus de l'Académie des Inscriptions* (1914), pp. 6–18, and *Bulletin de Correspondance Hellénique*, 44 (1920), p. 412.

6 Westward from Smyrna

CLAZOMENAE: J. M. Cook, *The Topography of Klazomenai* in *Archaiologike Ephemeris* (1953–54).
TEOS: Béquignon and Laumonier in *Bulletin de Correspondance Hellénique* (1925), pp. 281 ff.
MYONNESUS: G. Hirschfeld in *Archäologische Zeitung*, 33, p. 30.
G. Weber in *Athenische Mittheilungen*, 29, p. 228.
LEBEDUS: G. Weber, loc. cit.
ERYTHRAE: H. Gaebler, *Erythrä* (Berlin, 1892).
G. Weber in *Athenische Mittheilungen*, 26, pp. 103 ff.
J. Keil in *Österreichische Jahreshefte*, XIII (1910) and XV (1912).
(Sibyl): K. Buresch in *Athenische Mittheilungen*, 17 (1894), pp. 16 ff.

7 Ephesus

J. T. Wood, *Discoveries at Ephesus* (London, 1877).
F. Miltner, *Ephesos* (Vienna, 1958).
ARTEMISIUM: D. G. Hogarth, *Excavations at Ephesus* (London, 1908).
BELEVI: Perrot and Chipiez, op. cit., pp. 273–7 (with errors).
F. Miltner, *Ephesos*, 10–12 (with references in note 12).
H. V. Morton, *In the Steps of St. Paul* (London and New York, 1936).

8 Colophon, Notium, Claros

COLOPHON: C. Schuchhardt in *Athenische Mittheilungen*, XI (1886), pp. 398 ff.
NOTIUM: Demangel and Laumonier in *Bulletin de Correspondance Hellénique* (1923), pp. 353 ff.
CLAROS: C. Schuchhardt in *Athenische Mittheilungen*, XI (1886), pp. 439 ff.
Macridy in *Österreichische Jahreshefte*, XV (1912), pp. 36 ff.
Macridy and Picard in *Bulletin de Correspondance Hellénique*, 39 (1915), pp. 33 ff.
Ch. Picard, *Ephèse et Claros* (Paris, 1923).
(French Excavation): Preliminary notices in *Anatolian Studies* (1951–60).

9 Priene

T. Wiegand and H. Schrader, *Priene* (Publication of the German excavations, Berlin, 1904).
M. Schede, *Die Ruinen von Priene*, 2nd edition (Berlin, 1964).
PANIONIUM: G. Kleiner in *Neue Deutsche Ausgrabungen* (Berlin, 1959), pp. 172–80.

10 Miletus

Milet I–III (Publication of the German excavations, Berlin, 1906–36).

11 Didyma

C. T. Newton, *Halicarnassus, Cnidus and Branchidae* (London, 1863).
B. Haussoullier, *Histoire de Milet et du Didymeion* (Paris, 1902).
Didyma (Berlin: Publication of the German excavations), Vol. I, Buildings (1941); Vol. II, Inscriptions (1958).

12 Myus and Magnesia

MYUS: Ruge in Pauly-Wissowa *Realencyclopädie* s.v. Myus.
MAGNESIA AD MAEANDRUM: C. Humann, etc., *Magnesia am Maeander* (Berlin, 1904).

13 Heracleia under Latmus

F. Krischen in *Milet*, III, 2.
G. E. Bean and J. M. Cook in *Annual of the British School at Athens*, 52 (1957), pp. 138–40.

14 Sardis

Earlier excavations: *Sardis*, by H. C. Butler and others.
New excavations: Preliminary reports in *Bulletin of the American Schools of Oriental Research* (1958 onwards).

It is obviously impossible for a bibliography of this sort to keep abreast with the latest discoveries and publications. Readers who wish to follow the most recent developments are best advised to consult the survey of current work in Asia Minor which appear in the archaeological periodicals. Particularly recommended are Professor Machteld Mellink's survey 'Archaeology in Asia Minor', which appears each year in the *American Journal of Archaeology*, and two accounts published in the *Archaeological Reports* of the *Journal of Hellenic Studies*. The first, for 1965–70, is by Professor J. M. Cook and D. J. Blackman: *Archaeological Reports* 1971, pp. 33–62. The second, for 1971–78, by S. Mitchell and A. W. McNicoll, *Archaeological Reports* 1979.

Index

Abdera, 107
Achaeus, at Sardis, 222
Achilles and the Tortoise, 93, 233
Acoustics in theatres, 112–13
Acrobatae at Ephesus, 135
Ada Tepe, 38, 42, 44
Aegira, 210
Aemilius, 93
Aeneas, 84
Aeolis, Aeolians, 2, 21, 70ff., 83ff., 151, 206–7
Aepytus, 161
Agamemnon, Baths of, 29, 30, 99
Agrippa, 142
Akçakaya, 44
Akkaya, 41
Akpınar, 31
Alalia, 92
Aleon, River, 125
Ales, River, 156
Alexander the Great: conquest of Persia, 9, 10, 73, 153, 178, 195, 208; refounds Smyrna, 22–3, 40; at Ephesus, 130, 132; at Clazomenae, 101, 102; at Miletus, 186; at Priene, 161, 162, 178; at Teos (?), 115
Alexandria: library of, 12, 51; science at, 12, 48, 231–2
Alurca, 42, 44
Alyattes, 4, 22, 27, 100, 184, 218, 219; tomb of, 228
Amazons, 1, 21, 78, 80, 84
Amisus, 4
Amphitheatres, 68
Amr ibn el-Ass, 51
Anacreon, 109
Anaxagoras, 103
Anaxenor, 208
Anaximander, 183–4
Anaximenes, 183
Androclus, 129
Antigonus, 11, 22, 107, 119, 186
Antioch, 140
Antiochus I, 46, 88
Antiochus: II, 149; III, 12–13, 23, 47, 93, 108–9, 112, 116, 131, 222, 227
Antoninus Pius, 132, 223, 225
Antony, Mark, 14, 15, 51, 132, 145, 208
Apellicon, 109
Apollo, 31, 66; Clarian, 22, 154, 156ff.; Delphinius, 188–9; of Didyma, 188, 192ff.; Gryneian, 80, 83ff.; of Myus, 205–6
Arap Dere, 44
Arcadiane at Ephesus, 140
Arcadius, 140
Arcesilaus, 88

Ardys, 4, 218
Ariarathes, 163
Aristagoras: of Cyme, 78; of Miletus, 6, 185
Aristarchus, 12
Aristides, Aelius, 24, 25, 29, 59ff., 70ff.
Aristodicus, 200
Aristonicus, 13, 49, 93, 98, 131
Aristophanes, 66, 138
Aristotle, 36, 101–3, 153, 216
Aristotle, library of, 50–1, 109–10
Artaxerxes, 9, 207
Artemidorus, 117
Artemis, 31; of Claros, 158–60; of Didyma, 192, 195; of Ephesus, 6, 129–30, 132ff., 160; of Magnesia, 208–10; of Sardis, 222ff.
Artists of Dionysus, 107–8, 112, 116–17, 119, 121
Asclepius, Asclepieum, 29, 48, 58–69, 70
Asia: Province of, 13–18, 49, 131, 208; Commonalty of, 16; 'Asian Vespers', 14
Assurbanipal, 218
Assyria, 218
Asylum, 68, 132, 197
Athena, temple of: at Heracleia, 214; at Larisa, 75; at Notium, 154; at Pergamum, 50; at Priene, 162–5
Athenaeus, 128
Athens, 6, 7, 9, 26, 45, 48, 66, 84, 88, 100, 103, 153, 161
Athletics, ancient, 16, 56, 172ff.
Attalid Kingdom, 11, 86, 186
Attalus: I, 11, 23, 46–7; II, 48, 50, 108, 131, 163; III, 13, 48–9, 98
Augustus, 15–16, 132, 142, 164
Avşar, 204
Axus, River, 125
Aydın, 210

Babylon, 3, 9, 10, 130
Bafa, 181, 211
Balat, 181
Ball Games, 261
Baths: of Agamemnon, 29; of Diana, 24–5; of Faustina, 189–91
Bayraklı, 21, 23, 25, 26, 27, 41, 71
Bee, at Ephesus, 135
Belevi: Mausoleum, 148–9; Tumulus, 149–50
Belkahve, 35, 39–40, 42
Bereket Ilâhesi, 31–3
Bergama, 57, 69, 90
Beş Parmak, Mt., 211
Bias, 161–2, 179, 183
Bin Tepe, 227–9
Birki Tepe, 81
Bithynia, 11, 16
Boğazköy, 182
Books in antiquity, 50–1
Bornova, fort at, 42
Bouleuterion, *see* Council House
Boxing, ancient, 174
Bozdağ, *see* Tmolus
Branchidae, 192ff.
Bricks, floating, 8
Broteas, son of Tantalus, 33, 39
Brothel, at Ephesus, 144
Brothers, the Two, 20
Brutus, 15
Bülbül Dağı, 137
Bulgurca, 121
Buruncuk, 73–4, 232

Caesar, Julius, 15, 132, 197
Caicus, River, 45

Calchas, 156
Candarlı, 87ff.
Candaules, 217
Caracalla, 16, 54, 132, 226
Caravan Bridge River, 24
Caria, 2, 9, 21, 49, 157, 182, 211–12
Caunus, 84
Cayster, River, 129, 130, 131
Celsus, library of, 141–2
Çeşme, 29
Chandler, Richard, 21, 71, 104, 179, 222
Chersiphron, 130
Chios, Chians, 3, 4, 92, 122–4, 157
Christianity, 18, 53, 68, 81, 133, 144–5, 198, 201, 222
Chyton, Chytrion, 99, 101–3
Cicada, 208
Çıfit Kale, 115
Cimmerians, 4, 130, 207, 219, 227
Claros, 134, 151, 155ff.
Clazomenae, 4, 97–8, 99ff., 219
Cleopatra, 10, 51, 145
Cnopus, 123
Çobanpınarı, 42, 44
Coddinus, Rock of, 33
Codex, 50–1
Codrus, sons of, 2, 90, 106, 123, 129, 204
Coinage, invention of, 6, 219
Colophon, Colophonians, 4, 99, 118, 151ff., 206, 208
Colour in architecture, 143
Constantine, 18, 200
Cook, J. M., 71, 74, 100, 102–3, 122
Corinth, 48, 157, 171
Corsica, 92
Corycus, Mt, 124
Cos, 2
Council House: at Heracleia, 214; at Miletus, 189; at Notium, 155; at Priene, 168–9
Crete, Cretans, 1, 123, 156–7, 182, 207
Croesus, 4, 6, 73, 100, 129, 130, 156, 161–2, 183, 184, 193–4, 200, 201, 218, 219–21
Cumaovası 121, 151, 154
Cunaxa, battle of, 9
Curetes, 135, 137, 144
Cybele (Cybebe), 26, 31, 33, 38, 47, 129, 135, 207, 223
Cyllene, 74
Cyme, 72ff., 90, 93, 97–8, 126, 130, 200
Cyprus, 101, 182
Cyrus: the Great, 6, 9, 73, 200, 219–21; the Younger, 9
Cyzicus, 15, 105

Dağkızılca, 33
Darius, 7, 10, 45, 78, 184–5, 195, 197
Decius, 145
Değirmendere, 154
Deinocrates, 130
Delian Confederacy, 7, 22, 73, 78, 80, 84, 85, 88, 93, 100, 107, 119, 124, 129–30, 152, 185, 205, 207
Delos, 65
Delphic Oracle, 97, 159, 194, 209–10, 217–18
Delphinium at Miletus, 188–9
Demeter, 35; at Pergamum, 55–6; at Priene, 169–70
Demetrius the silversmith, 133, 139, 144
Diana, *see* Artemis
'Diana's Baths', 24–5

Didyma, 134, 157, 160, 192ff., 224
Didymeia, 202
Diet, Turkish, 204–5
Dio of Prusa, 197
Diocletian, 198
Diodorus, 97, 178, 180, 205
Diodorus Pasparos, 54
Dionysus, 145, 277; temple of, at Myus, 206; at Pergamum, 54; at Teos, 107–8, 110; Artists of, 107–8, 112, 116, 117, 119, 121; at Claros, 159
Discus-throwing, 174
Doğanbey, 116
Dogs, 152, 208
Domitian, 103–4, 139
Dorians, 1–2
Draco, Mt, 41
Drama, 108, 138–9, 165, 166, 185, 210

Earthquakes, 26, 28, 80, 107, 144, 164, 225
Ecbatana, 10
Echedorus, story of, 61
Eğridere, 71
Egypt, 10, 51, 57–8, 73, 130, 145, 183, 218
Egyptian deities, *see* Isis; Serapis
Elagabalus, 223
Elaea, 85ff., 100
Elea, Eleatics, 92, 233
Electrum coinage, 93
Eleusinian Mysteries, 55
Elgin Marbles, 194
Emiralem, 35, 71
Emmerich, Catherine, 147–8
Emperor-worship, 16, 56, 112, 189
Endymion, 212ff.
Enkomi, 182
Ephesus, 4, 14, 78, 107, 108, 118, 119, 128ff., 153, 185, 224
Ephesus, Council of, 141, 146
Ephorus, 79, 102
Epidaurus, 59, 61
Eratosthenes, 12, 231–2
Erythrae, Erythraeans, 4, 11, 88, 90–1, 122ff., 130, 178
Eski Foça, 90, 93–4
Essenes, 135
Eti Baba, 33–5
Etruria, 218, 234
Euclid, 12
Eumenes I, 46; II, 13, 47–9, 50, 55, 56, 131
Euripides, 103, 138
Eusebius, 146
Examyes, 182

Faustina: the Elder, 223, 225; the Younger, 189
Fimbria, 15, 68, 88
Flaccus, 15
Flavia Melitine, 63
Flying Arrow, 233
Foça, Eski, 90, 93–4
Foot-races, ancient, 173, 202

Galatia, *see* Gauls
Galen, 50, 59, 62, 86
Games, 218 (*and see* Athletics)
Gaugamela, battle of, 10, 195
Gauls, 11, 46–7, 53, 73, 195
Germanicus, at Claros, 157, 160
Geta, 226
Gibbon, Edward, 18
Gladiators, 17, 68
Golden Fleece, 219
Goths, 18, 197
Gövdelin, 42
Granicus, battle of, 10
Greek, 16, 141, 225

Gryneum, 80, 83ff., 160
Gugu of Luddi, 218
Gümüş Dağı, 207–8
Güzelçamlı, 179
Güzelhisar River, 81
Gygaea, Lake, 218, 227
Gyges, 4, 22, 30, 152, 184, 207, 217–18, 219; Tomb of, 228–9
Gymnasium: at Ephesus, of Vedius, 137; 'Girls' gymnasium', 145; at Lebedus, 121; at Pergamum, 56–7; at Priene, 175–6; at Sardis, 226; at Teos, 113–14

Hadrian, 63, 112, 131, 157, 197; temple of, at Ephesus, 143
Halesus, River, 156
Halicarnassus, 9, 130
Halka Pınar, 24–5, 70
Halys, River, 183, 219
Hamilton, William John, 107, 110, 113, 114, 126
Hannibal, 12, 48
Harpagus, at Phocaea, 92
Hecataeus, 117, 184
Hecate, 142, 152
Hecatomnos, 186
Hellanicus, 88
Hellenistic architecture, 17, 23, 54–5, 139, 165ff., 192
Hellenistic science, 12, 231
Hellenistic sculpture, 48
Heracleia under Latmus, 211ff.
Heracles (Hercules), 56, 122, 126
Heraclides, 12
Heraclitus, 183
Hermes, 56, 177
Hermocrates, 60
Hermogenes, 110, 209
Hermus, River, 20, 35, 70–1, 74, 98, 219
Herodotus, 2, 18–19, 20, 21, 33–5, 92, 93, 123, 130, 151, 178, 181, 182, 184, 185, 194, 195, 218, 220, 223, 228
Herophile, 124–5, 156
Herostratus, 130
Hesiod, 79
Hestia Boulaea, 144
Hierapolis, 76
Hipparchus, 12
Hippi Islands, 125
Hippias, 153
Hippocrates, 59
Hipponax, 228
Hippothous, 72
Histiaeus, 184–5
Hittites, 1, 21, 31, 33–5, 78, 182, 219
Hogarth, D. G., 134
Homer, 1, 2–3, 21, 24, 25, 26, 32, 72, 74, 79, 162, 178, 182, 209, 216, 218
Horace, 119
Housing, at Priene, 176–7
Hygieia, 63–4, 66

Iasus, 105
Ida, Mt, 99, 124
Ildır, 122, 123, 125, 127
Ilıca, 127
Imbat, 20, 23, 107, 121
Incir Ada, 95
India, 10
Ionia, 49
Ionian: civilization, 2ff., 21–2, 79, 109, 119, 204; migration, 2, 91, 99, 129, 161, 182; philosophy, 3, 103, 183–4; revolt, 6–7, 93, 100, 184–5, 195, 223
Ionian League, 73, 151, 161, 179
Ipsus, battle of, 11

Isis, temple of, 79
Issus, battle of, 10
Isthmian Sanctuary, 171–2

Javelin-throwing, 174
Jerome, 146
Joggled arch, 28
Julian, Emperor, 198
Julius Caesar, 15, 132, 197
Jumping, ancient, 174–5
Justinian, 133
Juvenal, 140

Kadife Kale, 20, 21, 28, 29
Kalabaktepe, 187
Kapıkırı, 211, 216
Kara Burun, 20
Karabel, 33–5, 228
Karagöl, 37, 71
Karakoç, 122
Karşıyaka, 71
Kazıkbağları, 86
Kemalpaşa, 33
Kemer Çayı, 24
King's Peace, 7, 9, 97, 101, 130
Kingship, 3, 16
Kısık, site of Lebedus, 119
Kızıl Avlu, 57–8
Kızılbahçe, 99
Kızılca, 41
Klazümen, 104
Knucklebones, 106, 218
Konya, 47

Labour disputes, 188
Labraynda, 216
Lade, battle of, 7, 93, 107, 119, 123–4, 161, 181, 185, 187, 205
Lagoras, 222
Lampsacus, 103, 204
Lampter, 94–6
Laodice, 112
Larisa, 72ff., 232
Latin, 16, 114, 141
Latmus: Mt., 211–12, 215; city, 212, 216
Latrine: at Ephesus, 137; at Pergamum, 65; at Priene, 177
Lebedus, 4, 107, 108, 116, 118–22, 204
Lelegians, 21
Lemnos, 80
Lesbos, 2
Lethaeus, River, 209
Leto, 31, 135, 158
Leucae, 97–8
Leucophrys, Leucophryene, 207, 208, 209, 250
Library, at Ephesus, 141–2; at Pergamum, 50–1; at Alexandria, 12, 51
Licinius, 200
Livy: on Myonnesus, 116–17; on Phocaea, 94–6; on Teos, 108–9, 115
Lycia, 10
Lydia, 4, 6, 22, 49, 97, 162, 217ff.; customs, 218; language, 225, 233–4
Lysimachus, 11, 22, 23, 28, 46, 107, 119, 130, 131, 137, 138, 153, 186

Macedonians, 9ff.
Macris, 109
Maeander, River, 2, 47, 118, 161, 162, 163, 181, 182, 187, 204, 205, 208, 212
Maeonians, 218
Magnes, story of, 207
Magnesia: ad Maeandrum, 134, 151, 204, 206ff.; ad Sipylum, 14, 38–40; battle of, 13, 47
Mahmut Dağı, 41

Malaria, 204–5
Maltepe at Pergamum, 69
Manisa, *see* Magnesia ad Sipylum
Manisa Daği, 20, 32, 71
Manto, 156
Marathon, 7
Marble, Teian, 115
Marcus Aurelius, 17, 189, 197
Mark Antony, *see* Antony
Marpessus, 124–5
Masons' marks, 54
Massalia (Marseilles), 91–2, 93
Mausoleum: at Halicarnassus, 9, 130, 164; at Belevi, 148–9
Mausolus, 9, 124, 185, 212, 216
Medes, 6
Medicine, ancient, 58ff.
Megabyxus, 135
Meles, River, 24, 25, 70, 157
Meles, king of Sardis, 220
Menemen, 21, 71
Menestheus, 85
Meryem Ana, 146–8
Mesate, Cape, 122
Midas, 4, 61, 97
Miletus, 4, 6, 7, 10, 11, 24, 78, 123, 130, 163, 181ff., 198, 202, 205, 219
Mimas, Cape, 20
Minoan Crete, 1, 187
Minos, 1
Mithridates VI, 14–15, 18, 23, 49, 88, 131, 132, 208
Mithridates, gate of, 142
Mopsus, 156
Morton, H. V., 128
Mother Goddess, *see* Cybele
Mudanya, 151
Museum at Ephesus, 140–1
Music, ancient, 221
Mussels, 85
Mycale, Mt, 178
Mycenaean civilization, 1–2, 3, 74, 182, 187
Myonnesus, 108, 113, 115–17
Myrcinus, 184–5
Myrina, 70, 77, 80ff.
Myrleia, 151
Mysia, 49
Mysteries, 55–6, 169–70
Myus, 4, 118, 182, 204–6

Namazgâh, 29
Namurt Limanı, 79
Nannus, story of, 91–2
Naulochus, 162, 163
Naustathmus, 94–6
Naxos, 185
Neileus, 182
Neleus, 109
Nemesis at Smyrna, 22
Neocorus, Neocorate, 132
Neonteichos, 72, 73–4
Nero, 131
Nicander, 160
Nicephorium, 68
Nicomedes, 46
Nif Dağı, 20
Niobe, 31–3
Notium, 151, 153, 154–5

Odeum, at Ephesus, 145; at Teos, 113
Ölüm Kayası, 42
Olympic Games, 17
Olympus, Mt, 20
Omar, Caliph, 51
Omphalos, 159
Oracle, 160, 201; of Claros, 22, 153, 156ff.; of Delphi, 97, 159, 194, 209–10, 217–18; of Didyma, 160 ,193ff.; of Gryneum, 84, 160

Orchomenus, 106
Orontes, River, 160
Orophernes, 163
Orphic religion, 55
Otomatik Tepe, 179
Oysters, 81, 84
Özbaşi, 204

Paches, 153
Pactolus, River, 219, 226
Pactyes, 200, 221
Pagus, Mt, 20, 21, 22, 24, 28, 45
Pamphylia, 10
Panaya Kapulu, 146–8
Panayır Dağı, 129, 130
Pancration, 174
Pandarus, story of, 61
Panionic League, 3, 6, 21–2, 23
Panionium, 90, 107, 162, 178–80
Panormus, 194, 197
Papyrus, 50–1
Parchment, 51
Parium, 123
Parmenio, 84
Pausanias, 18, 22, 32, 33, 36, 37, 38, 39, 84, 99, 101, 106, 122, 129, 152, 153, 160, 192, 195, 205–6
Pax Romana, 15, 17
Pelasgians, 72, 78, 88
Peloponnesian War, 7, 84, 152
Pelops, 35ff.
Pentathlon, 174–5
Pergamum, 11, 14, 15, 18, 23, 29, 45–69, 70, 85–6, 88, 160
Pericles, 103
Perseus of Macedonia, 48
Persian Wars, 6–7, 73, 161–2
Persians, 6ff., 45, 84, 92, 97, 107, 129–30, 149, 152, 153, 184–5, 187, 200, 226
Phallus stones, 96, 228
Pharnaces, 48
Philetaerus, 11, 46, 55, 88
Philip V of Macedon, 9, 12, 205
Philostratus, 108
Philotas, 161
Phocaea, 4, 90ff., 157
Phocis, 90, 91
Phriconis, 72
Phrygia, Phrygians, 4, 49, 97, 157, 219
Piasus, story of, 72
Pion, Mt, 129, 131, 142, 145
Pionius, 26
Pirates, 15, 157, 195
Pisidia, 157
Pitane, 80, 87ff.
Plague, 18
Plastene, Mother, 36ff.
Plataea, 195
Plato, 103, 235
Platonic Academy, 88
Pliny the Elder, 18, 26, 73, 80, 84, 88, 98, 101, 102, 104, 115, 125, 152, 157–8, 210
Plutarch, 135
Polichna, 100
Polycarp, 26, 28
Pompey the Great, 14, 15
Pontus, 11, 157
Poseidon Heliconius, 178, 179
Pramnian Wine, 25
Priene, 3–4, 11, 161ff., 182, 202, 208, 234
Proscenium, use of, 166
Prusias, 48
Ptolemaic Egypt, 10, 131, 186
Ptolemais, 119
Ptolemy: I, 10, 142; II, 119
Pulcheria, 146
Pydna, battle of, 48
Pyrrhus, 106
Pytheos, 164

Pythicus, River, 81

Quintus of Smyrna, 32, 33

Resinated Wine, 26
Rhegium, 92
Rhodes, 2, 130
Roman: citizenship, 16; government of Asia, 12–18, 23; occupation of Asia, 12, 47–9, 93, 108–9, 116–17, 131
Rome, deified, 14, 23
Royal Road, 227

St Charalambos, tomb of, 39–40
St John, 133, 146–7
St John of Damascus, 146
St Paul, at Ephesus, 133, 139, 147
Salamis, 172, 204
Salaries, 114
Samos, 4, 208
Sancaklı Kalesi, 38, 42
Sandoces, 78
Sarapis, *see* Serapis
Sardis, 4, 6, 7, 9, 14, 134, 161, 217ff., 234
Satan, Throne of, 53
Satraps, 6
Scholasticia, Baths of, 144
Schools, ancient, 114
Science, ancient, 12, 183–4
Scopelianus, 103
Scythia, 184
Sebastopolis, 80
Seferihisar, 107
Selçuk, 133
Selene, 212
Seleucid Kingdom, 11, 186
Seleucus: I, 10, 195, 200; II, 23; Alexandrian scientist, 12
Selinus, River, 57
Serapis, 57–8, 142–3
Sesostris, 33, 35
Setaneios, epithet of Dionysus, 112
Seven Sages, 183
Seven Sleepers of Ephesus, 145–6
Seven Wonders of the World, 130
Severus Alexander, 18
Şeytan Hamamı, 96
Sibyl, 124–5, 156
Sıçan Adası, 127
Sığacık (Sığacak), 106–7, 114
Sinope, 4
Sipylus, Mt., 20, 32, 35, 36
Smyrna, 2, 3, 4, 14, 20–30, 34–5, 39ff., 45, 70–1, 100, 104, 107, 127, 128, 160, 219
Socrates, 45, 103
Solon, 6, 183, 220
Sophocles, 32
Sparta, 7, 45, 84, 152
Stadium: at Didyma, 202–3; at Ephesus, 137–8; at Magnesia, 210; at Miletus, 189; at Pergamum, 57, at Pitane, 89; at Priene, 170ff.; at Sardis, 227; at Smyrna, 28
Stark, Freya, 74, 81, 106, 211
Strabo, 18, 22, 23, 30, 72, 73, 74, 77, 79, 83, 84, 88, 89, 99, 102–3, 109, 110, 119, 129, 131, 135, 137, 151, 162, 178, 195, 196, 205, 209, 219
Street-lighting, 140
Sulla, 14, 15, 110
Sundial at Claros, 159
Susa, 10
Sybarites, 152
Syria, 10, 11, 15, 149, 160

Tachos, 97, 98
Tacitus, on Claros, 157–8, 159, 160
Tanagra, 83
Tantalus, 21, 35; city of, 36–7, 40; lake of, 36–7; tomb of, 27, 28, 36–9, 228
Tartessus, 91
Taş Kule, 96–7
Taş Liman, 86
Taş Suret, 31–3, 39–40, 78
Telesphorus, 63, 66, 67
Teloneia, 163
Temaşalık Burnu, 85
Temnus, 74
Teos, 4, 90–1, 106ff., 118, 119, 124, 130, 152, 180
Tepekule, 21, 26–7
Texier, Ch., 37–8
Thales, 3, 107, 179–80, 182, 183, 191
Theatre: at Clazomenae, 104–5; at Cyme, 79, 126; at Ephesus, 138–9; at Erythrae, 126; at Heracleia, 214; at Magnesia, 210; at Miletus, 126, 188; at Notium, 155; at Pergamum, 53, 63–4; at Pitane, 89; at Priene, 126, 165ff.; at Sardis, 227; at Smyrna, 28; at Teos, 112–13, 126; at Tralles, 210
Themistocles, 172, 204–5, 207
Theodosius I, 143–4; Edict of, 198; II, 145–6
Theophrastus, 109
Thibron, 73, 207–8, 232
Thorax, Mt, 207, 208
Thucydides, 152, 178, 207
Tiberius, 80, 82, 132, 157, 160, 222
Tigranes, 15
Tire, 33, 35, 148
Titnaeus, River, 81
Tmolus, Mt., 218, 219
Torbalı, 33
Tos, 228
Trajan, 17, 197; fountain of, 144
Tralles, 210
Trojan War, 1, 2, 10, 29, 53, 72, 84, 85, 156, 182
Troy VIIa, 1
Turunçlar, 161

Üç Tepeler, 97
Ulucak, 71
Ürkmez, 119, 121, 122
Urla, 99, 102
Uzun Dere, 24

Varro, 51
View from theatre, 113
Virgil, 84
Virgin Mary, 133; church of, 140–1; house of, 146–8
Vitruvius, 126, 141

Wine in antiquity, 25–6, 104
Wrestling, ancient, 173–4

Xanthus, River, 79
Xenophanes, 183
Xenophon, 9, 45, 207, 232
Xerxes, 7, 78, 195
Xingi, site of Lebedus, 119
Yamanlar Dağı, 35, 37, 42, 71
Yanık Köy, 73–4, 76–7, 233
Yarıkkaya, 40
Yığma Tepe, 69

Zeno, 92–3, 233
Zeus, at Pergamum, 51–3, 54; at Sardis, 223; Zeus-Asclepius at Pergamum, 63
Zeytindağ, 86